Institutional Legacies of Violent Conflict

UNU World Institute for Development Economics Research (UNU-WIDER) was established by the United Nations University as its first research and training centre and started work in Helsinki, Finland, in 1985. The mandate of the institute is to undertake applied research and policy analysis on structural changes affecting developing and transitional economies, to provide a forum for the advocacy of policies leading to robust, equitable, and environmentally sustainable growth, and to promote capacity strengthening and training in the field of economic and social policymaking. Its work is carried out by staff researchers and visiting scholars in Helsinki and via networks of collaborating scholars and institutions around the world.

United Nations University World Institute for Development Economics Research – UNU-WIDER
Katajanokanlaituri 6B, 00160 Helsinki, Finland
www.wider.unu.edu

Institutional Legacies of Violent Conflict

Development and State-Building in the Shadow of Wartime Institutional Change

Edited by

PATRICIA JUSTINO

A study prepared by the United Nations University World Institute for Development Economics Research (UNU-WIDER)

UNU WIDER

OXFORD
UNIVERSITY PRESS

OXFORD
UNIVERSITY PRESS

Great Clarendon Street, Oxford, OX2 6DP,
United Kingdom

Oxford University Press is a department of the University of Oxford.
It furthers the University's objective of excellence in research, scholarship,
and education by publishing worldwide. Oxford is a registered trade mark of
Oxford University Press in the UK and in certain other countries.

World Institute for Development Economics Research of the United Nations University
(UNUWIDER), Katajanokanlaituri 6 B, 00160 Helsinki, Finland

Published in the United States of America by Oxford University Press
198 Madison Avenue, New York, NY 10016, United States of America

British Library Cataloguing in Publication Data
Data available

Library of Congress Control Number: 2026933362

ISBN 9780197904046

DOI: 10.1093/9780197904077.001.0001

Printed and bound by
CPI Group (UK) Ltd., Croydon, CR0 4YY

The manufacturer's authorized representative in the EU for product safety is
Oxford University Press España S.A. of Parque Empresarial San Fernando de Henares,
Avenida de Castilla, 2 – 28830 Madrid (www.oup.es/en or product.safety@oup.com).
OUP España S.A. also acts as importer into Spain of products made by the manufacturer.

MIX
Paper | Supporting
responsible forestry
FSC® C013604
FSC
www.fsc.org

Acknowledgements

This book brings together a diverse set of contributions that examine how governance is enacted, contested, and reshaped in settings affected by violent conflict. It is anchored in the conviction that understanding post-conflict governance requires looking beyond formal institutions and state-centric frameworks, to the everyday practices, networks, and arrangements that structure authority on the ground. The volume reflects the efforts of several researchers working across disciplines, geographies, and methodological traditions, united by a shared interest in how people navigate governance in the shadow of war.

As the editor of this volume, I had the privilege of curating and working closely with an extraordinary group of scholars whose research forms the core of this book. Their contributions—empirically rich, theoretically grounded, and policy-relevant—shed light on the complex institutional landscapes that emerge during and after violent conflict. Together, the chapters trace how wartime institutions persist into the post-conflict period, how local and national actors negotiate power in contested environments, and how historical legacies shape the capacity for reconstruction and reform.

My interest in the themes explored in this volume has developed over many years of conducting research, designing policy, and engaging with the lived realities of governance in fragile and conflict-affected contexts. Trained as a development economist, my work has consistently focused on understanding how institutions function under conditions of violence, inequality, and political instability. I have had the privilege of working with multilateral organizations, including the United Nations, and the World Bank, and of collaborating with local researchers and policymakers in regions marked by protracted conflict. Through this work, I have come to appreciate the complexity and adaptability of local governance arrangements, and the importance of grounding theoretical frameworks in empirical realities. This book reflects not only a scholarly interest, but a commitment to bringing greater analytical and policy attention to the actors and institutions that emerge when conventional governance structures break down.

My work at the Institute of Development Studies (IDS) and, more recently, at UNU-WIDER, has provided the institutional foundation to pursue these questions through interdisciplinary and empirically grounded approaches. As co-founder and co-director of the Household in Conflict Network, I have been privileged to collaborate with a global community of researchers committed to advancing knowledge on how conflict affects individuals, households, and institutions. This book builds on that tradition, bringing together insights from diverse settings to explore how governance is reconfigured in times of disruption and transition.

The process of editing this volume has been both intellectually enriching and personally meaningful. I am deeply grateful to all of the chapter authors, whose commitment to this project and openness to dialogue made the editorial process a true collaboration. Their work pushes the boundaries of how we think about governance in conflict and post-conflict contexts, and I have learned immensely from each contribution.

I would also like to acknowledge the many colleagues and interlocutors who have shaped this book indirectly through discussions, comments, and encouragement over the years. Particular thanks go to Ana Arjona, Laia Balcells, Tilman Brück, Ana María Ibáñez, Stathis Kalyvas, and Philip Verwimp, whose collaborations over the years have had a lasting impact on my thinking. I am also grateful to the UNU-WIDER team, especially Dominik Etienne, Aino Hiltunen, Sami Husa, Iina Kuuttila, Eeva Nyyssönen, Ruby Richarson, Laura Saavedra-Lux, Ricardo Santos, Anna Toppari, Leeni Varis, Annett Victorero, and Lumi Young, for their logistical and intellectual support throughout the preparation of this volume. Kit Rickard and Margherita Bove provided excellent research assistance at various stages of the project that generated this volume.

I extend my sincere thanks to Siméon Rapin at UNU-WIDER's publication team for his outstanding work in managing the compilation and production of this volume, and to the editorial team at Oxford University Press for their guidance, responsiveness, and professionalism throughout. Their support ensured that this volume could reach the broad academic and policy audience for whom it is intended.

Finally, I would like to acknowledge the many individuals and communities—often in extraordinarily difficult circumstances—who shared their experiences with the researchers whose work appears in this volume. This book is for them. It is an attempt to document, analyse, and amplify the ways in which governance is lived, shaped, and contested far beyond the boundaries of formal institutions.

Patricia Justino
Director, UNU-WIDER
Helsinki, May 2026

Contents

List of figures

List of tables

List of abbreviations

ACLED	Armed Conflict Location and Event Data
ALRMP	Arid Lands Resource Management Project
AMLO	Andrés Manuel López Obrador
ANC	African National Congress
ANUC	National Peasant Union
AUC	Autodefensas Unidas de Colombia
CCNPP	Citizen's Charter National Priority Programme
CDD	community-driven development
CDDO	Community-Driven Development Organization
CDR	community-driven reconstruction
CJNG	Cártel Jalisco Nueva Generación
CNDD-FDD	National Council for the Defense of Democracy – Forces for the Defense of Democracy
CNDP	National Congress for the Defence of the People
CPA	Comprehensive Peace Agreement
DANE	National Department of Statistics
DRC	Democratic Republic of the Congo
DTO	Drug trafficking organization
ELCA	Colombian Longitudinal Survey conducted by the Universidad de los Andes
EPLF	Eritrean People's Liberation Front
EPRDF	Ethiopian People's Revolutionary Democratic Front
FARC	Fuerzas Armadas Revolucionarias de Colombia
FIIA	Finnish Institute of International Affairs
FRODEBU	Front for Democracy in Burundi
FTLRP	Fast Track Land Reform Programme
HDZ	Croatian Democratic Union
HTS	Hayat Tahrir al-Sham
IDEAM	Colombian Institute of Hydrology, Meteorology, and Environmental Studies
IDP	internally displaced person
INEGI	Instituto Nacional de Estadística y Geografía
INLA	Irish National Liberation Army
IPLO	Irish People Liberation Organization
IRA	Irish Republican Army
IRR	incidence rate ratio
ISI	Islamic State in Iraq
IV	instrumental variable

JACs	Juntas de Acción Comunal
JaN	Jabhat al-Nusra
KDP	Kecematan Development Programme
KLA	Kosovo Liberation Army
LDK	Democratic League of Kosovo
LTTE	Liberation Tigers of Tamil Eelam
MAPS	Mapping Attitudes, Perceptions, and Support
MDC	Movement for Democratic Change
MILF	Moro Islamic Liberation Front
MNLF	Moro National Liberation Front
MoE	Ministry of Education
NGO	non-governmental organization
NPFL	National Patriotic Front of Liberia
NRM	National Resistance Movement
NSA	Non-State Actor
NSP	National Solidarity Programme
OLS	Ordinary least squares
PAIAMEX	Political Assassinations, Intimidation and Actors in Mexico
PAIGC	African Party for the Independence of Guinea and Cape Verde
PAN	Partido Acción Nacional
PDET	Programs for Development with a Territorial Focus
PEMEX	Petróleos Mexicanos
PPE	personal protective equipment
PRI	Partido Revolucionario Institucional
PSNI	Police Service Northern Ireland
RCT	randomized controlled trial
RPF	Rwandan Patriotic Front
RUC	Royal Ulster Constabulary
SIDA	Swedish International Development Cooperation Agency
SIGAR	Special Inspector General for Afghanistan Reconstruction
SNM	Somali National Movement
SOA	Super Output Area
SPLA	Southern People's Liberation Army
SSG	Syrian Salvation Government
SSR	security sector reform
TNA	Tamil National Alliance
TPLF	Tigray People's Liberation Front
UCDP	Uppsala Conflict Data Program
UN	United Nations
UNMISS	UN Mission in South Sudan
UNU-CPR	Centre for Policy Research
UP	Patriotic Union
USC	United Somali Congress
WHO	World Health Organization

ZANU	Zimbabwe African National Union
ZANU-PF	ZANU-Patriotic Front
ZAPU	Zimbabwe African People's Union
ZILIWACO	Zimbabwe Liberators and War Collaborators Association
ZNLWVA	Zimbabwe National Liberation War Veterans Association

Notes on contributors

Kristin M. Bakke is a Professor of Political Science and International Relations, University College London, and associate editor for the *Journal of Peace Research*. Her research interests include states' responses to opposition within their borders, dynamics of violence, wartime legacies, and geopolitical attitudes. She is the author of *Decentralization and Intrastate Struggles: Chechnya, Punjab, and Québec* (Cambridge University Press, 2015).

Sarah Zukerman Daly is an Associate Professor of Political Science at Columbia University. She is the author of *Organized Violence After Civil War: The Geography of Recruitment in Latin America* (Cambridge University Press, 2016) and *Violent Victors: Why Bloodstained Parties Win Postwar Elections* (Princeton University Press, 2022). She has published widely in the fields of international relations and comparative politics, with a particular focus on war and peace, democracy, organized crime, and geopolitics.

Adam Day is the Head of UN University Centre for Policy Research's Geneva Office and holds adjunct faculty positions at Columbia University and the Geneva Graduate Institute. With more than a decade of experience in UN peacekeeping, his early research focused on peace and security (*States of Disorder*, Oxford University Press 2021). More recently, he has focused on emerging risks from science and technology, serving as the Research Lead for the Secretary-General's Scientific Advisory Board. His most recent book, *The Forever Crisis* (Routledge 2025), applies complexity science to global risks.

Marta Furlan is a research consultant for international human rights organizations. Her research focuses on armed groups, civil conflicts, and violence against women and children. She is passionate about the use of participatory research methods and the inclusion of local knowledge systems in the formulation of sustainable solutions. She has published in leading peer-reviewed journals on violent non-state actors and published a book with Columbia University Press on the dynamics of Salafi-jihadist rebel governance.

Margarita Gáfaro is the Director of the Center for Sectoral Production and Trade Studies (CEPCO) at the Banco de la República in Cali. Her research lies at the intersection of development and agricultural economics, with a particular focus on the functioning of land, credit, and output markets in rural areas of developing countries.

Marine Gassier is a political scientist with a PhD from Sciences Po Paris. Her research examines rebel governance and political changes during and after civil wars in West and East Africa. Using mixed methods, she studies how armed groups govern territories and their lasting impact on societies. Her work contributes to understanding conflict dynamics and post-war political development in these regions.

Roxana Gutiérrez-Romero is a Professor of Policy and Quantitative Methods at the School of Business and Management, Queen Mary University of London. Her research focuses on the political economy of development, emphasizing the impacts of violence, inequality, and governance failures in Latin America and Africa. She has published widely in development economics, particularly on the long-term consequences of conflict, electoral dynamics, and the role of governance in shaping development outcomes.

Ana María Ibáñez is the Vice President for Sectors and Knowledge at the Interamerican Development Bank. Her research focuses on microeconomic analysis of internal conflict, migration, and rural development.

Patricia Justino is a Professor of Development Economics and a leading expert on political violence and development. She is the Director of UNU-WIDER and Professorial Fellow (on leave) at the Institute of Development Studies, UK. She has led major research programmes funded by the European Commission, the UK Economic and Social Research Council (ESRC), and the UK Department for International Development (DFID), and has advised several international organizations, including UN agencies and the World Bank. She holds a MPhil in Economics from Cambridge University and a PhD in Economics from London University. She has held visiting positions at Harvard University (2007–09) and the European University Institute (2017), among others.

Shelley Liu is an Assistant Professor of Public Policy and Political Science at Duke University. Her research focuses on how political and institutional contexts affect citizen-state relations, and how citizens in turn shape the state-building process. Her first book, *Governing After War: Rebel Victories and Postwar Statebuilding* (OUP 2024), examines how rebel groups organize themselves, transition into government, and engage in state-building after they win war.

Kit Rickard is a Senior Researcher at the Centre for Security Studies, ETH Zürich. He completed his PhD in political science at University College London. His research focuses on conflict, legacies of war, international relations, and research methods.

Cyrus Samii is a Professor of Politics at New York University. He researches strategies for post-conflict reconstruction and institutional innovation in war-affected and emergency contexts. He is also an expert in methods for quantitative policy evaluation and causal inference. He has published widely in political science, statistics, economics, and public policy.

Abbey Steele is an Associate Professor of political science at the University of Amsterdam. She researches civil wars, civilian displacement, and state-building. Her book, *Democracy and Displacement in Colombia's Civil War* (2017, Cornell University Press), explains how democratic reforms led armed groups to engage in political cleansing in Colombia. She has collaborated with USAID and UNDP to study state- and peace-building initiatives in Colombia, and her work has been published in the *American Political Science Review*, the *Journal of Peace Research*, and *Comparative Politics*.

Michael Weintraub is an Associate Professor in the Department of Political Science and Global Studies and Director of the Center for the Study of Security and Drugs (CESED) in the Department of Economics at Universidad de los Andes in Bogotá, Colombia. His research focuses on crime, political violence, and drug policy in Latin America. He has published in the *American Journal of Political Science, American Political Science Review, Journal of Politics, Nature Human Behaviour*, among other outlets. He has been a Visiting Scholar at the Harvard Kennedy School and is an Invited Researcher with J-PAL's Humanitarian Protection Initiative and the Displaced Livelihoods Initiative, and a member of the Evidence in Governance and Politics (EGAP) network.

PART I

CONCEPTUALIZING

A New Research Agenda

1

Institutional legacies of violent conflict

A new research agenda

Patricia Justino

1.1 Introduction

One of the most critical challenges in international development today is to understand how best to support peace, security, economic recovery, and legitimate political authority in countries affected by political instability and violent conflict—where almost 2 billion people live. While poverty has been reduced across the globe since 1990, it has increased in conflict-affected countries with the gap between peaceful and conflict-affected countries widening in recent years (World Bank 2020, 2024). The OECD estimates that fragile and conflict-affected countries will host 86 per cent of the world's extreme poor by 2023 (OECD 2022). Almost 70 per cent of those suffering from acute hunger live in countries experiencing violent conflict and instability, such as Afghanistan, the Democratic Republic of Congo, Ethiopia, Nigeria, South Sudan, Sudan, Syria, and Yemen (World Bank 2020; World Food Programme 2022). According to the UNHCR, at the end of June 2024, there were 122.6 million forcibly displaced people in the world, the largest number on record. Over 87 per cent of these displaced populations live in low- and middle-income countries, some fragile countries themselves (UNHCR 2024).

These numbers represent an unprecedented rise in human insecurity since World War II. In response, several governments have earmarked substantial portions of their aid budgets to support stability, peace, and state-building interventions in conflict-affected countries, even if overall development budgets are being reduced (Hoeffler and Justino 2023; Gisselquist et al. 2025). At the global level, the UN Sustainable Development Goals—specifically Goal 16—aim to reduce all forms of violence, and to work with governments and communities to find lasting solutions to conflict and insecurity. Yet, interventions to reduce the risk and impact of conflict have at best had mixed results (Crost et al. 2014; Blattman and Ralston 2015; Justino 2019). Despite peace and stability being central to the prosperity of countries and their citizens, we continue having limited understanding of

Patricia Justino, *Institutional legacies of violent conflict*. In: *Institutional Legacies of Violent Conflict*. Edited by: Patricia Justino, Oxford University Press. © United Nations University World Institute for Development Economics Research (UNU-WIDER) (2026). DOI: 10.1093/9780197904077.003.0001

how and why violent conflicts persist in modern times, how and why their legacies endure across time, and what can be done at the policy and practical levels to create better prospects for economic development and sustainable peace in post-conflict countries. This edited volume seeks to fill these gaps in knowledge and inform policy.

The volume brings together studies on the long-term legacies of wartime institutional changes to investigate how institutional dynamics that develop during violent conflicts shape state-building and economic development trajectories in the long run. The central hypothesis driving this volume is that the persistence of violent conflicts, their legacies, and the effectiveness of conflict interventions are shaped by the different socio-political dynamics and complex processes of institutional change that take place *during* the conflict. These complex dynamics are grounded on how local political authorities (including both state and non-state actors) behave, compete, and make decisions, how different governance structures produce or limit the use of violence and interact with civilian populations, and how territories and populations are ruled and controlled.

Violent conflicts are defining historical experiences that bring about fundamental change within societies, restructuring social, political, and economic order. This has important implications for states in their pursuit of peace and economic development. In fact, most of the armed conflicts we observe today are a reflection or extension of conflicts countries experienced in the past and their institutional legacies (Strand and Hegre 2021). Rebuilding conflict-affected societies requires understanding about what has been destroyed and what has been replaced—but also about what has been created during armed conflict and its legacies over time.

The volume highlights two conceptual shifts along which we aim to advance knowledge and increase the potential policy impact of this research. First, the volume brings together research that considers not just the formation of institutions during wartime—either by rebel groups or other armed actors, including the state and civilians—but also its long-term legacies. A growing body of research in political science and economics has documented how institutions and order emerge in the midst of civil wars and other violent conflicts. However, only recently have researchers turned their attention to their consequences, especially for long-term state-building, peace, and economic recovery. Yet, these long-term dynamics shape the process of building a functioning state that is able to deliver governance, prosperity, and sustained peace.

The second conceptual shift is the emphasis on civilian agency in the formation of wartime institutions. Much of the existing literature has focused on how institutional change emerges in conflict areas from the competition between rebel groups and the state military for territorial control. However, institutional change is also substantially shaped by interactions between armed groups and civilians.

These interactions, we argue, are key to understanding the long-term legacies and the persistence of violent conflict because they affect the distribution of different power configurations and patterns of wartime dynamics, arguably two central conditions explaining the long-term risk and impact of violent conflicts and the prospects for sustaining peace and economic recovery.

The idea that conflict is inherent to state-building is not new. Wars have long been identified as important catalysers of state formation, with warfare and mobilization for warfare being at the heart of the emergence of modern nation states (Tilly 1975). However, evidence on the transformation of social, economic, and political institutions in regions affected by civil wars and other violent conflicts today, and its ensuing political and economic legacies, is only now emerging. This is largely because conflict-affected settings have been understood in the literature as forms of state 'collapse', state 'failure', or 'limited' statehood. However, the collapse of the state is rarely accompanied by the collapse of governance and order: places where the state is not present are rarely ungoverned. As noted by Huang (2016: 3), the post-conflict setting is not an institutional '*tabula rasa* in which actors, whether domestic or international, can realize their vision of a new state from scratch'.

More often than not, state collapse is accompanied by the emergence of new institutions and organizations as myriad actors (rebel groups, militias, paramilitary groups, warlords, gangs, mafia, drug trafficking factions, private security providers, and vigilante groups) replace key state functions, govern, and create social, market, and political institutions to control territories, finance their operations, and gain the support of local populations (Mampilly 2011; Justino 2012, 2019; Arjona 2016; Staniland 2012, 2021; Stewart 2018; Mampilly and Stewart 2021; Shesterinina 2021). In these settings, armed groups, civilians, and state and non-state actors interact, fight, compete, and negotiate. Conflicts destroy but also generate or strengthen other forms of social, political, and economic organization and breed new forms of governance, identities, and societal organization that may be overlooked in the rush of the international community to build new states and institutions. We observed this in the case of Syria, where civil society groups emerged early in the conflict to provide public services in rebel-held urban areas, or in the case of the Islamic State, which in line with the behaviour of many non-state armed groups across the world provided substantial public service provision and infrastructure (Revkin and Ahram 2020; Revkin 2021). These are important dynamics which are likely to affect post-conflict state-building, economic recovery, and political development—consequently affecting how post-conflict states are able to effectively break cycles of poverty and violence. These legacies are also instrumental for how elites pursue political objectives after war, as well as how third parties (such as the international community) engage in building peace and economic prosperity.

1.2 From armed conflict to institutional change: political order and wartime governance

The idea that states are shaped by how institutions emerge and change at critical historical junctures has a long pedigree.[1] Several studies have discussed how modern developed societies have transitioned from violence and instability to inclusive political regimes through processes of institutional change at key historical transition points.[2] Wars are some of the most important transition points in the history of modern states. Charles Tilly (1975, 1992) famously argued that the formation of nation states in Europe was motivated by the need to collect revenue that would sustain ongoing warfare. This need provided, in turn, the incentives for political leaders to develop institutions to control and govern local populations and levy taxes to sustain the war effort, in exchange for protection and the provision of public goods. The ability of political authorities to collect revenue and provide security and public goods demonstrated, in turn, their capacity to govern over a territory and its population (Besley and Persson 2009; Bates 2008a, 2008b; Tilly 1992; Wimmer 2018), giving rise to the establishment of a social contract between rulers and citizens (Levi 1988; Bates et al. 2002; Acemoglu and Robinson 2006), and helping to forge national identities (Tilly 1992). These bureaucracies evolved into today's modern European states (Levi 1988; Tilly 1992; Olson 1993).

More recently, an emerging body of literature has provided important insights into the formation of political order and structures of state-like governance in areas where the government is violently contested, and different non-state armed political groups compete to hold the monopoly of violence in areas under their military control.[3] Kalyvas' (2006) pioneering study of the logic of violence in civil war conceptualized the emergence of political order in areas where one group exercises full territory control as groups favour order over disorder when the need to punish rivals and obtain information is reduced. Staniland (2012) defines a typology of wartime political orders shaped by the interaction between types of territorial control by armed groups in wartime (segmented, where groups control territory, or fragmented, where territorial contestation dominates) and level of cooperation between the state and an insurgent group (active, passive, or nonexistent). Different combinations of these two variables—territorial control and armed group cooperation—generate six possible wartime political orders: shared

[1] See Tilly (1975), Bates (1983, 2008b), Young (1994), Herbst (2000), Acemoglu et al. (2001, 2013), Boone (2003), Fukuyama (2004, 2012), North et al. (2009), and Wimmer (2018).

[2] Pioneering studies include Boix (2003), Acemoglu and Robinson (2006, 2012), Wimmer and Min (2006), North et al. (2009), and Besley and Persson (2011), among others.

[3] See, among others, Young (1994), Reno (1999, 2002), Pool (2001), Jackson (2003), Kasfir (2005), Kalyvas (2006), Stokke (2006), Cramer (2007), Menkhaus (2007), Bates (2008a), Kalyvas et al. (2008), Raeymaekers et al. (2008), Raeymaekers (2010), Mampilly (2011), Mampilly and Stewart (2021), Risse (2011), Ahmad (2015), Arjona et al. (2015), Arjona (2016), Sanchez de la Sierra (2020), and Staniland (2012, 2021).

sovereignty, spheres of influence, clashing monopolies, collusion, tacit coexistence and guerrilla disorder.[4] Arjona (2016) introduces the role of civilians in political order formation and discusses the advent of two forms of social order during wartime as a result of negotiations between non-state armed groups and civilians. In the first type of social order, rebelocracy (or the rule of rebels), rebel groups govern civilians and impose norms of behaviour and conduct. The second type, aliocracy (or the rule of others), is characterized by minimal interference of armed groups in civilian affairs. These types of order, or alternative situations of disorder, are shaped by the time horizons of armed groups and the quality of pre-existing local institutions before the arrival of the group to the community. More recently, Mampilly and Stewart (2021) have developed a typology of six rebel political institutional arrangements, including martial law, partial subjugation, status quo (more or less inclusive), and transformative (more or less inclusive). Each of these institutional arrangements is defined by variation across the ways in which power is shared between rebel groups and locals, the integration of civilians in rebel institutional arrangements, the degree to which groups transform pre-existing institutions, and levels of civilian influence over decision-making. Each institutional arrangement is, in turn, shaped by the interaction between the ideological position of rebel groups, their strategic objectives, and local conditions.

In broad terms, the core insight of these different frameworks is the fact that wartime political orders are shaped by how armed groups make decisions about governing based on their strategic objectives and interactions they engage in with civilians. These typologies are thus valuable to understanding the emergence of different constellations of wartime politics beyond the traditional conflation of wartime with violence—which is only one part of the dynamics of an internal armed conflict.

This literature focuses largely on insurgent (rebel) groups in civil wars, but its theoretical predictions apply also to other non-state armed actors such as militias, paramilitary groups, vigilantes, and similar groups (Jentzsch et al. 2015). In parallel, scholars have studied the emergence of state apparatus in *de facto* states (Florea 2020; Risse 2011), as well as the emergence of social and political order in what is sometimes described as 'ungoverned spaces', such as those ruled by Mafia-type groups (Gambetta 1996; Rolla and Justino 2022), prison gangs (Skarbek 2011, 2014), pirate organizations (Leeson 2007, 2009), and urban slum gangs (Venkatesh 2008, 2009; Blattman et al. 2020; Lessing 2021). This literature deals with the emergence of forms of self-governing structures to ensure the enforcement of property rights and the protection of (illegal) business interests in areas under the control of criminal organizations, but where the state is ultimately the main authority and enforcer of such authority (Skaperdas and

[4] In a follow-up book, Staniland (2021) condenses these into four armed orders established between armed groups and the state: alliance, limited cooperation, containment, and total war.

Syropoulos 1997; Arias 2017; Lessing 2021). This is in contrast with the civil war literature where the authority of the state is fragmented and contested, and alternative Leviathans emerge in controlled areas.[5]

The study of 'rebel governance' has in recent years become a central area of inquiry in conflict studies and political science (Mampilly 2011; Arjona et al. 2015; Arjona 2016), and more recently in development economics (Gáfaro et al. 2014; Justino and Stojetz 2019; Ibáñez et al. 2019; Bandiera et al. 2022). Civil wars are fought between the government of a state and non-state armed actors seeking to overthrow the government or secede from the state. State and non-state armed actors are typically divided by a master cleavage along economic, political, social, or cultural dimensions that pit those who want to retain the status quo against those who challenge it. Both generally employ political violence to coerce the other side into conceding concessions. While the master cleavage is between an assumed unitary government and one or more non-state armed groups (Bakke et al. 2012), there is local variation in how they interact (Kalyvas 2006; Staniland 2021). The ability of both sides to employ violence is often a function of their territorial control and popular support. Territorial control is ensured by the coercion, collaboration, or active support of civilians in areas under their rule. However, there are important differences in armed group–civilian relations within areas of armed group control. Arjona (2016) documents how, for some civilians, life under armed actors has clear rules that regulate conduct, but this does not apply to all. Equally, Mampilly and Stewart (2021) show how armed groups may incorporate civilians into governance institutions in some places, but in others there is no civilian involvement. The field of 'rebel governance' has emerged as an attempt to explain these differences (Arjona et al. 2015).

Non-state armed groups create forms of governance in wartime through processes of 'absorption, assimilation, or replacement' (Podder 2014). During conflict, armed groups often repurpose or develop the rules that citizens are expected to obey, and citizens turn to wartime institutions for public goods, to ensure their security, or to adjudicate disputes. The most basic public goods are usually ensuring local order by enforcing conflict mechanisms and protecting property rights, but wartime governance by armed groups also includes the ways in which civilians are included in agenda-setting and decision-making processes. Governance by armed groups in wartime is, thus, best understood as a spectrum, where minimal governance might aim to provide local order while high levels of governance, founded on the development or co-optation of advanced institutions, provide public goods such as education and healthcare (Mampilly 2011; Revkin 2021),

[5] A large body of literature has also documented the role of non-state institutions as service providers in contexts of weak or fragile states (see Helmke and Levitsky 2004). These institutions include NGOs, civil society organizations, citizen collective action, traditional leaders, and other similar civic organizations. In contrast to armed groups, these informal institutions are not driven by governing intentions and operate largely within state structures or alongside them.

courts and police (Sivakumaran 2009; Loyle 2021), and even elections (Kasfir 2005; Cunningham et al. 2021).

The development of 'insurgent', 'rebel', 'shadow', or 'de facto' states serves multiple purposes. The main aim is often to foster civilian support by enhancing the legitimacy of armed group rule (Duyvesteyn 2017; Podder 2017). For civilians, armed groups are visible in their ability to provide local order and physical security, which in turn becomes a major source of support for the group (Wickham-Crowley 1992; Podder 2014). Armed groups may also provide governance and create institutions to demonstrate their political goals and signal their ability to rule in a post-conflict setting to their constituents (Stewart 2018), vis-à-vis the state (McColl 1969), and to foreign states and organizations (Coggins 2015; Huang 2016). Legitimacy, in turn, boosts recruitment and active support in terms of resources such as shelter, food, and information (Mampilly 2011; Daly 2016). Once they have ensured the protection of constituents under their rule, non-state armed groups establish institutions to regulate economic affairs, which allow them to create new ways of financing their organization and ensuring their survival (Kasfir 2015; Reno 2015). These include but are not restricted to tax collection and extortion (Revkin 2021; Mampilly 2021), and direct involvement in narcotrafficking (Wickham-Crowley 2015). While there is variation in the formality of the institutions and the extent of civilian involvement, chaos during conflict is seldom the norm—there are spaces where the state has little or no authority, but they are rarely ungoverned.

1.3 Why wartime institutions matter: long-term legacies

Understanding wartime institutional change—which results from the interactions between armed groups and civilians in wartime—is important because it will profoundly shape the legacies of violent conflicts, including how economies recover, societies and polities rebuild, and peace is sustained. Recent research on conflict dynamics has significantly advanced understanding of the economic, social, and political consequences of violent conflict to local populations, especially with respect to exposure to different forms and intensity of violence (Verwimp et al. 2019). Violence exposure affects individual and household economic preferences (Voors et al. 2012), collective action (Bauer et al. 2016), and political attitudes (Balcels 2012). It deteriorates, sometimes in irreversible ways, human capital accumulation (Justino et al. 2014), deters investment (Besley and Mueller 2012), and introduces enormous uncertainty (Shesterinina 2021). Many of these effects last over many years after the conflict ends (Balcells 2012; Justino et al. 2014; Lupu and Peisakhin 2017), leading to a perpetuation of vicious cycles of insecurity and poverty (Justino 2009) and the possible reignition of violence (Kalyvas 2006).

This literature has, for the most part, focused on the legacies of violence, leaving unexplored other dynamics of conflicts beyond the exercise of violence. The literature on 'rebel governance' has emerged to address this gap, by documenting the emergence of political order in conflict areas. This has led to important advances discussed above in our understanding of the realities of conflict zones. As a result, we are also starting to better understand the legacies of wars beyond violence exposure, such as the legacies of social transformation during conflicts (Wood 2008; Bateson 2017), of wartime civilian resistance and mobilization (Huang 2016; Osorio et al. 2019), of ex-combatants' and civilian exposure to armed group governance (Ibáñez et al. 2019; Justino and Stojetz 2019; Arjona et al. 2022; Grasse et al. 2022), of wartime public goods provision in secessionist conflicts (Stewart 2018), and of wartime social control (Bakke and Rickard in this volume, Chapter 5).

Taken together, this incipient literature[6]—upon which this volume builds—shows that, during violent conflicts, armed actors do not just rely on coercive means to exert control but establish different forms of interactions with civilians that give rise to political order and new institutions, with important ramifications for state building after war. The structures and relationships created during wartime tend to remain intact even if violent interaction has come to an end. This allows myriad armed actors to retain control over certain populations and continue to implement governance strategies. Even after rebel victory, the state's ability to regain the monopoly over violence depends on whether local elites had been co-opted or replaced to rule during conflict (Gassier in this volume, Chapter 8). If armed groups sought a strategy of co-optation, this reinforced the status and bargaining power of local faction leaders and power brokers. This makes it more difficult for the post-conflict governments to enforce their rule after war, specifically if the interests and priorities of local elites diverge from those of the post-war government. Conversely, when armed groups have displaced local power structures during war and replaced them with their own strong organizations, post-war governments led by those actors are better positioned to mitigate the risks of fragmentation and re-armament, impose their rule, and even conduct successful elections (Daly in this volume, Chapter 10). But, even in the absence of diverging interests, wartime networks may prove to be an obstacle to the consolidation of peace as these governance systems were made to sustain warfare and benefit those involved. This is well illustrated in the case of South Sudan, where networks stretch across the rebel army, traditional leaders, and powerbrokers and are extremely resilient but also prone to corruption and patronage. Even after rebel victory, these networks are not easily replaced through external efforts to create 'good governance' (Day in this volume, Chapter 11).

[6] Many of the studies cited in this section were generated as part of UNU-WIDER's project on the 'Institutional Legacies of Violent Conflict', which gave rise to this volume.

If post-war governments are not run by rebels, governments appear to be inclined to retake control by focusing efforts to increase state capacity in previously insurgent-controlled territory or areas where state authority was contested as to prevent future threats to state authority (Kreiman 2022). While such efforts can be fruitful, wartime networks are surprisingly resilient and can allow non-state armed groups to remain active post-conflict. Particularly, wartime economic networks that established ties with the civilian population help rebels to sustain the capacity to conduct attacks against the state even if the state's coercive state capacity and investment increased (Saavedra-Lux 2024). During peacetime, these networks often remain an important driver of economic activity and secure local livelihoods. This generates necessary civilian support for the respective insurgent group to successfully contest the state's claim on the monopoly on violence. These non-state governance structures become exceptionally relevant in times of crisis as armed groups harness external shocks, such as the COVID-19 pandemic or climatic shocks, as an opportunity to retake or consolidate control (O'Neil 2023). Their ability to successfully offer extensive responses to crisis is, however, shaped by their capacity to deliver assistance or enforce certain rules (Furlan in this volume, Chapter 9).

The state also establishes policies and power structures during warfare. Forms of state repression, in particular, have lasting consequences for state building and political and economic development. While experiences of state repression can increase political participation in the long run once democratic rule had been established (Balcells and Villamil 2023), structures of repression often survive the end of conflict—regardless of countries (partially) transitioning to democracy. Governments have been shown to rely on these structures and employ state-affiliated irregular militias or co-opted local elites to repress protests (Berman et al. 2023; Krakowski and Schaub 2022; Bakke and Rickard in this volume, Chapter 5). These trends hamper the path to peace and sustainable development as they prevent the emergence or consolidation of legitimate state authority.

These works provide a narrative about the importance of the nature and form of wartime institutional transformation as a key determinant of political and developmental trajectories post-conflict. State-building and development interventions need to be guided by an understanding of the viability and continued presence of wartime institutional structures after war, as well as their long-term legacies. There are several reasons for why this is the case. First, the interactions between armed groups and civilians that gave rise to such wartime institutions determine how different population groups may perceive the legitimacy of different forms of authority and different political actors and, eventually, how these relationships may shape the nature of the state in the post-conflict period (Bates et al. 2002; Snyder and Bhavnani 2005; Justino et al. 2013). Second, wartime institutions are central to understanding the potential for an armed group to transition from a military organization involved in armed fighting to an organization with the capacity to provide public goods and services, collect revenue in legitimate and accountable ways, represent and manage competing interests across different social groups, maintain peace, and uphold the rule of law in the aftermath of the conflict (Mampilly 2011). Third, political orders and their governance structures built during conflicts tend to persist well after the end of fighting (Mann 1986; Tilly 1992; Kalyvas et al. 2008), shaping the strength and level of authority exercised by new governments and opposition groups in the post-conflict period and the level of support they can expect from local populations and different social groups they may or may not represent (Justino 2009; Mampilly 2011). As a result, a better understanding of the institutional legacies of war allows us to better identify challenges and opportunities to support more autonomous and sustainable forms of state-building.

1.4 Roadmap to the volume

The book is organized into four parts. The first part starts with a chapter by Patricia Justino, which lays out the theoretical framework underpinning this volume's approach to understanding legacies of wartime institutional change. The chapter explores how governance structures established by armed groups during civil wars influence post-war state-building trajectories. It develops the concept of wartime governance—how armed groups rule civilians and control territory—and discusses how wartime governance creates bureaucratic and institutional capacity that shapes post-conflict political outcomes. The chapter identifies six possible post-war state-building trajectories: stable democracy, weak democracy, stable autocracy, fragmented rule, contested autocracy, and durable disorder. These outcomes depend on two key factors: the institutional capacity of wartime governance (how well-armed groups govern territory), and the nature of wartime social contracts (how civilians interact with armed rulers). Strong governance with inclusive civilian engagement increases the likelihood of stable democracy, while fragmented or violent governance often leads to autocracy or disorder. The chapter bridges micro-level studies on armed group behaviour with macro-level theories of state formation to highlight how wartime institutions—such as taxation, security provision, and public service delivery—persist in post-conflict states, shaping their stability and political regime.

This conceptual framework is complemented by the next chapter, where Margarita Gáfaro, Ana María Ibáñez, and Patricia Justino model theoretically the strategies used by armed groups to control (when possible) local civic organizations, and the responses of civilian populations to the actions of armed groups. The chapter focuses on how pre-existing local institutional capacities shape the governance strategies of armed groups during conflict. Communities with robust institutional frameworks often force armed groups to adopt less coercive and more collaborative strategies. Conversely, in areas where institutions were weak prior to the conflict, armed groups exert dominance and coercion. These dynamics are not limited to the wartime period; they shape post-conflict civic engagement. For instance, communities with strong pre-war institutions often recover faster, with higher levels of political participation and organizational resilience. Alongside the first chapter, this study sets the stage for the volume by illustrating the foundational role of local institutions in determining how conflicts evolve and their long-term legacies.

Studying the long-term legacies of wartime institutional change matters because it allows us to further understand core concepts of political science, sociology, and economics, including how wars shape state capacity, the monopoly of violence, the social contract, and the political and economic behaviour of citizens. Part II of this volume shows how variation in several of these outcomes can be traced to wartime institutional change. Building on the Colombian context, Chapter 4, by Abbey Steele and Michael Weintraub, explores how rebel and paramilitary governance structures influence both formal and informal political participation post-conflict. Contrary to assumptions that armed group control undermines political engagement, the authors find that areas governed by both anti-state rebels and pro-state paramilitaries experienced higher levels of political participation. Governance structures that provided public goods and services, even when coercive, left institutional footprints that fostered mobilization. These findings challenge conventional wisdom and suggest that governance during conflict can create pathways for civic engagement and political reorganization in post-conflict societies. In Chapter 5, Kristin M. Bakke and Kit Rickard turn to the interaction between institutional change and norm formation in wartime and examine the enduring impact of anti-informing norms developed during the Troubles in Northern Ireland. These norms, created to discourage collaboration with state forces, have had long-term effects on community trust and social cohesion. Even decades after the conflict, these norms perpetuate divisions within communities, hindering collective action and effective governance. The analysis underscores how social dynamics during conflict create lasting institutional and cultural legacies that shape post-conflict governance. Roxana Gutiérrez-Romero follows up on this finding in Chapter 6 in the case of criminal governance in Mexico. The chapter investigates how criminal organizations adapt to state interventions, co-opting local and national institutions to maintain their power. Unlike traditional rebel groups, drug trafficking organizations embed themselves within state governance structures, diversifying their operations to survive. These adaptations not only perpetuate cycles of violence but also reshape governance, leaving legacies of corruption and instability. The findings highlight how governance dynamics during conflict are not limited to state–rebel interactions but also extend to criminal organizations, with implications for governance and political stability.

Taken together, the chapters in part II of the volume demonstrate the importance of accounting for the interaction between armed actors and civilians during the conflict to uncover both the positive and negative legacies of wartime institutional change. While the Colombian case identifies where the effects of wartime institutional change could be harnessed to build state capacity and promote economic development, the Northern Ireland and Mexico cases emphasize that wartime institutional change can undermine state–society relations long after conflict nominally ends.

Part III consists of four chapters on post-war state-building in the shadow of important wartime institutional legacies. These chapters complement Part II by focussing on how (former) armed actors in post-war society can harness the legacies of wartime institutional change to improve prospects for peace and stability, but equally, to pursue conflict-era objectives, which risk plunging the state back into war. In Chapter 7, Shelley Liu concentrates on the specific case of Zimbabwe. This chapter examines how Zimbabwe's ZANU-PF leveraged wartime civilian networks to consolidate power after independence. These networks, initially built during the liberation war, were repurposed to maintain political dominance in the post-war period. The chapter explores how these networks evolved in response to internal and external pressures, including party fragmentation and international sanctions. While these networks provided stability, they also entrenched authoritarian rule and corruption, illustrating the dual-edged nature of wartime legacies. Marine Gassier extends similar arguments to Ethiopia and Somalia in Chapter 8. Ethiopia's relatively stable transition is attributed to inclusive wartime governance that engaged local actors, fostering broad-based support for the post-conflict regime. In contrast, Somalia's exclusionary and fragmented wartime governance perpetuated instability, undermining state-building efforts. The chapter demonstrates how the inclusion or exclusion of local power structures during conflict affects post-conflict stability and the risk of conflict recurrence.

These long-term institutional legacies shape how political actors respond to shocks in the post-war period. In Chapter 9, Marta Furlan situates rebel governance in the context of the COVID-19 pandemic. During that period, armed groups all over the world, from insurgent groups in the Sahel to criminal gangs in Rio's favelas, played important roles in providing protective equipment and convincing people to vaccinate. This chapter focuses on the variation of responses of three armed groups across the Middle East: the Hayat Tahir al-Sham in Syria, the Houthis in Yemen, and Hamas in Gaza. The analysis highlights how governance capacity, financial resources, and strategic goals influenced their responses. For instance, armed groups with strong governance systems and access to resources were better able to manage public health crises, using these efforts to bolster their legitimacy. The chapter underscores the adaptability of wartime governance structures to external shocks and their implications for post-conflict state-building.

In Chapter 10, Sarah Zukerman Daly turns to the consequences of wartime institutional change for political outcomes. The chapter explores the long-term political consequences of ethnic wars, focusing on how wartime governance and alliances shape voter behaviour in post-conflict societies. The findings reveal that political alignments are influenced by the nature of wartime alliances and the outcomes of ethnic conflicts. Former rebel groups that provided governance during the war are often able to secure political power in the post-conflict period, leveraging their wartime legitimacy. The chapter highlights the interplay between wartime governance and post-war political dynamics.

The volume argues throughout that understanding the institutional legacies of war is important because it allows us to better identify the challenges and opportunities for external and internal interventions that improve the prospects for peace, stability, and economic development in the post-war period. In Chapter 11, Adam Day circles back to a key question asked in Part I of this volume: why have recent efforts of state-building in post-conflict countries failed to produce positive results? The chapter critiques international state-building efforts, arguing that their failures often stem from a disregard for pre-existing governance ecosystems. By imposing externally driven models, these interventions undermine local governance structures and fail to address the complexities of post-conflict societies. The chapter advocates for an 'ecosystems approach' that recognizes the complexities of local governance arrangements and builds on existing structures rather than attempting to replace them. Cyrus Samii provides, in Chapter 12, a more positive view of external state-building interventions in post-conflict settings, with a focus on community-driven reconstruction (CDR) programmes. Drawing on extensive empirical evidence from multiple post-conflict settings, the chapter demonstrates how CDR programmes empower local actors by placing decision-making power in the hands of communities. These programmes build on existing local governance structures, fostering resilience, accountability, and adaptability. Unlike top-down approaches, which often fail to address the unique needs of local populations, CDR programmes leverage the trust and knowledge of community members to implement sustainable development initiatives. The chapter also highlights the challenges of scaling up CDR programmes, particularly in contexts where state institutions remain weak or resistant to decentralization. Despite these challenges, the evidence presented strongly supports the conclusion that localized, participatory approaches may be more effective in fostering long-term stability and governance capacity.

The final chapter brings together the findings highlighted in Parts II, III, and IV to discuss the prospects for state-building in post-conflict countries. The various book chapters show clearly, and from different angles, the institutional complexity of post-war environments, where legacies of wartime institutional change can be used by different actors to both promote and undermine peace, stability, and economic development. Understanding these complex processes may provide, in turn, entry points for state-building and governance options in post-conflict countries, especially with respect to the institutional capacity of governments formed in the immediate post-conflict period and the strength of social contracts formed between ruling elites and ordinary citizens emerging from wars.

References

Acemoglu, D., S. Johnson, and J. Robinson (2001). 'The Colonial Origins of Comparative Development: An Empirical Investigation'. *American Economic Review*, 91: 1369–1401. https://doi.org/10.1257/aer.91.5.1369

Acemoglu, D., and J. Robinson (2006). *Economic Origins of Dictatorship and Democracy*. Cambridge: Cambridge University Press. https://doi.org/10.1017/CBO9780511510809

Acemoglu, D., and J. Robinson (2012). *Why Nations Fail: The Origins of Power, Prosperity and Poverty*. New York: Crown.

Acemoglu, D., J. Robinson, and R. Santos (2013). 'The Monopoly of Violence: Evidence from Colombia'. *Journal of the European Economic Association*, 11(S1): 5–44. https://doi.org/10.1111/j.1542-4774.2012.01099.x

Ahmad, A. (2015). 'The Security Bazaar: Business Interests and Islamist Power in Civil War Somalia'. *International Security* 39(3): 89–117. https://doi.org/10.1162/ISEC_a_00187

Arias, E. (2017). *Criminal Enterprises and Governance in Latin America and the Caribbean*. New York: Cambridge University Press. https://doi.org/10.1017/9781316650073

Arjona, A. (2016). *Rebelocracy: Social Order in the Colombian Civil War*. Cambridge: Cambridge University Press. https://doi.org/10.1017/9781316421925

Arjona, A., N. Kasfir, and Z. Mampilly (eds). (2015). *Rebel Governance in Civil War*. Cambridge: Cambridge University Press. https://doi.org/10.1017/CBO9781316182468

Arjona, A., A. M. Ibáñez, J. C. Cárdenas, and P. Justino (2022). 'The Legacies of Wartime Institutions on Citizens' Preferences for the Rule of Law'. forthcoming.

Bakke, K. M., K. G. Cunningham, and L. J. Seymour (2012). 'A Plague of Initials: Fragmentation, Cohesion, and Infighting in Civil Wars'. *Perspectives on Politics*, 10(2): 265–283. https://doi.org/10.1017/S1537592712000667

Balcels, L. (2012). 'The Consequences of Victimization on Political Identities: Evidence from Spain'. *Politics & Society*, 40(3): 311–347.

Balcells, L., and F. Villamil (2023). 'The Legacies of Authoritarian Repression on Civil Society'. WIDER Working Paper 1/2023. https://doi.org/10.35188/UNU-WIDER/2023/309-3

Bandiera, A., L. Dinarte-Diaz, J. M. Jimenez, S. Rozo, and M. Sviatschi (2022). 'Rebel Governance and Development: The Persistent Effects of Guerrillas in El Salvador'. Policy Research Working Paper 10222. World Bank, Washington, DC. https://doi.org/10.1596/1813-9450-10222

Bates, R., A. Grief, and S. Singh (2002). 'Organizing Violence'. *Journal of Conflict Resolution*, 46(5): 599–628. https://doi.org/10.1177/002200202236166

Bates, R. (1983). *Essays on the Political Economy of Rural Africa*. Cambridge: Cambridge University Press. https://doi.org/10.1017/CBO9780511558740

Bates, R. (2008a). 'Probing the Sources of Political Order'. In S. N. Kalyvas, I. Shapiro, I. and T. Masoud, T. (eds), *Order, Conflict, and Violence*. Cambridge: Cambridge University Press.

Bates, R. (2008b). *When Things Fell Apart: State Failure in Late-Century Africa.* Cambridge: Cambridge University Press. https://doi.org/10.1017/CBO9780511790713

Bateson, R. (2017). 'The Socialization of Civilians and Militia Members: Evidence from Guatemala'. *Journal of Peace Research*, 54(5): 634–647. https://doi.org/10.1177/0022343317721812

Bauer, M., C. Blattman, J. Chytilová, J. Henrich, E. Miguel, and T. Mitts (2016). 'Can War Foster Cooperation?' *Journal of Economic Perspectives*, 30(3): 249–274. https://doi.org/10.1257/jep.30.3.249

Berman, C., K. Clarke, and R. Majed (2023). 'Theorizing Revolution in Democracies: Evidence from the 2019 Uprisings in Lebanon and Iraq'. WIDER Working Paper 51/2023. https://doi.org/10.35188/UNU-WIDER/2023/359-8

Besley, T., and H. Mueller (2012). 'Estimating the Peace Dividend: The Impact of Violence on House Prices in Northern Ireland'. *American Economic Review*, 102(2): 810–833. https://doi.org/10.1257/aer.102.2.810

Besley, T. and T. Persson (2011). *Pillars of Prosperity: The Political Economics of Development Clusters.* Princeton, NJ: Princeton University Press. https://doi.org/10.2307/j.ctt1d2dmcd

Besley, T., and T. Persson (2009). 'The Origins of State Capacity: Property Rights, Taxation and Politics'. *American Economic Review*, 99(4): 1218–1244. https://doi.org/10.1257/aer.99.4.1218

Blattman, C., G. Duncan, B. Lessing, and S. Tobón (2025). 'Gang Rule: Understanding and Countering Criminal Governance'. *The Review of Economic Studies*, 92(3): 1497–1531. https://doi.org/10.1093/restud/rdae079

Blattman, C., and L. Ralston (2015). 'Generating Employment in Poor and Fragile States: Evidence from Labor Market and Entrepreneurship Programs'. https://doi.org/10.2139/ssrn.2622220

Boix, C. (2003). *Democracy and Redistribution.* Cambridge: Cambridge University Press. https://doi.org/10.1017/CBO9780511804960

Boone, C. (2003). *Political Topographies of the African State. Territorial Authority and Institutional Choice.* New York: Cambridge University Press. https://doi.org/10.1017/CBO9780511615597

Coggins, B. (2015). 'Rebel Diplomacy: Theorizing Violent Non-State Actors' Strategic Use of Talk'. In A. Arjona, N. Kasfir, and Z. Mampilly (eds), *Rebel Governance in Civil War.* Cambridge: Cambridge University Press. https://doi.org/10.1017/CBO9781316182468.005

Cramer, C. (2007). *Violence in Developing Countries: War, Memory, Progress.* Bloomington, IN: Indiana University Press. https://doi.org/10.2979/4802.0

Crost, B., J. Felter, and P. Johnston (2014). 'Aid Under Fire: Development Projects and Civil Conflict'. *American Economic Review*, 104(6): 1833–1856. https://doi.org/10.1257/aer.104.6.1833

Cunningham, K. G., R. Huang, and K. M. Sawyer (2021). 'Voting for Militants: Rebel Elections in Civil War'. *Journal of Conflict Resolution*, 65(1): 81–107. https://doi.org/10.1177/0022002720937750

Daly, S. Z. (2016). *Organized Violence After Civil War: The Geography of Recruitment in Latin America.* Cambridge: Cambridge University Press. https://doi.org/10.1017/CBO9781316412350

Duyvesteyn, I. (2017). 'Rebels & Legitimacy: An Introduction'. *Small Wars & Insurgencies*, 28(4–5): 669–685. https://doi.org/10.1080/09592318.2017.1322337

Florea, A. (2020). 'Rebel Governance in De Facto States'. *European Journal of International Relations*, 26(4): 1004–1031. https://doi.org/10.1177/1354066120919481

Fukuyama, F. (2004). *State-Building: Governance and World Order in the 21st Century*. Ithaca, NY: Cornell University Press.

Fukuyama, F. (2012). *The Origins of Political Order: From Pre-Human Times to the French Revolution*. London: Profile Books.

Gáfaro, M., A. M. Ibáñez, and P. Justino (2014). 'Local Institutions and Armed Group Presence in Colombia'. HiCN Working Paper 178, The Households in Conflict Network. Brighton: IDS. https://doi.org/10.35648/20.500.12413/11781/ii162

Gambetta, D. (1996). *The Sicilian Mafia: The Business of Private Protection*. Cambridge, MA: Harvard University Press.

Gisselquist, R., P. Justino, and A. Vaccaro (2025). *Fragile Aid: Development Cooperation in Weak States and Conflict Contexts*. Oxford: Oxford University Press. https://doi.org/10.1093/oso/9780198960287.001.0001

Grasse, D., R. Sexton, and A. Wright (2022). 'The Logic and Impacts of Rebel Public Services Provision: Evidence from the Taliban Courts in Afghanistan'. Working paper. https://static1.squarespace.com/static/53fc9eb3e4b01bd08e4a58ba/t/620ec3db76a6ae5a0576bb34/1645134812784/Afghanistan-Courts-GSW.pdf (retrieved on 28 March 2022).

Helmke, G., and S. Levitsky (2004). 'Informal Institutions and Comparative Politics: A Research Agenda'. *Perspectives on Politics*, 2(4): 726–740. https://doi.org/10.1017/S1537592704040472

Herbst, J. (2000). *States and Power in Africa. Comparative Lessons in Authority and Control*. Princeton, NJ: Princeton University Press.

Hoeffler, A., and P. Justino (2023). 'Aid and Fragile States'. In R. Desai, S. Devarajan, and J. Tobin (eds), *Elgar Handbook of Aid and Development*. Oxford: Oxford University Press. https://doi.org/10.4337/9781800886810.00020

Huang, R. (2016). *The Wartime Origins of Democratization: Civil War, Rebel Governance, and Political Regimes*. Cambridge: Cambridge University Press. https://doi.org/10.1017/CBO9781316711323

Ibáñez, A. M., J. Arteaga, J. C. Cárdenas, A. Arjona, and P. Justino (2019). 'The Effects of Wartime Institutions on Households' Ability to Cope with Shocks: Evidence for Colombia'. WIDER Working Paper 84/2019. Helsinki: UNU-WIDER. https://doi.org/10.35188/UNU-WIDER/2019/720-0

Jentzsch, C., S. Kalyvas, and L. Schubiger (2015). 'Militias in Civil Wars'. *Journal of Conflict Resolution*, 59(5): 755–769. https://doi.org/10.1177/0022002715576753

Justino, P., and W. Stojetz (2019). 'Civic Legacies of Wartime Governance'. WIDER Working Paper 104/2019. Helsinki: UNU-WIDER. https://doi.org/10.35188/UNU-WIDER/2019/740-8

Justino, P., M. Leone, and P. Salardi (2014). 'Short-and Long-Term Impact of Violence on Education: The Case of Timor Leste'. *The World Bank Economic Review*, 28(2): 320–353. https://doi.org/10.1093/wber/lht007

Justino, P., T. Brück, and P., Verwimp (eds), (2013). *A Micro-Level Perspective on the Dynamics of Conflict, Violence and Development*. Oxford: Oxford University Press. https://doi.org/10.1093/acprof:oso/9780199664597.001.0001

Justino, P. (2009). 'Poverty and Violent Conflict: A Micro-Level Perspective on the Causes and Duration of Warfare'. *Journal of Peace Research*, 46(3): 315–333. https://doi.org/10.1177/0022343309102655

Justino, P. (2012). 'War and Poverty'. In M. Garfinkel and S. Skaperdas (eds), *Handbook of the Economics of Peace and Conflict*, pp. 676–705. Oxford: Oxford University Press. https://doi.org/10.1093/oxfordhb/9780195392777.013.0027

Justino, P. (2019). 'Governance Interventions in Conflict-Affected Countries'. *Journal of Development Studies*, 55(7): 1364–1378. https://doi.org/10.1080/00220388.2018.1487053

Kalyvas, S., I. Shapiro, and T. Masoud (2008). *Order, Conflict, and Violence*. Cambridge: Cambridge University Press. https://doi.org/10.1017/CBO9780511755903

Kalyvas, S. N. (2006). *The Logic of Violence in Civil War*. Cambridge: Cambridge University Press. https://doi.org/10.1017/CBO9780511818462

Kasfir, N. (2015). 'Rebel Governance – Constructing a Field of Inquiry: Definitions, Scope, Patterns, Order, Causes. In A. Arjona, N. Kasfir, and Z. Mampilly (eds), *Rebel Governance in Civil War*, pp. 21–46. New York: Cambridge University Press. https://doi.org/10.1017/CBO9781316182468.002

Kasfir, N. (2005). 'Guerrillas and Civilian Participation: The National Resistance Army in Uganda, 1981–86'. *The Journal of Modern African Studies*, 43(2): 271–296. https://doi.org/10.1017/S0022278X05000832

Krakowski, K., and M. Schaub (2022). 'Elite Murder and Popular Resistance: Evidence from Post-World War II Poland'. WIDER Working Paper 148/2022. Helsinki: UNU-WIDER. https://doi.org/10.35188/UNU-WIDER/2022/281-2

Kreiman, G. (2022). 'The Incursion of Leviathan: Wartime Territorial Control and Post-Conflict State Capacity, Evidence from Perú'. WIDER Working Paper 136/2022. Helsinki: UNU-WIDER. https://doi.org/10.35188/UNU-WIDER/2022/269-0

Lessing, B. (2021). 'Conceptualizing Criminal Governance'. *Perspectives on Politics*, 19(3): 854–873. https://doi.org/10.1017/S1537592720001243

Leeson, P. (2009). *The Invisible Hook: The Hidden Economics of Pirates*. Princeton, NJ: Princeton University Press.

Leeson, P. (2007). 'An-arrgh-chy: The Law and Economics of Pirate Organization'. *Journal of Political Economy*, 115(6): 1049–1094.

Levi, M. (1988). *Of Rule and Revenue*. Berkeley, CA: University of California Press.

Loyle, C. E. (2021). 'Rebel Justice During Armed Conflict'. *Journal of Conflict Resolution*, 65(1): 108–134. https://doi.org/10.1177/0022002720939299

Lupu, N., and L. Peisakhin (2017). 'The Legacy of Political Violence Across Generations'. *American Journal of Political Science*, 61(4): 836–851. https://doi.org/10.1111/ajps.12327

Mampilly, Z. (2011). *Rebel Rulers*. Ithaca, NY: Cornell University Press.

Mampilly, Z. (2021). 'Rebel Taxation. Between Moral and Market Economy'. In N. Di Cosmo, D. Fassin, and C. Pinaud (eds), *Rebel Economies: Warlords, Insurgents, Humanitarians*. Lanham, MD: Rowman & Littlefield.

Mampilly, Z., and M. A. Stewart (2021). 'A Typology of Rebel Political Institutional Arrangements'. *Journal of Conflict Resolution*, 65(1): 15–45. https://doi.org/10.1177/0022002720935642

Mann, M. (1986). *The Sources of Social Power: A History of Power from the Beginning to A. D. 1760*. New York: Cambridge University Press. https://doi.org/10.1017/CBO9780511570896

McColl, R. W. (1969). 'The Insurgent State: Territorial Bases of Revolution'. *Annals of the Association of American Geographers*, 59(4): 613–631. https://doi.org/10.1111/j.1467-8306.1969.tb01803.x

Menkhaus, K. (2007). 'Governance without Government in Somalia: Spoilers, State Building, and the Politics of Coping'. *International Security*, 31(3): 74–106. https://doi.org/10.1162/isec.2007.31.3.74

North, D., J. Wallis, and B. Weingast (2009). *Violence and Social Orders: A Conceptual Framework for Interpreting Recorded Human History*. New York: Cambridge University Press. https://doi.org/10.1017/CBO9780511575839

OECD (2022). *States of Fragility 2022*. Paris: OECD Publishing. https://doi.org/10.1787/c7fedf5e-en

Olson, M. (1993). 'Dictatorship, Democracy and Development'. *American Political Science Review*, 87(3): 567–576. https://doi.org/10.2307/2938736

O'Neil, S. (2023). 'Armed Group Opportunism in the Face of Recent Crises: COVID-19 and Climate Change'. WIDER Working Paper 58/2023. Helsinki: UNU-WIDER. https://doi.org/10.35188/UNU-WIDER/2023/366-6

Osorio, J., L. Schubiger, and M. Weintraub (2019). 'Legacies of Resistance: Mobilization Against Organized Crime in Mexico'. *Comparative Political Studies*, 54(9): 1565–1596. https://doi.org/10.1177/0010414021989761

Podder, S. (2014). 'State Building and the Non-State: Debating Key Dilemmas'. *Third World Quarterly*, 35(9): 1615–1635. https://doi.org/10.1080/01436597.2014.970864

Podder, S. (2017). 'Understanding the Legitimacy of Armed Groups: A Relational Perspective'. *Small Wars & Insurgencies*, 28(4–5): 686–708. https://doi.org/10.1080/09592318.2017.1322333

Pool, D. (2001). *From Guerrillas to Government: The Eritrean People's Liberation Front*. Athens, OH: Ohio University Press.

Raeymaekers, T. (2010). 'Protection for Sale? War and the Transformation of Regulation on the Congo-Ugandan Border'. *Development and Change*, 41(4): 563–587. https://doi.org/10.1111/j.1467-7660.2010.01655.x

Raeymaekers, T., K. Menkhaus, and K. Vlassenroot (2008). 'State and Non-State Regulation in African protracted Crises: Governance without Government?' *Afrika Focus*, 21(2): 7–21. https://doi.org/10.21825/af.v21i2.5045

Reno, W. (1999). *Warlord Politics and African States*. Boulder, CO: Lynne Rienner Publishers. https://doi.org/10.1515/9781685853822

Reno, W. (2002). 'The Politics of Insurgency in Collapsing States'. *Development and Change*, 33(5): 837–858. https://doi.org/10.1111/1467-7660.t01-1-00251

Reno, W. (2015). 'Predatory Rebellions and Governance: The National Patriotic Front of Liberia, 1989'. In A. Arjona, N. Kasfir, and Z. Mampilly (eds), *Rebel Governance in Civil War*. Cambridge: Cambridge University Press. https://doi.org/10.1017/CBO9781316182468.013

Revkin, M. R., and A. Ahram (2020). 'Perspectives on the Rebel Social Contract: Exit, Voice, and Loyalty in the Islamic State in Iraq and Syria'. *World Development*, 132: 104981. https://doi.org/10.1016/j.worlddev.2020.104981

Revkin, M. (2021). 'Competitive Governance and Displacement Decisions Under Rebel Rule: Evidence from the Islamic State in Iraq'. *Journal of Conflict Resolution*, 65(1): 46–80. https://doi.org/10.1177/0022002720951864

Risse, T. (2011). *Governance Without a State? Policies and Politics in Areas of Limited Statehood*. New York: Columbia University Press.

Rolla, P., and P. Justino (2022). 'The Social Consequences of Organized Crime'. WIDER Working Paper 106/2022. Helsinki: UNU-WIDER. https://doi.org/10.35188/UNU-WIDER/2022/240-9

Sanchez de la Sierra, R. (2020). 'On the Origins of States: Stationary Bandits and Taxation in Eastern Congo'. *Journal of Political Economy*, 128(1): 32–74. https://doi.org/10.1086/703989

Saavedra-Lux, L. (2024). 'Quid Pro Quo: How the Wartime Economy Shapes the Violent Contestation of the State after War'. WIDER Working Paper 45/2024. Helsinki: UNU-WIDER. https://doi.org/10.35188/UNU-WIDER/2024/507-3

Snyder, R., and R. Bhavnani (2005). 'Diamonds, Blood and Taxes: A Revenue-Centered Framework for Explaining Political Order'. *Journal of Conflict Resolution*, 49(4): 563–597. https://doi.org/10.1177/0022002705277796

Shesterinina, A. (2021). *Mobilizing in Uncertainty: Collective Identities and War in Abkhazia*. Ithaca, NY: Cornell University Press. https://doi.org/10.1080/17449057.2022.2063477

Sivakumaran, S. (2009). 'Courts of Armed Opposition Groups: Fair Trials or Summary Justice?' *Journal of International Criminal Justice*, 7(3): 489–513. https://doi.org/10.1093/jicj/mqp039

Skaperdas, S., and Syropoulos, C. (1997). 'The Crisis of the Tax State'. In Gianluca Fiorentini and Sam Peltzman (eds), *The Economics of Organized Crime*. New York: Cambridge University Press.

Skarbek, D. (2014). *The Social Order of the Underworld: How Prison Gangs Govern the American Penal System*. Oxford: Oxford University Press. https://doi.org/10.1093/acprof:oso/9780199328499.001.0001

Skarbek, D. (2011). 'Governance and Prison Gangs'. *American Political Science Review*, 105: 702–716. https://doi.org/10.1017/S0003055411000335

Staniland, P. (2012). 'States, Insurgents, and Wartime Political Orders'. *Perspectives on Politics*, 10(2): 243–264. https://doi.org/10.1017/S1537592712000655

Staniland, P. (2021). *Ordering Violence: Explaining Armed Group-State Relations from Conflict to Cooperation*. Ithaca, NY: Cornell University Press. https://doi.org/10.7591/cornell/9781501761102.001.0001

Stewart, M. (2018). 'Civil War as State-Making: Strategic Governance in Civil War'. *International Organization*, 72(1): 205–226. https://doi.org/10.1017/S0020818317000418

Stokke, K. (2006). 'Building the Tamil Eelam State: Emerging State Institutions and Forms of Governance in LTTE-Controlled Areas in Sri Lanka'. *Third World Quarterly*, 27(6): 1021–1040. https://doi.org/10.1080/01436590600850434

Strand, H., and H. Hegre (2021). 'Trends in Armed Conflict, 1946–2020'. *Conflict Trends*, 3. Oslo: PRIO. https://www.prio.org/publications/12756.

Tilly, C. (1992). *Coercion, Capital and European States, AD 990-1992*. Oxford: Blackwell.

Tilly, C. (1975). 'Reflections on the History of European State Making'. In C. Tilly (ed.) *The Formation of National States in Western Europe*. Princeton, NJ: Princeton University Press.

UNHCR (2024). *Mid-Year Trends 2024*. United Nations High Commissioner for Refugees. https://www.unhcr.org/mid-year-trends-report-2024.

Venkatesh, S. (2008). *Gang Leader for a Day: A Rogue Sociologist Takes to the Streets*. London: Penguin Press.

Venkatesh, S. (2009). *Off the Books: The Underground Economy of the Urban Poor*. Cambridge, MA: Harvard University Press. https://doi.org/10.2307/j.ctv260712v

Verwimp, P., P. Justino, and T. Brück (2019). 'The Microeconomics of Violent Conflict'. *Journal of Development Economics*, 141: 102297. https://doi.org/10.1016/j.jdeveco.2018.10.005

Voors, M., E. E. M. Nillesen, P. Verwimp, E. H. Bulte, R. Lensink, and D. P. Van Soest (2012). 'Violent Conflict and Behaviour: A Field Experiment in Burundi'. *American Economic Review*, 102(2): 941–964. https://doi.org/10.1257/aer.102.2.941

Wickham-Crowley, T. P. (1992). *Guerrillas and Revolution in Latin America*. Princeton, NJ: Princeton University Press. https://doi.org/10.1515/9780691190204

Wickham-Crowley, T. P. (2015). 'Del Gobierno de Abajo al Gobierno de Arriba... and Back: Transitions to and from Rebel Governance in Latin America, 1956–1990'. In A. Arjona, N. Kasfir, and Z. Mampilly (eds), *Rebel Governance in Civil War*, pp. 47–73. Cambridge: Cambridge University Press. https://doi.org/10.1017/CBO9781316182468.003

Wimmer, A., and B. Min (2006). 'From Empire to Nation-State: Explaining Wars in the Modern World, 1816–2001'. *American Sociological Review*, 71(6): 867–897. https://doi.org/10.1177/000312240607100601

Wimmer, A. (2018). *Nation Building: Why Some Countries Come Together While Others Fall Apart*. Princeton, NJ: Princeton University Press. https://doi.org/10.1515/9781400888894

Wood, E. J. (2008). 'The Social Processes of Civil War: The Wartime Transformation of Social Networks'. *Annual Review of Political Science*, 11: 539–561. https://doi.org/10.1146/annurev.polisci.8.082103.104832

World Bank (2020). *Fragility and Conflict: On the Front Lines of the Fight Against Poverty*. Washington, DC: The World Bank.

World Bank (2024). *Poverty, Prosperity, and the Planet Report: Pathways Out of the Polycrisis*. Washington, DC: The World Bank.

World Food Programme (2022). *Global Report on Food Crises – 2022*. Rome: World Food Programme. https://www.wfp.org/publications/global-report-food-crises-2022.

Young, M. C. (1994). *The African Colonial State in Comparative Perspective*. New Haven, CT: Yale University Press.

2
Wartime governance and state-building trajectories in post-conflict societies

Patricia Justino

I do know that there is no greater necessity for men who live in communities than that they be governed, self-governed if possible, well-governed if they are fortunate, but in any event, governed.

(Walter Lippmann, quoted in Huntington 1968: 2)

2.1 Introduction

Considerable resources are committed annually to state-building interventions in post-conflict countries.[1] These interventions tend to have mixed results:[2] countries emerging from civil wars remain at risk of violent conflict for long periods of time, while others transition to more stable political regimes.[3] This is not a new phenomenon. In 1968, Samuel Huntington wrote about the 'modernizing countries of Asia, Africa, and Latin America', characterized by 'increasing ethnic and class conflict, recurring rioting and mob violence, [and] frequent military coups d'état' (1968: 2–3). Some of the countries Huntington mentioned, such as Turkey, Thailand, Vietnam, Indonesia and South Korea, went on to establish politically stable states. Some evolved into stable democracies and some into

[1] An earlier and very preliminary version of this chapter entitled 'Implications of Wartime Institutions for State-Building in Post-Conflict Countries' was circulated as a background paper for the World Development 2017 and funded by the World Bank. The author is grateful to comments from Edouard Al-Dahdah, Luis Filipe Lopez Calva, and participants at workshops and seminars where various parts of this chapter were presented at the University of Göttingen, Maryland University, University of Cambridge, University of Toronto, University of Navarra, Institute of Development Studies, UNU-WIDER, World Bank, Swedish International Development Cooperation Agency (SIDA), Centre for Policy Research (UNU-CPR), Finnish Institute of International Affairs (FIIA), UK Foreign, Commonwealth Development Office (FCDO), Households in Conflict Network annual workshops at the University of Gottingen (2021) and the Paris School of Economics (2019), and the 2021 American Political Science Association annual meeting.

[2] See reviews in King and Samii (2014) and Justino (2018, 2019).

[3] According to a widely cited study, six out of ten post-conflict countries relapse into conflict during the ten years after the end of the initial conflict (Collier et al. 2008).

Patricia Justino, *Wartime governance and state-building trajectories in post-conflict societies*. In: *Institutional Legacies of Violent Conflict*. Edited by: Patricia Justino, Oxford University Press. © United Nations University World Institute for Development Economics Research (UNU-WIDER) (2026). DOI: 10.1093/9780197904077.003.0002

resilient autocracies. Many others—such as Syria, Sudan, Iraq, Central African Republic, the Democratic Republic of the Congo (DRC), Pakistan, and most of Central America—continued to endure cycles of violence and conflict. Why? What explains this variation in the political trajectories of war-torn countries in the aftermath of violent conflict?

Several theories have been put forward to account for why post-conflict countries remain in or relapse into internal armed conflict. These include, among others, unequal and ineffectual patterns of economic and institutional development pursued in the post-conflict period (Walter 2004; Hegre and Nygård 2015), the deepening of ethnic antagonism in the aftermath of civil wars (Fearon 2004; Cederman et al. 2013), the type of peace agreement and post-war political settlement that is negotiated (Toft 2010; Driscoll 2015), whether civil wars end due to a military victory or a negotiated settlement (Fortna 2004; Toft 2010), and the effects of state and peacebuilding interventions by the international community (Autesserre 2010; Berdal and Zaum 2012; Doyle and Sambanis 2000, 2006; Fortna 2008; Paris 2004; Walter 2004). Some studies have also analysed how and why some countries are able to maintain peace and establish the seeds of democracy in the aftermath of civil wars, whereas others become stable autocracies. For instance, Wantchekon and Neeman (2002) and Wantchekon (2004) argue that the end of civil wars may result in democracy when citizens prefer a system that protects them against expropriation and their productive actions under democracy generate benefits for the warring elites.

Many of the existing theories have in common a focus on how conflicts end: the ways in which internal armed conflicts terminate and the interventions implemented at that point explain how post-conflict contexts evolve. All the factors above undoubtedly shape how (some) states are (re)built after civil wars.[4] However, the prevailing focus of existing theories of post-war state-building on how civil wars end has one important limitation: intentionally or not, these theories implicitly assume that state institutions in post-conflict countries are built in a blank slate. But, in reality, civil wars generate new institutions as armed actors, civilians, and myriad state and non-state actors and organizations interact, fight, compete, and negotiate (Arjona 2016; Justino 2012, 2013). These institutions are likely to shape post-conflict outcomes. To date, we have, however, limited knowledge about how institutional change in wartime shapes post-war societies and states. There are a few notable exceptions: Wood (2008) and Huang (2016) trace post-war democratization processes to wartime social mobilization of civilians, whereas Levitsky and Way (2022) discuss how governments born out of violent

[4] For instance, military victories may facilitate more effective post-war governance and trajectories towards either democratic or autocratic stability (Licklider 1995, Fortna 2004, Doyle and Sambanis 2006, Toft 2010). These effects may, in turn, be shaped by the actions of external actors and aid flows (Hoeffler and Justino 2024, Huang and Sullivan 2021).

revolutionary movements tend to result in durable authoritarian regimes. But what shapes these diverse trajectories in state-building formation?

This chapter explores an important form of wartime institutional transformation that may explain multiple state-building pathways—the forms of governance exercised by armed groups in wartime. The core argument is that civil wars generate within themselves bureaucratic and institutional capacity—through how armed groups govern territories and civilians within them—that shape how and what states are built in the post-war period.

Wartime governance is a widespread phenomenon. Although areas affected by internal armed conflicts tend to be portrayed in the media and public discourse as anarchic, disordered, and ungoverned, observations from the field show that this is not always (if ever) the case (Kalyvas et al. 2008; Mampilly 2011; Justino 2013; Arjona 2016; Ibáñez et al. 2024). These are areas where state authority is contested resulting in the fragmentation—but not necessarily the collapse—of social and political order. In such settings, different political (armed) actors, from rebel groups to existing government actors, adopt myriad governing strategies in their attempts to control territories and populations within them, including local security provision, building infrastructure, setting up systems of administration, mediating access to, and in some cases providing, public goods, imposing revenue-extracting systems, and regulating markets.

Some of these governing strategies result in stable forms of political order amidst the wider conflict. For instance, the *Fuerzas Armadas Revolucionarias de Colombia* (FARC) controlled and ruled over almost forty per cent of the Colombian territory at the height of the civil war, financing the construction of roads, provided medical services, and offered a range of justice and conflict adjudication processes (Arjona 2016; Ibáñez et al. 2024). Hezbollah provide hospitals, health centres, schools, orphanages, supermarkets, and gas stations, among other services that reach large numbers of communities in southern Lebanon (Flanigan 2008; Heger and Jung 2017). Justice and local conflict resolution provision was also at the heart of the expansion of Naxal rebels in India (Kennedy 2014). The Liberation Tigers of Tamil Eelam (LTTE) in Sri Lanka established a fully functioning parallel state in northern and eastern parts Sri Lanka, providing education and health care, sometimes in collaboration with the government (Stokke 2006; Flanigan 2008; Mampilly 2011). Other armed groups exercising 'state like' functions include the Taliban across large swathes of Afghanistan during the Karzai and Ghani regimes, and the Islamic State (IS) in Syria, Iraq, and surrounding areas, among many others. In these contexts, insurgent groups become the *de facto* ruling authority in the territories they control (Weinstein 2007; Mampilly 2011; Arjona et al. 2015; Arjona 2016; Justino and Stojetz 2018; Sanchez de la Sierra 2020). Outside rebel-controlled areas, existing governments continue to operate, albeit in (non-contested) parts of the national territory, often alongside pro-government militia, paramilitary groups, and other pro-government armed actors.

The main aim of this chapter is to build across and synthesize several literature strands to propose a theoretical framework outlining the pathways through which these forms of wartime governance may affect trajectories of state-building in the aftermath of civil wars and the factors shaping those pathways. To do so, the chapter bridges across two literatures that have largely remained disconnected: a growing literature at the micro level on the organization of violence, the emergence of political orders in conflict contexts, and the local dynamics of armed conflicts, and an older macro-level literature on state formation and nation-building. The chapter maps out and defines the characteristics of six possible state-building trajectories: stable democracy, weak democracy, stable autocracy, fragmented authoritarian rule, contested autocracy, and durable disorder. These different state-building trajectories are determined by two dimensions of wartime governance: how armed groups gain the ability to govern (i.e., how they build their *wartime institutional capacity*) and how they govern (i.e., the characteristics of *wartime social contracts* between armed groups and civilians). The level of wartime institutional capacity of armed groups shapes the probability of the group pursuing either a more democratic or more autocratic trajectory towards state-building in the post-war period. The type of wartime social contracts (whether collective, restrictive, or violent) determines the stability and cohesion of each state-building trajectory. State-building in the post-conflict period refers, in turn, to the development and implementation of institutions and arrangements to protect property rights, offer public goods and services, and manage social conflicts and external and internal threats, shocks, and volatility in ways that avoid violence and emanate from and are consolidated by legitimate public authority (North et al. 2009).

This chapter uses these theoretical arguments to better understand the long-term institutional legacies of wartime governance for state-building. Brief discussions of specific case studies are used to illustrate the arguments, rather than provide causal empirical evidence, and hopefully to pave the way for future more systematic data collection and empirical analysis on the long-term legacies of wartime governance and other wartime institutional dynamics.

2.2 Wartime governance: concepts and definitions

Wartime governance is defined as the way in which different armed political actors control, protect, and rule over a given territory during a civil war, regulate markets and communities, establish alliances or compete over power and resources, and manage civilian relations across different social groups. These actors include insurgent groups but also the state military and other groups associated to either the rebels or the state military, including militias, paramilitary groups, military juntas, warlords, and vigilante groups. Wartime governance is formed of two dimensions. The first is the level of institutional capacity of the group or, in other words, its 'infrastructural power' (Mann 1988), which is dependent on the strength and length of territorial control. The second is how armed groups interact with and govern civilians or, in other words, the shape of 'wartime social contracts'. Wartime refers to the period of fighting during civil wars,[5] whereas post-conflict or post-war refers to the period after a peace agreement or outright victory by one of the parties in the conflict—recognizing that the end of a conflict may not be necessarily associated with the end of violence. Wartime governance differs from peacetime governance in that policies and practices to rule obey military objectives and involve the use or threat of violence by those that rule.

Forms of wartime governance. Wartime governance can take on different forms ranging from the ad-hoc participation of armed groups in civilian affairs (Arjona 2016; Kaplan 2017; Ibáñez et al. 2024), the capture or co-option of local institutions for strategic purposes (Gáfaro et al. 2014; Gassier 2021; Ch et al. 2018; Raleigh and De Bruijne 2017), symbiotic relations between rebel and state groups (Staniland 2014, 2021), and being the *de facto* ruler (Mampilly 2011; Arjona 2016). Wartime governance can be exercised in specific territories by one group alone, under duopoly arrangements or through a variety of contracts, bargains, and alliances between several groups, including the state. When territory control is absolute, it is likely that one group will oversee the most important decisions with respect to governing that territory. In many cases, the state may be almost completely absent and its institutions (when they exist in the first place) are replaced, captured, or co-opted by the ruling armed group (Arjona 2016; Gáfaro et al., Chapter 3 of this volume; Gassier 2021; Mampilly and Stewart 2021). The incumbent government and its military may at times become a competing authority in some of these contexts (Kalyvas 2006), or rule indirectly via paramilitary groups, militia, and other armed political actors under its support (Marchais et al. 2018; Muchlinski 2021). Often, insurgent groups, state actors, paramilitaries, militia, and other groups interact, forge alliances, negotiate, and bargain—in addition to fighting to control territories and populations (Staniland 2021).

Wartime governance can involve a range of activities, including the regulation and operation of markets, the support of livelihoods, the provision of health and education services, the regulation of disputes and criminal activity, and the dispensation of justice. The activities exercised under wartime governance vary substantially across conflicts, groups, and even across time in the same conflict and within the same group. Typically, groups who exercise political authority in defined territories provide some public goods and services, ranging from security to health care, education, and local dispute resolution. Some limit the provision

[5] The theoretical framework proposed in the chapter applies largely to civil wars. External or internationalized wars are outside the scope of the chapter as wartime institutional dynamics in these settings will be largely shaped by external actors and geopolitical considerations not included in the framework. Throughout the chapter, the terms 'civil war' and 'internal armed conflict' are used interchangeably.

of goods and services to individuals and households in areas under their control to facilitate recruitment and information (Berman and Laitin 2008; Lewis 2020), whereas others provide public goods more widely to support state-building objectives (Heger and Jung 2017), particularly related to secessionism (Stewart 2018). Adjudication of disputes and conflict resolution are usually prominent components of wartime governance (Arjona 2016; Heger and Jung 2017; Loyle and Binningsbø 2018; Loyle 2020; Ibáñez et al. 2024). Some studies have also documented the participation of armed groups in elections in wartime, both in direct ways by standing as a political party or putting forward their own candidates, or indirectly through backing, bribing, co-opting, and intimidating local and national politicians (Dunning 2011; Matanock 2017; Matanock and Staniland 2018).

Aims of wartime governance. Armed groups exercise forms of governance with different (often simultaneous) purposes, including the need to raise revenue to finance wartime strategies (Reno 2011), as a form of increasing their institutional reach (Weinstein 2007), as a way of exercising political authority, controlling territory, and excluding rivals (Metelits 2009), as a symbol of legitimacy, power, ideology, and identity between the armed group and civilians (Mampilly 2011), and to facilitate internal organization dynamics (Weinstein 2007) and gather information and intelligence (Kalyvas 2006; Berman et al. 2011; Lewis 2020). All these purposes serve, in broad terms, to provide military advantage to a group over other competing groups. Like other incipient forms of nation states across history (Wimmer 2018), the ability to provide security and public goods broadly signals, in turn, the capacity of the armed group to rule and manage state functions in the post-conflict period (Kalyvas 2006; Mampilly 2011).

Determinants of wartime governance. The forms, strength, and duration of wartime governance are shaped by several factors including the strength and nature of pre-existing institutions in the communities where armed groups arrive (Arjona 2016), the levels of competition between different political actors (Kalyvas 2006), the time horizons of different factions and how long the group expects to stay in a certain area (Arjona 2016; Sanchez de la Sierra 2020), and the sources of external financing available to the group (Snyder and Bhavnani 2005; Weinstein 2007; Huang and Sullivan 2021). The decisions of armed groups to establish order and exercise governance are shaped not only by competition between key political actors and external relations but also by the choices, perceptions, behaviour, and motivations of civilians living in conflict areas (Nordstrom 1997; Justino 2013; Balcells and Justino 2014; Verwimp et al. 2019; Revkin 2020b) and their ability to coordinate and exercise collective action (Arjona 2016; Kaplan 2017; Rubin 2019; Breslawski 2021). Forms of interaction by civilians include establishing strategic social, economic, and political alliances with armed actors, adapting livelihoods to existing economic opportunities (which sometimes may be illegal), and negotiating with a variety of local powerful actors that often change as the conflict evolves (Wood 2008; Verwimp et al. 2019). Through these interactions, some communities support armed groups by voluntarily providing food, shelter, labour, recruits, and information. Other communities live under forced control by armed groups. Others resist armed groups openly and sometimes successfully (Arjona 2016; Kaplan 2017; Krause 2018).

Wartime, peacetime and criminal governance. Four key characteristics distinguish wartime governance from governance in peaceful times and from other forms of governance, such as those exercised by organized crime groups. First, wartime governance, independently of which group exercises it, operates under the threat of violence. Violence can be overt with armed groups engaging in combat with each other and against civilians, or covert whereby there is a clear understanding that armed groups will resort to violence when opposed. Violence can also be targeted towards specific individuals, groups, and physical targets, or be indiscriminate (Kalyvas 2006). In either case, violence is a key element to how wartime forms of governance are exercised and political orders are maintained in war zones. Second, wartime governance is often provided by actors and bureaucracies without recognized sovereignty (Kasfir 2015), alongside or in contestation of the incumbent government, itself a party of the conflict. But incumbent governments also adapt their forms of governance during wartime to respond to military aims, including outsourcing their governance functions to other armed actors, such as paramilitary groups and pro-government militias and vigilante groups. These state and proto-state forms of rule are part of this chapter's definition of wartime governance.[6] Third, wartime governance is provided by groups with political goals of 'competitive state-building' (Kalyvas 2006) and who hold territory (Kasfir 2015) during the war and where, for at least some time, the group exercises the monopoly of violence. This distinguishes the concept of wartime governance from governance exercised by criminal groups who typically operate under 'duopolies of violence' where the final authority lies with the state (Skaperdas and Syropoulos 1997; Lessing 2020). Fourth, wartime governance emerges to create political order. Political order facilitates revenue mobilization and, like criminal groups, armed groups involved in governance do so to extract resources. Many regulate illegal markets and extort financial contributions. But armed groups also tax populations in kind or financially in exchange for exercising state-like functions,[7] and to facilitate local recruitment (Daly 2016), improve the ability of armed groups to gather valuable information and loyalty (Kalyvas 2006; Berman et al. 2011; Lewis 2020), exclude rivals (Metelits 2009), and to strengthen authority, secure territory, and ensure civilian loyalty (Hoffmann at al. 2016;

[6] This extends the definition wartime governance beyond rebel governance, although a few studies of rebel governance have also taken into consideration the ruling roles of groups and organizations associated to the state such as paramilitary groups and militias (Arjona 2016).

[7] Criminal organizations may also tax directly those in the areas under their control (like small business) but this is usually not their main source of financing as amounts tend to be small and generally limited to businesses and not households (Lessing 2020).

Revkin 2020a; Mampilly and Thakur 2024). In other words, armed groups govern as a way of exercising and/or ensuring political authority and signalling to the population their ability to function as a state and gain legitimacy in their eyes. The ability and willingness to govern, in turn, distinguishes 'state-like' armed groups from criminal bands or other extractive organizations. To do so, groups co-opt or build new institutions, including legislative bodies (such as parliaments), judicial and legal systems, health and education systems, civilian councils, and sometimes diplomatic wings (Arjona 2016; Loyle 2020; Mampilly 2011; Mampilly and Stewart 2021; Staniland 2021). These wartime governance institutions have several important functions: they establish boundaries to the power exercised by local political (armed) authorities vis-à-vis local communities, shape shifting economic, social and political alliances, and frame the norms, behaviour and beliefs of local populations. Some wartime governing institutions are temporary due to shifts in power between different competing actors in given localities. Others endure into the post-conflict period. The next sections analyse how these forms of governance and the institutions that emerge from them shape post-war state-building trajectories.

2.3 From wartime governance to post-war state-building: a typology of trajectories

Much progress has been made over the last decade to understand the emergence of wartime social and political orders (Kalyvas 2006; Kalyvas et al. 2008; Mampilly 2011; Staniland 2014; Arjona et al. 2015; Arjona 2016; Mampilly and Stewart 2021). Much less is known about their consequences and long-term implications. Throughout history, several armed groups have transitioned into political parties, with varied degrees of success, including FRELIMO and RENAMO in Mozambique, the MPLA in Angola, the FMNL in El Salvador, the Maoists in Nepal, Hezbollah in Lebanon, Hamas in Palestine, the SPLM/A in South Sudan, and FRETILIN in East Timor (Manning 1998, de Zeeuw 2008; McDonough 2008; Ishiyama and Batta 2011; Pearce 2012). In some cases, like South Sudan, the DRC, Somalia, Yemen, and Afghanistan, among others, armed fighting and instability hindered processes of state-building and inclusive governance in the aftermath of civil wars. Other winning armed groups in countries like Angola, Mozambique, Rwanda, Uganda and Zimbabwe, for instance, have been able to form stronger state institutions and stable post-war governance systems under authoritarian regimes (Levitsky and Way 2012).[8] Autocracies that emerged from revolutionary

[8] Several scholars have observed that rebel victories—as was the case with almost all the examples above—lead to the establishment of long-lasting authoritarian regimes, especially among those groups that built strong cohesion during armed struggle (McDonough 2008, Levitsky and Way 2012). According to Toft (2010), between one-fifth and one-third of civil wars have resulted in rebel victories.

movements appear more stable than others (Levitsky and Way 2022). In a smaller set of countries, more democratic processes have prevailed (Huang 2016). These examples illustrate the wide variation in state-building processes experienced in countries moving from civil wars in modern times and their implications for the political regimes adopted by post-conflict countries. It is, however, unclear what explains this variation in how former military groups become the state and follow particular forms of political organization. This chapter focuses on understanding the extent to which governance structures set in place during civil wars, and their resulting institutions may establish the foundations for different trajectories of state-building and political regimes in the aftermath of civil wars. Several stylized facts from broad literatures on conflict dynamics and state-building allow the definition of six broad types of state-building and political regime trajectories in countries emerging from civil wars: from conflict to stable or weak democracy, from conflict to stable or contested autocracy, and from conflict to fragmented rule or durable disorder.

2.3.1 From conflict to (stable or weak) democracy

The first trajectory is that towards democratic states. Power-sharing arrangements, managed elite bargains, democratic elections, and decentralization processes are all mechanisms used by states and the international community to support the establishment of democratic trajectories in post-conflict countries. The overarching motivation of these interventions is to replicate the liberal democracy trajectories followed by the USA in the aftermath of the American Civil War, or the war-rooted historical emergence of nation-states in Western European, and consolidated after WWII (Tilly 1992), towards strong, accountable, inclusive, and legitimate democracies, where programmatic politics dominate over patronage or identity politics. States following this trajectory are ruled by governments that 'choose to employ force to protect rather than prey upon their citizens and when citizens choose to disarm, leaving it to the government to protect their lives and property' (Bates 2008: 22).

As shown in a large literature, democratic trajectories are largely dependent on how the new post-war governments credibly commit to non-predatory behaviour, the upholding of the social contract and govern over the whole country (Olken 2007). Overall, trajectories towards democracy may be more likely when winning elites at the end of war choose to adopt institutional reforms based on inclusive political competition (Acemoglu and Robinson 2006; North et al. 2009; Slater 2010). This requires the establishment of institutions that enable governments to accommodate multiple redistributive demands and, at the same time, constrain the power of ruling elites. There are few examples of countries in the post-Cold War period that moved from armed conflict to stable and consolidated democracies. There is, however, evidence that some post-war countries followed political trajectories that resulted in improved democratic outcomes. Wantchekon and Neeman (2002), Wantchekon (2004), and Huang (2016) discuss how between one-third and half of states that emerged from civil wars after 1950 improved their democratic scores in the Polity scale. These include Northern Ireland, Peru, Uganda, Nepal, Mozambique and Guatemala, among others. All these states include elements of democratic governance and democratic institutional-building process, albeit with large variation in the strength of such institutions.[9]

One defining characteristic of a democracy is the enactment of regular free and fair elections. There is some evidence that the establishment of early elections and processes of democratization in the immediate aftermath of civil wars may improve citizens' trust in the new government and support legitimacy and accountability of new state institutions (Hegre et al. 2001). Many of these efforts at early elections are, however, fraught with renewed violence fomented by ethnic, economic, and political competition, persistent mistrust between opposing groups and poorly organized institutional transitions, such as demobilization, disarmament and reintegration programs and power sharing agreements (Collier and Vicente 2012; Dowd et al. 2020; Durant and Weintraub 2014). Elections may also take place in wartime, as discussed in the previous section. In these cases, there is not much evidence that elections may lead onto peace agreements and better democratic outcomes in the post-war period. Instead, 'rather than being a solution to conflict, electoral strategies are often another means of waging war' (Matanock and Staniland 2018: 712) (see also Matanock 2017).

The overall evidence for the emergence of *stable democracies* in modern post-conflict countries that follow the European and Northern American models is thus not encouraging. There is nonetheless evidence that some post-conflict states have made progress in establishing *weak democracies* whereby inclusivity principles dominate but are not expanded widely across the country. This is achieved by governments in incipient democracies expanding political concessions, providing public goods to the overall population (instead of limiting those to patronage systems) and allowing competitive, multiparty democratic elections.

2.3.2 From conflict to (stable or contested) autocracy

The second type of trajectory results in states often characterized by strong but extractive, predatory, and authoritarian forms of governance. These countries tend to be effective in avoiding the re-ignition of open internal armed conflict and (sometimes) promoting economic development, at times over long periods

[9] One paradoxical example is Colombia, where internal armed conflict between the state, guerilla groups, and paramilitary groups has co-existed since the aftermath of *La Violencia* in the 1950s with fairly robust democratic institutions.

of time, if the power hold of elites and their alliances remain strong (Slater 2010; Levitsky and Way 2022). Historically, this has been the most common case of transition from war to state-building in modern civil wars. Liu (2023) identifies 11 countries in Africa which moved from war to peace since 1945 with some degree of success: Angola, Burundi, Chad, Côte d'Ivoire, Eritrea, Ethiopia, Mozambique, Namibia, Rwanda, Uganda, and Zimbabwe. In most of these countries, the same ruling party has been in power since the end of the war, and opposition parties, when allowed to exist, have limited pathways towards winning elections and presiding over a peaceful transfer of power. In Mozambique, the opposition party and former rebel group RENAMO has built at times convincing electoral opposition to the ruling FRELIMO (Manning 1998), whereas in Ethiopia, the power of the Tigray People's Liberation Front (TPLF) was reduced in recent years, giving rise to a new violence outbreaks.[10] In Uganda, the Museveni government built a decentralized structure of local councils, elected in every village, which made decisions about village-level issues and managed local conflict resolution mechanisms. These were moulded on the 'resistance councils' built by Museveni's National Resistance Movement during Uganda's 1981–1986 civil war to facilitate recruitment and ensure the supply of food and information to the NRM (Kasfir 1998). Similar forms of local organization were also established by the Eritrean People's Liberation Front (EPLF), which formed the basis for Eritrea's post-war government (Pool 2001), and the ZANU movement in Zimbabwe (Levitsky and Way 2012; Liu 2023). However, democratic institutions in these countries are at most incipient and volatile and, in many cases, some of the seemingly participatory structures set in place have largely served to strengthen the power of authoritarian rulers (Kasfir 1998; Liu 2023). Nonetheless, strong and far-reaching governance institutions and local forms of decentralized politics have supported economic development and stability in many of these countries (Levitsky and Way 2022).

Although some of above-mentioned countries have built strong and stable governments, many with far-reaching and efficient bureaucracies and state institutions, the threat of violence remains high and credible, as illustrated by recent events in Burundi, Ethiopia, Mozambique, Uganda, and Zimbabwe. This threat remains because myriad actors outside central elite bargains may be able to make use of their networks to exercise violence to access or maintain power. In fact, the threat of violence is in itself an integral part of the way in which governance takes place in countries under this state-building trajectory (North et al. 2009). Levels of violence and instability, however, vary considerably across this set of countries, and across time, depending on the hold elites have over political power, what bargains and arrangements are set in place between the centre and the periphery, and

[10] For earlier accounts of the TPLF, see Tadesse and Young (2003). For an analysis of recent events, see https://foreignpolicy.com/2020/12/18/the-war-in-tigray-is-a-fight-over-ethiopias-past-and-future/.

how internal and external factors may affect the power balance between these different groups (Christia 2012; Slater 2010; Justino 2018; Levitsky and Way 2022). Given the permanent potential for contestation, countries in this second type of state-building trajectory invest largely in security and tend to have a strong military and police apparatus. There is also typically large variation in the reach of state institutions reflecting the regime's military priorities, internal elite networks and interests, the involvement of outside interests, and how different factions are aligned with external interests and networks. The basic institutions of governance, such as rule of law, public goods provision, and security, are generally restricted to certain population groups and based on systems of monetized patronage (e.g., based on ethnic or kinship relations). This is particularly the case when building institutional capacity to govern in wartime and post-war goes hand in hand with instrumentalizing social identities as a way of mobilizing populations to support the war effort and the political ambitions of ruling elites in the post-war period (Horowitz 2003).

Under these systems of patronage, local powerful actors establish symbiotic relationships with the parties that control the central state by delivering votes and economic advantages (Acemoglu et al. 2006). State-citizen relations are based on these strategic alliances with the central regime and state capacity is often (but not always) limited to certain regions and enclaves. When this is the case, there is the widespread use of hybrid political orders in periphery regions to maintain stability (such as forms of indirect rule) (Marchais et al. 2018). In some cases, such alliances will result in *stable autocracies* with low levels of violence and based on mutually beneficial elite bargains and shared values and ideology (Slater 2010; Levitsky and Way 2012), many resulting from violent revolutionary movements that generated cohesion and loyalty among the ruling elites, a strong coercive apparatus, and the destruction of alternative opposition (Levitsky and Way 2022). In other cases, unstable elite bargains whereby powerful political actors antagonize, resist, and contest existing political settlements may result in *contested autocracies*, where the threat of violence remains high, elite alliances are shaped by the balance of military strength between factions, and governance outside the centre is maintained by repression (McDonough 2008; Slater 2010).

2.3.3 From conflict to fragmented rule or durable disorder

The third type of state-building trajectory results in states characterized by fragmented forms of political authority that remain in place after the formal end of violent conflicts, resulting in vicious cycles of state weakness and violent conflict. Examples include, among others, South Sudan after secession from Sudan, Somalia, Yemen, and the DRC. In some of these cases, violent conflict may or may not be overt, but violence is prevalent and central authority is largely absent. It is, however, important to note that political fragmentation may not equate anarchy and disorder. In many of these countries, elements of relatively stable forms of governance may emerge at the sub-national level, as reported, for instance, in Sanchez de la Sierra (2020) and Raeymaekers (2010) in parts of eastern DRC. This happens when local armed groups are able to establish local monopolies of violence or stable elite alliances for a certain period of time and in specific areas (see Titeca and de Herdt 2011; Kalyvas 2006; Mampilly 2011; Titeca 2011). Overall, despite occasional pockets of (short-lived) stability, these trajectories of state-building are largely characterized by what Staniland (2021) defined as 'armed politics', where political processes are dominated by fragmented elite power and hostility between different players, and where relations with citizens are weak, volatile, and based on shifting alliances. I define these contexts as situations of *fragmented rule*, where ruling authorities have weak institutional capacity, high levels of informality dominate economic and political relations, and violence is used as a way of groups establishing power, albeit for limited periods of time (Richards 2005; Boyle 2014). Relations between ruling groups and civilians are generally one-way without the emergence of any discernible form of stable social contract. Relations with international order are also fragmented and fraught, tap into external illicit financial and arms flows, and are highly vulnerable to external shocks and interventions. Examples include warlord enclaves of governance (e.g. Somalia), which are fairly stable across time but do not amount to a centralized state—and may even work actively to discourage the emergence of such centralized state. However, some of these sub-national polities have been able to provide the basic functions of the state, albeit at local levels, as described in Menkhaus (2007). Fragmented rule can easily slip into situations of *durable disorder*, where no discernable durable form of governance emerges, alliances quickly dissolve, and indiscriminate violence against civilians is common. These are Richards (2005)'s 'no peace no war' situations where political authority is left in the hands of bandits with no infrastructural power or durable authority over territories or populations.

2.4 Wartime governance, state-building, and political regime trajectories

What explains the transition of conflict-affected countries into the different forms of state-building outlined above? The literature so far has largely focused on explaining state formation in conflict-affected settings as a product of interventions implemented at the end of a conflict. The different constellations of power sharing, contestation, and alliance described above are not, however, solely the product of a peace agreement or a negotiated settlement at the end of the war. They have their roots in the conflict itself. This section theorizes the conditions under which wartime governance shapes the emergence of each state-building trajectory. I focus on two key conditions. The first condition—wartime institutional capacity—is defined as the ability of armed groups to govern, which is shaped by two key variables: territorial control and institutional reach. This condition allows us to define two types of armed groups. The first group type is characterized by strong wartime institutional capacity. These are groups able to maintain dominance in competition with other groups by ensuring sovereignty and large institutional reach over substantial parts of the national territory and during significant time periods in wartime. The second type includes groups that operate during wartime under fragmented territorial control, with limited institutional scope or reach. Wartime institutional capacity will, in turn, shape the ability of the winning armed group in the post-war period to establish a reasonably stable trajectory towards state-building. The exact form of such (in)stability is determined by the second condition—wartime social contracts. These are defined by how armed groups in delimited territories rule over civilians in wartime. Wartime social contracts can take three distinct forms: collective, restrictive, and violent.

Before proceeding, it is important to note that the theoretical framework discussed below does not explain how wartime governance may lead to regimes of democracy, autocracy, or fragmentation, but rather how variation in wartime governance may place a specific country on a *trajectory* towards each of these outcomes. This distinction has empirical implications: studying trajectories means estimating the probability of a given combination of wartime institutional capacity and wartime social contracts to generate changes in scores of democracy or autocracy in the post-war period across time rather than focusing on estimating outcomes in terms of absolute values in a given year. Three other caveats are also in order. First, it is to note that countries that start on one trajectory will not necessarily stay in it, and elements of each type can also co-exit at certain times. For instance, as discussed, countries under fragmented authority include many intractable conflicts, but, in many cases, pockets of stability emerge in what appears to be a messy and violent context. How this happens will depend on how state and non-state actors (and sometimes civilians) interact, negotiate, and agree on power sharing arrangements that are beneficial for each depending on own strategic objectives. Second, the democratic trajectories experienced in Western Europe and Northern America happened over centuries of breakouts of war, bargaining, and negotiation. Throughout most of their existence, these states followed trajectories of autocracy (North et al. 2009). It is thus unreasonable to expect that countries emerging from recent civil wars establish immediate trajectories towards democracy in the short term. The task of this section is to identify what wartime dynamics may make these trajectories *more or less likely* in the longer term. Third, the trajectories outline above should not be judged on being better or worse than each other. For instance, it is not immediately obvious that countries characterized by fragmented authority may necessarily be worse off than those under autocratic

Table 2.1 Typology of post-war state-building and regime trajectories

Wartime social contracts	Wartime institutional capacity	
	Strong	**Limited**
Collective	Stable democracy	Weak democracy
Restrictive	Stable autocracy	Fragmented rule
Violent	Contested autocracy	Durable disorder

regimes since citizens may prefer the multitude of orders that characterize fragmented authority trajectories than living under a strong repressive state. The main takeaway point is that state-building is a complex and chaotic process. No liner pathways are possible, and compromise and flexibility are needed. However, to better understand what these compromises might entail, it is useful to identify what factors or combination of factors may shape these ideal stylized pathways. These are summarized in Table 2.1 and discussed in more detail below.

2.4.1 Wartime institutional capacity

The strength of the wartime institutional capacity of a given armed group is determined in relation to other groups who may contend for access to *de facto* local power (including the incumbent government and armed groups associated to it) and may vary depending on various internal factors, such as the level of cohesion of the ruling group, and interests resulting from changes in local economic, social, and political environments. Civil wars have been portrayed as a form of competitive state-building (Kalyvas 2006; Staniland 2012). These forms of competition vary in form, ranging from antagonism and fighting to alliances and degrees of cooperation (Christia 2012; Staniland 2017). Competition between groups is often about how much of the national territory can be controlled and ruled effectively by a given armed group and for how long. The duration of territorial control shapes, in turn, the institutional capacity of the group. Institutional capacity is not possible without some degree of territorial control because territorial control defines a specific constituency, allows for some measure of stability and certainty, and facilitates access to resources. Kalyvas (2006) distinguishes between segmented control and fragmented control. Institutional capacity may be built under fragmented territorial control (Albert 2022), but is unlikely to last long or amount to sustainable forms of wartime governance. Armed groups are more likely to build institutional capacity under forms of segmented control, where armed groups hold sovereignty over portions of the national territory for meaningful lengths of time, thereby adjusting their time horizons accordingly (Arjona 2016). The expectation is that strong power holdings over territories where control continues over the long term may result in stronger wartime institutional capacity, which in turn may eventually ensure that the winning faction is able to transition into organizations with higher capacity to provide public goods and maintain stability in the aftermath of the conflict—either as a democracy or an autocracy.

The institutions build by armed groups to interact with and govern civilians in wartime take a variety of forms, including elective legislative bodies, local governing authorities, judicial and legal systems, structures for the provision of public goods and services, civilian councils, and diplomatic wings (Mampilly 2011; Arjona 2016; Loyle 2020). The form and operation of these institutions is shaped by both the ideological positions of the armed group and their wartime strategic objectives (Gassier 2021; Mampilly and Stewart 2020), with large variation across armed groups and across the duration of the conflict. For instance, the ZANU in Zimbabwe and FRELIMO in Mozambique had cells in almost every village at the end of their wars (Levitsky and Way 2012), whereas others like SPLM in South Sudan built impressive structures on paper which never took off in reality (Mampilly and Stewart 2020).

Armed groups build their institutional and organizational capacity in a number of ways. Some groups replace the state in the control of prior government institutions and keep them for similar purposes, such as revenue extraction, social service provision, and security provision, among others. For instance, Gáfaro et al. (2014, Chapter 3 of this volume) report how the FARC and paramilitary groups in Colombia appropriated local decision-making institutions for their own purposes, including influence over local elections and local political processes. Other groups operate institutions and organizations that run in parallel with the state apparatus and sometimes in collusion with (or at least without being contested by) state organizations. Secession movements are likely to favour this strategy to signal their ability to govern in the post-war period. That was the case of the LTTE in Sri Lanka, which ran an almost parallel state in some areas under their control (Mampilly 2011), sometimes alongside the state in some areas (Stokke 2006). The madrassas education system set in place by the Taliban and associated groups in Afghanistan and Pakistan was run in parallel to the state education system (Hanif et al. 2019), whilst the Karzai government in Afghanistan incorporated several warlords and their fiefdoms within government structures with varied levels of success (Mukhopadhyay 2014).

The incumbent government may exercise governance functions via implicit or explicit indirect rule implemented by quasi-government armed actors, such as paramilitary groups and militia, or in 'live-and-let-live' forms of engagement with insurgent groups. One example is the influential 'people's courts' rolled out by Maoist groups in Nepal (Loyle 2020). Similar justice-dispensing activities also took place areas under Naxalite influence in India where armed groups provide justice and public goods to rural populations where the state rarely exercised (or showed much interest in exercising) their functions (Kennedy 2014). The Taliban also operated an equally widespread system of courts and dispute adjudication (Giustozzi 2014).

In other cases, armed groups destroy previous institutions and bureaucracies and implement new ones that better serve their wartime objectives. Examples include the villagization programs implemented in Zimbabwe (and Mozambique), whereby civilians were moved to new communities under the full control of rebel groups (Liu 2023), and how the Tigray People's Liberation Front in Ethiopia transformed local power structures in ways that allowed military gains and civilian support across the territory (Gassier 2021). These new institutional settings generally rely on social networks and groups that supported the formation of the armed group initially and carry on strengthening their position during wartime through systems of patronage and kinship or other social and ideological ties. These ties are important to access reliable information, ensure protection from competing factions or sub-factions that may emerge as the conflict develops, and strengthen loyalty within the organization.

Choices made by armed groups with respect to institution-building in wartime have implications for state-building trajectories in the post-conflict period. Mann (1986) describes how state formation is shaped by the ability of certain rulers to effectively govern populations and regions through 'infrastructural powers'. These 'infrastructural powers' are different across the various institutional choices outlined above. Successful attempts at exercising state functions in areas under territorial control during wartime—either by appropriating existing state institutions or building alternative ones—may well lead into state-building trajectories towards some form of democracy or more stable forms of autocracy. Stokke (2006: 1024) shows that in the case of the LTTE before their military destruction by government troops, 'the LTTE state institutions contain authoritarian and technocratic tendencies that provide a certain administrative efficiency but prevent democratic accountability. On the other hand, they are also rooted in and committed to the rights, welfare and development of the Tamil community on whose behalf the militant and political struggles have been waged. [...] this combination of autonomy and embeddedness gives the emerging state a substantial degree of administrative capacity. This may provide an institutional basis for a more democratic relationship between the LTTE and citizens in northeast Sri Lanka'.

These complex trajectories towards inclusive democracies and/or strong autocracies are likely to hinge on sound institutional capacity and wide reach across the territories ruled in wartime, whereby public goods and services are provided to the entire population under rule in an effort to win hearts and minds, gather information, facilitate recruitment, and increase the opportunity cost of defection to opposing factions. In addition, the accumulation of experience with state-like institutions in a certain locality may result in stronger incentives for improved state capacity and effective governance in the long term (Alesina and Fuchs-Schündeln 2007; Depetris-Chauvin 2015).

When wartime institutional capacity is limited, ruling (armed) elites may rely on closer kinship, social networks, and alliances via patronage links and parochial politics, without attempting to expand their institutional capacity beyond their centres of power. In these cases, institutional capacity and reach is limited to the centre and may continue to be so in the post-conflict period, with areas outside the direct control of the new government (remote, mountainous areas, areas inhabited by different ethnic groups, or porous borders, for instance) being characterized by fragmented rule or outright political disorder. If the periphery is contested by local actors or splitter factions, central authorities may choose to govern in two ways. The first is by providing club goods to certain ethnic or other groups that may support them and exclude everyone as a way of 'dividing and ruling'. Governments may also govern those outside central alliances through forms of indirect rule whereby local strongmen represent the central state, thereby creating more stable autocracies. In this case, central authorities will transfer private goods to local elites to leverage their local political power (Marchais et al. 2018) or may devolve the provision of public goods to sub-national actors (Muchlinski 2021). One potential weakness with these approaches is that these may become sources of rebellion against the ruling elites (see Goodwin 2001; Wickham-Crowley 1992; Cederman et al. 2013), which in turn may move incipient autocracies into fragmented rule.

An alternative strategy is to govern through repression in areas of limited institutional capacity. This approach is the most likely to result in trajectories to durable disorder, whereby different power holders attempt to control local population by force or through forced displacement—rather than building stronger institutional capacity to govern. Unsuccessful attempts at governance that backfire, such as was the case of the SPLM in South Sudan (Podder 2014), may also place countries into durable disorder trajectories (Bueno de Mesquita et al. 2005). For instance, in the case of Somalia, the inability of the central government to govern across clan interests, especially in nomadic areas, and end clan-based conflicts led eventually to state collapse (Laitin and Samatar 1987; Wimmer 2018).

The strength of the wartime institutional capacity of an armed group allows us to draw hypotheses about state capacity and the scope of its institutions in the post-war period. However, this is not a sufficient condition to distinguish whether stable democracies or stable autocracies will emerge under strong wartime institutional capacity, whether limited wartime institutional capacity will lead to weak forms of democracy or to fragmented rule, or when fragmented rule may slide into durable disorder. To do so, we need to bring into play a key actor in conflict settings: civilians. Once territorial control is established and the group achieves a certain level of institutional capacity, it may choose to exercise wartime governance by engaging in co-option, alliances, bargains, and negotiations with local communities to maximize stability and their longevity (Tilly 1992; Cederman et al. 2013; Raleigh and De Bruijne 2017). These actions produce a set of power relations between those that govern and the different communities that are governed at different times during the conflict that, under certain conditions, may amount to a social contract or at least a social compact that may shape state–citizen relations in the post-war period.

2.4.2 Wartime social contracts

Understanding the social and institutional dynamics and legacies of civil wars implies understanding interactions not only between governments and armed groups—a type of inquiry that has dominated to date the study of civil wars—but also between these competing warring factions and the civilian population. These interactions are defined by two key factors: the provision of public goods and services and the management of violence against civilians. The interaction between the type of public goods provision and management of violence against civilians shapes, in turn, levels of legitimacy and compliance of civilians towards different armed groups and the mobilization of civilians either for or against armed groups in wartime—arguably key factors in how state-building trajectories will evolve in the post-conflict period.

This section defines three forms of wartime social contracts. The first are *collective social contracts*, whereby governance encompasses civilians both inside and outside the armed group's immediate networks. Collective social contracts are generally characterized by low levels of violence against civilians once territories are controlled. They are also often accompanied by efficient and inclusive provision of security and public goods and services, allowing the armed group to establish strong linkages with civilians and thus increase their perceived legitimacy by local communities, possibly beyond controlled areas. Armed groups who exercise these forms of collective, more inclusive rule are also often able to mobilize civilians to act in support of their cause in wartime, with civilians being incorporated into the running of local affairs and in decision-making processes within the territories controlled by the group.

The second category includes *restrictive social contracts*, whereby governance by armed groups is limited to the provision of private and club goods and services. As a result, social contracts are limited to kinship, patronage links, and social networks of the armed group, leading to limited legitimacy and compliance outside the centre of power. Civilian mobilization is discouraged or violently repressed, but pockets of civilian rebellion are likely to remain active. Selective violence may be used against such groups or networks outside the elite settlement.

The third category includes *violent social contracts*, where governance is exercised under the threat or direct use of violence. These forms of civilian rule are characterized by large levels of indiscriminate violence against civilians outside periods or spaces of (sporadic) shared control by armed groups. Armed groups

Table 2.2 Wartime social contracts

	Collective	Restrictive	Violent
Public goods provision	Inclusive	Club goods	Limited
Violence against civilians	Limited	Selective	Indiscriminate
Legitimacy and compliance	Widespread	Based on patronage systems	Limited
Civilian mobilization	Strongly supportive of group	Repressed with persistent pockets of rebellion	Highly repressed using indiscriminate violence

under this category are generally largely unable or uninterested in providing public goods and services beyond security. Table 2.2 illustrates these three categories of wartime social contracts.

Provision of public goods and services.[11] One key aspect of wartime governance is the provision of public goods and services to civilians, including security, health, education, legal and judicial services, and infrastructure. Citizen support for political authority is known to be strongly shaped by the effective and inclusive provision of public goods (Weber 1976; Wimmer 2018). Recent studies have examined how armed groups provide public goods during wartime and the consequences of these activities for their survival during and after civil wars. Security is a particularly important public good in these contexts. Daly (2019) argues that groups that show better capacity to provide security to citizens may also be preferred in post-conflict elections. Groups that provide public goods may also be more likely to successfully negotiate peace deals and avoid the threat of spoilers (Heger and Jung 2017), and secessionist groups are more successful when they provided public goods in wartime (Stewart 2018). Grasse et al. (2022) show the Taliban courts reduced the frequency of disputes and increased citizen approval towards Taliban rule in districts where they were in operation, which may partially explain Taliban's swift takeover of Afghanistan after the US and NATO withdrawal of military forces in 2021. By contrast, the authority of ruling armed groups may be undermined when public goods provision is ineffective or limited. For instance, armed group policies that may damage or close down local markets, such as policies of agricultural self-sufficiency followed by the *Sendero Luminoso* at various stages of their rule in Peru, and attacks to infrastructure, as performed by the FMLN in El Salvador in the

[11] Public goods and services are defined in the economics sense as goods and services, which are non-excludable and non-rivalrous, i.e., no one can be prevented from accessing or using them and their use by one person does not exclude access or availability to others.

1980s, contributed to loses in authority by the groups (Wickham-Crowley 1992; Wood 2003).

A large literature has discussed the importance of inclusive versus exclusive provision of public goods, services, and policies to the establishment of effective social contracts (see Acemoglu and Robinson 2006). In wartime, some armed groups provide inclusive public goods effectively to the entire population under their control (and even beyond) (Heger and Jung 2017; Stewart 2018). This strategy may support post-war state-building strategies towards (stable or weak) democracy because it allows ruling (armed) elites in wartime to extend their networks and alliances beyond their immediate circle and across larger areas of potential support (Wimmer 2018). Other groups only provide private or club goods (Berman and Laitin 2018). Reno (2011) describes these groups as 'parochial rebels', more likely to see the state as a prize to be won and a source of revenue and political influence—a view that is unlikely to change should the group win the war and take over the state. These groups may become successful at establishing stable autocracies with lasting, centralized power when elite bargains are mutually beneficial and last (Slater 2010; Driscoll 2015). Political fragmentation will dominate when elite bargains fail or are too volatile and groups are unable to build institutional capacity. In either case, limiting the provision of goods and services to private or club goods is unlikely to establish the seeds of democracy, although it may support stable autocracies when groups created strong institutional capacity in wartime.[12]

Violence against civilians. Another key aspect of wartime governance—and an important feature that distinguishes it from governance in peaceful contexts—is the management of violence against civilians during the period of rule (Justino 2018). Exercising governance in these contexts implies making decisions about the use of violence and repression for different purposes.[13] Armed groups facing information asymmetries tend to resort to indiscriminate forms of violence to control valuable resources, take over areas of strategic interest to the war effort, displace or kill the opposition, and control the behaviour of civilians (Kalyvas 2006). As access to information improves, armed groups may use more selective forms of violence or reduce the use of violence and repression of civilians.[14] Repression by violent means may also be deemed unnecessary as armed groups gain local support

[12] To note that the provision of public goods and services is useful to improve institutional capacity and social contracts in both democracies and autocracies. Better infrastructure, lower levels of violence, and stronger social contracts improve market exchange, diffusion of ideas, and information and accumulation of human capital—all necessary conditions for the consolidation of democracy. But they also improve the ability of rulers to send security forces to marginalized areas where contention risks may be highest, strengthen the ability of armed groups to use forms of selective violence more efficiently thanks to better monitoring of populations outside the immediate patronage networks, and facilitate better access resource-rich areas (Müller-Crepon et al. 2020).

[13] For reviews of the literature on violence against civilians in civil wars and its consequences, see Justino (2009, 2012) and Balcells and Stanton (2021).

[14] Kalyvas (2006) has shown how the use of indiscriminate or selective violence is endogenous to territorial control and levels of contestation with opposing factions.

or, at least, engage in mutually beneficial arrangements with local communities (Arjona 2016).

Repression comes at a cost because policing and targeting civilians requires manpower and intelligence and may trigger organized rebellion against the group, forcing it to fight on several fronts (Kasfir 2015; Arjona 2016; Kaplan 2017). Insurgent groups may nonetheless engage in predatory behaviour and exercise violence and repression against civilians when they are defeated in combat and lose territory (Wood 2014), or when they have access to external endowments in the form of natural resources or international financial and military support, which reduce their need to win hearts and minds (Weinstein 2007).

Armed groups with stronger internal organization and a strong central authority are more able to manage the use of violence against civilians (Kalyvas 2006; Staniland 2014). The restrained use of violence may win civilian support. For instance, Wood (2003) describes how the restrained use of violence by the FMLN during the El Salvador civil war resulted in strong support from civilian networks which, in turn, weighted in the peace settlement negotiations. In contrast, the increasingly strong use of force against civilians by the *Sendero Luminoso* in Peru resulted is weakened support by civilians and eventually their dismissal as an alternative political force (Starr and Wood 2017). In Iraq, civilian casualties caused by insurgents increased information flows from civilians to the state military about insurgent activities, whereas government-induced casualties reduced such sharing of information (Shaver and Shapiro 2021).

The restrained—or more selective—use of violence and repression may be more likely to support more stable (democratic or autocratic) political orders when armed groups progressively reduce the use of indiscriminate violence as they gain stronger control over territories, strengthen their rule over civilian populations and/or muster local support. As argued in Kalyvas (2015: 119), '[t]he more extensive the geographical scope of control exercised by a rebel group, the fuller the expression of its political identity on the institutions of rebel rule. Conversely, limited and tenuous territorial control correlates with more openly coercive practices'. The widespread of violence against civilians may result in trajectories towards contested autocracies where violence and repression are intrinsic components of how autocrats with strong institutional capacity at the centre rule over marginal parts of the territory where alliances with local authorities are weak and fraught with mistrust. Indiscriminate violence is a component of trajectories towards durable disorder, where arbitrary attacks of civilians and violent clashes between competing armed groups with weak institutional capacity dominate the political landscape.

Legitimacy and compliance. Many actors engage in battles over legitimacy in conflict-affected contexts: state and non-state armed groups in conflict settings are typically concerned not only with military struggle, but also work to delegitimize competing groups and mobilize mass support by establishing alternate legitimate political order (Mampilly 2011; Wickham-Crowley 1992). Perceptions about the legitimacy of forms of wartime governance, and ensuing political orders, are in turn shaped by how revenue extraction is used in exchange for protection, public goods, and other state-like functions, with highly coercive forms of wartime governance unlikely to be associated with positive perceptions of legitimacy (Bates 1983; Goodwin 2001; Podder 2014). Legitimacy is likely to be higher towards armed groups that exercise more inclusive forms of governance and public goods provision in wartime and restrain the use of coercion and repression. For instance, Wickham-Crowley (1992) and Goodwin (2001) discuss how rebel revolutionary movements were more likely to muster civilian support and gain legitimacy in Latin America in areas where governments exercised terror and repression towards their citizens. Kubota (2017) shows that civilian identity (Tamil versus Sri Lankan) in northern and eastern areas of Sri Lanka is considerably shaped by how local populations perceive the legitimacy of state-like functions performed by the LTTE during the war.

Improved legitimacy and capacity by armed groups may also ensure that civilians do not leave recently controlled territories, as Revkin (2020b) shows for the case of the Islamic State in Mosul, and may also strengthen ties between armed group commanders and local communities in the post-war period (Martin 2020). Perceptions of legitimacy about the state-like roles of armed groups during wartime are also important because they define state–military–citizen relations in the post-war period. For instance, Levitsky and Way (2012) show how ex-ZANU combatants remained loyal to Robert Mugabe throughout the post-war years in Zimbabwe despite serious cycles of economic downturns, given the ZANU party's organization 'around non-material sources of cohesion, such as ideology, ethnicity, or bonds of solidarity rooted in a shared experience of violent struggle' (pp. 870).

The nature of the relationship between civilians and ruling political actors can also be examined through the lens of compliance, and whether it is consensual or coercive (Revkin and Ahram 2020). While legitimacy reflects the perceptions of citizens about the right of competing authorities to rule, compliance refers to the degree of freedom civilians have to obey such rules. In some cases, civilians comply freely with the norms and regulations imposed by armed groups in wartime; in other cases, they resent and resist them. Often, they are coerced into complying with rules and norms. A variety of factors explains this variation in compliance, including the strength of territorial control (Kalyvas 2006), how the ideologies and interest of armed groups and civilians are aligned (Weinstein 2007; Gutierrez Sanin and Wood 2014), the extent to which armed groups have the bureaucratic capacity to enforce norms and regulations, extract revenues, and provide public good and security in return (Azam and Mesnard 2003; Centeno 2002), and perceptions of fairness about how competing political actors charge taxes and decide on the different amounts levied across different populations and businesses (Ahmad 2015; Hoffmann et al. 2016; Revkin 2020a; Mampilly and Thakur 2024).[15]

In general, the more legitimacy civilians confer to one group, the more likely they are to comply with rules imposed by the group and the more likely it will be for a country to initiate state-building trajectories towards inclusive democracy (Huang 2016), or stable autocracies (Levitsky and Way 2012, 2022). Groups that sustain legitimacy in the eyes of those they govern are also more likely to be viewed as legitimate by other states should they become the governing authority in the post-conflict period (for instance, via elections held as part of peace agreements) (Heger and Jung 2017). Strong power holdings combined with restricted levels of legitimacy and coercive compliance will likely result in 'contested autocracy' state-building trajectories, which may fold into more fragmented rule when facing external economic or political shocks (Slater 2010; Levitsky and Way 2012).

Civilian mobilization. Civilian collaboration and the mobilization of civilians to support own agendas has been often a major concern for warring factions intending on winning an internal armed conflict and controlling territories (Guevara 1968; Laqueur 1976; Kalyvas 2006). As such, civilian mobilization is likely to shape state-building trajectories. Acemoglu and Robinson (2017) theorize how the emergence of weak, despotic, or inclusive states arises from the type of relationship established between governing elites and ordinary citizens. Asymmetries of power that favour ruling elites over civil society will result in despotic states. Strong civil societies in the presence of weak authority result in weak and fragmented states. Inclusive states originate from endogenous processes whereby strong state capacity and strong civil society reinforce each other. This is particularly the case when civil society is formed of civic organizations able to bridge across ethnic, linguistic, and cultural divides (Wimmer 2018; Aghajanian et al. 2020).

In contexts of war, the net effect of strong civic organizations on state-building trajectories will depend on the effects of wartime governance on local civic life and how civilians are mobilized and integrated within the war effort of different factions. This relationship is formally theorized in Gáfaro et al. (2021), who show how the strength of civic society in the aftermath of violent conflict is shaped by political or economic alliances between armed groups and civilian populations during wartime. The strength of community collective action and social cohesion is also in turn a key determinant of the type and depth of governance systems implemented by armed groups locally (Rubin 2019; Breslawski 2021), and within-community social and economic structures (Justino 2022). Some armed

[15] Compliance can also be sought via the use of symbols like flags and anthems, which facilitate the identification of civilians with the warring faction that rules them (Mampilly 2011), or through mythical narratives used to consolidate values and beliefs and ensure civilian engagement (Nordstrom 1997, Hoffmann 2015).

groups engaged in the use of wartime governance often attempt to rule and govern over local populations through the capture of existing civic organizations or the establishment of new ones (Wood 2008; Kaplan 2017). For instance, Ch et al. (2018) show how both paramilitary and guerilla groups in Colombia make use of their *de facto* power at the local level to capture local tax and property rights organizations. In some cases, civilian institutions may be co-opted and incorporated into wartime governance structures, with sometimes civilians running some aspects of their operations (Mampilly 2011; Kaplan 2017; Mampilly and Stewart 2021). This may be the case in particular when armed groups and civilians share pre-war social ties and mutual support (Staniland 2014), or when the aims of civilians and armed groups are (or become) ideologically aligned, as was the case of the African Party for the Independence of Guinea and Cape Verde (PAIGC), led by Amilcar Cabral, who 'introduce[d] a participatory, inclusive system of governance that represented a fundamental divergence from colonial subjugation' (Mampilly and Stewart 2020: 22). In other cases, armed groups capture existing civic organizations to facilitate social control. Civilians may also resist the presence and control of armed groups, by creating resistance movements or civil defence groups (Kalyvas 2006; Krause 2018; Petersen 2001; Wood 2003). As a response to resistance, armed groups may, in turn, inhibit the functioning of local civic organizations to prevent civil resistance movements or co-opt local organizations by replacing their leaders (Gáfaro et al. 2021).

Civilian agency shapes these complex processes of institutional capture and institution-building in ways that will also determine the behaviour of civil society in the aftermath of conflicts. Inclusive and strong civic organizations that may have risen from resistance movements or from strong movements that supported insurgent or incumbent coalitions in the post-conflict period may potentially support state-building trajectories towards inclusive democracy. Wood (2000) illustrate how pressures from civil society lead to incumbent governments in El Salvador and South Africa agreeing to negotiate with insurgents. This resulted eventually in trajectories of both countries towards more inclusive democracies because 'sustained mobilization by poor and working-class people transformed key interests of economic elites, leading to pressure on the state to compromise with the insurgents, thereby strengthening regime moderates over hard-liners with the result that negotiated transitions to democracy followed' (Wood 2001: 863). As argued also by Huang (2016: 2), 'what may initially be a wartime choice on the part of rebel groups on how to engage with the people in their milieu has the force to catalyze regime change at the center once the war has come to an end' (see also Wantchekon 2004). Such 'pressure from below' can also reduce the opportunity costs of institutional reforms by elites because it increases the political costs of not conceding to demands (i.e., the potential loss of future political power) (Acemoglu and Robinson 2006; North et al. 2009). As noted by Slater (2010: 5), 'internal contention can "make the state" [...] when it takes especially threatening and challenging forms'.

Civilian mobilization and collective action in the immediate aftermath of violent conflicts can also be key in shaping what society and state are to emerge from the war. For instance, Chenoweth and Stephan (2011) show that civilian resistance, particularly in the form of nonviolent movements, can generate durable democracies and reduce the likelihood of post-conflict countries returning to civil war.

Trajectories towards autocracies are likely to emerge from the support of strategic alliances formed during wartime with specific population groups or specific local elites—at the cost of excluding non-supporters outside these patronage and kinship relations and repressing any form of dissent. For instance, Liu (2023) describes how the ZANU group in Zimbabwe courted civilian supporters to build local organizational capacity. This led to the creation of informal governing institutions that provided security, rule of law, and the provision of public goods. These institutions persisted once the ZANU party won the elections, ensuring the continuation of clientelist electoral politics in the post-war period (see also Levitsky and Way 2012). Where civilians' views were suppressed, the same patterned continued in the post-war period in ways that entrenched autocratic trajectories. As described in (Liu 2023: 3), 'political intimidation and state-sponsored violence against civilians is still disproportionately concentrated in districts that were historically pro-ZANU wartime strongholds [...]. Citizens living in these districts have significantly less political choice, express greater doubts towards voting and election outcomes, and report greater fear towards political participation. In short, the institutional and social legacies of war have facilitated ZANUPF's post-war dominance.' The manipulation of ethnic identities and the mobilization of civilians along ethnic lines to support war efforts may further strengths these processes of social and political exclusion in the post-war period, whereby political power is only extended to those within the alliances that form restrictive rule. However, civil wars may also reshape social and political identities in ways that overcome cultural cleavages and may lead to social change.

2.5 The legacies of wartime governance: a new research agenda?

Several seminal studies published in the last decade have analysed why and how political order and governance structures emerge in conflict zones (Kalyvas 2006; Kalyvas et al. 2008; Mampilly 2011; Staniland 2014; Arjona et al. 2015). However, only recently have scholars started to pay attention to the long-term implications of these important wartime institutional dynamics for how states build institutional capacity, rebuild social contracts, maintain stability in the post-war period, and establish political regimes. This chapter offered a new theoretical framing to explore six distinct state-building trajectories of post-conflict countries—stable democracy, weak democracy, stable autocracy, fragmented rule, contested autocracy, and durable disorder—each shaped by variation in forms of wartime governance. The chapter defines the concept of wartime governance as a key determinant of state-building trajectories and distinguishes it from other forms of governance, such as governance exercised in peacetime and forms of governance provided by criminal organizations.

This theoretical framework highlights two dimensions of wartime governance that shape these distinct state-building trajectories. The first is how armed groups compete during wartime to gain authority and capacity to rule over territories that may convey them power and military advantage—i.e. their wartime institutional capacity. The second is how armed groups rule and interact with civilian populations in areas they control during wartime, and subsequent civilian responses in conveying legitimacy and support to (or resist and repel) the armed group, effectively shaping 'wartime social contracts'. Identifying these two factors offers entry points to future empirical analysis and data collection on key forms of institutional change that take place during conflicts and on how to trace the legacies of these factors to post-conflict political, social, and economic dynamics. These mechanisms offer, in addition, important micro-foundations grounded on endogenous conflict dynamics to explain macro-level state-building processes.

This framework generates some fundamental questions about the nature of state formation and the organization of society and politics in the aftermath of civil wars. In particular, the theoretical framework proposed in this chapter helps to illustrate how civil wars may generate within themselves bureaucratic and institutional capacity that may, under certain conditions, be harnessed in the post-war period to build autonomous states capable of governing. Countries emerging from conflict are more likely to follow a trajectory of state-building towards inclusive democracy when they managed to control territory for long time periods (which ensured the efficient provision of public goods and services), govern over and established legitimate social contracts with local populations for a long period of time, and were able to build strong bureaucracies with wide institutional reach. Forms of wartime governance that faced large swings in territorial control, depended on specific alliances and the provision of club goods, and limited their operations to certain areas are more likely to follow into forms of contested autocracy. Large levels of competition between armed groups for territorial and political control, challenges in establishing social contracts with local (fragmented) civil society, and weak internal organization and institutional capacity are likely to result in trajectories towards fragmented rule or durable disorder orders.

The framework and arguments developed in the chapter open important directions for future research. The first is on the consequences of wartime political orders, especially over the longer term. Although a large body of research has mapped out the origins of wartime political orders in a variety of settings, less is known about its long-term consequences. This chapter focuses on one aspect of wartime political order (how armed groups govern) but other dynamics may matter too, including interactions between armed groups and external actors, cross border spillovers and the role of ideology. Second, the chapter offers a theoretical framework to better understand how wartime governance may place countries under different post-war state-building trajectories but leaves open questions about the sustainability of such trajectories: what trajectories may better support economic recovery and the social reintegration of civilians and combatants in the post-war period? How do different state-building trajectories shape and are shaped by changes in social and political norms during and after civil wars? How do different state-building trajectories affect the duration of peace and possible re-ignition of conflict and violence? Third, the theoretical framework proposed in the chapter raises additional questions about the determinants and evolution of political orders in wartime. While we are starting to get a good grasp on how different political orders emerge and their characteristics, we know much less about how they evolve and change over time. The typology proposed in this chapter illustrates how variation in wartime governance pushes a country towards a certain type of state-building trajectory. But once a country enters a specific state-building trajectory, what explains whether it stays on course, changes from one trajectory to another, or even relapses into armed violence once more? Possible explanations may include the role of political and economic shocks in the post-conflict period, shifts in aid priorities, the level and type of external financing support, and the role of geopolitical alliances. Finally, assessing the validity of the proposed theoretical framework requires compiling new data on variation in different forms of wartime governance across countries and conflicts, at the sub-national level and across time, as well as operationalize 'state-building trajectories' as a dependent variable. This is a daunting but not impossible task, as attested by several papers in this volume.

References

Acemoglu, D., and J. Robinson (2017). 'The Emergence of Weak, Despotic and Inclusive States', NBER Working Paper 23657. Cambridge, MA: NBER. https://doi.org/10.3386/w23657

Acemoglu, D., and J. Robinson (2006). *Economic Origins of Dictatorship and Democracy*. Cambridge: Cambridge University Press. https://doi.org/10.1017/CBO9780511510809

Aghajanian, A., P. Justino, and J. P. Tranchant (2020). 'Riots and Social Capital in Urban Maharashtra', WIDER Working Paper 42/2020. Helsinki: UNU-WIDER. https://doi.org/10.35188/UNU-WIDER/2020/799-6

Ahmad, A. (2015). 'The Security Bazaar: Business Interests and Islamist Power in Civil War Somalia'. *International Security*, 39(3): 89–117. https://doi.org/10.1162/ISEC_a_00187

Albert, K. (2022). 'What Is Rebel Governance? Introducing a New Dataset on Rebel Institutions, 1945–2012'. *Journal of Peace Research*, 59(4): 622–630. https://doi.org/10.1177/00223433211051848

Alesina, A., and N. Fuchs-Schündeln (2007). 'Goodbye Lenin (or Not?): The Effect of Communism on People's Preferences'. *American Economic Review*, 97(4): 1507–1528. https://doi.org/10.1257/aer.97.4.1507

Arjona, A., A. M. Ibáñez, J. C. Cárdenas, and P. Justino (2022). 'The Legacies of Wartime Institutions on Citizens' Preferences for the Rule of Law', forthcoming.

Arjona, A., N. Kasfir, and Z. Mampilly (2015). *Rebel Governance in Civil War*. New York: Cambridge University Press. https://doi.org/10.1017/CBO9781316182468

Arjona, A. (2016). *Rebelocracy: Social Order in the Colombian Civil War*. New York: Cambridge University Press. https://doi.org/10.1017/9781316421925

Autesserre, S. (2010). *The Trouble with the Congo: Local Violence and the Failure of International Peacebuilding*. New York: Cambridge University Press. https://doi.org/10.1017/CBO9780511761034

Azam, J. P., and A. Mesnard (2003). 'Civil War and the Social Contract'. *Public Choice*, 115(3–4): 455–475. https://doi.org/10.1023/A:1024265631528

Balcells, L., and J. Stanton (2021). 'Violence Against Civilians During Armed Conflict: Moving Beyond the Macro- and Micro-Level Divide'. *Annual Review of Political Science*, 24: 2.1–2.25. https://doi.org/10.1146/annurev-polisci-041719-102229

Balcells, L., and P. Justino (2014). 'Bridging Micro and Macro Approaches on Civil Wars and Political Violence: Issues, Challenges and Way Forward'. *Journal of Conflict Resolution*, 58(8): 1343–1359. https://doi.org/10.1177/0022002714547905

Bates, R. (2008). 'Probing the Sources of Political Order'. In S. N. Kalyvas, I. Shapiro, and T. Masoud (eds), *Order, Conflict, and Violence*. Cambridge: Cambridge University Press. https://doi.org/10.1017/CBO9780511755903.003

Bates, R. (1983). *Essays on the Political Economy of Rural Africa*. Cambridge: Cambridge University Press. https://doi.org/10.1017/CBO9780511558740

Berdal, M., and D. Zaum (2012). *Political Economy of State-Building: Power After Peace*. London: Routledge. https://doi.org/10.4324/9780203101308

Berman, E., and D. Laitin (2008). 'Religion, Terrorism and Public Goods: Testing the Club Model'. *Journal of Public Economics*, 92(10–11): 1942–1967.

Berman, E., and D. Laitin (2018). 'Religion, Terrorism and Public Goods: Testing the Club Model'. *Journal of Public Economics*, 92(10): 1942–1967. https://doi.org/10.1016/j.jpubeco.2008.03.007

Berman, E., J. Shapiro, and J. Felter (2011). 'Can Hearts and Minds Be Bought? The Economics of Counterinsurgency in Iraq'. *Journal of Political Economy*, 119(4): 766–819. https://doi.org/10.1086/661983

Boyle, M. (2014). *Violence After War: Explaining Instability in Post-Conflict States*. Baltimore: Johns Hopkins University Press. https://doi.org/10.1353/book.29443

Breslawski, J. (2021). 'The Social Terrain of Rebel Held Territory'. *Journal of Conflict Resolution*, 65(2–3): 453–479. https://doi.org/10.1177/0022002720951857

Brück, T., P. Justino, and P. Verwimp (2009). 'The Analysis of Conflict: A Micro-Level Perspective'. *Journal of Peace Research*, 46(3): 307–314. https://doi.org/10.1177/0022343309102654

Bueno de Mesquita, B., A. Smith, R. M. Siverson, and J. D. Morrow (2005). *The Logic of Political Survival*. Cambridge, MA: MIT Press.

Cederman, L.-E., K. Gleditsch, and H. Buhaug (2013). *Inequality, Grievances, and Civil War*. Cambridge: Cambridge University Press. https://doi.org/10.1017/CBO9781139084161

Centeno, M. (2002). *Blood and Debt: War and the Nation-State in Latin America*. University Park: Penn State University Press.

Ch, R., J. Shapiro, A. Steele, and J. F. Vargas (2018). 'Endogenous Taxation in Ongoing Internal Conflict: The Case of Colombia'. *American Political Science Review*, 112(4): 996–1015. https://doi.org/10.1017/S0003055418000333

Chenoweth, E., and M. Stephan (2011). *Why Civilian Resistance Works: The Strategic Logic of Nonviolent Conflict*. New York: Columbia University Press.

Christia, F. (2012). *Alliance Formation in Civil Wars*. New York: Cambridge University Press. https://doi.org/10.1017/CBO9781139149426

Collier, P., and P. Vicente (2012). 'Violence, Bribery, and Fraud: The Political Economy of Elections in Sub-Saharan Africa'. *Public Choice*, 153(1–2): 117–147. https://doi.org/10.1007/s11127-011-9777-z

Collier, P., A. Hoeffler, and M. Söderbom (2008). 'Post-Conflict Risks'. *Journal of Peace Research*, 45(4): 461–478. https://doi.org/10.1177/0022343308091356

Daly, S. Z. (2019). 'Voting for Victors: Why Violent Actors Win Postwar Elections'. *World Politics*, 71(4): 747–805. https://doi.org/10.1017/S0043887119000091

Daly, S. Z. (2016). *Organized Violence After Civil War: The Geography of Recruitment in Latin America*. New York: Cambridge University Press. https://doi.org/10.1017/CBO9781316412350

Depetris-Chauvin, E. (2015). 'State History and Contemporary Conflict: Evidence from Sub-Saharan Africa'. Working Paper available at SSRN. https://doi.org/10.2139/ssrn.2679594

de Zeeuw, J. (ed.) (2008). *From Soldiers to Politicians: Transforming Rebel Movements After Civil War*. Boulder, CO: Lynne Rienner. https://doi.org/10.1515/9781626373495

Dowd, C., P. Justino, R. Kishi, and G. Marchais (2020). 'Comparing "New" and "Old" Media for Violence Monitoring and Crisis Response: Evidence from Kenya'. *Research & Politics*, 7(3): 1–9. https://doi.org/10.1177/2053168020937592

Doyle, M., and N. Sambanis (2006). *Making War and Building Peace: United Nations Peace Operations*. Princeton, NJ: Princeton University Press. https://doi.org/10.1515/9781400837694

Doyle, M., and N. Sambanis (2000). 'International Peacebuilding: A Theoretical and Quantitative Analysis'. *American Political Science Review*, 94(4): 779–801. https://doi.org/10.2307/2586208

Driscoll, J. (2015). *Warlords and Coalition Politics in Post-Soviet States*. New York: Cambridge University Press. https://doi.org/10.1017/CBO9781107478046

Dunning, T. (2011). 'Fighting and Voting: Violent Conflict and Electoral Politics'. *Journal of Conflict Resolution*, 55(3): 327–339. https://doi.org/10.1177/0022002711400861

Durant, T. C., and M. Weintraub (2014). 'How to Make Democracy Self-Enforcing After Civil War: Enabling Credible Yet Adaptable Elite Pacts'. *Conflict Management and Peace Science*, 31(5): 521–540. https://doi.org/10.1177/0738894213520372

Fearon, J. (2004). 'Why Do Some Civil Wars Last So Much Longer Than Others?' *Journal of Peace Research*, 41(3): 275–301. https://doi.org/10.1177/0022343304043770

Flanigan, S. (2008). 'Nonprofit Service Provision by Insurgent Organizations: The Cases of Hizballah and the Tamil Tigers'. *Studies in Conflict and Terrorism*, 31(6): 499–519. https://doi.org/10.1080/10576100802065103

Fortna, V. P. (2008). *Does Peacekeeping Work? Shaping Belligerents' Choices After Civil War*. Princeton, NJ: Princeton University Press. https://doi.org/10.1515/9781400837731

Fortna, V. P. (2004). *Peace Time: Cease-Fire Agreements and the Durability of Peace*. Princeton, NJ: Princeton University Press. https://doi.org/10.1515/9780691187952

Gáfaro, M., A. M. Ibáñez, and P. Justino (2022). 'Community Organization and Armed Group Behaviour: Evidence from Colombia'. WIDER Working Paper 2022-2. Helsinki: UNU-WIDER. https://doi.org/10.35188/UNU-WIDER/2022/133-4

Gáfaro, M., A. M. Ibáñez, and P. Justino (2014). 'Local Institutions and Armed Group Presence in Colombia'. HiCN Working Paper 178. The Households in Conflict Network. https://doi.org/10.35648/20.500.12413/11781/ii162

Gassier, M. (2021). Anatomies of Rebellion: Determinants and Implications of Rebel Modes of Local Engagement. PhD Thesis, Sciences Po, Paris.

Giustozzi, A. (2014). 'The Taliban's "Military Courts"'. *Small Wars & Insurgencies*, 25(2): 284–296. https://doi.org/10.1080/09592318.2014.903638

Goodwin, J. (2001). *No Other Way Out: States and Revolutionary Movements, 1945–1991*. New York: Cambridge University Press. https://doi.org/10.1017/CBO9780511812125

Grasse, D., R. Sexton, and A. Wright (2022). 'The Logic and Impacts of Rebel Public Services Provision: Evidence from the Taliban Courts in Afghanistan'. https://static1.squarespace.com/static/53fc9eb3e4b01bd08e4a58ba/t/620ec3db76a6ae5a0576bb34/1645134812784/Afghanistan-Courts-GSW.pdf (accessed 28 March 2022).

Guevara, E. (1968). *Guerrilla Warfare*. New York: Vantage Books.

Gutierrez Sanin, F., and E. J. Wood (2014). 'Ideology in Civil War: Instrumental Adoption and Beyond'. *Journal of Peace Research*, 51(2): 213–226. https://doi.org/10.1177/0022343313514073

Hanif, S., H. A. Majid, and F. Shaheen (2019). 'Religious Extremism, Religiosity and Sympathy Toward the Taliban Among Students Across Madrassas and Worldly Education Schools in Pakistan'. *Terrorism and Political Violence*. https://doi.org/10.1080/09546553.2018.1548354

Heger, L., and D. Jung (2017). 'Negotiating with Rebels: The Effect of Rebel Service Provision on Conflict Negotiations'. *Journal of Conflict Resolution*, 61(6): 1203–1229. https://doi.org/10.1177/0022002715603451

Hegre, H., and H. Nygård (2015). 'Governance and Conflict Relapse'. *Journal of Conflict Resolution*, 59(6): 984–1016. https://doi.org/10.1177/0022002713520591

Hegre, H., T. Ellingsen, S. Gates, and N. P. Gleditsch (2001). 'Toward a Democratic Civil Peace? Democracy, Political Change, and Civil War, 1816–1992'. *American Political Science Review*, 95(1): 33–48. https://doi.org/10.1017/S0003055401000119

Hoeffler, A., and P. Justino (2024). 'Aid and Fragile States'. In R. Desai, S. Devarajan, and J. Tobin (eds), *Elgar Handbook of Aid and Development*, pp. 225–246. Cheltenham: Edward Elgar Publishing. https://doi.org/10.4337/9781800886810.00020

Hoffmann, K. (2015). 'Myths Set in Motion: The Moral Economy of Mai Mai Governance'. In A. Arjona, N. Kasfir, and Z. Mampilly (eds). *Rebel Governance in Civil War*, chapter 8. New York: Cambridge University Press.

Hoffmann, K., K. Vlassenroot, and G. Marchais (2016). 'Taxation, Stateness and Armed Groups: Public Authority and Resource Extraction in Eastern Congo'. *Development and Change*, 47(6): 1434–1456. https://doi.org/10.1111/dech.12275

Horowitz, D. L. (2003). *The Deadly Ethnic Riot*. Berkeley, CA: University of California Press.

Huang, R., and P. Sullivan (2021). 'Arms for Education? External Support and Rebel Social Services'. *Journal of Peace Research*, 58(4): 794–808. https://doi.org/10.1177/0022343320940749

Huang, R. (2016). *The Wartime Origins of Democratization: Civil War, Rebel Governance, and Political Regimes*. New York: Cambridge University Press. https://doi.org/10.1017/CBO9781316711323

Huntington, S. P. (1968). *Political Order in Changing Societies.* New Haven, CT: Yale University Press.
Ibáñez, A. M., J. Arteaga, J. C. Cárdenas, A. Arjona, and P. Justino (2024). 'The Long-Term Economic Legacies of Rebel Rule in Civil War: Micro Evidence from Colombia'. *Journal of Conflict Resolution*, 68(9): 1825–1855. https://doi.org/10.1177/00220027231170569
Ishiyama, J., and A. Batta (2011). 'Swords into Plowshares: The Organizational Transformation of Rebel Groups into Political Parties'. *Communist and Post-Communist Studies*, 44: 369–379. https://doi.org/10.1016/j.postcomstud.2011.10.004
Justino, P., and W. Stojetz (2018). 'On the Legacies of Wartime Governance'. HiCN Working Paper 263. The Households in Conflict Network.
Justino, P., T. Brück, and P. Verwimp (2013). *A Micro-Level Perspective on the Dynamics of Conflict, Violence and Development.* Oxford: Oxford University Press. https://doi.org/10.1093/acprof:oso/9780199664597.001.0001
Justino, P. (2022). 'Revisiting the Links Between Economic Inequality and Political Violence: The Role of Social Mobilization'. WIDER Working Paper 2022-19. Helsinki: UNU-WIDER. https://doi.org/10.35188/UNU-WIDER/2022/150-1
Justino, P. (2019). 'Governance Interventions in Conflict-Affected Countries'. *Journal of Development Studies*, 55(7): 1364–1378. https://doi.org/10.1080/00220388.2018.1487053
Justino, P. (2018). 'The Need to Be Governed: Governance and Violence in Conflict Contexts'. *Economics of Peace and Security Journal*, 13(1): 5–11. https://doi.org/10.15355/epsj.13.1.5
Justino, P. (2013). 'Micro-Level Dynamics of Conflict, Violence and Development: A New Analytical Framework'. In P. Justino, T. Brück, and P. Verwimp (eds), *A Micro-Level Perspective on the Dynamics of Conflict, Violence and Development.* Oxford: Oxford University Press. https://doi.org/10.1093/acprof:oso/9780199664597.001.0001
Justino, P. (2012). 'War and Poverty'. In M. Garfinkel and S. Skaperdas (eds), *Handbook of the Economics of Peace and Conflict*, pp. 676–705. Oxford: Oxford University Press. https://doi.org/10.1093/oxfordhb/9780195392777.013.0027
Justino, P. (2009). 'Poverty and Violent Conflict: A Micro-Level Perspective on the Causes and Duration of Warfare'. *Journal of Peace Research*, 46(3): 315–333. https://doi.org/10.1177/0022343309102655
Kalyvas, S., I. Shapiro, and T. Masoud (2008). *Order, Conflict, and Violence.* Cambridge: Cambridge University Press. https://doi.org/10.1017/CBO9780511755903
Kalyvas, S. (2015). 'Rebel Governance During the Greek Civil War, 1942–1949'. In A. Arjona, N. Kasfir, and Z. Mampilly (eds), *Rebel Governance in Civil War.* New York: Cambridge University Press. https://doi.org/10.1017/CBO9781316182468.006
Kalyvas, S. (2006). *The Logic of Violence in Civil Wars.* Cambridge: Cambridge University Press. https://doi.org/10.1017/CBO9780511818462
Kaplan, O. (2017). *Resisting War: How Communities Protect Themselves.* New York: Cambridge University Press. https://doi.org/10.1017/9781316671887
Kasfir, N. (2015). 'Rebel Governance—Constructing a Field of Inquiry: Definitions, Scope, Patterns, Order, Causes'. In A. Arjona, N. Kasfir, and Z. Mampilly (eds), *Rebel Governance in Civil War.* New York: Cambridge University Press. https://doi.org/10.1017/CBO9781316182468.002
Kasfir, N. (1998). 'African Ambiguities: "No-Party" Democracy in Uganda'. *Journal of Democracy*, 9(2): 49–61. https://doi.org/10.1353/jod.1998.0029

Kennedy, J. (2014). 'Gangsters or Gandhians? The Political Sociology of the Maoist Insurgency in India'. *India Review*, 13(3): 212–234. https://doi.org/10.1080/14736489.2014.937268

King, E., and C. Samii (2014). 'Fast-Track Institution Building in Conflict-Affected Countries? Insights from Recent Field Experiments'. *World Development*, 64: 740–754. https://doi.org/10.1016/j.worlddev.2014.06.030

Krause, J. (2018). *Resilient Communities: Non-Violence and Civilian Agency in Communal War*. Cambridge: Cambridge University Press. https://doi.org/10.1017/9781108675079

Kubota, Y. (2017). 'Imagined Statehood: Wartime Rebel Governance and Post-War Subnational Identity in Sri Lanka'. *World Development*, 90: 199–212. https://doi.org/10.1016/j.worlddev.2016.09.007

Laitin, D., and S. Samatar (1987). *Somalia: Nation in Search of a State*. Boulder, CO: Westview.

Laqueur, W. (1976). *Guerrilla: A Historical and Critical Study*. Boston, MA: Little, Brown.

Lessing, B. (2020). 'Conceptualizing Criminal Governance'. *Perspectives on Politics*, 19(3): 854–873. https://doi.org/10.1017/S1537592720001243

Levitsky, S., and L. Way (2022). *Revolution & Dictatorship: The Violent Origins of Durable Authoritarianism*. Princeton, NJ: Princeton University Press. https://doi.org/10.1515/9780691223575

Levitsky, S., and L. Way (2012). 'Beyond Patronage: Violent Struggle, Ruling Party Cohesion, and Authoritarian Durability'. *Perspectives on Politics*, 10(4): 872–874. https://doi.org/10.1017/S1537592712002861

Lewis, J. I. (2020). *How Insurgency Begins: Rebel Group Formation in Uganda and Beyond*. Cambridge: Cambridge University Press. https://doi.org/10.1017/9781108855969

Liu, S. (2023). 'Legacies of Victimization: Evidence from Forced Resettlement in Zimbabwe'. WIDER Working Paper 12/2023. Helsinki: UNU-WIDER. https://doi.org/10.35188/UNU-WIDER/2023/321-5

Loyle, C. (2020). 'Rebel Justice During Armed Conflict'. *Journal of Conflict Resolution*, 65(1): 108–134. https://doi.org/10.1177/0022002720939299

Loyle, C., and H. Binningsbø (2018). 'Justice During Armed Conflict: A New Dataset on Government and Rebel Strategies'. *Journal of Conflict Resolution*, 62(2): 442–466. https://doi.org/10.1177/0022002716655441

Mampilly, Z., and S. Thakur (2024). 'Rebel Taxation as Extortion or a Technology of Governance? Telling the Difference in India's Northeast'. *Comparative Political Studies*, 58(3): 462–493. https://doi.org/10.1177/00104140241237472

Mampilly, Z., and M. A. Stewart (2021). 'A Typology of Rebel Political Institutional Arrangements'. *Journal of Conflict Resolution*, 65(1): 15–45. https://doi.org/10.1177/0022002720935642

Mampilly, Z. (2011). *Rebel Rulers: Insurgent Governance and Civilian Life During War*. Ithaca, NY: Cornell University Press.

Mann, M. (1986). *The Sources of Social Power: A History of Power from the Beginning to A.D. 1760*. New York: Cambridge University Press.

Mann, M. (1988). *States, War and Capitalism*. Oxford: Basil Blackwell.

Manning, C. (1998). 'Constructing Opposition in Mozambique: Renamo as a Political Party'. *Journal of Southern African Studies*, 24(1): 161–189. https://doi.org/10.1080/03057079808708571

Marchais, G., R. Sanchez de la Sierra, and S. Henn (2018). 'Indirect Rule in Armed Conflict: Theoretical Insights from Eastern DRC'. IDS Working Paper 510. Brighton: IDS.

Martin, P. (2020). 'Commander-Community Ties After Civil War'. *Journal of Peace Research*, 58(4): 778–793. https://doi.org/10.1177/0022343320929744
Matanock, A., and P. Staniland (2018). 'How and Why Armed Groups Participate in Elections'. *Perspectives on Politics*, 16(3): 710–727. https://doi.org/10.1017/S1537592718001019
Matanock, A. (2017). *Electing Peace: From Civil Conflict to Political Participation*. Cambridge: Cambridge University Press. https://doi.org/10.1017/9781316987179
McDonough, D. (2008). 'From Guerrillas to Government: Post-Conflict Stability in Liberia, Uganda and Rwanda'. *Third World Quarterly*, 29(2): 357–374. https://doi.org/10.1080/01436590701806921
Menkhaus, K. (2007). 'Governance Without Government in Somalia: Spoilers, State Building, and the Politics of Coping'. *International Security*, 31(3): 74–106. https://doi.org/10.1162/isec.2007.31.3.74
Metelits, C. (2009). *Inside Insurgency: Violence, Civilians, and Revolutionary Group Behavior*. New York: New York University Press.
Mukhopadhyay, D. (2014). *Warlords, Strongman Governors, and the State in Afghanistan*. New York: Cambridge University Press. https://doi.org/10.1017/CBO9781139161817
Müller-Crepon, C., P. Hunziken, and L.-E. Cederman (2020). 'Roads to Rule, Roads to Rebel: Relational State Capacity and Conflict in Africa'. *Journal of Conflict Resolution*, 65(2–3): 563–590. https://doi.org/10.1177/0022002720963674
Muchlinski, D. (2021). 'Swords and Ploughshares: Property Rights, Collective Action, and Nonstate Governance in the Jewish Community of Palestine 1920–1948'. *American Political Science Review*, 115(4): 1373–1387. https://doi.org/10.1017/S0003055421000526
Nordstrom, C. (1997). *A Different Kind of War Story*. Philadelphia, PA: University of Pennsylvania Press.
North, D., J. Wallis, and B. Weingast (2009). *Violence and Social Orders: A Conceptual Framework for Interpreting Recorded Human History*. New York: Cambridge University Press. https://doi.org/10.1017/CBO9780511575839
Olken, B. (2007). 'Monitoring Corruption: Evidence from a Field Experiment in Indonesia'. *Journal of Political Economy*, 115(2): 200–249. https://doi.org/10.1086/517935
Paris, R. (2004). *At War's End: Building Peace After Civil Conflict*. New York: Cambridge University Press. https://doi.org/10.1017/CBO9780511790836
Pearce, J. (2012). 'Control, Politics and Identity in the Angolan Civil War'. *African Affairs*, 111: 442–465. https://doi.org/10.1093/afraf/ads028
Petersen, R. (2001). *Resistance and Rebellion: Lessons from Eastern Europe*. Cambridge: Cambridge University Press. https://doi.org/10.1017/CBO9780511612725
Podder, S. (2014). 'Mainstreaming the Non-State in Bottom-Up Statebuilding: Linkages Between Rebel Governance and Post-Conflict Legitimacy'. *Conflict, Security and Development*, 14(2): 213–243. https://doi.org/10.1080/14678802.2014.889878
Pool, D. (2001). *From Guerrillas to Government: The Eritrean People's Liberation Front*. Athens, OH: Ohio University Press.
Raeymaekers, T. (2010). 'Protection for Sale? War and the Transformation of Regulation on the Congo-Ugandan Border'. *Development and Change*, 41(4): 563–587. https://doi.org/10.1111/j.1467-7660.2010.01655.x
Raleigh, C., and K. De Bruijne (2017). 'Where the Rebels Dare to Tread: A Study of Conflict Geography and Co-option of Local Power in Sierra Leone'. *Journal of Conflict Resolution*, 61(6): 1230–1260. https://doi.org/10.1177/0022002715603767
Reno, W. (2011). *Warfare in Independent Africa*. New York: Cambridge University Press. https://doi.org/10.1017/CBO9780511993428

Revkin, M. R. (2020a). 'What Explains Taxation by Resource-Rich Rebels? Evidence from the Islamic State in Syria'. *Journal of Politics*, 82(2): 757–764. https://doi.org/10.1086/706597

Revkin, M. R. (2020b). 'Competitive Governance and Displacement Decisions Under Rebel Rule: Evidence from the Islamic State in Iraq'. *Journal of Conflict Resolution*, 65(1): 46–80. https://doi.org/10.1177/0022002720951864

Revkin, M. R., and A. Ahram (2020). 'Perspectives on the Rebel Social Contract: Exit, Voice, and Loyalty in the Islamic State in Iraq and Syria'. *World Development*, 132: 104981. https://doi.org/10.1016/j.worlddev.2020.104981

Richards, P. (ed.) (2005). *No Peace, No War: An Anthropology of Contemporary Armed Conflicts*. Oxford: James Currey.

Rubin, M. (2019). 'Rebel Territorial Control and Civilian Collective Action in Civil War: Evidence from the Communist Insurgency in the Philippines'. *Journal of Conflict Resolution*, 64(2–3): 459–489. https://doi.org/10.1177/0022002719863844

Sanchez de la Sierra, R. (2020). 'On the Origins of States: Stationary Bandits and Taxation in Eastern Congo'. *Journal of Political Economy*, 128(1): 32–74. https://doi.org/10.1086/703989

Shaver, A., and J. Shapiro (2021). 'The Effect of Civilian Casualties on Wartime Informing: Evidence from the Iraq War'. *Journal of Conflict Resolution*, 65(7–8): 1337–1377. https://doi.org/10.1177/0022002721991627

Skaperdas, S., and C. Syropoulos (1997). 'The Crisis of the Tax State'. In G. Fiorentini and S. Peltzman (eds), *The Economics of Organized Crime*. New York: Cambridge University Press.

Slater, D. (2010). *Ordering Power: Contentious Politics and Authoritarian Leviathans in Southeast Asia*. New York: Cambridge University Press. https://doi.org/10.1017/CBO9780511760891

Snyder, R., and R. Bhavnani (2005). 'Diamonds, Blood and Taxes: A Revenue-Centered Framework for Explaining Political Order'. *Journal of Conflict Resolution*, 49(4): 563–597. https://doi.org/10.1177/0022002705277796

Staniland, P. (2012). 'States, Insurgents and Wartime Political Orders'. *Perspectives on Politics*, 10(2): 243–264.

Staniland, P. (2021). *Ordering Violence: Explaining Armed Group-State Relations from Conflict to Cooperation*. Ithaca, N.Y.: Cornell University Press. https://doi.org/10.7591/cornell/9781501761102.001.0001

Staniland, P. (2014). *Networks of Rebellion: Explaining Insurgent Cohesion and Collapse*. Ithaca, NY: Cornell University Press.

Staniland, P. (2017). *Ordering Violence: Explaining Armed Group-State Relations from Conflict to Cooperation*. Ithaca N.Y.: Cornell University Press.

Starr, E., and E. J. Wood (2017). 'The Agrarian Legacies of Latin American Civil Wars in Comparative Perspective'. Unpublished manuscript, Yale University.

Stewart, M. (2020). 'Rebel Governance: Military Boon or Military Bust?' *Conflict Management and Peace Science*, 37(1): 16–38. https://doi.org/10.1177/0738894219881422

Stewart, M. (2018). 'Civil War as State-Making: Strategic Governance in Civil War'. *International Organization*, 72(1): 205–226. https://doi.org/10.1017/S0020818317000418

Stokke, K. (2006). 'Building the Tamil Eelam State: Emerging State Institutions and Forms of Governance in LTTE-Controlled Areas in Sri Lanka'. *Third World Quarterly*, 27(6): 1021–1040. https://doi.org/10.1080/01436590600850434

Tadesse, M., and J. Young (2003). 'TPLF: Reform or Decline?' *Review of African Political Economy*, 30(97): 389–403. https://doi.org/10.1080/03056244.2003.9659773

Tilly, C. (1992). *Coercion, Capital and European States, AD 990–1992*. Oxford: Blackwell.
Titeca, K. (2011). 'Access to Resources and Predictability of Armed Rebellion: The FAPC's Short-Lived "Monaco" in Eastern Congo'. *Africa Spectrum*, 46(2): 43–70. https://doi.org/10.1177/000203971104600202
Titeca, K., and T. De Herdt (2011). 'Real Governance Beyond the "Failed State": Negotiating Education in the Democratic Republic of the Congo'. *African Affairs*, 110(439): 213–231. https://doi.org/10.1093/afraf/adr005
Toft, M. (2010). *Securing the Peace: The Durable Settlement of Civil Wars*. Princeton, NJ: Princeton University Press. https://doi.org/10.1515/9781400831999
Verwimp, P., P. Justino, and T. Brück (2019). 'The Microeconomics of Violent Conflict'. *Journal of Development Economics*, 141: 1–6. https://doi.org/10.1016/j.jdeveco.2018.10.005
Verwimp, P., P. Justino, and T. Brück (2009). 'The Analysis of Conflict: A Micro-Level Perspective'. *Journal of Peace Research*, 46(3): 307–314. https://doi.org/10.1177/0022343309102654
Walter, B. (2004). 'Does Conflict Beget Conflict? Explaining Recurring Civil War'. *Journal of Peace Research*, 41(3): 371–388. https://doi.org/10.1177/0022343304043775
Wantchekon, L., and Z. Neema (2002). 'A Theory of Post-Civil War Democratization'. *Journal of Theoretical Politics*, 14(4): 439–464. https://doi.org/10.1177/095162902774006822
Wantchekon, L. (2004). 'The Paradox of "Warlord" Democracy: A Theoretical Investigation'. *American Political Science Review*, 98(1): 17–33. https://doi.org/10.1017/S0003055404000978
Weber, E. (1976). *Peasants into Frenchmen: The Modernisation of Rural France, 1870–1914*. Stanford, CA: Stanford University Press. https://doi.org/10.1515/9780804766036
Weinstein, J. (2007). *Inside Rebellion: The Politics of Insurgent Violence*. New York: Cambridge University Press. https://doi.org/10.1017/CBO9780511808654
Wickham-Crowley, T. (1992). *Guerrillas and Revolution in Latin America: A Comparative Study of Insurgents and Regimes Since 1956*. Princeton, NJ: Princeton University Press. https://doi.org/10.1515/9780691190204
Wimmer, A. (2018). *Nation Building: Why Some Countries Come Together While Others Fall Apart*. Princeton, NJ: Princeton University Press. https://doi.org/10.1515/9781400888894
Wood, E. J. (2008). 'The Social Processes of Civil War: The Wartime Transformation of Social Networks'. *Annual Review of Political Science*, 11: 539–561. https://doi.org/10.1146/annurev.polisci.8.082103.104832
Wood, E. J. (2003). *Insurgent Collective Action and Civil War in El Salvador*. New York: Cambridge University Press. https://doi.org/10.1017/CBO9780511808685
Wood, E. J. (2001). 'An Insurgent Path to Democracy: Popular Mobilization, Economic Interests and Regime Transition in South Africa and El Salvador'. *Comparative Political Studies*, 34(8): 862–888. https://doi.org/10.1177/0010414001034008002
Wood, E. J. (2000). *Forging Democracy from Below: Insurgent Transitions in South Africa and El Salvador*. Cambridge: Cambridge University Press.
Wood, R. (2014). 'From Loss to Looting? Battlefield Costs and Rebel Incentives for Violence'. *International Organization*, 68(4): 979–999. https://doi.org/10.1017/S0020818314000204

PART II

THE LEGACIES OF WARTIME GOVERNANCE

3

Civic participation in civil war

Armed group presence and civilian responses in Colombia

Margarita Gáfaro, Ana Maria Ibáñez, and Patricia Justino

3.1 Introduction

Armed groups entering new territories need to find strategies to control them and the populations within.[1] Groups with large military capacity may choose to exercise social and territorial control through violent coercion. Groups with less military capacity, or those who intend to signal to local populations their ability to govern, may prefer to restrain the use of violence and, instead, resort to co-opting and organizing civilians to gain the necessary strength and authority to effectively contest opposing factions and control key territories.

One common way in which armed groups ensure the control of local communities is by capturing and co-opting local institutions that organize community daily life. By doing so, armed groups take over local organizations, replace local leaders, and make use of their structures to ensure the indoctrination and compliance of local civilians. The capture and co-optation of local institutions during wars has been well documented, ranging from the capture of civic organizations by the Nazi and Fascist parties in Germany and Italy during the Second World War (Riley 2005; Satyanath et al. 2017) to more modern civil wars (Wood 2008; Mampilly 2011; Arjona 2016; Kaplan 2017; Arjona et al. 2019). Civilians, in turn, make use of community organizations to support armed groups when their ideology and strategic goals align. Others may organize themselves to resist and repel them and maintain their autonomy (Arjona 2016; Kaplan 2017; Krause 2018). These complex interactions between armed groups and civilians during wartime

[1] We would like to thank Ana Arjona, Andrew Foster, Stathis Kalyvas, Anja Sautmann, Michael Weintraub, and participants of the 9th Annual Meeting of the Households in Conflict Network at UC Berkeley and of seminars and workshops at the Universidad de los Andes, Northwestern University, Yale University, University of Colorado at Denver, the Institute of Development Studies, the UK Department for International Development, and UNU-WIDER for valuable comments and suggestions. We are grateful to Laura Montenegro, Maria Alejandra Arias, Paola Poveda, Natalia Moreno, and Sonia Monroy for excellent research assistance, and to Robert Karl for kindly sharing data on parliamentary fiscal transfers with us.

Margarita Gáfaro, Ana Maria Ibáñez, and Patricia Justino, *Civic participation in civil war*. In: *Institutional Legacies of Violent Conflict*. Edited by: Patricia Justino, Oxford University Press. © United Nations University World Institute for Development Economics Research (UNU-WIDER) (2026). DOI: 10.1093/9780197904077.003.0003

affect the course of the war and may lead to different pathways of recovery, state-building, and the consolidation of democracy in the post-conflict period (Wood 2008; Huang 2016). However, to date, we have only a rudimentary understanding of how armed groups shape local social organization in wartime: What are the implications of armed group war strategies for the organization of local communities? What is the effect of armed groups on civic participation in community organizations? How does civic participation change when exposed to the presence of armed groups? The aim of this chapter is to address these questions.

Community organizations are central to how people come together to achieve common societal goals in the absence of well-functioning state institutions, especially in areas outside power centres (Ostrom 1990; La Ferrara 2002).[2] Participation in civic organizations—defined as the membership and involvement of individuals in organizations and activities that constitute the 'civil society' (Lancee and van de Werfhorst 2012: 1167)—is also a determinant of how social movements and collective action emerge and are organized (Putnam 1993), both key conditions for how post-war societies recover, build state capacity, and maintain peace (Wood 2000; Wantchekon and Neema 2002; Wantchekon 2004; Huang 2016; Blair et al. 2022; and see Chapter 4 in this volume).

Several studies have investigated the effect of civil wars on community organization in the post-war period. In a much-cited paper, Bellows and Miguel (2009) show that individuals in households victimized during the 1991–2002 civil war in Sierra Leone were more likely to report attendance of community meetings, voting, and joining social and political groups in the immediate post-war period. In Northern Uganda, Blattman (2009) finds that young people forcibly recruited into the Lord's Resistance Army report higher levels of voting and community leadership. Voors et al. (2012) show that violence exposure during the 1993–2003 civil war in Burundi is associated with increased self-reported participation in community organizations, as well as more altruistic behaviour in a set of experiments. Similar results are reported in Tajikistan (Cassar et al. 2013), Nepal (Gilligan et al. 2014), and across a sample of European countries where individuals reported exposure to both WWII and violent conflicts in their regions in the 1990s and 2000s (Grosjean 2014). Overall, this literature finds evidence for a 'phoenix effect', whereby exposure of individuals to violence in wartime generates greater civic engagement in the post-war period, when compared to others not affected by violence. This effect is generally interpreted as evidence for increases in pro-social behaviour as a result of exposure to violence in wartime (Bauer et al. 2016).

[2] A large literature has documented the importance of local community organizations in developing countries, including their roles in the management of common resources, as informal credit and economic support networks and in the allocation of resources and decision-making over local development structures (Ostrom 1990; Putnam 1993; Bardhan 2005). Well-studied examples include the Colombian *Juntas de Acción Comunal*, formed of voluntary members (Kaplan 2017) and the *Panchayats* in India, formed of elected community members (Pande et al. 2007). Throughout the chapter, 'community organizations' or 'civic organizations' are used interchangeably. A community refers in broad terms to a village or *vereda* in the case of Colombia.

However, civil wars generate other legacies beyond violence, including forms of institutional change that may shape local social organization (Kalyvas 2006; Arjona 2016; Justino 2013; see also Chapter 2 in this volume). It is, therefore, possible that greater post-war civic participation may not be an expression of pro-social behaviour, but rather a response to new institutions driving civic participation in wartime for other reasons (as, for instance, strategic war objectives by armed groups) that may last beyond the end of the conflict.

An emerging literature has shown how institutional war dynamics beyond violence—which foster the emergence of social and political order in wartime—may explain changes in community organization. Two studies are of particular relevance. Arjona (2016) focuses on the interactions between armed groups and civilians and discusses the advent of two forms of social order during wartime. In the first type, rebelocracy (or the rule of rebels), rebel groups govern civilians and impose norms of behaviour and conduct. The second type, aliocracy (or the rule of others), is characterized by minimal interference of armed groups in civilian affairs. These types of order are shaped by the time horizons of armed groups and the quality of pre-existing local institutions before the arrival of the group to the community. Mampilly and Stewart (2021) develop a typology of six rebel political institutional arrangements: martial law, partial subjugation, status quo (more or less inclusive), and transformative (more or less inclusive). Each of these institutional arrangements is defined by variation in how power is shared between rebel groups and local citizens, the integration of civilians into rebel group institutional arrangements, the degree to which groups transform pre-existing institutions, and levels of civilian influence over decision-making. In broad terms, the core insight of these two frameworks is the fact that wartime political orders are shaped by how armed groups make decisions about governing based on their strategic objectives and interactions they engage in with civilians.[3] This literature has largely focused on explaining the emergence of political order, rather than its operation and consequences. We build on these studies and analyse in this chapter one aspect of how wartime political order is built—the control of local community organizations by armed groups. We ask how the presence of armed groups shapes local participation in community organizations and what armed group strategies may explain variation in observed participation.[4] To do so, we build a new theoretical framework to formally model the choices faced by armed groups and civilians with respect to

[3] Staniland (2021) also defines new typologies of wartime political orders, whereby political orders are shaped by the interaction between types of territorial control by armed groups in wartime and levels of cooperation between the state and insurgent groups. These typologies do not consider explicitly the role of civilian agency.

[4] Other aspects of political order, documented in an emerging literature on 'rebel governance', include the provision of public goods, construction of infrastructure, implementation of legal and justice systems, and, sometimes, the establishment of parallel parliament-type structure, local elections, and diplomatic wings (Mampilly 2011; Arjona et al. 2015; Arjona 2016; Loyle and Binningsbø 2018; Stewart 2018). Control of community organizations is arguably one of the institutional arrangements needed for armed groups to exercise effective rebel governance.

the organization of local communities. The model predictions are then tested for the case of Colombia.

The theoretical model explores the interplay between the strategies used by armed groups towards local organizations and the response of the local population to these strategies. A community characterized by a predetermined level of institutional capacity is assessed by the armed group in terms of its attractiveness for the general war strategy and aims of the group. Once it is present in the community, the group decides to capture local organizations as a mechanism to control the population (dominance strategy) or decides not to interfere in community-driven organizations (libertarian strategy).[5] The gains of capture for the armed group increase with the share of the population that participates in these organizations (because they can influence and control more people), while its costs are fixed.[6] The local population observes the actions of the armed group and chooses whether to participate or not in local organizations. Capture by the armed group decreases the utility of participation in communities with strong pre-existing institutional capacity due to, for instance, loss of agency and autonomy as armed groups take control over organizations previously run by civilians. There may also be a possible increased risk of victimization as armed groups may want to eliminate organization members who are perceived as hostile (Arjona 2016; Kaplan 2017). Conversely, capture by armed groups increases the utility of participation in communities with weaker pre-existing institutional capacity since participation to show obedience and compliance to the armed group may reduce a possible risk of violence (Kalyvas 2006). Armed groups may also now provide services and goods that were before absent or provided inefficiently by weak institutions (Rubin 2019). In equilibrium, the armed group will only capture organizations with a sufficiently high level of pre-existing institutional capacity, where it can reach (and thus influence) a sufficiently large share of the population through these organizations.

We extend the model to allow for civilian agency in the use of local organizations. If local citizens support the armed group, they will allow the group to make use of community organizations for their strategic or ideological purposes.

[5] It is to note that this chapter does not aim to offer an alternative typology of local political orders; it offers a typology of choices faced by armed groups with respect to one arguably key aspect of wartime governance—building local organizations. Armed groups may be more likely to adopt a dominance strategy in areas where they establish systems of rebelocracy (Arjona 2016) or transformative political institutional arrangements (Mampilly and Stewart 2021). However, dominance strategies through co-option of community organizations may still be possible in contexts of Arjona's aliocracy or Mampilly and Stewart's partial subjugation or status quo arrangements when, for instance, civilians do not use community organizations as means of outright rebellion. Under those forms of political order, such co-opted organizations may facilitate relations between armed groups and civilians from afar by providing a place to, for instance, share information or resources.

[6] Note that the number of individuals in a community organization does not define the institutional capacity of the organization or its effectiveness. Armed groups derive higher utility from larger organizations because they can reach more individuals to either support their cause or, at the very least, comply with their local governance arrangements.

If local citizens oppose the group, they may make use of community organizations as a collective mechanism of resistance towards the dominance of the armed group. Resistance increases the cost of capture of community organizations to the armed group. If the armed group anticipates effective resistance in communities with pre-existing strong institutional capacity, it will adopt a libertarian position. Otherwise, it will adopt a dominance strategy. Heterogeneity in the predictions of the model about the participation effects of the armed group in equilibrium allows us to infer, theoretically, what armed group strategy may explain observed changes in civilian participation in community organizations. This is useful because identifying armed group behaviour empirically in wartime is challenging.

It is to note that the model is necessarily a simplification of the complex and non-linear processes of exchange and negotiation established by armed groups and civilians in war zones. It also conveys a stepwise decision-making process that, in reality, may be much messier as on-the-ground realities respond to changes in military gains/losses and shifts in military and political power. However, the model offers a theoretical framework to identify what armed group behaviour may explain individual civic participation in wartime, which we believe is useful to understand how different configurations of local social organization may define the course of the conflict and its aftermath.

We test the effect of changes in armed group presence on changes in individual participation in community organizations across categories of pre-existing institutional capacity using a longitudinal dataset conducted in Colombia in 2010, 2013, and 2016 in 224 rural communities. Participation in community organizations is defined broadly to include the engagement of community members in local organizations that collectively address issues relevant to the organization, operation, and governance of local communities. In the case of Colombia, these include a variety of local social and political groups, rural cooperatives, and, especially, village councils (the *Juntas de Acción Comunal* or JACs). Institutional capacity is defined by the level of efficacy and legitimacy of community organizations to regulate and structure community life and exercise collective action (Arjona 2016; Rubin 2019). As a new attempt to measure pre-existing institutional capacity at the community level, we compiled information from public records on parliamentary fiscal transfers from the National Congress to community organizations in rural communities in 1977, a mechanism used by the government of Colombia to strengthen local organizations as part of the decentralization process initiated around that time.[7] This measure captures the fiscal capacity of local community organizations, which is a central aspect of overall institutional capacity (Besley and Mueller 2021).

[7] We thank Robert Karl for sharing these data with us.

The main empirical strategy exploits the panel structure of the data to estimate the effects of changes in the presence of armed groups (and within communities) on changes in individual participation in local organizations between survey waves. We control for individual and municipality-wave fixed effects and time-variant community characteristics.[8] We find that changes in the presence of armed groups in any given community between survey waves increase the participation in community organizations of individuals living in communities with low pre-existing institutional capacity and reduce the participation of individuals in local organizations in communities with high pre-existing institutional capacity. These results embody theoretical expectations of a dominance equilibrium, whereby armed groups capture local organizations for strategic war purposes.

This analysis offers a significant contribution to how we understand the operation and consequences of order and control in conflict areas, by building an integrated theoretical framework to study how civic participation changes in conflict areas. The strategies followed by armed groups with respect to local community organizations and the responses by civilians may, in turn, offer a basis to better understand the effectiveness of political orders in wartime communities. The focus on civic participation is especially important because changes in how communities are organized in wartime may lead to different pathways of institutional change in the post-conflict period. Greater capture and co-option of institutions by armed groups may facilitate their consolidation of power, strengthen their institutional capacity, and hinder the ability of civilians to exercise autonomy and collective action in the aftermath of war. Greater resistance by civilians may reduce the institution-building capacity of rebel groups and increase the capacity of communities for mobilization and collective action, which may, in turn, increase the likelihood of democratization in post-conflict countries (Wood 2000; Huang 2016).

3.2 Theoretical model

Armed actors opt for a variety of strategies when attempting to control local populations: from victimizing, displacing, and looting to capturing or creating local institutions for the provision of public goods and security, the organization and control of local markets and political structures, and the enforcement of social norms. To this purpose, insurgent groups make use of existing local community organizations or build new ones to better exercise control of territories they have gained (Arjona 2016; Kaplan 2017; Rubin 2019; Blair et al. 2022).

[8] As an alternative specification, we propose, later in the chapter, an instrumental variable that exploits the changes in the presence of armed groups in rural communities caused by the peace negotiations between the Colombian government and the Fuerzas Armadas Revolucionarias de Colombia. We conduct, in addition, robustness checks on potential biases due to sample selection and sorting induced by individual migration and show that our main results are robust across these tests.

Civilians may join various forms of collective action to either collaborate with armed groups or resist them (or other behaviours in between). Even if opposing the armed group, some individuals may endure the presence of the group by obeying their rules and joining community organizations built for the purpose of governing civilians and gaining legitimacy and support.[9] Others may choose to resist by using community organizations to coordinate collective action such as, for instance, forming armed defence groups (Arjona 2016; Petersen 2001; Wood 2003).

The effect of these complex interactions on local social organization has remained weakly understood at both theoretical and empirical levels. Below, we present a model that outlines the decision-making process of armed groups with respect to local organizations, and the participation choices of rural residents when the armed group establishes itself in the community. All proofs for the propositions of the model are shown in Appendix A.

3.2.1 General set-up of the model

We start with a rural community with a continuum of agents of mass 1 denoted by sub-index i. For simplicity, we assume that only one armed group is present in the community.[10] There is an infinite number of time periods, which we denote by t. At every period, the armed group makes choices about whether to establish a presence in the community and about the strategy it adopts regarding local organizations (capture or not). Once rural residents observe the choices made by the armed group, they decide whether to participate in community organizations. The community has a pre-existing level of institutional capacity, $s \in S$, which is fixed and does not depend on time-varying choices of agents in the community.[11] We assume that pay-offs are realized at the end of every period and depend only on the contemporaneous actions of the rural residents and the armed group. Figure 3.1

[9] Local populations may also resort to armed groups for physical and economic protection, especially when the state is weak, inadequate, or abusive (Goodwin 2001; Justino 2009, 2013; Kalyvas and Kocher 2007).

[10] This is a simplifying assumption in order to keep the model tractable. In reality, communities in wartime may face more than one armed group who compete with each other through military means or through a variety of contracts, bargains, and alliances. One of these groups may be the state. In most cases being considered in the chapter, the state is relatively absent in contested areas. In other cases, the state and its military may become a competing authority, or attempt to rule indirectly via paramilitary groups, militia, and other proxy political actors. One way of thinking about the simpler set-up of the model is to envisage a setting where territory control by that armed group is either absolute or likely to be absolute. In contexts of military competition, armed groups may delay decisions over the control of local organizations until territorial control is ensured.

[11] Institutional capacity has two components: one determined by long-run outcomes and another that depends on the short-run decisions of community members. While the latter component is the main endogenous variable in our model, we simplify the model by assuming the former to be exogenous. This assumption is justified by our interest in short-term community responses to the presence of armed groups.

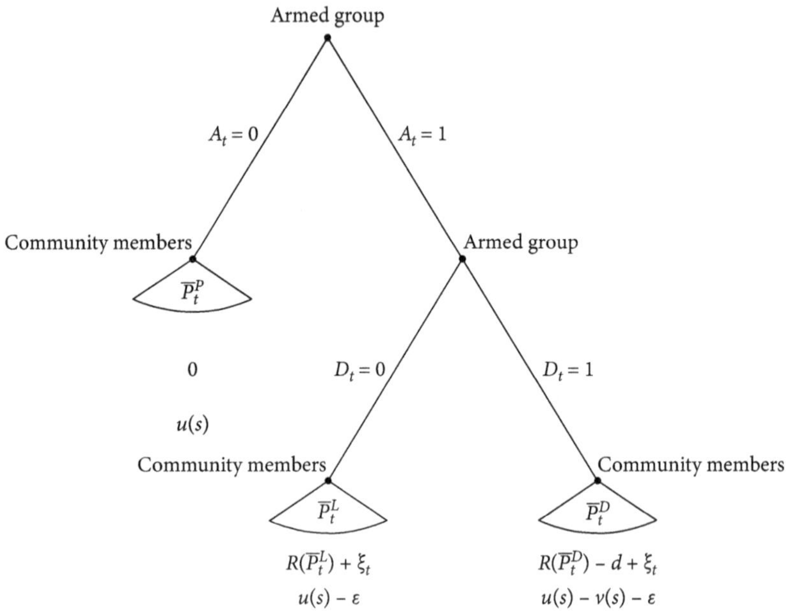

Figure 3.1 Armed group and community members: choices and pay-offs
Note: The figure depicts the structure of the game proposed in the theoretical framework; see text for more details.

depicts the choices of the armed group and of community members in the form of an extensive game representation.

3.2.2 To capture or not: armed group choices

At the beginning of every period, the armed group assesses the attractiveness of a given rural community. This attractiveness depends on the stage of the war, pre-determined community characteristics (such as geographical location, resource endowments, or the ideological or political alignment of their members) that may contribute to the war strategy of the group, and the long-term objectives of the group (for instance, to govern or not). For simplicity, we assume that the attractiveness of the community at time t can be summarized by the index ξ_t. The armed group observes ξ_t and decides whether to establish a presence in the community. We denote the choice of presence by the armed group by $A_t = \{0, 1\}$, where $A_t = 1$ if present at time t. Without loss of generality, we normalize the index such that $A_t = 1$ if $\xi_t \geq 0$.

Once present in the community, the armed group gains full information about the preferences of community members and levels of pre-existing institutional capacity. With this information, the armed group decides about the type of strategy it will adopt towards community organizations. One choice is to capture or co-opt community organizations that will allow the group to control local populations and the territory and establish more effective systems of governance by taking advantage of existing structural arrangements and successful organizational techniques (Riley 2005; Wood 2008; Arjona 2016; Satyanath et al. 2017). The capture and control of organizations allow armed groups to establish their own governance systems, exercise political authority, control territory, and gather information and revenue (Kalyvas 2006; Mampilly 2011; Arjona 2016). Throughout this section, we refer to this strategy as a *dominance strategy* towards community organizations, or *capture*. Alternatively, the armed group may seek to gain the support of civilians by not interfering in community organizations. We refer to this as a *libertarian strategy* towards community organizations.

Let $D_t = 1$ if the armed group adopts a dominance strategy towards community organizations and $D_t = 0$ otherwise.[12] We assume that the gains of capture for the armed group increase with the share of rural residents that participate in these organizations, since this represents the share of residents the armed group can reach—and hopefully bring to their side or ensure compliance—through the capture of local community organizations. Let $\overline{P}_t$ be the share of rural residents that participate in community organizations at time t. The gains from capture are determined by the function $R(\overline{P}_t)$, which is continuous, differentiable, and monotonically increasing. We assume that capture generates a cost d for the armed group. The armed group adopts a dominant strategy, $D_t = 1$, if $R(\overline{P}_t) > d$.

3.2.3 Participation in community organizations: civilian choices

Rural residents observe the behaviour of the armed group and decide whether to participate in community organizations. This decision depends on the utility they derive from participating, relative to not participating. We refer to the latter as their outside option.[13] We denote the participation decision by $p_{it} = \{0, 1\}$, with $p_{it} = 1$ if individual i participates at time t. We assume that the presence of the armed group in the community decreases the utility of rural residents by a constant factor, ϵ, regardless of individual participation in community organizations. This decrease in utility reflects a general risk of victimization, the imposition of taxes, rules of

[12] For simplicity, we assume that a dominance strategy implies capturing all community organizations (or that there is only one organization in the community). It is possible that armed groups may choose to co-opt only a few organizations, and that not all organizations may be prone to being captured. However, it is unlikely that there will be much of such variation in small units of analysis like Colombian *veredas*, for instance.

[13] Outside options may be limited in conflict zones and often the opportunity costs of leaving the control of armed groups may be higher than remaining under their influence (Justino 2009; Kalyvas and Kocher 2007).

behaviour, ideological disagreement, and other economic and social costs associated with the presence of armed actors in the community. We also assume that the utility from participating in local organizations is identical across individuals in the community and depends on (i) the pre-existing institutional capacity of the community, s, and (ii) the dominance strategy of the armed group in the case of presence D_t.

Let W_t represent the utility for residents of participating in community organizations at time t. This utility can be written as:

$$W(s; A_t, D_t) = u(s) - v(s) A_t D_t - \epsilon A_t \tag{1}$$

with u and v increasing and continuously differentiable. The function u captures the direct utility of participating in community organizations. We assume that this utility increases with the level of the community's pre-existing institutional capacity because collective action might be more successful in communities with stronger institutions. The function v represents the cost or benefit for community members of participating in organizations that have been captured by the armed group. We assume that this cost increases with pre-existing institutional capacity, as the risk of victimization and loss of agency due to the capture of the organization by the armed group may be higher for politically active individuals in institutionally stronger communities.[14] In communities with low pre-existing institutional capacity, there may be gains from participation due to lower risk of victimization (as individuals show compliance by participating in community organizations captured by the group) or more effective provision of public goods by the armed group. Assumption 1 summarizes these ideas.

Assumption 1. *Functions u and v are monotonically increasing and continuously differentiable functions that satisfy the following properties:*

i. $u' > 0,\ v' > 0,$ *and* $u' > v'$ *for all* $s \in S$
ii. $u(s) > 0$ *for all* $s \in S$
iii. $\exists\, \bar{s} \in S$ *such that for* $s \in S,\ v(s) \leq 0$ *if* $s \leq \bar{s}$ *and* $v(s) > 0$ *if* $s > \bar{s}$

The first part of Assumption 1 implies that pre-existing institutional capacity always increases the overall utility of participation, despite higher utility losses from armed group capture in communities with pre-existing stronger institutional capacity. The second part of the assumption implies that rural residents always derive positive utility from participation in community organizations in the absence of the armed group. The last part of the assumption implies that if pre-existent institutional capacity in the community is sufficiently low, the dominance of armed groups makes participation more attractive.

[14] For example, Prem et al. (2022) document the selective targeting and killing of social leaders in Colombia engaged in successful organizations.

Rural residents make their participation choices by taking into account their reservation utility in case of not participating, which is given by:

$$\overline{U}_i = \overline{u}_i - \epsilon A_t \tag{2}$$

This reservation utility has an idiosyncratic component, $\overline{u}_i$, which depends on individual characteristics and represents a heterogeneous utility that each community member would get in case of not being involved in local organizations. We assume that $\overline{u}_i$ is independent and identically distributed within the community, with the cumulative distribution function G. The reservation utility also has a common component for all community members, capturing the common utility losses resulting from the presence of armed groups in the community ϵ.

Every period, rural residents participate in community organizations ($p_{it} = 1$) if the utility of participation exceeds their reservation utility:

$$W(s; A_t, D_t) \geq \overline{U}_i \tag{3}$$

3.2.4 Equilibrium

In every period, the equilibrium is characterized by the participation choices of community members, p^*_{it}, armed group presence, A^*_t, and dominance strategy of the armed group, D^*_t, such that

$$p^*_{it} = \begin{cases} 1 \text{ if } W(s; A^*_t, D^*_t) \geq \overline{U}_i \\ 0 \text{ otherwise} \end{cases} \tag{4}$$

$$A^*_t = \begin{cases} 1 \text{ if } \xi_t \geq 0 \\ 0 \text{ otherwise} \end{cases} \tag{5}$$

$$D^*_t = \begin{cases} 1 \text{ if } R\left(Pr\left(\overline{U}_i \leq W(s; A^*_t = 1, D^*_t = 1)\right)\right) > d \\ 0 \text{ otherwise} \end{cases} \tag{6}$$

We define three types of equilibria depending on the presence of the armed group in the community and its strategy towards community organizations: dominance, libertarian, and peaceful. Below, we outline what civic participation we may expect under each equilibrium.

Dominance equilibrium

Dominance equilibrium takes place at time t if the armed group is present in the community, $A^*_t = 1$, and captures community organizations, $D^*_t = 1$. In this case, average participation is given by:

$$\overline{P}^D_t = E[p^*_{it} | A^*_t = 1, D^*_t = 1, s] = Pr\left(\overline{U}_i \leq u(s) - v(s)\right) \tag{7}$$

Libertarian equilibrium

Libertarian equilibrium takes place at time t if the armed group is present in the community, $A_t^* = 1$, but does not capture community organizations, $D_t^* = 0$. In this case, average participation is given by:

$$\overline{P}_t^L = E[p_{it}^*|A_t^* = 1, D_t^* = 0, s] = Pr(\overline{u}_i \leq u(s)) \tag{8}$$

Peaceful equilibrium

Peaceful equilibrium takes place at time t if the armed group is not present in the community. In this case, average participation is given by:

$$\overline{P}_t^P = E[p_{it}^*|A_t^* = 0, s] = Pr(\overline{u}_i \leq u(s)) \tag{9}$$

The following proposition compares average participation in the peaceful equilibrium with participation in the two alternative equilibria in which the armed group is present in the community.

Proposition 1. *For every time period t and r, we have*

i. $\overline{P}_t^L - \overline{P}_r^P = 0$
ii. *If* $s \leq \bar{s}$, *then* $\overline{P}_t^D - \overline{P}_r^P \geq 0$
iii. *If* $s > \bar{s}$, *then* $\overline{P}_t^D - \overline{P}_r^P < 0$

Proof. See appendix.

Proposition 1 implies that the effect of the dominance strategy adopted by armed groups on average participation depends on the pre-existing institutional capacity of the community. If pre-existing institutional capacity is sufficiently low, average participation under dominance is greater than average participation when the armed group is not present in the community. By contrast, if pre-existing institutional capacity is sufficiently high, the adoption of a dominance strategy by the armed group will reduce average participation compared with the peaceful equilibrium. For example, some individuals may remove themselves from local organizations for fear of being targeted or are removed forcibly by the armed groups and replaced by more compliant leaders (Kaplan 2017).

The type of equilibrium that takes place in the community depends on the attractiveness assessment by the armed group, and on whether the armed group adopts a dominance strategy when it establishes itself in the community. The latter depends on the participation of community members in local organizations relative to the cost of capture. If attractiveness assessment $\xi_t \geq 0$, then there is a dominance equilibrium if and only if:

$$R(E[p_{it}^*|A_t^* = 1, D_t^* = 1]) = R(Pr(\overline{u}_i \leq u(s) - v(s))) > d \tag{10}$$

Since $u(s) - v(s)$ is increasing in s and R is monotonically increasing, $R(Pr(\overline{u}_i \leq u(s) - v(s)))$ is also increasing in s. The expression in equation (10) implies that the armed group will adopt a dominance strategy if pre-existing institutional capacity is sufficiently high, such that an appropriately large share of rural residents can be reached through the capture of community organizations. The armed group will also always capture community organizations if the cost of doing so, d, is sufficiently low relative to s. In Proposition 2, we formalize this argument and define the effect of armed group presence on average participation, taking into account the optimal capture strategy of the armed group, which varies with the pre-existing institutional capacity of the community and the cost of dominance.

Proposition 2. *Let $\hat{s}$ be a level of pre-existing institutional capacity such that $R(Pr(\overline{u}_i \leq u(\hat{s}) - v(\hat{s}))) = d$. Then,*

i.
$$\text{If } s \leq \hat{s} \Rightarrow R(Pr(\overline{u}_i \leq u(s) - v(s))) \leq d \Rightarrow D_t^*|_{\xi_t \geq 0} = 0$$
$$\text{If } s > \hat{s} \Rightarrow R(Pr(\overline{u}_i \leq u(s) - v(s))) > d \Rightarrow D_t^*|_{\xi_t \geq 0} = 1 \qquad (11)$$

ii. *For a lower d, the threshold of pre-existing institutional capacity for dominance in the community ($\hat{s}$) is lower.*

Proof. See appendix.

Proposition 2 implies that if the pre-existing institutional capacity of the community is above (below) the threshold $\hat{s}$, then it is optimal for the armed group to adopt a dominance (libertarian) strategy. The participation response to the presence of an armed group in the community would then depend on the dominance strategy of the armed group (determined by the magnitude of s relative to $\hat{s}$) and how participation is affected by dominance (determined by the magnitude of s relative to $\bar{s}$).

Proposition 3

i. If $s > \max\{\hat{s}, \bar{s}\}$, *then a dominance equilibrium takes place whenever the armed group is present in the community, and average participation decreases in the presence of the armed group:* $E[p_{it}^* | A_t^* = 1, s] - E[p_{it}^* | A_t^* = 0, s] < 0$.

ii. If $s \leq \max\{\hat{s}, \bar{s}\}$, *either a dominance or a libertarian equilibrium can take place when the armed group is present, and average participation is non-decreasing in the presence of the armed group:* $E[p_{it}^* | A_t^* = 1, s] - E[p_{it}^* | A_t^* = 0, s] \geq 0$.

Proof. See appendix.

Proposition 3 implies that if the community has sufficiently high pre-existing institutional capacity ($s > \max\{\hat{s}, \bar{s}\}$), the armed group will adopt a dominance strategy and participation will decrease with the presence of the armed group. If pre-existing institutional capacity is not sufficiently large ($s \leq \max\{\hat{s}, \bar{s}\}$), the equilibrium would depend on the magnitude of $\hat{s}$ relative to $\bar{s}$. In particular, when $\hat{s} \geq \bar{s}$, there is always a libertarian equilibrium. By contrast, when $\hat{s} < \bar{s}$ and $\hat{s} < s \leq \bar{s}$, there is a dominance equilibrium.

Proposition 1 implies that we will observe changes in the participation of community members across time, depending on the presence of the armed group in each period. Proposition 3 also implies that if the pre-existing institutional capacity of the community is below $\max\{\hat{s}, \bar{s}\}$, participation does not decrease in the presence of the armed group. Whether the armed group adopts a dominance strategy or not in this case depends on the size of s relative to $\hat{s}$. According to the first part of Proposition 2, if $s > \hat{s}$, then the armed group captures community organizations. According to the second part of Proposition 2, if the cost of dominance is low, the threshold of pre-existing institutional capacity that will determine the adoption of a dominance strategy becomes low too, increasing the likelihood that $s > \hat{s}$.

3.2.5 Civilian resistance

The propositions above implicitly assume the compliance of civilians across all three equilibria. In this section, we consider the possibility that civilians join local organizations as a way of resisting the dominance of the armed groups. Civilians may adopt open or hidden ways to resist armed groups. Open resistance methods include armed defence groups, such as the Kamajor in Sierra Leone or paramilitary groups in El Salvador, Peru, and Colombia (Brockett 1990; Wood 2003, 2008). Covert resistance methods include acting as informants for opposing factions, undermining the activities of the groups, or forming hidden resistance groups (Arjona 2016; Petersen 2001; Wood 2003), such as the Lithuanian resistance against Soviet occupation in the 1940s (Petersen 2001), the actions of grassroots resistance movements against ETA in the Spanish Basque country (Funes 1998), and peasant resistance ('*rondas campesinas*') against Sendero Luminoso in Peru (Fumerton 2001). We modify the expression in equation (1) to incorporate the effect of resistance on the utility of individuals participating in local organizations:

$$W(s; A_t, D_t) = u(s) - (v(s) - r(s))A_tD_t - \epsilon A_t \tag{12}$$

where function r captures the role of resistance in mitigating the negative effects of dominance by the armed group. We modify Assumption 1 as follows:

Assumption 2. *The functions u, v, and r are increasing and continuously differentiable functions that satisfy the following properties:*

i. $u' > 0,\ v' > 0,$ *and* $r' > 0,\ u' > v' - r'$ *for all* $s \in S$
ii. $u(s) > 0, v(s) > 0, r(s) > 0, r(s) > v(s)$ *for all* $s \in S$

The first part of Assumption 2 implies that the utility of participation increases with pre-existing institutional capacity. The second part implies that resistance is more effective in communities with stronger pre-existing institutional capacity. However, even in communities with low pre-exiting institutional capacity, resistance may allow communities to mitigate the potential negative effects of capture by armed groups. Individual i participates in community organizations if:

$$u(s) - (v(s) - r(s)) A_t D_t \geq \overline{u}_i \tag{13}$$

Resistance by the community increases the cost of capture for the armed group. We define the cost function, $d(\overline{P}_t)$, as monotonically increasing with $d'' > 0$. Thus, in equilibrium, the armed group captures the organization if:

$$R(Pr(\overline{u}_i \leq u(s) - v(s) + r(s))) > d(Pr(\overline{u}_i \leq u(s) - v(s) + r(s))) \tag{14}$$

Proposition 4. *If there exists a* $\vec{s}^{\tau} \in S$ *such that* $R(Pr(\overline{u}_i \leq u(\vec{s}^{\tau}) - v(s) + r(\vec{s}^{\tau}))) = d(Pr(\overline{u}_i \leq u(\vec{s}^{\tau}) - v(\vec{s}^{\tau}) + r(\vec{s}^{\tau})))$, *then we have the following:*

i. *If* $s > \vec{s}^{\tau}$, *a libertarian equilibrium emerges whenever the armed group is present in the community, and average participation does not change with the presence of the armed group:* $E[p^*_{it} | A^*_t = 1, s] - E[p^*_{it} | A^*_t = 0, s] = 0.$
ii. *If* $s \leq \vec{s}^{\tau}$, *a dominance equilibrium emerges and average participation increases with the presence of the armed group:* $E[p^*_{it} | A^*_t = 1, s] - E[p^*_{it} | A^*_t = 0, s] > 0.$

Proof. See appendix.

Proposition 4 implies that if the community has sufficiently high pre-existing institutional capacity, then the armed group anticipates the effectiveness of resistance and adopts a libertarian strategy. In this case, average individual participation in community organizations does not change with the presence of armed groups. On the other hand, if pre-existing institutional capacity is below the threshold $\vec{s}^{\tau}$, individual participation in community organizations increases as a form of resistance to the dominance of the armed group. This increase in participation may not be high enough to dissuade the armed group from capturing local organizations.

As a response to resistance, armed groups may in turn inhibit the functioning of local collective organizations to prevent civil resistance movements or alienate support for the opponent group.

Overall, the model we outline above allows us to infer theoretically what armed group strategy may explain observed changes in civilian participation in community organizations. Under a libertarian strategy, the individual participation of rural residents in community organizations should not change with armed group presence in the community when compared to communities where armed groups are not present. By contrast, an armed group dominance strategy implies that we should observe a reduction in individual participation in civic organizations in communities with high pre-existing institutional capacity and an increase (or no change) in participation in civic organizations in communities with low pre-existing institutional capacity. If civilians use local organizations as a form of resistance against armed groups, in equilibrium, we should not observe changes in individual participation in local organizations in communities with strong pre-existing institutions but should observe an increase in participation in communities with low pre-existing institutional capacity.

3.3 The Colombian context

Colombia has been characterized by profound forms of institutional transformation as a result of decades of armed conflict since 1940. The conflict originated in the first half of the twentieth century due to a struggle between the two main political parties, the Liberals and the Conservatives. This period, known as *La Violencia*, ended in 1958 with a power-sharing agreement between the two parties, which excluded leftist movements. Peasant organizations that emerged during the late period of *La Violencia* turned into liberal left-wing guerrilla groups during the early 1960s, after the incomplete implementation of a peace process (Karl 2017; Sánchez and Meertens 1983). The emergence of the illegal drug trade intensified the conflict in the 1970s and 1980s by providing resources to left-wing guerrilla groups and promoting the creation of private armies to protect drug barons and some large landowners from guerrilla attacks (Sánchez and Palau 2006; Gutiérrez and Barón 2005). The conflict then expanded from isolated areas to areas with an abundance of natural resources and economic dynamism, and aggressions against the civil population escalated sharply. The paramilitary demobilization in 2003, along with an increase in public efforts to improve the provision of national security, resulted in a reduction in levels of violence. In 2016, a peace agreement with the Fuerzas Armadas Revolucionarias de Colombia (FARC), the largest guerrilla group in the country, demobilized more than 13,000 combatants. However, violence persists in parts of the country as the

National Liberation Army, FARC splinter groups, and illicit drug trade groups continue to operate.

The presence of a range of armed groups and their strategic objectives strongly influenced local organizations during the civil war. Guerrilla and paramilitary groups regulated day-to-day matters, controlled movements of the population, and undertook governance functions in regions under their control (Arjona 2016; Grupo de Memoria Histórica 2010, 2011; Gutiérrez and Barón 2005; Ronderos 2014). To do so, armed actors co-opted local organizations (Arjona 2016), aided by the decentralization process that started in 1988 and facilitated a closer relationship between local authorities and armed groups (Sánchez and Palau 2006). Armed actors sought to directly influence elections and frequently audited local authorities to enforce their own governance programs (Grupo de Memoria Histórica 2010; Ronderos 2014). Guerrilla groups also used some religious and productive organizations, as well as trade unions, to disseminate their political agenda. In many places, armed groups entered communities by influencing the actions of the JACs, forcing local community members to attend JAC sessions and coercing their members into participating in public works. Paramilitary groups, in particular, used the JACs to construct infrastructure, disseminate their rules of social behaviour, and collect valuable information for war activities (Ronderos 2014).

These strategies debilitated many social networks and community organizations. Armed actors instilled fear among the population and deliberately targeted community leaders and some organizations to force collaboration. Willingness to participate in community organizations or collective activities decreased in many communities. Fear and the risk of aggression for anyone perceived as collaborators with opponent groups generated mistrust among the population. Many households retreated to private life and restricted social interactions. The destruction of infrastructure, land mines, and compulsory confinement created further physical obstacles to collective activities (Grupo de Memoria Histórica 2010).

At the same time, some communities devised creative strategies to avoid total control over their organizations and collective life by armed actors. Communities created new organizations with an apparent non-political purpose, such as sports, religious, and cultural organizations, to avoid targeting. Massive protests relying on religious signs were organized after the occurrence of overt human rights violations by armed groups. Direct negotiations between armed groups and community representatives took place to ease rules of conduct, request mercy for threatened community members, and prevent asset seizure. In some cases, armed groups faced civil resistance in communities with strong organizations (Kaplan 2017). In subsequent sections, we explore empirically these complex interactions between armed groups and local institutions in conflict-affected areas in Colombia.

3.4 Data and empirical strategy

Our main dataset is the Colombian Longitudinal Survey conducted by the Universidad de los Andes (ELCA).[15] It includes a sample of 10,800 households: 6000 in urban areas and 4800 in rural areas, over three panel waves (a baseline collected in 2010 and two follow-ups in 2013 and 2016). In this chapter, we use the rural sample, since the conflict in Colombia has mostly taken place in the rural areas. The rural sample of the ELCA is representative of small agricultural producers in four micro-regions: Atlantic, Central, Coffee-Growing, and South. Within each region, municipalities and communities were randomly chosen. The baseline sample includes 17 municipalities and 224 rural communities (each covering between 500 and 1000 inhabitants). In every subsequent wave, enumerators resurveyed all households and, if the household had split off or migrated, tracked the household core group in their new households or host communities. This core group comprises the head, spouse, and children under nine years old in 2010 (Table 3.D.1 in Appendix D).[16] The attrition rate after three waves in 2016 was 13.5 per cent. We complement the ELCA surveys with data from the CEDE Municipality Panel on the presence of FARC in ELCA municipalities before the first survey wave, and data on total rainfall between survey rounds from the Colombian Institute of Hydrology, Meteorology, and Environmental Studies (IDEAM) to build various control variables.

3.4.1 Measuring participation in community organizations and armed group presence

Our main dependent variable, individual participation in community organizations, was extracted from the ELCA household questionnaire. The household questionnaire collected detailed information on individual participation in community organizations for household heads and their spouses, among other socioeconomic variables. Participation in community organizations includes membership, meeting attendance, or leading local organizations including trade unions; work cooperatives and producer guilds; religious, cultural, educational, environmental, and security groups; local political parties; and village councils (the JACs). About 30 per cent of individuals in our sample participate in local organizations, and average participation is higher in communities with a presence of armed actors (Table 3.D.3 in the Appendix D).

[15] See https://encuestalongitudinal.uniandes.edu.co/es.

[16] This number may increase between rounds due to household divisions and decrease due to attrition or death.

Information on armed group presence was compiled from ELCA's rural community questionnaire conducted among community leaders. The questionnaire elicited information on public infrastructure, economic conditions, social interactions, and conflict dynamics in the community, including the presence of armed groups. Figure 3.2 shows the share of ELCA communities in which armed groups are present over time. We define a dummy variable equal to 1 if an armed group was present in the community in the year of the survey or within two years before that. For 2013 and 2016, this corresponds to the presence of armed groups between rounds. Between 2002 and 2004, 16.5 per cent of communities had armed groups present. This share decreased to 6.8 per cent between 2008 and 2010 and to 1.4 per cent after 2013, as the Colombian conflict reduced in intensity.

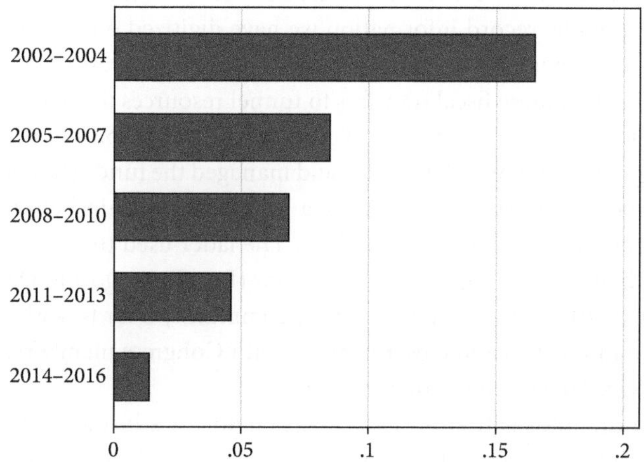

Figure 3.2 Armed group presence in ELCA communities across time
Source: Authors' calculations based on ELCA data; data on armed group presence between 2002 and 2010 come from baseline survey, while data on presence between 2011 and 2013 and between 2014 and 2016 come from 2013 and 2016 follow-ups, respectively.

3.4.2 Measuring pre-existing institutional capacity

To test the theoretical model, we need information about levels of pre-existing institutional capacity (i.e., institutional capacity before the arrival of the group in the community). This is not an easy concept to measure. Local community organizations in many rural areas in developing countries are often formed as a response to the absence of the state. As a result of this absence, local formal and informal organizations, such as community councils, cooperatives, religious councils, peasant associations, and other social and political groups, emerge to regularize and organize economic affairs and social life in the community. Institutional capacity of local community organizations may thus be strongest when the state is absent. However, in some cases, some of these organizations may be supported by the state as a form of enlarging their institutional reach. This was the case of village councils or JACs in Colombia. These community organizations are voluntarily created by community residents and have been central to local community organization and governance across Colombia. They were initially formed after the period of *La Violencia* to improve the reach of the state, but this process was not consistent or systematic. This strategy was only picked up properly after the decentralization process in the 1980s, when the JACs became the most important form of civic organization in the country (Zamosc 1986). Currently, there are over 45,000 JACs in Colombia (Sánchez Castañeda and Vargas Prieto 2017).

We measure pre-existing institutional capacity across communities in the ELCA sample using public record information we have digitized on the distribution of the value of parliamentary transfers from the National Congress in 1977. Congress members relied on these fiscal transfers to funnel resources for public investment in their regions. In rural areas, the allocation of these resources generally took place through the JACs, which received and managed the funds (Rodríguez Valero and Maldonado Gómez 2020), creating a direct relationship between community organizations and Congress members. The latter used these relationships to strengthen their political support in the regions (Leal Buitrago and Dávila Ladrón de Guevara 1990). We thus expect stronger community boards, with the capacity to mobilize more voters and closer contacts with Congress members, to be more likely to receive larger and steadier transfers.

To match the information on fiscal transfers to JACs in the 1970s with communities today, we matched the names and geographical locations of the ELCA communities with the public records on parliamentary transfers. We were able to do this for all baseline communities for which we have the exact name and geographical location. This exercise allows us to compute a measure of pre-existing institutional capacity for all non-migrants and migrants living in baseline ELCA communities (see Table 3.D.1 in Appendix D).[17] According to the data we compiled, 48 per cent of communities in the sample did not receive any transfers during this period. We define these as communities with low pre-existing institutional capacity. Twenty-five per cent of the communities received up to 20,000 Colombian pesos (COP) in 1977 (equivalent to 8.5 times the minimum wage in 1977[18]). We define these as communities with intermediate levels of institutional capacity. Twenty-seven per cent received a transfer of between COP20,000 and 230,000 (equivalent to between 8.5 and 98.3 times the minimum wage). These are communities defined as having high pre-existing institutional capacity

[17] Further details about the sources of information and the matching procedure are provided in Appendix B.

[18] The minimum wage in 1977 was 2340 COP per month.

(Figure 3.D.1 in Appendix D).[19] Table 3.D.2 in Appendix D shows that communities defined as having strong pre-existing institutional capacity benefit from a stronger presence of public institutions overall today. Communities with intermediate levels of pre-existing institutional capacity are more likely to have armed groups present (see Figure 3.3). These communities, as well as communities with high pre-existing institutional capacity, experience a sharp decrease in armed group presence after 2010. By 2014, armed groups are only present in communities with low pre-existing institutional capacity.

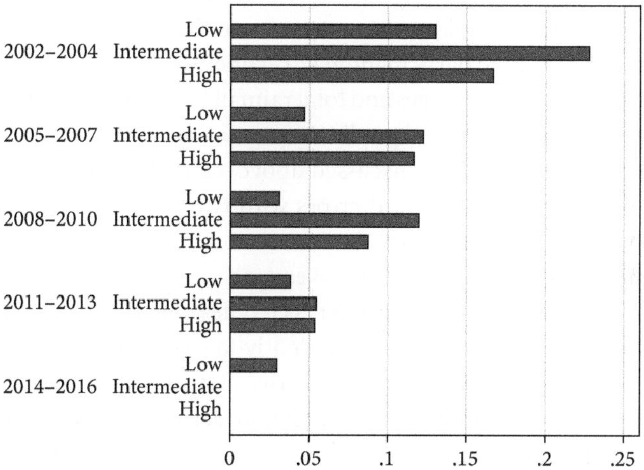

Figure 3.3 Armed group presence in ELCA communities, by pre-existing institutional capacity

Source: Authors' calculations based on ELCA data and public records on parliamentary transfers; data on armed group presence between 2002 and 2010 are compiled from the ELCA baseline survey; data on presence between 2011 and 2013 and between 2014 and 2016 are compiled from the 2013 and 2016 ELCA follow-ups, respectively; low, intermediate, and high pre-existing institutional capacities correspond to terciles of the distribution of parliamentary transfers in 1977.

3.4.3 Empirical strategy

We start by estimating empirically the effect of armed group presence on individual participation in local organizations with the following equation:

$$P_{i,c,m,r} = \alpha_i^s + \gamma_{m,r}^s + \beta^s A_{c,m,r} + \Theta^s X_{i,c,m,r} + \epsilon_{i,c,m,r} \tag{15}$$

[19] The thresholds we use are equivalent to the terciles of the distribution of transfers, taking into account the density of the distribution at 0. Even though the theoretical model uses two categories of institutional capacity (high and low), Figure 3.D.1 shows a concentration of high transfers among a small number of communities, many that receive almost no transfers, and a concentration of medium transfer levels among all other communities. In the appendix, we show that our results are robust to alternative thresholds.

where $P_{i,c,m,r}$ takes the value of 1 if individual i (household head or spouse) in community c of municipality m and wave r participates in local organizations. α_i^s and $\gamma_{m,r}^s$ are individual and municipality-wave fixed effects. $A_{c,m,r}$ takes the value of 1 if armed groups were present in the community between rounds.[20] $X_{i,c,m,r}$ are individual, household, and community controls found in previous literature to be strong determinants of individual civic participation (e.g. Verba et al. 1995). Individual and household controls include age, sex, years of education, number of household members, number of children under five years of age, and a wealth index. Community controls include (i) time to reach the municipal urban centre and total number of households, as remoteness and the size of the community can affect the feasibility of civic participation; (ii) economic conditions of the community (proxied by agricultural wages and total rainfall between rounds); and (iii) the number of public institutions and public investment, which proxy for overall state institutional capacity, which, as discussed above, can affect the strength of local organizations. We estimate standard errors with two-way clustering at the community and municipality-wave level to allow for individual errors to be correlated within communities and municipality waves.

We split the sample of communities across terciles of parliamentary transfers in 1977 and estimate equation (15) independently for each sample, $s = \{q_1, q_2, q_3\}$. Table 3.D.4 in Appendix D reports descriptive statistics for the individual and household variables included in the regression across our three categories of pre-existing institutional capacity.[21]

As discussed, since we do not directly observe the actions of the armed groups in each community, we cannot estimate directly parameters $\bar{s}$ and $\hat{s}$ of the theoretical model. However, the model framework allows us to infer that observing a positive or null coefficient estimate for communities in the lowest tercile of parliamentary transfers, $\beta^{q_1} \geq 0$, together with a negative coefficient for communities in the highest tercile, $\beta^{q_3} < 0$, would indicate the adoption of a dominance strategy by the armed group. In contrast, a null effect in communities with pre-existing high institutional capacity, $\beta^{q_3} = 0$, together with a positive coefficient in communities with pre-existing weak institutional capacity, $\beta^{q_1} > 0$, would provide evidence of a resistance equilibrium.

Our identification assumption is that by controlling for individual fixed effects and time-specific shocks at the municipality level, the exposure of individuals to armed groups in a certain period is orthogonal to time-specific shocks that determine participation in community organizations. Violations of this identification assumption would emerge if, for example, within municipalities, armed groups systematically target areas with an increased number of community organizations.

[20] For the 2010 survey round, we computed the presence of armed groups between 2008 and 2010.

[21] As shown in the appendix, in the theoretical framework, the thresholds $\bar{s}$ and $\hat{s}$ can generate a partition of S in three categories; these can represent the three groups of communities that we explore here. However, since we cannot estimate $\bar{s}$ and $\hat{s}$, the choice of thresholds here is arbitrary.

Although we cannot entirely rule out this possibility, we explore further, in the section below, the correlation between the presence of armed groups and time-varying characteristics of communities that might be correlated with local organizations. We also test below the validity of the results in relation to potential selection biases.

3.5 Empirical results

What is the effect of an armed group presence on individual participation in community organizations in rural Colombia and what armed group strategy may explain that effect? Columns 1–3 of Table 3.1 present the results of the estimation of equation (15) with community fixed effects. Each column includes the sample of communities in each tercile of the distribution of parliamentary transfers in 1977. In communities with high pre-existing institutional capacity, the presence of armed groups between waves is associated with a reduction in individual participation in community organizations (by 0.122 percentage points). The coefficient estimate for communities with low and intermediate pre-existing institutional capacity is not statistically significant. However, as shown, we cannot rule out an effect that is positive and large in magnitude in these samples.

Columns 4–6 present the results for our preferred specification, which controls for individual fixed effects. For communities in the highest tercile of parliamentary transfers, the coefficient estimate for the presence of armed groups is negative, statistically significant, and similar in magnitude to the estimate controlling for community fixed effects (−0.119), representing a 43 per cent reduction in the average of individual participation in community organizations when an armed group is present in the community.

Taken together, the results above show that armed group presence between survey waves resulted in a substantial reduction in individual participation in community organizations in communities with pre-existing high institutional capacity before the arrival of the group, and an increase in participation in communities with pre-existing low institutional capacity. Based on the theoretical model, we interpret these results above as strongly indicative that, on average, armed groups across ELCA communities largely adopted a strategy of organization capture when present in the rural communities.

3.5.1 Confounding effects

One possible confounding effect of the results above is the incidence of violence in each community. As discussed in Kalyvas (2006), violence typically intensifies when two groups contest the same territory but is likely to decline when one

Table 3.1 Effect of armed group presence on participation in community organizations

	Pre-existing institutional capacity					
	Low (1)	**Intermediate** (2)	**High** (3)	**Low** (4)	**Intermediate** (5)	**High** (6)
Armed group presence between waves	0.031	0.028	-0.122^{***}	0.021	0.050	-0.119^{**}
	(0.035)	(0.057)	(0.043)	(0.045)	(0.066)	(0.051)
	[−0.040 to 0.101]	[−0.088 to 0.145]	[−0.208 to -0.036]	[−0.069 to 0.111]	[−0.086 to 0.185]	[−0.222 to -0.015]
Observations	7976	3828	5038	7976	3828	5038
R-squared	0.163	0.132	0.162	0.592	0.557	0.592
Fixed effects (FE)	Community	Community	Community	Individual	Individual	Individual
Controls	Yes	Yes	Yes	Yes	Yes	Yes
Mean dep. var.	0.308	0.294	0.276	0.308	0.294	0.276

Note: Standard errors with municipality-year and individual cluster in parentheses, 95 per cent confidence interval in square brackets; all estimations include municipality-year dummies and control variables: age, age squared, sex, years of education, number of household members, number of children under five, wealth index, time to reach municipal urban centre, total number of households in the community, total rainfall between rounds, presence of public institutions in the community, and investments in public infrastructure between rounds; pre-existing institutional capacity defined as terciles of 1977 parliamentary transfers to the community; for the baseline survey, presence between waves corresponds to the presence of armed groups between 2008 and 2010; $^{***}p < 0.01$, $^{**}p < 0.05$, $^{*}p < 0.1$.

armed group becomes hegemonic, leading to full control of the territory and its population. The negative coefficients we observe in participation in communities with stronger pre-existing institutional capacity might thus be driven by an escalation of violence: individuals may decide to reduce their participation in community organizations not because of the dominance strategy adopted by an armed group, but due to an increase in violence caused, for instance, by two or more groups (or the armed group and the state) competing for control of what may be perceived as an attractive community to them. To explore if this was the case, we estimated alternative specifications in which we controlled for dummy variables that indicate whether the household experienced instances of violence between survey waves, and for an indicator of violent shocks in the community. We define violent shocks in the community as those clearly related to conflict, such as homicides, illegal land seizures, and kidnappings. Table 3.2 presents the results for the estimation with individual fixed effects. We continue to observe a negative and statistically significant effect of armed group presence on participation in communities with pre-existing strong institutional capacity. When we consider household-level exposure to violence, the coefficient estimate is similar in magnitude to our baseline estimate. When we include community-level exposure to violence, the coefficient is smaller in magnitude, yet the difference is not statistically significant. In these communities, there is a negative but not statistically significant association between individual participation in community organizations and exposure of the household to violent shocks. These results suggest that part of the negative effect of armed group presence on individual participation in community organizations might occur through a dissuasive effect of violence. However, a direct negative effect of armed group presence on individual participation remains, suggesting that the capture of local organizations by armed groups occurs not only through violence. It is to note that the coefficient estimates for household exposure to violence in communities with low and intermediate levels of pre-existing institutional capacity are positive, although not statistically significant. This result might be consistent with the dominance mechanism in our theoretical model, whereby participation in communities with weak institutional capacity may signal obedience towards a violent armed group, preventing higher levels of victimization.

3.5.2 Validity of results

Despite the array of rich controls we use in the regressions above, it is possible that our results may still be driven by other factors or affected by sample biases. We conduct two tests in this subsection to assess the potential effect of selection into migration as well as armed group selection. We test further the validity of the main results by replacing the estimation strategy above with an instrumental variable (IV) approach.

Table 3.2 Effect of armed group presence on participation in community organizations: controlling for violent shocks

Variables	Pre-existing social capital					
	Low (1)	Intermediate (2)	High (3)	Low (4)	Intermediate (5)	High (6)
Presence between rounds	0.021	0.050	−0.119**	0.025	0.051	−0.075*
	(0.045)	(0.066)	(0.051)	(0.048)	(0.072)	(0.043)
	[−0.070 to 0.112]	[−0.086 to 0.186]	[−0.222 to −0.016]	[−0.071 to 0.122]	[−0.096 to 0.198]	[−0.162 to 0.013]
Household violent shock	0.045	0.030	−0.068			
	(0.062)	(0.104)	(0.087)			
	[−0.080 to 0.169]	[−0.184 to 0.243]	[−0.244 to 0.108]			
Community violent shock: any				−0.024	−0.004	−0.074
				(0.026)	(0.039)	(0.044)
				[−0.076 to 0.029]	[−0.085 to 0.076]	[−0.163 to 0.015]
Observations	7969	3826	5036	7976	3828	5038
R-squared	0.592	0.558	0.592	0.592	0.557	0.593
FE	Individual	Individual	Individual	Individual	Individual	Individual
Controls	Yes	Yes	Yes	Yes	Yes	Yes
Mean dep. var.	0.308	0.294	0.276	0.308	0.294	0.276

Note: Standard errors with municipality-year and individual cluster in parentheses, 95 per cent confidence interval in square brackets; all estimations include municipality-year dummies and control variables: age, age squared, sex years of education, number of household members, number of children under five, wealth index, time to reach municipal urban centre, total number of households in the community, total rainfall between rounds, presence of public institutions in the community, and investments in public infrastructure between rounds; pre-existing institutional capacity defined as terciles of 1977 parliamentary transfers to community; for the baseline survey, presence

Migration

Selection into migration is a potential source of threat to our empirical strategy. Colombia has one of the highest rates of internal displacement in the world. The decision to move or stay in a community might be related to both the presence of armed groups and participation in community organizations. Individual migration might result in two sources of bias in our context. First, we do not observe the full set of community variables for migrants in host communities that are not in the baseline, which may cause a sample selection bias in our estimates. Second, even if we observe both participation and the community characteristics of migrants, because migration occurred before the baseline survey or because the household moved between waves to a baseline ELCA community, neither these communities nor the individuals that we observe in these communities are a random sample of the population. Our coefficient estimates for the population parameters, β^s, with this sample would be biased due to individual sorting. The coefficient estimates will be overestimated if those who are more likely to participate in community organizations when armed groups are present are also more likely to stay in communities with armed group presence. For instance, supporters or people allied with one armed group might prefer to stay in communities controlled by that group and participate in organizations to obtain benefits or protection. The coefficient estimates will be underestimated if those who are more likely to participate when armed groups are present are also more likely to relocate to communities without armed groups. Members of civil resistance movements or threatened community leaders might be in this group.

We make use of the panel structure of our data to explore the correlation between the decision to migrate and community and individual characteristics, taking into account individual and municipality-wave fixed effects. We estimate the following equation:

$$M_{i,c,m,r} = \alpha_i^s + \gamma_{m,r}^s + \mu^s A_{c,m,r} + \Theta^s X_{i,c,m,r-1} + \nu_{i,c,m,r} \tag{16}$$

where $M_{i,c,m,t}$ takes the value of 1 if individual i migrated from community c between waves r and $r-1$, $A_{c,m,r}$ is the presence of armed groups in the community between waves; $X_{i,c,m,r-1}$ is the individual and community characteristics prior to migration.

Columns 1–3 of Table 3.3 show that the presence of armed groups does not have a statistically significant effect on the likelihood of migration between waves in any of the samples that we consider. In columns 4–6, we control for an indicator of individual participation in local organizations before migration. The coefficient estimate for participation in the three samples is again not statistically significant, suggesting that there is no systematic correlation between participation and migration. As a final robustness check, we follow Lee (2009) to estimate bounds to the

Table 3.3 Migration rounds and presence of armed groups

	Pre-existing institutional capacity					
	Low (1)	**Intermediate** (2)	**High** (3)	**Low** (4)	**Intermediate** (5)	**High** (6)
Armed group presence between waves	−0.017	−0.094	−0.034	−0.015	−0.096	−0.032
	(0.036)	(0.133)	(0.102)	(0.036)	(0.133)	(0.106)
	[−0.091 to 0.056]	[−0.374 to 0.186]	[−0.243 to 0.174]	[−0.088 to 0.058]	[−0.376 to 0.183]	[−0.249 to 0.185]
Participation any ($t-1$)				0.014	-0.015	0.035
				(0.017)	(0.028)	(0.021)
				[−0.020 to 0.048]	[−0.075 to 0.045]	[−0.009 to 0.078]
Observations	4598	1940	2802	4504	1916	2762
R-squared	0.670	0.637	0.670	0.669	0.639	0.664
FE	Individual	Individual	Individual	Individual	Individual	Individual

Note: Standard errors with municipality-year and individual cluster in parentheses, 95 per cent confidence interval in square brackets; all estimations include municipality-year dummies and control variables are lagged: age, age squared, sex years of education, number of household members, number of children under five, wealth index, time to reach municipal urban centre, total number of households in the community, total rainfall between rounds, presence of public institutions in the community, and investments in public between rounds; pre-existing institutional capacity defined as terciles of 1977 parliamentary transfers to community; for the baseline survey, presence between rounds corresponds to the presence of armed groups between 2008 and 2010; $^{***}p < 0.01$, $^{**}p < 0.05$, $^{*}p < 0.1$.

effect of the presence of armed groups on participation in local organizations, taking into account sample selection due to migration or any other source of attrition. Our results in Appendix C show that the upper bounds for the effects in strong communities are still negative, reinforcing our main result.

Armed group selection

One key assumption in the theoretical model and in our empirical strategy is that armed groups select communities based on an assessment of the attractiveness of the community to the group. This attractiveness depends on how predetermined community variables interact with time-varying conditions during the war that are exogenous to the community. However, rural communities across the country (with and without armed group presence) may differ systematically in terms of their history of violence, development of local institutions, local markets, and geographical characteristics. These differences might result in communities that are systematically more attractive to armed groups. Using the data collected in the community questionnaire, we construct two groups of variables that account for: (i) socioeconomic conditions at the time of the survey, and (ii) events that took place in the community between waves. Tables 3.D.5 and 3.D.6 in Appendix D show a number of differences in individual (age), household (young children and household members), and community characteristics (distance to urban centres and average rainfall) across communities with and without armed group presence.

We regress the indicator for armed group presence between waves on the two groups of community variables. First, we control for lagged socioeconomic characteristics of the community in the year of the survey,[22] such as the number of households in the community, the presence of public institutions, the value of agricultural wages, and the time to reach the municipal urban centre. Second, we include investments in public infrastructure and total rainfall between waves. We control for community and municipality-wave fixed effects. This specification allows us to check if baseline community characteristics are correlated with the presence of armed groups between rounds. In alternative specifications, we do not include the fixed effects and include time-invariant community characteristics, such as the tercile of parliamentary transfers and the historical presence of armed groups in the community, to explore the correlation between armed group presence and time-invariant community characteristics. Table 3.D.7 in Appendix D reports the results of these exercises and shows that, when we include community fixed effects, the presence of armed groups is not correlated with other time-varying characteristics of the community, which reassures us about the validity of our identification assumptions.

[22] When we look at presence between 2010 and 2013, this corresponds to community characteristics in 2010. For presence between 2013 and 2016, it refers to community characteristics in 2013.

Instrumental variable estimation

As an additional robustness check, we instrument the presence of armed groups in the community. We exploit the fact that in September 2016, the Colombian government and FARC signed a peace agreement that involved the demobilization of FARC troops. The agreement was signed after four years of negotiations between the parties. We expect these negotiations to induce a reduction in the presence of FARC members in rural communities, particularly near the end of the agreement. This reduction may be stronger in demobilization camps located around communities closer to urban centres, where compliance with the agreement may be easier to verify. We use data at the municipality level on the presence of FARC before the peace negotiations to construct an IV as follows:[23]

$$Peace_{c,m,r} = FARC_m \times Post_r \times distance_{cm}$$

where $FARC_m$ takes the value of 1 if FARC members were present in municipality m in 2006, $Post_r$ takes the value of 1 for the 2016 wave, and $distance_c$ is the distance between the community and the municipality urban centre in 2010. Caution must be taken about the exclusion restriction of the IV given that the peace agreement involved broad prior consultation across the Colombian society, which may have affected community organizations via other routes besides the presence of armed groups. To (partially) address this possibility, we estimate a two-stage least squares regression with community and municipality-wave fixed effects. We control, in alternative specifications, for individual fixed effects instead of community fixed effects. Our identification assumption is that the peace agreement affected participation in community organizations only through its effects on the presence of armed groups after 2016, once we take into account municipality-wave-specific effects and community fixed effects.

Table 3.4 presents the results of the IV estimation. First-stage estimates are presented in Table 3.D.8 in Appendix D. We find a larger negative effect of the presence of armed groups in communities with high pre-existing institutional capacity. We also find that the positive coefficient for participation in communities with pre-existing weak institutional capacity is now statistically significant (albeit at 10 per cent level). We are aware that this IV strategy may not fully rule out all threats to the exclusion restriction and, thus, these results must be interpreted with some caution. However, when taken together, all robustness tests reinforce our interpretation of a dominance strategy by armed groups across sampled communities in Colombia in the period under consideration.

[23] Note that these data come from the CEDE Municipality Panel. The ELCA did not collect information on the identity of the armed groups in the community, and we are thus unable to identify what armed group (FARC, paramilitary, or other) is present in each ELCA community across the survey waves.

Table 3.4 Instrumental variable estimates

	Pre-existing institutional capacity					
	Low (1)	**Intermediate** (2)	**High** (3)	**Low** (1)	**Intermediate** (2)	**High** (3)
Armed group presence between waves	0.237	−0.011	−0.579*	0.386*	0.232	−0.422**
	(0.218)	(0.198)	(0.316)	(0.211)	(0.294)	(0.212)
Observations	7976	3828	5038	7976	3828	5038
FE	Community	Community	Community	Individual	Individual	Individual
Controls	Yes	Yes	Yes	Yes	Yes	Yes
F—first stage	33.36	2.725	11.38	26.22	1.681	8.714

Note: Standard errors with municipality-year cluster in parentheses; all estimations include municipality-year dummies and control variables: age, age squared, sex years of education, number of household members, number of children under five, wealth index, time to reach municipal urban centre, total number of households in the community, total rainfall between waves presence of public institutions in the community, and investments in public infrastructure between waves; pre-existing institutional capacity defined as terciles of 1977 parliamentary transfers to community; for the baseline survey, presence between waves corresponds to the presence of armed groups between 2008 and 2010; ***$p < 0.01$, **$p < 0.05$, *$p < 0.1$.

3.6 Conclusion

Wars change local institutions and the organization of local communities in dramatic ways. This chapter analysed an important aspect of this change by examining the effect of armed group presence on local collective organizations in Colombia—arguably a key determinant of the strength of civic society and prospects for democracy in the post-conflict period. Based on a new theoretical model, we explored whether observed increased participation of civilians in community organizations when armed groups are present in their communities may be driven by communities organizing themselves to resist or counteract the influence of armed actors, or by armed actors capturing organizations and impose stronger control over the population by coercing their participation. The results show that changes in the presence of armed groups in any given community increases the participation in local organizations of individuals in communities with low pre-existing institutional capacity and reduces the participation in local organizations of individuals in communities with high pre-existing institutional capacity. This result is consistent with the theoretical predictions of a dominance/capture equilibrium.

These results contribute significantly to a better understanding of the links between armed conflict and institutional change by showing how, in the case of Colombia, local organizations were manipulated by armed groups to advance and cement their war strategies and political objectives. The theoretical framework also allows us to identify conditions under which alternative equilibria—libertarian or resistance—may be prevalent in other conflicts. This is an important contribution to the literature because different equilibria in how armed groups deal with local community organizations in wartime may lead to different pathways of institutional change in the post-conflict period. Capture strategies of the type identified in Colombia may signal a stronger institutional capacity for the group but lower capacity for collective action among civilians. The prevalence of a resistance equilibrium may lead to stronger forms of democratization from below in the post-conflict period (Huang 2016).

This analysis also has important policy implications. The Colombian results point to the need for some caution about current policy agendas that target aid to post-conflict communities in the hope of strengthening local institutions, governance, and social cohesion. If the type of institutional capture we observe in Colombia is also present in other countries, post-conflict community-level interventions may well reinforce war dynamics and the power of armed groups and their allies, thereby creating potential sparks for conflict reignition. Communities that benefit from resistance-type processes during wartime may experience more positive results from these policy interventions, though much more research is needed to document such cases and the implications of different equilibria proposed by the model for state-building and development processes in the long term.

The results also have implications for the ongoing peace process in Colombia, where real democratic outcomes will require serious investment by the Colombian government to create and support strong and independent local civic organizations that can overcome the capture of local organizations by armed groups during the conflict. This will not be an easy task.

3.7 Appendix

A. Model proofs

Proof of Proposition 1. Since pay-offs are realized every period, pre-existing institutional capacity and rural residents' preferences are fixed, and ξ_t is independent and identically distributed, then, conditional on s, armed group presence, dominance, and participation are independent across time. Therefore, for every t and r:

$$\overline{P}_t^D = \overline{P}_r^D$$
$$\overline{P}_t^L = \overline{P}_r^L$$
$$\overline{P}_t^P = \overline{P}_r^P$$

Moreover, from equations (8) and (9),

$$\overline{P}_t^L = Pr\left(\overline{u}_i \leq u\left(s\right)\right) = \overline{P}_t^P$$

and from equations (7) and (9),

$$\overline{P}_t^D = Pr\left(\overline{u}_i \leq u\left(s\right) - v\left(s\right)\right) \geq Pr\left(\overline{U}_i \leq u\left(s\right)\right) = \overline{P}_t^P$$
$$\Leftrightarrow -v\left(s\right) \geq 0$$
$$\Leftrightarrow \; s \leq \overline{s}$$

Proof of Proposition 2. Part 1 follows from $R\left(Pr\left(\overline{u}_i \leq u\left(s\right) - v\left(s\right)\right)\right)$ being monotonically increasing in s. For part 2, since $R' > 0$ and $u\left(s\right) - v\left(s\right)$ is increasing on s, then $R\left(Pr\left(\overline{u}_i \leq u\left(s\right) - v\left(s\right)\right)\right)$ is also increasing on s. Thus, for every $\hat{d}_o > \hat{d}$, there is $\hat{s}_o > \hat{s}$ such that $R\left(Pr\left(\overline{u}_i \leq u\left(\hat{s}_o\right) - v\left(\hat{s}_o\right)\right)\right) = \hat{d}_0$; and for $\hat{d}_o < \hat{d}$, there is $\hat{s}_o < \hat{s}$ such that $R\left(Pr\left(\overline{u}_i \leq u\left(\hat{s}_o\right) - v\left(\hat{s}_o\right)\right)\right) = \hat{d}_0$.

Proof of Proposition 3. Note that for $\hat{s} \geq \overline{s}$:

1. If $s < \overline{s} \leq \hat{s}$, then $D_t^*|_{\xi_t \geq 0} = 0$ and $E\left[p_{it}^* | A_t^* = 1, s\right] - E\left[p_{it}^* | A_t^* = 0, s\right] = 0$
2. If $\overline{s} \leq s \leq \hat{s}$, then $D_t^*|_{\xi_t \geq 0} = 0$ and $E\left[p_{it}^* | A_t^* = 1, s\right] - E\left[p_{it}^* | A_t^* = 0, s\right] = 0$
3. If $\overline{s} \leq \hat{s} < s$, then $D_t^*|_{\xi_t \geq 0} = 1$ and $E\left[p_{it}^* | A_t^* = 1, s\right] - E\left[p_{it}^* | A_t^* = 0, s\right] < 0$

And for $\hat{s} < \bar{s}$:

1. If $s \leq \hat{s} < \bar{s}$, then $D_t^*|_{\xi_t \geq 0} = 0$ and $E\left[p_{it}^* | A_t^* = 1, s\right] - E\left[p_{it}^* | A_t^* = 0, s\right] = 0$
2. If $\hat{s} < s \leq \bar{s}$, then $D_t^*|_{\xi_t \geq 0} = 1$ and $E\left[p_{it}^* | A_t^* = 1, s\right] - E\left[p_{it}^* | A_t^* = 0, s\right] \geq 0$
3. If $\hat{s} < \bar{s} < s$, then $D_t^*|_{\xi_t \geq 0} = 1$ and $E\left[p_{it}^* | A_t^* = 1, s\right] - E\left[p_{it}^* | A_t^* = 0, s\right] < 0$

Proof of proposition 4. Since R and d are monotonically increasing in $\overline{P}$, and $\overline{P}$ is monotonically increasing in s, if there exists $\bar{s}' \in S$ such that $R(Pr(\overline{u}_i \leq u(\bar{s}') - v(s) + r(\bar{s}'))) = d(Pr(\overline{u}_i \leq u(\bar{s}') - v(\bar{s}') + r(\bar{s}')))$, then $R(\overline{P}) - d(\overline{P})$ satisfies the single crossing property. For $s \leq \bar{s}'$, $D_t^*|_{\xi_t \geq 0} = 1$ and $E[p_{it}^* | A_t^* = 1, s] = Pr(\overline{u}_i \leq u(s) - v(s) + r(s)) > Pr(\overline{u}_i \leq u(s)) = E[p_{it}^* | A_t^* = 0, s]$. For $s > \bar{s}'$, $D_t^*|_{\xi_t \geq 0} = 0$ and $E[p_{it}^* | A_t^* = 1, s] = Pr(\overline{u}_i \leq u(s)) = Pr(\overline{u}_i \leq u(s)) = E[p_{it}^* | A_t^* = 0, s]$.

B. Matching records of parliamentary transfers with ELCA communities

We digitized official information on parliamentary transfers available in the Annals of the National Congress. This information contains the name and municipality of the recipient, the amount of the transfer, and the purpose of the funds. If the recipient is a JAC, the name of the community (*vereda*) is specified. First, we match ELCA communities with communities in the public records by name and municipality. Since communities are not official jurisdictions, their names might have changed over time. To reduce mismeasurement due to variations in the names of communities, we follow a two-step procedure. First, we use a fuzzy merge algorithm to match names in the ELCA data with names in the Congress records. With this procedure, we were able to find ninety-one ELCA communities in the Congress Annals. Second, we use the GPS coordinates of the communities to identify alternative names of these communities based on a map of *veredas* available in the National Department of Statistics (DANE). We then apply the fuzzy merge algorithm to match these alternative names with the Congress records. In this step, we were able to match twenty-seven additional communities.

C. Sample selection and bounds on treatment effects

We follow Lee (2009) to estimate bounds on the effect of the exposure to armed groups on participation in local organizations. We present the analysis only for communities in the highest tercile of parliamentary transfers, since we aim to check if sample selection is inducing the negative and statistically significant effect that we find in these communities. We compute the change in participation and individual exposure to armed groups between rounds for each individual in the sample. As a baseline for the analysis, we estimate the first-differences equations:

$$\Delta P_{i,c,m,r} = \beta^{+}\Delta A_{c,m,r} + \epsilon^{+}_{i,c,m,r} \text{ if } \Delta A_{c,m,r} \geq 0$$

$$\Delta P_{i,c,m,r} = \beta^{-}\Delta A_{c,m,r} + \epsilon^{-}_{i,c,m,r} \text{ if } \Delta A_{c,m,r} \leq 0$$

The change in exposure to armed groups can take three possible values: $\Delta A_{c,m,r} = -1$ if armed groups left the community between rounds, $\Delta A_{c,m,r} = 0$ if the presence of armed groups did not change, and $\Delta A_{c,m,r} = 1$ if armed groups arrived between rounds. We independently estimate the effect of a positive and a negative $\Delta A_{c,m,r}$, taking as the control group individuals who did not experienced changes in their exposure to armed groups, $\Delta A_{c,m,r} = 0$. We then follow Lee (2009) to compute bounds on β^{+} and β^{-}.

Table 3.C.1 First-differences estimates and Lee bounds in strong communities

	Coefficient (S.E.)	Lower bound (S.E.)	Upper bound (S.E.)	n
Panel A: 2013–2010, 2016–2013				
β^{-}	−0.091 (0.058)	−0.106 (0.053)	−0.077 (0.053)	3201
β^{+}	−0.033 (0.012)	−0.0332 (0.116)	−0.0323 (0.116)	3073
Panel B: 2013–2010				
β^{-}	−0.123 (0.036)	−0.138 (0.059)	−0.112 (0.056)	1696
β^{+}	−0.101 (0.028)	−0.112 (0.118)	−0.091 (0.116)	1634
Panel C: 2013–2016				
β^{-}	−0.001 (0.067)	−0.074 (0.104)	0.058 (0.100)	1505
β^{+}	–	–	–	

Note: Sample includes only communities with high pre-existing institutional capacity; $\beta^{+}$is not identified for 2013–2016 because there is no arrival of armed groups in communities during this period; S.E. = standard error.

Table 3.C.1 presents the results for the whole period and for each follow-up round individually. Overall, we find negative upper bounds for the effects of armed group presence on participation in local organizations. Note that since there is a sharp reduction in the presence of armed groups after 2013, for the last period, we do not have observations with $\Delta A_{c,m,r} = 1$, and we cannot identify β^{+}.

D. Additional figures and tables

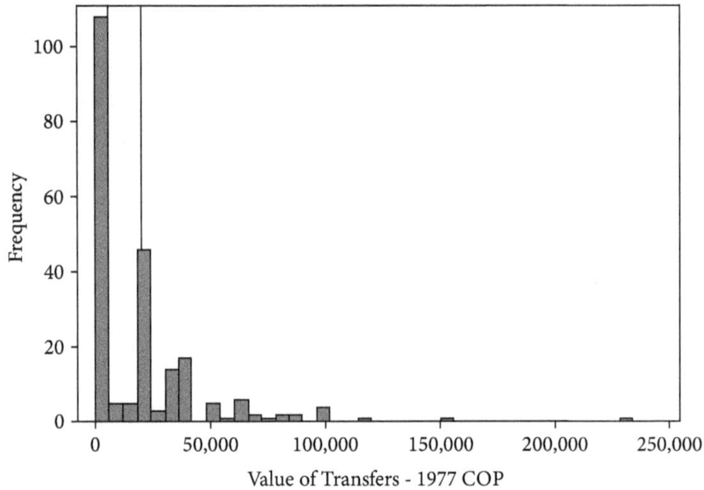

Figure 3.D.1 Distribution of parliamentary transfers in 1977 across ELCA communities

Source: Authors' calculations based on ELCA data and public records on parliamentary transfers.

Table 3.D.1 Sample size by survey round

	Round		
	2010	2013	2016
All household heads and spouses	7562	7664	6590
Migrants		1258	894
Migrants with community information		515	486
Migrants with community and 1977 parliamentary transfers information		348	412

Note: Migrants are defined as those individuals who report a change in their community of residence between survey waves.

Table 3.D.2 Baseline community characteristics in 2010, by pre-existing institutional capacity

	Pre-existing institutional capacity		
	Low (1)	Intermediate (2)	High (3)
Value of parliamentary transfers (1977 COP)	0.00 (0.00)	18,404.07 (3641.55)	54,769.70 (34,546.21)
Time to urban centre (hours)	0.61 (0.44)	0.92 (0.83)	0.74 (0.61)
Number of households in community	85.61 (78.24)	92.76 (94.36)	87.68 (92.43)
Public institutions	2.06 (1.72)	2.39 (1.63)	2.50 (2.07)
Public institutions: childcare	0.24 (0.51)	0.13 (0.38)	0.43 (0.65)
Public institutions: schools	1.55 (1.12)	1.98 (1.20)	1.70 (1.28)
Public institutions: health facilities	0.06	0.09	0.10
Average annual rainfall between waves	7.50 (0.34)	7.57 (0.40)	7.55 (0.28)
Droughts	0.53	0.40	0.46
Log daily agricultural wage	9.59 (0.42)	9.87 (0.14)	9.67 (0.35)
Years of armed group presence 2001–2007	0.59 (1.33)	1.16 (2.05)	0.81 (1.55)
Community residents help each other	0.95	0.88	0.96
Infrastructure investments between waves: education	0.36	0.38	0.37
Infrastructure investments between waves: transport and communication	0.65	0.76	0.47
Infrastructure investments between waves: other	0.12	0.18	0.12
Community violent shock: any	0.09	0.28	0.05
Community violent shock: kidnapping	0.00	0.06	0.00
Community violent shock: land eviction	0.01	0.02	0.00
Community violent shock: homicides	0.08	0.24	0.05
Observations	108	56	60

Note: Low, intermediate, and high pre-existing institutional capacities correspond to terciles of the distribution of parliamentary transfers in 1977; 'public institutions' refers to the total number of public institutions of different categories available in the community; childcare and schools can take values between 0 and 2 and 0 and 4, respectively, corresponding to the number of public institutions that provide different types of educational and childcare services; health facilities is a dummy variable for the presence of health facilities in the community.

Table 3.D.3 Participation in local organizations across armed group presence

	Whole sample	Armed group presence: Yes	Armed group presence: No	
	(1)	(2)	(3)	(4)
Participation	0.30	0.39	0.30	***
Observations	16,842	640	16,202	

Note: Armed group presence in the community is defined as a dummy variable for the presence of armed groups in the year of the survey or within two years before the survey; column 4 presents the test for mean differences across the sample with and without armed group presence; ***p < 0.01, **p < 0.05, *p < 0.1.

Table 3.D.4 Descriptive statistics of main individual and household variables across pre-existing institutional capacity

	Pre-existing institutional capacity		
	Low	Intermediate	High
	(1)	(2)	(3)
Panel A: Household head and spouse variables			
Meeting attendance	0.29	0.27	0.25
Hold leadership position	0.14	0.13	0.11
Age	47.07	46.24	46.43
	(13.50)	(13.39)	(13.65)
= 1 if male	0.48	0.48	0.48
Years of education	4.53	4.63	4.64
	(3.54)	(3.50)	(3.61)
Panel B: Household variables			
Children under five	0.47	0.48	0.48
	(0.76)	(0.75)	(0.76)
Number of household members	4.62	4.59	4.56
	(2.09)	(2.03)	(2.01)
Wealth index	0.12	−0.12	−0.12
	(2.71)	(1.86)	(2.24)
Household violent shock	0.01	0.01	0.01
Observations	10,131	4900	6150

Note: Low, intermediate, and high pre-existing institutional capacities correspond to terciles of the distribution of parliamentary transfers in 1977.

Table 3.D.5 Descriptive statistics of main individual and household characteristics across armed group presence

Mean (std dev.)	Armed group presence			
	Whole sample (1)	Yes (2)	No (3)	(4)
Panel A: Household head and spouse characteristics				
Age	47.42	45.94	47.48	***
	(12.84)	(12.53)	(12.85)	
= 1 if male	0.48	0.49	0.48	
Years of education	4.52	4.61	4.51	
	(3.48)	(3.50)	(3.48)	
Observations	16,842	640	16,202	
Panel B: Household characteristics				
Children under five	0.42	0.53	0.42	***
	(0.71)	(0.79)	(0.71)	
Number of household members	4.43	4.84	4.41	***
	(2.00)	(2.17)	(1.99)	
Wealth index	−0.01	−0.11	−0.00	
	(2.34)	(2.78)	(2.32)	
Household violent shock	0.01	0.02	0.01	
Observations	9700	363	9337	

Note: Armed group presence in the community is defined as a dummy variable for the presence of armed groups in the year of the survey or within two years before the survey; column 4 presents the test for mean differences across the sample with and without armed group presence; ***$p < 0.01$, **$p < 0.05$, *$p < 0.1$.

Table 3.D.6 Descriptive statistics of main community variables across armed group presence

Mean (std dev.)	Armed group presence			
	Whole sample (1)	Yes (2)	No (3)	(4)
Time to urban centre (hours)	0.68	1.25	0.66	***
	(0.55)	(0.86)	(0.52)	
Number of households in community	89.77	68.52	90.72	
	(85.21)	(41.81)	(86.54)	
Public institutions: childcare	0.29	0.19	0.29	
	(0.57)	(0.40)	(0.57)	

continued

Table 3.D.6 *continued*

Mean (std dev.)	Armed group presence			
	Whole sample (1)	Yes (2)	No (3)	(4)
Public institutions: health facilities	0.08	0.15	0.07	
Public institutions: schools	2.04 (1.11)	2.07 (1.47)	2.03 (1.10)	
Infrastructure investments between waves: education	0.37	0.48	0.36	
Infrastructure investments between waves: transport and communication	0.69	0.56	0.70	
Infrastructure investments between waves: other	0.15	0.07	0.15	
Log daily agricultural wage	9.87 (0.38)	9.81 (0.23)	9.87 (0.39)	
Average annual rainfall between waves	7.40 (0.37)	7.64 (0.30)	7.38 (0.37)	***
Community violent shock: any	0.19	0.48	0.18	***
Community violent shock: kidnapping	0.06	0.11	0.06	
Community violent shock: land eviction	0.04	0.07	0.04	
Community violent shock: homicides	0.16	0.37	0.15	***
Observations	631	27	604	

Note: Armed group presence in the community is defined as a dummy variable for the presence of armed groups within two years before the survey; column 4 presents the test for mean differences across the sample with and without armed group presence; $^{***}p < 0.01$, $^{**}p < 0.05$, $^{*}p < 0.1$; childcare and schools can take values between 0 and 2 and 0 and 4, respectively, corresponding to the number of public institutions that provide different types of educational and childcare services; health facilities is a dummy variable for the presence of health facilities in the community.

Table 3.D.7 Armed group presence between waves and community variables

	No FE	Municipality-wave FE	Municipality-wave & community FE
	(1)	(2)	(3)
Time to urban centre (hours) ($t-1$)	0.032* (0.017)	0.025 (0.016)	0.005 (0.031)
Number of households in community ($t-1$)	0.000 (0.000)	−0.000 (0.000)	−0.000 (0.000)
Public institutions: childcare ($t-1$)	−0.016 (0.013)	−0.032 (0.024)	−0.026 (0.023)

	No FE	Municipality-wave FE	Municipality-wave & community FE
	(1)	(2)	(3)
Public institutions: health facilities (t – 1)	0.001 (0.022)	−0.009 (0.022)	−0.007 (0.070)
Public institutions: schools (t – 1)	−0.012* (0.007)	−0.006 (0.008)	−0.025 (0.017)
Average annual rainfall between waves (t – 1)	−0.011 (0.022)	−0.037 (0.077)	−0.067 (0.169)
Average annual rainfall between waves	0.041 (0.026)	0.066 (0.084)	0.299 (0.210)
Infrastructure investments between waves: education (t – 1)	0.004 (0.008)	−0.004 (0.007)	−0.025 (0.020)
Infrastructure investments between waves: transport and communication (t – 1)	0.034 (0.024)	0.023 (0.024)	0.028 (0.032)
Infrastructure investments between waves: other (t – 1)	−0.020** (0.010)	−0.016 (0.011)	−0.030 (0.026)
Log daily agricultural wage (t – 1)	−0.034 (0.032)	0.031 (0.049)	0.156 (0.138)
Pre-existing institutional capacity: intermediate	−0.009 (0.021)	−0.030 (0.022)	
Pre-existing institutional capacity: high	−0.007 (0.017)	0.003 (0.016)	
Years of armed group presence 2001–2007	0.011 (0.006)	0.015* (0.009)	
Constant	0.117 (0.426)	−0.499 (0.712)	−3.135 (2.791)
Observations	382	382	382
R-squared	0.053	0.168	0.593
FE	No	municipality-year	municipality-year and community
Mean dep. var.	0.0236	0.0236	0.0236

Note: Ordinary least squares (OLS) estimation with presence of armed groups between waves as dependent variable; standard errors with community clusters in parentheses; sample includes a balanced panel of 191 communities in 2013 and 2016 for which we have information on lagged community characteristics; armed group presence between waves takes the value of 1 if armed groups were present at least one year between waves, including the survey year; ***$p < 0.01$, **$p < 0.05$, *$p < 0.1$.

Table 3.D.8 First stage: instrumental variables estimates

	Pre-existing institutional capacity					
	Low (1)	**Intermediate** (2)	**High** (3)	**Low** (1)	**Intermediate** (2)	**High** (3)
$FARC_m \times Post_r$ $\times\ distance_{cm}$	-0.369^{***} (0.064)	-0.098^{*} (0.059)	-0.285^{***} (0.084)	-0.367^{***} (0.072)	−0.095 (0.073)	-0.305^{***} (0.103)
Observations	7976	3828	5038	7976	3828	5038
FE	Community	Community	Community	Individual	Individual	Individual
Controls	Yes	Yes	Yes	Yes	Yes	Yes

Note: Standard errors with municipality-year cluster in parentheses; all estimations include municipality-year dummies and control variables: age, age squared, sex years of education, number of household members, number of children under five, wealth index, time to municipal urban centre, total number of households in the community, total rainfall between waves, the presence of public institutions in the community, and investments in public infrastructure between waves; pre-existing institutional capacity defined as terciles of 1977 parliamentary transfers to community; for the baseline survey, presence between waves corresponds to the presence of armed groups between 2008 and 2010; $^{***}p < 0.01$, $^{**}p < 0.05$, $^{*}p < 0.1$.

References

Arjona, A. M. (2016). *Rebelocracy: Social Order in the Colombian Civil War.* New York: Cambridge University Press. https://doi.org/10.1017/9781316421925

Arjona, A. M., N. Kasfir, and Z. Mampilly (2015). *Rebel Governance in Civil War.* New York: Cambridge University Press.

Arjona, A., J. Camilo Cárdenas, A. M. Ibáñez, and J. Arteaga Vallejo (2019). 'The Effects of Wartime Institutions on Households' Ability to Cope with Shocks'. WIDER Working Paper 84/2019. Helsinki: UNU-WIDER. https://doi.org/10.35188/UNU-WIDER/2019/720-0

Bardhan, P. (2005). *Scarcity, Conflicts, and Cooperation.* Cambridge, MA: MIT Press.

Bauer, M., C. Blattman, J. Chytilová, J. Henrich, E. Miguel, and T. Mitts (2016). 'Can War Foster Cooperation?' *Journal of Economic Perspectives*, 30(3): 249–274. https://doi.org/10.1257/jep.30.3.249

Bellows, J., and E. Miguel (2009). 'War and Local Collective Action in Sierra Leone'. *Journal of Public Economics*, 93(11–12): 1144–1157. https://doi.org/10.1016/j.jpubeco.2009.07.012

Besley, T., and H. Mueller (2021). 'Fiscal Capacity and State Fragility'. In R. Chami, R. Espinoza, and P. J. Montiel (eds), *Macroeconomic Policy in Fragile States*, pp. 235–270. Oxford: Oxford University Press. https://doi.org/10.1093/oso/9780198853091.003.0009

Blair, R., M. Moscoso, A. Vargas Castillo, and M. Weintraub (2022). 'Preventing Rebel Resurgence after Civil War: A Field Experiment in Security and Justice Provision in Rural Colombia'. *American Political Science Review*, 116(4): 1258–1277. https://doi.org/10.1017/S0003055422000284

Blattman, C. (2009). 'From Violence to Voting: War and Political Participation in Uganda'. *American Political Science Review*, 103(2): 231–247. https://doi.org/10.1017/S0003055409090212

Brockett, C. D. (1990). *Land, Power and Poverty: Agrarian Transformation and Political Conflict in Central America.* Boulder, CO: Westview Press.

Buitrago, F. L., and A. D. L. De Guevara (2010). *Clientelismo: el sistema político y su expresión regional.* Universidad de los Andes.

Cassar, A., P. Grosjean, and S. Whitt (2013). 'Legacies of Violence: Trust and Market Development'. *Journal of Economic Growth*, 18(3): 285–318. https://doi.org/10.1007/s10887-013-9091-3

Daly, S. Z. (2016). *Organized Violence after Civil War: The Geography of Recruitment in Latin America.* New York: Cambridge University Press. https://doi.org/10.1017/CBO9781316412350

Fumerton, M. (2001). 'Rondas Campesinas in the Peruvian Civil War: Peasant Self-Defence Organisations in Ayacucho'. *Bulletin of Latin American Research*, 20(4): 470–497. https://doi.org/10.1111/1470-9856.00026

Funes, M. (1998). 'Social Responses to Political Violence in the Basque Country: Peace Movements and their Audience'. *Journal of Conflict Resolution*, 42(4): 493–510. https://doi.org/10.1177/0022002798042004005

Gilligan, M., B. Pasquale, and C. Samii (2014). 'Civil War and Social Cohesion: Lab-in-the-Field Evidence from Nepal'. *American Journal of Political Science*, 58(3): 604–619. https://doi.org/10.1111/ajps.12067

Goodwin, J. (2001). *No Other Way Out: States and Revolutionary Movements, 1945–1991.* Cambridge: Cambridge University Press. https://doi.org/10.1017/CBO9780511812125

Grosjean, P. (2014). 'Conflict and Social and Political Preferences: Evidence from World War II and Civil Conflict in 35 European Countries'. *Comparative Economic Studies*, 56(3): 424–451. https://doi.org/10.1057/ces.2014.2

Grupo de Memoria Histórica (2010). *Silenciar la democracia. Las masacres de Remedios y Segovia, 1982–1997*. Bogotá: Taurus Editores.

Grupo de Memoria Histórica (2011). *San Carlos: Memorias del éxodo en la guerra*. Bogotá: Taurus Editores.

Gutiérrez, F., and M. Barón (2005). 'Re-stating the State: Paramilitary Territorial Control and Political Order in Colombia (1978–2004)'. Working Paper 66. London: London School of Economics.

Huang, R. (2016). *The Wartime Origins of Democratization: Civil War, Rebel Governance, and Political Regimes*. New York: Cambridge University Press. https://doi.org/10.1017/CBO9781316711323

Justino, P. (2009). 'Poverty and Violent Conflict: A Micro-Level Perspective on the Causes and Duration of Warfare'. *Journal of Peace Research*, 46(3): 315–333. https://doi.org/10.1177/0022343309102655

Justino, P. (2013). 'Research and Policy Implications from a Micro-Level Perspective on the Dynamics of Conflict, Violence and Development'. In P. Justino, T., Brück, and P. Verwimp (eds), *A Micro-Level Perspective on the Dynamics of Conflict, Violence and Development*. Oxford: Oxford University Press. https://doi.org/10.1093/acprof:oso/9780199664597.001.0001

Justino, P. (2019). 'Governance Interventions in Conflict-Affected Countries'. *Journal of Development Studies*, 55(7): 1364–1378. https://doi.org/10.1080/00220388.2018.1487053

Justino, P., and W. Stojetz (2019). 'Civic Legacies of Wartime Governance'. WIDER Working Paper 104/2019. https://doi.org/10.35188/UNU-WIDER/2019/740-8

Kalyvas, S. N. (2006). *The Logic of Violence in Civil War*. New York: Cambridge University Press. https://doi.org/10.1017/CBO9780511818462

Kalyvas, S. N., and M. A. Kocher (2007). 'How "Free" is Free Riding in Civil Wars? Violence, Insurgency, and the Collective Action Problem'. *World Politics*, 59: 177–216. https://doi.org/10.1353/wp.2007.0023

Kaplan, O. R. (2017). *Resisting War: How Communities Protect Themselves*. New York: Cambridge University Press. https://doi.org/10.1017/9781316671887

Karl, R. (2017). *Forgotten Peace: Reform, Violence and the Making of Contemporary Colombia*. Oakland, CA: University of California Press. https://doi.org/10.1525/california/9780520293922.001.0001

Krause, J. (2018). *Resilient Communities: Non-Violence and Civilian Agency in Communal War*. Cambridge: Cambridge University Press. https://doi.org/10.1017/9781108675079

La Ferrara, E. (2002). 'Inequality and Group Participation: Theory and Evidence from Rural Tanzania'. *Journal of Public Economics*, 85(2): 235–273. https://doi.org/10.1016/S0047-2727(01)00102-5

Lancee, B., and H. G. Van de Werfhorst (2012). 'Income Inequality and Participation: A Comparison of 24 European Countries'. *Social Science Research*, 41(5): 1166–1178. https://doi.org/10.1016/j.ssresearch.2012.04.005

Leal Buitrago, F., and A. Dávila Ladrón de Guevara (2010). *Clientelismo: El Sistema Político y su Expresión Regional*. Bogotá: Ediciones Uniandes – Universidad de los Andes.

Lee, D. S (2009). 'Training, Wages, and Sample Selection: Estimating Sharp Bounds on Treatment Effects', *Review of Economic Studies*, 76(3): 1071–1102. https://doi.org/10.1111/j.1467-937X.2009.00536.x

Loyle, C. and H. Binningsbø (2018). 'Justice during Armed Conflict: A New Dataset on Government and Rebel Strategies'. *Journal of Conflict Resolution*, 62(2): 442–466. https://doi.org/10.1177/0022002716655441

Mampilly, Z. (2011). *Rebel Rulers: Insurgent Governance and Civilian Life during War.* Ithaca, NY: Cornell University Press.

Mampilly, Z. and M. Stewart (2021). 'A Typology of Rebel Political Institutional Arrangements'. *Journal of Conflict Resolution*, 65(1): 15–45. https://doi.org/10.1177/0022002720935642

Ostrom, E. (1990). *Governing the Commons: The Evolution of Institutions for Collective Action.* New York: Cambridge University Press.

Pande, R., T. Besley, and V. Rao (2007). 'Political Economy of Panchayats in South India'. *Economic & Political Weekly*, 42(8): 661–66.

Petersen, R. (2001). *Resistance and Rebellion: Lessons from Eastern Europe.* Cambridge: Cambridge University Press. https://doi.org/10.1017/CBO9780511612725

Prem, M., A. Rivera, D. Romero, and J. Vargas (2022). 'Selective Civilian Targeting: The Unintended Consequences of Partial Peace'. *Quarterly Journal of Political Science*, 17(3): 317–354. https://doi.org/10.1561/100.00020088

Putnam, R. D. 1993. *Making Democracy Work.* Princeton, NJ: Princeton University Press.

Riley, D. (2005). 'Civic Associations and Authoritarian Regimes in Interwar Europe: Italy and Spain in Comparative Perspective'. *American Sociological Review*, 70(2): 288–310. https://doi.org/10.1177/000312240507000205

Rodríguez Valero, L. A., and N. Maldonado Gómez (2020). 'Las Políticas Distributivas en Colombia: De los Auxilios Parlamentarios a las Partidas de Inversioón Social Regional o Mermelada Tóxica'. *Revista de la Facultad de Derecho y Ciencias Políticas Universidad Ponticia Bolivariana*, 50(1320): 1–28. https://doi.org/10.18566/rfdcp.v50n132.a01

Ronderos, M. T. (2014). *Guerras Recicladas. Una Historia Periodística del Paramilitarismo en Colombia.* Bogotá: Editorial Aguilar.

Rubin, M. (2019). 'Rebel Territorial Control and Civilian Collective Action in Civil War: Evidence from the Communist Insurgency in the Philippines'. *Journal of Conflict Resolution*, 64(2–3): 459–489. https://doi.org/10.1177/0022002719863844

Sánchez Castañeda, J. M., and A. Vargas Prieto (2017). 'Incidencia de las Juntas de Accion Comunal en el Desarrollo Local en Areas de Influencia de Proyectos de Hidrocarburos'. *Equidad & Desarrolo*, 27: 195–212.

Sánchez, F., and M. Del Mar Palau (2006). 'Conflict, Decentralization and Local Governance in Colombia, 1974–2004'. Documento CEDE 2180. Bogotá: Universidad de los Andes.

Sánchez, G., and D. Meertens (1983). *Bandoleros, Gamonales y Campesinos: El Caso de la Violencia en Colombia.* Bogotá: El Áncora Ed.

Satyanath, S., N. Voigtlaender, and H.-J. Voth (2017). 'Bowling for Fascism: Social Capital and the Rise of the Nazi Party'. *Journal of Political Economy*, 125(2): 478–526. https://doi.org/10.1086/690949

Staniland, P. (2021). *Ordering Violence: Explaining Armed Group-State Relations from Conflict to Cooperation.* Ithaca, NY: Cornell University Press. https://doi.org/10.7591/cornell/9781501761102.001.0001

Stewart, M. (2018). 'Civil War as State-Making: Strategic Governance in Civil War'. *International Organization*, 72(1): 205–226. https://doi.org/10.1017/S0020818317000418

Verba, S., K. L. Schlozman, and H. E. Brady (1995). *Voice and Equality: Civic Voluntarism in American Politics.* Cambridge, MA: Harvard University Press. https://doi.org/10.2307/j.ctv1pnc1k7

Voors, M., E. Nillesen, P. Verwimp, E. Bulte, R. Lensink, and D. Van Soest (2012). 'Violent Conflict and Behavior: A Field Experiment in Burundi'. *American Economic Review*, 102(2): 941–964. https://doi.org/10.1257/aer.102.2.941

Wantchekon, L., and Z. Neema (2002). 'A Theory of Post-Civil War Democratization'. *Journal of Theoretical Politics*, 14(4): 439–464. https://doi.org/10.1177/095162902774006822

Wantchekon, L. (2004). 'The Paradox of 'Warlord' Democracy: A Theoretical Investigation'. *American Political Science Review*, 98(1): 17–33. https://doi.org/10.1017/S0003055404000978

Weinstein, J. M. (2007). *Inside Rebellion: The Politics of Insurgent Violence*. Cambridge: Cambridge University Press. https://doi.org/10.1017/CBO9780511808654

Wood, E. J. (2000). *Forging Democracy from Below: Insurgent Transitions in South Africa and El Salvador*. New York: Cambridge University Press.

Wood, E. J. (2003). *Insurgent Collective Action and Civil War in El Salvador*. Cambridge: Cambridge University Press. https://doi.org/10.1017/CBO9780511808685

Wood, E. J. (2008). 'The Social Processes of Civil War: The Wartime Transformation of Social Networks'. *Annual Review of Political Science*, 11: 539–561. https://doi.org/10.1146/annurev.polisci.8.082103.104832

Zamosc, L. (1986). *The Agrarian Question and the Peasant Movement in Colombia: Struggles of the National Peasant Movement (1967–1981)*. Cambridge: Cambridge University Press. https://doi.org/10.1017/CBO9780511558948

4

Rebel governance and political participation

Abbey Steele and Michael Weintraub

4.1 Introduction

Rebels, militias, and criminal groups all govern civilians[1]. Armed group governance includes the provision of security, dispute resolution, tax collection, establishment of schools and hospitals, and political representation (e.g., Arjona 2015; Arjona et al. 2015; Mampilly and Stewart 2020). For example, the Islamic State in Iraq and Syria sought to create a legal system to resolve disputes among citizens and between civilians and the newly established Islamic state government between 2014 and 2017 (Revkin and Ahram 2020). Half a world away, the African Party for the Independence of Guinea and Cape Verde (PAIGC) provided education and healthcare, and also held elections (Stewart 2020).

Yet armed groups approach governance in different ways. Some replace local governing authorities upon assuming local rule, while others work with existing decision-makers to govern jointly (Vargas Castillo 2019). Some armed groups impose draconian, illiberal policies that run counter to local preferences, while others implement rules adopted via participatory mechanisms, akin to democratic representation, in ways that reflect local customs and beliefs (e.g., Kasfir 2005). Because armed group governance may transform local decision-making, alter expectations about what would-be governors can and should do, and/or legitimate existing state institutions, we expect that how armed groups govern has important

[1] The survey analysed here was developed and implemented in collaboration with Marianne Dahl, Helga Malmin Binningsbø, Håvard Mokleiv Nygård, and UNDP Colombia. The survey firms SEI and Proyectamos handled data collection. We thank the UNDP staff, and especially Pablo Ruiz, Camilo Sánchez Meertens, Jessica Faieta, and Tamara Simao for their support of the project. The conclusions and analyses reported here are solely the responsibility of the authors. We thank Sebastián Pantoja Barríos, Dayanna Erazo, Peder Landsverk, and Tora Sagård for excellent research assistance. Versions of this chapter have been presented at the Conflict Research Society annual meeting 2019, Latin American Peace Science conference 2021, University of British Columbia political science department, Amsterdam Conflict Research Network, and the 2022 UNU-WIDER Puzzle of Peace conference. We thank Juan Masullo and Megan Stewart for helpful feedback. We are grateful for financial support from the Norwegian Ministry of Foreign Affairs and the Research Council of Norway (grants nr: 275400 and 250441), and from the UNU-WIDER project Institutional Legacies of Violent Conflict. The survey received approval from the Ethics Committee at Universidad de los Andes.

Abbey Steele and Michael Weintraub, *Rebel governance and political participation*. In: *Institutional Legacies of Violent Conflict*. Edited by: Patricia Justino, Oxford University Press. © United Nations University World Institute for Development Economics Research (UNU-WIDER) (2026). DOI: 10.1093/9780197904077.003.0004

consequences for how local citizens experience politics. These varied experiences should, in turn, shape decisions about how civilians mobilize and participate in politics, even once conflict wanes or ends entirely.

We argue that governing strategies adopted by armed groups during civil war affect how citizens choose to engage politically in post-conflict environments, with potentially significant consequences for the health of democratic politics. We conceptually disaggregate formal from informal political participation. Formal engagement, in which individuals participate in politics through the state, and informal engagement, in which individuals join civil society organizations or engage in protest, are important because civil wars represent contests over the rules of the game and the legitimacy of state institutions. How armed group governance affects political participation should shed light on core questions about political engagement, democratic stability, and the robustness of civic life in post-war settings.

Differences in armed group governance and the kinds of mobilization that armed groups incentivize, encourage, or prohibit should affect the preferences and behaviours of individuals even after the conflict ends. We argue that two dimensions of armed group rule intersect and shape individuals' political engagement. The first is the armed group's position relative to the state. Armed groups can either fight against state authority or reinforce it. Rebels engage in competitive state-building over and against the state, while pro-government militias and paramilitaries pursue actions to buttress the state's counterinsurgency efforts. The second dimension is the governance ideology of the group. Armed groups can either embrace a 'shared' or 'centralized' governance ideology. A shared governance ideology includes civilians in governance at the local level, while a centralized one excludes civilians and imposes top-down rule.

Armed groups aligned with the state will encourage civilian participation in formal state institutions. Where pro-state armed groups also embrace a shared governance ideology, incorporating pre-existing communal institutions into their governing strategy, we expect an increase in informal political participation as well. In contrast, we expect anti-state rebels that rule with a shared governance ideology to channel political action away from formal channels, to avoid legitimizing the state in areas they control. These groups will encourage political participation through other means. When anti-state rebels hold a centralized governance ideology, in contrast, we expect lower levels of political participation, whether formal or informal.

We test this argument in Colombia, drawing on a novel, large-scale survey conducted as part of the Mapping Attitudes, Perceptions, and Support (MAPS) project (Weintraub et al. 2021). In 2016, the Colombian government and the country's largest rebel group, the Revolutionary Armed Forces of Colombia (FARC-EP), signed a peace agreement after nearly five decades of conflict. In late 2019, we fielded a survey in 16 regions of Colombia targeted for peace agreement implementation, determined based on historic exposure to violence and levels of poverty. These 'Programs for Development with a Territorial Focus' (PDETs, for its Spanish acronym) cover a massive area of the country: at 411,029 km^2, they represent 36 per cent of all Colombian territory and, when taken together, are larger than Norway. The MAPS survey is representative at the level of each of the 16 PDETs, allowing us to draw inferences about each and make comparisons among them.[2] The total number of respondents was 12,052 individuals, making ours among the largest surveys deployed to study the implementation of Colombia's peace agreement, and the only survey of which we are aware that is representative at the PDET level. The vast geographic coverage, combined with a sampling strategy that intentionally targeted areas deeply affected by conflict, means that our survey is uniquely suited to answer research questions related to armed group governance. To minimize potential threats to inference, our statistical models include fixed effects at the municipal level, as well as a battery of covariates at the individual level.

We find partial support for our hypotheses. While governance by pro-state paramilitaries increased formal participation, so too did governance by the FARC-EP. Exposure to insurgent governance only increased *some* forms of informal participation—such as protest activity, belonging to a victims' organization, and belonging to communal village councils. And those exposed to paramilitary governance were *also* more likely to participate informally, including via protests, participation in activist groups, and victims' organizations. Given this mixed support for our hypotheses, we test alternative explanations as well, although we do not find support for these alternatives either. Following this brush-clearing empirical exercise, we provide a roadmap for future research on related questions.

This chapter contributes to multiple bodies of research. First, we contribute to the literature on rebel governance (e.g., Arjona 2016; Arjona et al. 2015; Cunningham and Loyle 2020; Loyle 2021; Mampilly 2011; Mampilly and Stewart 2020; van Baalen 2021). Second, we contribute to a large and rapidly expanding literature on the legacies of armed conflict (Balcells 2012; Costalli and Ruggeri 2015; Grandi 2013; Lupu and Peisakhin 2017; Osorio et al. 2019; Wood 2008). Third, we contribute to work on political participation and social mobilization in weakly institutionalized democracies and post-conflict spaces (e.g. Bratton 1999). In particular, on this last point, we conceptually disaggregate forms of political engagement and test our theoretical expectations by leveraging micro-level public opinion data in Colombia.

4.2 Theoretical framework

Institutions—the rules of the game that structure human interactions (North and Weingast 1989)—shape decisions about how citizens participate in their

[2] In August 2020, two new PDETs—both within Bogotá—were approved. Our survey does not include these two new subregions.

communities, and influence citizen preferences over policy processes and outcomes. The institutions that armed groups establish or adapt during conflict are likely to do the same. But does armed group governance during war leave a lasting impact on individuals' political preferences and behaviour? If so, what changes does armed group governance produce?

We follow Arjona et al. (2015: 3) in defining rebel governance as 'the set of actions that insurgents engage in to regulate the social, political, and economic life of non-combatants during civil war'.[3] Governance can vary across multiple dimensions: for example, Arjona (2016) distinguishes between rebelocracy and aliocracy, depending upon how much relative power the rebel group or the community retains in governance arrangements, as well as the breadth of governance adopted by rebels. Armed groups' engagement in communal affairs can also vary in terms of how coercive and illiberal or responsive and democratic that engagement is. Mampilly and Stewart (2020) characterize the qualities of different political institutions adopted by armed groups and argue that armed groups decide which institutions to construct in a stepwise fashion, in part influenced by the community itself.

Other studies examine variation in governance across rebel groups or between different civil war settings (Huang 2016; Mampilly 2011; Revkin 2019; Stewart 2018; Vargas Castillo 2019).[4] Differences between armed groups might produce meaningful variation across communities—and, we think, individuals—long after the rebel rule has ended. We draw on this work to develop testable hypotheses connecting armed group governance to individual-level decisions about political participation.

4.2.1 Political participation

When deciding whether and how to participate in politics in post-conflict spaces, individuals have multiple options available to them.[5] We conceive of these as broadly falling into two types: formal and informal engagement. Formal engagement involves participating in state-based institutions, such as voting or contacting an elected official (e.g. Bratton 1999).[6] Informal engagement occurs outside of, and

[3] While early work focused on actions taken by *rebels*, studies are no longer limited to insurgents who compete with state governance, but also include reactionary paramilitary and militia groups (Kasfir et al. 2017) and criminal actors (Blattman et al. 2021), and we include such groups when we refer to 'rebel' governance.

[4] van Baalen (2020) considers 'responsiveness' of armed groups' governance across armed groups, communities, and *segments* of the population. Revkin (2021) also finds differences across population segments' perceptions of governance within Mosul.

[5] Not all options may be available to all individuals, given the persistent threat of violence and differing access to tools of mobilization.

[6] Ley (2018) and Berens and Dallendörfer (2019) refer to similar types of engagement as 'electoral' and 'non-electoral'. We choose 'formal' and 'informal' to capture engagement with state institutions and non-state political organizations and actions.

is often antagonistic towards, the state. We consider membership in civil society organizations and participating in protests or strikes as core examples of informal participation.

Formal engagement and informal engagement also differ in the degree to which engagement is independent or collective. Formal channels of engagement tend to be independent, while informal channels are more likely to be collective. For example, although decisions about whether to vote may be influenced by other community members' decisions to do so (Eubank et al. 2019; Rolfe 2012), the act of voting itself does not require significant interpersonal or communal coordination. On the other hand, informal participation, including forming or mobilizing non-governmental organizations for political action, requires overcoming significant collective action problems, particularly in environments where participation might be met with violence (Kuran 1991; Siegel 2009).

We believe that these dimensions of participation are substantively important. The extent to which individuals participate in formal (democratic) channels likely has an impact on the health of democratic states. In states that have experienced civil wars, it is normatively desirable for regions most afflicted by violence to be represented in national debates about peace-building and post-war politics that most affect them. Informal participation, in the form of civil society engagement and collective protest or strikes, is arguably equally important for influencing the course of post-war states and politics, as an active civil society can help tame repressive governments while providing channels for radical ideas to flourish and gain popular acceptance.

4.2.2 Our argument

How does rebel governance influence informal and formal political participation? We focus on two key dimensions that interact in theoretically meaningful ways: the position of an armed group vis-à-vis the state—whether it is 'anti-state' (rebels) or 'pro-state' (paramilitaries or militias)—and its approach to incorporating community members into its governing practices.

We begin with *position vis-à-vis the state*. Armed groups can either be nominally or formally aligned with the state—complementing its coercive capacity—or against it. Rebel groups that seek to overthrow the government, or secede from a given polity, are the clearest examples of anti-state armed actors, while 'rearguard' paramilitary forces that use local ties to determine who has collaborated with rebels are clear examples of pro-state armed actors. Others fall on a spectrum somewhere in between: organized criminal groups that collude with state authorities to capture rents are, in one sense, against the state, committing illicit acts formally punished under the penal code, but sustained cooperation between state officials and organized criminal groups to violate the law belies that anti-state designation. We argue below that an armed group's position affects the kinds of activities permitted and encouraged within the territory that an armed group rules, with consequences for citizens' political participation in the long run.

The second dimension is the approach an armed group takes to community involvement in governance: it is either a shared project between the community and the armed group or it stems from top-down rules that community members are obliged to follow.[7] Shared governance creates 'shared understandings such as a normative expectation that communal authority should lead through consultation processes with the community, notions of order and cleanliness of public space, and communitarian and egalitarian logics in addressing collective affairs' (Vargas Castillo 2019: 211).

Consultations with community members may become more frequent, and communicating preferences more common. While armed groups may imply punishment for not joining communal organizations, or even openly demand participation, in shared governance arrangements, the armed group is not directly responsible for implementing governance actions.

Table 4.1 outlines the intersection of the two dimensions of armed group governance (position vis-à-vis the state and governance ideology) and our expectations about political participation. When shared governance is pursued by an armed group that opposes the state (upper left-hand box), we expect citizens will participate more informally.[8] Because anti-state rebel groups engage in competitive state-building, we anticipate that civilians exposed to governance by these groups will be socialized to reject the legitimacy of formal state institutions and will instead, in the long term, seek to participate in politics via informal channels. Civilians exposed to state-aligned armed group governance should, on average, be encouraged to participate in formal channels of participation. At the same time, individuals who experience shared governance should be more likely to hold beliefs that collective forms of organizing are both desirable and effective for achieving political ends. As a result, we expect them to be more open or inclined, on average, to participate in associations and other collective forms of organization, and be more willing to assume costs associated with participating in these ways.

[7] These types of rule would both fall under what Arjona (2016) terms 'rebelocracy', which involves extensive intervention in community life. Here, we distinguish *how* that intervention takes place and, as such, do not address what Arjona calls 'aliocracy', in which community affairs are delegated to community leaders and in which armed groups refrain from shaping economic, political, and social life.

[8] Our theoretical expectations differ from Huang (2016), who reasons that contentious politics are more likely following wars during which civilians have sustained contact with insurgent groups, given that insurgent groups will expose civilians to new ideas about politics, and may lead to mass organizing against the state. We argue that insurgents do not only need to provide an alternative to the state's vision of governance, but also to embrace an ideology that promotes alternative modes of political participation.

Table 4.1 Armed group governance and political participation

Community involvement in governance	Position	
	Anti-state	**Pro-state**
Shared	+ informal	+ formal and informal
Centralized	– formal and informal	+ formal

When an anti-state armed group embraces a centralized governance ideology (lower left-hand box)—'an administrative arrangement where armed group agents rule social life directly' (Vargas Castillo 2019: 51)—we expect individuals will be less engaged in both formal and informal modes of participation. Centralized governance emphasizes rule-following rather than shared decision-making, with rules that are 'pre-baked' and enforced by the armed group. Such an approach to political organization would not be amenable to bottom-up, informal participation, given that organizational vehicles for participation are either actively depressed or simply not encouraged. The armed group's opposition to state institutions should, as described above, likewise disincentivize formal participation.

In contrast, when a state-aligned armed group embraces centralized governance (lower right-hand box), we expect that the armed group will endorse rules for formal political participation and encourage individuals to follow them.[9] Centralized governance may involve coercion to prompt participation in formal state institutions, including mandating voting in elections. Pro-state, centralized rule will also discourage anti-status quo political activities, even those that are only adjacent to insurgent organizing tactics, such as protests or strikes. For this reason, we argue that those living under this governance arrangement are unlikely to participate informally in politics.

Finally, armed groups aligned with the state that embrace shared governance (upper right-hand box) are likely to have increased formal and informal political participation. Norms, beliefs, and preferences to increase participation will be cultivated under shared governance practices, regardless of the armed group's position relative to the state. State-aligned armed groups should encourage participation via state-based channels of participation to legitimate government-aligned processes of participation. Compared to individuals from communities that do not experience any such endorsement or organizing, we expect these individuals, on average, will engage through multiple participatory channels.

[9] For pro-state armed groups in autocratic settings without formal institutions for participation, we may not see an increase in political participation. However, the majority of autocracies now hold elections (Gandhi and Lust-Okar 2009).

Each of the changes occasioned by armed group governance—which relate to the scope, depth, and texture of local political life under armed groups—should generate changes in attitudes and behaviour for ordinary citizens. The broad argument is that an armed group governing in a collaborative way with the community is likely to encourage *informal* participation by citizens on average. In contrast, governance by pro-state armed groups is more likely to foster *formal* participation, whether or not the form of governance is centralized or shared.

We recognize that governance is not always exclusive: multiple armed groups may seek to rule over the same populations simultaneously, or they may do so sequentially (e.g., Kasfir et al. 2017; Mampilly and Stewart 2020). Here, we agree with Vargas Castillo (2019): the aggregate effect of multiple rulers is likely to undermine the impact of one form of rule over another and, as a result, we should observe weaker relationships between governance type and political engagement outcomes in the presence of multiple would-governors.

4.3 Colombian context

The Colombian civil war dates to the formation of the FARC in the mid-1960s. Until the 1980s, the group remained peripheral, developing a strong presence in several remote areas but rarely confronting state forces.[10] In the 1980s, the FARC expanded its role in the cocaine trade, eventually entering into conflict with El Mexicano, a member of the Medellín cartel, over taxation of coca crops. This confrontation with militias affiliated with the cartel eventually evolved into the revival of counterinsurgent militias (Ronderos 2014). Though the FARC participated in peace talks in the early 1980s and formed a legal political party as a result, it did not demobilize, but rather increased in strength throughout the decade. In the 1990s, the FARC expanded its territorial presence, oftentimes confronting the Colombian armed forces directly.

Counterinsurgent militias unified under a federation known as the *Autodefensas Unidas de Colombia* (AUC) in 1997 and succeeded in ousting the FARC from many regions through bloody incursions involving massacres and mass displacement (Steele 2017). Over time, the armed forces became more effective at fighting the FARC, sometimes in tandem with the AUC. Beginning in the early 2000s, the military began targeting high-ranking FARC members for assassination. After losing several leaders, the FARC entered into secret talks with the Santos administration in 2010.

[10] In the early 1970s, a group broke away from the FARC to found the M-19, whose leaders explicitly disagreed with the FARC about how to take the war effort forward: they argued for, and pursued, an urban front. The brief summary of the conflict that we provide here focuses on the FARC, but several other insurgent groups formed over this time period as well.

Between 2012 and 2016, government and FARC representatives and international guarantors negotiated the contents of a peace agreement that comprised five core pillars (plus details regarding the implementation of the agreement): agrarian/land reform, political participation, illicit crops, transitional justice and reparations for victims, and demobilization and reincorporation of ex-combatants. The peace agreement was signed by the parties on 26 September 2016, but failed by a slim margin to win popular support in a plebiscite on 2 October 2016. The parties returned to the negotiating table to discuss the petitions of political leaders who led opposition to the plebiscite and then signed a modified agreement in November 2016.[11] As of April 2021, there were 13,087 ex-members of the FARC-EP engaged in reincorporation following disarmament via the 2016 peace agreement.

The ELN also formed in the early 1960s, inspired by the Cuban revolution and dedicated to Guevara's *foquismo* approach to guerrilla warfare. The ELN is less centralized than the FARC, which some observers link to its failure to remain in peace talks with the government. Most recently, peace talks were called off in January 2019. The group remains active on the Venezuelan border, particularly Catatumbo and Arauca, and in Chocó.

4.3.1 Rebel governance in Colombia

Non-state armed groups intervened in civilians' lives to varying degrees across Colombian communities (Arjona 2016). Variation in governance practices also exists across armed groups (Vargas Castillo 2019). The FARC and the ELN operated in collaboration with existing forms of political authority—exhibiting polycentric governance alongside communal village boards or *Juntas de Acción Comunal* (JACs) where they controlled territory—while paramilitaries generally sought to eradicate pre-existing forms of political decision-making locally—imposing more centralized forms of governance.[12]

Paramilitary groups also engaged in governance (Arjona 2016; Robinson 2013; Ch et al. 2018). However, paramilitary blocks were aligned with the state and regional elites, and often worked through state institutions for the benefit of these elites. Governance at the community level was more centralized than what their insurgent counterparts pursued: paramilitaries enforced a 'zero tolerance policy towards petty criminality' while also directly offering conflict resolution services for disputes among neighbours, instead of using existing communal

[11] The Santos administration subsequently required approval from a court to accept the agreement through a 'fast-track' legislative process. Though it was approved by the court, it stalled in Congress. Nearly five years later, Congress is still in the process of amending and adopting laws to implement the peace agreement.

[12] Though see Larratt-Smith (2020).

vehicles to do so (e.g. Vargas Castillo 2019, 249–251). Measures of social control—including restrictions on movement and curfews—were also commonly imposed and enforced directly by paramilitaries.

4.3.2 Political engagement in Colombia

Opportunities for political participation in Colombia have shifted over time and in relation to the ongoing war. In spite of the conflict, Colombia is one of the most durable democracies in Latin America. Nevertheless, between 1958 and 1982, the democracy was a consociational one, dominated by the Liberal and Conservative political parties who alternated power mechanically every four years. Presidents appointed governors, who then appointed municipal mayors. Some argued that the exclusionary and top-down political system fuelled the twin insurgencies, because it could not sufficiently accommodate a broader range of political preferences (Pécaut 1989). During the 1982 peace talks with the FARC, this interpretation was embraced and political reforms were adopted to address it. The FARC founded a legal political party in 1985, the Patriotic Union (UP), whose candidate for president in the 1986 elections won 4 per cent of the national vote. In 1988, municipalities began holding direct elections for mayors—another reform stemming from the peace talks. Though the FARC initially embraced electoral participation, following a wave of assassinations and mass displacements perpetrated by counterinsurgent militias, it abandoned this strategy, and in the 1990s, it forbade electoral participation in areas it controlled (Steele 2017). The UP stopped contesting elections in 2002. Despite the UP's exit from formal politics, uneven protections for electoral participation, and high levels of clientelism in some regions, new political parties proliferated in the 1990s following the adoption of a new constitution in 1991. Electoral participation rates in Colombia during this period were roughly comparable to those in other democracies.

In terms of political engagement beyond formal state channels, civil society organizations and unions expanded after the return to democracy in 1957. Government repression of student activists and unions under the Turbay administration (1978–1982) led many to join the insurgency. In the late 1980s, the Catholic Church and human rights activists began agitating for greater attention to the violence that social leaders and union members faced in peripheral regions of the country (Tate 2007). Social leaders seeking reparations and land restitution for victims have frequently been targeted with lethal violence, at a pace that has accelerated since the signing of the 2016 peace agreement with the FARC (Prem et al. 2018). In spite of the history of violence against activists, Colombia has a vibrant civil society that is frequently vocal in its criticism of the state.

The division of formal and informal political engagement blurs in some domains, such as the JACs and civil society organizations like the National Peasant

Union (ANUC). Both were formed by the state in the early 1960s in order to engage more peasants and secure land reforms, although these innovations did not work as planned (e.g. Albertus and Kaplan 2013). JACs are elected bodies located within municipalities that have some say in the governance of rural communities and form the axis of local governance in rural communities (Blair et al. 2022). However, in some regions where armed groups were active, JACs were targeted for infiltration (Ch et al. 2018; Eaton 2006; Vargas Castillo 2019), while in other cases, insurgent groups used the JACs to help govern or collaborated with them to do so. As a result, those who experienced rebel governance would be unlikely to view the JACs as formal state institutions.[13]

4.3.3 Testable implications of the theory in Colombia

The FARC and ELN, as described above, were both anti-state rebel groups that embraced shared governance, albeit with slightly different implementations. In contrast, pro-state paramilitary blocks largely applied centralized forms of governance. We expect that those who experienced rebel governance under the FARC or ELN are more likely to be politically engaged through informal channels than those who did not. We expect that those who experienced pro-state, centralized rule via paramilitary governance are more likely to be politically engaged through formal channels than those who did not. Finally, we anticipate that those who experienced armed group rule by multiple types of groups are less likely to be politically engaged through formal and informal channels than those who did not experience governance by multiple groups. Note that because of the configurations of position vis-à-vis the state and governance ideology in the Colombian case, we are unable to test all four combinations described in Table 4.1.

4.4 Empirical strategy

4.4.1 Survey data

We test our hypotheses using data from a novel survey that we conducted in 2019. The first surveys were administered in January 2019, in two PDETs—Arauca and Tolima—the former on the Venezuelan border and deeply affected by Colombia's largest remaining rebel army, the ELN, and the latter the birthplace of the FARC. After making adjustments to the survey instrument, we conducted surveys in the remaining 14 PDETs between October and December 2019.

[13] We also suspect that many who did not experience rebel governance would likewise be unlikely to view them this way.

The sample included the *cabecera municipal*, or municipal seats, and the *centros poblados* or slightly more urbanized villages—consisting of at least 20 homes—for each municipality.[14] Within *centros poblados*, field coordinators randomly selected blocks ('manzanas') for enumerators to visit. Within selected blocks, the enumerator walked around to identify the type of structures contained within each block, including inhabited residences, abandoned homes, empty lots, or businesses. The enumerator then entered this information into a hand-held device. Given the types of properties observed, and the sample size required, the software randomly selected households to be surveyed among the universe of inhabited residences on each block. Within the household, the aim was to speak with a member of the household who was an adult and at home at the time. Enumerators aimed for gender parity in the sample of each block, but this depended on availability. Table 4.2 displays descriptive statistics for our sample; more detail about the data collection process can be found in Appendix A. The total number of survey respondents was 12,052 individuals. Figure 4.1 shows the distribution of our respondents at the municipal level.

Table 4.2 Descriptive statistics

Variable	Mean	SD	Min	Max	N
Formal participation dummy	0.77	0.42	0	1	12,052
Informal participation dummy	0.26	0.44	0	1	12,052
FARC only governance	0.13	0.34	0	1	12,052
ELN only governance	0.05	0.22	0	1	12,052
Paramilitary only governance	0.36	0.48	0	1	12,052
All governance	0.14	0.35	0	1	12,052
FARC and paramilitary governance	0.09	0.29	0	1	12,052
FARC and ELN governance	0.03	0.18	0	1	12,052
ELN and paramilitary governance	0.01	0.12	0	1	12,052
No armed governance	0.46	0.50	0	1	12,052
Contact leader	0.17	0.37	0	1	12,052

[14] The 'dispersed' rural population was not included: it would have been prohibitively costly given that no sampling frame exists for such areas.

Variable	Mean	SD	Min	Max	N
Contact politician	0.20	0.40	0	1	12,052
Vote plebiscite	0.49	0.50	0	1	12,052
Vote legislative	0.64	0.48	0	1	12,052
Protest	0.09	0.28	0	1	12,052
Activist group	0.12	0.33	0	1	12,052
Victims Org	0.06	0.24	0	1	10,335
JAC	0.11	0.31	0	1	10,335
Female	0.57	0.50	0	1	12,052
Age	3.38	1.61	1	6	12,052
Work	0.53	0.50	0	1	12,052
Study	0.04	0.19	0	1	12,052
Domestic tasks and other	0.49	0.50	0	1	12,052
Education	2.18	1.49	0	6	12,052

Estimation

We use an ordinary least squares (OLS) estimator. We include a set of individual-level controls for age, level of education, gender, a set of dummies for employment status (employed, student, and domestic worker), and whether an individual lives in a municipal centre or a village. To soak up any unmeasured heterogeneity at the municipal level, we also include municipal-level fixed effects.[15] In all models, we use population weights that reflect the municipal population size per PDET and rural–urban divide, based on the 2018 census.

All dependent and independent variables are operationalized at the individual level. Our core dependent variables are formal and informal political engagement. To measure formal political engagement, we take two approaches. First, we construct a dummy variable that takes a value of 1 if an individual responded affirmatively to having engaged in *any* of the following activities: (1) contacted a community leader in the prior six months; (2) contacted a politician in the prior six months; (3) voted in the 2016 plebiscite on the peace agreement; or (4) voted in the 2018 legislative elections. More than 76 per cent of the sample take a value of 1 on this variable, driven chiefly by affirmative answers to the voting questions:

[15] Following Abadie et al. (2017), we do not cluster standard errors given our use of fixed effects and the fact that our core interest is not in treatment heterogeneity.

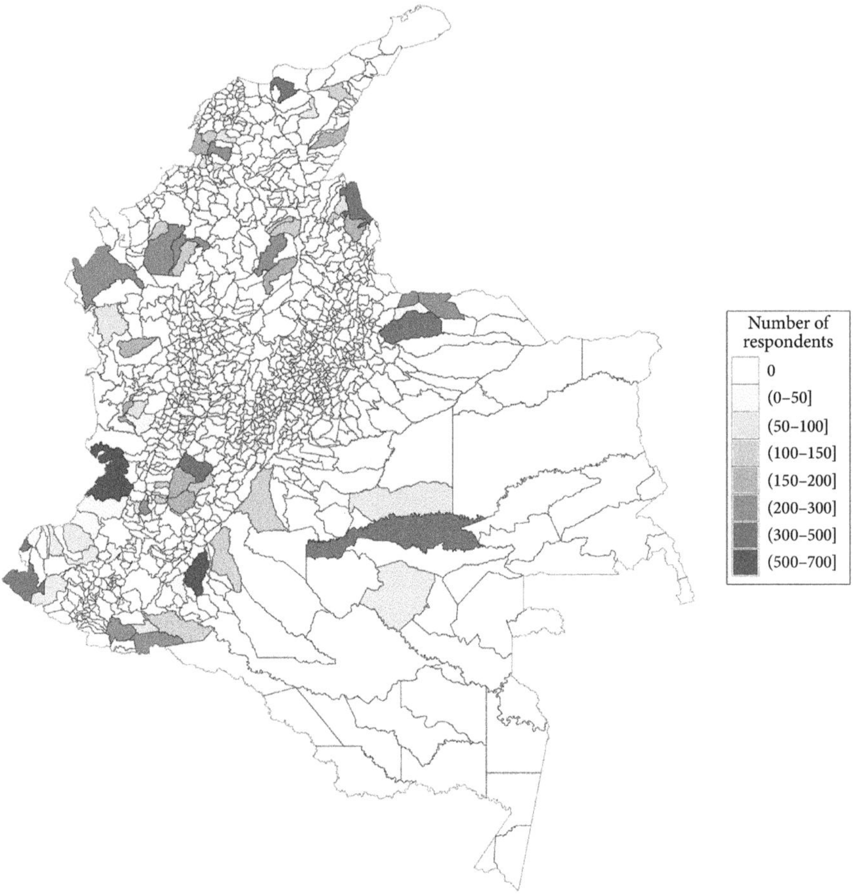

Figure 4.1 Distribution of respondents in the MAPS sample in each municipality

49 per cent report having voted in the plebiscite, while nearly 64 per cent report having voted in legislative elections. Second, we estimate the effects of armed group governance on each of these individual components.

To measure informal political engagement, we take a parallel approach. First, we construct a dummy variable that takes a value of 1 if an individual responded affirmatively to having engaged in *any* of the following activities: (1) participated in a protest in the prior six months; (2) was a member of an NGO; (3) was a member of a victims' group or citizen platform organization; or (4) was a member of a JAC. Although JACs were originally launched by the state in the 1960s (Kaplan 2017), they typically functioned autonomously and were frequently co-opted by rebel groups (e.g., Karl 2017; Peñaranda Currie et al. 2021, 4; Vargas Castillo 2019, 196–220). We code JAC membership as informal engagement, although our results are not sensitive to this decision. Approximately 26 per cent of respondents take a value of 1 on the informal participation dummy variable. A total of 12 per cent

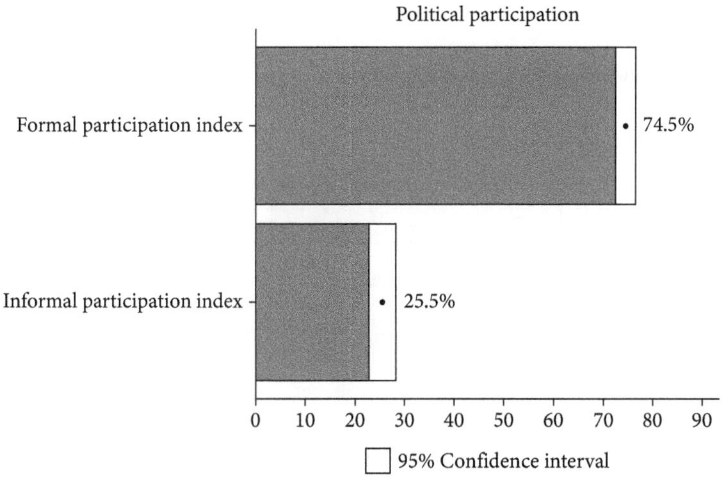

Figure 4.2 Formal and informal participation in the MAPS sample
N = 12,052
Source: MAPS 2019 survey PNUD/PRIO

report having participated in an activist group, while 11 per cent report participation in a JAC. Second, as above, we test the effects of armed group governance on each of these individual components. Figure 4.2 shows the distribution of the formal and informal participation dummy variables, using the population survey weights described and displaying 95 per cent confidence intervals.

Our core independent variables measure self-reported exposure to different forms of armed group governance. We ask whether, prior to the signing of the 2016 peace agreement, one or more of the following groups was 'in charge' in respondents' communities: FARC, ELN, and paramilitaries. Respondents were provided the opportunities to respond yes or no to each.[16] Based on the answer to these questions, we create a set of dummy variables for each respondent, depending upon whether they reported FARC-only governance (8.7 per cent of the sample); ELN-only governance (4.2 per cent); paramilitary-only governance (38.2 per cent); FARC and ELN governance (3.5 per cent); FARC and paramilitary governance (9 per cent); ELN and paramilitary governance (1.5 per cent); or governance by all three (12.8 per cent). The reference category for these regressions is reporting no armed group governance at all (5548 respondents, or 48.9 per cent of the sample), which most likely corresponds to state-provided governance but may also capture the absence of *any* authority locally. The percentage of respondents reporting no armed group governance is broadly consistent across regions, ranging from a minimum of 3.41 per cent in Sur de Bolívar to a maximum of 9.19 per cent in Cuenca del Caguan and Piedemonte Caqueteño. The overall distribution of the

[16] Don't know/refuse to answer were also options provided to respondents.

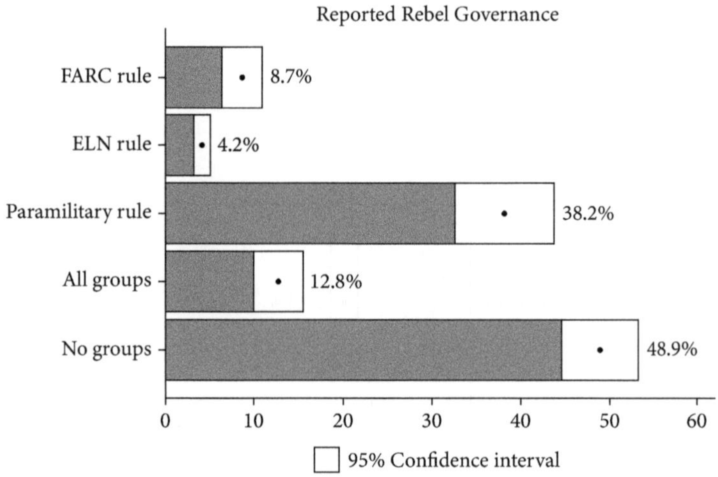

Figure 4.3 Reported armed group governance in the MAPS sample
N = 12,052
Source: MAPS 2019 survey PNUD/PRIO

armed group governance variables can be found in Figure 4.3 (for legibility, we exclude some multiple armed group categories).

The geographic distribution of these armed group governance variables can be found in Figure 4.4, where we also distinguish between respondents living in more urban areas (municipal capitals) and rural areas (hamlets). For these purposes, we exclude migrants and internally displaced persons (IDPs), an issue to which we return below. The patterns lend credence to our survey measure of armed group governance: in traditional FARC strongholds such as Ariari-Guayabero, for example, more than 50 per cent of respondents report FARC-only governance. The same holds for areas of traditional ELN control, as in Arauca on the Venezuelan border, and in some areas of the Pacific Coast. Finally, the area around Montes de María, Córdoba, and Bolívar all clearly show significant paramilitary governance. Nor do we see massive differences in responses across rural and urban areas. In short, we believe that the survey responses are likely a reasonable measure for armed group governance.

At the same time, we acknowledge that measuring armed group governance is difficult and subject to potential measurement error. For example, there may be significant dispersion within communities in how individuals report on armed group governance. To determine how consistent individual responses are with community responses, we construct indices measuring the probability that an individual respondent's answer to each armed group governance question matches that provided by others in her community. For each individual respondent, we take the number of respondents indicating that a given group (either FARC,

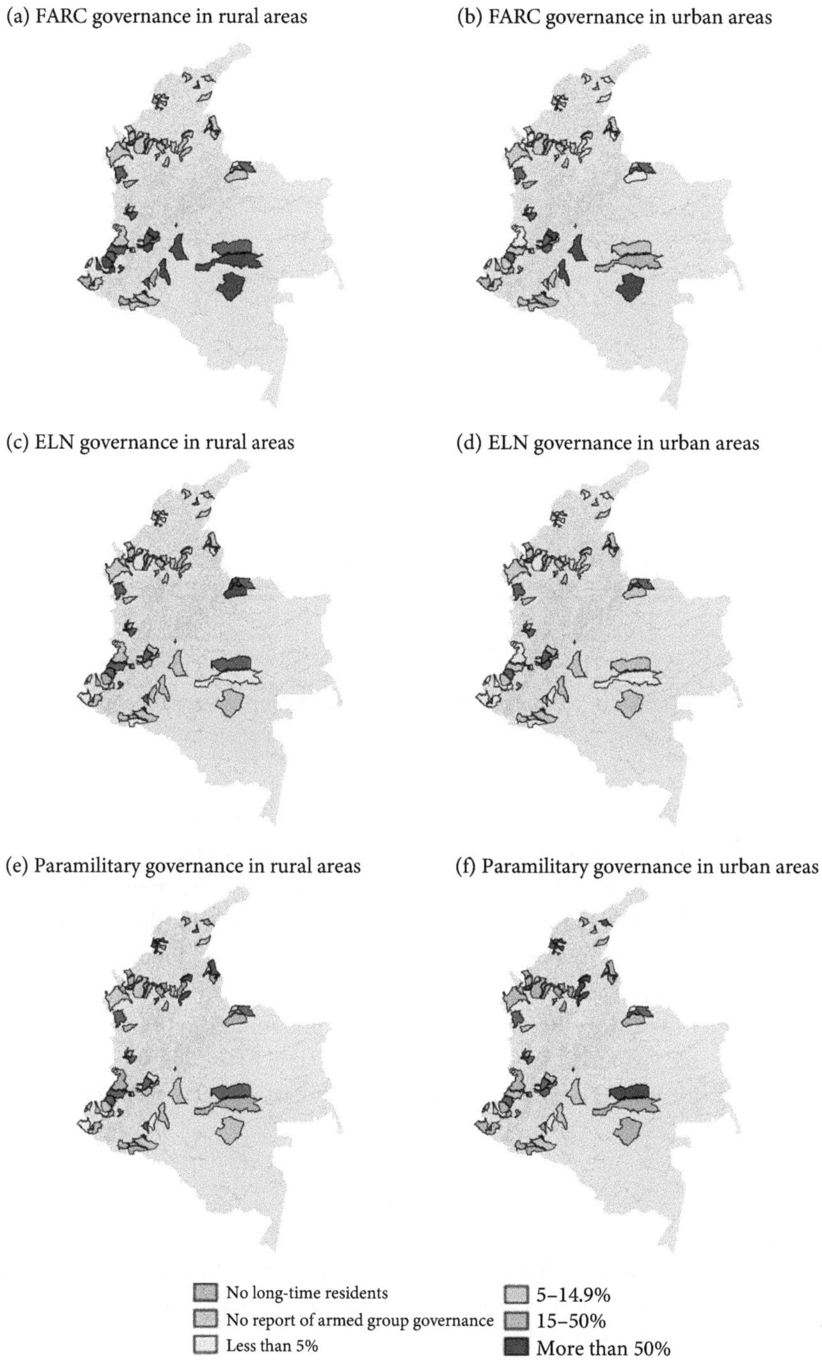

Figure 4.4 Maps of armed group governance using survey data

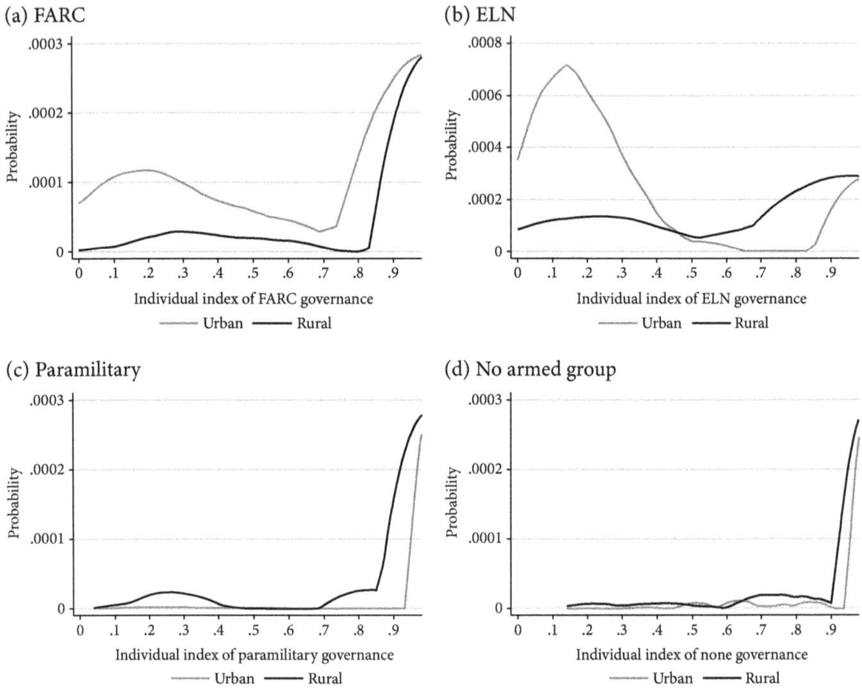

Figure 4.5 Consistency in responses regarding armed group governance using survey data

ELN, or paramilitaries) ruled in their community and divide it by the number of individuals reporting the most-reported group in their community. For example, if we surveyed ten individuals in a rural hamlet and only one mentioned ELN governance while the rest chose paramilitaries, the ELN index for that respondent would be 1/9, and 1 for the other respondents in the hamlet. Figure 4.5 reveals a high degree of consistency in responses about armed group governance across both rural and urban areas for the FARC (panel a), paramilitaries (panel c), and no armed group rule (panel d). Results for the ELN (panel b) are noisier, potentially because ELN rule was more rare and geographically concentrated (see Figure 4.4).

4.5 Limitations

Our study is not without limitations. First, the statistical relationships we uncover may be driven by the endogeneity of armed group choices, both about which communities they opt to rule and what governing strategies they adopt (Gáfaro et al. 2022). If armed groups choose to rule communities that already have preferences aligned with rules they subsequently use to govern, then governance is epiphenomenal. We think this is unlikely, given that armed group decisions about governance strategies are frequently made on the basis of ideological commitments or ultimate goals, rather than local 'matches' between armed group preferences and local attitudes. Decisions about which communities to rule are the product of complex calculations about pre-existing state strength, arms and drug trafficking routes, and more.

Second, if individual survey respondents choose where to live based on past or current armed group governing patterns, the relationships we uncover may not be causal. To counter this possibility, we include a rich set of individual-level control variables, as well as municipality fixed effects to soak up unmeasured heterogeneity across municipalities, but we cannot rule this out definitively. To probe its plausibility, we run robustness checks that exclude both victims of forced displacement and anyone who has moved from their place of birth.

Third, we are unable to measure with precision the length of armed group rule experienced by each respondent, nor how much time has elapsed between the reported armed group rule and our outcomes of interest.

4.6 Results

4.6.1 Weak evidence that insurgent governance increases informal participation

Table 4.3 provides the main results for the effect of armed group governance on our informal engagement binary measure (column 1), as well as the disaggregated outcomes: protests (column 2), membership in NGOs (column 3), membership in other civil society organizations (column 4), and membership in the JACs (column 5). We find evidence that self-reported exposure to rebel governance increases informal participation. We observe a 13.7 per cent increase in informal participation for those exposed to FARC-only governance (0.270) when compared to those not exposed to any armed group governance (0.237), although this is only statistically significant at $p < 0.10$. We see a statistically significant effect for paramilitary-only governance (0.298), which increases informal participation by 25.5 per cent when compared to the baseline of no armed group governance. Finally, those reporting that all groups governed—nearly 14 per cent of the total sample—are 21 per cent less likely (0.188) than the baseline to report informal participation. The disaggregated components of informal participation in columns 2–5 of Table 4.3 show that FARC-only governance increased protest and membership in victims' organizations. In contrast, the large increases in informal participation stemming from paramilitary-only governance are—quite surprisingly—driven chiefly by protest activity, participation in an activist group, and (weakly) participation in victims' organizations.

Table 4.3 Informal participation and armed group governance

	(1) Informal Participation Dummy	(2) Protest	(3) Activist Group	(4) Victims Org.	(5) JAC Member
FARC only governance	0.04 (0.02)	0.03** (0.01)	0.02 (0.02)	0.02* (0.01)	0.02 (0.01)
ELN only governance	0.03 (0.04)	0.05 (0.04)	−0.00 (0.02)	−0.02 (0.01)	0.02 (0.02)
Paramilitary only governance	0.07*** (0.02)	0.04** (0.01)	0.04* (0.02)	0.02* (0.01)	0.00 (0.01)
All governance	−0.05* (0.02)	−0.04* (0.02)	−0.02 (0.02)	−0.01 (0.01)	0.00 (0.01)
FARC and paramilitary governance	−0.00 (0.02)	−0.01 (0.02)	−0.01 (0.02)	−0.00 (0.02)	0.02 (0.01)
FARC and ELN governance	−0.05 (0.05)	0.00 (0.05)	−0.04 (0.03)	0.02 (0.02)	−0.03 (0.02)
ELN and paramilitary governance	−0.08 (0.05)	−0.07+ (0.04)	−0.01 (0.04)	−0.01 (0.03)	−0.01 (0.02)
Constant	0.07+ (0.04)	−0.01 (0.03)	0.01 (0.02)	−0.06*** (0.01)	0.05* (0.02)
N	12,052	12,052	12,052	12,052	12,052

Notes: Effects of armed group governance on an informal participation dummy (column 1) and the components of informal participation (columns 2-5). All specifications include municipal fixed effects, as well as individual respondent controls (gender, age, educational attainment, and dummies for employment). ***$p < 0.01$, **$p < 0.05$, *$p < 0.1$.

4.6.2 Armed group governance tends to increase formal participation

Table 4.4 provides results for the effect of armed group governance on our formal engagement binary measure (column 1), as well as the formal engagement disaggregated outcomes: contacting community leaders (column 2) or politicians (column 3), and voting in the 2016 peace accord plebiscite (column 4) and the 2018 legislative elections (column 5). We observe a 12.5 per cent increase in formal participation for those exposed to FARC-only governance (0.793) when compared to those who experienced no armed group governance (0.705). We see a 9.4 per cent increase in formal participation for those exposed to paramilitary governance

Table 4.4 Formal participation and armed group governance

	(1) Formal Participation Dummy	(2) Contact Community Leader	(3) Contact Politician	(4) Plebiscite Vote	(5) Legislative Vote
FARC only governance	0.09*** (0.02)	0.09*** (0.02)	0.08*** (0.02)	0.08*** (0.02)	0.07** (0.02)
ELN only governance	0.02 (0.05)	0.10*** (0.03)	0.07* (0.03)	0.02 (0.05)	0.01 (0.05)
Paramilitary only governance	0.07*** (0.02)	0.03+ (0.02)	0.09*** (0.01)	0.08* (0.03)	0.07** (0.03)
All governance	0.02 (0.03)	0.03 (0.02)	−0.03 (0.02)	0.02 (0.03)	0.01 (0.03)
FARC and paramilitary governance	0.04+ (0.02)	0.05+ (0.03)	0.00 (0.02)	0.06* (0.03)	0.04+ (0.02)
FARC and ELN governance	0.03 (0.04)	0.00 (0.03)	−0.01 (0.05)	0.10* (0.05)	0.02 (0.05)
ELN and paramilitary governance	−0.02 (0.03)	−0.00 (0.03)	−0.07 (0.04)	−0.04 (0.04)	0.01 (0.03)
Constant	0.35*** (0.04)	0.00 (0.03)	0.01 (0.02)	−0.01 (0.05)	0.19*** (0.05)
Individual-level controls	✓	✓	✓	✓	✓
Municipal FEs	✓	✓	✓	✓	✓
N	12,052	12,052	12,052	12,052	12,052

Notes: Effects of armed group governance on a formal participation dummy (column 1) and the components of formal participation (columns 2–5). All specifications include municipality fixed effects, as well as individual respondent controls (gender, age, educational attainment, and dummies for employment). ***$p < 0.01$, **$p < 0.05$, *$p < 0.1$.

only (0.771) when compared to those without exposure to any armed group governance. We also find evidence that individuals who report having experienced FARC and ELN governance were 4.6 per cent more likely to participate formally. All of these effects are statistically significant at conventional levels. These patterns are broadly consistent when looking at the disaggregated components of formal participation in columns 2–5 of Table 4.4: the effects of FARC-only governance and paramilitary-only governance are not driven by any one outcome.

In Appendix H, we consider possible heterogeneous treatment effects (HTEs) of armed group governance on political participation. We find relatively modest effects: women who experienced paramilitary-only governance appear to participate less via informal channels when compared to men, while women who experienced ELN and paramilitary governance are more likely to participate via informal channels when compared to men. Some of these effects may be due to differential reporting of armed group governance by gender: indeed, we show in Appendix H that women are less likely to report some kinds of armed group governance than men. In Figures 4.A.1, 4.A.2, 4.A.3, 4.A.4, 4.A.5, 4.A.6, 4.A.7, and 4.A.8 we also consider HTEs by education but find no evidence that education modulates the effect of armed group governance on participation.

4.6.3 Measurement issues related to sample composition: IDPs and non-native-born populations

Our results may suffer from a problem of ecological inference, given that a high proportion of our sample are IDPs (55 per cent). To evaluate whether IDPs were affected differently by rebel governance than long-term residents, we take two steps. First, in Table 4.5, we compare results that include IDPs (columns 1 and 3) and those that exclude them (columns 2 and 4). Second, in Table 4.6, we compare models that include all respondents (columns 1 and 3) and only those who were born in the same municipality where the survey was administered (columns 2 and 4). Our results are broadly consistent regardless of whether we exclude IDPs or migrants, although the effects appear to be attenuated when excluding IDPs.

Table 4.5 Internally displaced persons (IDPs)

	(1)	(2)	(3)	(4)
	Formal Participation Dummy	**Formal Participation Dummy, No IDPs**	**Informal Participation Dummy**	**Informal Participation Dummy, No IDPs**
FARC only governance	0.09*** (0.02)	0.07* (0.03)	0.04 (0.02)	0.02 (0.03)
ELN only governance	0.02 (0.05)	0.13+ (0.07)	0.03 (0.04)	−0.03 (0.07)
Paramilitary only governance	0.07*** (0.02)	0.09** (0.03)	0.07*** (0.02)	0.07*** (0.02)
All governance	0.02 (0.03)	−0.00 (0.05)	−0.05* (0.02)	−0.07* (0.03)
FARC and paramilitary governance	0.04+ (0.02)	0.02 (0.03)	−0.01 (0.02)	−0.02 (0.03)

	(1) Formal Participation Dummy	(2) Formal Participation Dummy, No IDPs	(3) Informal Participation Dummy	(4) Informal Participation Dummy, No IDPs
FARC and ELN governance	0.04	−0.07	−0.05	0.05
	(0.04)	(0.08)	(0.05)	(0.10)
ELN and paramilitary governance	-0.02	0.03	-0.08	-0.09
	(0.03)	(0.06)	(0.06)	(0.07)
Education	0.06***	0.07***	0.05***	0.04***
	(0.00)	(0.01)	(0.00)	(0.01)
Constant	0.35***	0.27***	0.07+	0.03
	(0.05)	(0.07)	(0.04)	(0.08)
Individual-level controls	✓	✓	✓	✓
Municipal FEs	✓	✓	✓	✓
N	12,052	4,830	12,052	4,830

Notes: Effects of armed group governance on a formal participation dummy (columns 1 and 2) and an informal participation dummy (columns 3 and 4), with IDPs included (columns 1 and 3) and without (columns 2 and 4). All specifications include municipal fixed effects, as well as individual respondent controls (gender, age, educational attainment, and dummies for employment). ***$p < 0.01$, **$p < 0.05$, *$p < 0.1$.

Table 4.6 Mobile respondents versus native municipal residents

	Formal	Formal, Native only	Informal	Informal, Native Only
FARC only governance	0.09***	0.08**	0.04	0.05+
	(0.02)	(0.03)	(0.02)	(0.03)
ELN only governance	0.02	-0.05	0.03	0.08
	(0.05)	(0.06)	(0.04)	(0.06)
Paramilitary only governance	0.07***	0.07***	0.07***	0.08***
	(0.02)	(0.02)	(0.02)	(0.02)
All governance	0.02	−0.00	−0.05*	−0.06+
	(0.03)	(0.03)	(0.02)	(0.03)
FARC and paramilitary governance	0.04+	-0.01	-0.01	-0.04
	(0.02)	(0.03)	(0.02)	(0.03)

continued

Table 4.6 *continued*

	Formal	Formal, Native only	Informal	Informal, Native Only
FARC and ELN governance	0.04 (0.04)	0.13+ (0.07)	−0.05 (0.05)	−0.03 (0.08)
ELN and paramilitary governance	−0.02 (0.03)	−0.06 (0.04)	−0.08 (0.06)	−0.11+ (0.06)
Education	0.06*** (0.00)	0.06*** (0.01)	0.05*** (0.00)	0.05*** (0.00)
Constant	0.35*** (0.05)	0.40*** (0.04)	0.07+ (0.04)	0.01 (0.05)
Individual-level controls	✓	✓	✓	✓
Municipal FEs	✓	✓	✓	✓
N	12,052	6,845	12,052	6,845

Notes: Effects of armed group governance on a formal participation dummy (columns 1 and 2) and an informal participation dummy (columns 3 and 4), with all respondents included (columns 1 and 3) and with only native-born municipal residents (columns 2 and 4). All specifications include municipal fixed effects, as well as individual respondent controls (gender, age, educational attainment, and dummies for employment). $^{***}p < 0.01$, $^{**}p < 0.05$, $^{*}p < 0.1$.

4.7 Discussion

Two findings do not conform to our expectations: exposure to FARC governance increased formal participation, and exposure to paramilitary governance increased informal participation. In this section, we consider potential explanations for these unexpected results.

4.7.1 Why does insurgent governance produce greater formal participation?

We find unexpectedly that insurgent governance is associated with higher participation. Why? Although we believe our coding of the FARC as 'anti-system' is accurate, the group was much more flexible in its *practices*.[17] How the FARC actually governed demonstrates the porous boundaries between the rebel and state institutions. For example, Peñaranda Currie et al. (2021: 7) describe how the FARC interfaced with the state in a frontier region where the former explicitly mobilized residents and local state institutions to build roads or achieve other

[17] See Wood (2010) and Parkinson (2021) for a discussion of practices.

collective ends, effectively 'legitimating the FARC as representatives who secured benefits from the state for their social bases'. Therefore, even though *rhetorically* the FARC positioned itself as a state adversary, it *used* the state to gain benefits and arguably showed residents in these territories that it was possible to do so, and how.

Along similar lines, Arjona (2016: 147) shows that where the state ruled, rebelocracy was higher, suggesting a symbiotic relationship with state institutions. Mampilly (2011) also demonstrates that armed groups competing with more institutionalized states were more likely to develop or co-opt these institutions. In terms of what we call 'formal participation', Arjona (2016) also finds that in '50% of all cases of rebelocracy, combatants intervened in local, regional, or national elections' (Arjona 2016: 186). Involvement in elections also changed over time: initially, the FARC opposed participating in elections, yet in the mid-1980s, it created a legal political party to contest elections. While the approach backfired—in part due to the extermination of party leaders and members—those living under FARC influence were mobilized to participate in future elections, and the FARC would later influence citizen decisions about whether and for whom to vote, just as paramilitaries did. For example, Arjona (2016, 186–187) shows that rebels told locals for whom they should vote in 22 per cent of cases of rebel rule, and banned voting in 40 per cent of cases. This active rebel intervention may have incentivized formal participation in ways that our theoretical framework elided.

The JACs—those communal institutions that the FARC used to co-administer territory in some places—were not entirely independent of the state, either: '[i]nterestingly, the JAC's success – at the expense of other forms of social organization such as labor unions, or the legally unrecognized "Colonization Committees" – was precisely because "it's a more legal form to make demands on the government," and "because we can solicit public works" (colonos cited in Cubides et al., 1986, 180)' (Peñaranda Currie et al. 2021: 4). This proximity to the state may have encouraged more formal political participation than what a revolutionary armed group might be expected to incentivize.

More anecdotally, the FARC socialized communities it ruled to know the Colombian constitution and specific laws that could be used to make legal claims against the state. The rebel group's willingness to cite Colombian law seems to indicate not that these rules were illegitimate, but that the state had failed to uphold its duty to citizens to properly enforce them.

Finally, the FARC's anti-state posture had one final but crucial pivot: the FARC accepted the legitimacy of the Colombian state in the 2016 peace agreement. While the group's territorial control had waned substantially by this point, such a recognition may have had an influence over those previously ruled by the group, ushering in final 'approval' by rebels and urging citizens to join participatory actions sanctioned and implemented by the state.

4.7.2 Why does paramilitary rule increase informal participation?

Does a similar gap between ideology and practice also exist on the paramilitary side, and might this explain the positive association between paramilitary governance and informal participation? In our theoretical framework, we reasoned that pro-state armed groups with a centralized approach to governance would produce greater participation via formal channels, and that a pro-state armed group that engaged in shared approaches to governance would increase both formal and informal political participation.

One difference between paramilitaries and the FARC is how decentralized the paramilitary alliance was: the AUC was an umbrella organization that unified pre-existing paramilitary blocs. As a result, the group likely featured more heterogeneity in ideology *and* governance practices across commanders, and therefore across their subordinates enforcing armed group rule. As Gutiérrez Sanín (2015) recounts, El Alemán, the former paramilitary commander of the Bloque Élmer Cárdenas of the AUC in Urabá, 'created a series of NGOs' that included 'leaders of community action boards', among other local community leaders. In other words, some commanders adopted more shared governance arrangements, which may have produced more informal political participation by citizens experiencing this kind of rule. Given the relative paucity of documentation related to paramilitary governance when compared to insurgent rule, however, this explanation is speculative and could be pursued in future work.

4.8 Conclusion

Armed group governance has diverse effects on local- and national-level politics, many of which likely transcend the conflict period (Huang 2016; Vargas Castillo 2019). Rebel, paramilitary, and criminal governance—depending on whether they challenge or seek to reinforce state authority, and how they do so—may either mobilize or depress ordinary citizens' political behaviour in the post-conflict period. Yet we know little about the impact that different forms of armed group governance have on political participation in post-conflict societies. This is a crucial omission, because most civil wars end in negotiated settlements, which typically include mechanisms for establishing or strengthening democratic competition and buttressing civic life (Matanock 2014).

Existing efforts to explain post-conflict political participation also fail to account for the rich and varied ways that armed groups govern communities they control. Most studies have focused on victimization and its impact on individuals' political participation: increasing citizens' likelihood of voting in elections (Blattman 2009), for example. But communities' interactions with armed groups should not be reduced to having suffered violence. The focus on violence may be an artefact of the comparative ease of measuring victimization, relative to other important concepts that are more difficult to proxy. Likewise, failure to study a broad range of outcomes related to participation threatens to generate misleading findings: are increases in turnout prompted by armed group behaviour also accompanied by greater engagement in communal affairs? Under what conditions do armed group governance decisions 'crowd out' allegiance to state authorities, by exposing individuals to previously unimagined governance possibilities? Under what conditions do they have the opposite effects, convincing civilians that the state is and should be the ultimate guarantor of rights?

The advantage of our simple theoretical approach is its applicability to a broad range of contexts, and its flexibility in accommodating shifts in armed groups' positions. Yet our hypotheses were not unambiguously supported by our empirical results. Instead, experience with armed group governance on average leads to more participation through both informal and formal channels. (The exception is reported rule by multiple armed groups, which depressed participation.) We account for these unexpected results primarily by re-evaluating our assessment of the armed groups' characteristics that we study here. Avenues for further research could include alternative ways of categorizing armed groups' governance approaches as well.

Another area for further work relates to the persistence or attenuation of effects over time, and defining the precise mechanisms through which persistence or attenuation occurs. A large literature has catalogued how beliefs, attitudes, and opinions constituted during transformative events are passed down over time (e.g., Balcells 2012; Charnysh and Peisakhin 2021; Lupu and Peisakhin 2017; Osorio et al. 2019). Acharya et al. (2018), for example, show how parent-to-child transmission of racial attitudes in the American South translated into durable political attitudes generations later, in the contemporary period. This typically requires either reliable 'transmission belts' that use existing organizational vehicles—such as the Catholic Church or schools—to instantiate, replicate, and transmit messages from one generation to the next, or the establishment of convincing incentives for one group to continue believing certain things, or continue engaging in certain behaviours. The latter, for example, would include significant symbolic or material benefits stemming from holding particular beliefs: if, in the conflict period, an armed group consistently rewarded particular attitudes that produced a set of behaviours, in the post-conflict period, citizens would likely hold those same attitudes and continue to undertake those same behaviours. Understanding the impact of armed group rule on post-conflict participation is both theoretically interesting and urgent for policy-makers: avoiding democratic backsliding and conflict relapse depends upon the creation of a healthy, participatory democracy capable of adjudicating differences and peacefully resolving disputes. Understanding the legacies of armed group rule should help identify places most at risk for democratic malaise, and assist policy-makers in reinvigorating participation in the aftermath of war.

4.9 Appendix

A. Heterogeneous treatment effects

In this section, we consider possible HTEs of armed group governance on political participation. We focus on gender and education.

A.1 Gender

Armed group governance may destabilize existing gender norms, with consequences for political behaviour. For example, Lazarev (2019) shows that in war-affected areas in Chechnya, gender hierarchies were more profoundly upended, leading women in those areas to seek redress from institutions that were (at least officially) more gender-equal. We might expect women who experienced FARC and ELN governance to be exposed to more norms of gender equality in terms of labour and political participation. As a result, women who experienced rebel governance may be more likely than their counterparts to report all kinds of participation.

We begin by asking whether women and men in our sample experienced self-reported armed group governance in similar proportions. To do so, we use simple *t*-tests; we find that women are less likely to report each kind of armed group governance (except ELN and paramilitary joint governance), differences that are statistically significant at conventional levels. These systematic gender-based differences in reporting could be due to multiple causes. Women may be less likely to directly experience armed group governance if armed groups prioritize

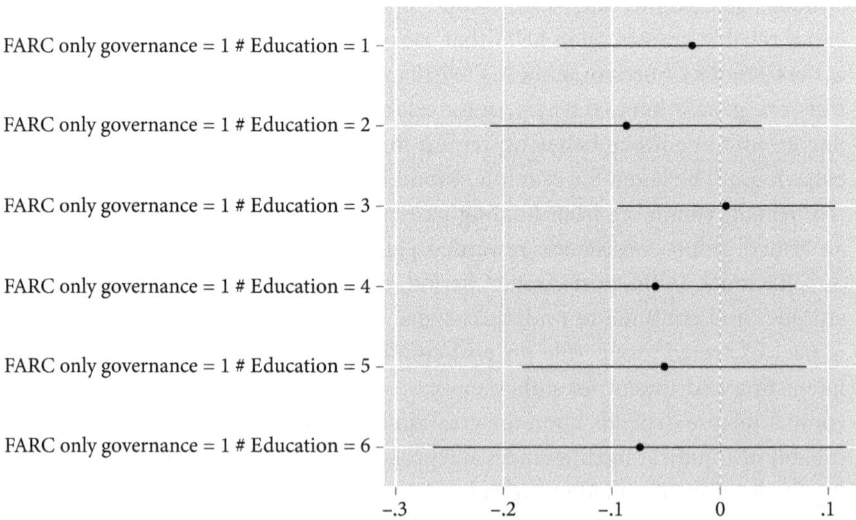

Figure 4.A.1 Effects of FARC governance and education on formal participation

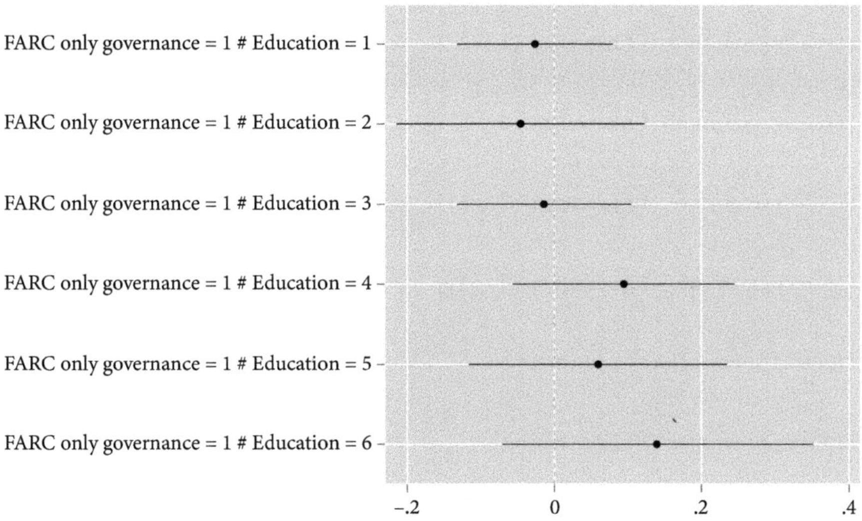

Figure 4.A.2 Effects of FARC governance and education on informal participation

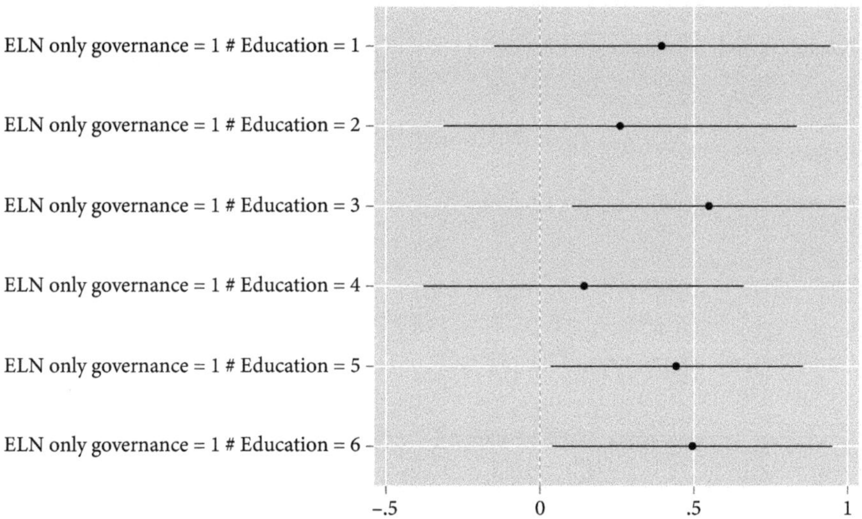

Figure 4.A.3 Effects of ELN governance and education on formal participation

male-dominated spaces for decision-making. Or women may be less likely to feel comfortable reporting armed group governance if they have more reasons to fear retribution from armed groups. This is an important avenue for future research.

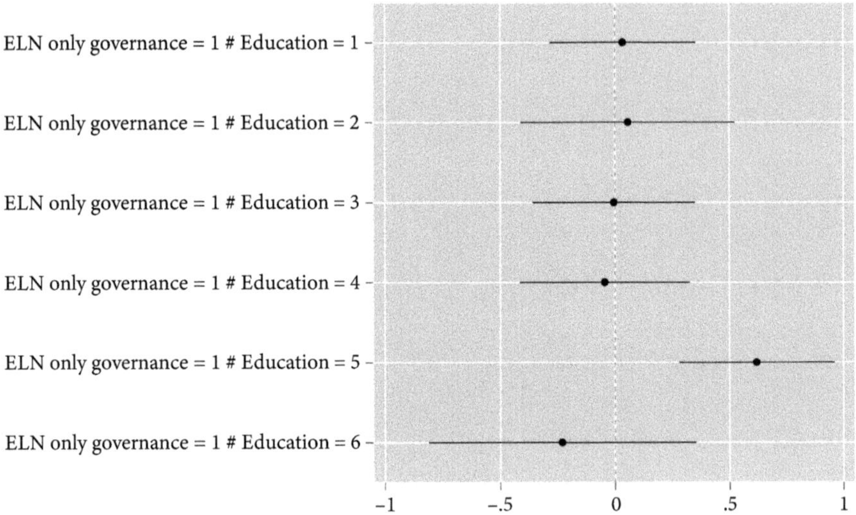

Figure 4.A.4 Effects of ELN governance and education on informal participation

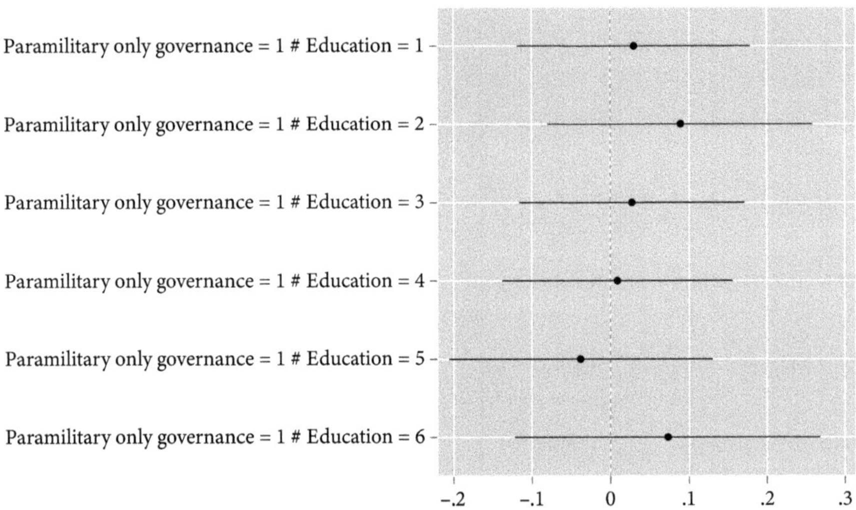

Figure 4.A.5 Effects of paramilitary governance and education on formal participation

Next, in Table 4.A.1 we ask whether the effects of armed group governance are stronger for men or women. We find relatively modest effects: women who experienced FARC-only governance appear to participate more via formal channels when compared to men. Women who reported FARC and ELN governance

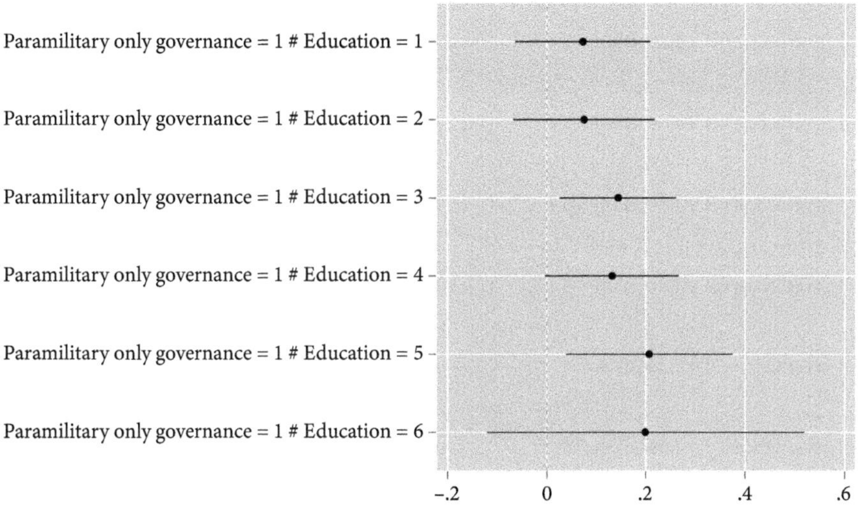

Figure 4.A.6 Effects of paramilitary governance and education on informal participation

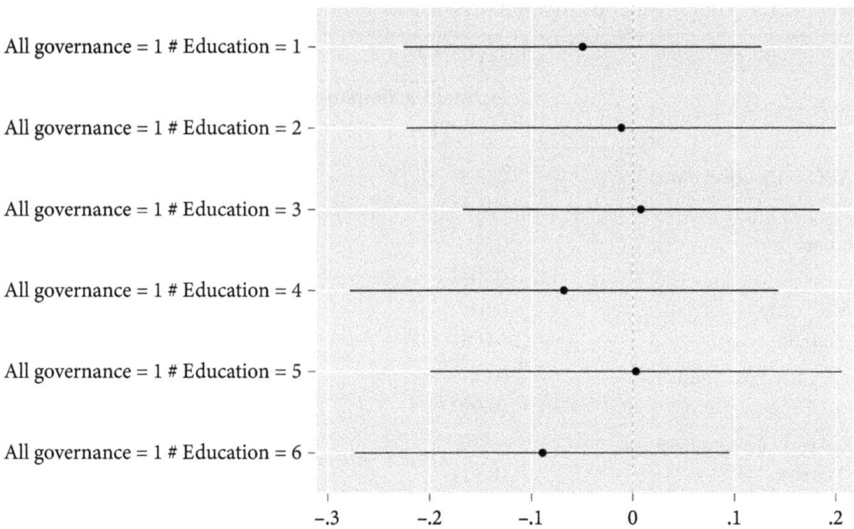

Figure 4.A.7 Effects of all group governance and education on formal participation

are more likely to participate via formal channels when compared to men. The other interaction terms are not statistically significant, indicating no differential effects of gender on participation depending upon armed group governance.

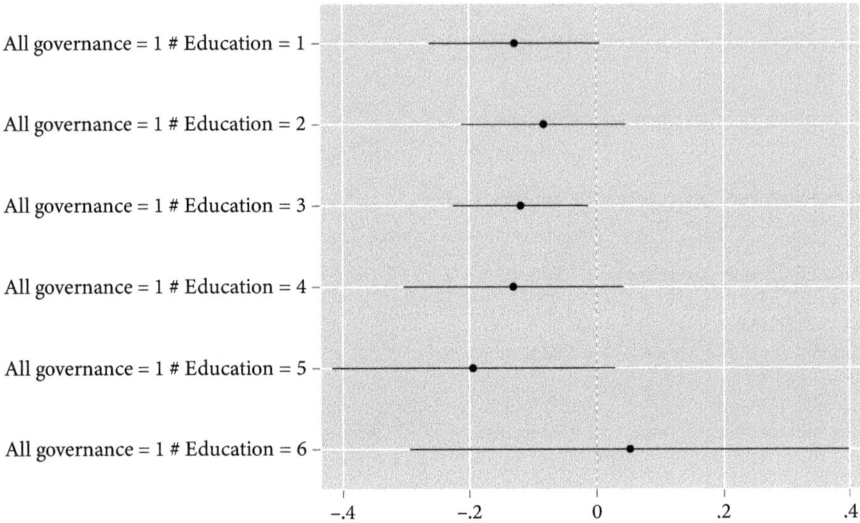

Figure 4.A.8 Effects of all group governance and education on informal participation

Table 4.A.1 Heterogeneous treatment effects by gender

	(1) Formal Participation Dummy	(2) Informal Participation Dummy
FARC only governance	0.07*	0.05
	(0.03)	(0.03)
Female	0.00	–0.04***
	(0.02)	(0.01)
FARC only governance × Female	0.03	–0.02
	(0.04)	(0.04)
ELN only governance	0.04	0.07
	(0.09)	(0.06)
ELN only governance × Female	–0.03	–0.07
	(0.11)	(0.06)
Paramilitary only governance	0.06+	0.10***
	(0.03)	(0.03)
Paramilitary only governance × Female	0.02	–0.07*
	(0.04)	(0.03)
All governance	0.01	–0.05
	(0.04)	(0.03)

	(1) Formal Participation Dummy	(2) Informal Participation Dummy
All governance	0.01 (0.04)	−0.05 (0.03)
All governance × Female	0.02 (0.04)	−0.00 (0.04)
FARC and paramilitary governance	0.05+ (0.03)	−0.02 (0.04)
FARC and paramilitary governance × Female	−0.03 (0.04)	0.02 (0.06)
FARC and ELN governance	0.02 (0.08)	−0.09 (0.06)
FARC and ELN governance × Female	0.03 (0.12)	0.09 (0.06)
ELN and paramilitary governance	0.01 (0.04)	−0.16* (0.06)
ELN and paramilitary governance × Female	−0.05 (0.08)	0.16* (0.07)
Constant	0.36*** (0.05)	0.06 (0.04)
N	12,052	12,052
Individual-level controls	✓	✓
Municipal FEs	✓	✓

Note: Heterogeneous treatment effects of armed group governance on a formal participation dummy (column 1) and an informal participation dummy (column 2). All specifications include municipal fixed effects, as well as individual respondent controls (gender, age, educational attainment, and dummies for employment). ***p < 0.01, **p < 0.05, *p < 0.1.

References

Abadie, A., S. Athey, G.W. Imbens, and J. Wooldridge (2017). 'When Should You Adjust Standard Errors for Clustering?'. Working Paper 24003. Cambridge, MA: National Bureau of Economic Research. https://doi.org/10.3386/w24003

Acharya, A., M. Blackwell, and M. Sen (2018). *Deep Roots*. Princeton, NJ: Princeton University Press. https://doi.org/10.23943/9781400889976

Albertus, M., and O. Kaplan (2013). 'Land Reform as a Counterinsurgency Policy: Evidence from Colombia'. *Journal of Conflict Resolution*, 57(2): 198–231. https://doi.org/10.1177/0022002712446130

Arjona, A. (2015). 'Civilian Resistance to Rebel Governance'. In A. Arjona, N. Kasfir, and Z. Mampilly (eds), *Rebel Governance in Civil War*. Cambridge: Cambridge University Press. https://doi.org/10.1017/CBO9781316182468

Arjona, A. (2016). *Rebelocracy: Social Order in the Colombian Civil War*. Cambridge: Cambridge University Press. https://doi.org/10.1017/9781316421925

Arjona, A., N. Kasfir, and Z. Mampilly (2015). 'Introduction'. In A. Arjona, N. Kasfir, and Z. Mampilly (eds), *Rebel Governance in Civil War*. Cambridge: Cambridge University Press. https://doi.org/10.1017/CBO9781316182468

Balcells, L. (2012). 'The Consequences of Victimization on Political Identities: Evidence from Spain'. *Politics & Society*, 40(3): 311–347. https://doi.org/10.1177/0032329211424721

Berens, S., and M. Dallendörfer (2019). 'Apathy or Anger? How Crime Experience Affects Individual Vote Intention in Latin America and the Caribbean'. *Political Studies*, 67(4),1010–1033. https://doi.org/10.1177/0032321718819106

Blair, R., M. Moscoso, A. Vargas, and M. Weintraub (2022). 'Preventing Rebel Resurgence After Civil War: A Field Experiment in Security and Justice Provision in Rural Colombia'. *American Political Science Review*, 116(4): 1258–1277. https://doi.org/10.1017/S0003055422000284

Blattman, C. (2009). 'From Violence to Voting: War and Political Participation in Uganda'. *American Political Science Review*, 103(2): 231–247. https://doi.org/10.1017/S0003055409090212

Blattman, C., G. Duncan, B. Lessing, and S. Tobón, S. (2021). 'Gang Rule: Understanding and Countering Criminal Governance'. Working Paper 28458. Cambridge, MA: National Bureau of Economic Research. https://doi.org/10.3386/w28458

Bratton, M. (1999). 'Political Participation in a New Democracy: Institutional Considerations from Zambia'. *Comparative Political Studies*, 32(5): 549–588. https://doi.org/10.1177/0010414099032005002

Ch, R., J.N. Shapiro, A. Steele, and J.F. Vargas (2018). 'Endogenous Taxation in Ongoing Internal Conflict: The Case of Colombia'. *American Political Science Review*, 112(4): 996–1015. https://doi.org/10.1017/S0003055418000333

Charnysh, V., and L. Peisakhin (2021). 'The Role of Communities in the Transmission of Political Values: Evidence from Forced Population Transfers'. *British Journal of Political Science*, 52(1): 238–258. https://doi.org/10.1017/S0007123420000447

Costalli, S., and A. Ruggeri (2015). 'Forging Political Entrepreneurs: Civil War Effects on Post-Conflict Politics in Italy'. *Political Geography*, 44: 40–49. https://doi.org/10.1016/j.polgeo.2014.08.008

Cunningham, K.G., and C.E. Loyle (2020). 'Introduction to the Special Feature on Dynamic Processes of Rebel Governance'. *Journal of Conflict Resolution*, 65(1), 3–14. https://doi.org/10.1177/0022002720935153

Eaton, K. (2006). 'The Downside of Decentralization: Armed Clientelism in Colombia'. *Security Studies*, 15(4): 533–562. https://doi.org/10.1080/09636410601188463

Eubank, N., G. Grossman, M. Platas, and J. Rodden (2019). 'Viral Voting: Social Networks and Political Participation'. *Quarterly Journal of Political Science*, 16(3): 265–284. https://doi.org/10.1561/100.00019092

Gandhi, J., and E. Lust-Okar (2009). 'Elections under Authoritarianism'. *Annual Review of Political Science*, 12: 403–422. https://doi.org/10.1146/annurev.polisci.11.060106.095434

Grandi, F. (2013). 'Why Do the Victors Kill the Vanquished? Explaining Political Violence in Post-World War II Italy'. *Journal of Peace Research*, 50(5): 577–593. https://doi.org/10.1177/0022343313480202

Gutiérrez Sanín, F. (2015). 'Conexiones Coactivas: Paramilitares Y Alcaldes En Colombia'. *Análisis Político*, 28(85): 131–157. https://doi.org/10.15446/anpol.v28n85.56251

Gáfaro, M., A.M. Ibánez, and P. Justino (2022). 'Community Organization and Armed Group Behaviour: Evidence from Colombia'. WIDER Working Paper 2022/2. Helsinki: UNU-WIDER. https://doi.org/10.35188/UNU-WIDER/2022/133-4

Huang, R. (2016). *The Wartime Origins of Democratization: Civil War, Rebel Governance, and Political Regimes*. Cambridge: Cambridge University Press. https://doi.org/10.1017/CBO9781316711323

Kaplan, O. (2017). *Resisting War: How Communities Protect Themselves*. Cambridge: Cambridge University Press. https://doi.org/10.1017/9781316671887

Karl, R.A. (2017). *Forgotten Peace: Reform, Violence, and the Making of Contemporary Colombia*. Berkeley, CA: University of California Press.

Kasfir, N. (2005). 'Guerrillas and Civilian Participation: The National Resistance Army in Uganda, 1981–86'. *Journal of Modern African Studies*, 43(2): 271–296. https://doi.org/10.1017/S0022278X05000832

Kasfir, N., G. Frerks, and N. Terpstra (2017). 'Introduction: Armed Groups and Multi-Layered Governance'. *Civil Wars*, 19(3): 257–278. https://doi.org/10.1080/13698249.2017.1419611

Kuran, T. (1991). 'Now Out of Never: The Element of Surprise in the East European Revolution of 1989'. *World Politics: A Quarterly Journal of International Relations*, 44(1): 7–48. https://doi.org/10.2307/2010422

Larratt-Smith, C. (2020). 'Navigating Formal and Informal Processes: Civic Organizations, Armed Nonstate Actors, and Nested Governance in Colombia'. *Latin American Politics and Society*, 62(2): 75–98. https://doi.org/10.1017/lap.2019.61

Lazarev, E. (2019). 'Laws in Conflict: Legacies of War, Gender, and Legal Pluralism in Chechnya'. *World Politics*, 71(4): 667–709. https://doi.org/10.1017/S0043887119000133

Ley, S. (2018). 'To Vote or Not to Vote: How Criminal Violence Shapes Electoral Participation'. *Journal of Conflict Resolution*, 62(9): 1963–1990. https://doi.org/10.1177/0022002717708600

Loyle, C.E. (2021). 'Rebel Justice during Armed Conflict'. *Journal of Conflict Resolution*, 65(1): 108–134. https://doi.org/10.1177/0022002720939299

Lupu, N., and L. Peisakhin (2017). 'The Legacy of Political Violence across Generations'. *American Journal of Political Science*, 61(4): 836–851. https://doi.org/10.1111/ajps.12327

Mampilly, Z.C. (2011). *Rebel Rulers: Insurgent Governance and Civilian Life during War*. Ithaca, NY: Cornell University Press.

Mampilly, Z., and M.A. Stewart (2020). 'A Typology of Rebel Political Institutional Arrangements'. *Journal of Conflict Resolution*, 65(1): 15–45. https://doi.org/10.1177/0022002720935642

Matanock, A. (2014). 'Militant Group Electoral Participation Dataset'. Presented at the Peace Science Society Annual Meeting, Philadelphia.

North, D., and B.R. Weingast (1989). 'Constitutions and Commitment: The Evolution of Institutions Governing Public Choice in Seventeenth-Century England'. *Journal of Economic History*, 49: 803–832. https://doi.org/10.1017/S0022050700009451

Osorio, J., L.I. Schubiger, and M. Weintraub (2019). 'Legacies of Resistance: Mobilization Against Organized Crime in Mexico'. *Comparative Political Studies*, 54(9): 1565–1596. https://doi.org/10.1177/0010414021989761

Parkinson, S.E. (2021). 'Practical Ideology in Militant Organizations'. *World Politics*, 73(1): 52–81. https://doi.org/10.1017/S0043887120000180

Peñaranda Currie, I., S. Otero-Bahamon, and S. Uribe (2021). 'What Is the State Made Of? Coca, Roads, and the Materiality of State Formation in the Frontier'. *World Development*, 141: 105395. https://doi.org/10.1016/j.worlddev.2021.105395

Prem, M., A.F. Rivera, D.A. Romero, and J.F. Vargas (2018). 'Killing Social Leaders for Territorial Control: The Unintended Consequences of Peace'. Working Paper 016385. Bogotá: Universidad del Rosario.

Pécaut, D. (1989). *Crónica de Dos Décadas de Política Colombiana 1968–1988*. Bogotá: Siglo Veintiuno.

Pérez-Cardona, S., R. Ch, J.F. Vargas, and M. Weintraub (2022). 'Let the Rebels Rule? Rebel Governance and Economic Development in Colombia'. *Working Paper 3*. Bogotá: Universidad de los Andes.

Revkin, M.R. (2019). 'What Explains Taxation by Resource-Rich Rebels? Evidence from the Islamic State in Syria'. *Journal of Politics*, 82(2): 757–764. https://doi.org/10.1086/706597

Revkin, M.R. (2021). 'Competitive Governance and Displacement Decisions under Rebel Rule: Evidence from the Islamic State in Iraq'. *Journal of Conflict Resolution*, 65(1): 46–80. https://doi.org/10.1177/0022002720951864

Revkin, M.R., and A.I. Ahram (2020). 'Perspectives on the Rebel Social Contract: Exit, Voice, and Loyalty in the Islamic State in Iraq and Syria'. *World Development*, 132: 104981. https://doi.org/10.1016/j.worlddev.2020.104981

Robinson, J.A. (2013). 'Colombia: Another 100 Years of Solitude'. *Current History*, 112(751): 43–48. https://doi.org/10.1525/curh.2013.112.751.43

Rolfe, M. (2012). *Voter Turnout: A Social Theory of Political Participation*. Cambridge: Cambridge University Press. https://doi.org/10.1017/CBO9781139058513

Ronderos, M.T. (2014). *Guerras Recicladas: Una Historia Periodística del Paramilitarismo en Colombia*. Bogotá: Aguilar.

Siegel, D.A. (2009). 'Social Networks and Collective Action'. *American Journal of Political Science*, 53(1): 122–138. https://doi.org/10.1111/j.1540-5907.2008.00361.x

Steele, A. (2017). *Democracy and Displacement in Colombia's Civil War*. Ithaca, NY: Cornell University Press. https://doi.org/10.7591/cornell/9781501713736.001.0001

Stewart, M.A. (2018). 'Civil War as State-Making: Strategic Governance in Civil War'. *International Organization*, 72(1): 205–226. https://doi.org/10.1017/S0020818317000418

Stewart, M.A. (2020). 'Rebel Governance: Military Boon or Military Bust?'. *Conflict Management and Peace Science*, 37(1): 16–38. https://doi.org/10.1177/0738894219881422

Tate, W. (2007). *Counting the Dead: The Culture and Politics of Human Rights Activism in Colombia*. Berkeley, CA: University of California Press.

van Baalen, S. (2020). 'Reconceptualising Rebel Rule: The Responsiveness of Rebel Governance in Man'. Program on Governance and Local Development Working Paper 34. Rochester, NY: Social Science Research Network. https://doi.org/10.2139/ssrn.3732277

van Baalen, S. (2021). 'Local Elites, Civil Resistance, and the Responsiveness of Rebel Governance in Côte d'Ivoire'. *Journal of Peace Research*, 58(5): 930–944. https://doi.org/10.1177/0022343320965675

Vargas Castillo, A. (2019). 'Legacies of Civil War: Wartime Rule and Communal Authority in Rural Colombia'. PhD dissertation. New Haven, CT: Yale University.

Weintraub, M., A. Steele, H. Mokleiv Nygård, M. Dahl, and H. Malmin BinningsbØ (2021). 'Introducing the Mapping Attitudes, Perceptions and Support (MAPS) Dataset on the Colombian Peace Process'. Working Paper. Bogotá: Universidad de los Andes.

Wood, E.J. (2008). 'The Social Processes of Civil War: The Wartime Transformation of Social Networks'. *Annual Review of Political Science*, 11: 539–561. https://doi.org/10.1146/annurev.polisci.8.082103.104832

Wood, E.J. (2010). 'Sexual Violence during War: Variation and Accountability'. In A. Smeulers and E. Van Sliedregt (eds), *Collective Crimes and International Criminal Justice: An Interdisciplinary Approach*. Antwerp: Intersentia.

5

'Ten pound touts'

Post-conflict trust and the legacy of counterinsurgency in Northern Ireland

Kit Rickard and Kristin M. Bakke

5.1 Introduction

What are the long-term impacts of violent conflict on local community trust? In particular, how do the dynamics of counterinsurgency tactics aimed at extracting information shape trust within local communities? We explore these questions in the context of Northern Ireland, a post-conflict society that, by many accounts, is a success story, as the armed conflict has not recurred. The 30-year long conflict known as 'the Troubles' erupted in 1968 and officially came to an end with the Good Friday Agreement in 1998. The armed conflict—which originated between, on one side, Republican paramilitary groups wanting to be part of the Republic of Ireland rather than the United Kingdom (politically, the Nationalist side) and, on the other side, Loyalist paramilitary groups aiming to maintain the status quo (politically, the Unionist side) and, from 1969, involved the British security forces—has not recurred, though low-level violence still persists in various forms. Moreover, as we show in this chapter, the conflict's legacies still characterize everyday life in Northern Ireland in ways that are likely to shape the very fabric of society: people's ability to trust others in their local community.

In any armed conflict, local information is key for both the state's forces and the non-state actors opposing it—the 'rebels' or 'insurgents'. Rebels rely on civilian support for resources, information, and cover, which they can foster both through coercion and fostering consent. As such, the state's counterinsurgency strategy may target rebel strongholds—areas where the rebels have significant local support—to extract information that can be used to identify and eliminate insurgents. In turn, in their strongholds, rebels may enforce strong anti-informing rules. Over time, these rules can become internalized norms and have sticky legacies. We propose that anti-informing norms have legacies specifically on community trust, as people remain on guard against others—even against their neighbours. Areas targeted by counterinsurgency tactics aimed at extracting information from the local population may, therefore, be more likely to have low levels of local

Kit Rickard and Kristin M. Bakke, *'Ten pound touts'*. In: *Institutional Legacies of Violent Conflict*. Edited by: Patricia Justino, Oxford University Press. © United Nations University World Institute for Development Economics Research (UNU-WIDER) (2026). DOI: 10.1093/9780197904077.003.0005

community trust, even long after a conflict nominally ends. A probing case study of the conflict in Northern Ireland shows how the British counterinsurgency mainly targeted Republican strongholds—predominantly Catholic neighbourhoods where paramilitary groups were embedded and maintained social control. We trace the emergence of strong anti-informing norms in these areas. In contrast to Loyalist strongholds in predominantly Protestant areas, in Republican strongholds, decades of infiltration and the experience of never knowing who was an informer have undermined internal cohesion. The endurance of anti-informing norms has had a detrimental legacy on local community trust, even long after the end of the war. Drawing on secondary sources, we show that the anti-informing norm remains strongly embedded in Catholic strongholds. In addition, an original survey fielded in 2022 reveals significant differences in local trust and views around informing between the two communities involved in the conflict.

Our findings have important implications for research on the legacies of civil war and rebel governance. First, we demonstrate that exposure to violence is just one of many important impacts that conflict can have on post-conflict society. The *norms* engendered by wars also have long-term legacies (Wood 2008). Second, while research on rebels' wartime governance is growing (for an overview, see Loyle et al. 2023), we draw attention to the state's strategies and tactics to counter these efforts and undermine insurgent support. Both rebel governance and the state's efforts to undermine it are likely to leave important post-conflict legacies.

5.2 Literature review: Armed conflict and post-war trust

Much research on conflict resolution and post-conflict societies has emphasized that among the key challenges facing societies that have experienced armed conflict are low levels of political trust (e.g. Lake 2010; De Juan and Pierskalla 2016; Bakke et al. 2014; Wong 2016; Fisk and Cherney 2017) and high distrust of the other 'side' in the struggle (e.g. Trew 1986; Bar-Tal 2000; Hewstone et al. 2006; Noor et al. 2008). Indeed, research on post-war institution building is often built on the (sometimes implicit) assumption that a central challenge to overcome is how to build institutions that can minimize distrust of both an unchecked state and the other side (cf. Lake and Rothchild 1996; Weingast 1998), for example by creating peace agreements that entail credible commitments (e.g. Walter 2002) or developing power sharing institutions (e.g. Roeder and Rothchild 2005). Similarly, conflict resolution efforts aimed at fostering contact between ordinary people from the (formerly) warring communities are built on the assumption that such contact can help build inter-group trust and break down stereotypes and strict us-versus-them boundaries (e.g. Maoz 2011). In Northern Ireland, central to the Good Friday Agreement was power sharing between Nationalist and Unionist political parties, and is today central to civic programs aimed at bringing together Catholic and Protestant children and young people.

Expectations from the literature when it comes to *intra*-group trust and local community cohesion are more mixed. On the one hand, research has shown that traumatic experiences such as wartime violence cause distress (e.g. Ringdal et al. 2007) and can have detrimental effects on people's trust in their fellow human beings (e.g. De Luca and Verporten 2015b; Rohner et al. 2013). To the degree that a war is characterized not only by fighting between the 'sides' but also within each side—as many conflicts are (e.g. Bakke et al. 2012)—it may have negative consequences for local community trust in the post-war period (Cassar et al. 2013). On the other hand, a growing body of work anchored in psychological research on 'pro-social growth' and 'altruism born from suffering' is challenging the conventional wisdom and suggesting that experiences of violence can inadvertently contribute to bonding and community cohesion (e.g. Blattman 2009; Bauer et al. 2016). Experiment-based studies, for example, have shown that people living in communities with the greatest exposure to violence were the most likely to invest in trust-based transactions (Gilligan et al. 2013; Gilligan et al. 2014). That is, research suggests that experiences of violence can have both negative and positive implications for community trust and cohesion.

The existing literature on the implications of armed conflict for trust has primarily been based on arguments about what the *violence* in an armed conflict does. A growing body of work has brought attention to how armed groups, to varying degrees, also engage in wartime *governance*, such as 'policing' and courts, educating children, or running hospitals (e.g. Sivakumaran 2009; Mampilly 2011; Arjona 2016; Duyvesteyn 2017; Podder 2017; Loyle et al. 2023), which may boost local-level legitimacy and, as such, have implications for local-level trust (Loyle and Onder 2023). Rebels may provide governance and create institutions to demonstrate their political goals and signal their ability to rule, both to their constituents (Stewart 2021; Revkin 2021) and foreign states and organizations (Coggins 2016; Huang 2016; Stewart 2018; McWeeney et al. 2023). While 'rebel rule' may boost the local legitimacy of the rebels, an unintended consequence is that strongholds become the targets of the state's counterinsurgency campaign. We explore how the state's counterinsurgency tactics may have enduring legacies on local trust.

5.3 Argument

5.3.1 Rebel strongholds and social control

Rebels are often militarily weaker than the state, and, thus, engage in guerrilla warfare, the distinguishing features of which are an avoidance of battles—which rebels may lose—and a heavy reliance on local knowledge and support to compensate for inferior numbers and weaponry (Wickham-Crowley 1992, 3). Armed groups seek to establish territorial control to mount a credible military challenge against an often much stronger state. While civilians within the territory are an important source of material support in the sense that they provide shelter, information, and recruits, they also pose significant military challenges. Key among these challenges is civilian defection, when discontented civilians 'collaborate with the state, providing crucial information and engaging in actions of sabotage against insurgent rule' (Mampilly 2011, 54; see also Arjona 2017). Faced with this challenge, insurgents can rely on violence to quell discontent and remove the 'disloyal' from the territory (Steele 2017), but sustained control by coercion is a costly strategy and 'rebels cannot fight wars effectively while holding a gun to the head of every civilian' (Arjona et al. 2016, 3; cf. Ahmad 1971, 8). It is less costly to control civilians with some level of consent. Indeed, as shown by a growing body of literature on rebel governance, rebels often pursue a variety of legitimation strategies (e.g. McColl 1969; Terpstra and Frerks 2017; McWeeney et al. 2023), including public goods provision to foster legitimacy and induce civilian collaboration. Equally, wartime order creates clear rules of conduct that facilitate the monitoring and punishment of civilian defection (Arjona 2016).

The most basic public good required by humans is personal security. To ensure security from internal and external threats, armed groups often seek to establish a monopoly of violence not dissimilar to states (cf. Weber 1958 (1919)). On the ground, however, armed groups rarely achieve a monopoly of violence. Instead, they often operate in areas of contested authority, with areas of military control overlapping with the state. Here, securing the loyalty of civilians is particularly important as civilian collaboration with the state risks significantly undermining local insurgent control and, ultimately, group survival. Indeed, Ahmad (1971, 10) notes that '(o)ne renegade can destroy a whole network in the area by informing the enemy who invariably tortures him to get the names of others'.

5.3.2 How does the state undermine rebel control?

Counterinsurgency scholars recognize that support to rebels is often crucial in determining the success of an insurgency. The literature identifies two main strategies available to states fighting insurgencies (Kilcullen 2010). The first is an 'enemy-centric' strategy that aims to destroy the network of rebels in the belief that by doing so, the problem disappears (e.g. Callwell 1896). The second and now more common approach is a 'population-centric' strategy and is closely linked to 'classical insurgency' (e.g. Galula 1964; Thompson 1966), an approach that was applied by Frank Kitson (1971) in Northern Ireland where he was a commander. Because insurgents require control over and support from the population to compel the government into concessions or military defeat, the state attempts to limit civilian support for insurgents. They do so by first gaining military control of an area (the 'clear and hold' strategy). Insurgents may still be present but not able to openly operate. The state then begins rolling out public goods to win over support from civilians (Stubbs 2011). As civilian support for the state increases, they begin to provide information on the identities and locations of insurgents, who are subsequently targeted and forced out of the community.

A successful counterinsurgency, thus, relies on both military and political responses. It is about winning the 'hearts and minds' of the civilian population. Operations to usurp local support for insurgents tend to include a mix of military and political strategy, but the main enemy-centric counterinsurgency tactic is to gather information that can be used to locate, identify, and ultimately eliminate insurgents. Information, which is often harboured by civilians, is, thus, a fundamental resource in irregular war (Kitson 1971). It is the contest over information that underpins Kalyvas's (2006) theory of selective violence as a joint process—'the political actors' attempts to deter individual defection, and individuals' decision to provide information to political actors' (ibid., 173; see also Balcells 2017). As noted by Podder (2017), information is the key resource held by the population and, in the eyes of the state fighting an insurgency, it needs to be controlled.

5.3.3 Anti-informing norms and local trust

But the rebels are not passive in this information struggle. The practice of 'necklacing' in South Africa, the 'Sourire Kabyle' in Algeria, and executions by the 'Nutting Squad' in Northern Ireland are all examples of brutal rebel tactics aimed at eliminating and dissuading informers and collaborators. While rules against informing may be initially brutally enforced, the use of coercion decreases as civilian compliance becomes quasi-voluntary (Podder 2017). Wartime institutions in rebel strongholds help ensure predictable behaviour through clear rules that are followed by civilians and enforced by insurgents. Over time, not only do the rules become well-known to civilians in these areas, but civilians also come to internalize shared concepts of how things should be done through a socialization mechanism (e.g. Bateson 2017; Checkel 2017). Therefore, unless the state manages to break the link between insurgents and the community, civilians in strongholds and contested areas become socialized into accepting these rules. Over time, they become internalized norms—socially defined and enforced standards of behaviour (Deaux and Wrightsman 1988). These norms are transmitted via informal socialization mechanisms among family and community members.

We expect that norms against informing lead to diminished levels of local community trust because awareness of informing is high among the civilian population and the devastating effects for the insurgency, especially over a long conflict, are well known.[1] While local norms are often sticky, we suggest that this is particularly the case for 'informing norms' for two reasons. First, when an armed conflict ends, the areas where local norms against informing are strongest are the same areas where elites will attempt to reintegrate or build the presence of the formal institutions of the state. However, the norms are likely to make this process particularly difficult. Second, armed actors that seek to continue to undermine state authority—be they political or criminal—are likely to take advantage of these norms, hence reinforcing them into the post-war era. In sum, we expect that a counterinsurgency strategy based on gathering information from civilians in stronghold areas will have long-term detrimental effects on local community trust. In areas heavily targeted by the state's counterinsurgency campaign, norms against informing are likely to develop, which can undermine local community trust long after a conflict nominally ends.

5.4 Research design

To evaluate the legacies of counterinsurgency on trust, we conduct a plausibility probe (Eckstein 1975) case study of the legacies of the conflict known as 'the Troubles' in Northern Ireland. Research on the local legacies of conflict faces important methodological challenges because areas controlled by rebel groups during conflict are often different to other areas, making comparisons difficult (cf. Walden and Zhukov 2020). Post-conflict Northern Ireland, however, offers the opportunity to compare areas with similar experiences of wartime order provided by armed groups and exposure to violence but that vary in terms of their relationship with the state. It is well suited to probe our theoretical expectations because non-state armed actors on both sides of the conflict provided rudimentary public goods in the form of informal 'justice' systems, yet it was primarily the Republican groups in predominantly Catholic urban areas that were the target of the extensive and decades-long counterinsurgency campaign by the British state. In contrast, Loyalist groups in predominantly Protestant urban areas were not, or less so, the targets of this campaign, and there is evidence of significant collusion between them and the state. The case, thus, provides variation in the relations between armed groups and the state, from 'clashing monopolies' in Catholic areas to 'collusion' in Protestant areas (cf. Staniland 2012).

We employ a mixed-methods research design. Our analysis is structured as follows: First, we present the case, discuss the extent and nature of social control in rebel strongholds, and outline the British counterinsurgency strategy. Second,

[1] Empirically, we examine this only in one case, but we note that, theoretically, we expect this to be the case whether the counterinsurgency ultimately is successful or not.

we trace the emergence of a norm against informing in predominantly Catholic areas, which, as the secondary literature shows, endures today. Third, we present the results of an analysis of a survey we conducted in 2022. We show how local community trust is significantly lower in former Republican stronghold compared to Loyalist strongholds. To demonstrate the role of a norm against informing, we show that people in former Republican strongholds are *still*—more than two decades after the armed conflict nominally ended—more fearful of being perceived as informers, which evidences the persistence of an anti-informing norm in these communities.

5.5 Counterinsurgency in Northern Ireland

5.5.1 The conflict known as 'the Troubles'

At the heart of the conflict, which emerged in the late 1960s, were economic difficulties faced by both the Catholic/Nationalist/Republican and Protestant/Unionist/Loyalist communities. The Unionist community, which historically had dominated economically, was hit by industrial stagnation. The Catholic community, particularly working-class Catholics, were aggrieved due to unemployment and long-term economic and political discrimination, most notably in housing provision and the gerrymandering of elections. Mobilization led to violent clashes between the two communities. The police, known as the Royal Ulster Constabulary (RUC), often sided with the Unionists and, therefore, became a symbol of an oppressive state for the Catholic community. By 1969, the British army was deployed to secure order. Though the army was initially welcomed by the Catholic community, it, too, became a symbol of an oppressive state due to its use of violence, most infamously during the 1972 peaceful protest march in Derry that became known as Bloody Sunday.[2]

5.5.2 Strongholds, 'no go' areas, and social control

When ethnic rioting broke out in 1968, paramilitary groups on both sides of the communal divide emerged and, to differing degrees, sought to exert social control within their communities. While paramilitary groups never truly disappeared after the Irish Civil War (1922–1923), historians generally agree that the Irish Republican Army (IRA) had lost touch with the Catholic community in Ulster by the 1960s (Bell 1997; Hanley and Millar 2010; Sanders 2011). The re-emergence

[2] Members of the Nationalist community call the city 'Derry' and members of the Unionist community call it 'Londonderry'. For simplicity, we will refer to 'Derry' henceforth.

of these groups[3] in urban working-class areas, and the swelling of their ranks during the 1970s, is often attributed to the strong-handed tactics employed by the state in response to civil right protests, violence against the Catholic community, and discriminatory policies such as internment (English 2003; Murphy 2015). Police violence towards Catholics led these communities to erect defensive barricades in the overwhelmingly working-class areas of Derry and Belfast (O'Dochartaigh 2005). These areas became 'no go' areas for the state. Republican paramilitary groups quickly became heavily involved in the local defence, largely due to a demand from the communities, and the 'no go' areas effectively came under the control of the Republican paramilitaries (English 2003; Hanley and Millar 2010). This community demand for the paramilitaries to step in was echoed in interviews we conducted in 2018.[4] These spaces became 'sanctuaries' (Feldman 1991), which came to be policed by local defence groups even after the barricades were dismantled. Indeed, once the army moved into Northern Ireland in 1969, the RUC was no longer deployed to police these areas, but the army did not engage in everyday policing. Loyalist groups also came to take on community 'policing' roles when they thought the state did not act quickly or go far enough. Hence, there was a policing vacuum that was filled by the paramilitary groups—both in Republican and Loyalist areas—and once it was filled, the areas became more or less inaccessible to the state.

The 'no go' areas were areas of high support for the paramilitary groups, which proved to be crucial for them to pursue the armed struggle. As noted by a former member of the Provisional IRA, Collins (1999, 225), 'without the community we were irrelevant. We carried the guns and planted the bombs, but the community fed us, hid us, opened their homes to us, turned a blind eye to our operations (...)'. Republican groups, therefore, attempted to foster and maintain popular support in predominately Catholic areas. Faced with the option of ensuring support through coercion or consent, Republican groups opted for the latter, partially due to the security risk of civilian collaboration. Indeed, as noted by Sluka (1989, 166), 'intimidation would be inherently counterproductive for the IRA and INLA, because it would alienate support and lead to an increase in the number of people prepared to give information to the Security Forces'.

The main public good provided by paramilitary groups was community 'policing'. As far as the rudimentary 'justice' system was concerned, paramilitary groups in both Republican and Loyalist communities developed a system

[3] The IRA split into several rival factions, including the Provisional, Official, Continuity, and Real IRA, as well as the Irish National Liberation Army (INLA) and the Irish People Liberation Organization (IPLO).

[4] We conducted 15 semi-structured interviews community members in areas affected by paramilitary violence and restorative justice organizations (including former paramilitaries). The fieldwork was funded by Research Council of Norway/Norges Forskningsråd (grant number 240446) and approved by the ethics committee at University College London (UCL).

of 'punishments' based on the seriousness of the offence under consideration (Monaghan and Mclaughlin 2006, 176), ranging from warnings, curfews, fines, acts of public humiliation, and punishment beatings to punishment shootings (such as kneecappings), expulsions, and assassinations (Silke 1998; 1999a).[5] These systems were also applied to individuals accused of informing (Dudai 2022).

5.5.3 The British counterinsurgency

The state's initial approach to emerging political violence in Northern Ireland was militaristic. Internment, which overwhelmingly targeted Republican communities (de Silva 2012, 94), was introduced on 9 August 1971, a day on which hundreds of people were arrested. The policy was a failure, resulting in increased intercommunal rioting and a growth in the membership of Republican paramilitary groups (English 2003). The British forces recognized that a military approach was not effective in quelling support for Republican paramilitaries and, instead, pursued a strategy of 'normalization' and 'criminalization' (Guelke 2007). They particularly targeted the Catholic 'no go' areas to undermine support for Republican groups and ultimately, reduce the groups' ability to inflict harm. Leahy (2020, 5) notes that the British forces required inside information from the IRA and the Republican community in which it was embedded in order to disrupt IRA activities, reducing it 'to a level at which it caused minimal disruption to political, social, and economic life in Northern Ireland'. Key tools in the latter were the reliance on informers.

There are three major sources of information: material indices, violent extraction, and consensual provision (Kalyvas 2006, 175). The British forces attempted to extract information in all forms, although they relied predominantly on consensual provision. The counterinsurgents recruited informers in the Republican movement, including in areas where Republican groups had high support, as well as within the ranks of the different Republican groups, notably the Provisional IRA but also other Republican groups, such as the Official IRA and the INLA. Informers at the higher echelons of the paramilitary groups became known as 'supergrasses'. People like Christopher Black in 1981, 'Stakeknife' in 2003, and Denis Donaldson in 2005 were top-level informants that wreaked havoc in the Republican movement. The British forces also relied on material indices gathered through a range of technologies—mostly photography and audio recordings—albeit to a lesser extent. As noted by Kirk-Smith and Dingley (2009, 558), 'an informant might be able to tell you more in five minutes than any other method, such as electronic surveillance or satellite images, could tell you in five months'. Indeed, the use of agents and informers was the 'primacy of counterinsurgency'

[5] On the provision of 'justice' by rebel groups more generally, see Sivakumaran (2009) and Loyle (2021).

(McGovern 2016, 293). According to a former Special Branch officer, William Matchet (2016), 60% of intelligence came from informers.

There was important regional variation in counterinsurgency strategies, especially between rural and urban areas. In the early years of the conflict, the IRA was well supported within its communities and 'remained elusive' in 'no go' areas (Leahy 2020, 39). As such, they would often make little to no attempt to conceal their identities (ibid.). And yet popular support for the IRA made intelligence hard to obtain. As the conflict progressed and the British forces regained a military footprint in the 'no go' areas through a 1972 military operation known as Operation Motorman, urban communities became challenges for the Republican groups. As paramilitary groups also recruited from these communities, insurgents often continued to live at home with their family (Soule 1989). The Special Branch aimed to recruit informers within or very close to the paramilitary organizations (Kirk-Smith and Dingley 2009, 556), which was easier in urban settings with tightknit communities (Taylor 2014). According to a British soldier (Leahy 2020, 149), certain features of urban areas made infiltration possible. Key among them was the compact nature of Republican estates in the cities, which allowed 'nosey neighbours' greater opportunities to spy on the IRA. Low-level informers, as opposed to the 'supergrasses', gathered the bulk of basic information in pubs, clubs, and the streets. The IRA Green Book (Melaugh 2023) specifically warns against the risks of 'loose talk' if members of the Provisional IRA drink too much alcohol. The British forces often recruited young, first-time criminals who were arrested and persuaded to become informants in exchange for dropping charges or reduced sentences (Soule 1989, 40; McGovern 2016). These became known as the 'ten pound touts' after an article in a prominent newspaper in West Belfast, the Andersonstown News, carried the phrase on its front page.

The British counterinsurgency aimed to collect information about the location, identities, and plans of Republican insurgents. They did this predominantly through the use of informants. In urban areas, informers were mostly low-level members of paramilitary groups or members of the community in which the groups were embedded. These places, such as Ardoyne and the Falls Road in Belfast, as well as the Creggan in Derry, were targeted by a British counterinsurgency campaign that relied heavily on the use of informers.

5.5.4 Collusion with Loyalist paramilitaries

Although Loyalist paramilitary groups also emerged from the intercommunal violence of the late 1960s, they were inherently different in their relationship with the state. Whereas Republican groups emerged to defend predominately Catholic communities, Loyalist groups emerged to protect the Union. This relationship fundamentally changed after the Anglo-Irish Treaty of 1985, when the British government shifted its historic alliance with the Unionist community in exchange for a stronger partnership with the Republic of Ireland, which still had a territorial claim on the six northern counties enshrined in its constitution (Todd 2011; Arthur and Jeffery 1988). Silke (1999b) shows a clear trend after the Anglo-Irish Agreement, with Loyalist groups increasingly partaking in so-called 'punishment attacks' and no longer cooperating with the RUC. According to a Loyalist paramilitary speaking in 2007, 'there was an absence of policing and when people needed help, they went to the paramilitaries who were the ones who could deliver instant justice because there was no formal connections or relationships with the police' (Byrne and Monaghan 2008, 64).

There is significant evidence of 'systematic and institutionalized' collusion between the British forces and Loyalist paramilitaries, which was particularly high in the 1980s and 1990s despite the growing distance between the state and loyalist groups (McGovern 2016, 297). Links between paramilitary groups and locally recruited state forces predate the conflict (Cochrane 2013), and there has long been suspicion of dual membership (Sluka 1989, 222; Collins and McGovern 1998). According to the *Report of the Patrick Finucane Review* (de Silva 2012, 253), there were 270 instances of assistance between members of the security forces and Loyalist paramilitaries in just the two years between 1987 and 1989, the most common form of which was 'targeting information on Republican terrorists'. Clearly, the relationship between the state and Loyalist communities was fundamentally different to the relationship between the state and Republican communities. While the state's counterinsurgency targeted Republican groups in their communities, it relied on Loyalist paramilitaries to eliminate Republican insurgents that it, as a liberal democracy, did not have the legal basis to do (Rolston 2005, see also Mitchell 2004). Despite significant intelligence sharing, members of Loyalist paramilitary organizations were pursued by the state and charged with terrorism. It is important to highlight that there was not a clear-cut cooperative relationship between the British forces and Loyalist paramilitaries.

For the purposes of this research, we are interested in how people's experience of counterinsurgency tactics differed across the main cleavage of the conflict. While the full scale of informing remains unknown—and neither Republican paramilitaries-turned-politicians nor the police have incentives to fully disclose such information (Dudai 2022, 55)—the 'operational difficulties' of infiltration can be investigated 'by studying IRA activity levels at the time' (Leahy 2020, 13). A very useful source is Michael McKeown's Post-Mortem database (2009), which includes an indicator for deaths due to 'informational collaboration' with the state. The bottom pane of Figure 5.1 shows the number of deaths coded as *internal security*, those who were paramilitary 'members, as well as non-members, whom [Republican or Loyalist groups][6] felt might be conveying information about them

[6] The Post-Mortem database outlines which specific groups were responsible for the deaths. We aggregate the different Republican and Loyalist groups.

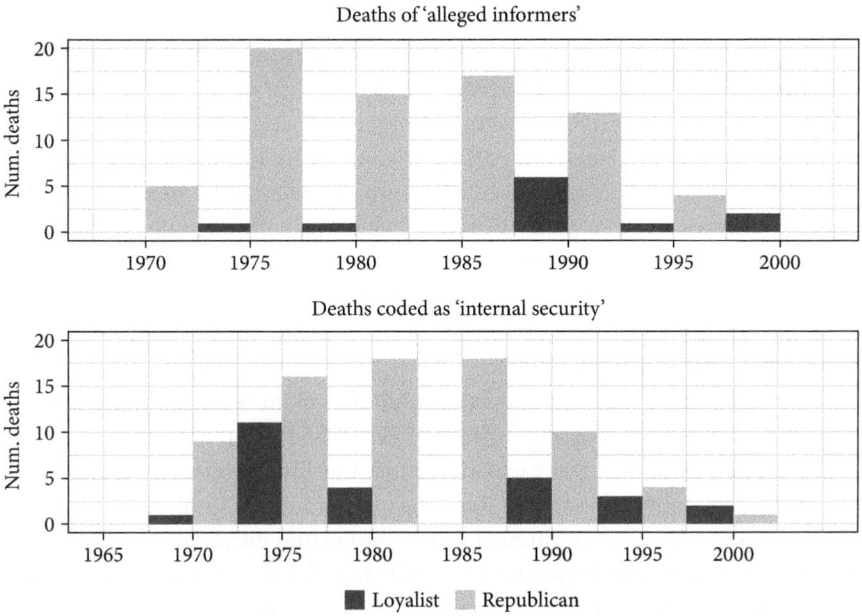

Figure 5.1 Punishment deaths coded as 'alleged informer'/'paramilitary informer' (top pane) and 'internal security' (bottom pane) in the Post-Mortem database (1968–2001)

Source: authors' illustration based on original Post-Mortem database by McKeown (2009).

to the security authorities' (McKeown 2009: 9). The top pane shows victims coded as *alleged* and *paramilitary informers*—people who were murdered by paramilitary groups as punishment for informing. Important for our purposes is that both panes demonstrate that Republican paramilitary groups targeted informants at a higher rate than Loyalist paramilitary groups.

In sum, the British counterinsurgency campaign relied heavily on the use of informers. While both Republican and Loyalist paramilitary groups were embedded in urban communities and provided limited governance in the form of informal 'justice' systems in their respective strongholds, the state focused its use of informers on Republican communities. Republican paramilitary groups were, as such, more likely to target and murder people suspected of informing.

5.5.5 The emergence of anti-informing norms

Insurgents generally rely on local populations to provide resources, information, and cover. This was also true in Northern Ireland, where Republican paramilitary groups sought to impose social control for political and military reasons.

Politically, these communities served to undermine the legitimacy of the state and 'de-normalizing' Northern Irish society (Bean 2012, 212). Practically and militarily, these areas provided Republican groups with sanctuary and became notorious as centres of IRA recruitment, organization, and arms concealment (Downey 1983). Compliance was particularly important due to the nature of the insurgency. The social control imposed on urban communities served not only political purposes, but also military ones, particularly in the ongoing information war between Republican groups and the British security forces. It was ensured through a combination of intimidation, punishment, and rewards, which also served to identify and eliminate informers or so-called 'touts' (Monaghan and McLaughlin 2006; Feldman 1991).

In the tightly knit, densely populated Catholic micro-societies, nothing was 'more despised than an informer' (Soule 1989, 40). Soule (1989) argues that, in a vicious circle dynamic, the backlash against the British informer system led to greater community support for Republican paramilitary groups. Indeed, the informer system led to de-legitimizing state authorities even further, creating a governance vacuum that Republican paramilitaries filled by performing 'normal police duties' (Soule 1989, 40). Crucially, the British counterinsurgency led to a strong social stigma against informing and the emergence of an anti-informing norm in Republican strongholds. The counterinsurgency relied heavily on informers and fostered an environment of distrust within Republican paramilitaries and their communities. According to a former member of the Provisional IRA, 'we were in total disarray... You didn't know who was a tout, or who was going to poison you' (cited in Leahy 2020, 143).

Dudai (2012; 2022) argues that informers became a 'folk devil' in certain communities during the conflict. 'Folk devils' create moral panics, whereby 'a condition, episode, person or group of persons emerge to become defined as a threat to societal values and interests' (Cohen 1972, 1). He claims that hostility to informers has 'continued almost unabated well into the peace-process years' because reconciliation—while possible across the ethnic divide—is still beyond the pale for communities and informers. Dudai (2012, 40) claims that informing is an 'intimate betrayal', especially because of the localized and close-knit nature of Republican groups and their urban communities (see also Williams and Leahy 2023).

The norm against informing enforces a standard of behaviour. Like all norms, it is sticky and has an enduring legacy on communities, but it might be particularly sticky due to the intimate nature of the betrayal in such tightknit communities. Indeed, according to Cochrane and Monaghan (2012, 20), 'a hatred and loathing of informants remains deep within the Republican psyche' (cf. Bar-Tal 2000). This norm is likely an important factor in explaining why post-war engagement with the police is 'viewed politically as contentious and problematic for some sections of the community' (Byrne and Jarman 2011, 447). The criminalization of paramilitary groups and the use of informers by the security forces during the conflict mean that 'in some areas even being seen talking to the police is still considered informing' according to a community worker interviewed by Topping and Byrne (2012, 47). Evidently, over a decade after the conflict nominally ended, there was still a stigma in sections of the community 'who perceived informing the police about crime as "touting"' (Byrne and Monaghan 2008, 65) or 'collaborating with the enemy' (Byrne and Monaghan 2008, 114). Writing more recently, Fr. Martin Magill, a Catholic priest in West Belfast, claimed that the principle of 'not touting' is deeply ingrained within society and that being a 'tout' is considered 'to this day despicable and not to be done'.[7] These norms are transmitted via informal socialization mechanisms among family and community members. The sharing of personal stories and anecdotes, songs about the Irish struggle (such as 'Kevin Barry', in which the hero is tortured by the British yet 'he would not tell the names of his brave comrades'), and 'touts will be shot' graffiti on walls are all part of this socialization process. While the transmission of these norms does not have to be localized—songs, for example, transcend locales—much of it is, as the control by paramilitaries during the conflict was very localized and has remained so in its aftermath (e.g. Rickard and Bakke 2021), often quite visible in painted curbsides, flags, and wall murals (e.g. Jarman 1998; Rolston 2003; Rickard et al. 2025).

In sum, in their counterinsurgency strategy in Northern Ireland, the British forces relied on informers, which created a norm against informing that endures to this day and, we argue, undermines local community trust. This norm developed particularly in Republican strongholds because these were the areas in which the British relied most heavily on informers.

5.6 Survey results

We argue that an anti-informing norm continues to undermine local trust in areas targeted by the counterinsurgency's heavy use of informants. To investigate this quantitatively, we draw on a face-to-face public opinion survey conducted in 2022.[8] The survey was fielded in areas that were strongholds during the conflict and where social control by paramilitary groups endures today in the form of so-called 'punishment attacks' (what the police calls 'paramilitary-style attacks'), including, most infamously, kneecappings. These are attacks directed at the groups' 'own' communities (ingroup attacks). Rickard and Bakke (2021)

[7] Fr. Magill's opinion piece, '"Touting" and the ethics of gathering information' appeared on Slugger O'Toole on 16 August 2018, available here: https://sluggerotoole.com/2018/08/16/touting-and-the-ethics-of-gathering-information/.

[8] This research was funded by the Research Council of Norway (FRIPRO), as part of the project 'Street-Level Autocrats: Individual Decisions with Collective Consequences' (grant no. 275404). The project is registered and has ethics approval from University College London (no.4931/002). The survey was fielded by Belfast-based Perceptive Insight.

show that there is a strong correlation between areas experiencing such present-day social control by armed groups and their social control during the conflict. We sampled census tract areas, known as Super Output Areas (SOAs), that are worst affected by paramilitary-style attacks between 2008 and 2018 (there are 890 SOAs in Northern Ireland, with an average population of 2000 people). To do so, we rely on data provided to us by the Police Service Northern Ireland (PSNI). This type of violence occurs across Northern Ireland, but clusters in urban SOAs such as Derry and Belfast, as shown in Figure 5.2. We selected the eight SOAs worst affected by Republican attacks (on average thirteen attacks per SOA over this period) and the eight SOAs worst affected by Loyalist attacks (on average ten attacks). We sampled a total of 512 respondents, which amounts to thirty-two per SOA.[9]

These areas include predominantly Catholic areas such as Ardoyne and Falls Park in Belfast, and the Creggan in Derry, and predominantly Protestant areas such as Shankill in Belfast and Love Lane in Carrickfergus. These areas were all 'no go' areas during the conflict, and they continue to experience paramilitary violence. That is, these areas are similar on key dimensions likely to affect community trust, but one half of them—the predominantly Catholic areas—were harder hit by the counterinsurgency campaign than the other half.

As a measure for local community trust, we ask people how much they trust 'people in your neighbourhood or village'. Respondents can state that they trust 'not at all', 'not very much', 'somewhat', or 'completely'. We treat all dependent variables as continuous variables and estimate linear regression models. The key independent variable is whether respondents live in a predominantly Protestant or Catholic neighbourhood.[10] Our expectation is that predominantly Catholic communities, which were more affected by the British counterinsurgency, are less likely to exhibit high levels of community trust. We also account for age, income, education, and gender, as well as personal experiences of violence, which—as noted in the literature review—has been linked to both social distrust and community cohesion.[11] All models include standard errors clustered at the SOA level to account for potential dependencies between observations.

Table 5.1 shows the main results of our analysis. Column 1 shows that respondents in predominately Catholic neighbourhoods are more likely to

[9] As part of the project, we also sampled similar areas that experience no or few paramilitary-style attacks. For the analysis here, we want to hold present-day violence constant; hence, we focus only on areas that experience high levels of such attacks.

[10] Our findings are unchanged if we rely on self-declared religion as our key independent variable. As the survey areas are highly ethnically homogenous, both variables correlate highly (Pearson correlation coefficient = 0.89).

[11] We code respondents as having personally experienced violence if they report that they were 'shot at (with either real or plastic bullets)' or experienced 'physical violence (beaten, tortured, or otherwise injured)' by either the army or the police. Over 19% of respondents report—30% in Catholic areas and 9% in Protestant areas—that they experienced violence.

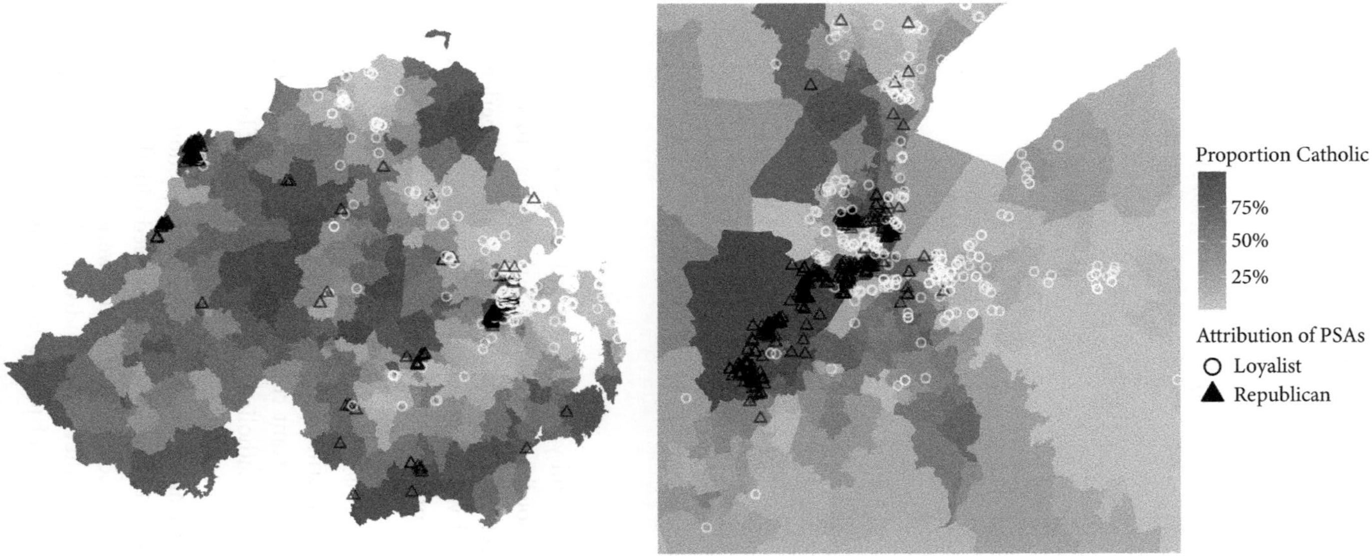

Figure 5.2 'Paramilitary-style attacks' (2008–2018) across Northern Ireland (left) and Belfast (right)

Note: census tracts (SOAs) are dark where there are high proportions of respondents who identify as Catholic according to the 2011 census. Icons indicate whether the PSNI suspect attacks were conducted by Republican (black triangles) or Loyalist (white circles) paramilitary groups. By definition, 'paramilitary-style attacks' are ingroup attacks, as collected and categorized by the PSNI.

Source: authors' illustration based on PNSI data and 2011 census data (Northern Ireland Statistics and Research Agency, NISRA). Maps generated in R using shapefiles from NISRA Open Data Boundaries.

Table 5.1 Results for community trust as the dependent variable

	Community trust	Community trust
Intercept	2.131^{***} (0.046)	1.804^{***} (0.153)
Catholic community	-0.290^{***} (0.066)	-0.272^{***} (0.070)
Experience violence		−0.095 (0.087)
Age		0.001^{+} (0.001)
Income		0.187^{***} (0.033)
Education		0.004 (0.030)
Gender (female)		-0.145^{*} (0.067)
Num.Obs.	491	479
R2	0.038	0.120
R2 Adj.	0.036	0.109
AIC	1095.9	1037.6

$^{+}p < 0.1$, $^{*}p < 0.05$, $^{**}p < 0.01$, $^{***}p < 0.001$.

report low levels of community trust compared to respondents in predominantly Protestant neighbourhoods. Column 2 shows that this finding holds with the inclusion of demographic controls and personal experiences of violence. Among the control variables, personal experiences of violence are associated with lower levels of community trust, although just 90% confidence levels, and women are less likely to report trusting people in their neighbourhood. Finally, wealthier people report higher levels of trust on average. While the experience of the counterinsurgency is not the only way in which predominately Catholic and Protestant communities differ, we argue that a norm against informing means that Catholic areas have lower levels of local community trust.

To assess whether a norm against informing persists in predominantly Catholic areas, we asked respondents to what extent they agreed with the statements 'people do not go to the police because they do not want to be seen as informers'. Respondents could reply that they 'strongly disagreed' to 'strongly agreed' on a five-point scale. The proportion of people in predominantly Catholic communities who strongly agree with the statement is four times higher (26%) than in predominantly Protestant communities (6%), while more people disagreed (25%) in Protestant communities compared to Catholic communities (16%).[12]

To control for confounding variables, we run linear regression models in which the dependent variable is the extent to which people disagree or agree with the statement. Table 5.2 shows the result of a linear regression model in which our key independent variable is whether respondents live in predominantly Catholic neighbourhoods. Results in Column 1 show that respondents in predominately Catholic areas are significantly more likely to agree to the statement. The finding is robust to additional controls. While the coefficient is slightly lower, the results in Column 2 show that the strongest predictor for support for the statement remains whether the area in which respondents live is predominantly Catholic.

Table 5.2 Results for informing is the dependent variable

	Informers	**Informers**
Intercept	3.037*** (0.077)	3.339*** (0.297)
Catholic community	0.600*** (0.112)	0.434*** (0.121)
Experience violence		0.323* (0.146)
Age		−0.001 (0.003)
Income		0.031 (0.060)
Education		−0.189*** (0.053)
Gender (female)		0.093 (0.116)
Num.Obs.	416	405
R2	0.065	0.110
R2 Adj.	0.063	0.097
AIC	1291.6	1248.8

$^{+}p < 0.1$, $^{*}p < 0.05$, $^{**}p < 0.01$, $^{***}p < 0.001$.

[12] We note that the share of respondents answering 'don't know' or refuse to answer is high at 21%. This number is higher in Catholic areas, where 26% of respondents do not answer the question compared to just 15% in predominantly Protestant areas. These levels indicate that the question may be sensitive and suffer from non-response bias. The fact that it is more sensitive in predominately Catholic areas indicates that it is here where the anti-informing norm may be strongest.

Among the controls, the only variables reaching statistical significance are personal experiences of violence and education. Generally, respondents who personally experienced violence are more likely to agree with the statement, while more educated people tend to disagree. For education, this association is unlikely due to greater knowledge about informing itself. Instead, it is more likely that respondents are referring to whether they themselves fear reporting, and so we may be capturing actual behaviour, not just the perception of other people's behaviour in their community.

In the accompanying appendix, we show that the results of the survey analyses are robust to a series of alternative model specifications. First, we show that, in line with our theoretical argument, our expectations hold only for community trust and not inter-group trust. Second, we note that predominantly Protestant and Catholic areas vary in other ways. To account for these differences, we include SOA-level control variables for income, crime, and community composition and run models with SOA-fixed effects. Third, we conduct a causal mediation analysis (Imai, Keele, and Tingley 2010) of the relationship between exposure to the British counterinsurgency, anti-informing norms, and communal trust. Finally, an important concern is whether there were systematic differences in levels of trust between Protestant and Catholic communities before the onset of the conflict, social control of armed actors, and British counterinsurgency. We attempt to overcome this in two ways. First, we run alternative model specifications with additional deprivation measures from the 1971 census. Second, we rely on a survey conducted in similar areas in 1966 to show that there are not systematic differences between Catholic and Protestant respondents for concepts related to trust. There is no perfect empirical strategy because there is no baseline survey on trust in these areas that pre-date the conflict. However, the combined results of the survey-based analyses provide additional empirical support to the expectation that local community support is lower in Republican than Loyalist 'stronghold' areas, and that this is likely driven by a norm against informing in Republican strongholds that were the primary targets of the state's counterinsurgency campaign.

5.7 Conclusion

Rebel groups often rely heavily on civilians during conflict, and governments recognize that rebel strength comes predominantly from their ability to strike and retreat into areas where they have local support. In asymmetric warfare, in which 'weaker' rebels are fighting 'stronger' states, greater access to information is often key to rebel survival and, ultimately, extracting concessions from the government. States' counterinsurgency strategies, thus, attempt to extract information from civilians in rebel strongholds. A growing body of work on rebel governance—informal wartime institutions—shows that rebels attempt to rule by consent. Commonly, rebels create institutions to foster civilian support and legitimize their rule, but also to deter and punish collaboration. One such institution is the strong norm and stigma against informing. Drawing on a mixed-methods research design, we show that these norms have long-lasting legacies on community trust with a controlled comparison of areas controlled by paramilitary groups during the conflict in Northern Ireland.

We trace how, during the conflict, paramilitary groups emerged on both sides of the main conflict cleavage. Both Republican and Loyalist groups established territorial control in relatively small urban communities, predominantly in Belfast and Derry. In these 'no go' areas, they established rudimentary forms of governance to fill a policing vacuum—informal 'justice' systems. However, the relationship between the paramilitary groups and the state was fundamentally different. The British forces mounted a three-decade-long counterinsurgency against Republican groups that relied heavily on the use of informers. In Republican strongholds, a strong norm against informing emerged, which we show endures long after the armed conflict nominally ended. Indeed, informers have emerged as a 'folk devil' in predominately Catholic communities during the conflict, which has endured to the present, potentially because informing is such an intimate betrayal in such close-knit communities (cf. Dudai 2022). To systematically assess the insights from the qualitative analysis, we rely on an original survey conducted in 2022 in areas that were Republican and Loyalist strongholds during the war. The results of our statistical analysis show that respondents who live in predominantly Catholic areas have, on average, lower levels of local community trust, underscoring the long-term legacy of a norm against informing. To explore whether this difference is, indeed, due to a persistent stigma against informing, a further analysis of the data shows that people in predominately Catholic areas are more likely to agree that people do not go to the police because they do not want to be seen as informers.

Our work makes several contributions to existing research. First, while there is a growing body of work on rebel governance, and public goods provision in conflict more generally, we draw attention to the state's strategies and tactics to counter these efforts and undermine insurgent support. Second, we join a small but growing body of work specifically interested in the legacies of institutional change during conflict. We show that institutional change during conflict may be due, jointly, to the armed strategies of rebel groups and the military strategy of state, which have enduring legacies on post-war society. We also make a contribution to understanding legacies of war in Northern Ireland and beyond. While there is some research on the reluctance of certain sections of society to turn to the police, we demonstrate the differences across communities, relying on quantitative analyses of original survey data across communities. Our findings can inform efforts to reintegrate the police into areas where the police was historically a symbol of oppression—areas that suffer from high levels of crime (e.g. Deglow 2022). Decades of fear in predominately Catholic communities led to a persistent norm and high levels of local community distrust, which may undermine post-conflict reconciliation. We believe this work has implications beyond the Northern Irish context. As noted by Dudai (2012, 39), there was a strong informer culture in South Africa after apartheid; in Algeria after independence from France; and in Norway after World War II. It is likely that norms against informing emerge in most conflicts in which rebels seek to establish territorial control (cf. Kalyvas 2006) and foster civilian support by providing governance (cf. Mampilly 2011). These dynamics are likely to extend beyond asymmetric conflicts. For instance, at the time of writing, Ukrainian forces have attempted to identify collaborators in territory regained from Russian invading forces (Callaghan 2022). Equally, across Russian-occupied territory, the Ukrainian army is building a system of informers and resistance fighters to undermine Russian control and identify military targets (Khurshudyan and Hrabchuk 2022). The conflict in Northern Ireland demonstrates detrimental effects of similar wartime military dynamics on local community trust, long after the conflict nominally ended.

Future work should consider the legacies of the rebel governance and counterinsurgency nexus. While our focus is on a case where a strong state has the capacity to target rebel strongholds, in cases where state capacity to target counterinsurgency across all rebel strongholds is limited, the legacies of rebel governance may depend on counterinsurgency strategies employed. Areas where insurgents develop wartime institutions may exhibit high levels of ingroup trust for several reasons. First, these areas are on the frontline of group antagonism. The effect of living under insurgent rule can foster strong ingroup favouritism through the experience of a shared struggle, and, similar to the legacies of ingroup bonding experienced by members of armed groups (e.g. Daly 2016; Nussio and Oppenheim 2014), it can have legacies that extend well beyond the official end of the conflict. Second, wartime institutions may ensure predictable behaviour through clear rules that are followed by civilians and enforced by insurgents, thus leading to higher levels of trust. However, our research shows that rebel strongholds are the natural targets of counterinsurgency campaigns, which can have negative implications for local community trust. Future work should consider the legacies of rebel governance in cases where counterinsurgency efforts vary.

5.8 Appendix

A. Robustness checks

A.1 Intergroup trust

Table 5.A.1 shows the results of a similar analysis to our main analysis (the results of which are shown in Table 5.1 in the manuscript). Here, however, we replace intercommunal trust with inter-group trust as the dependent variable.

Table 5.A.1 Results of a linear regression analysis in which intergroup trust is the dependent variable

	Intergroup trust	Intergroup trust
Intercept	1.464^{***} (0.052)	0.684^{***} (0.198)
Catholic community	0.010 (0.076)	0.101 (0.080)
Experience violence		-0.310^{**} (0.102)
Age		0.006^{**} (0.002)
Income		0.105^{**} (0.039)
Education		0.142^{***} (0.035)
Gender (female)		−0.084 (0.077)
Num.Obs.	461	448
R2	0.000	0.097
R2 Adj.	−0.002	0.085
AIC	1126.5	1058.4

$^{+}p < 0.1$, $^{*}p < 0.05$, $^{**}p < 0.01$, $^{***}p < 0.001$.

Respondents were asked how much they trust 'People from another community background'. There is no statistically significant difference between respondents in predominantly Catholic or Protestant communities, which we would expect given the theory. The key difference in trust between the communities is communal trust, not intergroup trust.

A.2 SOA-level controls and SOA fixed effects

Table 5.A.2 shows the results of our main analysis with the inclusion of additional SOA-level controls. In columns 1 and 4, we include income deprivation measured in 2015–2016,[13] crime rates measured in 2011–2016,[14] and total number of paramilitary-style assaults measured in 2008–2018. As we sample thirty-two respondents from sixteen SOAs, the data are clustered in space and may be hierarchical. To account for potential interdependencies in the data, we cluster

[13] Income deprivation is measured as the proportion of the population living in households whose equivalized income is below 60% of the Northern Irish median (NIMDM 2017).

[14] The crime rate is the rate of violence, sexual offence, robbery, and public order by the total population of the SOA according to the 2011 census (including non-resident workplace population) (NIMDM 2017).

Table 5.A.2 Results of main models with additional SOA-level controls and fixed effects

	Community trust	Community trust	Community trust	Informers	Informers	Informers
Intercept	1.630*** (0.325)	1.861*** (0.521)	1.840*** (0.204)	0.424 (0.536)	6.885*** (0.941)	3.030*** (0.321)
Catholic community	−0.363*** (0.088)	−0.224** (0.085)	−0.583** (0.198)	0.478*** (0.141)	0.239+ (0.137)	1.990*** (0.317)
Experience violence	−0.105 (0.087)	−0.105 (0.089)	−0.111 (0.086)	0.196 (0.134)	0.213 (0.143)	0.166 (0.126)
Age	0.001+ (0.001)	0.001* (0.001)	0.002* (0.001)	−0.001 (0.003)	0.000 (0.003)	−0.002 (0.003)
Income	0.192*** (0.033)	0.196*** (0.036)	0.123** (0.040)	0.008 (0.055)	−0.024 (0.061)	0.000 (0.061)
Education	0.006 (0.030)	0.019 (0.031)	0.028 (0.031)	−0.135** (0.048)	−0.177*** (0.053)	−0.180*** (0.050)
Gender (female)	−0.162* (0.068)	−0.174* (0.069)	−0.159* (0.068)	−0.013 (0.106)	0.104 (0.113)	0.013 (0.102)
Income deprivation (2017)	0.739 (1.017)			14.874*** (1.597)		
Crime rate (2017)	−0.003 (0.002)			0.003 (0.004)		
Total Para. attacks (2008-2018)	0.020 (0.018)			0.052+ (0.029)		

continued

Table 5.A.2 *continued*

	Community trust	Community trust	Community trust	Informers	Informers	Informers
Prop. unemployed men (1971)		0.508 (0.902)			10.807*** (1.557)	
Prop. male population (1971)		−0.349 (0.993)			−8.742*** (1.817)	
Num.Obs.	479	448	479	405	381	405
R2	0.129	0.125	0.175	0.271	0.223	0.378
FE	N	N	Y	N	N	Y
R2 Adj.	0.112	0.109	0.139	0.254	0.207	0.346
AIC	1038.9	965.2	1034.7	1174.1	1131.1	1131.7

$^{+}p < 0.1$, $^{*}p < 0.05$, $^{**}p < 0.01$, $^{***}p < 0.001$.

standard errors. In columns 2 and 4, we include two controls from the 1971 Northern Irish census (Shuttleworth and Lloyd 2009). First, we control for the proportion of unemployed men at the SOA level in 1971. Our finding on community trust is robust (column 2). However, our main finding for the norm around informing is statistically significant at just 90% confidence intervals. We note that there are important limitations with using census data collected during conflict, as outlined by Adida et al. (2023). Finally, Table 5.A.2 also shows the results of the main analysis with the inclusion of SOA fixed effects (columns 3 and 6). The main results for both models on trust and norms around informing are robust to this alternative model specification. In sum, we note that our main results are robust to several alternative model specifications.

A.3 Causal mediation analysis

Causal mediation analysis allows us to establish whether the norm against informing is a possible causal mechanism underpinning low levels of community trust. To conduct a mediation analysis, we adopt the mediation approach by Imai, Keele, and Tingley (2010) and Imai, Keele, and Yamamoto (2010). Specifically, our outcome of interest is communal trust measured by respondents' answers to how much they trust 'people in your neighbourhood or village' on a four-point scale from 'not at all' to 'completely'. The treatment variable is whether respondents reside in an area that was historically a Republican or Loyalist stronghold. The mediating variable is respondents' support for the statement 'people do not go to the police because they do not want to be seen as informers' on a five point-scale from 'strongly disagreed' to 'strongly agreed'. Table 5.A.3 shows the results of the mediation analysis.

Consistent with our theoretical expectations, agreeing with an anti-informing statement mediates (−0.03, p <0.05) the relationship between community and

Table 5.A.3 Results of a causal mediation analysis between community, informing norms, and communal trust

	Estimate	95% upper CI	95 % lower CI	p-value
Mediated effect	−0.027	−0.063	0.00	0.042*
Direct effect	−0.261	−0.414	−0.10	0.004***
Total effect	−0.288	−0.438	−0.13	0.00***
% effect mediated	0.091	0.004	0.28	0.042*

$^{+}p < 0.1$, $^{*}p < 0.05$, $^{**}p < 0.01$, $^{***}p < 0.001$.

Nonparametric Bootstrap Confidence Intervals with the Percentile Method

communal trust. This finding suggests that respondents who live in areas that were republican strongholds during the conflict will agree more with a norm against informing, which accounts in part for lower levels of communal trust.

A.4 Accounting for pre-war levels of trust

An important concern with our main analysis concerns whether systematic differences in levels of trust between Protestant and Catholic communities pre-date the conflict, the social control of armed actors, and the British counterinsurgency. This is often a plight for research on the legacies of conflict (e.g. Walden and Zhukov 2020). In the absence of a plausibly natural experiment, one can rarely know whether people or communities of interest—in our case, predominantly Catholic urban communities—were targeted in ways that were related to trust levels that pre-date the war, i.e. there is non-random treatment assignment which can undermine causal inference. Our research design relies on the assumption that Loyalist and Republican communities, mainly due to the social control of armed actors and exposure to violence during the conflict, are similar. However, it could be that there were lower levels of trust in Catholic communities which, interacting with social control by armed actors, led to lower levels of post-war trust. To evaluate whether pre-war levels of trust were different across communities, we rely on an original household survey conducted by the Belfast City Planning Department before the onset of the war.[15]

The survey, fielded between June and July 1966, interviewed housewives (N = 1588) in six deprived urban areas of Belfast that had been selected for redevelopment: Sandy Row, Donegall Pass, Cromac, Shankill, and Albertbridge. There are important limitations in analysing these data. First, we do not have information on the areas in which respondents were surveyed for privacy and security reasons. Areas can only be differentiated by a randomly generated number. This means that we cannot directly compare areas surveyed in 2022 to those surveyed in 1966. Second, most areas were predominantly Protestant. Indeed, all areas contained between 16 and 20% Catholic respondents. The survey pre-dates the displacement caused by ethnic rioting in 1968, and so these percentages are high compared to similar measures in the same areas today. It is, therefore, still possible that levels of trust were systematically different in majority Catholic areas. Third, we do not have the same questions on trust and norms around informing that we asked in 2022. Instead, we rely on measures that approach similar underlying concepts. Taken together, these limitations make direct comparisons between opinions recorded in 1966 and those recorded in 2022 impossible. However, they do allow us to check whether the levels of concepts related to trust were systematically different between Catholic and Protestant respondents before the

[15] The UK Data Service digitized the records for our analysis.

Table 5.A.4 Results of regression analyses comparing Catholic and Protestant respondents in deprived urban communities before war onset

	Neighbours not as friendly as other places	**Importance of good neighbours**	**Importance of privacy**
Protestant	−0.082 (0.234)	−0.002 (0.044)	−0.060 (0.042)
No religion	−0.798 (0.552)	0.033 (0.164)	0.116 (0.131)
Other religion	−0.272 (0.382)	−0.045 (0.074)	−0.048 (0.074)
Household income	−0.077* (0.032)	−0.012+ (0.007)	0.014* (0.006)
Family members living in district	0.300 (0.186)	0.038 (0.033)	0.011 (0.033)
Num.Obs.	1507	1541	1550
R2		0.006	0.010
R2 Adj.		−0.003	0.001
AIC	1002.4	2934.5	2936.3

+p < 0.1, *p < 0.05, **p < 0.01, ***p < 0.001.
All models include district fixed-effects.

conflict in similar areas that were sampled in 2022—economically-deprived and urban neighbourhoods.

To do so, we run three regression models. All models include controls for income, whether respondents have family members living in the same district, and district fixed effects. The results are shown in Table 5.A.4. The key independent variable is self-declared religion, with Catholic as the reference category. Asked whether neighbours are too friendly or not as friendly as in other places, Protestant respondents were not more or less likely to report that neighbours were more friendly (results for the logit regression are shown in column 1). Asked how important good neighbours were to them, once more there is no statistically significant difference between respondents of different religions (results for a linear regression are shown in column 2). Finally, asked how important it was to be private, Protestant respondents were not more or less likely to support highly rate the importance of privacy (results for a linear regression are shown in column 3). While these dependent variables do not directly measure local community trust, we would expect them to correlate highly. Any differences in responses between Catholic and Protestant respondents would indicate varying levels of trust. In the absence of any differences in these questions, we conclude that levels of trust were not systematically different between Catholic and Protestant respondents before the conflict.

References

Adida, C. L., J. M. Brown, G. C. McCord, and P. McLachlan. (2023). 'Diversity and Violence during Conflict Migration: The Troubles in Northern Ireland'. *Political Science Research and Methods*, 11(3): 451–467. https://doi.org/10.1017/psrm.2022.36

Ahmad, E. (1971). 'Revolutionary War and Counter-Insurgency'. *Journal of International Affairs*: 1–47.

Arjona, A. (2016). *Rebelocracy*. Cambridge: Cambridge University Press. https://doi.org/10.1017/9781316421925

Arjona, A. (2017). 'Civilian Cooperation and Non-cooperation with Non-state Armed Groups: The Centrality of Obedience and Resistance'. *Small Wars & Insurgencies*, 28(4–5): 775–778. https://doi.org/10.1080/09592318.2017.1322328

Arjona, A., N. Kasfir, and Z. C. Mampilly (2016). *Rebel Governance in Civil War*. Cambridge: Cambridge University Press.

Arthur, P., and K. Jeffery (1988). *Northern Ireland since 1968*. 2nd ed. Oxford: Blackwell.

Bakke, K. M., K. G. Cunningham, and L. J. Seymour (2012). 'A Plague of Initials: Fragmentation, Cohesion, and Infighting in Civil Wars'. *Perspectives on Politics*, 10(2): 265–283. https://doi.org/10.1017/S1537592712000667

Bakke, K. M., J. O'Loughlin, G. Toal, and M. D. Ward (2014). 'Convincing State-builders? Disaggregating Internal Legitimacy in Abkhazia'. *International Studies Quarterly*, 58(3): 591–607. https://doi.org/10.1111/isqu.12110

Balcells, L. (2017). *Rivalry and Revenge*. Cambridge: Cambridge University Press. https://doi.org/10.1017/9781316392737

Bar-Tal, D. (2000). 'From Intractable Conflict Through Conflict Resolution to Reconciliation: Psychological Analysis'. *Political Psychology*, 21(2): 351–365. https://doi.org/10.1111/0162-895X.00192

Bateson, R. (2017). 'The Socialization of Civilians and Militia Members: Evidence from Guatemala'. *Journal of Peace Research*, 54(5): 634–647. https://doi.org/10.1177/0022343317721812

Bauer, M., C. Blattman, J. Chytilová, J. Henrich, E. Miguel, and T. Mitts (2016). 'Can War Foster Cooperation?'. *Journal of Economic Perspectives*, 30(3): 249–274. https://doi.org/10.1257/jep.30.3.249

Bean, K. (2012). '"New Dissidents Are But Old Provisionals Writ Large"? the Dynamics of Dissident Republicanism in the New Northern Ireland'. *The Political Quarterly*, 83(2): 210–218. https://doi.org/10.1111/j.1467-923X.2012.02300.x

Bell, J.B. (1997). *The Secret Army: The IRA*. Piscataway, NJ: Transaction Publishers.

Blattman, C. (2009). 'From Violence to Voting: War and Political Participation in Uganda'. *American Political Science Review*, 103(2): 231–247. https://doi.org/10.1017/S0003055409090212

Byrne, J., and N. Jarman (2011). 'Ten Years After Patten: Young People and Policing in Northern Ireland'. *Youth & Society*, 43(2): 433–452. https://doi.org/10.1177/0044118X10383542

Byrne, J., and L. Monaghan (2008). *Policing Loyalist and Republican Communities: Understanding Key Issues for Local Communities and the PSNI*. Belfast: Institute for Conflict Research.

Callaghan, L. (2022). 'Russian "Collaborators" Rounded Up as Ukraine Reasserts Control Over Tense, Divided Region'. *The Times*, 13 November. Available at: https://www.thetimes.co.uk/article/russian-collaborators-rounded-up-as-ukraine-reasserts-control-over-tense-divided-region-d3r28vkgj (accessed 5 December 2022).

Callwell, C. E. (1896). *Small Wars: their Principles and Practice.* London: HM Stationery Office.

Cassar, A., P. Grosjean, and S. Whitt (2013). 'Legacies of Violence: Trust and Market Development.' *Journal of Economic Growth*, 18(3): 285–318. https://doi.org/10.1007/s10887-013-9091-3

Checkel, J. T. (2017). 'Socialization and Violence: Introduction and Framework.' *Journal of Peace Research*, 54(5): 592–605. https://doi.org/10.1177/0022343317721813

Cochrane, M. (2013). 'Security Force Collusion in Northern Ireland 1969–1999: Substance or Symbolism?'. *Studies in Conflict & Terrorism*, 36(1): 77–97. https://doi.org/10.1080/1057610X.2013.739080

Cochrane, M., and R. Monaghan (2012). 'Countering Terrorism Through the Use of Informants: The Northern Ireland Experience.' *Behavioral Sciences of Terrorism and Political Aggression*, 4(1): 26–40. https://doi.org/10.1080/19434472.2011.631346

Coggins, B. L. (2016). 'Rebel Diplomacy: Theorizing Violent Non-state Actors' Strategic Use of Talk.' In A. Arjona, N. Kasfir, and Z. Mampilly (eds), *Rebel Governance in Civil War.* Cambridge: Cambridge University Press. https://doi.org/10.1017/CBO9781316182468.005

Cohen, S. (1972). *Folk Devils and Moral Panics: The Creation of the Mods and Rockers.* Abingdon: MacGibbon and Kee.

Collins, E., and M. McGovern (1998). *Killing Rage.* London: Granta Books.

Cronin, M., and L. O'Callaghan (2015). *A History of Ireland.* Second Edition. London: Bloomsbury.

Daly, S. Z. (2016). *Organized Violence After Civil War: The Geography of Recruitment in Latin America.* Cambridge: Cambridge University Press. https://doi.org/10.1017/CBO9781316412350

Deaux, K., and L. S. Wrightsman (1988). *Social Psychology.* Pacific Grove, CA: Pacific Grove.

Deglow, A. (2022). 'Losing Hearts and Minds: Civil Conflict, Counterinsurgency Policing and Postwar Crime in Insurgent Strongholds.' *Terrorism and Political Violence*, 35(2): 370–389. https://doi.org/10.1080/09546553.2021.1931139

De Juan, A., and J. H. Pierskalla (2016). 'Civil War Violence and Political Trust: Microlevel Evidence from Nepal.' *Conflict Management and Peace Science*, 33(1): 67–88. https://doi.org/10.1177/0738894214544612

De Luca, G., and M. Verpoorten (2015a). 'Civil War, Social Capital and Resilience in Uganda.' *Oxford Economic Papers*, 67(3): 661–686. https://doi.org/10.1093/oep/gpv036

De Luca, G., and M. Verpoorten (2015b). 'Civil War and Political Participation: Evidence from Uganda.' *Economic Development and Cultural Change*, 64(1): 113–141. https://doi.org/10.1086/682957

de Silva, D. S. (2012). *The Report of the Patrick Finucane Review.* London: The Stationery Office.

Downey, J. (1983). *Them and Us.* Dublin: Ward River Press.

Dudai, R. (2012). 'Informers and the Transition in Northern Ireland.' *The British Journal of Criminology*, 52(1): 32–54. https://doi.org/10.1093/bjc/azr055

Dudai, R. (2018). 'Underground Penality: The IRA's Punishment of Informers.' *Punishment & Society*, 20(3): 375–395. https://doi.org/10.1177/1462474517701302

Dudai, R. (2022). *Penalty in the Underground: The IRA's Pursuit of Informers.* Oxford: Oxford University Press. https://doi.org/10.1093/oso/9780198759409.001.0001

Duyvesteyn, I. (2017). 'Rebels & Legitimacy: An Introduction.' *Small Wars & Insurgencies*, 28(4–5): 669–685. https://doi.org/10.1080/09592318.2017.1322337

Eckstein, H. (1975). 'Case Study and Theory in Political Science'. In F. I. Greenstein and N. W. Polsby (eds), *Handbook of Political Science*. Boston, MA: Addison-Wesley.

English, R. (2003). *Armed Struggle: A History of the IRA*. London: Pan Macmillan.

Feenan, D. (2002). 'Researching Paramilitary Violence in Northern Ireland'. *International Journal of Social Research Methodology*, 5(2): 147–163. https://doi.org/10.1080/13645570110045972

Feldman, A. (1991). *Formations of Violence: The Narrative of the Body and Political Terror in Northern Ireland*. Chicago, IL: University of Chicago Press. https://doi.org/10.7208/chicago/9780226240800.001.0001

Fisk, K., and A. Cherney (2017). 'Pathways to Institutional Legitimacy in Postconflict Societies: Perceptions of Process and Performance in Nepal'. *Governance*, 30(2): 263–281. https://doi.org/10.1111/gove.12208

Galula, D. (1964). *Counterinsurgency Warfare: Theory and Practice*. Westport, CT: Praeger Security International.

Gilligan, M. J., E. N. Mvukiyehe, and C. Samii (2013). 'Reintegrating Rebels into Civilian Life: Quasi-experimental Evidence from Burundi'. *Journal of Conflict Resolution*, 57(4): 598–626. https://doi.org/10.1177/0022002712448908

Gilligan, M. J., B. J. Pasquale, and C. Samii (2014). 'Civil War and Social Cohesion: Lab-in-the-Field Evidence from Nepal'. *American Journal of Political Science*, 58(3): 604–619. https://doi.org/10.1111/ajps.12067

Guelke, A. (2007). 'The Northern Ireland Peace Process and the War Against Terrorism: Conflicting Conceptions?'. *Government and Opposition*, 42(3): 272–291. https://doi.org/10.1111/j.1477-7053.2007.00224.x

Hanley, B., and S. Millar (2010). *The Lost Revolution: The Story of the Official IRA and the Workers' Party*. London: Penguin UK.

Hewstone, M., E. Cairns, A. Voci, J. Hamberger, and U. Niens (2006). 'Intergroup Contact, Forgiveness, and Experience of "the Troubles" in Northern Ireland'. *Journal of Social Issues*, 62(1): 99–120. https://doi.org/10.1111/j.1540-4560.2006.00441.x

Huang, R. (2016). 'Rebel Diplomacy in Civil War'. *International Security*, 40(4): 89–126. https://doi.org/10.1162/ISEC_a_00237

Imai, K., L. Keele, and D. Tingley. (2010). 'A General Approach to Causal Mediation Analysis'. *Psychological Methods*, 15(4): 309–334. https://doi.org/10.1037/a0020761

Imai, K., L. Keele, and T. Yamamoto. (2010). 'Identification, Inference and Sensitivity Analysis for Causal Mediation Effects'. *Statistical Science*, 25(1): 51–71. https://doi.org/10.1214/10-STS321

Jarman, N. (1998). 'Painting Landscapes: The Place of Murals in the Symbolic Construction of Urban Space'. In A. Buckley (ed.), *Symbols in Northern Ireland*. Belfast: Institute of Irish Studies, Queen's University.

Kalyvas, S. N. (2006). *The Logic of Violence in Civil War*. Cambridge: Cambridge University Press. https://doi.org/10.1017/CBO9780511818462

Kilcullen, D. (2010). *Counterinsurgency*. Oxford: Oxford University Press.

Kirk-Smith, M., and J. Dingley (2009). 'Countering Terrorism in Northern Ireland: The Role of Intelligence'. *Small Wars & Insurgencies*, 20(3–4): 551–573. https://doi.org/10.1080/09592310903027132

Kitson, F. (1971). *Low Intensity Operations*. London: Faber and Faber.

Khurshudyan, I., and K. Hrabchuk (2022). 'Stealthy Kherson Resistance Fighters Undermined Russian Occupying Forces'. *The Washington Post*, 18 November. Available at: https://www.washingtonpost.com/world/2022/11/18/kherson-resistance-partisans-russia-occupation/ (accessed 5 December 2022).

Lake, D. A. (2010). 'Building Legitimate States After Civil Wars'. In C. Hartzelll and M. Hoddie (eds), *Strengthening Peace in Post-civil War States: Transforming Spoilers into Stakeholders*. Chicago, IL: University of Chicago Press. https://doi.org/10.7208/chicago/9780226351261.003.0002

Lake, D. A., and D. Rothchild (1996). 'Containing Fear: The Origins and Management of Ethnic Conflict'. *International Security*, 21(2): 41–75. https://doi.org/10.1162/isec.21.2.41

Leahy, T. (2020). *The Intelligence War Against the IRA*. Cambridge: Cambridge University Press. https://doi.org/10.1017/9781108767033

Loyle, C. E. (2021). 'Rebel Justice During Armed Conflict'. *Journal of Conflict Resolution*, 65(1): 108–134. https://doi.org/10.1177/0022002720939299

Loyle, C. E., K. G. Cunningham, R. Huang, and D. F. Jung (2023). 'New Directions in Rebel Governance Research'. *Perspectives on Politics*, 21(1): 264–276. https://doi.org/10.1017/S1537592721001985

Loyle, C. E., and I. B. Onder. (2023). 'The Legacies of Rebel Rule in Southeast Turkey'. *Comparative Political Studies*, 57(11): 1771–1803. https://doi.org/10.1177/00104140231204223

Mampilly, Z. C. (2011). *Rebel Rulers*. Ithaca, NY: Cornell University Press.

Matchett, W. (2016). *Secret Victory: The Intelligence War that Beat the IRA*. Otley: WRM Consultancy Limited.

Maoz, I. (2011). 'Does Contact Work in Protracted Asymmetrical Conflict? Appraising 20 Years of Reconciliation-aimed Encounters Between Israeli Jews and Palestinians'. *Journal of Peace Research*, 48(1): 115–125. https://doi.org/10.1177/0022343310389506

McColl, R.W. (1969). 'The Insurgent State: Territorial Bases of Revolution'. *Annals of the Association of American Geographers*, 59(4): 613–631. https://doi.org/10.1111/j.1467-8306.1969.tb01803.x

McGarry, J., and B. O'Leary. (1995). *Explaining Northern Ireland: Broken Images*. Hoboken, NJ: Wiley-Blackwell.

McGovern, M. (2016). 'Informers, Agents and the Liberal Ideology of Collusion in Northern Ireland'. *Critical Studies on Terrorism*, 9(2): 292–311. https://doi.org/10.1080/17539153.2016.1175274

McKeown, M. (2009). 'Post-Mortem: An Examination of the Patterns of Politically Associated Violence in Northern Ireland'. Conflict Archive on the Internet (CAIN). http://cain.ulst.ac.uk/victims/mckeown/mckeown01.pdf (accessed 5 December 2022).

McWeeney, M., K. G. Cunningham, and L. Bauer. (2023). 'Rebel Actors and Legitimacy Building'. *International Politics*, 62: 269–290. https://doi.org/10.1057/s41311-023-00493-1

Melaugh, M. (2023). 'Text of Irish Republican Army (IRA) "Green Book" (Book I and II)'. Conflict Archive on the Internet (CAIN). Available at https://cain.ulster.ac.uk/othelem/organ/ira/ira_green_book.htm.

Mitchell, N.J. (2004). *Agents of Atrocity: Leaders, Followers and Violation of Human Rights in Civil Wars*. London: Palgrave Macmillan. https://doi.org/10.1057/9781403973696

Monaghan, R., and S. McLaughlin (2006). 'Informal Justice in the City'. *Space and Polity*, 10(2): 171–186. https://doi.org/10.1080/13562570600921667

Murphy, J. (2015). 'Tracking Change in Northern Ireland Policing: Temporal Phases and Key Themes'. *Policing: An International Journal of Police Strategies and Management*, 38(1): 117–131.

NIMDM. (2017). *Northern Ireland Multiple Deprivation Measure 2017*. Belfast: The Northern Ireland Statistics and Research Agency (NISRA). https://www.nisra.gov.uk/statistics/deprivation/northern-ireland-multiple-deprivation-measure-2017-nimdm2017

Noor, M., R. J. Brown, and G. Prentice (2008). 'Precursors and Mediators of Intergroup Reconciliation in Northern Ireland: a New Model'. *British Journal of Social Psychology*, 47(3): 481–495. https://doi.org/10.1348/014466607X238751

Nussio, E., and B. Oppenheim (2014). 'Anti-social Capital in Former Members of Non-state Armed Groups: A Case Study of Colombia'. *Studies in Conflict & Terrorism*, 37(12): 999–1023. https://doi.org/10.1080/1057610X.2014.962438

O'Dochartaigh, N. (2005). *From Civil Rights to Armalites: Derry and the Birth of the Irish Troubles*. London: Palgrave Macmillan. https://doi.org/10.1057/9780230006041

Parkinson, S. E. (2013). 'Organizing Rebellion: Rethinking High-risk Mobilization and Social Networks in War'. *American Political Science Review*, 107(3): 418–432. https://doi.org/10.1017/S0003055413000208

Podder, S. (2017). 'Understanding the Legitimacy of Armed Groups: A Relational Perspective'. *Small Wars & Insurgencies*, 28(4–5): 686–708. https://doi.org/10.1080/09592318.2017.1322333

PSNI (Police Service of Northern Ireland) (2021). *Police Recorded Security Situation Statistics*. Belfast: Northern Ireland Statistics and Research Agency (NISRA).

Revkin, M. R. (2021). 'Competitive Governance and Displacement Decisions Under Rebel Rule: Evidence from the Islamic State in Iraq'. *Journal of Conflict Resolution*, 65(1): 46–80. https://doi.org/10.1177/0022002720951864

Rickard, K., G., Hollenweger, S. Weber, and K. M. Bakke (2025). 'Contentious Rituals and Intergroup Relations: Parading in Northern Ireland'. *British Journal of Political Science*, 55(e135): 1–25. https://doi.org/10.1017/S0007123425100835

Rickard, K., and K. M. Bakke (2021). 'Legacies of Wartime Order: Punishment Attacks and Social Control in Northern Ireland'. *Security Studies*, 30(4): 603–636. https://doi.org/10.1080/09636412.2021.1976822

Ringdal, G. I., K. Ringdal, and A. Simkus (2007). 'War-related Distress Among Kosovar Albanians'. *Journal of Loss and Trauma*, 13(1): 59–71. https://doi.org/10.1080/15325020701741781

Roeder, P. G., and D. S. Rothchild (2005). *Sustainable Peace: Power and Democracy After Civil Wars*. Ithaca, NY: Cornell University Press.

Rohner, D., M. Thoenig, and F. Zilibotti (2013). 'Seeds of Distrust: Conflict in Uganda'. *Journal of Economic Growth*, 18(3): 217–252. https://doi.org/10.1007/s10887-013-9093-1

Rolston, B. (2003). 'Changing the Political Landscape: Murals and Transition in Northern Ireland-. *Irish Studies Review*, 11(1): 3–16.

Rolston, B. (2005). '"An Effective Mask for Terror": Democracy, Death Squads and Northern Ireland'. *Crime, Law and Social Change*, 44(2): 181–203. https://doi.org/10.1007/s10611-006-9007-7

Sanders, A. (2011). *Inside the IRA: Dissident Republicans and the War for Legitimacy*. Edinburgh: Edinburgh University Press. https://doi.org/10.1515/9780748646043

Shuttleworth, I. G. and C. D. Lloyd. (2009). 'Are Northern Ireland's Communities Dividing? Evidence from Geographically Consistent Census of Population Data, 1971–2001'. *Environment and Planning A: Economy and Space*, 41(1): 213–229. https://doi.org/10.1068/a40163

Sivakumaran, S. (2009). 'Courts of Armed Opposition Groups: Fair Trials or Summary Justice?'. *Journal of International Criminal Justice*, 7(3): 489–513. https://doi.org/10.1093/jicj/mqp039

Silke, A. (1998). 'Motives of Paramilitary Vigilantism in Northern Ireland'. *Low Intensity Conflict & Law Enforcement*, 7(2): 121–156.

Silke, A. (1999a). 'Rebel's Dilemma: The Changing Relationship Between the IRA, Sinn Féin and Paramilitary Vigilantism in Northern Ireland'. *Terrorism and Political Violence*, 11(1): 55–93. https://doi.org/10.1080/09546559908427495

Silke, A. (1999b). 'Ragged Justice: Loyalist Vigilantism in Northern Ireland'. *Terrorism and Political Violence*, 11(3): 1–31. https://doi.org/10.1080/09546559908427514

Sluka, J. A. (1989). *Hearts and Minds, Water and Fish: Support for the IRA and INLA in a Northern Irish Ghetto*. Stamford, CT: Jai Press.

Soule, J. W. (1989). 'Problems in Applying Counterterrorism to Prevent Terrorism: Two Decades of Violence in Northern Ireland Reconsidered'. *Studies in Conflict & Terrorism*, 12(1): 31–46. https://doi.org/10.1080/10576108908435759

Staniland, P. (2012). 'States, Insurgents, and Wartime Political Orders'. *Perspectives on Politics*, 10(2): 243–264. https://doi.org/10.1017/S1537592712000655

Steele, A. (2017). *Democracy and Displacement in Colombia's Civil War*. Ithaca, NY: Cornell University Press.

Stewart, M. A. (2018). 'Civil War as State-making: Strategic Governance in Civil War'. *International Organization*, 72(1): 205–226.

Stewart, M. A. (2021). *Governing for Revolution: Social Transformation in Civil War*. Cambridge: Cambridge University Press. https://doi.org/10.1017/9781108919555

Stubbs, R. (2011). 'From Search and Destroy to Hearts and Minds: the Evolution of British Strategy in Malaya 1948–60'. In D. Marston and C. Malkasian (eds), *Counterinsurgency in Modern Warfare*. London: Bloomsbury Publishing.

Taylor, P. (2014). *The Provos: The IRA and Sinn Fein*. London: A&C Black.

Terpstra, N., and G. Frerks (2017). 'Rebel Governance and Legitimacy: Understanding the Impact of Rebel Legitimation on Civilian Compliance with the LTTE rule'. *Civil Wars* 19(3): 279–307.

Thompson, S. R. (1966). *Defeating Communist Insurgency*. Westport, CT: F.A. Praeger.

Todd, J. (2011). 'Public Opinion and Persuasion'. In A. Aughey and C. Gormley (eds), *The Anglo-Irish Agreement: Rethinking its Legacy*. Manchester: Manchester University Press.

Toolis, K. (1995). *Rebel Hearts: Journeys within the IRA's Soul*. London: Picador.

Topping, J., and J. Byrne (2012). 'Paramilitary Punishments in Belfast: Policing Beneath the Peace'. *Behavioral Sciences of Terrorism and Political Aggression*, 4(1): 41–59. https://doi.org/10.1080/19434472.2011.631349

Trew, K. (1986). 'Catholic-Protestant Contact in Northern Ireland'. In M. Hewstone and R. Brown (eds), *Contact and Conflict in Intergroup Encounters*. Oxford: Basil Blackwell.

Walden, J., and Y. M. Zhukov (2020). 'Historical Legacies of Political violence'. *Oxford Research Encyclopedia of Politics*.

Walter, B. F. (2002). *Committing to Peace: The Successful Settlement of Civil Wars*. Princeton, NJ: Princeton University Press.

Weber, M. (1958). 'Politics As a Vocation'. In H. H. Gerth and C. W. Mills (Trans.), *Essays in Sociology*. Oxford: Oxford University Press

Weingast, B. R. (1998). 'Constructing Trust: The Political and Economic Roots of Ethnic and Regional Conflict'. In V. Haufler, K. Soltan, and E. Uslaner (eds), *Institutions and Social Order*. Ann Arbor, MI: University of Michigan Press.

Wickham-Crowley, T. P. (1992). *Guerrillas and Revolution in Latin America: a Comparative Study of Insurgents and Regimes Since 1956*. Princeton, NJ: Princeton University Press.

Williams, E. Leah., and T. Leahy (2023). 'The 'Unforgivable'?: Irish Republican Army (IRA) Informers and Dealing with Northern Ireland Conflict Legacy, 1969-2021'. *Intelligence and National Security* 38(3): 470–490.

Wong, P. H. (2016). 'How Can Political Trust Be Built After Civil Wars? Evidence from Post-conflict Sierra Leone'. *Journal of Peace Research*, 53(6): 772–785. https://doi.org/10.1177/0022343316659334

Wood, E. J. (2008). 'The Social Processes of Civil War: The Wartime Transformation of Social Networks'. *Annual Review of Political Science*, 11: 539–561. https://doi.org/10.1146/annurev.polisci.8.082103.104832

6

Killing for control

How drug traffickers capture the state and expand their criminal economies

Roxana Gutiérrez-Romero

6.1 Introduction

Drug trafficking organizations (DTOs) have not merely expanded their geographic reach; they have embedded themselves within the political and economic fabric of many nations.[1] These groups systematically infiltrate state institutions—co-opting politicians, military leaders, customs agents, border patrol officers, and prosecutors, among many others. By co-opting these key actors, they repurpose state structures to consolidate control over critical zones essential for resource extraction and their broader strategic objectives. Mexico offers a compelling case study of how this weaponization of governance exacerbates violence and instability. Since the onset of the militarized 'war on drugs' in 2006, the country has seen over 350,000 homicides as criminal groups continue to dispute territory amid mounting enforcement pressures. These groups have also diversified their operations into extortion, human trafficking, oil theft, and small-scale drug trafficking, among many other crimes, as documented in several earlier studies (Battiston et al. 2024; Magaloni et al. 2020; Moncada 2022; Trejo and Ley 2020). However, a particularly underexplored driver of this crisis is the surge of political violence—a phenomenon with profound implications for governance and public policy, analysed here.

Over 500 politicians have been assassinated in Mexico since 2000, with most killings occurring in recent years (Gutiérrez-Romero and Iturbe 2024). Earlier studies had documented only a fraction of these assassinations, focusing on the onset of the war on drugs. These studies attributed these earlier cases to inter-cartel rivalries, self-defence, cartel territorial disputes, or refusals by politicians to share municipal tax revenues with drug cartels (Blume 2017; Hernández Huerta

[1] I acknowledge funding from the United Nations University World Institute for Development Economics Research and the Global Challenges Research Fund (RE-CL-2021-01). I also thank the United Nations Office on Drugs and Crime for providing access to satellite data on sampling areas where opium poppy crops are present.

Roxana Gutiérrez-Romero, *Killing for control*. In: *Institutional Legacies of Violent Conflict*. Edited by: Patricia Justino, Oxford University Press. © United Nations University World Institute for Development Economics Research (UNU-WIDER) (2026). DOI: 10.1093/9780197904077.003.0006

2020; Ponce et al. 2022; Trejo and Ley 2021). However, my recent work has demonstrated that, over the last two decades (2000–2021), the political assassinations have been closely tied to the rent-seeking and retaliatory violence strategies used by DTOs (Gutiérrez-Romero and Iturbe 2024). These patterns are particularly evident in the targeting of political candidates in municipalities near oil pipelines, which are vital to DTOs involved in gasoline theft and criminal governance. Incumbent mayors, serving as heads of local police forces often co-opted by DTOs, are especially vulnerable to retaliation following the arrests or killings of organized crime members. Former mayors, too, face significant risks, likely stemming from their past associations with criminally strategic regions.

Building on these earlier insights, here I develop and empirically test a theory of criminal territorial governance, revealing how DTOs use targeted strategies to capture state authority. By subverting electoral processes and deploying retaliatory violence—including the assassinations of politicians and their families—these organizations manipulate national security policies to serve and diversify their criminal interests. In doing so, they consolidate their criminal and economic control over state institutions and local communities. To uncover the causal mechanisms behind these dynamics, I use an instrumental variable approach, moving beyond anecdotal accounts to analyse the impact of government crackdowns on DTOs' strategies.

The analysis contributes to the literature on criminal governance in three significant ways. First, it provides compelling evidence of how DTOs deploy retaliatory violence to respond to state actions that threaten their survival. Beyond the visible assassinations of politicians, DTOs orchestrate broader campaigns of intimidation targeting the families and close collaborators of political figures. Drawing on a comprehensive database of political violence, I analyse the assassinations of 156 family members of politicians and 19 close collaborators between 2000 and 2021, where the intent was to send a message to the politicians themselves.

Second, the findings reveal the counterintuitive effects of crackdowns on organized crime on voter turnout and party loyalty during 2000–2021. Arrests and killings of organized crime members by authorities escalate lethal violence against politicians, their families, and close collaborators. In contrast, the destruction of drug laboratories or illicit crops provokes non-lethal intimidation directed at local politicians. Despite these acts of violence and coercion, both types of crackdowns result in increased voter turnout, with drug destruction in particular bolstering support for incumbents, reflecting public approval of state efforts to combat organized crime. However, areas with clear evidence of opium poppy cultivation, as identified through satellite data, show lower voter participation, suggesting that dependency on illicit economies may suppress civic engagement.

Finally, I propose the crime diversification hypothesis. This argues that once DTOs adapt to enforcement pressures and co-opt local authorities to establish their criminal governance, they strategically diversify their criminal operations to maximize profitability. I show that extortion, small-scale drug trafficking, and disappearances increasingly mark this shift; yet their distribution is far from random or generalized across the country. These forms of violence and coercion are more concentrated in regions where resources offer strategic opportunities for extraction. Areas near oil pipelines used for oil theft have become centres of criminal innovation, reflecting calculated adaptation.

Paradoxically, as DTOs expand into fuel theft and extortion, other illicit activities may decline as a calculated strategy. An example of this is car theft, which has declined nationally by 34% since its peak in 2018—unlikely as a result of improved law enforcement but rather because DTOs have prioritized other crimes. Stealing vehicles would undermine the demand for gasoline—critical to their profits—making it strategically advantageous to suppress car theft in areas where fuel theft dominates.

This analysis then traces the full cycle of criminal governance. It demonstrates how DTOs co-opt government officials and law enforcement to influence policies and protect their operations. When these arrangements are disrupted by state actions—such as arrests and drug eradications—DTOs retaliate with political violence to maintain control. While civilians are not the primary targets of such political violence, they endure its lasting effects: rising crime, weakened institutions, and the deep integration of criminal networks into local governance.

6.2 Towards a theory of criminal governance

At the core of DTOs' governance strategies lies a calculated equilibrium between bribery (*plata*) and coercive violence (*plomo*). These tactics, as theorized by a few studies already, are not mutually exclusive but complementary (Alesina et al. 2019; Dal Bó et al. 2006). DTOs deploy them based on local conditions, balancing incentives and threats to achieve compliance. In regions where state institutions are functional but fragile, bribery often takes precedence.

However, bribery loses its efficacy in competitive environments, when political actors resist co-operation, or when state interventions directly threaten DTOs' operations. Political violence often escalates around election periods (Alesina et al. 2019). Criminal organizations aim to influence candidate selection by forming alliances with favourable candidates or intimidating rivals through coercive tactics. The primary goal of this pre-electoral violence is to gain control over the incoming government and its policies (Daniele and Dipoppa 2017; Durán-Martínez 2008; Ponce et al. 2022). Additionally, post-electoral violence can serve as a means of coercion against politicians who do not uphold previous agreements or who take actions that threaten the interests of the criminal organizations (Dal Bó et al. 2006).

6.2.1 Drivers and targets of political violence

Alongside bribes, DTOs also strategically deploy targeted intimidation. As I argued in an earlier co-authored article (Gutiérrez-Romero and Iturbe 2024), DTOs use political violence in Mexico primarily targeting local political actors—candidates, incumbent mayors, and former officials—for two main reasons. First, *rent-seeking violence* is deployed to secure access to high-value resources. In Mexico, regions surrounding oil pipelines have become focal points for large-scale fuel theft, a criminal enterprise that generates profits rivalling those of narcotics trafficking. In these areas, DTOs seek to influence electoral outcomes by coercing or eliminating candidates who threaten their access to lucrative rents.

Second, *retaliatory violence* is used to punish political actions that disrupt DTOs' operations. Incumbent mayors, who serve as the heads of municipal police forces, are particularly vulnerable. DTOs systematically bribe municipal police forces, co-opting them not just to evade detection but to turn them into enforcers of their criminal agendas. This entanglement between local law enforcement and organized crime amplifies the strategic value of mayors. Despite their pivotal roles in local governance, mayors lack meaningful authority over state or federal security strategies, making them expendable targets whose removal sends a powerful message while minimizing federal repercussions. Their assassinations serve a dual purpose: warning higher-level officials of the costs of opposing DTOs while targeting lower-ranking officials whose deaths rarely provoke significant federal consequences.

Here, I extend the earlier retaliatory violence hypothesis by providing new evidence on the strategic targeting of politicians. Political assassinations are only the most visible aspect of DTOs' intimidation. More subtle forms of coercion, such as threats, attacks on families, and public humiliation, are often used to enforce compliance while avoiding public scrutiny. A critical question is what conditions drive DTOs to escalate from non-lethal intimidation to lethal violence.

I hypothesize that the scale of economic losses suffered by DTOs determines the intensity of their responses. Minor disruptions, such as localized revenue losses derived from the destruction of illegal drugs, are likely to result in non-lethal intimidation aimed at political actors. In contrast, existential threats—such as the arrest or killing of DTO members—provoke lethal violence, targeting not only politicians but also their families and close collaborators as both retaliation and a deterrent to future interference.

6.2.2 Impact of criminal governance on voting behaviour

Electoral manipulation often includes the use of violence directed at voters. In earlier work, I hypothesized that organized crime in Mexico uses a cost-effectiveness strategy during elections by targeting politicians rather than civilians.

Violence against civilians to influence elections is risky; it undermines electoral legitimacy and destabilizes the political arrangements criminal actors rely on. Moreover, the secrecy of the ballot makes direct voter intimidation both costly and inefficient. As a result, DTOs focus on controlling the candidate pool, coercing or eliminating rivals while supporting candidates aligned with their interests. This strategy allows criminal organizations to exert influence over governance without the widespread disruption associated with voter manipulation. This mechanism explains the negligible impact of political violence on voter turnout during elections from 2000 to 2021 (Gutiérrez-Romero and Iturbe 2024).

Here, I show other ways in which organized crime can affect elections. For instance, voters in regions tied to opium poppy cultivation may perceive that the contest for power is resolved long before ballots are cast, rendering elections symbolic rather than decisive. This perception can undermine the perceived effectiveness of voting and ultimately be reflected in lower voter turnout. The results section provides evidence of this dynamic.

6.2.3 Criminal diversification

The ultimate objective of criminal governance extends beyond dominating the narcotics trade; it seeks to embed itself within local economies and political systems as part of a broader strategy of territorial control and governance. This involves the systematic use of coercion, including the assassination of politicians, to secure control over lucrative rents. Once these criminal cells have consolidated their criminal governance, they will diversify their activities to sustain profitability and territorial exploitation. This diversification is visible in their expansion of multiple crimes, including *narcomenudeo* (local drug retail) and extortion.

Extortion, in particular, has become a cornerstone of DTOs' revenue model. Through *pago de piso* (protection payments), DTOs impose taxes on businesses, agricultural producers, and households. Far from being isolated acts of opportunism, these practices constitute a system of economic extraction that integrates DTOs into the everyday economic life of the territories they govern across several countries in Latin America (Moncada 2022). Other examples include the imposition of 'shadow taxes' by mafias in Sicily, the control of natural resources such as diamonds by rebel groups in Africa, and the taxation of agricultural producers in Colombia (Balletta and Lavezzi 2023; Gambetta 1996; Olsson 2007; Vélez-Torres and Méndez 2022).

Crime diversification, however, is not arbitrary; it reflects a strategic geographic logic. In the crime diversification hypothesis I advance, DTOs prioritize regions critical to their operations. In the Mexican case, these are areas surrounding oil pipelines, which serve as hubs for large-scale fuel theft. These regions offer significant logistical and economic advantages, enabling DTOs to maximize economies of scale and deepen territorial control.

Crime diversification often leads to a reallocation of resources, resulting in the suppression of some crimes to stabilize higher-return activities. Evidence of this diversification and simultaneous displacement of crime is presented in the following sections.

6.3 Setting: from modest narcotics player to leading smuggler

Mexico's narcotics trade emerged from humble beginnings, rooted in marijuana farming and small-scale opium production. Today, Mexican DTOs have evolved into global enterprises, controlling complex supply chains. These criminal organizations have not functioned entirely outside the state; rather, they have forged alliances with state institutions to entrench and expand their power. Under the Partido Revolucionario Institucional's (PRI; Institutional Revolutionary Party) dominance (1929–2000), this arrangement consisted of DTOs paying bribes to state actors and operating within tacit boundaries, thereby minimizing public violence and respecting territorial divisions. In return, the PRI ensured non-interference and enforced adherence to these informal rules.

This '*pax mafiosa*', however, was neither stable nor durable. External shocks, such as US-led anti-drug campaigns in the 1960s, revealed its fragility. Efforts to eradicate opium and marijuana cultivation in Mexico's Golden Triangle disrupted established networks, forcing traffickers to decentralize their operations into other regions such as Guadalajara. By the 1980s, changes in the global cocaine trade, spurred by US enforcement crackdowns in the Caribbean, elevated Mexico to a central position in the supply chain. Mexican DTOs became indispensable intermediaries, using tunnels, vehicles, and even light aircraft and submarines to outmanoeuvre authorities.

The resulting influx of wealth empowered DTOs to reshape their relationships with the state. No longer limited to bribing local officials, traffickers began bypassing traditional networks, paying direct 'taxes' to key figures within political and enforcement hierarchies (Hernández 2014: 69). This consolidation of influence further blurred the boundaries between criminal enterprise and state authority, entrenching DTOs as key players within Mexico's political economy.

6.3.1 Fragmentation and adaptation

In the late 1990s, the democratization process, marked by the rise of competitive political parties, fragmented the state's capacity to manage its relationships with DTOs. What had once been a system of negotiated coexistence gave way to one of violent contestation. The 2000 presidential victory of Vicente Fox of the Partido Acción Nacional (PAN; National Action Party) further disrupted the dynamics with DTOs. The gradual fragmentation of political power weakened the coordination between federal, state, and municipal governments, leaving criminal organizations without the predictable system of patronage and control.

Felipe Calderón's contested 2006 presidential election marked a turning point in Mexico's criminal economy. Facing a legitimacy crisis after his polarizing victory, Calderón declared a war on drugs, framing it as a state-building effort to reassert authority over contested territories. Backed by the US-funded Mérida Initiative, his administration deployed the military to target cartel leadership. However, this decapitation strategy splintered the cartels, creating factions that fought for control over increasingly contested criminal economies. The rise of the Zetas, composed of elite military defectors, epitomized this transformation. Their reliance on militarized tactics, extreme violence, and psychological warfare changed the dynamics of organized crime. The backlash of militarization is evident in the trend of homicide rates. In 2006, Mexico stood out as one of the safest countries in the Americas, with a homicide rate of less than 10 per 100,000 inhabitants (Wainwright 2017). By 2012, that figure had more than doubled.

DTOs expanded even further under the administration of Enrique Peña Nieto from the PRI. He temporarily reduced the arrests and killings of major drug kingpins. However, overall, there was a continued decline in the arrests of members of organized crime, broadly defined. This trend appeared to have temporarily reduced homicide rates, but soon the violence returned with a vengeance. The surge of violence, as explained in the next section, was driven by policy reforms to gasoline prices, which drew DTOs into large-scale oil theft operations.

6.3.2 Criminal innovation and predation

The rise of large-scale oil theft, commonly referred to as *huachicol*, stands as one of the most striking examples of criminal diversification by DTOs, evolving into a central pillar of their operations.

Decades of corruption, underinvestment, and declining oil production weakened the production capacity of Petróleos Mexicanos (PEMEX), Mexico's state-owned energy giant and major contributor to public finances. Felipe Calderón's administration introduced gradual fuel subsidy reductions, framed as necessary for fiscal stability. Enrique Peña Nieto's 2013 constitutional reforms liberalized the energy market, allowing private investment and moving fuel prices closer to global benchmarks. By 2015, domestic fuel prices began to unexpectedly rise more frequently, culminating in the 2017 *gasolinazo*, when gasoline prices spiked by up to 20%, triggering widespread protests.

Attracted by the profitability of the market, DTOs capitalized on PEMEX's vulnerabilities, bribing employees to access pipeline maps and schedules and securing protection from local officials. The Cártel Jalisco Nueva Generación (CJNG; Jalisco New Generation Cartel) emerged as a dominant player, using violence to control pipeline routes and eliminate competitors. The CJNG's aggressive expansion into states like Puebla, Querétaro, Hidalgo, and Guanajuato brought it into direct conflict with local criminals, and the Cártel de Santa Rosa de Lima.

There are no fine-grained data on oil theft in Mexico, but the government has released information on the number of clandestine taps detected in pipelines used to extract gasoline and diesel. These taps reveal a sharp, organized response by DTOs, who quickly moved their operations towards fuel theft after the onset of the war on drugs (Gutiérrez-Romero and Iturbe 2024). It is estimated that about 90% of stolen fuel is distributed to local gas stations and local companies, while only about 10% is sold directly to individual customers (Stevenson 2017).

The 2018 presidential election of Andrés Manuel López Obrador (AMLO), representing the newly formed Morena party, brought renewed attention to Mexico's ongoing crisis of violence. He promised to reduce violence with his 'hugs, not bullets' policy, emphasizing social programmes over military confrontation with DTOs. His policy appeared to aim at establishing another *pax mafiosa*, but it backfired. The ultimate failure of his six-year administration is demonstrated in the nearly 200,000 homicides officially recorded, making it the deadliest administration in modern Mexican history.

Another failure of AMLO's administration was its inability to curtail oil theft. Despite early efforts, such as shutting down pipelines and deploying military personnel to safeguard vital infrastructure, oil theft persisted and even expanded to an industrial scale. Criminal networks reportedly reaped annual revenues of approximately $5.2 billion from this activity (Arzate 2023). The proliferation of oil theft contributed to broader changes in criminal dynamics.

Analysing long-term trends in crime is complicated, as municipal-level data in Mexico have only been systematically available since 2015 for most crimes due to methodological changes. Despite these limitations, there are some notable patterns. Retail drug sales (*narcomenudeo*) have offered DTOs a reliable source of income as they moved beyond exclusive dependence on US-bound narcotics (Figure 6.1.a). Methamphetamines, fentanyl, and new synthetic drugs have flooded neighbourhoods both in the United States and Mexico.

As shown in Figure 6.1.b, overdose deaths, although still relatively low in Mexico, have been rising since the onset of the war on drugs, with a noticeable acceleration in recent years. This trend points to an increasing prevalence of domestic drug consumption.

Extortion became another pillar of economic diversification (Figure 6.1.a). In Michoacán, DTOs turned agriculture into a captive industry. Avocado, berry, and lemon farmers faced demands at every stage of production: planting, harvesting, and transportation. These commodities rank among Mexico's most profitable agricultural exports, making them prime targets for organized crime. This form of extortion has extended to other regions, leaving entire sectors vulnerable to coercion.

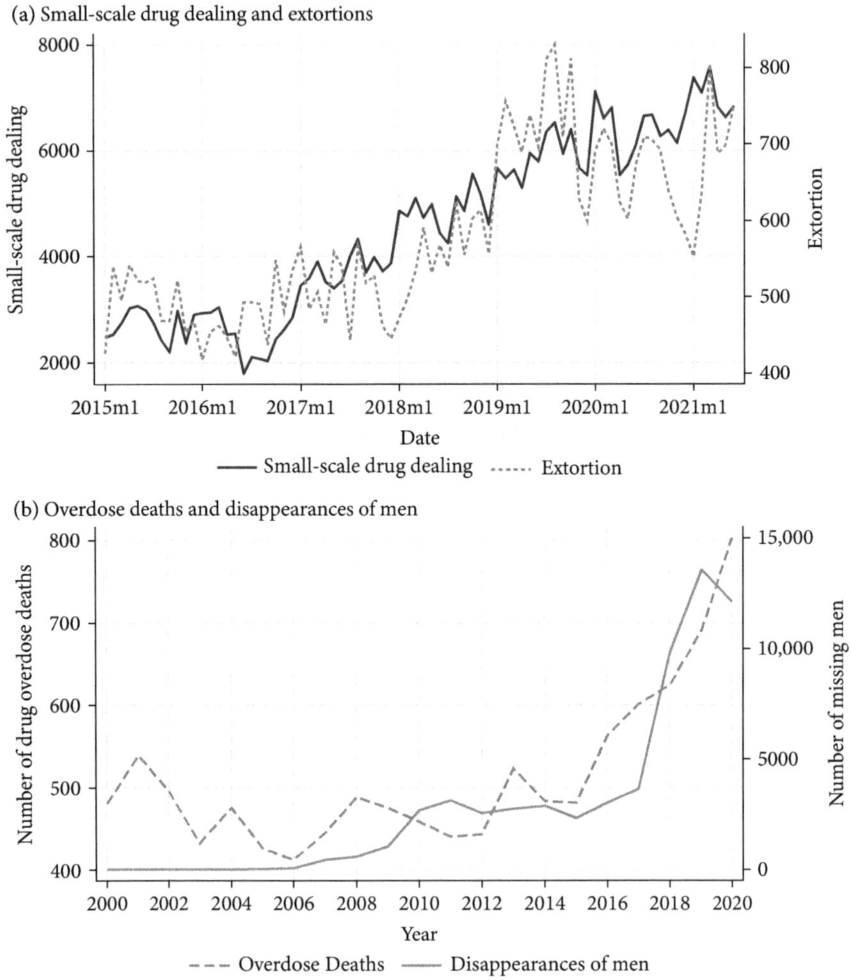

Figure 6.1 Rise of other crimes, overdose deaths, and disappearances of men

Source: Author's estimates based on data from Secretariado Ejecutivo del Sistema Nacional de Seguridad Pública (2024) and the Registro Nacional de Personas Desaparecidas y No Localizadas (2022).

The reach of criminal organizations into the local economy created a shadow system of governance that operated with brutal efficiency. One of the most troubling consequences has been the dramatic rise in disappearances. Over 70% of the 117,000 officially reported disappearances involve young adult men, with cases soaring since 2018 (Figure 6.1.b).[2]

[2] Women account for 30% of disappearances, often driven by a wider range of motives, including domestic violence and femicides. I explore this issue in greater depth in a separate study (Gutiérrez-Romero 2024b).

6.3.3 The dynamics of political violence

In parallel with crime, political violence grew. During the 1980s and 1990s, political violence included some isolated and targeted political assassinations of members of opposition groups, particularly in Michoacán (Calderón Molgóra 1994). The dynamics of political violence radically changed with the onset of the war on drugs.

To gain a deeper understanding of political violence, I use the 'Political Assassinations, Intimidation and Actors in Mexico' (PAIAMEX) dataset—a project co-authored in an earlier study (Gutiérrez-Romero and Iturbe 2024). Covering the years from 2000 to 2021, it primarily integrates media reports that document political assassinations and non-lethal forms of intimidation against politicians.

Unlike the sporadic political violence of earlier decades, PAIAMEX reveals a distinct pattern: political assassinations are deliberate tools of governance. Figure 6.2 illustrates the stark distribution of victims, overwhelmingly composed of mayors in office, former mayors, and municipal candidates. PAIAMEX also reveals both overt political violence and the subtler mechanisms of intimidation that sustain control. Between January 2000 and June 2021, 156 relatives and 19 close collaborators of politicians were murdered, often in their presence, delivering chilling warnings designed to enforce compliance. Additionally, the database records 281 instances of non-lethal intimidation directly targeting politicians.

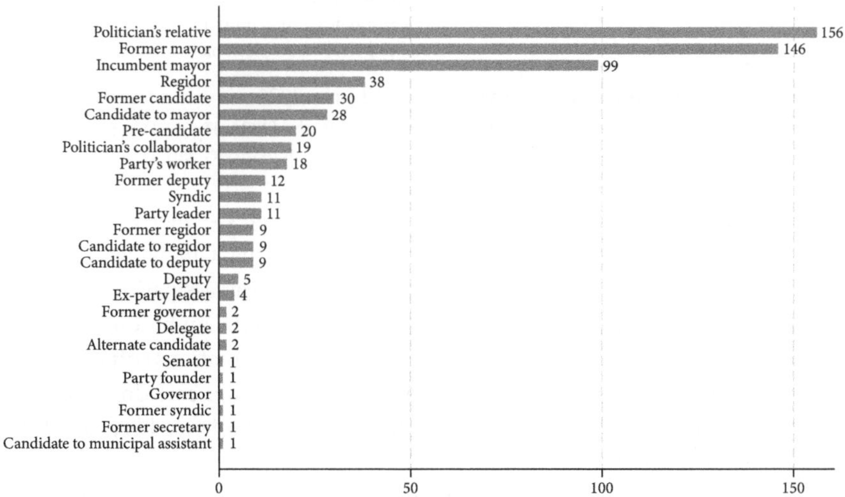

Figure 6.2 Political assassinations in Mexico, January 2000 to June 2021, PAIAMEX

Source: Author's estimates based on data from PAIAMEX, collected by Gutiérrez-Romero and Iturbe (2024).

To my knowledge, no individual has been held accountable for these crimes. However, over 80% of the assassinations were carried out using high-calibre firearms—a signature of organized crime's methods—frequently executed by convoys of heavily armed operatives.

The evolution of political assassinations provides further evidence of the involvement of criminal organizations (Figure 6.3). Political assassinations rose sharply in the mid-2000s, aligning with the intensification of Mexico's drug war. As documented in Gutiérrez-Romero and Iturbe (2024) initially, opposition politicians were disproportionately targeted, reflecting their lack of state protection. Over time, however, figures from all major parties became vulnerable.

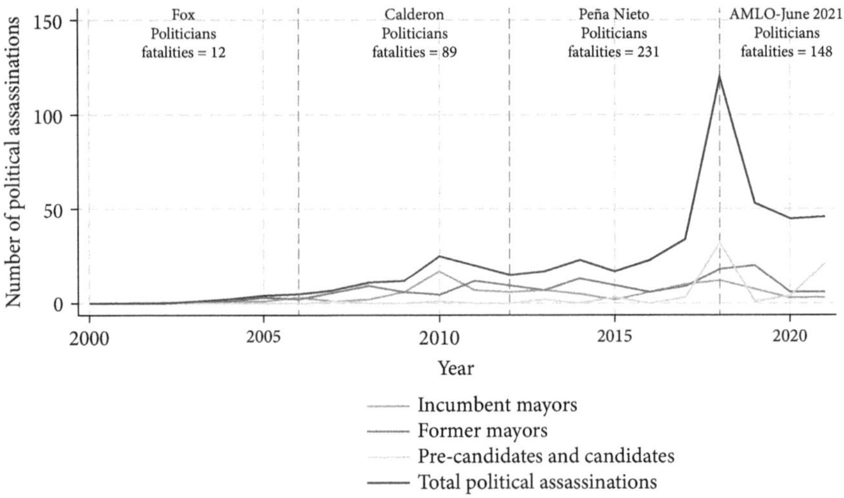

Figure 6.3 Political assassinations over time until June 2021

Source: Revised and reproduced from Gutiérrez-Romero and Iturbe (2024: Figure 4), under a CC-BY-NC 4.0 license (https://creativecommons.org/licenses/by-nc/4.0/deed.en)

The geography of these killings is equally telling. Ten states—Guerrero, Oaxaca, Veracruz, Michoacán, Puebla, Estado de México, Chihuahua, Guanajuato, Jalisco, and Tamaulipas—account for 75% of all recorded political assassinations. Each of these regions reveals a distinct nexus of violence and criminal ambition. In Guerrero, for example, a state central to opium production, assassinations coincide with the eradication of illicit crops and competition for trafficking corridors. Puebla, once relatively peaceful, has emerged as a focal point of violence because of its critical role in the fuel-theft economy.

Perhaps the most compelling evidence of organized crime's involvement lies in the geographic distribution of these crimes over the past two decades. As illustrated in Figure 6.4, these incidents are concentrated in municipalities located near the country's oil pipeline network and in areas where oil theft has been documented. In some coastal regions, these pipelines intersect with zones of illegal cultivation, creating a unique convergence that has facilitated crime diversification.

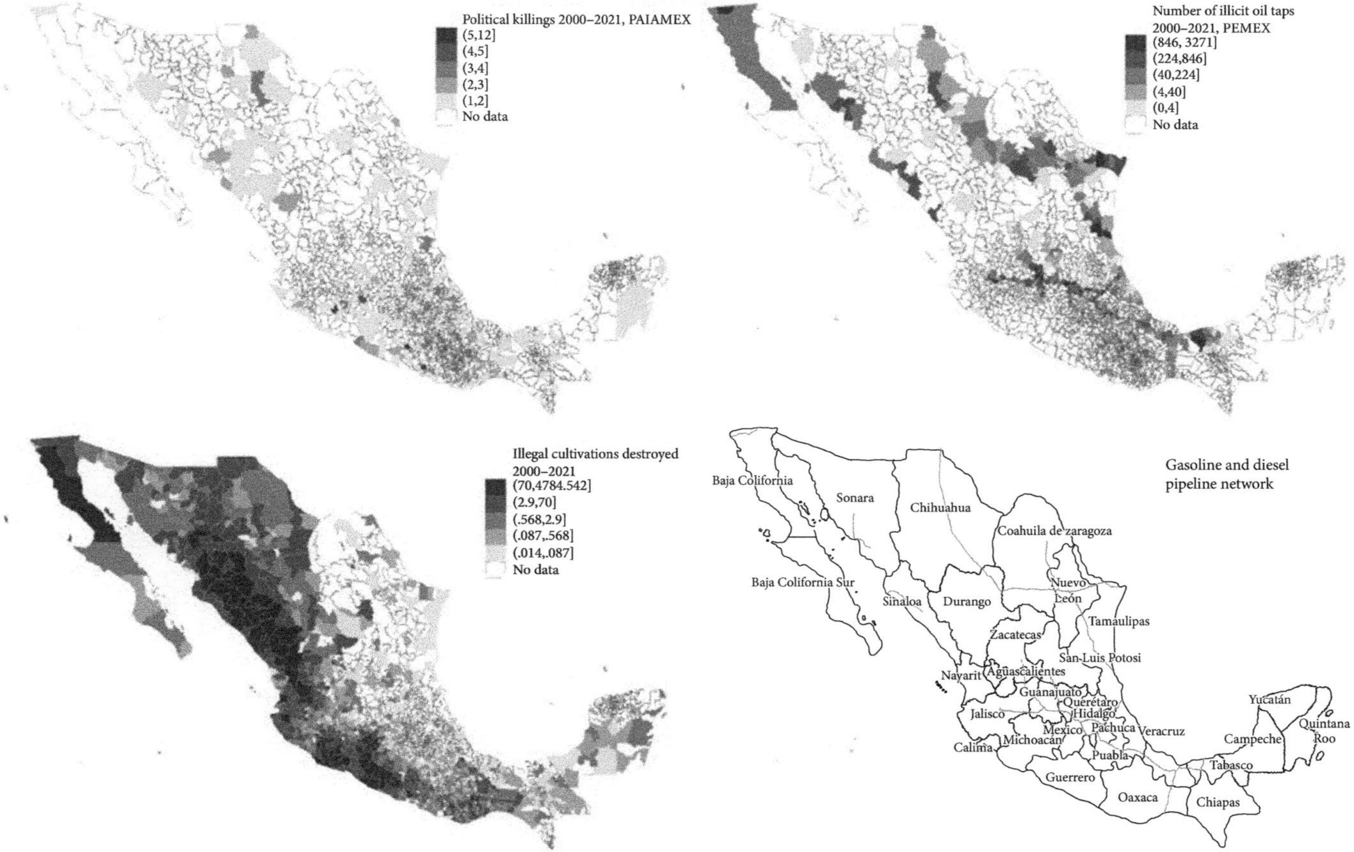

Figure 6.4 Political assassinations, oil theft, and destruction of illegal cultivations, 2000–2021

Source: Reproduced from Gutiérrez-Romero and Iturbe (2024: Figure 7), under a CC-BY-NC 4.0 license (https://creativecommons.org/licenses/by-nc/4.0/deed.en)

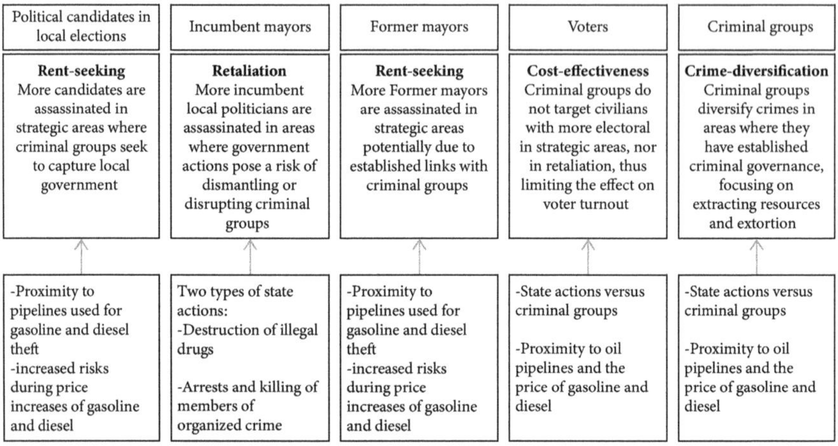

Figure 6.5 Hypotheses

Source: Revised and reproduced from Gutiérrez-Romero and Iturbe (2024: Figure 9), under a CC-BY-NC 4.0 license (https://creativecommons.org/licenses/by-nc/4.0/deed.en)

In the next sections, I will test the hypotheses elaborated in Section 2. As a recap, Figure 6.5 summarizes the hypotheses about the primary motivations behind political assassinations, the likely effects on voter behaviour, and the strategies used by criminal groups.

6.4 Data

To test the rent-seeking, and retaliation hypotheses, I rely on PAIAMEX. The dataset on political violence is aggregated monthly at the municipal level. It spans over two decades, from January 2000 to June 2021.

The cost-effectiveness hypothesis, I turn to the Armed Conflict Location and Event Data (ACLED) Project. This database has records of incidents of electoral violence and the number of fatalities related to such violence (Raleigh and Dowd 2016). From these data, available from 2018 to 2021, I exclude attacks on politicians. Voter turnout and vote share by competing parties in municipal elections from 2000 to 2021 are drawn from all the electoral institutes nationwide. I also consider the margin of victory.

To investigate the crime diversification hypothesis, I draw on three data sources. The first is the official crime statistics compiled by the Secretariado Ejecutivo del Sistema Nacional de Seguridad Pública (2024, Secretary of the National Public Security System), focusing on small-scale drug dealing (commonly referred to as *narcomenudeo*), extortion, and car theft. Unfortunately, a change in the methodology for recording crime in 2015 limits the availability of historical data at the municipal level for many crimes. However, it is possible to obtain longer-term statistics for extortion, beginning in 2011. For small-scale drug dealing and car theft, the analysis covers the period from 2015 to 2021, with data aggregated at the monthly level. Although no official statistics exist for overdose deaths in Mexico, publicly available death certificate records provide a useful alternative. These records include causes of death, allowing me to identify cases linked to drug abuse, whether accidental or intentional. Additionally, I examine the number of men reported as disappeared, drawn from the Registro Nacional de Personas Desaparecidas y No Localizadas (2022, National Registry of Missing and Unlocated Persons).

The government does not release information on oil theft at the municipal level. To sidestep this limitation, I measure the distance from each municipality to the nearest oil pipeline, as well as the monthly local market prices of gasoline and diesel. Oil pipelines were built long before Mexico's drug conflict. Fuel prices fluctuate along international markets, introducing an exogenous element to the analysis.

To examine government crackdowns, I track whether authorities (any of them) destroyed illicit crops, dismantled drug laboratories, or seized illegal drugs within a given municipality and month. I create an overall dummy indicator to represent whether a municipality had implemented any drug-related interventions. Separately, I include data on the number of arrests and killings of organized crime members carried out by all types of security authorities in the country.

The analysis also accounts for broader patterns of violence by incorporating municipal homicide rates per 100,000 people from 2000 to 2021. These figures are sourced from Instituto Nacional de Estadística y Geografía (INEGI; National Institute of Statistics and Geography). I also include municipal revenue data adjusted for inflation, supplemented by satellite-derived nightlight intensity as a proxy for local wealth. Additional details for all variables can be found in Gutiérrez-Romero (2025).

6.5 Method

To investigate how government interventions targeting organized crime contribute to political assassinations, I adopt a panel fixed-effects Poisson estimator. This is shown in Equation (1). This approach is ideal for analysing rare events such as political killings, as it handles count data with many zero observations while remaining robust under various data dispersion conditions (Wooldridge 1999).

$$E(y_{it}|\, d_{it-1},\, a_{it-1}, x_{it}, \beta_i) = \beta_i exp\,(d_{it-1}\beta_1 + a_{it-1}\beta_2 + x_{it}\beta_3) + u_{it} \qquad (1)$$

The analysis examines monthly counts of assassinated politicians—pre-candidates, incumbents, and former mayors—as well as their relatives and collaborators, across Mexican municipalities from January 2000 to June 2021. These types of assassinations are analysed separately, along with non-lethal intimidation acts, represented by y_{it}. The error term is denoted by u_{it}.

I examine whether government crackdowns, specifically the destruction of illicit drugs, are denoted by d_{it-1}. This is a dummy variable indicating whether the municipality destroyed any illegal crops, seized illegal drugs from organized crime, or dismantled laboratories to produce synthetic drugs. Additionally, a_{it-1} captures the number of arrests and killings of members of organized crime, at the municipality level, by any of the country's security forces. Both of these variables are lagged by one month to establish a clear sequence of events and reduce potential feedback effects where crackdowns could respond to prior violence rather than cause it.

Equation (1) includes a range of municipal characteristics, denoted by the vector x_{it-1}. These are indicators of economic opportunity, such as the ratio of proximity to fuel pipelines to local gasoline and diesel prices, as well as political alignment across levels of government, whether the same party controlled the municipality, state governorship, and presidency during the month analysed. Additionally, I add the lagged homicide rate, municipal revenue, and nightlight intensity as a proxy for economic activity. The homicide rate is from the previous month. To prevent double counting, I exclude political assassinations and the killings of organized crime members by authorities from this rate. The model accounts for heterogeneity by clustering standard errors at the municipal level.

6.5.1 Addressing endogeneity

An important concern is endogeneity—unmeasured factors that might simultaneously drive both government crackdowns and political violence. To address this, I use a two-stage pseudo-maximum likelihood fixed-effects Poisson estimator (Mullahy 1997).

In the first stage, I model the suspected endogenous variables—the destruction of illicit drugs d_{it-1}, and the arrests or killings of organized crime members a_{it-1}—on the vector of excluded instruments z_{it-1}. Since both suspected endogenous variables are rare events, I use fixed-effects Poisson regression to estimate the first-stage regressions. I use three instruments: the ratio of historical flows of Chinese people migrating to Mexico to local corn prices, proximity to ports interacted with cocaine prices in the United States, and the interaction of the percentage of mountainous terrain in municipalities with the heroin prices in the United States.

The first instrument connects the legacy of early twentieth-century migration of Chinese people to Mexico with the economic conditions of contemporary farmers. During the 1930s, immigration laws in the United States restricted migration of Chinese people, prompting many to migrate south to Mexico. This influx brought opium poppy seeds and knowledge of opium production. As Murphy and Rossi (2020) show, these areas have evolved into strongholds for DTOs. By integrating the historical settlement patterns of Chinese migrants with current corn prices, this instrument captures a distinctive interplay of historical inertia and economic volatility that informs state interventions. When corn prices decline, the incentive to engage in illegal drug cultivation increases, while simultaneously reducing the probability of state crackdowns to avoid major social unrest. In contrast, when corn prices are high, farmers are more reliant on legal crops, and state crackdowns are more likely to intensify.

The second instrument allows me to identify the timing and locations where government crackdowns are most likely to occur. Proximity to ports, which are crucial conduits for international trade, is often important for trafficking as well. Higher drug prices increase the probability that Mexican criminal organizations will violently compete for control over smuggling routes (Castillo et al. 2020; Gutiérrez-Romero 2024a). Therefore, when cocaine prices rise, smuggling routes become more lucrative, and criminal groups are more likely to escalate their activities, along with government crackdowns to curb the violence.

Similarly, the third instrument interacts the percentage of mountainous terrain in municipalities with the size of the retail heroin market in the United States. Mountainous areas have historically provided refuge for illicit activities, offering the seclusion necessary for opium poppy cultivation and heroin production. When heroin prices rise, production and distribution increase, leading to more violence along with more government crackdowns to contain it, particularly the arrests or killings of organized crime members. All these instruments meet the exclusion criteria for validity, as they shape the intensity and timing of crackdowns without directly affecting political violence.

$$d_{it-1} = \varphi_i \exp\left(z_{it-1}\varphi_1 + x_{it}\varphi_2\right) + e_{1it-1} \tag{2}$$

$$a_{it-1} = \pi_i \exp\left(z_{it-1}\pi_1 + x_{it}\pi_2\right) + e_{1it-1} \tag{3}$$

The second stage uses predictions from the first stage, $\hat{d}_{it-1}$, and $\hat{a}_{it-1}$ to assess the causal effects of government actions on political violence. This is shown in Equation (4), where v_{it} denotes the error term.

$$y_{it} = \delta_i \exp\left(\hat{d}_{it-1}\delta_1 + \hat{a}_{it-1}\delta_2 + x_{it}\delta_3\right) + v_{it} \tag{4}$$

6.6 Results

To begin, I examine the factors driving political violence in Mexico over the past two decades.[3] The results of the regressions are reported as incidence rate

[3] For brevity, I omit presenting all the estimates from the Poisson fixed-effects estimations, which do not account for potential endogeneity and are, therefore, prone to bias. However, these estimates can be found in Gutiérrez-Romero (2025).

ratios (IRRs). An IRR of 1 suggests no impact, while an IRR greater than 1 indicates an increase, and an IRR less than 1 signals a decrease in the expected number of political assassinations for each unit increase in the corresponding covariate. An alternative way to interpret this coefficient is to compute the expected percentage change in political assassinations by using the formula [(IRR coefficient−1)×100] for each unit increase in the covariate.

Appendix Table 6.A.1 addresses endogeneity concerns by presenting the first-stage results of the instrumental variable regression, offering a more robust framework for causal inference. The first-stage instrumental variable regression findings reveal that the instruments are statistically significant, relevant, and consistent with theoretical expectations. Regions historically reliant on drug trafficking—shaped by the legacy of Chinese immigrants introducing opium poppy cultivation techniques—are less likely to face government crackdowns during periods of low corn prices, as economic hardship forces farmers to turn increasingly to drug production. In such times, the government appears reluctant to intervene, wary of exacerbating rural instability. In contrast, and consistent with expectations, areas with strategic importance for organized crime—such as proximity to ports or mountainous terrain—experience a significant increase in arrests and killings of criminal members when US drug prices rise.

Table 6.1 provides the results of the instrumental variable fixed-effects Poisson estimator, alongside tests for endogeneity. These tests strongly support the instrumental variable specifications as the more reliable approach. The results remain consistent when focusing exclusively on arrests of organized crime members, rather than combining arrests and killings. For simplicity and clarity, I present these two forms of crackdowns, arrests and killings of members of organized crime, together in the analysis.

To begin with, I focus on the rent-seeking hypothesis. This hypothesis posits that areas rich in economic resources, particularly areas vulnerable to extraction or exploitation, are more susceptible to political violence targeting candidates. The results align with this view: pre-candidates and confirmed local candidates are significantly less likely to face assassination if they are competing for municipalities far from oil pipelines. That is why its IRR coefficient is below 1 and statistically significant. That is, a unit increase in the ratio of the distance to oil pipelines to the average price of gasoline and diesel results in an 88% reduction [(0.119−1)×100] in the expected number of assassinations of candidates.

By the same token, their risk of political assassination increases if these candidates are contending in areas near oil pipelines targeted for large-scale oil theft, particularly during periods of rising gasoline and diesel prices. Similarly, former mayors, as shown in Column 3 of Table 6.1, also face an increased risk of political assassination if they governed areas near oil pipelines. According to independent analysts, this heightened risk stems from their co-optation by organized crime during their incumbency, leaving them entangled in criminal networks and business ties even after leaving office (Mejía 2021). These alleged

	(1)	(2)	(3)	(4)	(5)	(6)
	Pre- and candidates	**Incumbent mayor**	**Former mayor**	**Non-lethal intimidating attacks on politicians**	**Politicians' relatives assassinated**	**Politicians' relatives and collaborators assassinated**
	Second-stage instrumental variable fixed-effects Poisson					
State actions against illegal drugs (destroyed cultivations, seized drugs, dismantled laboratories) in the previous month	44.141 (112.548)	0.739 (1.623)	13.905 (23.174)	22.363** (28.284)	12.349 (26.310)	5.660 (11.287)
Number of members of organized crime arrested or killed in the previous month	1.205 (0.584)	2.470*** (0.705)	0.746 (0.211)	1.740** (0.402)	1.700* (0.503)	1.851** (0.529)
Distance to the oil pipeline divided by the average price of gasoline and diesel	0.119** (0.116)	0.873 (0.122)	0.614*** (0.092)	0.299*** (0.070)	0.551*** (0.109)	0.512*** (0.104)
Homicide rate in the previous month (excluding criminals and political assassinations)	1.040 (0.035)	0.998 (0.011)	1.001 (0.007)	0.996 (0.011)	0.997 (0.008)	0.998 (0.008)
Political coordination: The municipality was ruled by the same party as its respective state and presidency	0.764 (2.394)	0.781 (1.268)	0.595 (0.309)	1.054 (0.337)	0.789 (0.318)	0.795 (0.317)
Annual income of the government municipal budget, in real terms	1.000 (0.000)	1.000 (0.000)	1.000 (0.000)	0.675 (0.192)	0.926 (0.343)	1.032 (0.333)
Annual nightlight in logarithm	0.376 (0.297)	2.413* (1.100)	0.623 (0.216)	1.000 (0.000)	1.000 (0.000)	1.000 (0.000)
Observations	8907	12,453	16,892	29,042	15,540	18,611
Wald χ^2	38.17	35.29	33.49	103.1	44.22	46.52
Log pseudo-likelihood	−161.4	−298.5	−424.9	−636.6	−439.7	−519.0
Endogeneity test	4.77	23.52	0.640	16.71	17.61	10.38
P-value	0.029	0.000	0.424	0.000	0.000	0.001

Source: Author's estimates.

businesses involve oil theft, along with other activities related to money laundering in such areas, including *narco-ranching*, which uses trading cattle to legalize money.

The findings suggest that elections, rather than disrupting criminal governance, serve to regenerate it, as criminal groups compete to secure their influence over new political actors. These groups do not thrive solely because of powerful drug kingpins commanding armies. Their dominance is rooted in their ability to infiltrate political systems, capturing politicians who provide protection and enable their activities.

A widely held belief in Mexico, which is revived with every political assassination, is that incumbent mayors are being targeted for refusing to share tax revenue with organized crime (Ferri and Zerega 2024). Over the 20 years analysed, I find no evidence that the size of a municipality's tax revenue is linked to political assassinations (Table 6.1). Instead, the main driver for the assassination of candidates, incumbents, and former mayors is undeniably their location in areas with a strong presence of organized crime, particularly near oil pipelines. However, oil pipelines are not the sole driver of political violence.

Table 6.1, Column 2, shows that the only statistically significant factor increasing the risk of assassination for incumbent mayors is the arrest or killing of organized crime members by authorities in the preceding month. Specifically, for each additional arrest or killing of members of organized crime, the expected number of assassinations increases by a factor of 2.47. This finding supports the retaliation hypothesis.

Table 6.1, Column 1, also shows that the risk of political assassination for pre-candidates and candidates is not linked to government crackdowns against organized crime. This is unsurprising, as these candidates have yet to assume power and, therefore, lack the authority to enact or obstruct policies affecting criminal organizations.

Interestingly, the destruction of illegal drugs, while representing a significant economic blow to these organizations, does not appear to drive the assassination of candidates, incumbent mayors, or former mayors. Instead, as shown in Column 4, such actions provoke other non-lethal forms of intimidation against politicians, suggesting that criminal groups prioritize coercion over outright political executions when seeking to counter the state for this type of crackdown. These tactics include explicit threats, such as the delivery of pig heads, the display of *narcomantas*—banners with intimidating messages displayed in public spaces—and shootings targeting the homes of politicians. Non-lethal intimidation of politicians also sees an increase following the arrests or killings of members of organized crime, as well as with proximity to oil pipelines (Column 4).

Different types of government crackdowns elicit varying responses from criminal organizations. For instance, the destruction of illegal drugs does not provoke other types of political assassinations, such as those targeting family members or collaborators of politicians. Thus, criminal organizations seem to resort to intimidation as an initial response to economic losses. However, political assassinations are predominantly triggered by the arrest or killing of members of organized crime. This pattern extends to the assassinations of politicians' relatives and close collaborators, as evidenced in Columns 5 and 6. Specifically, the expected number of such politically linked assassinations increases by a factor of 1.8 for every additional organized crime member arrested or killed by authorities (Column 6). Furthermore, the findings also reveal that the assassinations of relatives and collaborators of politicians are consistently more likely to occur near oil pipelines. This reinforces the notion that such acts are strategically motivated by the economic stakes tied to territorial control.

The findings also demonstrate that political assassinations and intimidation in Mexico are not driven by partisan allegiance. The model presented in Table 6.1 tests whether the politician's party aligns with that of the state governor and the president. I tested various approaches to examine the role of partisan affiliation, but none of the specifications produced statistically significant results. These results reveal the pragmatic and opportunistic nature of organized crime in Mexico.

Political violence stems from motives distinct from those driving other forms of criminal violence. To explore this distinction, the model incorporates the previous month's homicide rate, excluding cases involving political assassinations or lethal actions against organized crime by government authorities. The results, presented in Table 6.1, reveal that homicide rates consistently fail to explain political assassinations. Instead, both non-lethal intimidation and political assassinations are strongly associated with the presence of organized crime, especially in regions affected by government crackdowns. These results suggest that political violence is a deliberate strategy by DTOs to establish and enforce systems of criminal governance.

6.6.1 Electoral violence and voting behaviour

To test the cost-effectiveness hypothesis, in an earlier study, I used ACLED, which has systematically tracked election-related violence in Mexico since 2018, a period marked by a significant rise in political assassinations (Gutiérrez-Romero and Iturbe 2024). I examined the number of electoral violence events targeting civilians and the number of civilian fatalities resulting from such violence. I exclude any events—lethal or otherwise—directed at political figures.

Given that electoral violence incidents are statistically rare events, I used a fixed-effects Poisson estimator. To address potential endogeneity concerns when testing the impact of government crackdowns on electoral violence, I used the same instrumental variable identification strategy outlined earlier.

The findings, as documented in earlier work, show that government crackdowns, whether through the destruction of illegal drugs or the arrest or killing of organized crime members by authorities, do not statistically significantly affect the number of electoral violence episodes targeting civilians or the number of civilian fatalities associated with such violence (Gutiérrez-Romero and Iturbe 2024). Supporting the cost-effectiveness hypothesis, state-led actions against criminal organizations are not associated with electoral violence directed at civilians. Similarly, the general homicide rate in municipalities (excluding the assassination of politicians and members of organized crime) shows no statistically significant association with incidents of electoral violence targeting civilians. The analysis also reveals that proximity to oil pipelines does not affect either of the indicators used for electoral violence targeting civilians. Furthermore, there is no link between electoral violence against civilians and municipalities' fiscal revenue.

In earlier work, I also documented the impact of political violence on electoral outcomes. Electoral outcomes are observed in every election, making panel fixed-effects the appropriate model rather than Poisson specifications. Because of the potential endogeneity arising from unobserved factors that could simultaneously influence government actions against criminal organizations and electoral results, panel fixed-effects were combined with instrumental variables. The first-stage results, presented in Gutiérrez-Romero and Iturbe (2024), instrumented whether the government destroyed illegal drugs and the number of organized crime members arrested or killed by authorities during the administration just ending. The instruments used include the interaction between a municipality's distance to the nearest port and US cocaine prices, as well as the interaction between US heroin prices and the percentage of mountainous terrain of the municipality. The rationale behind these choices is that changes in drug prices abroad affect the profitability of trafficking in Mexico, which, in turn, influences government enforcement actions, especially in areas of strategic geographic significance.

The second-stage instrumental variable results show that voter turnout remains largely unaffected by the general homicide rate, excluding political assassinations or killings of organized crime members by authorities during the electoral cycle leading up to election day (Gutiérrez-Romero and Iturbe 2024). For a unit increase in the homicide rate, voter turnout declines by 0.018 percentage points, a rather small yet statistically significant effect.

As anticipated, for every political assassination, there is a small reduction in voter turnout of 1.62 percentage points, and it is only statistically significant at the 10% level. This finding aligns with the cost-effectiveness hypothesis, which suggests that political violence predominantly targets politicians rather than civilians, thereby causing minimal disruption to overall voter participation.

For every political assassination at the municipal level, there is a boost in the margin of victory by approximately 3 percentage points. This slight increase in the vote share difference between the two leading parties suggests that voters may consolidate their support for a particular party in response to such events. However, this does not result in a statistically significant change in the probability of the incumbent party being re-elected, indicating that the effects of political violence on electoral outcomes are nuanced and do not inherently favour incumbent parties.

Another indication that criminals do not retaliate against civilians is the observed increase in voter turnout following government crackdowns during the 20 years analysed. For every increase in arrests or killings of organized crime members by authorities, voter turnout is boosted by approximately 1.8 percentage points. This trend suggests that such crackdowns galvanize civic engagement, reinforcing the notion that a strong stance against organized crime resonates positively with the electorate.

In the case of actions targeting illegal drug operations, they not only boost voter turnout—by approximately 7 percentage points—but they also significantly increase the probability of the incumbent party's re-election, raising their probability of victory by 40 percentage points. This suggests that voters tend to reward governments that take decisive action against organized crime, rather than those that tolerate or ignore its presence.

One may wonder whether the observed increase in voter turnout and re-election rates hints at electoral manipulation, such as ballot stuffing. While the available data do not allow for a direct test of this possibility, indirect evidence provides useful insights. In an earlier study, voting behaviour in areas near opium poppy drug cultivation, identified through satellite imagery, was examined (Gutiérrez-Romero and Iturbe 2024). The analysis revealed that these regions experience slightly lower voter turnout—around 1.4 percentage points less—than areas without such activity. This suggests that zones engaged in opium production may naturally exhibit reduced levels of electoral participation. Furthermore, the findings imply that anti-drug enforcement could enhance voter participation in areas where organized crime's dominance might otherwise suppress political participation.

Building on that analysis, here I examine whether voter turnout is any different in areas with confirmed illegal drug cultivation where there were also government crackdowns.

The presence of illegal cultivation is determined using satellite data spanning 2015–2019, a period that includes the 2018 general election—one of the most violent in the country's history. The regression is confined to the period 2015–2019, constrained by the availability of satellite data.

The results indicate that voter turnout is increased by nearly 7 percentage points in areas with confirmed opium poppy cultivation that experienced crackdowns against drugs, compared with areas without recorded cultivation data and without such crackdowns. Voter turnout remains unaffected in areas with opium poppy drug cultivation when they experience the arrests or killings of organized crime members by the authorities. Neither of these types of crackdowns enhances nor diminishes the probability of the incumbent party's re-election, suggesting a neutral impact on incumbency re-election chances.

6.6.2 Legacies of drug trafficking on crime

So far, I have analysed how organized crime establishes criminal governance, often overriding the preferences of civilians who aim to elect leaders with a strong stance against crime. I now turn to analyse how crime evolves once criminal governance is firmly established.

Table 6.2 tests the crime diversification hypothesis. I do so for municipalities, examining crimes on a monthly basis during the periods denoted in Table 6.2, depending on their availability. Since crimes are not rare events, I use a panel fixed-effects specification to analyse the role of government crackdowns alongside geographic proximity to oil pipelines.

To address endogeneity concerns with government crackdowns, I use the same identification strategy with instrumental variables as in the baseline results. The first-stage instrumental variable regression is presented in Appendix Table 6.A.1. The instruments, which capture external shocks to US drug markets along areas with a tradition of drug trafficking, allow for a more accurate assessment of the causal impact of government interventions. These instruments are statistically significant and exhibit expected signs. There is also evidence of endogeneity. Hence, the instrumental variable results in Table 6.2 should be preferred to the panel fixed-effects.

The findings suggest that dismantling criminal cells through targeted crackdowns can reduce these crimes, with impacts often observable within a month. For every member of organized crime arrested or killed by authorities, small-scale drug dealing (*narcomenudeo*) cases decrease by 1.33, and extortion cases decline by 0.035 (Table 6.2, Columns 1 and 4). However, this trend does not apply to all types of crime. For every organized crime member arrested or killed by authorities, car theft increases by nearly three vehicles stolen. This suggests that dismantling criminal groups may force remaining members into lower-skill crimes, such as car theft.

Other government crackdowns yield similarly mixed outcomes. The destruction of illegal drugs in the previous month results in three additional official cases of small-scale drug dealing and 0.33 more extortion cases, as shown in Columns 1 and 4. At the same time, it significantly reduces car theft, with nearly 19 fewer vehicles stolen. This suggests that eliminating large drug shipments and laboratories—primarily intended for international markets—forces criminal groups to diversify. The loss of merchandise drives them towards local markets,

	(1)	(2)	(3)	(4)	(5)
	Small-scale drug dealing, 2015–2021	**Overdose deaths, 2000–2020**	**Disappearances of men, 2015–2021**	**Extortion, 2011–2021**	**Car theft, 2015–2021**
	Second-stage instrumental variable panel fixed-effects				
State actions against illegal drugs (destroyed cultivations, seized drugs, dismantled laboratories) in the previous month	3.352***	0.007	0.704***	0.333***	−19.052***
	(0.987)	(0.004)	(0.105)	(0.045)	(0.896)
Number of members of organized crime arrested or killed in the previous month	−1.335***	−0.000	−0.145***	−0.035***	2.863***
	(0.410)	(0.001)	(0.026)	(0.008)	(0.256)
Distance to the oil pipeline divided by the average price of gasoline and diesel	−0.459***	−0.001***	−0.139***	−0.038***	1.293***
	(0.079)	(0.000)	(0.012)	(0.005)	(0.069)
Homicide rate in the previous month (excluding criminals and political assassinations)	0.021***	0.000	0.001***	−0.001***	0.029***
	(0.005)	(0.000)	(0.000)	(0.000)	(0.002)
Political coordination: The municipality was ruled by the same party as its respective state and presidency	−0.966**	0.000	−0.274***	−0.028***	1.732***
	(0.400)	(0.001)	(0.026)	(0.007)	(0.186)
Annual income of the government municipal budget, in real terms	1.439***	0.002	−0.073***	−0.065***	3.834***
	(0.286)	(0.001)	(0.021)	(0.009)	(0.230)
Annual nightlight in logarithm	0.000***	0.000***	0.000	0.000***	0.000***
	(0.000)	(0.000)	(0.000)	(0.000)	(0.000)
Constant	25.756*	0.005	4.488***	1.097***	−77.147***
	(13.860)	(0.023)	(0.888)	(0.264)	(7.789)
Observations	633,648	633,648	108,906	633,648	633,648
Log pseudo-likelihood	−426,865	104,518	−199,606	−221,761	−400,892
Endogeneity test	6.500	5.070	3.370	30.890	354.100
P-value	0.011	0.024	0.067	0.000	0.000

Source: Author's estimates based on death certificates released by INEGI, crime figures released by Secretariado Ejecutivo del Sistema Nacional de Seguridad Pública (2024), and disappearances released by Registro Nacional de Personas Desaparecidas y No Localizadas (2022).

increasing small-scale drug sales and extortion as alternative revenue streams while deprioritizing other crimes such as car theft.

A natural question arises: how has drug addiction evolved in Mexico now that small-scale drug trafficking has risen? Reliable statistics on drug addiction are scarce. However, I find no significant relationship between the destruction of illegal drugs and overdose deaths, whether examining the entire period from 2000 to 2020 (Table 6.2, Column 2) or focusing on data since 2015 (results not shown in Table 6.2). This suggests that the destruction of drug shipments has little impact on overdose deaths. This insight is important. Supply-side measures, such as targeting drug shipments or production, do little to address the public health crises driven by widespread drug use. Addressing these challenges requires strategies focused on prevention, treatment, and harm reduction, rather than relying solely on interdiction efforts.

Another important finding is the higher frequency of small-scale drug dealing, disappearances, and extortion in areas near oil pipelines. Figure 6.6 illustrates some of the marginal effects already shown in Table 6.2 but projected at different distances from oil pipelines. Municipalities closer to oil pipelines, given the average fuel prices during the analysed period, report more cases of small-scale drug dealing (Figure 6.6.a) and male disappearances (Figure 6.6.b). The only exception is car theft (Figure 6.6.c).

Car theft serves as a telling example of how criminality evolves in regions dominated by organized crime. During the administration of Peña Nieto, this type of crime surged, reaching its peak in 2018. However, by 2021, it had declined by 34%, falling slightly below the levels observed at the beginning of the series. While this decline could be interpreted as a success of the incumbent Morena administration, it is also closely tied to the diversification of organized crime operations. DTOs shifted their focus to more lucrative activities such as extortion, oil theft, and small-scale drug dealing. Stealing vehicles would reduce the demand for gasoline, which is essential for their profits. Therefore, it would be strategically beneficial to suppress car theft in areas where fuel theft is prevalent.

Figure 6.6.c shows that car theft was reduced in areas dominated by *huachicol* (large-scale oil theft operations) while remaining prevalent in municipalities farther from oil pipelines. Car theft has increased in Morelos, Oaxaca, and Quintana Roo at the southern border. In these areas, DTOs face reduced risks and costs, as stolen vehicles can be quickly and discreetly moved across international borders. Additionally, other hotspots closer to Mexico City have experienced a rise in car theft, driven by the high profitability of selling stolen vehicles and auto parts to the extensive urban markets.

Another key finding is the role of political coordination in reducing crime. When local, state, and federal authorities share the same political affiliation, small-scale drug dealing, disappearances of men, and extortion are reduced (see Table 6.2, Columns 1, 3, and 4). This alignment appears to enhance the ability of

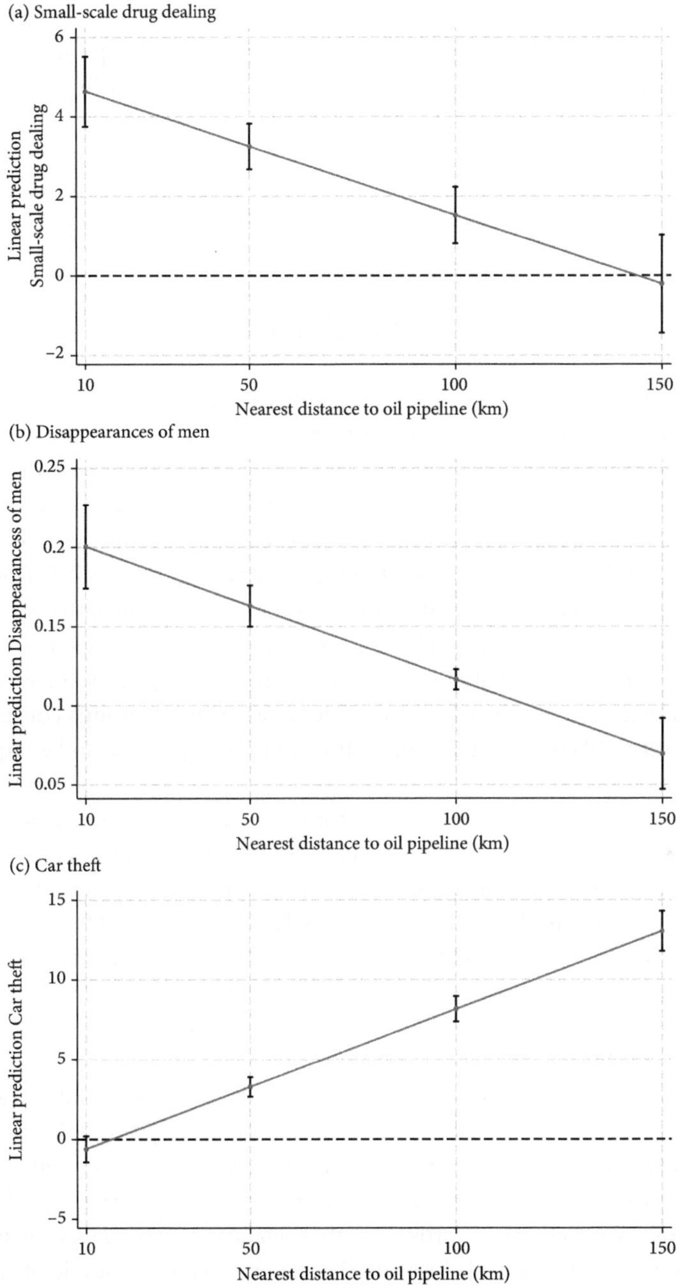

Figure 6.6 Marginal effects of distance to the oil pipeline, given the average price of gasoline and diesel

Source: Author's estimates based on crime statistics released by Secretariado Ejecutivo del Sistema Nacional de Seguridad Pública (2024) and disappearances released by Registro Nacional de Personas Desaparecidas y No Localizadas (2022).

governments to implement cohesive policies and coordinate enforcement efforts, weakening the grip of organized crime in these areas. The exceptions to this are overdose deaths (where there is no association with political coordination) and car theft (where such coordination boosts car theft). The positive association found for car theft may be related to the fact that once criminals move the stolen vehicles abroad or quickly dismantle the cars, it is easy to evade capture, no matter how coordinated authorities are within the country.

6.7 Conclusion

This study examined the evolving dynamics of criminal governance, exploring its historical roots, drivers, and the most lethal manifestations of political violence. It also addressed the broader consequences for citizens, including rising crime, economic underdevelopment, and the erosion of democratic institutions.

Demand from global markets and the enforcement strategies of the war on drugs have fundamentally reshaped the local economies in which DTOs operate. In Mexico, what began as modest, localized narcotics production evolved into a central hub of the international drug trade, bolstered by the tacit complicity of political actors and security forces. This transition reshaped local governance, marked by escalating levels of political violence as criminal groups consolidated their authority and enforced their interests in a more fragmented and competitive political landscape.

Political assassinations in Mexico, far from being random acts of violence, follow clear patterns tied to the strategic interests of criminal organizations. More than 500 politicians have been assassinated, as well as 156 family members of politicians and at least 19 of their close collaborators since 2000, with a sharp increase after 2017. The geographic concentration of these assassinations reveals that criminal groups prioritize regions with high-value economic resources, particularly those linked to oil pipelines that generate profits on par with those from narcotics trafficking.

This form of criminal governance is characterized by integration into local political and economic systems, achieved in part through targeted violence against political candidates to secure incoming local governments. In such settings, government crackdowns against organized crime, such as the arrest or killing of members of organized crime, provoke lethal retaliatory acts against incumbent politicians, their families, and close associates, perpetuating the cycle of criminal governance.

Another key contribution is the revelation that political assassinations orchestrated by DTOs undermine democratic accountability—not by deterring voter turnout, but by fundamentally distorting the pool of viable candidates and the policies they are willing to pursue. These targeted killings dictate who can safely run for office and who stands a chance of winning. By eliminating candidates who oppose their agendas or resist co-optation, criminal groups transform electoral processes into tools for consolidating their influence.

Finally, I showed the multiple burdens imposed on civilians under criminal governance. This system allows criminal organizations to evolve into quasi-governmental entities, exerting territorial control not only for illicit purposes but also to enforce compliance and regulate local economies. Unlike earlier portrayals of DTOs focused on the drug trade, here I show these organizations manage a diversified portfolio of crimes while influencing political processes to secure their dominance. This explains why, in areas rich with rent-seeking opportunities, such as oil theft zones, several crimes rise and levy extortion payments with more frequency than in other faraway areas.

This diversification of criminal portfolios is strategic, prioritizing profitable ventures while de-emphasizing others that can be outsourced to peripheral actors or relocated to less contentious areas. Criminal diversification inevitably generates an economy of violence, where competition among rival groups triggers distinct patterns of conflict and retaliation across territories. Responding to state pressure to curb overt displays of violence, these organizations increasingly rely on disappearances as a tactic to avoid public backlash, project an illusion of state control, and solidify their grip on local governance.

The implications of these findings are profound. DTOs do not simply coexist with governance systems; they actively transform them. By embedding themselves within local political and economic structures, these organizations leave a lasting legacy of deep human suffering, economic stagnation, and democratic erosion.

6.8 Appendix

Table 6.A.1 First-stage regression of Tables 6.1 and 6.2—panel fixed-effects Poisson and incidence rate ratios

	(1)	(2)
	State's actions against drugs	**Members of organized crime arrested or killed**
Log Chinese population in the area in the 1930s divided by the average price of corn in the previous quarter	0.772*** (0.034)	0.424*** (0.135)
Distance to the nearest port multiplied by the annual price of cocaine in the United States per kilogramme	1.012*** (0.002)	1.106*** (0.014)

continued

Table 6.A.1 *continued*

	(1) State's actions against drugs	(2) Members of organized crime arrested or killed
Log percentage of mountainous territory multiplied by the annual price of heroin in the United States	0.893** (0.045)	25.990*** (13.579)
Distance to the oil pipeline divided by the average price of gasoline and diesel	1.077*** (0.011)	1.075 (0.053)
Homicide rate in the previous month (excluding criminals and political assassinations)	1.002*** (0.000)	1.005 (0.004)
Political coordination: the municipality was ruled by the same party as its respective state and presidency	0.972 (0.028)	0.476*** (0.129)
Annual income of the government municipal budget, in real terms	1.000*** (0.000)	1.000 (0.000)
Annual nightlight in logarithm	1.218*** (0.028)	0.619** (0.126)
Observations	301,898	90,329
Log pseudo-likelihood	−89141	−17034
Wald χ^2	267.2	177.6
Excluded instruments		
Log pseudo-likelihood	−98,662	−17,989
Wald χ^2	22.63	122.4

Source: Author's estimates based on actions against drug trafficking organizations according to SEDENA, SEMAR, the national guard, and the federal police.

References

Alesina, A., S. Piccolo, and P. Pinotti (2019). 'Organized Crime, Violence, and Politics'. *The Review of Economic Studies*, 86(2): 457–499. https://doi.org/10.1093/restud/rdy036

Arzate, E. (2023). *Acabar Con El Huachicol, Promesa Incumplida* [Ending the Huachicol: Unfulfilled Promise]. *Forbes*, 3 July. https://forbes.com.mx/acabar-con-el-huachicol-promesa-incumplida/ (accessed March 2025).

Balletta, L., and A. M. Lavezzi (2023). 'The Economics of Extortion: Theory and the Case of the Sicilian Mafia'. *Journal of Comparative Economics*, 51(4): 1109–1141. https://doi.org/10.1016/j.jce.2023.05.003

Battiston, G., G. Daniele, M. Le Moglie, and P. Pinotti (2024). 'Fuelling Organised Crime: The Mexican War on Drugs and Oil Theft'. *The Economic Journal*, 134(663): 2685–2711. https://doi.org/10.1093/ej/ueae047

Blume, L. R. (2017). 'The Old Rules No Longer Apply: Explaining Narco-Assassinations of Mexican Politicians'. *Journal of Politics in Latin America*, 9(1): 59–90. https://doi.org/10.1177/1866802X1700900103

Calderón Molgóra, M. A. (1994). *Violencia Política y Elecciones Municipales* [Political Violence and Municipal Elections]. Zamora. Instituto Mora.

Castillo, J. C., D. Mejía, and P. Restrepo (2020). 'Scarcity Without Leviathan: The Violent Effects of Cocaine Supply Shortages in the Mexican Drug War'. *Review of Economics and Statistics*, 102(2): 269–286. https://doi.org/10.1162/rest_a_00801

Dal Bó, E., P. Dal Bó, and R. Di Tella (2006). '"*Plata o Plomo?*": Bribe and Punishment in a Theory of Political Influence'. *American Political Science Review*, 100(1): 41–53. https://doi.org/10.1017/S0003055406061995

Daniele, G., and G. Dipoppa (2017). 'Mafia, Elections and Violence Against Politicians'. *Journal of Public Economics*, 154: 10–33. https://doi.org/10.1016/j.jpubeco.2017.08.004

Durán-Martínez, A. (2008). *The Politics of Drug Violence: Criminals, Cops and Politicians in Colombia and Mexico*. Oxford: Oxford University Press.

Ferri, P., and G. Zerega. (2024). '*Alejandro Arcos: Los Cabos Sueltos Del Asesinato Del Alcalde de Chilpancingo*' [Alejandro Arcos: The Loose Ends of the Murder of the Mayor of Chilpancingo]. *El País*, 13 November. https://elpais.com/mexico/2024-10-13/los-cabos-sueltos-del-asesinato-del-alcalde-de-chilpancingo.html (accessed March 2025).

Gambetta, D. (1996). *The Sicilian Mafia: The Business of Private Protection*. Cambridge, MA: Harvard University Press.

Gutiérrez-Romero, R. (2024a). 'Drug Trafficking Fuels Violence Leading to Mass Emigration: The Case of Guatemala'. *Economic Modelling*, 131: 106595. https://doi.org/10.1016/j.econmod.2023.106595

Gutiérrez-Romero, R. (2024b). 'Femicide Laws, Unilateral Divorce, and Abortion Decriminalization Fail to Stop Women's Killings in Mexico'. Arxiv Working Paper.

Gutiérrez-Romero, R., and N. Iturbe (2024). 'Causes and Electoral Consequences of Political Assassinations: The Role of Organized Crime in Mexico'. *Political Geography*, 115: 103206. https://doi.org/10.1016/j.polgeo.2024.103206

Gutiérrez-Romero, R. (2025). 'From drug trafficking to state capture: The dynamics of criminal governance, political violence, and crime diversification'. UNU-WIDER Working Paper Number 19/25.

Hernández, A. (2014). *Narcoland: The Mexican Drug Lords and Their Godfathers*. London: Verso Books.

Hernández Huerta, V. A. (2020). 'Candidates Murdered in Mexico: Criminal or Electoral Violence?'. *Política y Gobierno*, 27(2): 1–28.

Magaloni, B., G. Robles, A. M. Matanock, A. Diaz-Cayeros, and V. Romero (2020). 'Living in Fear: The Dynamics of Extortion in Mexico's Drug War'. *Comparative Political Studies*, 53(7): 1124–1174. https://doi.org/10.1177/0010414019879958

Mejía, D. (2021). 'Interview with Rubén Salazar, Director of Etellekt Consultores'. Mexico: Noticias 7 a.m. https://www.youtube.com/watch?v=X-mYheSbZ4o

Moncada, E. (2022). *Resisting Extortion*. Cambridge: Cambridge University Press. https://doi.org/10.1017/9781108915328

Mullahy, J. (1997). 'Instrumental-Variable Estimation of Count Data Models: Applications to Models of Cigarette Smoking Behavior'. *Review of Economics and Statistics*, 79(4): 586–593. https://doi.org/10.1162/003465397557169

Murphy, T. E., and M. A. Rossi (2020). 'Following the Poppy Trail: Origins and Consequences of Mexican Drug Cartels'. *Journal of Development Economics*, 143: 102433. https://doi.org/10.1016/j.jdeveco.2019.102433

Olsson, O. (2007). 'Conflict Diamonds'. *Journal of Development Economics*, 82(2): 267–286. https://doi.org/10.1016/j.jdeveco.2005.07.004

Ponce, A. F., R. Velázquez López Velarde, and J. Sáinz Santamaría (2022). 'Do Local Elections Increase Violence? Electoral Cycles and Organized Crime in Mexico'. *Trends in Organized Crime*, 25(1): 37–57. https://doi.org/10.1007/s12117-019-09373-8

Raleigh, C., and C. Dowd (2016). *Armed Conflict Location and Events Data (ACLED) Codebook*. Armed Conflict Location & Event Data Project. https://acleddata.com/knowledge-base/codebook/ (accessed March 2025).

Registro Nacional de Personas Desaparecidas y No Localizadas (2022). Gobierno de México. https://versionpublicarnpdno.segob.gob.mx/Dashboard/Index (accessed March 2025).

Secretariado Ejecutivo del Sistema Nacional de Seguridad Pública (2024). Datos Abiertos de Incidencia Delictiva. Gobierno de México. https://www.gob.mx/sesnsp/acciones-y-programas/datos-abiertos-de-incidencia-delictiva (accessed March 2025).

Stevenson, M. (2017). 'Gasoline Thieves Are Out of Control and Deadly in Mexico'. *Associated Press*, 14 July. https://apnews.com/general-news-d6529c484f1d4262bfc660453f011bb4 (accessed March 2025).

Trejo, G., and S. Ley (2020). *Votes, Drugs, and Violence: The Political Logic of Criminal Wars in Mexico*. Cambridge: Cambridge University Press. https://doi.org/10.1017/9781108894807

Trejo, G., and S. Ley (2021). 'High-Profile Criminal Violence: Why Drug Cartels Murder Government Officials and Party Candidates in Mexico'. *British Journal of Political Science*, 51(1): 203–229. https://doi.org/10.1017/S0007123418000637

Vélez-Torres, I., and F. Méndez (2022). 'Slow Violence in Mining and Crude Oil Extractive Frontiers: The Overlooked Resource Curse in the Colombian Internal Armed Conflict'. *The Extractive Industries and Society*, 9: 101017. https://doi.org/10.1016/j.exis.2021.101017

Wainwright, T. (2017). *Nacronomis*. London: Penguin Random House.

Wooldridge, J. M. (1999). 'Distribution-Free Estimation of Some Nonlinear Panel Data Models'. *Journal of Econometrics*, 90(1): 77–97. https://doi.org/10.1016/S0304-4076(98)00033-5

PART III

WARTIME INSTITUTIONAL LEGACIES AND POST-WAR STATE-BUILDING

7

Varieties of insecurity and rebel–civilian ties across time

Evidence from post-war Zimbabwe

Shelley Liu

7.1 Introduction

Existing research has examined how rebels govern across different regions, both within and across countries, highlighting how they interact with civilians, create informal governing structures, and maintain social control during conflicts (Arjona 2016; Mampilly 2012; Stewart 2018; Huang 2016; Cunningham et al. 2021; Revkin 2021). Only more recently have scholars begun to explore the *post-war implications* of rebel governance, both in war's immediate aftermath (Liu 2024b; Martin 2021; Thaler 2018) and in the long term (Liu 2024a; Loyle and Onder 2024; Haass and Ottmann 2022). Notwithstanding this more recent body of work, understanding the aftermath of these conflicts, and in particular linking its short-term effects to longer term legacies, remains a critical yet understudied dimension of rebel governance.

This chapter examines how organized ties with civilian supporters on the ground influence post-war politics when rebels win control of the state. I argue that the relationship between organized civilian supporters and a ruling party after war depends in major part on the *varieties of insecurity* that the rebel victor faces as the new ruling party, and the governance challenges that potentially threaten their hold on power. Further, rebel victors are likely to face multiple instances of insecurity across time. I investigate three distinct scenarios, which commonly affect the stability of a ruler's hold over power. First, rebel victors may confront existential insecurity stemming from lingering wartime rivals, meaning that they face an *external* challenge in the form of a counter-revolution or a return to civil war. This is particularly common across post-war contexts, where various armed factions seek to regroup and return to resume conflict (Walter 2004; Mason et al. 2011). Second, rebel victors potentially face *internal* challenge from splits within the rebel government or ruling coalition, threatening intra-party cohesion.

Shelley Liu, *Varieties of insecurity and rebel–civilian ties across time*. In: *Institutional Legacies of Violent Conflict*. Edited by: Patricia Justino, Oxford University Press. © United Nations University World Institute for Development Economics Research (UNU-WIDER) (2026). DOI: 10.1093/9780197904077.003.0007

These splits may emerge either between the political and military wings of the movement (Martin 2022; Meng and Paine 2022) or between different political factions in the government that have different tastes for ideology, policy, and reform (Atlas and Licklider 1999; Daly 2014; Roeder 2005). Third, the primary challenge to the rebel victor may be *electoral* in nature: the victorious rebel party faces no existential threat in the form of violent overthrow, but may fear being voted out of power by the opposition party's civilian base (Haass and Ottmann 2022; Liu 2024a).

The type of challenge with which the rebel victor is most acutely concerned will condition how rebel governance and rebel–civilian ties shape the post-war political landscape at specific points in time. In addition, rebel victors' strategies with respect to their organized civilian base may change across time as new forms of challenge take primacy within domestic politics. In instances where victors grapple with existential insecurity from external rivals, rebel–civilian ties should serve as one integral component of the rebel victor's broader state-building strategy to exert control, stabilize the state, and consolidate power (Liu 2022). In such cases, rebel–civilian ties in victor strongholds may be used to tamp down demands for greater redistribution from the state, freeing up the ruling party to concentrate its resources on insecure regions. Alternatively, where internal party disagreements may weaken party cohesion, the ruling party may use the strength of rebel–civilian ties between communities and specific former commanders as a heuristic for selecting strategically optimal individuals for co-optation, thereby reducing coup threats and strengthening the ruling party overall (Meng and Paine 2022). Finally, where the victor's primary concern is electoral insecurity, rebel–civilian ties—along with rebel institutions and informal structures—may be repurposed as efficient party brokers, offering a cost-effective means of maintaining control without resorting to broader state-building initiatives (Liu 2024a; Haass and Ottmann 2022).

I illustrate and substantiate these arguments through a comprehensive examination of four decades of rebel victor rule in Zimbabwe after the end of the Zimbabwe Liberation War in 1979. During the Liberation War, two anti-colonial rebel parties—the Zimbabwe African National Union (ZANU) and the Zimbabwe African People's Union (ZAPU)—fought for the country's independence from the eastern and western borders of the country, respectively. During this time, both engaged in rebel governance and formed significant rebel–civilian ties within areas that they operated; however, ZANU's mass mobilization efforts across Zimbabwe's rural regions using Maoist tactics proved to be especially effective in organizing civilians across different communities and galvanizing them to aid the war effort. Where ZANU succeeded in implementing these strategies, its rebel governance structures—from local party cells (village committees), to groups of youth collaborators (mujibas), to the politicization of traditional community events (pungwes)—were useful not only during war for exerting control over the broader civilian population, but also was socialized and institutionalized into political processes after war in a variety of ways.

Following Zimbabwe's independence in 1979, ZANU emerged as victorious during its first post-war elections in 1980 under the party name ZANU-Patriotic Front (ZANU-PF). The party has subsequently won control of the government in every election since: first under wartime leader Robert Mugabe as president, and then more recently under Emmerson Mnangagwa, a former ZANU combatant and Mugabe's long-time ally. Throughout its post-war rule, the ruling party has faced varying threats that shifted over time, ranging from electoral uncertainties during election periods, to existential challenges posed by wartime rivals, to internal party concerns posed by former liberation war veterans who demanded greater compensation for their wartime sacrifices. Across each of these forms of insecurity, ZANU's ties to its civilians shaped the nature of politics and policymaking in a variety of ways. Ultimately, both the nature of politics—shaped by rebel governance strategies—and the expansion of various rebel institutions themselves come together to help explain the political party's long-term hold over Zimbabwean politics.

By analysing the historical trajectory of rebel governance and the evolving nature of rebel–civilian ties across different regions in Zimbabwe, this chapter aims to provide one account of how these factors intricately shape post-war politics based on the security and electoral constraints that the ruling party faced. It contributes to a broader body of literature on rebel politicization and organizational structures during war (Wood 2008; Arjona 2016; Mampilly 2012; Stewart 2021) and how such wartime processes affect post-war effects politics, state capacity, and party-building (Thaler 2018; Huang 2016; Martin 2022; Liu 2022, 2024b; Schwartz 2020). Particularly where rebels have had success in organizing civilians (Wood 2000), exerting social control (Sánchez De La Sierra 2020; Balcells 2011), and engaging in service provision (Revkin 2021; Stewart 2018), such activities are likely to have substantial post-war effects on politics and the organization of the state. This ought to be especially true in cases of rebel victory (Lyons 2016; Meng and Paine 2022; Daly 2022; Liu 2024a), as the revolutionary regime durability literature has also theorized (Levitsky and Way 2022; Lachapelle et al. 2020); however, this chapter contends that such durability is achieved is explained not only through elite-level politics but also the organization of pro- and anti-government forces at a subnational level (Liu 2022). This organizational capacity, which connects the party to community-level affairs, speak in particular to literature on clientelism through community and extra-party ties in new or developing democracies in post-conflict states (Haass and Ottmann 2022; Taylor et al. 2017; Bowles et al. 2020).

7.2 Theory

A large literature has explored how armed groups govern during war—balancing coercion with public goods provision—by forming ties with civilians (Martin 2021; Liu 2022) and establishing parallel institutions to exert control over local communities (Arjona 2016; Breslawski 2021; Mampilly and Stewart 2021; Loyle et al. 2023).[1] While these costly governing strategies may not increase the likelihood of rebel victory, they often reflect rebel group strategies for demonstrating state-building and governance capacity (Stewart 2018, 2021).

Rebel governance strategies vary, but not all persist after rebels gain power post-war (Kasfir 2024). Rather, due to continued insecurity post-war, rebel victors are more likely to rely on the coercive elements of their wartime rule to continue to retain control once they have captured power (Liu 2024a). I focus specifically on the wartime ties with civilians as a major building block for successful rebel governance, and explore how different *varieties of insecurity* may re-activate these ties for the continuation of post-war social control. In this section, I first describe the varieties of insecurity that rebel victors may face once in power, as well as the timing of such insecurity in the post-war landscape. I then outline predictions for how rebel victors leverage their wartime ties in rebel-governed areas for exerting control at a national level after war.

7.2.1 Varieties of insecurity

Following rebel victory, whether through a military victory or through a political (electoral) victory, rebel groups come into power to form the new post-war government. The government may be ruled entirely by a single rebel party, such as in Angola, Uganda, Eritrea, and Rwanda, or it may be ruled through a nominal coalition of rebel groups where one is the clear dominant victor, such as in Zimbabwe or South Africa. Regardless of the structure of the new government however, threats to the rebel victors' position in power are not eliminated simply by winning war and political control—they continue to face various major threats to their hold over power due to the polarized and fragile nature of the post-war peace. In short, beyond various forms of low-level violence that remain from war or emerge from new sources (Bara et al. 2021),[2] rebel victors must

[1] While initial research suggested the importance of *territorial* control (Kalyvas 2006), increasingly scholars argue for the role of *social* control for successful rebel governance (Liu 2024b).

[2] It should be noted that other forms of violence are likely to exist in tandem with external and internal threats, including criminal, militia, or communal violence occurring in the post-war landscape. However, while such violence weakens the state and state capacity, in most cases, they do not pose outright threats to the rebel victor's position in power.

also contend with major challenges that—if managed poorly—may result in their overthrow (Mason et al. 2011).

I explore three major forms of insecurity that threaten rebel victors' rule: (1) violence from external rivals, (2) violence from internal divisions, and (3) peaceful transfer of power due to electoral politics. While this is certainly not an exhaustive list of threats to the rebel victors' consolidation of power—e.g. interstate warfare, such as the Eritrean-Ethiopian War, is also a major form of insecurity not explored fully here—these three forms of insecurity are sufficiently broad to apply to a wide range of challenges to incumbent power across states.

First, violence from *external rivals*, and specifically from counter-rebellions or other armed groups discontent with the rebel victor's new position in power, poses an existential threat to the new regime's survival. This is particularly likely to happen shortly after the end of civil war, where the risk of return to outright war in the fragile post-war context is already high (Walter 2004; Call 2012). While rebel victories tend to remain more stable in the long run (Mason et al. 2011; Toft 2010; Meng and Paine 2022), they too are susceptible to civil war recurrence as they face violent challenges from ex-government forces, from other wartime rivals where more than one armed group contested for the state, or even from newly created armed groups dissatisfied with the rebel regime's ascent to power.

The threat of civil war recurrence is a major cause of concern for rebel victories: as Liu (2024b) finds, 75% of the rebel victories (15 of 20) in sub-Saharan Africa faced violent rivals within two years of coming into power. These come in various forms, and often within the same country. Take, for example, the National Resistance Movement (NRM)'s rebel victory in 1986. Not only did the former government's forces become armed challengers against the new NRM government, but new rebel groups emerged from ex-government-supporting regions of rural Uganda as the new government was still working to consolidate control over the state (Lewis 2020). Rebel victors in Rwanda, Angola, and Liberia faced similar concerns as they continued to contend with rival armed groups that they had technically defeated to end the civil war. The possibility of violent overthrow is problematic for rebel regimes in other continents as well, including cases such as the Sandinistas in Nicaragua and the Khmer Rouge in Cambodia, among others.

Beyond civil war recurrence, rebel victors are also threatened by challenges from within their own organization: like all governments and ruling coalitions, rebel victors are vulnerable to party splits and coups. Despite seizing power, *internal* factionalization can hinder the consolidation of authority and introduce intra-party weakness—particularly dangerous when other forms of external challenges are also taking place concurrently. To be clear, the existing literature has found that rebel victors are particularly resistant to internal splits in comparison to other post-war governments, for various reasons. Levitsky and Way (2022) and Lyons (2016), for example, point to ideological or organizational cohesion and shared experiences during war as being instrumental for keeping ex-rebel governments cohesive after war; Meng and Paine (2022) argue that rebel victors are adept at power-sharing between the civilian and military wings, resulting in a cohesive elite alliance between the political party and the defence sector.

Despite rebel victors' broader successes at minimizing the likelihood of intra-party challenges, these challenges still occur with some frequency. For example, Martin (2022) finds that militaries where commanders do not sustain strong ties to particular communities outside of the rebel movement are more likely to remain loyal to the political party, while those with strong ties have greater opportunities to defect. Variation across victorious groups is also implicit in Levitsky and Way's (2022) analysis of why some revolutions are more durable than others. Notably, unlike civil war recurrence—which tends to happen quickly after war has ended—internal threats often take longer to manifest (see Liu 2024b), possibly for several reasons. First, and particularly where movements are cohesive during war, discontent from within the party may take longer to manifest as policy decisions are made and implemented. For example, discontent ex-combatants in Zimbabwe only began to threaten violence against the ruling party over a decade after independence, largely due to unkept wartime promises. Alternatively, factions within the party may be more likely to appear only once the ruling party is weakened by other challenges—such as in the case of Charles Taylor's presidency following the First Liberian Civil War.

Finally, rebel victors may be threatened electorally: even if they have consolidated power by eliminating potential armed rivals and have sustained organizational cohesion from within, they may still be susceptible to being voted out of power. Both the conflict termination and reconstruction processes often involve setting up elections for democratic and institutional reform (Lyons 2004; Sisk 2009; Matanock 2017). These may be an integral part of peace agreement provisions, such as in Burundi or South Africa; or they may be set up after conflict termination by the ruling party, such as in Uganda or Rwanda. Rebel victors often have an incentive to comply with, or set up new, electoral institutions for strategic reasons such as democratizing while strong to increase domestic and international support, address intra-party factions, or attracting greater foreign aid from donors (Riedl et al. 2020).

Rebel victors are often stronger than their opponents at the outset of conflict termination, particularly as people are more likely to vote for parties that are militarily the strongest (Daly 2022). Yet, even strong ruling parties that enjoy significant popular support are susceptible to electoral defeat down the line (Riedl et al. 2020). The African National Congress (ANC) in South Africa is the most recent example of this: the anti-apartheid party sustained dominance at the polls for three decades before eventually losing its electoral majority during the 2024 elections due to popular discontent over government performance. To guard against losing power at the polls, ruling rebel parties are more likely to become competitive authoritarian regimes (Levitsky and Way 2010): they weaken opposition parties, cultivate fear among constituents, and hold elections on uneven playing fields to prevent being ousted through electoral processes (Young 2019; Liu 2024a; van Baalen 2024).

7.2.2 Rebel–civilian ties under different forms of insecurity

Through rebel governance, rebel groups build locally embedded social networks (i.e. rebel–civilian ties) and establish informal institutions to exert social control. Once a rebel group comes into power, these networks and institutions may be mobilized in different ways, depending not just on the *threats* that the new government faces but also on *where* they were able to successfully govern during war. Where rebel governance was well-established, their local ties and governing institutions are likely to be stronger. However, in regions where their wartime governing projects were incomplete or where the population resisted rebel control, these rebel–civilian ties are weaker or may not exist at all. Wartime ties offer different resources for post-war governance, allowing the new government to adapt to the types of insecurity it encounters. In other words, in managing dissent within the country, rebel–civilian ties play a dual role: providing a means of controlling populations outside of its strongholds while also helping to address internal tensions from within supportive populations.

As previously explained, the rebel victor may predominantly face violent threats from *external rivals* once coming into power, which, if left unmanaged, is likely to expand into a return to civil war. These threats are likely to emerge in rival territory—where rivals are more embedded among their own supporters and can, therefore, most easily galvanize for support to resume conflict (Liu 2022). To suppress a potential counter-rebellion and contain conflict, the rebel victor should prioritize security and military operations in rival-held areas. However, overcommitting resources to these efforts creates a dilemma. Neglecting other parts of the state could increase civilian grievances, as they may expect investments in development. This dissatisfaction could bolster political support for the counter-rebellion. Then, if military operations cannot contain rivals quickly, the threat of civil war may spread beyond rival territory, especially if civilian discontent is already high.

To minimize this possibility, the rebel victors may rely on their wartime civilian ties in two ways: for *organization* and for *politicization*. First, a rebel victor may leverage its greater wartime organizational capacity to mobilize collective action for development and security—a core component of rebel governance during war. Just as rebel groups relied on civilian ties to secure support for security and goods provision during the war, these same networks can facilitate grassroots reconstruction efforts post-war. This approach lowers costs and fosters loyalty to the rebel victor, potentially reducing the state's resource burden. Second, the rebel victor may mobilize key civilian supporters to extend politicization campaigns into unorganized areas. This mirrors wartime strategies, using grassroots organizing to consolidate social control and expand support into previously unpoliticized localities.

Hypothesis 1. *Where the threat to power is violence from external rivals, the rebel victor minimizes conflict spread across the country by using its wartime ties to organize and politicize communities.*

Alternatively, where the rebel victor faces threats *internal* to the rebel party, it aims to prevent a coup attempt that may successfully result in its overthrow. Unlike insecurity from external rivals, which is managed through state-building strategies, internal factionalism requires balancing between different elites within the party who may be most successful in motivating defection and mounting a credible threat. Meng and Paine (2022), in particular, point to rebel victors' success in sharing power between civilian politicians and military elites through Minister of Defence appointments as an important coup-proofing strategy.

Extending this logic further, rebel–civilian ties may partially help the victor to determine *which* military elites to promote to minimize coup risks. As Martin (2022) argues, military commanders' likelihood of choosing defection vs. loyalty increases with the strength of their ties to local communities through rebel governance: commanders that failed to form strong and long-lasting rebel–civilian ties were more likely to remain obedient to the political party whereas those who had an independent base of support posed a greater threat to the victors' civilian wing. If this is the case, rebel victors ought to focus internal co-optation on these particular military elites for two reasons. First, because they command the greatest risks, their promotion would help to reduce the likelihood of a successful coup. Second, however, these military elites are also poised to bring the greatest benefit: if well-connected military elites with strong local bases of support are re-integrated into the ruling party, then these elites' local civilian ties—over whom they exert significant social control—are likely to be useful for consolidating power further.

Hypothesis 2. *Where the threat to power is internal to the party, the rebel victor strengthens party control through coup-proofing by promoting potential defectors that sustain greatest ties with civilians.*

Finally, once the consolidation of power has occurred and the existential threat of war has subsided, the rebel victor faces decreasing incentives to expand its influence. Under this scenario, power is sustained not through conflict prevention, but through the successful implementation of clientelistic state control—specifically, using vote-buying or intimidation tactics that can fragment challengers and win votes (Nichter 2008; Stokes et al. 2013). In short, once stability has been reasonably established in a post-conflict state, rebel parties begin to act much like other parties in developing countries that successfully retain power through electioneering. This cost-effective strategy helps maintain control and counter electoral threats, showcasing the adaptable nature of these relationships in navigating the complex post-war political landscape.

If rebel–civilian ties and rebel governing institutions are used for coercive clientelism, then there is path dependence from wartime rebel control to post-war state control (Haass and Ottmann 2022; Liu 2024a). War acts as a critical juncture through which social and power relations are upturned and reformed (Wood 2008): in areas where the rebel government had maintained institutions of governance and control during war, its embeddedness in local rural communities becomes a powerful tool for maintaining power through intimidation, vote-buying, and voter suppression under electoral politics. These behaviours would most affect the rebel victor's wartime strongholds, where these ties were strongest during war. This outcome has negative implications for sustained democratization under rebel victory: despite increased civilian politicization and democratic behaviour in the short run after war (Huang 2016), the long-run political control stemming from wartime institutions ought to decrease the likelihood of authentic and meaningful political participation.

Hypothesis 3. *Where the threat to power is electoral competition, the rebel victor uses its wartime ties to control voting behaviour through intimidation and coercion, predominantly within strongholds.*

7.2.3 Summary

Figure 7.1 summarizes the different varieties of insecurity that rebel victors face, and the hypothesized ways through which rebel–civilian ties may be used to help the victor to sustain control and retain power. In the subsequent section, I next turn to the Zimbabwean case to provide evidence for each of these channels throughout different periods in its post-independence history.

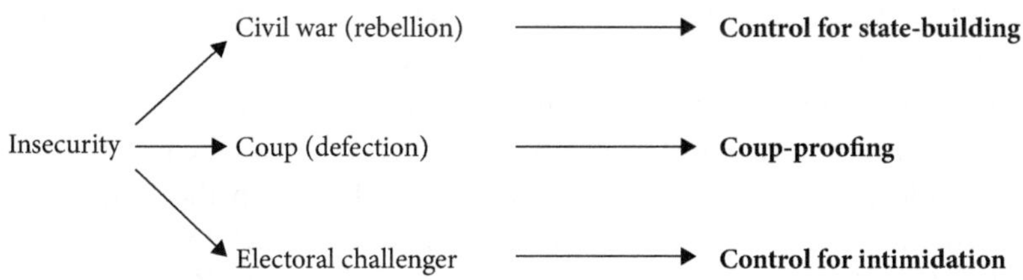

Figure 7.1 Varieties of insecurity
Source: Author's illustration.

7.3 Rebel governance and Zimbabwe's Liberation War

Zimbabwe's independence movement began as a political effort both within and beyond its borders but shifted to a military struggle in the 1970s to intensify resistance against colonial rule. The Zimbabwe Liberation War (1972–1979) involved two anti-colonial rebel groups, the ZAPU and the ZANU, each with its own military wing. Although ZANU initially split from ZAPU as a minor faction, it came to dominate the military struggle during the war. After independence, ZANU's political party, ZANU-PF, secured an overwhelming electoral victory in Zimbabwe's first post-independence elections in 1980.

ZANU's successes can be at least partially attributed to the strategies that the rebel party and its military wing used to exert social control over civilian communities in eastern Zimbabwe *during war*. This section explores three of its rebel governance strategies and outlines how these strategies were expanded heterogeneously across the country.

7.3.1 Strategies to exert wartime control

ZANU's rebel governance strategies were rooted in Maoist principles of a People's War: guerrilla warfare featuring separate military and political wings, with strength drawn from a broad and highly politicized civilian base. Once mobilized, civilians enabled the rebel party to remain embedded in local communities while also serving as a secondary support system for military activities, such as providing reconnaissance, cooking and washing, hiding weapons, and other day-to-day activities. To sustain this structure, ZANU prioritized establishing local party cells to organize civilians and launched political education campaigns to mobilize them through ideology and nationalism.

Yet, to ensure the continued cooperation of such a large number of people across rural Zimbabwe was a difficult task, which necessitated greater collaboration with key civilians on the ground. Two forms of rebel–civilian ties emerged. First, ZANU strategically organized mujibas—small groups of youth collaborators—who became the direct line of contact with local communities. Mujibas played a crucial role in guerrilla warfare by bridging the communication gap between hidden ZANU military bases in the country and the general population: while the locations of these bases were intended to be confidential, mujibas were entrusted with this sensitive information, and ZANU members relied on them to relay messages and information between communities and other sympathetic institutions (such as the church). They also had 'a *policing* function as watchdogs of the ZANU controlled [localities], supervising the entry and exit of people' (Cliffe et al. 1980: 52). This system allowed rebels to maintain operational security while also being able to influence and mobilize the broader community for information, supplies, and secondary support (Murambiwa 2014).

Second, local village committees—-community-level party cells—emerged as a major informal rebel governing institution during the Liberation War. Village committees were made up of older members in the community and were tasked with the key responsibility of gathering resources for the war effort and sustaining social control over civilian affairs within the communities. Village committees (in communication with mujibas) were the ones who organized civilians to provide secondary support for rebel soldiers. Village committees existed in a wider hierarchical structure that made up the ZANU's civilian wing, wherein several village-level committees reported to a base committee, which in turn was overseen by district committees and, ultimately, provincial committees (Jeche 2014). Cliffe et al. (1980: 50–51) write about some committees that were particularly developed:

> While there was no widespread restructuring of production, the committees did provide the impetus for some self-help. In the field of health, for example, instruction in hygiene was given, the necessity of building latrines and pits to store the rubbish was stressed and in the last few months of the war, local clinics were set up in some areas...

Third, mujibas and village committee members would help the rebels to organize—and ensure community attendance—at all-night pungwes, which were traditional all-night community events that became sites of mandatory rebel-led gatherings for mass politicization during the Liberation War. Where wartime pungwes were organized, ZANU political commissars would educate the community about the independence and liberation, socialism, and nationalism; community members were instructed to sing songs of liberation and were socialized into the practices of the broader liberation movement. Pungwes, however, were also sites of rebel control beyond education: it was during these events that mujibas would identify 'sellouts' in the community—i.e. those who were suspected of aiding the colonial regime—to be punished by ZANU members (Kwenda 2014).

Table 7.1 summarizes ZANU's rebel–civilian engagement during the Liberation War. While rebels attempted to broker such rebel–civilian relations throughout all

Table 7.1 ZANU's wartime rebel–civilian engagement

	Civilians	Function	Structure
Mujibas (Collaborators)	Youths	Intelligence, communication	Small groups
Village Committees	Older generation	Logistics, bureaucracy	Village, base district, province
Pungwes	Entire community	Politicization	Singing, drinking, denunciations

Source: Author's elaboration.

areas in which they militarily operated, these types of rebel–civilian institutions were successfully implemented primarily within a fraction of the areas—which became ZANU's wartime strongholds. Where the ZANU rebels were able to broker these rebel–civilian relationships, it exerted social control over civilian lives through these wartime supporters who played their roles as intermediaries between the rebel group and the community.

7.4 Varieties of insecurity in post-independence Zimbabwe

Post-independence, Zimbabwe's ruling party ZANU-PF faced all three forms of insecurity described previously: external, internal, and electoral insecurity. These periods in the country's history, therefore, allow me to investigate their use of their wartime rebel governing strategies to reduce post-war threats to their power. I highlight four periods in particular. First, from 1979 to 1980, the party engaged in pre-election campaigning where it faced an *electoral challenger*. Second, from 1980 to 1987, ZANU-PF faced post-independence insecurity from its wartime rivals, and thus it feared a return to *civil war*. Third, threats internal to the political party ballooned from 1990 to 2008, and ex-combatants credibly threatened a *coup*. Finally, from 1999 onward, the ruling party has faced major *electoral challengers* every election period.

7.4.1 Pre-election campaigning (1979–1980)

Following the Lancaster House agreement signed in December 1979, the newly independent Zimbabwe began preparing for its first elections that would take place between February and March of 1980. Despite initial agreements to run as one party, the two liberation parties contested the elections separately as ZANU-PF and PF-ZAPU and became the two main competitors for these first elections.[3] During the campaign period, ZANU-PF's wartime rebel–civilian ties proved to be exceptionally helpful during the first election period. As Hypothesis 3 would expect, the rebel party relied on these wartime endowments to engage in electioneering, and often did so using a combination of politicization and coercion within its strongholds to ensure obedience from the local population while preventing the opposition party from free access to conduct their own campaign activities.

As part of the peace process, combatants from the two rebel armies were required to assemble in cantonment sites for demobilization, while the parties' civilian leadership conducted nationwide campaigns for the 1980 elections.

[3] Two other parties—the colonial Rhodesian Front supported by white voters, and the United African National Council led by Bishop Abel Muzorewa—also contested.

The policy aimed to reduce the risk of electoral violence and prevent armed combatants from participating directly in the campaigns. This led to serious concerns, however, that demobilizing and gathering at cantonment sites would leave the rebel parties vulnerable to sudden security threats. Additionally, combatants feared that their gathering in specific sites would make themselves easy targets for retaliatory violence from the former colonial party and army.

ZANU combatants avoided these concerns by relying on their wartime civilian ties. They did so by colluding with trusted mujibas, who would surrender themselves to demobilization processes as combatants while the actual combatants themselves went free. Observers estimated that over a quarter of ZANU combatants failed to comply, and instead ZANU demobilization camps were filled by mujibas (P. Ndlovu 2012). This strategy was particularly useful not only for retaining security forces who could respond if the peace process went poorly: it was useful also for electioneering because it allowed combatants and wartime political commissars—who were not supposed to be campaigning at all—to return to their wartime operational areas and work once again in conjunction with the wartime civilian supporters to campaign at the grassroots level. As one former ZAPU combatant noted, 'ZANU from word go they had seven thousand commissars, trained commissars who were being infiltrated into the country. Even toward the elections seven thousand were outside and doing the party work' (Nkiwane 2012).

Within communities themselves, mujibas and village committees continued to be instrumental for exerting control. Continuing their wartime functions, they kept a watchful eye on citizens in the communities and campaigned on their behalf. Most critically, they supported ZANU combatants in sidelining PF-ZAPU politicians, effectively barring them from campaigning in ZANU's wartime strongholds. As one former ZAPU politician explained (Dabengwa 2012):

> [. . .] at a certain stage when ZANU decided to say there were no-go areas, there were certain areas in the country where they would not allow political party to participate in . . . and those are the areas where [ZANU combatants] had had a strong presence. [. . .] [ZAPU] actually made a very strong protest [. . .] to say that we can't call that free and fair election where you have one party refusing people to come and campaign in the areas where their forces are.

The resulting vote shares for the two political parties in each province are presented in Table 7.2. The table also indicates whether that province was a ZANU stronghold during war. Noticeably, ZANU's wartime strongholds had significantly higher percentages of votes for ZANU-PF; more importantly, these vote shares could not be attributed solely to ethnic voting. During the war, ZANU recruited primarily from the Shona ethnic group while ZAPU recruited from the Ndebele ethnic group—which undoubtedly played a large role in the resulting vote shares. Yet, Mashonaland West and Midlands provinces both voted for ZANU-PF at lower

Table 7.2 Votes for main parties

	ZANU wartime stronghold	ZANU-PF votes	PF-ZAPU votes
Manicaland	✓	84.1%	1.6%
Mashonaland Central	✓	83.8%	2.3%
Mashonaland East	✓	80.5%	4.6%
Mashonaland West		71.9%	13.4%
Matabeleland North		10.0%	79.0%
Matabeleland South		6.7%	86.4%
Midlands		59.7%	27.1%
Masvingo	✓	87.3%	1.9%

Source: Vote shares from Tevera (1989); wartime stronghold data from Liu (2022).

proportions than their Shona ethnic composition would suggest. Party leaders attributed this to the lack of grassroots mobilization due to a lack of wartime rebel–civilian ties: while the party set up formal party machinery in Mashonaland West and Midlands to campaign during the elections, these formal structures were not as effective as the informal structures for control that ZANU was able to embed within communities during war (Cliffe et al. 1980).

7.4.2 Post-independence insecurity (1980–1987)

After winning the first post-independence elections, the ruling party ZANU-PF faced domestic insecurity from its wartime rivals. ZAPU combatants and civilian supporters viewed the election results as illegitimate, largely due to ZANU's campaign tactics, which included violating ceasefire terms and restricting free movement. Further, while ZAPU leaders did occupy some positions of power within the government, and many ZAPU combatants were integrated into the army, a substantial proportion of its former combatants still advocated against full demobilization in case of violence from ZANU-PF. As a result, 'ZAPU was deeply suspicious of ZANU, believing that no true will of the people was reflected in the election result. ZANU, apparently, feared ZAPU, presumably because of its continuing military strength...' (M. Ndlovu 2012: 91). This deep mistrust between the two parties escalated tensions at all levels of government and society, spanning the ruling civilian leadership, the military, and the broader civilian population nationwide.

ZANU-PF would point to two concrete incidents, in 1981 and 1982, as evidence of external threats to its power. First, ZAPU soldiers integrated into the national army fomented a small uprising in the Entumbane barracks in 1981. These barracks were located in territories that were ZAPU wartime strongholds, meaning that it was already difficult for ZANU-PF to sustain complete control. In 1982, a large collection of weapons were found on ZAPU-owned farms, which ZANU-PF took as clear evidence of a mounting security threat. In response, the ruling party purged the government of PF-ZAPU politicians and began preparing for a return to violence. Meanwhile, ZAPU ex-combatants deserted the military *en masse* and joined their other wartime fighters to launch a low level guerrilla campaign from the Matabeleland provinces, which had long supported ZAPU.

ZANU-PF responded to these threats with mass violence against its civilians living in the Matabeleland provinces. The Gukurahundi massacres, which were carried out by the Fifth Brigade army from 1983 to 1986, killed an estimated 20,000 civilians who were labelled as ZAPU dissident supporters simply by co-ethnicity. At the same time, Zimbabwe's National Army carried out counterinsurgency efforts to eliminate combatants themselves, while the Zimbabwe National Police, along with ZANU-PF youth members, used coercion and intimidation to prevent conflict spread beyond Matabeleland.

While state forces and paramilitary forces were deployed to eliminate external threats in rival terrain, ZANU-PF's wartime ties to local communities, along with their wartime institutions, played a significant role in post-war politics. As I next explain, they helped the ruling party to consolidate power by *sustaining control* in strongholds (Hypothesis 1), which became necessary under the tense post-war political landscape as well as greater demands for resources within both the development and security sectors:

Resource constraints

As is common with post-conflict reconstruction, post-war Zimbabwe struggled with resource constraints to rebuild the nation. This was exacerbated by three major (though not exhaustive) factors. First, public infrastructure and goods were severely ill equipped to accommodate the majority Black Zimbabwean population under the colonial regime, which predominantly met the needs of the White population. Addressing these disparities became a priority for the new government, which focused on expanding education, healthcare, and infrastructure, particularly in rural communal areas where most Black Zimbabweans lived. Second, ZANU-PF's wartime promises extended beyond independence and Black majority rule; the party had also pledged widespread land reform, as the country's most productive lands remained concentrated in the hands of wealthy White farmers due to colonial policies. Post-independence, the ruling party worked towards this promise through the 'willing buyer willing seller' policy, in which the government would buy land from White landowners who were willing to sell (Chilunjika and Uwizeyimana 2015). Despite promises of assistance from the British government to compensate white landholders, and despite very few farmers actually being willing to sell their land, buying land at full market value proved to be resource intensive. Third, the threat of return to conflict in the Matabeleland provinces pushed the ruling party to spend more on security forces—army and paramilitary—diverting funds from its development projects elsewhere in the country.

ZANU-PF, during Zimbabwe's first decade of independence, sought to tackle development challenges across the country by relying on bureaucratic professionalism and efficiency. Yet, it was unable to keep up with the resource demands from projects it had conceived, while the large hopeful population pushed their new government to make good of its wartime and election promises. At its face, development did not immediately threaten the ruling party's power; however, in combination with a growing insurgency and distrusting population in the West, ZANU-PF's inability to meet civilian demands threatened to increased support for the opposition—which would then exacerbate the need for resources within the security sector. In other words, resource constraints and external rivals were simultaneously threatening ZANU-PF's consolidation of power, and thus, political factors undoubtedly shaped how the ruling party engaged in resource allocation across priorities and territories.

To address resource constraints, ZANU-PF promoted self-help, urging communities to take an active role in reconstruction and development by partially providing for their own needs rather than relying solely on government resources. This strategy drew on practices from wartime rebel governance, where village committees had been instrumental in mobilizing community cooperation and fostering collective action (Cliffe et al. 1980). In the first few years after war, village committees both collected and disbursed aid to community members in need (Kriger 1991); throughout the rest of the decade, ZANU-PF continued to rely on them to co-produce local development. Within the healthcare sector for example, rural women were trained as Village Health Workers to work either as a volunteer or while receiving a small stipend; this program eased pressures on the government to pay the extensive costs of healthcare expansion, which was already straining budgets at the time (Sanders 1990). The role of self-help and co-producing development was most evident in education, a sector in which ZANU-PF enjoyed massive success in the first decade after independence. Where communities could be galvanized to engage in self-help for fundraisers and manpower, the government was able to rely on them to engage in school construction and expansion with less resource inputs from the government (Ministry of Education, NAZ 1983). A ZANU-PF ex-combatant put this succinctly (author interview[4]):

> When the government began to develop, began to build the schools, there was not enough budget... The news reached the war veterans who said 'no problem!

[4] Author interview conducted in Harare, 2017.

> Let the government pay teachers with the budget. We will organize the parents to build the schools' . . . Remember when I told you of the organization [during the war]?

Ultimately, the ethos of self-help, through community organizations such as village committees, were instrumental for allowing the ruling party to sidestep the threats of resource constraints in development. It also freed up national budgets for security spending in the West to tackle ex-ZAPU dissidence in the Matabelelands.

Social control

Beyond engaging citizens in self-help to loosen budget constraints, rebel–civilian ties were also particularly important for maintaining social control over the population. Kriger (1991: 215), for example, details this clearly in various districts that had been under strong ZANU-PF control during the war. Immediately after the war, it was already clear that the institutions left over from wartime would continue to retain their coercive elements:

> Seemingly influenced by guerrilla courts, some party committees took it on themselves to punish people who did not obey party rules. A man who experienced such party justice took the matter to the Mutoko magistrate's court. His crime was that he did not obtain permission to visit an area. Monitoring visitors to an area was a wartime hangover from guerrilla instructions to villagers to watch people, especially those new to an area, to detect potential 'sell-outs'.

For the years following the war, the political mood after war was one of national reconciliation and unity—at the expense of allowing for criticism against the new ruling party. The decade after war saw major changes as the new government sought to implement policies and projects based on its own visions of development. Beyond education expansion, the government also rolled out policies such as large vaccine campaigns, substantially curbing traditional leaders' powers, and attempting to implement different strategies for more efficient land allocation. These changes were not always popular with communities, who oftentimes experienced these new government directives as major impositions on their lives and livelihoods. In addition, while the ethos of self-help was broadly popular, citizens consistently made demands for greater resources as they noted that some parts of the country were greater beneficiaries of government funding. The previously mentioned Village Health Workers program is one such example: to make up for a lack of major clinics, the Village Health Workers program was meant to train a large number of civilians to work as volunteer health workers in rural communities and, therefore, to take the strain off of the national health system. Yet, while VHWs in some were indeed volunteers, VHWs in other areas were paid a stipend—leading to general dissatisfaction among those who had not been offered payment (Sanders 1990).

Where ZANU-PF sustained greater embeddedness within local communities, such complaints were largely stifled by newly elected party cells and newly appointed bureaucrats who had previously played important roles in the Liberation War (Liu 2024b). While people living in ZANU-PF strongholds expected their homes and communities—which were badly affected by the war—to benefit during the reconstruction period, they were largely disappointed by government inaction (Kwenda 2014). However, civilians were not allowed to speak out against the ruling party where party structures had been long embedded into the community. Fear of dissent, and of being seen as an opposition party supporter, was common:

> In some districts, including parts of Mutoko, people refused food aid, also fearing that it had come from another party and would get them in trouble later. When I asked questions about the new resettlement programme, which did not meet many villagers' expectations, or ZANU-PF, many people simply refused to answer or said 'one cannot say anything bad about the party', by which they implied that it was foolish to ask them what they felt about policies (Kriger 1991: 219).

In short, while the national government preached participatory politics, reconciliation, and self-help, community-level politics through local party officials did not operate in line with those goals. Instead, wartime strongholds became sites of intense political and social control as local party officials helped the ruling party to consolidate power across the nation.

7.4.3 Internal threats and ex-combatant demands (1990–2008)

By the late 1980s, having largely consolidated power over the country by eliminating civil war threat in opposition-supporting areas, ZANU-PF turned to internal consolidation of power through coup-proofing in the face of potential defection from within its base (Hypothesis 2).

Initial pressures came from the war veterans, who had been combatants during the Liberation War but had since been demobilized as part of the political transition process in 1980. Although various commanders were rewarded after conflict with high-ranking positions in the army or government, rank-and-file ex-combatants found themselves with little prospects during the first decade of independence. Many ex-combatants had hoped to join the Zimbabwe National Army, but were not eligible based on age and education requirements. Demobilization pay was relatively meagre—a one-time payment of Z$400 in 1980, and another lump sum of Z$4400 a few years later—and there were few reintegration services or job training opportunities beyond it due to lack of resources and government capacity to implement programs for the overwhelming number of ex-combatants eligible for them. Ten years after independence in 1990, around 25,000 ex-combatants were still jobless and were struggling with poverty and poor mental health (Hove and Mutanda 2014).

While external threats to ZANU-PF's rule in the 1980s demanded greater internal cohesion and loyalty from the armed forces and demobilized combatants, when threats subsided, ex-combatant dissatisfaction with the ruling party became particularly salient once again. Discontent war veterans became increasingly vocal about their demands in the 1990s and fissures between veterans and ZANU-PF politicians grew stronger. Sadomba (2008: 81) writes about ex-combatant power and connection with civilians in Masvingo, a staunch ZANU-PF stronghold since the war:

> In Masvingo, War Veterans mobilised peasants to vote against the ZANU-PF Politburo choice of candidate in primaries leading to the 1990 general elections. In a nationally publicised showdown between Shuvai Mahofa and Cosmas Gonese (a War Veteran) the Politburo candidate lost the primaries, humiliating the ruling party in what was seen as a head-on conflict between a War Veteran-peasant alliance and the ruling clique...
>
> The War Veterans continued with their tactic of organising peasants as their power base to challenge the ruling oligarchy, a tactic applied until [the late 1990s]. With this tactic the War Veterans' movement expanded beyond ex-combatants, drawing in peasants, youths and other political interests.

Particularly contentious was the issue of land reform: as previously explained, ZANU-PF initially attempted to roll out land reform through a willing-buyer-willing-seller system wherein white farmers who were willing to sell their land would find the government to be a willing buyer at market price. This land was meant to be redistributed to Black Zimbabweans. Yet, meaningful land reform was slow to materialize during the first two decades—resulting in substantial frustration among ex-combatants. In particular, they had expected to be beneficiaries of land reform given their wartime service per the government's eligibility requirements for land allocation, which indicated that land would go to the landless poor, war refugees, and war veterans. Yet, substantial portions of the already-insufficient lands were reallocated to party supporters, predominantly those living within ZANU-PF strongholds (Kriger 2007).

The Zimbabwe National Liberation War Veterans Association (ZNLWVA) became a powerful platform for ex-combatants to express their grievances. Established in 1990 to advocate for ex-combatant welfare, the organization quickly mobilized former fighters for collective action. Within just a few years, the

ZNLWVA successfully used violence to pressure the ruling party into implementing reforms, including the War Veterans Act of 1992, which established a War Veterans Board, and the War Victims Compensation Act of 1993, which provided compensation to ex-combatants injured during the war (Musemwa 2011).[5] Violent ex-combatant protests during the Heroes Day demonstration in 1997 extracted even greater compensation from the government but not sustainable program, including a large lump sum payment of $Z50,000 and a monthly pension of Z$2,000, which hastened Zimbabwe's economic decline due to the unbudgeted expense.

ZANU-PF's contention with the ZNLWVA and the war veterans were further complicated by electoral challenges occurring in parallel. In 1999, the first meaningful political opposition emerged to become a major challenger in electoral politics (to be explained further later). The Movement for Democratic Change (MDC), led by union leader Morgan Tsvangirai, was able to rally substantial support from urban Zimbabwe and the youth population seeking for political change. The MDC had early successes, including a strong showing at both the parliamentary and presidential elections; it also successfully campaigned against a proposed constitutional change in 2000, which would have greatly benefitted the ruling party had it passed.

In short, by the turn of the century, ZANU-PF faced *both* ex-combatant discontent and a viable opposition party, which required it to increase the intensity of its coercion and control over the civilian population. In particular, ex-combatants' ability to wield violence and to galvanize rural communities within ZANU-PF strongholds was problematic for the party's survival; the opposition MDC's ability to campaign in the cities, as well as in areas outside of ZANU-PF strongholds, compounded the ruling party's concerns.

To respond to both of these threats, ZANU-PF passed and implemented the Fast Track Land Reform Programme (FTLRP) in July 2000, a major land reform that would allow the government to expropriate land from White farmers for redistribution. The FTLRP also allowed for *co-optation* to reduce coup threat: ZANU-PF empowered War Veterans under the ZNLWVA to lead the charge in expropriation, resulting in major violent land grabs and squatting across the nation. This strategy was economically poorly conceived, but politically expedient for two intertwined reasons. First, despite FTLRP's initial criteria for land allocation, the program resulted in ZANU-PF's supporters gaining a substantial amount of land, including both the political and military elite alongside ZNLWVA leaders who controlled the ex-combatants (International Crisis Group 2007). The land

[5] As Musemwa (2011: 123) writes, 'The government's gesture was therefore not simply an altruistic measure but one into which it had been cajoled by a series of protests led by the intemperate war veteran leader Chenjerai 'Hitler' Hunzvi who at one time laid siege to President Mugabe's party offices with disgruntled war veterans.'

occupations, therefore, greatly increased ex-combatants' power in society and tied the welfare of important players in Zimbabwean politics directly to both the land issue and also to ZANU-PF in particular.

Second, FTLRP renewed the wartime organizational capacity that ZANU-PF uses to perpetuate its control. As Matondi (2012: 214) writes about the Fast Track Farms that emerged from FTLRP, social organization was 'influenced by politicization, which resulted in power struggles, the creation of personality cults based on political connections or liberation war credentials.' In particular, ex-combatants were able to organize the rural civilian base to organize for occupation in the first place, and in ways that mimicked wartime rebel governance (Moyo and Yeros 2005). Further, because ex-combatants led the land occupations, this ultimately gave the ex-combatants substantial say over community affairs and allowed them to also organize social relations in the new Fast Track Farms. Thus, in conjunction with increasing ex-combatant wealth and power in society, the creation of the new Fast Track Farms also allowed the ruling party to ensure that 'political participation became a major determinant of influencing social order,' wherein political participation among citizens—much like wartime politicization—often meant involuntary engagement with pro-government community-level institutions and organizations (Matondi 2012).

As strong evidence of Hypothesis 2, FTLRP successfully bound ex-combatants to ZANU-PF. Ex-combatants sought to sustain the ruling party's power for their own economic benefit, thereby reducing the likelihood of internal dissent, while ZANU-PF relied on them to maintain control over rural populations. This dynamic has had far-reaching consequences for civilian life well beyond the peak of the land occupations in the 2000s. Because the ex-combatants' organizational strength was in part rooted in their ties to civilian communities—and because this organizational strength was derived from wartime strategies—the result was an illiberal socio-political structure that further entrenched ZANU-PF's power over rural civilians. From the early 2000s onward, the ZNLWVA became a clearly partisan organization, one on which ZANU-PF heavily relied to retain control over local communities where the ZNLWVA had strong ties (i.e. wartime strongholds), particularly during election campaigns.

Ultimately, by bringing the military and war veterans closer to the ruling faction within ZANU-PF as well, the party had successfully sidestepped the possibility of a coup from potential defectors. As a 2007 report noted: 'war veterans, who campaign for Mugabe in the party and the countryside at election time, have been formally constituted as a reserve force under defence ministry control, with a monthly wage. Their loyalty and that of the military would make it difficult for ZANU-PF dissidents to stage a successful coup against Mugabe' (International Crisis Group 2007). This continued to be true until a decade later.

7.4.4 Insecurity at the polls (1999–ongoing)

As briefly explained in the previous section, ZANU-PF once again began to face insecurity through a new electoral challenger beginning in 1999. After eliminating ZAPU in the late 1980s, the ruling party had enjoyed uninterrupted support for over a decade due to a lack of political challengers despite growing political discontent within the country. In 1999, the opposition movement coalesced around the MDC, an urban and labour union-based party that sought to contest for elections and install a new generation of young leaders into national politics. The MDC was exceptionally successful from the outset: during the 2000 parliamentary elections, the young party won almost 50% of the seats despite credible allegations of state-sponsored vote coercion. In 2002, the MDC's party candidate, Morgan Tsvangirai won 42% of the presidential vote. These vote shares were a substantial shift from ZANU-PF's prior electoral challengers: during the prior election cycle—the 1995 parliamentary elections and the 1996 presidential elections—the largest opposition party won only 7% and 5%, respectively.

The opposition party performed even better in the harmonized 2008 elections. The MDC-Tsvangirai (MDC-T) party[6] won the plurality of parliamentary seats (99 seats, to ZANU-PF's 97), while Tsvangirai emerged with a higher vote share during the first round of the presidential elections (47% to Mugabe's 43%). These results led to two outcomes: the MDC-T alleged major vote coercion and rigging during the first round of the presidential election and subsequently boycotted the runoffs; due to the MDC-T's success in parliamentary elections, ZANU-PF and MDC-T formed a Government of National Unity in February 2009, with Mugabe as president and Tsvangirai as prime minister.

Since the rise of the MDC—and particularly after the disastrous 2008 election results—ZANU-PF has increased both its covert and overt violence during election campaign periods. To be clear, these behaviours had been present since the first post-independence elections in 1980, as previously noted: even despite winning a comfortable majority across each election, ZANU-PF had used a combination of intimidation and vote-buying to keep constituents in line each electoral cycle (Kriger 2005). Its successes in using these strategies—both in terms of *how* they are carried out but also *where* they are carried out—are a direct reflection of rebel–civilian tie-formation during war and the legacies of how these ties facilitated post-war control through the institutionalization of wartime roles, relationships, and practices.

In other words, although ZANU-PF's strategies for sustaining control have shifted over the years, similarities to wartime strategies are clearly evident.

[6] In 2005, the MDC split two factions, the MDC-Tsvangirai and the MDC-Ncube, due to leadership disputes.

Voter intimidation and vote-buying are carried out by agents of the state, who reproduce wartime institutions from key positions of power in society (Liu 2024a). During war, mujibas and village committees organized local society and held pungwes for politicization; today, ZANU-PF supporters who occupy similar wartime roles, along with party cells, continue to do the same in various ways.

Wartime roles

The explicit use of youth militias in politics has carried on from the end of conflict until today, although they have taken different forms over the years. While the original cohort of mujibas were directly involved in the electoral strategy at independence, they have undoubtedly since aged out of playing such roles. Yet, it is their *roles* that have been institutionalized into politics, reflecting how wartime rebel–civilian ties and governance structures are perpetuated in post-war politics—even if the individuals themselves changed. After being elected into power, the newly formed ZANU-PF youth wing has been instrumental in ensuring support for ZANU-PF during every general election. ZANU-PF took it further in 2000 with the creation of the National Youth Service, more commonly known as the Green Bombers, which acted as a ZANU PF youth militia formed for the purposes of vote coercion. The Green Bombers was formed by ZANU-PF's Minister for Gender, Youth, and Employment, who had been a former mujiba during the war and sought to recreate a youth militia that would 'foster "patriotism", as founded on memories of the liberation struggle, among youth who had not experienced the war' (Ndlovu-Gatsheni and Willems 2009). Even later in 2010, the ruling party formed the youth organizations Chipangano and Upfumi Kuvadiki for the purposes of sustaining control and electioneering.

Beyond youth militias, organizations like the Zimbabwe Liberators and War Collaborators Association (ZILIWACO) and the Zimbabwe National Liberation War Veterans Association (ZNLWVA) still exist to carry out voter intimidation and exist explicitly with a pro-government orientation. For example, the secretary general of ZILIWACO recently asked: 'The million-dollar question to ask is do we need opposition political parties in a liberated Africa. Let us reflect our foundations which are liberations platforms of Africa as this gathering' (The Zimbabwe Mail 2021). ZILIWACO's vice-chairperson also noted: 'being a war collaborator is not about age. It's all about what has been stated and written down to indicate what constitutes a mujibha or chimbwido' (The Sunday Times 2019). Such sentiments highlight the continued influence of wartime rebel–civilian ties in post-war politics.

Party organization

During war, village committees were functionally ZANU party apparatuses as formally indicated in the party's internal documentation (Bhebe 1999); after war, similar structures were formally institutionalized as ZANU-PF party cells within communities to continue ensuring deep party control in everyday life. As one ZANU ex-combatant and current-day politician explained when speaking about the Liberation War's effects on current-day politics: 'You don't go into a village in Zimbabwe and slip in without people knowing who you are. They report [you]... People are too organized' (author interview[7]).

During election periods, party workers are particularly relevant for ensuring control: they force civilians to attend pungwes to repoliticize them with liberation music and rhetoric, and have held war re-enactments in key sites (LeBas 2006). Harkening back to wartime strategies, these are held in conjunction with the previously mentioned youth militias, who use these pungwes as an opportunity to now identify and eliminate MDC supporters who were then 'beaten in public or snatched away to secret detention centres that specialized in crude forms of torture' (Bratton and Masunungure 2008: 51).

Further, because ZANU-PF derives most of its votes from its wartime strongholds, these are also the areas that see the most organized and consistent voter coercion and intimidation. It is in these areas that the legacies of wartime rebel–civilian ties and wartime institutions are still the most salient; these areas are also where the ruling party has exerted strong social and political control from the very beginning, and therefore continue to exert outsized influence today. Bratton and Masunungure (2008: 51–52) write:

> The targets of intimidation were not so much the solid MDC strongholds in the cities and the southwest, but politically contested areas in the country's middle belt and northeast where, in the first round of the election, voters had swung away from ZANU-PF and toward the MDC. The object of electoral cleansing was to create 'no-go zones' (note again the guerrilla-insurgency terminology) where the ZANU-PF monopoly could be enforced at the local level through the direct and demonstration effects of violence.

In short, it is no coincidence that opposition parties, which had little access to ZANU-PF strongholds even during the 1980 elections, still today derive most of their strength from areas where ZANU-PF was unable to engage in rebel governance during war. While some inroads have been gained in Manicaland province (a ZANU-PF stronghold from wartime), opposition parties today still predominantly win their support predominantly from western Zimbabwe. In part because of ZANU-PF's deep rural penetration during the war through rebel governance, opposition parties are also far more successful in urban cores today as well.

[7] Author interview conducted in Harare, December 2017.

7.5 Conclusion

This chapter has explored the varieties of insecurity that rebel victors face once they come into power, and how each form of insecurity may subsequently the victors' strategies for consolidating power. In particular, I focus on the continuation of rebel governance strategies from wartime and argue that the organization of rebel–civilian ties during war may be reproduced in different ways post war—depending on the threats to the ruling party's position in power. Where victors face *external* insecurity from wartime rivals and thus the potential for a renewed civil war, rebel–civilian ties complement other state-building strategies by artificially reducing civilian demands on ruling party resources. Where victors face *internal* insecurity—from within the party—it engages in coup-proofing by paying off its own members, but prioritizes those with particularly strong rebel–civilian ties as these ties not only heighten insecurity but also strengthen party control if successfully co-opted. Finally, where the victor primarily faces *electoral* insecurity at the polls, rebel–civilian ties may be repurposed as party brokers—a cheaper strategy for maintaining control than broader statebuilding.

I illustrate the argument through Zimbabwe's post-independence politics, during which the independence-seeking rebel group ZANU has continuously ruled as the ZANU-PF political party. Since independence in 1979, ZANU-PF has faced all three forms of insecurity: From 1979 to 1980, it contested and won its first national elections (electoral insecurity); then, from 1980 to 1987, it then feared a return to civil war as ex-combatants and civilians loyal to its wartime rivals, ZAPU, grew discontent with its rule. While ZAPU was eliminated by 1987, ZANU-PF then faced its third threat: from 1990 to 2008, internal challenges from its loyal ex-combatants—who demanded to be paid off for their wartime sacrifices—increased in severity as the ZNLWVA's founding substantially bolstered their collective action. Overlapping these internal threats was yet another electoral threat by a new opposition party, the MDC (1999 onwards).

Throughout each of these periods, ZANU-PF's strategies for eliminating threats to its power consistently drew from its wartime tactics of politicization, organization, and control. At its core, each strategy involved suppressing the demands of those within its wartime strongholds by leveraging its deep-rooted presence in these areas. However, the manifestation of this approach varied depending on the type of insecurity faced. When greater resources were needed to counter external challengers, the rebel–civilian ties in wartime strongholds helped reduce resource demands by promoting self-help through politicization and coercion. In cases where the party feared violent defection from ex-combatants, it rewarded war veterans and ZNLWVA leaders, who were both dangerous and useful due to their networks and connections to civilian communities. Lastly, during periods of electoral uncertainty, ZANU-PF once again relied on its wartime strongholds as sites of organized coercion and intimidation to secure adequate voter turnout.

Of course, it should be noted that parts of the country that were not under ZANU control during war were *also* subject to various strategies for consolidating power, and these often were also violent and coercive as the ruling party sought to dismantle local institutions and collective action potential opposing their rule. However, because its power had—since war—been derived from its rural base in eastern Zimbabwe, organized social control after war continues to be strongest in these areas as wartime strategies are reproduced most efficiently and effectively in these regions.

References

Atlas, P. M., and Licklider, R. (1999). 'Conflict Among Former Allies After Civil War Settlement: Sudan, Zimbabwe, Chad, and Lebanon'. *Journal of Peace Research*, 36(1): 35–54. https://doi.org/10.1177/0022343399036001004

Arjona, A. (2016). *Rebelocracy*. Cambridge: Cambridge University Press. https://doi.org/10.1017/CBO9781316421925

Balcells, L. (2011). 'Continuation of Politics by Two Means: Direct and Indirect Violence in Civil War'. *Journal of Conflict Resolution*, 55(3): 397–422. https://doi.org/10.1177/0022002711400865

Bara, C., Deglow, A., and van Baalen, S. (2021). 'Civil War Recurrence and Postwar Violence: Toward an Integrated Research Agenda'. *European Journal of International Relations*, 27(3): 913–935. https://doi.org/10.1177/13540661211006443

Bhebe, N. (1999). *The ZAPU and ZANU Guerrilla Warfare and the Evangelical Lutheran Church in Zimbabwe*. Gweru: Mambo Press.

Bowles, J., Larreguy, H., and Liu, S. (2020). 'How Weakly Institutionalized Parties Monitor Brokers in Developing Democracies: Evidence from Postconflict Liberia'. *American Journal of Political Science*, 64(2): 223–239. https://doi.org/10.1111/ajps.12500

Bratton, M., and Masunungure, E. (2008). 'Zimbabwe's Long Agony'. *Journal of Democracy*, 19(4): 41–55. https://doi.org/10.1353/jod.0.0024

Breslawski, J. (2021). 'The Social Terrain of Rebel Held Territory'. *Journal of Conflict Resolution*, 65(2–3): 453–479. https://doi.org/10.1177/0022002720951857

Call, C. T. (2012). *Why Peace Fails: The Causes and Prevention of Civil War Recurrence*. Washington, DC: Georgetown University Press. https://doi.org/10.1353/book14243

Chilunjika, A., and Uwizeyimana, D. E. (2015). 'Shifts in the Zimbabwean Land Reform Discourse from 1980 to the Present'. *African Journal of Public Affairs*, 8(3): 130–144.

Cliffe, L., Mpofu, J., and Munslow, B. (1980). 'Nationalist Politics in Zimbabwe: The 1980 Elections and Beyond'. *Review of African Political Economy*, 7(18): 44–67. https://doi.org/10.1080/03056248008703424

Cunningham, K. G., Huang, R., and Sawyer, K. M. (2021). 'Voting for Militants: Rebel Elections in Civil War'. *Journal of Conflict Resolution*, 65(1): 81–107. https://doi.org/10.1177/0022002720937750

Dabengwa, N. (2012). *Transcript of Interview with Dumiso Dabengwa*. AL3291/B03, conducted by Mary Ndlovu on 7 July 2011, SAHA Collection AL3291 – The ZAPU/Zenzo

Nkobi Oral History Project Collection. South African History Archive (SAHA). Available at: https://www.saha.org.za/collections/AL3291/b03.htm (accessed on 9 April 2021)

Daly, S. Z. (2014). 'The Dark Side of Power-sharing: Middle Managers and Civil War Recurrence'. *Comparative Politics*, 46(3): 333–353. https://doi.org/10.5129/001041514810943027

Daly, S.Z. (2022). *Violent Victors: Why Bloodstained Parties Win Postwar Elections (Vol. 196).* Princeton, NJ: Princeton University Press. https://doi.org/10.2307/j.ctv2nnv4zm

Haass, F., and Ottmann, M. (2022). 'The Effect of Wartime Legacies on Electoral Mobilization after Civil War'. *The Journal of Politics*, 84(3): 1322–1336. https://doi.org/10.1086/718976

Hove, M., and Mutanda, D. (2014). 'Revisiting the Welfare of War Veterans in Zimbabwe'. *Scholars Journal of Arts, Humanities and Social Sciences*, 2(1): 116–128.

Huang, R. (2016). *The Wartime Origins of Democratization: Civil War, Rebel Governance, and Political Regimes.* Cambridge: Cambridge University Press. https://doi.org/10.1017/CBO9781316711323

International Crisis Group. (2007). *Zimbabwe: A Regional Solution?* ICG Africa Report no. 132.

Jeche, A. (2014). *Interview, 26 August.* Capturing Fading National Memory, National Archives of Zimbabwe, Oral History Department.

Kalyvas, S. N. (2006). *The Logic of Violence in Civil War.* Cambridge: Cambridge University Press. https://doi.org/10.1017/CBO9780511818462

Kasfir, N. (2024). 'Legacies of Victors Rebel Governance'. *Civil Wars*, online 19 March 2014(early view): 1–27. https://doi.org/10.1080/13698249.2024.2318686

Kriger, N. J. (1991). *Zimbabwe's Guerrilla War: Peasant Voices.* Cambridge: Cambridge University Press. https://doi.org/10.1017/CBO9780511895869

Kriger, N. J. (2005). 'ZANU (PF) Strategies in General Elections, 1980-2000: Discourse and Coercion'. *African Affairs*, 104(414): 1–34. https://doi.org/10.1093/afraf/adi007

Kriger, N. J. (2007). 'Liberation from Constitutional Constraints: Land Reform in Zimbabwe'. *SAIS Review of International Affairs*, 27(2): 63–76. https://doi.org/10.1353/sais.2007.0034

Kwenda, H. (2014). *Interview, 26 August.* Capturing Fading National Memory, National Archives of Zimbabwe, Oral History Department.

Lachapelle, J., Levitsky, S., Way, L. A., and Casey, A. E. (2020). 'Social Revolution and Authoritarian Durability'. *World Politics*, 72(4): 557–600. https://doi.org/10.1017/S0043887120000106

LeBas, A. (2006). 'Polarization as Craft: Party Formation and State Violence in Zimbabwe'. *Comparative Politics*, 38(4): 419–438. https://doi.org/10.2307/20434010

Levitsky, S., and Way, L. (2010). *Competitive Authoritarianism: Hybrid Regimes after the Cold War.* Cambridge: Cambridge University Press. https://doi.org/10.1017/CBO9780511781353

Levitsky, S., and Way, L. (2022). *Revolution and Dictatorship: The Violent Origins of Durable Authoritarianism.* Princeton, NJ: Princeton University Press. https://doi.org/10.1515/9780691223575

Lewis, J. I. (2020). *How Insurgency Begins: Rebel Group Formation in Uganda and Beyond.* Cambridge: Cambridge University Press. https://doi.org/10.1017/9781108855969

Liu, S. (2022). 'Control, Coercion, and Cooptation: How Rebels Govern after Winning Civil War'. *World Politics*, 74(1): 37–76. https://doi.org/10.1017/S0043887121000174

Liu, S. (2024a). 'Coercive Legacies: From Rebel Governance to Authoritarian Control'. *The Journal of Politics*, 86(4): 1129–1145. https://doi.org/10.1086/729947

Liu, S. (2024b). *Governing after War: Rebel Victories and Post-war Statebuilding*. Oxford: Oxford University Press. https://doi.org/10.1093/oso/9780197696705.001.0001

Loyle, C. E., Cunningham, K. G., Huang, R., and Jung, D. F. (2023). 'New Directions in Rebel Governance Research'. *Perspectives on Politics*, 21(1): 264–276. https://doi.org/10.1017/S1537592721001985

Loyle, C. E., and Onder, I. B. (2024). 'The Legacies of Rebel Rule in Southeast Turkey'. *Comparative Political Studies*, 57(11): 1771–1803. https://doi.org/10.1177/00104140231204223

Lyons, T. (2004). 'Post-conflict Elections and the Process of Demilitarizing Politics: The Role of Electoral Administration'. *Democratization*, 11(3): 36–62. https://doi.org/10.1080/1351034042000238167

Lyons, T. (2016). 'From Victorious Rebels to Strong Authoritarian Parties: Prospects for Post-war Democratization'. *Democratization*, 23(6): 1026–1041. https://doi.org/10.1080/13510347.2016.1168404

Mampilly, Z. (2012). *Rebel Rulers: Insurgent Governance and Civilian Life during War*. Ithaca, NY: Cornell University Press. https://doi.org/10.7591/9780801462979

Mampilly, Z., and Stewart, M. A. (2021). 'A Typology of Rebel Political Institutional Arrangements'. *Journal of Conflict Resolution*, 65(1): 15–45. https://doi.org/10.1177/0022002720935642

Martin, P. (2021). 'Commander–Community Ties after Civil War'. *Journal of Peace Research*, 58(4): 778–793. https://doi.org/10.1177/0022343320929744

Martin, P. (2022). 'Insurgent Armies: Military Obedience and State Formation after Rebel Victory'. *International Security*, 46(3): 87–127. https://doi.org/10.1162/isec_a_00427

Mason, T. D., Gurses, M., Brandt, P. T., and Michael Quinn, J. (2011). 'When Civil Wars Recur: Conditions for Durable Peace after Civil Wars'. *International Studies Perspectives*, 12(2): 171–189. https://doi.org/10.1111/j.1528-3585.2011.00426.x

Matanock, A. M. (2017). *Electing Peace: From Civil Conflict to Political Participation*. Cambridge: Cambridge University Press. https://doi.org/10.1017/9781316987179

Matondi, P. B. (2012). *Zimbabwe's Fast Track Land Reform*. London: Bloomsbury Publishing. https://doi.org/10.5040/9781350224209

Meng, A., and Paine, J. (2022). 'Power Sharing and Authoritarian Stability: How Rebel Regimes Solve the Guardianship Dilemma'. *American Political Science Review*,: 1–18. https://doi.org/10.1017/S0003055422000296

Ministry of Education, NAZ (1983). *Ministry of Education Report, 1983*. National Archives of Zimbabwe.

Moyo, S., and Yeros, P. (2005). *Reclaiming the Land: The Resurgence of Rural Movements in Africa, Asia and Latin America*. London: Zed Books. https://doi.org/10.5040/9781350222175

Murambiwa, A. (2014). *Interview, 27 August*. Capturing Fading National Memory, National Archives of Zimbabwe, Oral History Department.

Musemwa, M. (2011). 'Zimbabwe's War Veterans: From Demobilisation to Re-mobilisation'. *Transformation: Critical Perspectives on Southern Africa*, 75(1): 122–131.

Ndlovu, M. (2012). *ZAPU Through Zenzo Nkobi's Lens*. Braamfontein: The South African History Archives (SAHA).

Ndlovu, P. (2012). *Transcript of interview with Parks Ndlovu*. AL3291/B15, conducted by Mary Ndlovu and Zephaniah Nkomo on 12 November 2010, SAHA Collection AL3291 – The ZAPU/Zenzo

Nkobi Oral History Project Collection. South African History Archive (SAHA). Available at: https://www.saha.org.za/collections/AL3291/b15.htm (accessed on 9 April 2021)

Ndlovu-Gatsheni, S. J., and Willems, W. (2009). 'Making Sense of Cultural Nationalism and the Politics of Commemoration under the Third Chimurenga in Zimbabwe'. *Journal of Southern African Studies*, 35(4): 945–965. https://doi.org/10.1080/03057070903314226

Nichter, S. (2008). 'Vote Buying or Turnout Buying? Machine Politics and the Secret Ballot'. *American Political Science Review*, 102(1): 19–31. https://doi.org/10.1017/S0003055408080106

Nkiwane, A. (2012). *Transcript of interview with Abraham Nkiwane*. AL3291/B20, conducted by Mary Ndlovu and Zephaniah Nkomo on 24 November 2010, SAHA Collection AL3291 – The ZAPU/Zenzo Nkobi Oral History Project Collection. South African History Archive (SAHA). Available at: https://www.saha.org.za/collections/AL3291/b20.htm (accessed on 9 April 2021)

Revkin, M. R. (2021). 'Competitive Governance and Displacement Decisions under Rebel Rule: Evidence from the Islamic State in Iraq'. *Journal of Conflict Resolution*, 65(1): 46–80. https://doi.org/10.1177/0022002720951864

Riedl, R. B., Slater, D., Wong, J., and Ziblatt, D. (2020). 'Authoritarian-led Democratization'. *Annual Review of Political Science*, 23(1): 315–332. https://doi.org/10.1146/annurev-polisci-052318-025732

Roeder, P. G. (2005). 'Power Dividing as an Alternative to Ethnic Power Sharing'. In P. G. Roeder, and D. Rothchild (eds), *Sustainable Peace: Power and Democracy after Civil Wars* (pp. 51–82). Ithaca, NY: Cornell University Press.

Sadomba, W. Z. (2008). *War Veterans in Zimbabwe's Land Occupations: Complexities of a Liberation Movement in an African Post-colonial Settler Society*. Wageningen: Wageningen University and Research.

Sánchez De La Sierra, R. (2020). 'On the Origins of the State: Stationary Bandits and Taxation in Eastern Congo'. *Journal of Political Economy*, 128(1): 32–74. https://doi.org/10.1086/703989

Sanders, D. (1990). 'Equity in Health: Zimbabwe Nine Years on'. *Journal of Social Development in Africa*, 5(1): 5–22.

Schwartz, R. A. (2020). 'Civil War, Institutional Change, and the Criminalization of the State: Evidence from Guatemala'. *Studies in Comparative International Development*, 55(3): 381–401. https://doi.org/10.1007/s12116-020-09312-7

Sisk, T. D. (2009). 'Pathways of the Political: Electoral Processes after Civil War'. In *The Dilemmas of Statebuilding* (pp. 210–238). London: Routledge.

Stewart, M. A. (2018). 'Civil War as State-making: Strategic Governance in Civil War'. *International Organization*, 72(1): 205–226. https://doi.org/10.1017/S0020818317000418

Stewart, M. A. (2021). *Governing for Revolution: Social Transformation in Civil War*. Cambridge: Cambridge University Press.

Stokes, S. C., Dunning, T., Nazareno, M., and Brusco, V. (2013). *Brokers, Voters, and Clientelism: The Puzzle of Distributive Politics*. Cambridge: Cambridge University Press. https://doi.org/10.1017/CBO9781107324909

Taylor, C., Pevehouse, J., and Straus, S. (2017). 'Perils of Pluralism: Electoral Violence and Incumbency in Sub-saharan Africa'. *Journal of Peace Research*, 54(3): 397–411. https://doi.org/10.1177/0022343316687801

Thaler, K. M. (2018). *From Insurgent to Incumbent: State Building and Service Provision after Rebel Victory in Civil Wars* (Unpublished doctoral dissertation). Harvard University.

The Sunday Times (2019). *Youth league gets support* [7 July 2019]. Available at: https://www.sundaynews.co.zw/youth-league-gets-support/

The Zimbabwe Mail (2021). *War Veterans Endorse Mnangagwa for 2023 Presidency* [26 May 2021]. Available at: https://www.thezimbabwemail.com/politics/war-veterans-endorse-mnangagwa-for-2023-presidency/

Toft, M. D. (2010). 'Ending Civil Wars: A Case for Rebel Victory?' *International Security*, 34(4): 7–36. https://doi.org/10.1162/isec.2010.34.4.7

van Baalen, S. (2024). 'Polls of Fear? Electoral Violence, Incumbent Strength, and Voter Turnout in Côte D'ivoire'. *Journal of Peace Research*, 61(4): 595–611. https://doi.org/10.1177/00223433221147938

Walter, B. F. (2004). 'Does Conflict Beget Conflict? Explaining Recurring Civil War'. *Journal of Peace Research*, 41(3): 371–388. https://doi.org/10.1177/0022343304043775

Wood, E. J. (2000). *Forging Democracy from below: Insurgent Transitions in South Africa and El Salvador*. Cambridge: Cambridge University Press.

Wood, E. J. (2008). 'The Social Processes of Civil War: The Wartime Transformation of Social Networks'. *Annual Review of Political Science*, 11(June): 539–561. https://doi.org/10.1146/annurev.polisci.8.082103.104832

Young, L. E. (2019). 'The Psychology of State Repression: Fear and Dissent Decisions in Zimbabwe'. *American Political Science Review*, 113(1): 140–155. https://doi.org/10.1017/S000305541800076X

8

Armed groups' modes of local engagement and post-conflict (in)stability

Insights from the Ethiopian and Somali civil wars

Marine Gassier

8.1 Introduction

Some governments emerging from civil conflicts manage to durably restore stability and create political conditions under which a sustainable peace can be achieved. In other cases, however, the efforts of post-conflict governments to assert their authority fail to consolidate the post-conflict order, and conflict resumes.[1] Existing perspectives on civil war recurrence emphasize that stability requires a military hegemon capable of deterring further challenges. They also suggest that the failure of many negotiated peace settlements can be tied to commitment problems preventing disarmament. Such analyses offer important insights into the determinant of civil war recurrence and matched observed trends: war recurrence is more likely after settlements than after government or rebel victories. At the same time, these arguments leave important patterns of variation unaddressed. Not all conflicts that end with a victory are followed by period of prolonged stability, and not all settlements fall apart. Understanding the threats that post-war governments may face even after the actors that took power proved capable of defeating their adversaries and identifying the resources that have allowed some of the governments that emerged from negotiated settlements to withstand the turbulences of the post-conflict period have important implications for the design of recovery and post-conflict state-building programmes.

This chapter first examines the specific processes through which the post-conflict order typically unravels, considering three mechanisms in particular: (i) the fragmentation of the ruling coalition or its constitutive entities, (ii) inadequate demobilization of non-state armed groups, and (iii) governments'

[1] I am also grateful to Patricia Justino and Yvan Guichaoua for their helpful comments and suggestions.

Marine Gassier, *Armed groups' modes of local engagement and post-conflict (in)stability*. In: *Institutional Legacies of Violent Conflict*. Edited by: Patricia Justino, Oxford University Press. © United Nations University World Institute for Development Economics Research (UNU-WIDER) (2026). DOI: 10.1093/9780197904077.003.0008

dependence on local power brokers. Focusing on the processes often involved in the resumption of conflict suggests that patterns of civil war recurrence depend in part on how wartime political processes have redistributed power between the central government and local power structures. When wartime politics has deconcentrated power to the benefit of local authority figures and social organizations, the coalitions underpinning post-conflict regimes, even those formed by victors, often have difficulties avoiding fragmentation, enforcing demobilization, and ruling autonomously. When, on the contrary, civil wars undermine local power structures, even if these wars end with negotiated settlements, post-war governments are better positioned to mitigate the risks of fragmentation and re-armament, and less reliant on fragile, costly alliances with local elites. The effect of conflict on the distribution of power between the central and the local level results from wartime modes of local engagement, and specifically from the dominant actors in a war establishing their support base by co-opting or transforming local power structures. When actors in a war replace existing power structures with new institutions at the local level, for instance replacing traditional leaders with revolutionary councils, they not only create conditions conducive to greater power concentration after the war but also develop, through the institutions they create, new levers of governance that post-war governments can capitalize on.

To assess this hypothesis, I use a new dataset documenting armed groups' local political practices to identify differences in the modes of local engagements of actors that took part in recurring versus non-recurring conflict. In addition, I compare the local political strategies of the dominant insurgent movements during the civil wars in Ethiopia (1974–1991) and Somalia (1981–1991). Through this comparison, I show how critical differences in their approaches contributed to the two countries' divergent trajectories, in each case after a rebel coalition ousted the incumbent regime.

8.2 Threats to post-conflict stability: existing perspectives

What sets apart post-war governments who establish stable political orders from those who fail to do so? Under what circumstances are civil conflicts most likely to resume? Dominant explanations for civil war recurrence have chiefly considered the role of two factors: (i) the ability of victors to deter new challenges and (ii) the ability of parties to a settlement to credibly commit to the terms negotiated. Both sets of explanations provide important insights into the conditions that can foster stability after a civil conflict. But they do not account for the full range of possible outcomes, failing to explain the resumption of civil conflicts even after a first phase that ended with a decisive victory, or the stability of some negotiated post-conflict political arrangements, even in the absence of enforcement mechanisms.

8.2.1 First type of threat: deterrence failure

Realist explanations for peace emphasize the need for a sovereign authority capable of achieving military hegemony, arguing that only such an authority can quell or durably deter further violent challenges. This perspective on the conditions for stability dates back to English philosopher Thomas Hobbes, who argued that a durable peace requires a military conquest capable of imposing a new social order (see Hobbes 2016 [1651]). There are multiple examples of such a process unfolding in recent or more distant history. In Sri Lanka, the successful military operations that the government launched between 2006 and 2009 allowed it to take control of the de facto capital city and of the military bases of the Liberation Tigers of Tamil Eelam (LTTE), thereby asserting its dominance over the insurgents. These operations killed thousands of civilians, but, unlike the peace agreement that had been signed in 2002, they ended a war that had started over 25 years ago when the LTTE explicitly admitted defeat in 2009 (Bhattacharji 2009). In some cases, victorious insurgents can establish a new, durable political order. In China, the Communist Party has controlled the country since the Red Army's victorious campaigns, waged between 1946 and 1949.

More generally, the type of security dilemma that can trigger the recurrence of civil conflicts is more likely to emerge in the absence of a clearly dominant military actor. Such conditions may prompt military actors to attempt to consolidate their position by taking steps to achieve military hegemony, or various subnational communities to determine that their security is a matter that they should take into their own hands. Different investigations, including Fearon's (2004) examination of the determinants of the duration of civil wars, suggest that conflicts are more likely to remain settled when they end with a military victory. Toft (2009) also finds that enduring peace is more likely after wars that end with one side's decisive victory. Nevertheless, to reach a more complete understanding of patterns of post-war stability, it is important to look beyond the military equilibrium that emerges at the end of a conflict. A war ending with the victory of one side may create conditions more favourable to stability. Nevertheless, it does not constitute a guarantee, nor a necessary condition for it to be achieved.

A war ending with one party defeating its adversaries may create conditions that are more favourable to stabilization, but it does not guarantee it. After Mujahideen troops moved into Kabul and the Soviet government of Najibullah collapsed in 1992, violent confrontations promptly resumed. A peaceful political order can fail to emerge even after government forces prevail over their challenges. In 1996, after seven years of brutal counterinsurgency campaign, the Indonesian government claimed to have fully eliminated the Free Aceh Movement. Three years later, the insurgents launched new attacks in spite of a growing presence of government forces. In Aceh, military successes failed to produce a sustainable order (Ansori 2012). These examples suggest that stability requires more than a sufficiently large power differential between victors and losers, and that deterrence failures do not fully explain the resumption of some conflicts after one side initially prevailed.

8.2.2 Second type of threat: misaligned incentives and commitment problems

Another way to make sense of patterns of civil war recurrence is to consider how actors capable of violence will resort to it when they perceive that such a strategy best serves their interests and abandon it when it is no longer the case. This type of incentive already plays an important role in the onset of civil conflict. For instance, Bates (2015) argues that, starting in the 1980s, violent conflicts multiplied in a range of countries in Africa, including Rwanda, Sudan, Liberia, and Congo, because the incentives of state elites changed. Economic volatility and democratization shortened their time horizons, prompting them to prioritize short-term gains, even if the pursuit of these gains turned violent and destabilized their country. Similar incentive-based mechanisms can also explain how conflict comes to end. Driscoll (2015) argues that warlords in Georgia and Tajikistan were aware that access to foreign aid depended on the stabilization of their countries. This incentive was enough to motivate them to forego violent competition for power and spoils and, instead, strike enduring bargains.

Peace settlements fail when some parties renege on the terms negotiated and opt to re-arm themselves to pursue more favourable ones, becoming peace 'spoilers' (Stedman 1997). Do such failures occur because the terms of these settlements do not offer a path preferable to violent struggle for all parties involved? Some studies suggest that this is the case, highlighting how flawed settlement terms can leave some core grievances unaddressed (Fortna 2003; Paris 2004), with inadequate power-sharing provisions being a common deficiency of these terms (Hartzell and Hoodie 2003). Other studies argue that while settlement terms that are misaligned with the incentives of some of the parties that negotiated them can trigger new rounds of violent conflict, settlements typically do not fail because negotiators could not agree on terms that were acceptable to all parties. Rather, settlements break down because even after an agreement that all prefer to war has been reached, actors cannot commit to complying with its terms. They do not want to disarm knowing that no institutions exist to force their adversaries to do the same (Walter 2002). Violence persists largely because of this insecurity (Toft 2009; Werner and Yuen 2005).

External enforcement can support stabilization. In Nepal, the implementation of the Comprehensive Peace Accord signed in 2006 between the government and the Unified Communist Party, which put an end to a ten-year conflict, has succeeded in part because of the direct involvement of the United Nations Mission in Nepal (Wagle and Jackson 2015). But the success of peace agreements does not appear to be entirely predicated on external enforcement. In El Salvador, the Peace Accords signed thirty years ago between the government and insurgents have also ended the civil war, and allowed for the conversion of the Farabundo Martí National Liberation Front from a rebel force into a political party (Sprenkels 2018). Söderberg Kovacs and Hatz (2016) find that of all the non-state actors who signed peace agreements between 1975 and 2011, about a third successfully transformed into political parties, meaning that they abandoned violent strategies and pursued power through non-violent means, primarily elections. Some but not all of these groups emerged after an intrastate peace agreement that involved third parties as mediators or signatories. However, these forms of involvement are not equivalent to guaranteed enforcement.

These trends suggest that mechanisms beyond reliance on external enforcement may be available to the governments established through negotiated settlements that can facilitate the emergence of a stable post-conflict order. Discussions of the determinants of civil war recurrence tend to focus on how conflicts ended and whether one side prevailed. They emphasize how victories are associated with deterrence effects that are absent when conflicts end with a settlement, and how settlements are always threatened by the insecurity of the parties that negotiated them. Such arguments highlight important mechanisms, and matched observed trends: conflict recurrence is less likely after a victory than after a negotiated settlement. Nevertheless, the connections between how a conflict (or its first phase) ended and the risk of recidivism should not be overstated. First, these differences can be subtle. Some victories are achieved not through military means but through successful negotiations that allow one side to induce defections among its opponents. Conversely, some settlements can operate as face-saving mechanisms in contexts where one party has clearly prevailed (Driscoll 2015). Furthermore, the explanatory power of arguments hinging on the implications of victories versus settlements remains limited. Cases of conflicts that ended with one side's clear victory can still vary considerably in their long-term evolution. So do cases of conflicts that ended with a negotiated settlement. Advancing our understanding of the drivers of post-war instability beyond deterrence failure and commitment problems requires zooming in on the specific processes through which the post-conflict order tends to unravel.

8.3 How the post-conflict order unravels: core processes

Three mechanisms are typically at the root of the disruptions that trigger new rounds of violence after the first phase of a conflict has ended: (i) the fragmentation of dominant actors in this conflict, (ii) unsuccessful processes of demobilization, and (iii) gaps in the government's capacity for governance that perpetuate its dependence on local actors. These processes preclude the concentration of power—both political and military—that stabilization requires. They not only reduce the likelihood of rival actors pursuing non-violent means of negotiation but can also give rise to new patterns of conflict.

8.3.1 Fragmentation

The fragmentation of insurgent groups can lower the threat that these groups pose to the regime in place. But governments facing fragmented insurgencies also have greater difficulties achieving uncontested victories or negotiating stable settlements. The enduring violence in Mindanao in the Philippines illustrates these challenges. In the late 1980s, the government of the Philippines engaged in negotiation with the original insurgent group, the Moro National Liberation Front (MNLF). However, this process failed to quell the violence largely because it did not include a splinter insurgent organization, the Moro Islamic Liberation Front (MILF), which had formed ten years earlier when the government had reneged on a previous agreement. Creating the conditions for negotiating a stable settlement proved to be an elusive quest, as the insurgent organizations in Mindanao further fragmented. While the MILF lowered its demands and started to pursue autonomy rather than full independence, a new radical splinter faction, known as the Bangsamaro Islamic Freedom Fighters, formed. Overall, peace agreements negotiated with Moro movements, including the MNLF and the MILF, have been particularly fraught because of weak cohesion of these groups and the repeated formation of splinter factions that characterizes the conflict (Latif et al 2020; Tajima 2010). As peace talks between the government and some of the armed groups operating in Mindanao were underway, other groups, including Abu Sayyaf, continued to emerge. There are currently at least three distinct jihadist groups operating in Mindanao (Hwang and Schulze 2018).

The fragmentation of insurgent movements leads to recurring conflicts, not only because of confrontation between government forces and new splinter factions but also because of rivalries pitting insurgent factions against each other. Using data on the organizational features of rebel groups and the evolution of civil wars, Ishiyama and Batta (2011) observe that 'organizationally incoherent' groups are associated with a greater likelihood of conflict resuming. This is in part because such groups may lack the ability to implement the provisions of the settlements they negotiated, leading to new rounds of conflict between the initial adversaries. But a substantial share of war recidivism is connected to insurgent organization splintering or formerly allied factions turning against each other. This is often the result of internal disagreements on post-conflict power-sharing or rent redistribution. Peace is then threatened by new patterns of internecine conflict.

Finally, this type of splintering does not befall only organizations that challenge the state. Organizations that have gained power may also break into rival faction, and such fragmentation can threaten the stability of the post-conflict order even more than disunity within insurgent factions. In South Sudan, a power struggle between two factions within the party in power—the Sudan People's Liberation Movement—triggered a new civil war in 2013, only two years after the country achieved independence. This war lasted over five years and led to severe food insecurity rising to the level of famine, while forces on all sides engaged in abusing civilians. To this day, peace has not been restored to South Sudan, even though over 12,000 peacekeepers have been deployed (Sundberg 2019). Overall, the multiple channels through which fragmentation can shatter the post-conflict order and trigger new patterns of conflict suggest that the risk of conflict recurrence is closely tied to the inability of initial adversaries to maintain their unity.

8.3.2 Failed demobilization

Failed or stalled demobilization is another important factor contributing to recurring cycles of conflict. It is one of the drivers of the enduring violence in the North Kivu province of the Democratic Republic of Congo. The National Congress for the Defence of the People (CNDP by its French acronym)—which has been engaged in the conflict since the mid-2000s—was established and led by Laurent Nkunda, a former officer of the Congolese Rally for Democracy (Goma faction) who had refused to see his troops integrated in the national army after 2003 (when the transitional government was formed) (Stearns 2007). In 2009, Nkunda was arrested and the remaining troops of the CNDP signed a peace agreement with the government, agreeing to join the national army. But four years later, hundreds of these fighters formed a new rebel group. Citing the government's failure to implement the peace agreement signed on 23 March 2009, it took the name M23. They turned against the government because they refused to redeploy in other parts of the country outside of Kivu (Broache 2014).

Disarmament, demobilization, and reintegration programmes have at times received considerable support from the international community, particularly around 2005 when new policy guidelines were developed (Hanson 2007). The goals of such programmes are clear: they aim to support stabilization by curtailing the coercive capacity of violent actors and to promote security by preventing former fighters from preying on civilians. But studies show that these programmes have been implemented with varying levels of success (Hanson 2007). Poor implementation, which means that political actors can easily revert to violent strategies, can be a prelude to war recidivism.

8.3.3 Dependence on local power brokers

Another important dimension that contributes to the fragility of post-war governments and to recurring conflict is the deficiencies of the state institutions, which induce post-war governments to outsource core governance functions to local power brokers. Post-conflict governments face two main tasks. First, to rebuild the country, they must provide a range of basic services. But they must do so without the benefits of state institutions that could organize and support this effort. Second, they must dismantle the violent institutions that challenged the state during the war. But these institutions can be the most effective structures operating in post-conflict states. In practice, it is not infrequent for post-war governments to rule by negotiating with local power structures as they lack the capacity to administer local communities directly. In some cases, the local power brokers that post-conflict governments negotiate with are traditional community leaders who have long been in their roles. In other cases, the war has dimmed the political relevance of traditional local elites, and new local power brokers have emerged. These could be former rebels and army commanders or the leaders of new illicit economic networks. Whether the local power brokers that post-conflict governments bargain with are well-established or relatively new actors, they are often the very organizations that not long ago had mobilized against the state (Themnér and Utas 2016).

These arrangements, and the limits on state autonomy that they impose, can undermine post-war stability in different indirect but consequential ways. First, maintaining these alliances is costly, which means there are fewer resources that post-war governments can allocate to recovery. This economic impact matters for stability: individuals who are dissatisfied with their own economic situation and local economic trends may be more likely to join armed groups (Walter 2004). Second, such alliances have a political impact: they may preclude meaningful political reforms and genuine opening of the political space. This matters because unyielding barriers to political participation can be another predictor of civil war recurrence (Walter 2004). The dependence of post-war governments on local elites also threatens stability in a direct manner. In such contexts, little can be done to prevent local power brokers to revert to violent strategies should the alliances they have negotiated with the government turn sour.

Civil war recurrence is more likely when dominant actors lack cohesiveness, when post-war governments are unable to enforce demobilization, and when these government rule through brokerage. On the contrary, stability necessitates that groups in power as well as their adversaries be able to preserve their unity, which makes it possible for demobilization plans to be executed. It also requires that post-war governments build up their capacity to rule autonomously. Existing perspectives on civil war recurrence emphasize the implications of the position of wartime adversaries relative to one another at the end of the conflict. Did a clear victor capable of militarily dominating its rivals emerge? Or can these adversaries credibly commit to a settlement? Considering the specific processes fostering or hindering post-war stabilities suggests that the redistribution of power between central and local actors matters as much as the distribution of power between adversaries.

8.4 The legacy of wartime modes of engagement with local power structures

What factors determine how vulnerable the political order emerging in the aftermath of civil conflicts is to fragmentation, how likely new governments are to enforce demobilization, and how dependent on local power brokers these governments tend to remain? I argue that the intensity of these threats to post-war stability depends in part on how the war has bolstered or undermined the position of the local power structures that compete with the state for social control. These local political processes are, in turn, conditioned by how dominant actors have engaged with these local structures. Civil conflicts in which main actors rely on local power structures to establish their support base tend to amplify the influence of these rivals of the state. In contrast, governments forming in the aftermath of civil conflicts—during which key actors replaced old power structures with new institutions—are better positioned to centralize power. The latter type of local wartime engagement creates conditions under which the post-war state can better preserve its unity, enforce agreements on disarmament, and can also rule with more autonomy.

8.4.1 Variation in wartime modes of engagement with local power structures

Insurgent groups, and actors at war more generally, differ in how they relate to local power structures as they emerge. Many rebel groups have leveraged existing local networks and hierarchies, as Staniland (2014: 23) argues in *Networks of Rebellion*, which shows how 'insurgent leaders construct organizations by trying to convert prewar social networks into wartime institutions'. In Myanmar's Shan state, the still active insurgency that emerged in 1958 had initially capitalized on the historical status of the members of the traditional local ruling dynasties, known as the Saophans (Lintner 1984). In South Sudan, the Sudan People's Liberation Army co-opted the same traditional chiefs that the colonial and post-colonial regimes had relied on to administer civilians in the territories it controlled (Öhm 2015). Across the continent, in Mali and Niger, the successive Tuareg insurgencies between 1960 and 2012 rallied around confederations led by traditional

Amenokals (Deycard 2012). But not all rebel groups have leveraged existing local power structures. A diverse set of insurgent movements have instead replaced these structures with new institutions. During the Second World War, the Viet Minh set up underground People's Revolutionary Committees throughout Northern and Central Vietnam. These committees were meant to replace the council of notables and their executive officers, the '*huong ca*', that dominated Vietnamese village structure under the colonial system (McQueen 1968). In Afghanistan, the Taliban started to set up a shadow government around 2003, with representatives down to the local level (Jackson 2018). In particular, by 2010, they had appointed over 500 judges in the provinces they controlled (Jackson 2018). In Colombia, the Revolutionary Armed Forces–People's Army (FARC by its Spanish acronym) also set up an alternate system of justice in many parts of the territories under their control. In some instances, they started to regulate market transaction and labour relations, including wages (Arjona 2016).

Various types of local power structures may be relevant to the political dynamics of conflict, including clans, tribes, kinship networks, political parties, religious institutions, traditional chieftaincies, gangs, and economic networks, licit or illicit. The examples outlined above reveal that the extent to which armed groups engage with such structures varies between actors and contexts. These distinct modes of engagement and their impact on the distribution of power across society constitute one of the critical political processes prompted by civil conflict. In some cases, civil wars bolster the capacity for influence and political power structures. In other conflicts, even well-established local power structures are overpowered by wartime organizations.

8.4.2 Effects on the stability of the post-war order

Whether the dominant actors in a war have leveraged or displaced local power structures is an important factor shaping the capacity of post-war regimes to centralize power. These structures can be conceived as rivals, competing sometimes with each other but particularly with the state for social control, that is, for the ability to set and enforce the rules of everyday life. Civil wars commonly change their standing relative to that of state institutions. This matters for the stability of the post-conflict state because the degree to which war has bolstered or undermined local power structures informs post-war regimes' ability to avoid fragmentation, enforce demobilization, and rule autonomously.

To better understand the connections between the modes of local engagement of dominant actors in a war and the likelihood of the post-conflict order unravelling, it is helpful to compare the relationships between the top leadership and field commanders in organizations that have co-opted local power structures and those that have replaced them. In the first type of relationship, rebel leaders form alliances with elites to capitalize on their legitimacy and capacity for influence. When mobilization is conducted through such alliances, the resulting organization typically retains high levels of internal differentiations, based on pre-war local political structures and identities, for instance reflecting the boundaries between different tribes, clans, regions, or religious affiliations. Because these local elites have an independent capacity for social control that dates back to the pre-war period, they cannot easily be replaced. Should rebel leaders try, they may lose the faction that these elites 'brought' with them. Crucially, these elites retain an exit option. If they find themselves at odds with the top leadership or if they determine that their alliance with the insurgent movement no longer serves them in the local arena, they may opt to depart. They may refuse to continue fighting, join a rival organization, or start a new one, which is how splinter factions form. Because in such organizations local elites hold on to their capacity for influence, the armed groups remain vulnerable to fragmentation both during and after the war. In contrast, when groups establish themselves by displacing local power structures, the resulting organization is more immune to this kind of risk. The field officers that are appointed to lead combat units or administer specific areas owe their authority over their men or the communities they are in charge of to the organization that put them in this role. More generally, status and influence are more impersonally defined in these groups, and individuals cannot retain them outside of the organization.

The immediate post-war period is a phase during which the cohesion of an armed group is tested. When an armed group's survival is no longer at stake, the solidarity between the different factions that constitute it can often subside (Woldemariam 2018). These groups must navigate intense internal competition, triggered by concerns over how the profits of peace are going to be shared not only between but also within groups. Such challenges can be more easily weathered by groups whose cohesion does not depend on the robustness of their alliances with local elites and the networks these elites control. When groups have developed autonomous organizational resources, the defection of mid-level commanders, who do not have a following loyal to them personally, does not constitute an existential threat, either to the wartime organization they have built or to the post-conflict regime.

For similar reasons, demobilization is also more difficult when the key actors in a conflict have leveraged rather than displaced local power structures. Such conflicts reinforce the political power of local elites, which they then remain eager to maintain in the aftermath of war. The dissolution of the combat units they control would undermine this power, and local elites in such contexts are likely to resist disarmament and demobilization efforts. When, on the contrary, armed groups replace local power structures with their own institutions, they create a system in which fighters and members are loyal to the organization itself rather than to specific figures and rules trump personal ties. Once the leadership commits to demobilization, it has both the legitimacy and the institutionalized chain of command required to enact it.

Finally, for post-war regimes to rule autonomously, they need to centralize power. But again, when these regimes have been established by groups that depend on the support of subnational elites, it is risky for them to attempt to wrestle power away from these elites who often control factions that have not disarmed. In contrast, armed groups that adopted strategies of transformation of local power structures have already weakened these elites, creating conditions more favourable to the centralization of power. Equally importantly, through the wartime institutions that these groups set up to consolidate their support base or maintain control of their territories, they have already developed the kind of organizational and administrative capacity that direct rule requires.

8.5 Preliminary empirical investigation

To investigate these connections between wartime modes of local engagement and conflict recurrence, I use novel data on the political practices of rebel groups and compare the rates of adoption across groups involved in conflicts that have recurred and conflicts that have not. A first challenge in implementing this comparison is to define conflict recurrence. This section describes the criteria used to do so as well as the rebel political practices documented. It then presents descriptive statistics on the differences in wartime modes of local engagement between groups involved in recurring versus non-recurring conflicts.

8.5.1 Documenting conflict recurrence and post-conflict instability

Instances in which a civil war was followed by a durable and secure peace are relatively easy to distinguish from cases in which countries' post-war trajectories have been more turbulent. But it is harder to make distinctions between cases characterized by varying degrees of instability. Should a brief period of peace followed by renewed violence be treated as a lull in a single conflict or an instance of recurrence? Similarly, should the overthrow of a short-lived government installed after the initial phase of a conflict be considered as an episode in an ongoing war or the beginning of a new one? How long should peace last before we can say that the post-war regime has achieved stability? For the purpose of this study, I adopted the following classification rules:

- A conflict has ended (and subsequent rounds of violence, therefore, mark the beginning of a new conflict) if a settlement was negotiated, a new regime was established, or the war is no longer coded as active in the Uppsala Conflict Data Programme dataset for at least two years.

- A post-conflict regime has secured a stable peace if there are no active conflicts for at least ten years.
- Cases in which the post-war regime has consolidated its power but a subnational conflict is still active are generally not treated as instances of war recurrence unless the subnational conflict constitutes an existential threat for the new regime.

In some cases, such as after the victory of the Khmer Rouge in Cambodia or the independence of Eritrea, the post-war regime appears stable, but engages in considerable violence against civilians. One limitation of the approach I follow here is that it does not distinguish between such instances and cases of actual peace and recovery. Examining the determinants of post-war regime violence is an important goal for future studies.

8.5.2 Documenting rebel modes of local engagement

Data on local political practices of armed groups

To capture differences in rebel modes of local engagement, I documented a range of practices that may allow rebel groups to either replace or co-opt local power structures. The dataset covers the political practices that some armed groups have adopted and that produced the most meaningful shifts in the distribution of power within communities in the territories they control, producing lasting impacts on local politics. More specifically, the dataset includes six variables documenting practices of political transformation that can allow rebel groups to transform local political systems, as well as two practices typically embraced by armed groups that have co-opted local power structures. Table 8.1 presents the practices of political transformation and political co-optation coded.

Table 8.1 Practices of political transformation and political co-optation

Variable	Coding criteria
Political transformation	
Attacks against old elites	A group is coded as having conducted attacks against local elites when they removed elites from their position or there are documented instances of elites fleeing rebel governance.
Creation of local councils	A group is coded as having created new local councils or institutions of representation when the literature documents instances of such institutions being established.

continued

Table 8.1 *continued*

Variable	Coding criteria
Reform of the judiciary system	A group is coded as having transformed local judiciary systems when it has introduced new courts, rules, processes, or personnel.
Redistribution of land	A group is coded as having redistributed land when either holders of large estates are expropriated and their assets reallocated, or collectivized holdings are constituted.
Social empowerment of groups treated as subalterns	A group is coded as having promoted new social norms when its discourse and institutions has enfranchised, at least in theory, groups that pre-war systems treated as subalterns (women, youth, minorities).
Systematic propaganda	A group is coded as having engaged in systematic propaganda if it has appointed specific agents in that role, or developed dedicated tools, trainings, or media to bring forth a new political system and extinguish the legitimacy of the old one.
Political co-optation	
Promotion of norms and identities tied to traditional structures	A group is coded as having promoted traditional norms when it has legitimized its struggle by appealing to tradition, norms of solidarity with one's in-group, and other obligations associated with a shared identity.
Mechanisms of indirect governance	A group is coded as having implemented mechanisms of indirect governance when it has delegated critical functions—such as the acquisition of material resources, recruits, or intelligence—to local elites.

Source: List of variables compiled by the author.

Sample selection and limitations of the dataset

These practices have been coded for a subset of the cases listed in the Non-State Actor (NSA) dataset, coded by Cunningham et al. (2013), which itself includes all insurgent organizations involved in civil conflicts since 1945. More specifically, I coded the practices of datasets that met the following criteria. First, the insurgent organizations had to be coded in the NSA dataset as having controlled territory during the war. Second, it had to meet at least one of following conditions: (i) its mobilization capacity (the size of the armed forces they could raise) matched or exceeded the capacity of the state; or (ii) the organization was active for at least two years. Applying these criteria yields a subset of 126 rebel organizations.

The resulting dataset has a number of limitations. Because rebellion is a clandestine activity, it can be difficult to ascertain and the range of practices that some insurgent organizations deployed is likely underestimated. Because overall more information is available—both in academic and non-academic publications—about conflicts that involved Western powers, this risk is greater for organizations involved in conflicts that did not. The dataset also does not capture variations over time or space in the political practices enacted.

More generally, an important limitation of the overall approach of this study is that it examines differences in the mode of engagement of insurgent groups only. State armed forces may also differ in their approaches to local power structures, and these differences also matter for the redistribution of power during the war. While an analysis built solely on the effect of insurgent strategies on local power structures can offer insights into how these processes shape the post-war order, the contributions of state wartime strategies of local engagement also merit attention.

8.5.3 Recurrence by type of conflict termination

This study builds on existing investigations of the determinants of civil war recurrence that emphasize how the likelihood of recurrence depends on how conflict ended. Table 8.2 presents the share of insurgent groups in the sample involved in a recurring conflict, by type of conflict termination.

When a group is involved in a conflict that ended with an agreement, it is also more likely to be involved in a conflict that recurred, particularly relative to groups involved in conflicts that ended with a government victory. This is also the case when groups were engaged in conflicts that ended in low activity (violence abated without any agreement being negotiated). These trends are in line with the argument that the resumption of violence is more likely after a

Table 8.2 Share of groups involved in recurring conflict, by type of conflict termination

Ending of conflict in which the group was involved	**Share of groups involved in recurring conflict (%)**
Agreement	38
Government victory	6
Rebel victory	20
Low activity	39
Overall	29

Source: Author's compilation based on a new dataset documenting rebel political practices.

settlement than after a victory. At the same time, many groups were involved in conflicts that ended with a settlement and did not recur, and others in recurring conflicts that followed government or insurgent victories. To determine the contribution that wartime modes of local engagement made to these patterns, I compare the practices of groups in recurring versus non-recurring conflicts, considering differences between groups involved in conflicts with similar types of ending. Table 8.3 shows these comparisons for practices of transformation and co-optation.

The average number of practices of transformation adopted is higher in groups involved in conflict that did not recur (1.93 practices adopted out of 6) than in groups involved in recurring conflicts, which is consistent with the hypothesis that wartime political processes that transform local power structures create conditions under which post-conflict order tends to be more resilient. This pattern is similar across conflicts with all types of ending. Conflicts that ended with a government victory are the exception, since the Free Aceh Movement, the only group involved in the only conflict that recurred after a government victory, set up new institutions before being defeated. Conversely, the average number of practices of co-optation is consistently greater among groups involved in recurring conflict

Table 8.3 Average number of practices of political transformation and co-optation

	Recurring versus non-recurring conflict	
	Conflict did not recur	**Conflict recurred**
Political transformation adopted (out of six practices coded)		
Agreement	1.60	0.00
Government victory	1.53	3.00
Rebel victory	3.42	0.00
Low activity	1.53	1.20
Overall	1.93	0.66
Political co-optation adopted (out of two practices coded)		
Agreement	0.27	0.89
Government victory	0.33	2.00
Rebel victory	0.25	2.00
Low activity	0.53	0.73
Overall	0.36	1.00

Source: Author's compilation based on a new dataset documenting rebel political practices.

(1 practice out of 2 coded for groups in recurring conflict versus 0.36 for groups in non-recurring conflict). This pattern also conforms with the hypothesis that when actors at war rely on local power structures, threats to the post-conflict order are heightened.

8.6 Insights from transitions from rebellion to government in Ethiopia and Somalia

The evolution of the post-war order in Ethiopia and Somalia after insurgent groups overthrew the incumbent regimes in each country illustrates the connections between the modes of local engagement of armed groups and the risk of conflict recurrence. In Ethiopia, a rebel coalition led by the Tigray People's Liberation Front (TPLF) overthrew the regime of the Derg. That same year, the two dominant armed groups at the time in Somalia—the United Somali Congress (USC) and the Somali National Movement (SNM)—ousted the regime of Siad Barre in Somalia. In spite of these parallel chronologies, the post-war trajectories of the two countries have been remarkably different. This is apparent in how international observers have characterized these two countries. Ethiopia was often referred to as 'bastion of stability' in the turbulent Horn of Africa, while Somalia has been seen as the archetype of a 'failed state'. These characterizations mask complex realities. Nevertheless, the post-war regime in Ethiopia was able to consolidate a new political order that lasted over two decades, while the successive governments that formed in Somalia after 1991 failed to assert their authority over most of the country's territory. This is in part because the dominant armed groups in the two conflicts adopted distinct modes of local engagement. During the war, the TPLF built an extensive governance infrastructure that replaced the old local elites and offered the victorious group the levers needed to rule autonomously. The SNM and the USC, on the other hand, enacted strategies of recruitment and local engagement that further empowered clan-based political structures, initiating a process that led to their own fragmentation.

8.6.1 The victorious Ethiopian insurgency

During the last stages of the war in Ethiopia, the TPLF created a coalition, the Ethiopian People's Revolutionary Democratic Front (EPRDF), that incorporated political organizations from the different provinces of the country. The TPLF formed this coalition not through alliances with existing armed groups, but by manufacturing its own allies. This was achieved largely by helping captured officers that the TPLF had rallied to its cause to establish their own organization. The leaders of these satellite parties were unlikely to leave the coalition as they owed their status to the central committee of the TPLF (Verhoeven 2016). The process through which the EPRDF consolidated its power was not always seamless, and led to clashes with established armed groups beyond the borders of Tigray. Nevertheless, this approach proved effective in fostering a cohesive, stable political settlement. These clashes did not put the existence of the regime at stake the way an internal defection would have (Vaughan 2015). The EPRDF governed from the end of the transition period in 1995 until its dissolution in 2021. The rebel forces and the combatant units who had fought for the Derg were successfully integrated to form one of the most effective armies on the continent. The EPRDF was also able to turn around the dire economic situation it had inherited from the Derg era. Fifteen years after the end of the war, Ethiopia was growing faster than any non-oil-dependent African economy (Lefort 2015). During this phase, the government was generating and attracting resources that could be allocated to poverty reduction programmes (Geiger and Goh 2012). These progresses were achieved even as productivity gains remained limited, because the state was autonomous enough to intervene strategically in the Ethiopian economy, without being primarily or exclusively concerned with protecting political alliances.

The achievements of the EPRDF government built on the TPLF's strategy of local engagement during the war in several ways. First, this strategy, combined with the reform enacted by the Derg, had considerably impaired the position of old subnational elites, creating a political vacuum that the EPRDF's governance system came to fill, or at least ensuring that these elites could not coordinate an effective resistance to the EPRDF's political project. Before the onset of the war, Tigray was under the control of local 'noble' landowners. After the coup that brought the Derg to power, these landowners launched a reactionary resistance movement (Clapham 1988). When the TPLF established its first base in Tigray, there were, in addition to this conservative rebellion, leftist insurgent groups operating in the area, which were also larger and better equipped. Despite its numerical inferiority, the TPLF treated both as rivals and rapidly came to engage in military confrontations with them until it successfully pushed them out of the region. By the early 1980s, the TPLF had become the dominant insurgent group in Tigray (Young 2006). The formation of the EPRDF can be seen as a continuation of this effort to expand without forming alliances with existing entities.

Second, once in power, the EPRDF built on two pillars of the wartime governance system that the TPLF had established while the conflict was still active: the election of village councils (known as '*baitos*') and the redistribution of land rights that these groups enacted (Young 2006). Once in power, the EPRDF replicated them in other parts of the country, systematically combining the process of local state-building with that of expanding the party. This allowed the TPLF-led ruling coalition to maintain its hegemonic political position for over two decades (Vaughan 2015). The reform of land rights, which the coalition continued to expand to other areas, also contributed to the stabilization of the country, as it meant that most demobilized fighters could be assigned a plot. Finally, during the internal crises that arose after they took power, the central committees of the TPLF and the EPRDF continued to rely on the practices and methods they had adhered to during the war, including the practice of 'criticism and self-criticism', and the procedures organizing their debates and public votes. This rule-based culture also helped create a context conducive to effective demobilization and preserve the committees' unity in the face of internal dissent.

8.6.2 The disintegration of the Somali insurgent movements

In Somalia, the insurgent movements who had fought against the regime of Siad Barre failed to take over the state. Rather, competition between these groups prompted a succession of new wars. While the nature of these wars has evolved, stability continues to be elusive in Somalia. The series of international interventions launched to improve security and rebuild state structures has largely failed to achieve their goals. This includes the humanitarian UN interventions conducted between 1992 and 1995, as well as the Ethiopian and African Union Mission to Somalia in 2006–2007 (Williams 2013). The disintegration of the early rebel groups led to the emergence of new forms of insurgencies, including a new generation of Islamist armed groups and militias.

In the north of the country, the SNM had emerged as an uncontested winner in 1991. Its leadership promptly declared the independence of Somaliland, a move that local communities supported. Yet, the emergence of an SNM-controlled government in Somaliland did not prevent the splintering of the organization. This fragmentation resulted in part from disagreement within its leadership on the issue of independence. The creation of an independent government for Somaliland was the preferred option of clan elders and guerrilla leaders who had closer ties to the organization's support base. Other members of the central committees favoured the formation of a national government based in Mogadishu in which they would have a prominent role (Compagnon 1998). Eventually, clan elders took over the government formation process in Somaliland, distributing roles based on clan affiliation. Mistrust and lack of funds soon precipitated a crisis, and the competition between clans turned violent following disputes around the demobilization process and the integration of the clan militias into a Somaliland army. This further undermined clan elders' control over ex-rebel forces, to such an extent that they could no longer prevent militias from turning against their own clan.

The USC is the other insurgent movement that played a role in the collapse of the regime of Siad Barre. Since its inception, it lacked organization coherence and could be best described as a loose coalition of sub-clans. Clashes multiplied between these factions as a result of the rivalries between leaders of the organizations, and particularly between Ali Mahdi Muhammad, who had been appointed interim president, and General Mohamed Farrah Aidid, who had been elected chairman of the organization (Compagnon 1998). The USC leadership also contributed to the violence and destruction in Mogadishu after the fall of the regime by condoning revenge killings against other clans. Like the leadership of the SNM, it had little control over its militias and was unable to prevent the looting of the national capital (Bakonyi 2009). The clan elites with whom these militias were affiliated lacked the authority to give demobilization orders that would be followed and, to preserve their position, resisted their dissolution anyway.

While the SNM initially attempted to rally supporters from different clans around an inclusive political project, both the SNM and the USC ended up organizing themselves around clan structures. Clan-based representation came to dominate all wartime politics and sub-clans armed themselves strategically to defend and improve their position under this new violent equilibrium. During the early history of the SNM, some of the founders of the organization sought to establish it as a structure open to diverse clans and pursue the establishment of an equally inclusive new political regime. However, the leadership of the SNM was soon divided between those who supported this project and those who prioritized bolstering the position of the Isaaq clan that dominated the movement. Efforts to ensure that the SNM would remain a multi-clan organization failed in part because of the incumbent regime's skill in fostering mistrust between clan-based factions and arming them against one another (Compagnon 1998). But these efforts were also abandoned relatively promptly because intra-clan solidarity proved to be a more effective lever of mobilization than appeals to broader political goals. In her work on patterns of violence in Somalia in the late 1980s, Bakonyi (2009: 6) explains how the SNM transitioned from a relatively small guerrilla movement into a large insurgency by 'embedding [itself] in the moral economy of the clan system'. SNM members were sent by their leadership to their particular sub-clan within the Isaaq clan-family to request support and remind them of their obligation to assist fellow clan members in distress (this obligation, primarily economic but may extend to political support, is sometimes referred to as '*Qaaraan*') After such an appeal has been made, supported elders and those who withhold support risk lasting damage to their reputation. Because elders played such a critical role in this process, the SNM's successful appeal to norms of solidarity within and between Isaaq sub-clans transformed the internal structure of the organization until its central committee included almost exclusively Isaaq clan elders. This also affected the movement's armed forces. The SNM's military wing had originally been established as an integrated force with a clear command structure. However, by the late 1980s, it had become 'a decentralized networks of Isaaq clan and sub-clan militias' (Bakonyi 2009: 8).

The result of these wartime political processes in Somaliland was the emergence of a governance system that shared some of the features of a modern bureaucracy, but remained dominated by traditional clan-based elements. The SNM had a written constitution, distinct departments, and codified procedures for decision making. But by the late 1980s, its leadership was dominated by clan elders. This dual structure was institutionalized when Somaliland declared its independence and became jointly governed by a House of Representatives and a House of Elders ('*Guurti*'). Bakonyi (2009: 2), who characterizes this trend as a 're-emergence of localized governance structures' highlights how it hinders any shift from clan-based political representation.

The internal structure of the USC largely followed the same clan-based blueprint as the SNM. The USC was created as the conflict was already active and its leaders never articulated a clear political programme (Ingiriis 2019). The military forces of the USC were composed of former army members of the Hawiye clan and other smaller Hawiye militias. With the weakening of the incumbent regime already visible, Hawiye sub-clan elders anticipated that the political influence of factions without their own may suffer in the future, and therefore they started to mobilize fighters from their constituency, which helped fuel the growth of the USC. But these were recruits over whom the USC top leadership had little authority. Bakonyi (2009) talks about a process of 'clanization' of the insurgent movements that was already well advanced when these movements advanced on the national capital. Compagnon (1998) suggests that the battle of Mogadishu was as much a showdown between Hawiye clan militias and Darood elements of the Somali army as it was a confrontation between state and insurgent forces. Insurgent strategies in Somalia reinforced the relevance of clan structures, exacerbating pre-existing fault lines, and ensuring that any government would remain beholden to the priorities of clan leadership.

8.7 Conclusion

Dominant arguments on the drivers of civil war recurrence tend to focus on the implications of how a conflict ended. They highlight the ability of victors who have achieved a hegemonic military position to deter further challenges and how commitment problems may undermine settlements. But the fact that countries can relapse into war even after a victory or achieve stability even after a settlement invites us to nuance and expand our understanding of the political processes that fuel recurring conflict or, on the contrary, support the emergence of stable post-war states.

By examining the specific processes through which post-conflict political order typically comes undone, and by exploring the connections between wartime modes of local engagement and patterns of conflict recurrence, this chapter suggests that the stability of the post-war order depends at least in part on whether the efforts of actors at war to consolidate their support base have empowered or weakened local elites.

The role of local elites, and particularly ex-rebel commanders, in shaping the post-war order has been a topic of debate among conflict scholars. Some arguments connect the resilience of 'warlords' to state failure. In contrast, others suggest that 'hybrid' forms of governance in which local leaders, traditional or not, play a substantive role may be more robust and more effective than the replacement of these forms of governance with institutions resulting from conventional state-building approaches. The findings from this study suggest that after conflicts characterized by political processes that reinforce local power structures and the influence of local elites, threats to the stability of the post-war regime are higher. But further research is needed to build a more comprehensive theory explaining variation in the redistribution of power between the central government and local power brokers during conflict, and how this redistribution may constrain or support sustainable state-building in the aftermath of conflict.

References

Ansori, M. (2012). 'From Insurgency to Bureaucracy: Free Aceh Movement, Aceh Party and the New Face of Conflict'. *Stability: International Journal of Security and Development*, 1(1): 31–44. https://doi.org/10.5334/sta.ah

Arjona, A. (2016). *Rebelocracy*. Cambridge: Cambridge University Press. https://doi.org/10.1017/9781316421925

Bakonyi, J. (2009). 'Moral Economies of Mass Violence: Somalia 1988–1991'. *Civil Wars*, 11(4): 434–454. https://doi.org/10.1080/13698240903403790

Bates, R. H. (2015). *When Things Fell Apart: State Failure in Late-Century Africa*. Cambridge: Cambridge University Press. https://doi.org/10.1017/CBO9781316423974

Bhattacharji, P. (2009). 'Liberation Tigers of Tamil Eelam (aka Tamil Tigers) (Sri Lanka, Separatists)'. Council on Foreign Relations. https://www.cfr.org/backgrounder/liberation-tigers-tamil-eelam-aka-tamil-tigers-sri-lanka-separatists (accessed 28 July 2018).

Broache, M. (2014). 'The International Criminal Court and Atrocities in DRC: A Case Study of the RCD-Goma (Nkunda Faction)/CNDP/M23 Rebel Group'. 1 September. http://dx.doi.org/10.2139/ssrn.2434703

Clapham, C. (1988). *Transformation and Continuity in Revolutionary Ethiopia*. Cambridge: Cambridge University Press.

Compagnon, D. (1998). 'Somali Armed Movements: The Interplay of Political Entrepreneurship and Clan-Based Factions'. In C. Clapham (ed.), *African Guerrillas*. Oxford: James Currey Press, pp. 73–90.

Cunningham, D. E., K. S. Gleditsch, and I. Salehyan (2013). 'Non-State Actors in Civil Wars: A New Dataset'. *Conflict Management and Peace Science*, 30(5): 516–531.

Deycard, F. (2012). 'Political Cultures and Tuareg Mobilizations: Rebels of Niger, from Kaocen to the Mouvement Des Nigériens Pour La Justice'. In Y. Guichaoua (ed.), *Understanding Collective Political Violence*. London: Palgrave Macmillan, pp. 46–64. https://doi.org/10.1057/9780230348318_3

Driscoll, J. (2015). *Warlords and Coalition Politics in Post-Soviet States*. Cambridge: Cambridge University Press. https://doi.org/10.1017/CBO9781107478046

Fearon, J. D. (2004). 'Why Do Some Civil Wars Last so Much Longer than Others?'. *Journal of Peace Research*, 41(3): 275–301. https://doi.org/10.1177/0022343304043770
Fortna, V. P. (2003). 'Scraps of Paper? Agreements and the Durability of Peace'. *International Organization*, 57(2): 337–372. https://doi.org/10.1017/S0020818303572046
Geiger, M., and C. Goh (2012). *Ethiopia Economic Update: Overcoming Inflation, Raising Competitiveness*. Washington, DC: World Bank. https://doi.org/10.1596/26771
Hanson, S. (2007). 'Disarmament, Demobilization, and Reintegration (DDR) in Africa'. *Council on Foreign Relations*. https://www.cfr.org/backgrounder/disarmament-demobilization-and-reintegration-ddr-africa (accessed 7 April 2022).
Hartzell, C., and M. Hoddie (2003). 'Institutionalizing Peace: Power Sharing and Post-Civil War Conflict Management'. *American Journal of Political Science*, 47(2): 318–332. https://doi.org/10.1111/1540-5907.00022
Hobbes, T. (2016) [1651]. 'Leviathan, or, The Matter, Form, and Power of a Common-Wealth Ecclesiastical and Civil'. In W. E. Engel, R. Loughnane, and G. Williams (eds), *The Memory Arts in Renaissance England: A Critical Anthology*. Cambridge: Cambridge University Press, pp. 218–220. https://doi.org/10.1017/CBO9781316091722.048
Hwang, J. C., and K. E. Schulze (2018). 'Why They Join: Pathways Into Indonesian Jihadist Organizations'. *Terrorism and Political Violence*, 30(6): 911–932. https://doi.org/10.1080/09546553.2018.1481309
Ingiriis, M. H. (2019). 'From Grievance to Greed in Somalia'. *Cahiers d'études africaines*, 235: 783–814. https://doi.org/10.4000/etudesafricaines.26951
Ishiyama, J., and A. Batta (2011). 'Rebel Organizations and Conflict Management in Post-Conflict Societies 1990–2009'. *Civil Wars*, 13(4): 437–457. https://doi.org/10.1080/13698249.2011.629873
Jackson, A. (2018). *Life under the Taliban Shadow Government*. London: Overseas Development Institute. Available at: https://odi.org/en/publications/life-under-the-taliban-shadow-government/ (accessed December 2022).
Latif, I. R., D. Mutiarin, and A. Nurmandi (2020). 'The Quality of Peace in Post-Conflict Situation: A Comparative Study Between Armed Conflicts in Aceh and Bangsamoro'. *Global: Jurnal Politik Internasional*, 22(2): 221–243. https://doi.org/10.7454/global.v22i2.430
Lefort, R. (2015). 'The Ethiopian Economy; the Developmental State vs. the Free Market'. In G. Prunier and É. Ficquet (eds), *Understanding Contemporary Ethiopia: Monarchy, Revolution and the Legacy of Meles Zenawi*, London: Hurst & Company, 357–394.
Lintner, B. (1984). 'The Shans and the Shan State of Burma'. *Contemporary Southeast Asia*, 5(4): 403–450. https://doi.org/10.1355/CS5-4B
McQueen, H. (1968). 'Vietnam—Villagers and Voters'. *The Australian Quarterly*, 40(4): 5–11. https://doi.org/10.2307/20634236
Öhm, M. (2015). *War and Statehood in South Sudan*. London: Bloomsbury Publishing. https://doi.org/10.5771/9783845258508
Paris, R. (2004). *At War's End: Building Peace After Civil Conflict*. Cambridge: Cambridge University Press. https://doi.org/10.1017/CBO9780511790836
Söderberg Kovacs, M., and S. Hatz (2016). 'Rebel-to-Party Transformations in Civil War Peace Processes 1975–2011'. *Democratization*, 23(6): 990–1008.
Sprenkels, R. (2018). *After Insurgency: Revolution and Electoral Politics in El Salvador*. Notre Dame, IN: University of Notre Dame Press. https://doi.org/10.2307/j.ctvpj7g2b
Staniland, P. (2014). *Networks of Rebellion: Explaining Insurgent Cohesion and Collapse*. Ithaca, NY: Cornell University Press.

Stearns, J. (2007). 'Laurent Nkunda and the National Congress for the Defence of the People (CNDP)'. *L'Afrique des Grands Lacs: Annuaire*, 2008: 245–267. Available at: https://medialibrary.uantwerpen.be/oldcontent/container2143/files/Publications/Annuaire/2007-2008/12-Nkunda.pdf (accessed December 2022).

Stedman, S. J. (1997). 'Spoiler Problems in Peace Processes'. *International Security*, 22(2): 5–53. https://doi.org/10.1162/isec.22.2.5

Sundberg, R. (2019). 'UN Peacekeeping and Forced Displacement in South Sudan'. *International Peacekeeping*, 27(2): 210–237. https://doi.org/10.1080/13533312.2019.1676642

Tajima, Y. (2010). *Understanding the Livelihoods of Former Insurgents: Aceh, Indonesia.* Washington, DC: World Bank. https://doi.org/10.1596/27784

Themnér, A., and M. Utas (2016). 'Governance through Brokerage: Informal Governance in Post-Civil War Societies'. *Civil Wars*, 18(3): 255–280. https://doi.org/10.1080/13698249.2016.1215639

Toft, M. D. (2009). *Securing the Peace: The Durable Settlement of Civil Wars.* Princeton, NJ: Princeton University Press. https://doi.org/10.1515/9781400831999

Vaughan, S. (2015). 'Federalism, Revolutionary Democracy and the Developmental State, 1991–2012'. In G. Prunier and É. Ficquet (eds), *Understanding Contemporary Ethiopia: Monarchy, Revolution and the Legacy of Meles Zenawi.* London: Hurst & Company, pp. 283–311.

Verhoeven, H. (2016). 'Behind the Violence in Ethiopia: Will Its Experiment with Ethnic Federalism Work?'. *Foreign Affairs*, 29 August. Available at: https://www.foreignaffairs.com/articles/ethiopia/2016-08-29/behind-violence-ethiopia (accessed 17 December 2020).

Wagle, G. S., and P. Jackson (2015). 'Lessons from Peace Processes: The Case of Nepal'. In P. Jackson (ed.), *Handbook of International Security and Development.* Cheltenham: Edward Elgar Publishing, pp. 420–441. https://doi.org/10.4337/9781781955536.00035

Walter, B. F. (2002). *Committing to Peace: The Successful Settlement of Civil Wars.* Princeton, NJ: Princeton University Press. https://doi.org/10.1515/9781400824465

Walter, B. F. (2004). 'Does Conflict Beget Conflict? Explaining Recurring Civil War'. *Journal of Peace Research*, 41(3): 371–388. https://doi.org/10.1177/0022343304043775

Werner, S., and A. Yuen (2005). 'Making and Keeping Peace'. *International Organization*, 59(2): 261–292. https://doi.org/10.1017/S0020818305050095

Williams, P. D. (2013). *AMISOM in Transition: The Future of the African Union Mission in Somalia.* RVI Nairobi Forum Briefing Paper, 13 February. Rift Valley Institute. https://riftvalley.net/sites/default/files/publication-documents/RVI%20Briefing%20Paper%20-%20AMISOM.pdf (accessed December 2022).

Woldemariam, M. (2018). *Insurgent Fragmentation in the Horn of Africa: Rebellion and Its Discontents.* Cambridge: Cambridge University Press. https://doi.org/10.1017/9781108525657

Young, J. (2006). *Peasant Revolution in Ethiopia: The Tigray People's Liberation Front, 1975–1991.* Cambridge: Cambridge University Press.

9

Rebel governance during COVID-19

Describing and explaining armed groups' response to the pandemic in the Middle East

Marta Furlan

9.1 Introduction

As COVID-19 spread worldwide, not only governments but also armed groups—especially those that control territories—were called to face the crisis. However, as will be noted in the first part of this chapter, our understanding of the responses implemented by armed groups to address the pandemic is limited. In fact, while a body of scholarly literature has been developing in recent years on armed groups' governance, academic knowledge is scarce when it comes to how armed groups respond to external shocks such as famines, droughts, natural calamities, and health emergencies. Thus, while great attention was devoted to states' responses to the coronavirus pandemic, much less attention was paid to non-states' responses. To be certain, there are some authors who have recognized the importance of studying rebel governance during COVID-19. However, why different armed groups responded to the crisis differently is a question that has remained largely unexplored.

As large swaths of territories throughout the Middle East are under the control of armed groups, this chapter seeks to understand the responses that armed non-state actors in the region adopted to address the pandemic. It aims to *describe* the different responses that different armed groups have implemented and *explain* why those armed groups have responded to the pandemic as they have. Answering those questions, in fact, seems relevant from an academic perspective as well as from a policy perspective. From an academic perspective, understanding the responses that armed groups adopt in face of external shocks is relevant to address a gap in knowledge. From a policy perspective, understanding the behaviour of armed groups during COVID-19 is relevant to inform effective approaches to those non-state actors in times of emergency.

The present chapter proposes to conduct a qualitative case study analysis of three ruling armed groups: Hayat Tahrir al-Sham (HTS) in north-western Syria, the Houthis in northern Yemen, and Hamas in Gaza. As I will explain in the third

Marta Furlan, *Rebel governance during COVID-19*. In: *Institutional Legacies of Violent Conflict*.
Edited by: Patricia Justino, Oxford University Press. © United Nations University World Institute
for Development Economics Research (UNU-WIDER) (2026). DOI: 10.1093/9780197904077.003.0009

part, the three groups were selected for the following reasons: they enjoy territorial control and provide some form of governance; they adopted different responses to COVID-19; they display differences when it comes to some factors commonly discussed in the literature to explain governance variation—ultimate goals, intensity of the conflict, financial resources, and previous governance experience. To collect data, reference will be made to a combination of primary sources and secondary sources.

Following the development of a relevant theoretical framework and following the study of HTS, the Houthis, and Hamas, I will proceed to argue that the intensity of the conflict does not appear to be a relevant explanatory factor, as it cannot account satisfactorily for the variation(s) observed across the three groups. Conversely, the groups' ultimate goals, the type of financial resources available to them, and their prior governance experience can explain the observed patterns of COVID-19 governance. In the last part, I will offer conclusive observations.

9.2 Violent non-state actors and COVID-19 governance: a lacuna

The years 2020 and 2021 were marked by the spread of the COVID-19 pandemic worldwide, which by September 2022 had taken the life of more than six million people.[1] As the virus spread, not only governments but also armed groups were called to address the health emergency. In many territories throughout the world, in fact, daily life is administered by armed non-state actors. As of 2020, between 50 and 60 million people worldwide were estimated to live under the full control of armed groups (Herbet and Drevon 2020).

However, still very little is known with respect to the responses implemented by armed groups to address the pandemic. In general, academic knowledge is limited when it comes to how armed groups respond to external shocks such as famines, droughts, natural calamities, and health emergencies (Mampilly 2009; Jackson and Aynte 2013; Walch 2014). The academic literature on rebel governance, in fact, has focused mostly on rebel responses to shocks that are related to the conflict—such as the emergence of ideological competition between among groups (Berti 2023); changes in the rebels' military fortunes (Kasfir 2005); variations in the rebels groups' control over territory and resources (Al-Tamimi 2015; Zelin 2016); changes of rebel leadership (Ladbury 2016); growing military pressures on the rebel proto-state (Al-Tamimi and McCants 2016; Hashim 2018); and the temporary cessation of hostilities (Mampilly 2015). Conversely, much less attention has been devoted to the relationship between governance and shocks unrelated to the conflict dynamics.

[1] Data from: https://www.worldometers.info/coronavirus/coronavirus-death-toll/.

Thus, while over the past two years and a half, studies have been devoted to states' responses to the coronavirus pandemic, much less attention has been paid to non-states' responses. To be certain, there are some scholars who have recognized the importance of studying rebel governance during COVID-19. For instance, Hockey and Jones (2020) were amongst the first ones to offer an analysis of the response to COVID-19 implemented by al-Shabaab. Adopting a comparative approach and extending the analysis to Hayat Tahrir al-Sham and the Taliban, I suggested in a previous article that emergencies are opportunities for rebels to present themselves as more credible and desirable rulers vis-à-vis the government (Furlan 2023). Similarly, Alijla (2021) looked into the responses of Hamas and Hezbollah, focusing on the groups' capacity to mobilize their constituency and rely on pre-existing welfare systems. Breslawski (2022) also mapped the responses adopted by different types of armed groups and interesting research was conducted by Felbab-Brown (2020) on Mexican drug cartels and their provision of COVID-19-related aid.

However, the question of why different groups have responded to the (same) crisis differently has remained largely unexplored. Yet, addressing this question seems of great relevance from an academic as well as from a policy perspective. From an academic perspective, understanding the responses that armed groups adopt in face of external shocks is relevant to address the lacuna currently existing in the scholarly knowledge. From a policy perspective, understanding the behaviour of armed groups during the current health emergency is relevant to ultimately inform effective approaches to those violent non-state actors. Considering that millions of people live under the control of armed groups, addressing those questions is most needed.

9.3 Assessing and explaining variation in COVID-19 responses

Reflecting on the responses that armed groups could implement to address an emergency such as the COVID-19 pandemic, I have built an *Emergency Response Continuum* (Figure 9.1) in which responses range from 'null' to 'extensive'. Null engagement is observed when a ruling armed group refrains from taking any measure aimed at addressing the emergency and/or undertakes detrimental actions. In the case of COVID-19, examples include the tendency of some armed groups to deny cases of infection, engage in disinformation campaigns, and promote conspiracy theories. Acknowledging the crisis but refusing to do anything about it, or being unable to do anything about it, also accounts for a 'null' response.

Moderate engagement is observed when a rebel ruler adopts preventive measures aimed at avoiding or containing the spread of the emergency. In the case of COVID-19, examples in this regard include closing traditionally crowded public spaces (e.g., markets), enforcing general lockdowns for a certain period of time, launching awareness campaigns on the virus, and spreading guidelines on how to behave to prevent its transmission. These information campaigns may take place through a variety of channels—billboards, radio announcements, social media, and murals. Significantly, these types of actions are relatively inexpensive for an armed group to take and quite accessible, as they involve a comparatively lower investment of resources and capacities with respect to the more pro-active measures that will be discussed below.

An extensive response, on the other hand, is observed when an armed group adopts responsive measures aimed at addressing the emergency. These measures may be carried out independently, through the armed group's own resources, or with the support of other actors such as international aid organizations, civil society organizations, and foreign governments. In the case of COVID-19, extensive measures may include the distribution of protective supplies and vaccines, the training of medical personnel, the creation of quarantine facilities, and the sterilization of public places. These actions are more expensive and challenging for an armed group to take, as they involve greater resources and capacities than preventive measures. Clearly, the costs and the challenges are even greater for armed groups that engage in those responses independently.

Null	**Moderate**	**Extensive**
No action	Preventive measures	Preventive measures
Disinformation		Responsive measures

Figure 9.1 Emergency response continuum

When attempting to explain why different armed groups opt for different strategies in their response to the COVID-19 emergency, reference to the literature on rebel governance suggests that the following factors are especially worthy of being investigated: the groups' ultimate goals, the intensity of the conflict in which the groups are engaged, the groups' prior governance experience, and the type of resources available to the groups.

The literature on rebel governance has identified a group's ultimate goals as one of the factors that might explain its propensity to engage in governance. Specifically, it has suggested that secessionist groups are particularly prone to invest extensive efforts in civilian administration. In fact, the long-term success of secessionist groups depends mostly on their capacity to acquire international legitimacy, as their seceded polity can be viable only if recognized internationally. Driven by this dependency on international recognition, they see governance as a desirable strategy to reach their objective (Mampilly 2015; Stewart 2018). Furthermore, secessionist groups are interested in civilian administration because they need to prove to the population of their envisioned state that if they were to secede they would indeed be capable of governing (Breslawski 2022). Similarly, ethno-nationalist groups have also been identified as inclined to invest in governance, because they face a pressing need to prove to their narrow ethno-nationalist constituency that they are ready to rule (Mampilly 2015). Conversely, non-secessionist groups, whose goal of capturing power at the centre is considerably less dependent on international recognition, and non-ethno-nationalist groups, whose political project targets the entire civilian population rather than a narrow sub-group thereof, are less incentivized to invest resources in governance and more prone to invest in the military effort.

Building on these arguments, I argue that secessionist groups and ethno-nationalist groups are more likely to engage in extensive governance efforts when faced with an external emergency such as COVID-19, because they need to prove to the international community and to their local constituency their credibility as rulers even in face of unprecedented challenges. Conversely, non-secessionist groups and non-ethno-nationalist groups are less likely to engage in extensive responses to external shocks, as they do not necessarily have to prove their governance capacity—neither to the international community nor to the local population.

According to the scholarly literature, another factor that might be responsible for a group's capacity and willingness to engage in governance is the intensity of the conflict. In fact, it is difficult for an armed group to engage in governing activities when it is fighting for its survival (Kasfir 2005). Armed groups that face military pressure have both less capacity and less interest in governance, as most of their resources (time, finances, and manpower) need to be directed to the battlefront (Al-Tamimi and McCants 2016). As suggested by Breslawski (2022), armed groups in high-intensity conflicts are also likely to face more frequent shifts in territorial control, which renders the benefits associated with governance less relevant and negatively affects the motivation to respond to public emergencies. Conversely, armed groups that enjoy periods of relative peace are more prone to invest resources in governance (Mampilly 2011).

I thus argue that armed groups fighting high-intensity conflicts are unlikely to engage in governance efforts even when faced with a crisis unrelated to the conflict such as COVID-19, because activities of warfare remain their priority. Differently, armed groups fighting low-intensity conflicts are more likely to engage in governance efforts when faced with sudden emergencies such as the current pandemic, as they can allow themselves to devote resources to non-military activities.

Another factor that might contribute to explaining why some armed non-state actors are more prone to engage in emergency responses than others is prior governance experience—both in absolute terms and, even more so, in the specific area of governance affected by the emergency. In other words, when a ruling armed group is faced with an emergency, its capacity to respond is likely to be impacted by the group's prior experience as governor. As noted by Mampilly (2015), in fact, when rebels engage in governance from scratch, they are less likely to do so effectively because they initially lack the necessary institutions and competencies. The only exception to this would be if the rebel group managed to co-opt pre-existing institutions and networks of governance—if these are existent at all. As similarly suggested by Alijla (2021), pre-pandemic experience in service provision was something that Hamas and Hezbollah could rely upon when addressing the COVID-19 emergency.

I thus argue that armed groups that prior to the arrival of COVID-19 were already engaged to some extent in the provision of healthcare are likely to have the capacity to respond to the pandemic in somewhat extensive ways. Conversely, armed groups that were not engaged in the provision of healthcare, or could provide healthcare only limitedly and poorly, are likely to lack the capacity to address the pandemic beyond, perhaps, a minimal response.

Finally, scholars have noted that a group's propensity to engage in governance is affected also by the resources available to it, as an armed organization with limited resources is unlikely to invest them in costly activities of administration (Kasfir 2015). Equally important, however, is the type of resources available. Specifically, rulers that depend on the civilian population to extract financial resources (e.g., taxation) have an interest to invest resources in governance. Conversely, rulers with access to financial resources that do not need the contribution of the civilian population to be extracted (e.g., foreign support) do not face the same incentive to engage in activities of governance that benefit the people (Mkandawire 2002; Moore 2004; Weinstein 2007; Conrad et al. 2022).

Therefore, I argue that groups that depend to some extent on the civilian population to extract resources are more prone to invest efforts in prompt and extensive governance responses when they are faced with emergencies that come to threaten the well-being of the population—and, by extension, the latter's capacity to engage in productive economic activities. Differently, armed groups that do not depend (or not significantly so) on civilians to extract financial resources are more likely to refrain from extensive governance efforts when faced with emergencies, as they are less affected by, and therefore less concerned with, the people's well-being.

9.4 Research questions, methodology, and data

As large swaths of territories throughout the Middle East are under the control of (mostly Islamist) armed groups, in this chapter, I focus on the Middle Eastern region. I aim to *describe* the different responses that different Islamist armed groups implemented to address COVID-19 and *explain* why they acted as they did. To answer these research questions, I conduct a qualitative case study analysis of Hayat Tahrir al-Sham in Syria (HTS), the Houthis in Yemen, and Hamas in Gaza.

I selected these three groups for the following reasons. First, they are instances of (Islamist) armed groups that at the time of the pandemic engaged in some form of (at least minimal) governance over some territories. HTS began to engage in governance around 2012 and acted as the hegemonic ruler of Idlib governorate and parts of Aleppo governorate between 2017 and 2024. The Houthis have been engaged in governance over the northern half of Yemen since late 2014. Hamas has been ruling over the Gaza Strip since 2007, when it took control of the territory militarily after a clear, yet contested, electoral victory. While the future of the Gaza Strip is currently surrounded by uncertainty, it seems unlikely that Hamas will return to its previous position of power. Second, a brief reading of the secondary literature suggests that the three groups adopted different responses to COVID-19, which makes them particularly instructive case studies to illuminate variation in armed groups' responses to emergencies. Third, the three groups display some relevant differences with respect to the potential explanatory factors that were discussed in the previous section.

To collect data, I combine primary and secondary sources to offer an account of governance by the three groups as accurate as possible. Specifically, I refer to the textual, audio, and video materials disseminated by the groups themselves. These primary sources are in Arabic and English and include administrative documents, newsletters, pamphlets, speeches, audio messages, videos, and pictures documenting the group's governance efforts. At the same time, I refer to the reports and articles produced by humanitarian organizations, aid agencies, humanitarian personnel, scholars, and journalists who have documented the governance experience of the three groups.

9.5 Hayat Tahrir al-Sham

Without going deeper into the history of the organization, it is worth remembering that HTS is the manifestation of what once was Jabhat al-Nusra (JaN). The latter was created in 2012 by the then leader of the Islamic State in Iraq (ISI) Abu Bakr al-Baghdadi as a small contingent led by Abu Mohammad al-Julani to be sent to Syria. The cell was assigned the task of penetrating the local insurgency and seizing territory (Lister 2016). Once in Syria, JaN became increasingly self-sufficient (Jones 2014). In the meantime, disputes with ISI over matters of leadership emerged and escalated until the final rupture that saw al-Baghdadi on one side and al-Julani and Ayman al-Zawahiri (al-Qaeda's leader) on the other.

After it brought under its control several territories across Syria, JaN opted to engage in some activities of governance to realize the goal of the group: overthrow the existing system led by President Bashar al-Assad and establish an Islamic emirate governed according to *sharia* (Al-Badawi et al. 2017). In 2017, the group led by al-Julani merged with others into Hayat Tahrir al-Sham and subsequently created the Syrian Salvation Government (SSG) as a civil authority through which to govern Idlib.

When coronavirus arrived in the Middle East in early 2020, HTS said in its *Iba'* newsletter that the virus had been sent by God to kill the disbelievers who 'shed the blood of Muslims all over the world.' (Al-Tamimi 2020). However, HTS also recognized the importance of addressing promptly the threat posed by COVID-19 and already in mid-March the SSG's Ministry of Health instructed civilians on preventive measures to adopt. The instructions were published on billboards and flyers.[2] During the month of Ramadan, specific instructions were also given to worshippers to prevent mosques from becoming places of contagion.[3]

As those preventive measures were promptly introduced, the Head of the SSG, Ali Keda, announced that 'we [the SSG] call on humanitarian organizations and the World Health Organization to share its responsibility in the liberated north [. . .]', thus revealing the government's renewed willingness and readiness to cooperate with other actors.[4] Significantly, this new approach towards international aid organizations had already been announced by al-Julani during an interview in January 2020: 'Our policy toward NGOs has changed. We are willing to facilitate the work of any organization that would like to return to work in Idlib, and we pledge non-interference. We will reconcile with any organization we've had problems with in the past if they are prepared to help the people here. [. . .]' (International Crisis Group 2020a).

Thanks to this greater cooperation with international organizations, in April 2021 HTS-controlled north-western Syria received 53,800 doses of coronavirus vaccines through the global vaccine-sharing platform COVAX. One month later, inoculations started (Reuters 2021; TRT World 2021; Alsayed 2021). As of August 2021, 55,000 doses of vaccines had been distributed in Idlib, with priority given to healthcare workers, the elderly, and people with chronic diseases (WHO 2021; Arab News 2021). In September 2021, there was an additional delivery of 358,000 vaccine doses (The New Arab 2021).

HTS also took other active steps. For instance, it conducted medical checks on all in-bound travellers at the border crossings with Turkey as well as sterilization of buses at the crossing stations (Enab Baladi 2020).[5] At the Bab al-Hawa crossing, a temporary quarantine centre where to isolate people who returned from Turkey with symptoms was also established (Enab Baladi 2020).[6] Additional quarantine

[2] 'Coronavirus and the Salvation Government – Hayat Tahrir al-Sham', 14 March 2020. *Jihadology*, blog by A. Y. Zelin. Available at: https://jihadology.net/coronavirus-and-the-salvation-government-hayat-tahir-al-sham/

[3] Ibid., 29 April 2020 entry.

[4] Ibid., 9 July 2020 entry.

[5] 'Coronavirus and the Salvation Government – Hayat Tahrir al-Sham', 13 April and 2 July 2020. *Jihadology*, blog by A. Y. Zelin. Available at: https://jihadology.net/coronavirus-and-the-salvation-government-hayat-tahir-al-sham/.

[6] Ibid., 23 April and 23 May 2020 entries.

centres were established in other areas and were regularly visited by the SSG's Minister of Health.[7] People who were required to self-isolate were provided with food baskets by the Ministry of Health.[8] Sterilization practices were also conducted in Idlib's mosques, police departments, and other public buildings.[9]

Importantly, emergency response teams created by HTS and the SSG visited ovens and markets, medical points, and refugee camps to monitor and enforce health directives.[10] During one such inspection, four ovens that had failed to implement the necessary measures were closed by the SSG's General Directorate of Trade and Supply in cooperation with the Ministry of Interior.[11] In other cases, markets were subjected to general closures.[12] In those markets that were kept open, the SSG's officials distributed gloves, masks, and informative brochures to sellers.[13]

Mosques, parks, wedding halls, swimming pools, restaurants, cafes, and playgrounds were also closed to prevent gatherings (Taneja 2020).[14] The Ministry of Education closed schools and universities and introduced on-line distance learning (Hifzy and Ghourabi 2020). One of HTS's Quranic schools released prerecorded course videos for children (Zelin 2020). In mid-July 2020, schools were reopened with proper preventive measures (distancing and compulsory use of masks and gloves) to allow students to take their final exams.[15] As far as mosques are concerned, a circular from the Minister of Endowments ordered mosque administrators to sterilize mosques, shorten sermons, maintain social distancing between worshippers, and impose masks during prayer.[16] It is noticeable that masks were distributed to worshippers at the entrance to mosques.[17]

Importantly, the above measures were regularly communicated by the SSG's Health Minister in official audio messages.[18] Similarly, the Director of the SSG's Public Relations Office held press conferences to inform the public and the media about the measures taken and the Minister of Health published regular reports on the number of new infections, deaths, and recoveries.[19] HTS's efforts notwithstanding, cases of infections were soaring in Idlib as of September and October 2021 (AFP 2021; Doctors Without Borders 2021). In late September, HTS

[7] Ibid., 6 June 2020 entry.
[8] "Ibid., 11 November 2020 entry.
[9] Ibid., 7, 12, 17, and 26 May as well as 25 and 30 November 2020 entries.
[10] 'Coronavirus and the Salvation Government – Hayat Tahrir al-Sham', 20 April, 14 July, and 13 December 2020. *Jihadology*, blog by A. Y. Zelin. Available at: https://jihadology.net/coronavirus-and-the-salvation-government-hayat-tahir-al-sham/.
[11] Ibid., 13 April 2020 entry.
[12] Ibid., 6, 7, 8, 9 April and 10 November 2020 entries.
[13] Ibid., 7 April 2020 entry.
[14] Ibid., 7 April, 16 and 23 September, and 20 October entries.
[15] Ibid., 12 July 2020 entry.
[16] Ibid., 10 July and 2 August 2020 entries.
[17] Ibid., 13 and 20 November, and December 2020 entries.
[18] 'Coronavirus and the Salvation Government – Hayat Tahrir al-Sham', 12 July 2020. *Jihadology*, blog by A. Y. Zelin. Available at: https://jihadology.net/coronavirus-and-the-salvation-government-hayat-tahir-al-sham/.
[19] Ibid., February 2021 entry.

and the SSG re-imposed temporary closures of schools, markets, swimming pools, playgrounds, wedding halls, and amusement parks. Restaurants were kept open for deliveries only (al-Kanj 2021).

9.6 The Houthis

In May 1990, southern and northern Yemen were united into a single state. The Zaydi Shias that had ruled northern Yemen since the ninth century became a minority and their areas were neglected by the government (Schmitz 2018). It was in this context that the Houthi movement was created as an expression of Zaydi interests (Schmitz 2018). When in early 2011 the Arab Spring arrived in Yemen, the Houthis joined popular opposition to President Ali Abdullah Saleh. The latter's replacement with Vice-President Abdrabbuh Mansur Hadi in February 2012 was met with criticism by the Houthis, who saw Hadi as representative of the old system. In addition to this, the National Dialogue Conference aimed at reconciling the parties failed to respond to the Houthis' political demands and territorial claims. In 2014, the Houthis aligned with Saleh and initiated an insurgency that saw the group overthrow the government (Schmitz 2018). Since late 2014, the Houthis have been the de facto governing authority in the northern half of Yemen (International Crisis Group 2014).

Yemen was among the last countries to announce the pandemic. The first confirmed case was declared on 10 April 2020 (Mugahed 2021). From that moment, the Houthis launched a disinformation campaign, declaring the virus an 'American conspiracy'. (Human Rights Watch 2021). In the words of the Houthi leader Abdulmalik al-Houthi, 'America bears the primary responsibility for COVID-19 epidemic [. . .]Americans have worked for years to benefit from the coronavirus and have worked to spread it in certain societies.' (Nasser et al. 2021).[20] Mohammed Ali al-Houthi, President of the movement's Revolutionary Council, made similar statements (ACAPS 2020: 4). The Houthis even organized public demonstrations of hostility towards the United States and Israel, accused of having created COVID-19 as a weapon of biological warfare (ACAPS 2020: 5).

To better control and manipulate information, Houthi authorities intimidated health workers, journalists, and even grave diggers to suppress information about the extent of the outbreak (Mugahed 2021). Thus, while two hospitals in Sana'a—Zayed Hospital and Kuwait Hospital—were receiving patients with COVID-19, doctors and family members of the deceased feared to speak openly because of threats of reprisal (Al-Rawhani 2020). Most dramatically, as part of their broader manipulation of the COVID-19 health emergency, the Houthis also

[20] Abulmalik's speech at: https://www.youtube.com/watch?v=8PfTemGCr_M [no longer accessible].

launched new recruitment campaigns among the youngsters, convincing them that joining the group was the only way not to contract the virus (Asharq Al Awsat 2021).

Poems explaining the rules of social distancing to reduce the spread of the virus were published and shared on pro-Houthi websites and social media. However, while trying to promote some medical advice those poems also sought to remind listeners that foreign adversaries—the United States, Israel, and the Saudi 'aggression'—rather than Houthi officials were to be blamed for the pandemic and for the difficulty of addressing it (Porter 2020; SABA 2020a,b,c).

Nonetheless, in February 2020, the Houthis allegedly established a Higher Ministerial Committee for Combating Epidemics to coordinate the response to COVID-19 and elaborate preventive measures (SABA 2020d). In the words of the Houthis' Minister of Health, Taha al-Mutawakkil, 'we depended on our Almighty Allah and we urged the people to take guidelines and awareness into their accounts and as the instructions issued by the Higher Ministerial Committee for Combating Epidemics, including proper nutrition to strengthen immunity and deal with a high responsibility to prevent the spread of the virus and limit its spread' (SABA 2020e).

Initially, the Houthi authorities reportedly gave indications to close schools, stop prayers at mosques, limit public gatherings, and regulate markets and shops (Ardemagni 2020a,b). They closed land borders with the government-controlled parts of Yemen and ceased all incoming flights (ACAPS 2020: 4; SABA 2020f). Later on, however, big mass events relevant to the Houthis' ideology were held: in October 2021, for instance, major rallies that attracted millions of people were organized in Sana'a and other Houthi-controlled cities to celebrate the anniversary of the birth of the Prophet Muhammad (SABA 2021a). Prior to that, Abdulmalik al-Houthi encouraged Yemenis to take to the streets and celebrate the seventh anniversary of the revolution that brought the group to power (SABA 2021b).

In 2021, as vaccines were distributed to Yemen through COVAX, the Houthis refrained from distributing the necessary doses throughout the areas under their control and from cooperating with the World Health Organization (WHO) in this regard (Human Rights Watch 2021). More specifically, the Houthi authorities initially agreed to accept 10,000 doses of vaccine, but the transfer was obstructed after they set as condition that the vaccines could only be distributed by the group without WHO supervision (Human Rights Watch 2021; Magdy 2021). This is coherent with the traditional practice of the group, which in mid-2020 blocked a large shipment of anti-COVID-19 personal protective equipment (PPE) (Human Rights Watch 2020). Thus, despite the Houthis' claims of having met with the WHO to discuss how to best address the pandemic (SABA 2020g), it does not seem that any real and significant effort has been made.

9.7 Hamas

As the First Intifada erupted in 1987, the Islamic Resistance Movement, better known by its acronym Hamas, was established as the armed wing of the Gaza-based branch of the Egyptian Muslim Brotherhood (Baracskay 2015). Its goal was to eliminate Israel and create an Islamic state over historical Palestine.[21] In 2005, Hamas participated in elections for the first time and in 2006 it won the legislative elections. However, its victory was not recognized by most of the international community (Natil 2011). A Palestinian civil conflict broke out until mid-June 2007, when Hamas established its own government in the Gaza Strip (Berti and Gutiérrez 2016; Brenner 2017).

When in the context of the COVID 19 pandemic, the government in Ramallah announced a state of emergency and enforced a total lockdown in early March 2020, Hamas refused to follow suit, arguing that the Gaza Strip had no cases. It was only on the evening of 21 March that Hamas confirmed the first two cases of coronavirus. The two infected people, as well as all those who had been in contact with them, were placed in quarantine (International Crisis Group 2020c). From there, Hamas proceeded to close markets, schools, mosques, restaurants, and prohibit large gatherings such as weddings. Working hours of non-essential businesses were also reduced to the minimum (Abuhabib et al. 2020; Sky News 2020). In April 2021, as cases rose, Hamas imposed a ten-day total lockdown on Gaza, with only essential businesses such as pharmacies, bakeries, and foodstores allowed to remain open (Khoury 2021). The imposition of the lockdown, however, did not come without controversies due to the precarious socio-economic conditions in Gaza: in the words of a Hamas official, 'one should remember that we're in the Gaza Strip, not in Israel or another developed country that provides its citizens with a safety net or with compensation for closed businesses' (Khoury 2021).

Quarantine was imposed on symptomatic and infected people returning to Gaza through the Rafah border crossing with Egypt and the Eretz border crossing with Israel (Palestinian Ministry of Health 2020a; Herzog and al-Omari 2020). The group also installed a temporary medical clinic at the Rafah crossing to conduct medical checks on inbound travellers and instruct those required to self-isolate (Palestinian Ministry of Health 2020b,c). Quarantine centres were also opened in hotels (Palestinian Ministry of Health 2020b). As it was the case with general lockdowns, the imposition of quarantine was also a challenging task for Hamas: as argued by the group's head in Gaza, Yahya Sinwar, 'when we [Hamas] decided to establish compulsory quarantine facilities for people returning to Gaza, we knew that it would be a difficult decision that would cause a lot of criticism against us' (Times of Israel 2020).

[21] The original charter of Hamas can be accessed at: https://avalon.law.yale.edu/20th_century/hamas.asp.

Faced with a major health crisis, al-Qassam Brigades—the armed wing of Hamas—also tried to play the role of a national army by participating in efforts to fight the pandemic. They contributed to the construction of two quarantine facilities and contributed to the sterilization of public spaces (Abdalfatah 2020). However, it has been reported by residents that Hamas also resorted to harsh tactics such as beatings, water cannons, and dirt barriers to keep people away from the streets (Mitnick 2020).

Besides the measures described above, the Ministry of Health in Gaza conducted training for medical personnel in hospitals and healthcare centres, including how to deal with suspected cases, how to transfer patients, and how to conduct sterilization (Palestinian Ministry of Health 2020d). Campaigns of awareness were also organized: the Health Education Department of the Ministry of Health printed 122,000 leaflets and 200 awareness posters (Palestinian Ministry of Health 2020d). In addition to that, Hamas urged mosques to use Friday sermons to inform and preach about coronavirus, its symptoms, and the importance of hygiene and social distancing from a religious point of view (Alijla 2021).

To address the crisis and deal with the limits of Gaza's healthcare system (Reuters 2020; AFP 2020), Hamas also engaged in some form of cooperation with Israel: it sent doctors, nurses, and lab technicians to Israel for training; samples were sent from Gaza to Israel for testing; Israel sent to the Strip 20 respirators, 300 testing kits, and 50,000 masks; doctors in Gaza and Israel shared data on the virus' spread (Tzoreff and Michael 2020; Abu Jahal 2020). Nonetheless, despite this collaboration on COVID-related issues, it is worth mentioning that, just as the Houthis blamed the 'Saudi aggression' for the effects of COVID-19 in northern Yemen, so Hamas put the blame for its difficulties in addressing the health emergency on the blockade imposed by Israel on the Strip (Palestinian Ministry of Health 2020e).

Besides Israel, Hamas cooperated also with international aid organizations and other governments. For instance, the UAE donated to Gaza a field hospital for the treatment of COVID-19 patients that was installed in Rafah city (Palestinian Ministry of Health 2021a). The WHO cooperated with Hamas' Ministry of Health to implement an advanced course for doctors (Palestinian Ministry of Health 2021b); the Turkish Red Crescent delivered medical supplies to the Ministry of Health (Palestinian Ministry of Health 2020f); the Palestinian government in Ramallah sent testing kits and sterilizers to the Strip (Sama News 2020).

In February 2021, the Gaza Ministry of Health launched a national vaccination campaign, starting with medical staff (Palestinian Ministry of Health 2021c). The Ministry of Health distributed Pfizer and AstraZeneca vaccines received through the COVAX program (Palestinian Ministry of Health 2021d). Up to 50,000 people have been inoculated thus far (Palestinian Ministry of Health 2021e).

9.8 HTS, the Houthis, and Hamas in the fight against COVID-19

Following the case studies above, I argue that the Houthis offered a COVID-19 governance response that can be regarded as 'null'. Conversely, HTS displayed a much greater engagement in COVID-19 response, which can be located between the 'moderate' and 'extensive' points along the proposed continuum. For its part, Hamas offered a COVID-19 governance response that can be coded as 'extensive'. The observations are summarized in Figure 9.2.

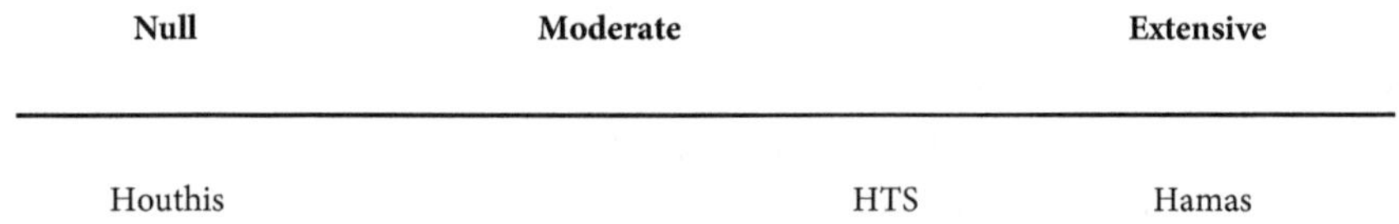

Figure 9.2 COVID-19 response by HTS, Houthis, and Hamas

Having described how HTS, the Houthis, and Hamas responded to the health emergency posed by COVID-19, I proceed here to explain the variations observed in the three groups' responses (summarized in Table 9.1). As I suggested before, when armed groups are faced with an unexpected crisis, their propensity to respond may depend on their ultimate goals and their dependency on domestic or international legitimacy. Specifically, secessionist and ethno-nationalist groups are expected to be more prone to engage in extensive activities of governance in times of crisis, as they regard this as a useful strategy to obtain the international recognition and domestic credibility on which their success depends. Conversely, non-secessionist and non-ethno-nationalist groups are expected to invest less in emergency governance.

These expectations find confirmation in the three case studies. Hamas has historically pursued the establishment of an internationally recognized Islamic state over Palestine (International Crisis Group 2006: ii; Al-Omari 2015; Michael and Dostri 2018). To reach its ambitious goal, it must prove its capacity to govern both to the Palestinian population over which it aspires to rule and to the international community by which it aspires to be recognized. Therefore, when faced with the health emergency posed by COVID-19, Hamas sought to offer an extensive response that would enhance its governance credentials both at home and abroad. As noted by Alijla (2021), Hamas' response to COVID-19 'was meant to send a message to the international community, but also to the local population, that it is capable of acting as a governing body [. . .]'.[22]

Similar considerations apply to HTS. When the group joined the Syrian insurgency, its goal was to overthrow the regime and establish an Islamic emirate for the Syrian people. Over time, HTS also aspired to obtain international recognition of

[22] See also Soliman (2021).

Table 9.1 Explaining variation in armed groups' COVID-19 response

Armed group	Explanatory factors				COVID-19 response
	Ultimate goal	Conflict intensity	Governance experience	Financial resources	
HTS	Islamic statelet in Idlib, internationally recognized	High	Moderate, but growing	Dependent on people	Moderate/ Extensive
Houthis	Central power in Yemen	High	Poor	Independent of people	Null
Hamas	Islamic state in Palestine, internationally recognized	Low	Significant and consolidated	Dependent on people	Extensive

its Islamic statelet in Idlib (Tsurkov n.d.). To reach this goal, HTS needed to prove to the Syrian population and to the international community its actual capacity to govern over the millions of people living under its rule. Thus, when COVID-19 spread throughout the country, the group sought to invest resources in a health-care response extensive enough that would testify its capacity to provide for the people.

The Houthis, for their part, aspire to capture power throughout Yemen (Zimmerman and Harnisch 2010; Albloshi 2016). However, they believe that conquering power in Yemen is not dependent upon international recognition or domestic legitimacy, but rather upon their capacity to conquer territories and consolidate victories (Feierstein and Abo Alasrar 2021; Sharp 2020). Therefore, they prioritize the military struggle and do not see the need to prove themselves as governors in the eyes of domestic and international audiences. As cases of COVID-19 were reported in Yemen, the Houthis lacked incentives to engage in extensive activities of governance—especially as doing so required redirecting resources away from a military effort perceived as crucial.

Besides ultimate goals, I suggested that the intensity of the conflict might also contribute to explaining a group's propensity to governance in times of emergency. Specifically, I suggested that groups engaged in low-intensity conflicts will be more prone to act as rulers with respect to groups engaged in high-intensity conflicts. In fact, the temporary cessation of hostilities allows the former to invest resources in governance without running risks in terms of survival.

This expectation, however, is only partially confirmed by the three case studies. Hamas, which invested in an extensive COVID-19 response, was engaged in a low-intensity conflict against Israel.[23] Therefore, when COVID-19 arrived in Gaza, Hamas could afford to invest resources in governance activities without risking that this would translate in military defeats on the battlefront. The Houthis, which engaged in null-to-minimum COVID-19 response, were fighting a high-intensity conflict against the Yemeni government.[24] Therefore, when COVID-19 arrived in Yemen, the Houthis could not afford to divert resources away from the military effort, as this would have offered an advantage to the enemy. However, HTS was also engaged in a high-intensity conflict against the Syrian regime and its allies.[25] Nonetheless, as COVID-19 spread, it decided to invest in a somewhat extensive COVID-19 response. These observations suggest that while a low level of conflict intensity might place an armed group in a better position to address an external emergency, this is not necessarily a *conditio sine qua non*. Armed groups engaged in high-intensity conflicts might still find incentives and ways to perform activities of governance even as they continue to be confronted by pressing military concerns.

In the discussion in the second part of this chapter, I suggested that a further factor that might contribute to explaining variation in armed groups' responses to external emergencies is a group's prior governance experience, especially in the area affected by the crisis. I suggested that groups with a poor experience as providers of healthcare would be less capable of engaging in extensive COVID-19 governance responses, while groups with a meaningful experience as providers of healthcare would have a greater capacity to address the pandemic.

This expectation is confirmed by the three case studies. Hamas had been engaged in practices of healthcare governance since conquering Gaza in 2007. It had been running hospitals and clinics and had been employing its own medical staff (Roy 2011: 217). It had also been cooperating and coordinating with many international humanitarian agencies, allowing them to run their clinics (Berti 2015). Therefore, when cases of COVID-19 began to be reported in Gaza, Hamas could benefit from its prior experience as provider of healthcare, relying on pre-existing medical personnel, hospitals and clinics, medical equipment, and cooperative relationships with external actors.

HTS had also been actively engaged in the provision of healthcare, even though less successfully and comprehensively than Hamas and for less extended time. Following the creation of the SSG, the government's Ministry of Health was charged with the task of managing Idlib's hospitals, pharmacies, and medical centres and regulating all healthcare matters (Hagedorn 2019). To be sure, provision of healthcare was far from ideal in HTS-controlled territories (International Crisis

[23] https://ucdp.uu.se/country/666 (Israel); https://ucdp.uu.se/actor/209 (Hamas). From Uppsala Conflict Data Program (UCDP), Department of Peace and Conflict Research.

[24] https://ucdp.uu.se/country/678 (Yemen [North Yemen]); https://ucdp.uu.se/conflict/230 (Yemen [North Yemen]: Government).

[25] https://ucdp.uu.se/country/652 (Syria); https://ucdp.uu.se/actor/6815 (HTS).

Group 2020b). Nonetheless, HTS and the SSG had been engaged in governance efforts that provided them with some degree of useful know-how once COVID-19 spread throughout north-western Syria. As the first cases were reported, HTS did not have to build its governance capacity from scratch but could rather refer to its prior experience and pre-existing structures.

Conversely, the Houthis have a poor experience as providers of healthcare. After taking over Sana'a, they did not invest in governance—and healthcare has probably been the area in which the limits of their governance have been most evident. Specifically, the Houthis had been unable (and uninterested) to pay salaries to medical workers and to address the shortage of medical equipment and drugs (Human Rights Watch 2021). They had also occupied and militarized hospitals to control medical services, and they had commandeered medical facilities to prioritize care to their members or supporters (PHR and Mwatana 2020). When COVID-19 arrived in northern Yemen, the Houthis were completely unprepared—unexperienced and under-resourced—to deal with the emergency. Their failure to act as providers of healthcare governance meant that when the pandemic arrived, there was no pre-existing experience or structure that they could refer to.

Finally, I suggested that the type of financial resources available to a group might also explain propensity to governance. Groups that depend on the population to extract resources are more incentivized to perform activities of civilian administration when confronted with an emergency that threatens the well-being of the people. Conversely, groups that do not depend on the population to extract resources are hardly incentivized to perform activities of civilian administration when an emergency comes and threatens the people's health and life.

This is confirmed by the case studies of Hamas, HTS, and the Houthis. Hamas used to derive many of its financial resources from the taxation of Gaza's population: the collection of fees on services such as birth certificates, water, shop licenses, and building permits; the collection of custom duties on goods that enter the Strip from Israel and Egypt; and the collection of taxes on activities of smuggling conducted through Gaza's underground tunnel network (Miller 2015; Jalal 2020). HTS also used to derive many of its financial resources from the collection of taxes from the local civilian population. It also collected fees at checkpoints and border crossings for the transit of goods and people and fees for the provision of services (International Crisis Group 2018, 2019; al-Zaraee and Shaar 2021; Eaton et al. 2019; SOHR 2020). In the words of an SSG official, '[m]ost of the [SSG's] resources come from taxes and royalties on citizens and organizations, as well as entry and exit fees [. . .].' (Nassar and Brignola 2019). Therefore, when COVID-19 spread throughout Gaza and Idlib, it became of paramount importance for Hamas and HTS to engage in an effective response that would protect civilians. A sick population, in fact, would not be able to engage in those economic activities that are the backbone of the taxation system of the two groups. Thus, as COVID-19 spread, Hamas and HTS were incentivized to engage in a governance response extensive enough that would allow to preserve their traditional patterns of financing, suddenly threatened by the pandemic.

The Houthis, conversely, derive most of their financial resources from the seizure of properties, bank accounts, and companies; appropriation of revenues and salaries of public employees; control over the Sana'a branch of Yemen's Central Bank; theft of humanitarian aid and sale thereof on the black market; and custom duties on incoming vessels at Hodeida and fees on ships for discharging their cargo (Salisbury 2017; The Arab Weekly 2020; Sana'a Center Economic Unit 2020; al-Iryani et al. 2021). Sustained by these financial revenues, when coronavirus arrived in Yemen, the Houthis lacked the incentives to engage in an even minimal response. In fact, the financial well-being of the organization is not dependent on the well-being of the civilian population and the latter's capacity to engage in economic activities.

9.9 Conclusion

As COVID-19 spread worldwide, not only governments but also armed groups in control of territories were called to address the crisis. Recognizing that little scholarly attention has been paid to the phenomenon, in this chapter I sought to explain armed groups' responses to the pandemic. I built a continuum of armed groups' governance responses to COVID-19 ranging from 'null' to 'extensive'. I then referred to the existing scholarship on non-state governance to identify the factors that might be most useful to illuminate governance variation in times of emergency. Following the study of HTS, the Houthis, and Hamas, I found that the intensity of the conflict does not appear to be a relevant explanatory factor. Conversely, the groups' ultimate goals and its dependency on domestic or international legitimacy, the type of financial resources available to the groups, and the groups' prior experience in (healthcare) governance explain the observed patterns of COVID-19 governance. More specifically, I found confirmation to the expectations that armed groups that aspire to obtain domestic or international recognition of their political system, armed groups that have prior experience in the area of governance affected by the crisis, and armed groups whose financial resources depend mostly on civilians are more likely to engage in moderate-to-extensive emergency governance.

Being this the first study to look in depth into armed groups' responses to COVID-19, future studies should test on other armed groups the arguments advanced here. Future studies should also look beyond the Middle East and include in the analysis groups ruling in other geographic regions. Focusing on non-Islamist groups will also allow to investigate whether doctrine might also contribute to different patterns of COVID-19 governance.

References

Abdalfatah, M. (2020). *COVID-19 Crisis: Business As Usual for Gaza?* London: Chatham House.

Abuhabib, A. A., S. N. Abu-Aita, C. Procter, and I. Al-Smeri (2020). 'Unique Situation of Gaza Strip Dealing with COVID-19 Crisis'. *International Journal of Infectious Diseases*, 100: 149–151. https://doi.org/10.1016/j.ijid.2020.08.070

Abu Jahal (2020). 'Hamas Quietly Allows Gaza Doctors to Get Covid-19 Training in Israel' *Al-Monitor*, 22 April 2020. Available at: https://www.al-monitor.com/originals/2020/04/gaza-doctors-coronavirus-training-israel-ramallah.html.

ACAPS (2020). *Covid-19 Impact on Yemen*. Risk Report, 23 March 2020.

AFP (2020). 'Coronavirus: Hamas Unable to Carry Out Covid-19 Tetsing in Gaza Due to Kit Shortage'. *AlArabiya*, 7 December. https://english.alarabiya.net/News/middle-east/2020/12/07/Coronavirus-Coronavirus-Hamas-unable-to-carry-out-COVID-19-testing-in-Gaza-due-to-shortage.

AFP (2021). 'Syria's Idlib Creports Spike in COVID-19 Cases'. *Al-Arabiya*, 13 September. https://english.alarabiya.net/coronavirus/2021/09/13/Syria-s-Idlib-reports-spike-in-COVID-19-cases.

Al-Badawi, E. et al. (2017). *Inside the Jihadi Mind: Understanding Ideology and Propaganda*. London: Tony Blair Institute for Global Change, p. 49.

Albloshi, H. H. (2016). 'Ideological Roots of the Houthi Movement in Yemen'. *Journal of Arabian Studies*, 6(2): 143–162. https://doi.org/10.1080/21534764.2016.1247522

Alijla, A. (2021). '"We Are in a Battle with the Virus": Hamas, Hezbollah, and Covid-19'. *Middle East Law and Governance*, 14: 101–113. https://doi.org/10.1163/18763375-14010001

al-Iryani, A., C. Coombs, and S. A. Salah (2021). 'Improving Relations Between Central State Institutions and Local Authorities'. White Paper, September 2021. Sana'a Center for Strategic Studies, pp. 14–15

al-Kanj, S. (2021). 'Northwest Syria Closes Schools, Markets to Slow Virus Spread'. *al-Monitor*, 26 September. https://www.al-monitor.com/originals/2021/09/northwest-syria-closes-schools-markets-slow-virus-spread.

Al-Omari, G. (2015). 'Hamas Ramps up its Quest for International Recognition'. Policy Analysis, 13 August. Washington, DC: The Washington Institute for Near East Policy.

Al-Rawhani, O. (2020). 'Houthi Coronavirus Coverup Unleashes Death, Suffering as Yemen Marks Eid'. 22 May. Sana'a Center for Strategic Studies.

Alsayed, G. (2021). 'Vaccine Campaign Begins amid Virus Surge in Rebel-held Syria'. *Associated Press*, 2 May. https://apnews.com/article/syria-europe-middle-east-coronavirus-health-bd6b38e4608915e91c7b5f3406211825.

Al-Tamimi, A. (2015). 'The Evolution in Islamic State Administration: The Documentary Evidence'. *Perspectives on Terrorism*, 9: 117–129.

Al-Tamimi, A. (2020). 'Jihadist Perspectives on Coronavirus Pandemic'. *Aymennjawad.org*, 25 March. http://www.aymennjawad.org/2020/03/jihadist-perspectives-on-coronavirus-pandemic.

Al-Tamimi, A., and W. McCants (2016). 'Experts weigh in (part 2): Is ISIS good at governing?' 3 February. Brookings Institution.

al-Zaraee, N., and K. Shaar (2021). 'The Economics of Hayat Tahrir al-Sham'. Middle East Institute, 21 June. https://www.mei.edu/publications/economics-hayat-tahrir-al-sham.

Arab News (2021). 'Inoculation Begins in Rebel-held Syria'. *Arab News*, 2 May. https://www.arabnews.com/node/1852196/middle-east.

Ardemagni, E. (2020a). 'How Yemen's Houthis Differ from Shia Militias in Dealing with Covid-19'. Commentary, 7 May. Italian Institute for International Political Studies (ISPI). https://www.ispionline.it/it/pubblicazione/how-yemens-houthis-differ-shia-militias-dealing-covid-19-25981.

Ardemagni, E. (2020b). 'Governance, De Facto Authority and Rebel Governance in Times of Covid-19'. Meomo. Washington, DC: The Project on Middle East Political Science (POMEPS).

Asharq Al Awsat (2021). 'Houthis Exploit Coronavirus Fears to Mobilize Recruitment'. *Asharq al-Awsat*, 17 March. https://english.aawsat.com/home/article/2184581/houthis-exploit-coronavirus-fears-mobilize-recruitment.

Baracskay, D. (2015). The Evolutionary Path of Hamas: Examining the Role of Political Pragmatism in State Building and Activism. *Terrorism and Political Violence*, 27: 520–536. DOI: 10.1080/09546553.2013.812035.

Berti, B. (2015). 'Non-State Actors as Providers of Governance: The Hamas Government in Gaza between Effective Sovereignty, Centralized Authority, and Resistance'. *Middle East Journal*, 69(1): 9–31. https://doi.org/10.3751/69.1.11

Berti, B. (2023). 'From Cooperation to Competition: Localization, Militarization and Rebel Co-governance Arrangements in Syria'. *Studies in Conflict and Terrorism*, 46(2): 209–227. https://doi.org/10.1080/1057610X.2020.1776964

Berti, B., and B. Gutiérrez (2016) Rebel-to-Political and Back? Hamas as a Security Provider in Gaza Between Rebellion, Politics and Governance. *Democratization*, 23: 1059–1076. DOI: 10.1080/13510347.2016.1170008.

Brenner, B. (2017). *Gaza under Hamas: From Islamic Democracy to Islamic Governance*. London: I.B.Tauris, pp. 142–148.

Breslawski, J. (2022). Armed Groups & Public Health Emergencies: A Cross-Country Look into Armed Groups' Responses to Covid-19. *Journal of Global Security Studies*, 7: ogab017.

Conrad, J., L. E. Reyes, and M. A. Stewart (2022). Revising Opportunism in Civil Conflict: Natural Resource Extraction and Healthcare Provision. *Journal of Conflict Resolution*, 66: 91–114. DOI: 10.1177/00220027211025597.

CSIS (2018). 'Hayat Tahrir al-Sham (HTS)'. Backgrounder. Washington, DC: Center for Strategic and International Studies. https://www.csis.org/programs/former-programs/warfare-irregular-threats-and-terrorism-program-archives/terrorism-backgrounders/hayat-tahrir.

Doctors Without Borders (2021). 'Northern Syria: Health System Overwhelmed in Most Severe COVID-19 Outbreak Yet'. News, 19 October. https://www.doctorswithoutborders.ca/article/northern-syria-health-system-overwhelmed-most-severe-covid-19-outbreak-yet

Eaton, T., C. Cheng, R. Mansour, P. Salisbury, J. Yazigi, and L. Khatib (2019). *Conflict Economies in the Middle East and North Africa*. London: Chatham House, the Royal Institute of International Affairs, pp. 34–35.

Enab Baladi (2020). 'Smuggling Breaks Coronavirus Preventive Measures in Northern Syria'. *Enab Baladi*, 9 May. https://english.enabbaladi.net/archives/2020/05/smuggling-breaks-coronavirus-preventive-measures-in-northern-syria/.

Feierstein, G., and F. A. Alasrar (2021). How Biden Can Help Yemen. *War on the Rocsk*. 15 July.

Felbab-Brown, V. (2020). 'Mexican Cartels Are Providing COVID-19 Assistance. Why that's Not Surprising'. Commentary, 27 April. Brookings Institution.

Furlan, M. (2023). 'Rebel Governance at the Time of Covid-19: Emergencies as Opportunities for Rebel Rulers'. *Studies in Conflict and Terrorism*, 46(8): 1440–1463. https://doi.org/10.1080/1057610X.2020.1816681

Hagedorn, E. (2019). 'Remaining Hospitals in Syria's Idlib Overwhelmed with Patients'. *The New Arab*, 8 October. https://english.alaraby.co.uk/english/indepth/2019/10/8/remaining-hospitals-in-syrias-idlib-overwhelmed-with-patients.

Hashim, A. (2018). *The Caliphate at War*. Oxford: Oxford University Press, pp. 240–241.

Herbet, I., and J. Drevon (2020). Engaging Armed Groups at the International Committee of the Red Cross: Challenges, Opportunities and Covid-19. *International Review of the Red Cross*, 102: 1021–1031. DOI: 10.1017/S1816383121000588.

Herzog, M., and G. al-Omari (2020). 'Coronavirus on the Israeli-Palestinian Scene (Part 2): The Gaza Strip'. PolicyWatch 3311, 1 May. The Washington Institute of Near East Policy. https://www.washingtoninstitute.org/policy-analysis/coronavirus-israeli-palestinian-scene-part-2-gaza-strip

Hifzy, K., and Y. Ghourabi (2020). 'Challenges in Implementing Distance Learning in Syria's Idlib amid Lack of Electronic Devices and Stable Internet Connection'. *Enab Baladi*, 18 May. https://english.enabbaladi.net/archives/2020/05/challenges-in-implementing-distance-learning-in-syrias-idlib-amid-lack-of-electronic-devices-and-stable-internet-connection/.

Hockey, C., and M. Jones (2020). The Limits of 'Shabaab-CARE': Militant Governance amid Covid-19. *CTC Sentinel*, 13: 33–39.

Human Rights Watch (2020). *Deadly Consequences: Obstruction of Aid in Yemen During Covid-19*. Report, September. New York: Human Rights Watch.

Human Rights Watch (2021). 'Yemen: Houthis Risk Civilians' Health in Covid-19'. News, 1 June. New York: Human Rights Watch.

International Crisis Group (2006). *Enter Hamas: The Challenges of Political Integration*. Middle East Report 49. Brussels: International Crisis Group.

International Crisis Group (2014). *The Huthis: From Saada to Sanaa*. Middle East Report 154. Brussels: International Crisis Group.

International Crisis Group (2018). 'Voices of Idlib'. 11 July.

International Crisis Group (2019). 'The Best of Bad Options for Syria's Idlib'. Middle East Report 197. Brussels: International Crisis Group.

International Crisis Group (2020a). 'The Jihadist Factor in Syria's Idlib: Conversation with Abu Muhammad al-Jolan'. Commentary, 20 February. Brussels: International Crisis Group.

International Crisis Group (2020b). *Silencing the Guns in Syria's Idlib*. Middle East Report 213. Brussels: International Crisis Group.

International Crisis Group (2020c). 'The Gaza Strip and COVID-19: Preparing for the Worst'. Crisis Group Middle East Briefing 75, 1 April. Gaza City/Jerusalem/Brussels: International Crisis Group.

Jackson, A., and A. Aynte (2013). Al Shabaab engagement with aid agencies. *Policy Brief.* Overseas Development Institute, 53.

Jalal, R. A. (2020). 'Hamas Hikes Taxes of Imports, Including from West Bank'. *Al-Monitor*, 30 January. https://www.al-monitor.com/originals/2020/01/cutoms-duties-taxes-hamas-erez-goods-gaza-west-bank-legal.html.

Jones, S. G. (2014). *A Persistent Threat: The Evolution of Al-Qaida and Other Salafi Jihadists.* RAND, pp. 7–24.

Kasfir, N. (2005). Guerrillas and Civilian Participation: The National Resistance Army in Uganda, 1981–1986. *Journal of Modern African Studies*, 43: 271–296. DOI: 10.1017/S0022278X05000832.

Kasfir, N. (2015). 'Rebel governance. Constructing a field of inquiry: Definitions, scope, patterns, order, causes'. In A. Arjona, N. Kasfir, and Z. Mampilly (eds), *Rebel Governance in Civil War.* Cambridge: Cambridge University Press, pp. 21–46. DOI: 10.1017/CBO9781316182468.002.

Khoury, J. (2021). 'Hamas Orders Lockdown in Gaza as Covid Infections Spike'. *Haaretz*, 7 April. https://www.haaretz.com/middle-east-news/.premium-hamas-orders-lockdown-in-gaza-as-covid-infections-spike-1.9691690.

Ladbury, S. et al. (2016). Jihadi Groups and State-Building: The Case of Boko Haram in Nigeria. *Stability: International Journal of Security and Development*, 5, 1–19.

Lister, C. (2016). *Profiling Jabhat Al-Nusra.* Analysis Paper no. 24. Brookings Institution.

Magdy, S. (2021). 'In Yemen's North, Houthis Face Virus with Outright Denial'. 13 August. Associated Press. https://apnews.com/article/middle-east-health-coronavirus-pandemic-united-nations-yemen-1d134157c61c85c844667613183ac1b3.

Mampilly, Z. (2009). 'A Marriage of Inconvenience: Tsunami Aid and the Unraveling of the LTTE and the GoSL's Complex Dependency'. *Civil Wars*, 11: 302–320. DOI: 10.1080/13698240903157545

Mampilly, Z. C. (2011). *Rebel Rulers.* Ithaca, NY: Cornell University Press, pp. 81–82.

Michael, K., and O. Dostri (2018). 'The Hamas Tightrope: Between Political Institutionalization and Armed Struggle'. *Strategic Assessment*, 21(3): 35–46.

Miller, E. (2015). 'New Hamas Import Tax Leaves Gaza Merchants Fuming'. *Times of Israel*, 21 April. https://www.timesofisrael.com/new-hamas-import-tax-leaves-gaza-merchants-fuming/.

Mitnick, J. (2020). 'In Gaza, Surge of Coronavirus Spurs Fears and a Jolt of Pragmatism'. *The Christian Science Monitor*, 10 September. https://www.csmonitor.com/World/Middle-East/2020/0910/In-Gaza-surge-of-coronavirus-spurs-fears-and-a-jolt-of-pragmatism.

Mkandawire, T. (2002). 'The Terrible Toll of Post-Colonial 'Rebel Movements' in Africa: Toward an Explanation of the Violence Against the Peasantry'. *Journal of Modern African Studies*, 40: 181–215. DOI: 10.1017/S0022278X02003889.

Moore, M. (2004). Revenues, State Formation, and the Quality of Governance in Developing Countries. *International Political Science Review*, 25: 297–319. DOI: 10.1177/0192512104043018.

Mugahed, R. (2021). *The Impact of the Covid-19 Pandemic on Yemeni Women.* Sana'a: Sana'a Center for Strategic Studies.

Nasser, S. et al. (2021). '"There is no Corona in Yemen: The Virus and the Vaccine are a Conspiracy"'. *Daraj*, 23 February. https://daraj.com/66867/ [no longer accessible].

Nassar, A., and J. Brignola (2019). '"From the Gutter to the Rain": Inside HTS' Takeover of Northwestern Syria'. *Syria Direct*, 25 February.https://syriadirect.org/news/from-the-gutter-to-the-rain-inside-hts-takeover-of-northwestern-syria/.

Natil, I. (2011). Hamas Between Militarism and Governance. *Journal of Conflict Transformation and Security*, 1: 151–163.

Palestinian Ministry of Health (2020a). 'Daily Report on Coronavirus', 27 March. https://www.moh.gov.ps/portal/27-3-2020daily-report-on-coronavirus-covid-19/.

Palestinian Ministry of Health (2020b). 'Daily Report on Coronavirus', 23 March. https://www.moh.gov.ps/portal/daily-report-on-coronavirus-covid-19-23-3-2020/.

Palestinian Ministry of Health (2020c). 'Abu Al-Reish Heads a Technical Ministerial Team to Pursue the Field Rafah Crossing Hospital, 16 March. https://www.moh.gov.ps/portal/abu-al-reish-heads-a-technical-ministerial-team-to-pursue-the-field-rafah-crossi ng-hospital/.

Palestinian Ministry of Health (2020d). 'Daily Report on Coronavirus', 22 March. https://www.moh.gov.ps/portal/wp-content/uploads/2020/03/Corona-Eng.-22-03.pdf.

Palestinian Ministry of Health (2020e). 'Daily Report on Coronavirus', 25 March. https://www.moh.gov.ps/portal/daily-report-on-coronavirus-covid-19-march-25-2020/

Palestinian Ministry of Health (2020f). 'MoH Gaza and Turkish Red Crescent Discussing Ways of Cooperation'. 11 November. https://www.moh.gov.ps/portal/moh-gaza-and-turkish-red-crescent-discussing-ways-of-cooperation/.

Palestinian Ministry of Health (2021a). 'United Arab Emirates Field Hospital to Arrive Soon'. 27 June. https://www.moh.gov.ps/portal/establishing-and-equipping-and-the-uae-field-hospital-for-covid-19-patients/.

Palestinian Ministry of Health (2021b). 'MoH and WHO Implements an Advanced Course for ICU Doctors'. 28 June. https://www.moh.gov.ps/portal/moh-and-who-implements-an-advanced-course-for-icu-doctors/.

Palestinian Ministry of Health (2021c). 'MoH Gaza Launches the National Covid-19 Vaccination Campaign'. 21 February. https://www.moh.gov.ps/portal/moh-gaza-launches-the-national-covid-19vaccination-campaign/.

Palestinian Ministry of Health (2021d). 'The Ministry of Health and WHO Have Begun Vaccination with the Pfizer and Astrazeneka Vaccine Provided by the Kovacs Foundation'. 28 March. https://www.moh.gov.ps/portal/the-ministry-of-health-and-the-who-have-begun-vaccination-with-the-pfizer-and-astrazenka-vaccine-provided-by-the -kovacs-foundation/.

Palestinian Ministry of Health (2021e). 'MoH Gaza Expands Covid-19 Vaccination Campaign to Reach 50000 People'. 22 June. https://www.moh.gov.ps/portal/moh-gaza-expands-covid-19-vaccination-campaigns-to-reach-50000-people/.

PHR and Mwatana (2020). *'I ripped the IV out of my arm and started running': Attacks on Healthcare in Yemen*. March. Physicians for Human Rights (PHR) and Mwatana for Human Rights (Mwatana). https://phr.org/our-work/resources/i-ripped-the-iv-out-of-my-arm-and-started-running-attacks-on-health-care-in-yemen/.

Porter, H. (2020). 'A Battle of Hearts and Minds: The Growing Media Footprint of Yemen's Houthis'. Commentary, Gulf International Forum. https://gulfif.org/a-battle-of-hearts-and-minds-the-growing-media-footprint-of-yemens-houthis/.

Reuters (2020). 'Coronavirus: Gaza Receives Vital Medical Aid as Hospitals Battle Raising Infections'. *AlArabiya*, 29 November. https://english.alarabiya.net/coronavirus/2020/11/29/Coronavirus-Coronavirus-Gaza-receives-vital-medical-aid-as-hospitals-battle-rising-infections.

Reuters (2021). 'First Batch of COVID-19 Vaccines Arrives in Northwest Syria'. *Reuters*, 1 April. https://www.reuters.com/world/middle-east/first-batch-covid-19-vaccines-arrive s-northwest-syria-2021-04-21/.

Roy, S. (2011). *Hamas and Civil Society in Gaza: Engaging the Islamist Social Sector*. Princeton, NJ: Princeton University Press.

SABA (2020a). 'Reopen Sana'a Airport Become Urgent Necessity: Report'. *SABA*, 27 December. https://www.saba.ye/en/news3121615.htm.

SABA (2020b). 'Holding Oil Ships by Aggression Coalition Undermines efforts to Confront Corona in Yemen'. *SABA*, 10 June. https://www.saba.ye/en/news3099225.htm.

SABA (2020c). 'Health Minister Holds Aggression Coalition Responsible for Spread of Epidemics in Yemen'. *SABA*, 2 May. https://www.saba.ye/en/news3095829.htm.

SABA (2020d). 'Epidemic Control Committee Discusses Procedures to Face any Developments of Coronavirus'. *SABA*, 5 September. https://www.saba.ye/en/news3108028.htm.

SABA (2020e). 'Health Ministry Succeeds in Reducing Repercussions of Coronavirus "COVID 19"'. *SABA*, 7 July. https://www.saba.ye/en/news3101978.htm.

SABA (2020f). 'Committee for Combating Epidemics Suspends Flights to Sanaa Airport for 2 Weeks'. *SABA*, 14 March. https://www.saba.ye/en/news3090760.htm.

SABA (2020g). 'FM Meets Resident Representative of World Health Organization'. *SABA*, 8 September. https://www.saba.ye/en/news3108354.htm.

SABA (2021a). 'Millions of Yemenis Celebrate on Prophet's Birthday Anniversary'. *SABA*, 19 October. https://www.saba.ye/en/news3160888.htm.

SABA (2021b). 'Revolution Leader Calls for Honorable Participation to Commemorate the 7th Anniversary of the Revolution'. *SABA*, 21 September. https://www.saba.ye/en/news3156635.htm.

Salisbury, P. (2017). 'Yemen: National Chaos, Local Order'. Research Chapter, 20 December. London: Chatham House, the Royal Institute of International Affairs.

Sama News (2020). 'Ramallah: The Ministry of Health Announces the Dispatch of a Shipment of Medical Aid to Gaza'. *Sama News*, 19 July [Arabic]. Available at: .الإخبارية سما - لغزة طبية مساعدات شحنة إرسال تعلن الصحة وزارة :الله رام

Sana'a Center Economic Unit (2020). 'Yemen Economic Bulletin: Tax and Rule – Houthis Move to Institutionalize Hashemite Elite with 'One-Fifth' Levy'. Analysis, 6 October. Sana'a Center for Strategic Studie. https://sanaacenter.org/publications/analysis/11628.

Schmitz, C. (2018). 'Yemen, the Forgotten Conflict'. Oasis website, 13 September. Milan: Oasis. https://www.oasiscenter.eu/en/war-in-yemen-who-is-involved.

Sharp, J. M. (2020). *Yemen: Civil War and Regional Intervention*. Congressional Research Service Report R43960. 8 December 2020 update.

Sky News (2020). 'Hamas Imposes a Curfew in Gaza after First Outbreak of Corona'. *Sky News*, *25* August 2020 [Arabic]. Available at: .عربية نيوز سكاي | لكورونا تفشّ أول بعد غزة في تجوّل حظر تفرض حماس

SOHR (2020). 'Islamic Terror Group Confiscating Christian-owned Properties in Syria'. 5 May. Syrian Observatory for Human Rights. https://www.syriahr.com/en/163224/.

Soliman, N. (2021). 'The New Jihadists and the Taliban Model'. Commentary, 20 December. Washington, DC: Carnegie Endowment for International Peace.

Stewart, M. (2018). Civil War as state-making: Strategic governance in Civil War. *International Organization*, 72: 1–31.

Taneja, K. (2020). 'Beware of terrorists offering COVID19 aid'. Expert Speak, 17 April. Observer Research Foundation.

The Arab Weekly (2020). 'Houthi Taxes Drain Funds from Already Impoverished Yemenis'. *The Arab Weekly*, 25 September. https://thearabweekly.com/houthi-taxes-drain-funds-already-impoverished-yemenis.

The New Arab (2021). 'North-west Syria Receives Covid-19 Vaccines amid Delta Variant Surge'. *The New Arab*, 7 September. https://english.alaraby.co.uk/news/northwest-syria-receives-covax-delivery-amid-delta-surge.

Times of Israel (2020). 'Hamas chief Threatens Israel over Ventilators for Coronavirus Patients'. *Times of Israel*, 2 April. https://www.timesofisrael.com/hamas-chief-threatens-israel-over-ventilators-for-coronavirus-patients/.

TRT World (2021). 'First Batch of Covid-19 Jabs Arrives in Northwest Syria'. *TRT World*, 22 April. https://www.trtworld.com/magazine/first-batch-of-covid-19-jabs-arrive-in-northwestern-syria-46124.

Tsurkov, E. (n.d.). 'Hayat Tahrir al-Sham (Syria)'. Guns and Governance: How Europe Should Talk with Non-state Armed Groups in the Middle East. European Council on Foreign Relations. https://ecfr.eu/special/mena-armed-groups/hayat-tahrir-al-sham-syria/ (accessed in 2020).

Tzoreff, Y., and K. Michael (2020). *The Corona Pandemic and the Palestinian Arena: The Significance for Israel.* Tel Aviv: Institute for National Security Studies.

Walch, C. (2014). Collaboration or Obstruction? Rebel Group Behavior During Natural Disaster Relief in the Philippines. *Political Geography*, 43: 40–50. DOI: 10.1016/j.polgeo.2014.09.007.

Weinstein, J. (2007). *Inside Rebellion.* Cambridge: Cambridge University Press, pp. 171–172.

WHO (2021). 'Updates on COVID-19 Vaccination in Syria, August 2021'. News. World Health Organization. http://www.emro.who.int/syria/news/updates-on-covid-19-vaccination-in-syria-august-2021.html?format=html.

Zelin, A. Y. (2016). '*The Islamic State's Territorial Methodology*'. Research Note.29. Washington, DC: The Washington Institute for Near East Policy.

Zelin, A. Y. (2020). '*The Jihadi-Backed Salvation Government and Covid-19 in Northwest Syria*'. Policy Analysis, 15 May. Washington, DC: The Washington Institute for Near East Policy.

Zimmerman, K., and C. Harnisch (2010). 'Profile: Al-Houthi Movement'. *Critical Threats*, 28 January 2010.

10
Political life after ethnic war

Sarah Zukerman Daly

10.1 Introduction

What explains political life after mass violence in ethnic war? What accounts for how voters cast their ballots in post-ethnic war elections? In the wake of ethnic conflict and the horrors of mass violence, societies are often left grappling with the daunting task of rebuilding their social and political fabric. The scars of such conflicts run deep, leaving communities divided. How do nations, torn apart by ethno-nationalist strife, chart a course towards political stability and reconciliation?

Elections in the aftermath of such conflicts are critical junctures that shape the course of a nation's recovery, reconciliation, and future. Understanding the factors that influence the behaviour of political actors and voters in these circumstances is essential for both scholars and policymakers seeking to promote peace, stability, and democratic governance in post-conflict societies.

Scholars of the political legacies of violence indicate how experiences of war and victimization may mobilize citizens and guide their vote choice for or against their perpetrators. However, we know less about how these patterns manifest specifically in contexts of ethnic conflict.

Scholarship on war's legacies in ethnic contexts suggests that, in the aftermath of ethnic violence, societies become defined by deep-seated ethnic cleavages and ethnic parties emerge as a consequence of ethno-nationalist sentiments and the need to protect the interests of particular ethnic groups. However, other scholars question the stylized way in which ethnic conflict is often portrayed and the assumption of a legacy of hardened identities; rather, they claim that institutions and interests can significantly shape identities and, in particular, guide whether war-ravaged populations vote on ethnic lines.

This study focuses on the first elections following ethnic war. I argue that the nature of the violent incompatibility between warring parties—whether government or territory—and the military outcomes of the war—victory, draw, or defeat—structures party and voter strategies and electoral performance in these elections. I demonstrate this theory by embedding illustrative case studies of ethnic

Sarah Zukerman Daly, *Political life after ethnic war*. In: *Institutional Legacies of Violent Conflict*.
Edited by: Patricia Justino, Oxford University Press. © United Nations University World Institute
for Development Economics Research (UNU-WIDER) (2026). DOI: 10.1093/9780197904077.003.0010

wars within an original cross-national database of founding post-war elections covering 1970–2015.

10.2 Existing scholarship

A proliferating literature on the political effects of violence counters traditional accounts of war as solely fomenting death and destruction. Instead, drawing on theory of post-traumatic growth,[1] recent studies have found glimmers of hope amidst the tragic growth industry of civil wars (Blattman 2009). Out of their devastation, at times, emerge victimized populations more likely to engage civically and participate politically (Bellows and Miguel 2009; Lupu and Peisakhin 2017). These findings present an encouraging silver lining. However, while they establish that victimization may prompt civic engagement and voting, they have tended to leave underexplored the question of for whom victimized populations vote.[2]

A few important exceptions tackle this key question. Focused on longer-term, intergenerational effects, scholars demonstrate that experiences of victimization drive individuals to vote against their perpetrators and for their perpetrators' adversaries (Balcells 2012; Lupu and Peisakhin 2017; Rozenas et al. 2017; Zhukov and Talibova 2018). This is consistent with expectations from psychology that posit that victims often feel the emotion of anger which sparks the action tendencies of revenge and punishment of the perpetrators (Elster 1999, 2004; Lerner and Tiedens 2006; Petersen and Daly 2010). Studying the immediate aftermath of war, Daly (2019, 2022a) instead finds that war outcomes influence whether victimized populations vote for or against parties that committed mass atrocities against the population.

Other scholars emphasize that not only the intensity but also the nature of the perpetrator and repertoires of violence can influence voting and preferences for punishment of victimizers (Kao and Revkin 2023; Levy 2022). Levy (2022) shows that voters in post-war elections may support perpetrator-candidates who violated less stringent norms, exhibited less agency, and maintained weaker ties to the victims. Kao and Revkin (2023) argue that the type of rebel collaboration rather than the rebel's social identity shapes attitudes towards revenge and forgiveness. However, significantly less is known about how conflict-created inter-group dynamics influence political participation, vote choice, and the manifestation of political legacies following ethnic as opposed to non-ethnic wars (Butt 2023; Hadzic et al. 2020).

[1] See, for example, Tedeschi and Calhoun (2004).

[2] Related scholarship studies the organizational transformation of rebel groups into political parties (Manning 2008; Sindre 2016; Söderberg Kovacs 2007); their governance records (Liu 2022; Lyons 2016; Martin et al. 2021; Thaler 2018); and their influence on peace (Brancati and Snyder 2012; Daly 2022b; Matanock 2017), democracy (Fortna and Huang 2012; Hartzell and Hoddie 2015; Levitsky and Way 2012), and public goods provision (Daly 2021; Flores and Nooruddin 2012).

10.2.1 Ethnicity, identity, and voting after conflict

One assumed war legacy maintained by an important body of literature is that violence solidifies ethnic group identities. While not all studies conclude that war inevitably leads to ethnic voting, many argue that protracted conflicts can create a sense of 'us versus them' antagonism among ethnic groups, making citizens more likely to vote along ethnic lines. Hadzic et al. (2020: 345), for example, argue that 'community-level experience with war-time violence solidifies ethnic identities, fosters intra-ethnic cohesion and increases distrust toward non-co-ethnics, thereby making ethnic parties the most attractive channels of representation and contributing to the politicization of ethnicity'. It is, therefore, anticipated that exposure to violence intensifies the prominence and division of ethnic identities. Indeed, during times of ethnic war, the stark differences between ethnic groups are accentuated. This may compel individuals to adopt and solidify their ethnic identities as a means of protection and coping, with important implications post-conflict.

Furthermore, amidst war-time ethnic violence, even individuals who were initially neutral may become compelled to align themselves with a particular group to gain advantages, seek security, or express moral outrage in response to the violence. As a result, people may tend to retreat into their respective ethnic communities. This phenomenon can reinforce individuals' identification with their ethnic group while simultaneously diminishing trust and interpersonal interactions among members of previously peaceful ethnic groups.

The collective memory of these events, along with deliberate efforts to exploit this memory in the aftermath of the conflict, can further solidify ethnic cohesion and prolong the endurance of heightened ethnic identities. This, in turn, may strengthen individuals' preferences for policies that favour their own ethnic group, as demonstrated in studies by Bar-Tal (2003) and Hadzic et al. (2020). As further noted by Alexander and Christia (2011), individuals often link their personal well-being closely to the fortunes of their ethnic community, which significantly influences their policy decisions. Consequently, this dynamic can lead to an increase in ethnically driven mobilization and voting patterns, as ethnic representatives are perceived as the most effective conduits for political representation, with ethnic parties seen as credible advocates best able to serve the interests of their respective ethnic groups. In sum, one widely purported war legacy is hardened identities, leading to ethnic voting in war's aftermath.

10.2.2 The institutional perspective

Other scholars argue, however, that whether ethnic voting occurs in general, or in particular after conflict, depends on institutions and interests. These shape which identity comes to the fore and whether citizens vote on ethnic lines. What is more, others challenge the very premise that violence necessarily hardens identities by questioning whether ethnic violence automatically follows a primordialist logic in practice.

The design of political institutions can have a profound impact on post-ethnic war politics. Institutions 'provide the context in which individuals interpret their self-interest and thereby define their policy preferences' (Steinmo 1989: 504). Power-sharing arrangements have been employed in various post-conflict societies to accommodate ethnic diversity and prevent renewed violence. Proportional representation institutions, its proponents argue, particularly when complemented with other elements of consociationalism (a grand coalition, segmental autonomy or federalism, and minority vetoes), can serve to dampen conflict in multi-ethnic states. These institutions fulfil multiple ethnic groups' security, political, and economic needs and thereby enable them to look to the government rather than to (illegal) sub-groups for protection and public goods. By providing representation and thus a stake at the centre, power-sharing produces guarantees and credible commitments for all ethnic groups.

Critics of power-sharing, however, argue that it fails to alter the incentive structure of politicians to cooperate across the ethnic divide as politicians remain beholden only to those who voted them into office: co-ethnics. Accordingly, these institutions may only further freeze ethnic identities into sharply defined cleavages, encouraging individuals to vote along ethnic lines and preventing the fluid, malleable process from producing new cross-cutting cleavages, which are favourable to stability and peace after conflict (Barry 1975; Horowitz 1985).

Bosnia, for example, adopted a system of ethnic quotas after the war. These quotas may have increased the overall level of ethnic voting by priming voters to think of political life in ethnic terms and by incentivizing parties to ground their appeals in ethnic identity (thus increasing the supply of ethnic parties).

Accordingly, scholars, most prominently Horowitz (1985, 1990, 1993), advocate instead for integrative institutions to encourage cooperation and accommodation between rival groups and break down the salience of ethnicity (Kasfir 1979; Reilly 2001). The goal of such electoral engineering is to increase intra-group competition and inter-group bargaining and coalitions. For this purpose, Horowitz (1985, 1991) recommends preferential voting systems designed to induce vote-pooling across ethnic divides. This approach thus offers the potential for fluid identities, floating voters, shifting multi-ethnic alliances, and temporary majorities. In effect, it provides the possibility for a non-ascriptive society and encourages the development of broad-based parties, thus shifting the focus of politics from ethnic issues to ones that concern all ethnic groups.[3] In sum, by this account, whether ethnic violence leads to ethnic voting depends on the nature of the institutions.

[3] Bose (2002) argues that the alternative voting system can become manipulated and therefore backfire. He describes how, in Bosnia, it actually 'precipitated a much higher degree of consolidation of the ethnic Serb electorate behind the SDS, an "extremist" party . . . than might otherwise have been the case' (Bose 2002: 232).

10.2.3 The role of interests

Others argue that not only institutions but also other economic and social conditions structure identity decisions. Individuals have many identities—some ethnic, some non-ethnic—with which they can identify politically (Posner 2005; Wilkinson 2004). These scholars argue that individuals are likely to identify with ethnic ones post war for the same reason that they do so in normal politics—because these identities best serve their political and economic opportunities and self-interests: material resources, power, and physical security (Kasfir 1979). If class, religion, ideology, gender, or another identity better serves individuals' self-interests, these identities will come to the forefront in political decision-making.

Individuals often identify on ethnic rather than, say, class lines because ethnicity is particularly well suited to serving rational interests. For elites, ethnic appeals are effective political resources for such agendas as constituency building, mobilization, outbidding intra-group competitors, economic scape-goating, or undermining transitions. For the masses, particular ethnic identifications arise as the most efficient response to individual needs to extract desired patronage goods (jobs, markets, and land) from the state because they facilitate collective action and aggregation of interests (Bates 1974). For many voters living in multi-ethnic societies, both in post-conflict and in non-post-conflict environments, ethnic identity can serve as an important factor in determining voters' decisions during elections (Conroy-Krutz 2013; Ferree 2006, 2011).

Voters in diverse contexts have proven more likely to cast their votes for co-ethnic candidates than for candidates from other ethnicities (Adida 2015; Bratton and Kimenyi 2008; Ferree 2006; Heath et al. 2015; Horowitz 1985; Hutchings and Valentino 2004; Posner 2005). Particularly, in information-poor environments, co-ethnicity can act as a signal for responsiveness, shared preferences, competence, and likely public goods provision for in-group members (Brady and Sniderman 1985; Butt 2023; Ferree 2011). It can also create bias in the evaluation of parties' past performance (Burgess et al. 2015; Butler and Broockman 2011; Carlson 2015; Kramon and Posner 2011). Adida et al. (2017), for example, demonstrate that voters tend to reward competent leaders when they share the same ethnicity, while they penalize underperforming leaders when they belong to a different ethnic group. Aha (2019) corroborates this finding by showing that ethnic minority parties in Central and Eastern Europe are less likely to face electoral consequences for economic shortcomings compared to their coalition partners due to the support of a steadfast ethnic voter base. If interests are best served by identifying on ethnic lines and choosing political representation on ethnic lines, voters will do so, according to this logic. However, such ethnic identification is not inevitable; accordingly, the effect of war-time violence on post-war politics will depend on voters' interests in war's aftermath.

10.2.4 Constructivist challenges

Finally, scholars question whether the violence, in fact, always follows a primordialist logic, as often assumed.[4] If not, identities may not be frozen in violence's aftermath. In certain ethnic wars, not all violence occurs along ethnic lines; rather, belligerents oftentimes commit violence against co-ethnics.[5] As a result, in the aftermath of such violence, the belligerents, even if constituted as ethnic parties, may need to seek the votes of populations they previously victimized.

A constructivist view further shows that not all ethnic kin necessarily support their co-ethnic belligerent. Many prefer non-violence, object to the violence committed, or support non-combatant parties. Furthermore, a constructivist rendering suggests that people hold multiple identities and, thus, in peacetime following these wars cleavages deactivated during the wars may resurface, or new overarching identities may make their way to the fore.

A constructivist account further means that societies that have experienced violent struggles in which individuals of different ethnic groups have mobilized against each other are not necessarily polarized along ethnic lines. For example, Bakke et al. (2009) map dimensions of social distance among 4000 survey respondents in Bosnia-Herzegovina and in the North Caucasus region of Russia. They do not find patterns of clear attitudinal cleavages among members of different ethnic groups. Dyrstad (2012), also studying the Balkans, similarly finds that ethnonationalism does not necessarily increase with ethnic civil war and that individual war-time exposure to violence is less important than expected in fomenting ethnic divides.

10.2.5 Theoretical contribution: violent incompatibility and war outcomes

In this chapter, I add two new dimensions to the debate on the political legacies of ethnic war: the nature of the violent incompatibility and military outcomes. I propose that whether the combatants contest government or territory and how the war ends—whether in government victory, rebel victory, or a draw—shape how parties run and how voters cast their ballots and with what electoral consequences. The key mechanism in the chapter's theory is whether the geography of the electorates becomes unitary or bifurcated, which influences whether the sides of the conflict will compete in the same elections, and whether they will

[4] On primordialism, see, for example, Burleigh (2014) and Kaplan (1994). On constructivism, see Abdelal et al. (2009), Chandra (2001, 2012), Posner (2004), and Waters (1999). On the institutionalist approach to ethnicity, see Laitin (1986).

[5] See Bakke et al. (2012), Christia (2012), Fjelde and Nilsson (2012), Kalyvas (2008), McLauchlin and Pearlman (2012), Rudloff and Findley (2016), and Staniland (2012).

compete for the same voters. I argue that conflict incompatibility and war outcomes guide the fluidity of voter allegiances after armed conflict, influence the overlap in belligerents' electorates, and shape whether belligerent successor parties are strategically compelled to seek votes from victimized populations. The nature of the incompatibility and military outcome also guide whether direct victims and conflict-affected citizens might vote for violent perpetrators. As such, I argue that war victors may win victimized citizens' votes after rebellions fought over government control by running as restrained Leviathans (Daly 2022a). In territorial rebellions, this pattern may also manifest, but co-ethnic voters of the losing belligerent tend not to cross the ethnic belligerent divide to reward non-co-ethnic war-winners with their ballots; instead, they cast their votes for non-belligerent parties. In turn, incompatibilities and war outcomes determine post-war electoral performance of belligerent and non-belligerent parties across different types of wars.

I first define the key terms. I then walk through the different scenarios, highlighting a variety of cases to illustrate the chapter's logic. Finally, I extract several observable implications which I test with cross-national data.

10.3 Key definitions

To define ethnic war, I adopt the classification of Cederman et al. (2010): wars are categorized as ethnic if they seek ethnic aims, predominantly recruit fighters among their leaders' own ethnic group, and forge alliances on the basis of ethnic affiliation.

I define war outcomes along a spectrum ranging from outright government victory (rebel defeat) to outright rebel victory (government defeat). In the middle are indecisive outcomes in which neither side wins the war outright, which I classify into two outcomes on the continuum. In the left-hand middle category, the war ends with the government winning the war, although the rebels' organization remains viable. I call this outcome 'relative government victory'. In the right-hand middle category are belligerents who end war at a draw or a 'mutually hurting stalemate'. These middle two categories might terminate in either (1) negotiated settlements that conclude the military behaviour of the parties through negotiated surrender (in cases of military asymmetry) or robust peace agreement (in cases of a draw), or (2) sustained ceasefires, truces, armistices, or some other mode of freezing that results in a cessation of hostilities and termination of military operations, but does 'not deal with the incompatibility' so as to resolve the underlying conflict (Daly 2022a: 23).

I define wars in which the incompatibility concerns the government as war over the 'type of political system, the replacement of the central government, or the change of its composition', following Uppsala Conflict Data Program (UCDP) coding. In contrast, in territorial rebellions, the casus belli concerns 'the status of a specified territory ... e.g., secession or autonomy' (Davies et al. 2024; Gleditsch et al. 2002). These tend to be fought by ethnically concentrated minorities against majority ethnic groups. They seek territory in which they can practice the right to self-determination and self-governance.

The chapter focuses on democratic elections after war. It adopts Schumpeter's minimalist characterization of democracy: 'The democratic method is that institutional arrangement for arriving at political decisions in which individuals acquire the power to decide by means of a competitive struggle for the people's vote' (Schumpeter 1976: 260). Under this definition, countries in which there is 'free competition for a free vote' are designated as democratic. I, therefore, exclude contexts in which no elections were held after war. I also exclude cases of elections in one-party states (Schumpeter 1976: 271). While it is clear that electoral choice-less choices are made under conditions of autocracy, sham democracy, and extreme repression, I aim to explain why there are voluntary votes for belligerent parties, even in democratic elections with viable competition. Electoral intimidation, fraud, and coercion can no doubt account for some of the abundant votes for tormentors, but this chapter's emphasis is not on these votes.

I define the *founding elections* as the first legislative, presidential, and regional elections following the termination of armed struggle. The chapter is about electoral performance. I follow Lupu (2015) and define the outcome—*electoral success*—as receiving a plurality of the vote, winning the first round, or attracting no less than one-third of the winning vote share. The cross-national analysis explores performance in lower-house legislative elections, which take place in all political systems, and which present lower barriers to participation.

I adopt Sartori's definition of a political party as 'any political group identified by an official label that presents at elections, and is capable of placing, through elections (free or non-free), candidates for public office' (Sartori 1976: 56). I assume that there are two types of parties after war: belligerent parties and non-belligerent parties. Belligerent or civil war successor parties are the post-war parties representing the ideological and organizational characteristics of the war-time armed organizations. A *government belligerent successor party* is defined as a political party, group, or organization that possessed authoritative control over the state's coercive apparatus during the conflict. In some cases, the government belligerent party is one that was active through the era of the conflict. In other cases, it is a post-war party that formally adopts the name, programme, or mantle of the government's armed forces, or the party whose platform and membership are most closely associated with the government belligerent's side.

The *rebel* is defined as the armed opposition organization. A *rebel successor party* is the political party formed by or around the rebel belligerent. It may be a previously existing party that represented the rebels during the conflict. If no conflict-era rebel party existed, the rebel belligerent successor is the party that formally adopts the name, programme, or mantle of the rebels, or is the party whose platform or membership is most closely associated with the rebels.

Non-belligerent parties are conflict-era parties or organizations that did not have a coercive apparatus and did not participate in the armed conflict, or they are new parties that emerged after the war and whose platforms and memberships do not represent the war-time armies. Such non-belligerent parties may be, for example, non-ethnic parties, where the conflict pitted violent ethno-nationalist parties against each other. They may be parties espousing peaceful self-determination in contexts of violent secessionism. They may represent opposition to authoritarian or democratic regimes in wars with rebel movements aimed at state takeover. They may have served in governing coalitions but lacked control of the coercive apparatus. They may be a new governing party that ended the war's brutalities and ushered in peace and that now, as electoral incumbents, seek re-election in founding post-war contests. Their defining feature is that they did not take part in the war as belligerents and do not have blood on their hands. An empirical tendency is that they frequently are more moderate than belligerents, whose social bases were forged in the polarizing, radical-rewarding, and outbidding environment of war (Daly 2022a).

Following Chandra (2004), I define an ethnic party as 'a party that overtly represents itself as a champion of the cause of one particular ethnic category or set of categories to the exclusion of others, and that makes such a representation central to its strategy of mobilizing voters' (Chandra 2004: 3).

10.4 War type and electoral outcomes

This section examines how different war types and outcomes shape electoral dynamics in post-conflict societies. I first analyse wars fought over government control, then wars over territory, illustrating each with case studies that demonstrate the mechanisms at work. The key distinction is whether electorates remain unitary (in government-focused conflicts) or become bifurcated (in territorial conflicts), and how this affects political strategies and voter behaviour, depending on the war outcomes.

10.4.1 Wars fought over government control

Following wars fought over government, irrespective of the war outcome, the electorate remains unitary. This means that the rebel and government belligerent parties usually contest the *same* elections and face a *common, national* constituency. They may be able to win votes only from their co-ethnic, hardcore supporters but, usually, there exists a larger pool of co-optable or swing voters that they need to attract in order to gain electoral victory. This constituency may be carved up ethnically, but the allegiances usually vary from hardcore to co-optable. The voters that remain in play, potentially willing to cross the ethnic divide with their ballots, create incentives for belligerents to seek the votes of the ethnicities that they ignored or even victimized during the war. I argue that, following draws—such as those in Burundi, Angola, and Mozambique—the belligerent parties will be likely to share the vote across the ethnic demography and the parties' success at convincing swing voters determines whether the vote is shared evenly or unevenly.

In cases of rebel victory—such as those in Rwanda, Zimbabwe, Ethiopia, and Liberia—and cases of government victory—such as those in Uganda and Sierra Leone—the electorate is similarly unitary. Given that the population will live under one government, to build legitimacy, prevent future conflict, and perform well against non-belligerent parties (which may have a good case to make with voters: arguing for their clean human rights records, and warning that belligerent parties will revictimize in the future), winning belligerents have incentives to reach across ethnic lines to seek the votes of those that they either ignored or victimized. I draw on cases from Rwanda, Burundi, Liberia, Mozambique, and Iraq to illustrate this dynamic.

In Rwanda, the internecine violence included rebel Tutsi brutality against Hutus and extremist Hutu genocide against Tutsis, but also an extremist Hutu genocide against moderate co-ethnic Hutus who did not side with the radical Hutu belligerent. The rebel Tutsi-RPF (Rwandan Patriotic Front) won the war. Victorious, hegemonic, and with an incontestable hold on political power, it could have embraced its violent past, offered security only to co-ethnics, and sought the votes only of co-ethnics, even though the Tutsis were a minority in Rwanda. Instead, in the campaign for the 2003 elections, the RPF sought to win the support of security, moderate, and victimized Hutu voters. It strategized to spin the war-time atrocities as one-sided, committed *only* by the extremist Hutu genocidaires (Brehm and Fox 2017). At the same time, it opted to mitigate its own violence as justified by its provision of security and peace. This worked; the RPF became 'credited by many Rwandans—Hutu and Tutsi alike—with having ended the 1994 genocide' (Meierhenrich 2006: 631). The RPF sought to translate its military success into a reputation for competence on future protection not only for Tutsis but also for Hutus. Lyons (2016: 176) writes of how, on the one hand, 'the defeat of genocidal forces by the Rwandan Patriotic Front provided RPF substantial initial endowments of legitimacy', while, on the other hand, its own past record of victimization against Hutus meant that 'the perceived ethnic character of the RPF raised doubts among some [swing Hutus] about the nature of their new protectors'. To sell itself as a prospective restrained sovereign for the whole Rwandan population, including its former adversary ethnic group and victims (IHS Global Insight 2003), the RPF decided to play the constructivist card and stretch its constituency from just Tutsis to an overarching Rwandan identity. To do so, it promoted a 'powerful' brand of Rwandan 'civic nationalism', constructing and elevating a new identity of 'national unity' based on territory to supplant the war-time cleavage of ethnicity (Kalinaki 2003), a process rendered easier by the ruling party's ability to ban discussions of ethnicity.[6] The RPF also allowed a moderate Hutu to assume the post of interim president. Meanwhile, the RPF undermined perceptions of its opponents' competence on security by claiming that they were prospective re-victimizers, likely to incite ethnic tensions and violence again. RPF commander and later president Paul Kagame explained that the people 'wanted security first of all. Even people who didn't know the RPF program in detail saw us as the party that would guarantee that [security]' (Kinzer 2008: 229). As a result, albeit in only minimally democratic, post-war elections, the Tutsi-RPF gained the vast majority of its large number of votes from swing Hutus, who fuelled its electoral landslide.[7]

In other post-ethnic war contexts in which warring parties had fought and recruited along ethnic lines for ethnic aims, it appears that security and swing voters surprisingly also existed. Belligerent parties similarly sought to persuade voters of their ability to consolidate peace in order to capture these votes across ethnic lines. Depending on their war outcome, they succeeded.

In Burundi, for instance, the Hutu-dominated National Council for the Defense of Democracy – Forces for the Defense of Democracy (CNDD-FDD) 'presented the party as the guardian against any possible threat to the [population's] security'. It sought to 'guarantee the security of the country's institutions in service to the *whole* Burundian nation', not just that of the majority Hutus (The Canadian Press 2003), by establishing a 'truly national army' with equal participation by Tutsis and Hutus (Nindorera 2012: 15). For a sustainable end to the war, Burundi's Hutus, therefore, voted nearly unanimously against their ethnic interests for quotas that would grant Tutsis—constituting only 15% of the population—half of the upper house of Congress and 40% of the lower house. In the 2005 elections, despite its past use of violence, Hutu belligerent successor party CNDD-FDD drew Hutu voters away from the non-belligerent Front for Democracy in Burundi (FRODEBU) party, and it also seems to have drawn some Tutsi voters—victims of that violence—to its side.[8] According to a voter in Bujumbura, 'For me this election means voting peace in the country' (Niyoyita 2005.

In Liberia, convicted war criminal Charles Taylor's National Patriotic Front of Liberia (NPFL) 'generated such brutality', taking the lives of one-tenth and displacing one-third of the pre-war population of 2.5 million (The Carter Center 1997). This violence was originally 'systematic and ethnically motivated', later becoming

[6] Nation may, in public expression, have supplanted ethnicity but, given incentives to falsify public beliefs, this may not have trickled down into people's lives and personal preferences (Kuran 1991).

[7] Hutus constituted approximately 83% of Rwanda's population (The Economist 2003).

[8] CNDD-FDD won approximately 60% of the vote, FRODEBU 22%, and the Tutsi-dominated UPRONA 7.21% (International Foundation for Electoral Systems 2005).

'arbitrary' in nature (Gerdes 2015: 448). To appeal to the broad electorate in the founding post-war election of 1997, including ethnic groups he had terrorized, Taylor attempted to project the image of a patriot and nationalist, described in one banner as 'Father of the Liberian Revolution'.[9] In trying to frame himself as all things to all men, he claimed Gola and Americo-Liberian ancestry, changed his middle name from Macarthur to Ghankay and, with elections looming, added another name, Jarkpana. Additionally, in late 1996, Taylor became a born-again Christian.[10] He attracted votes across ethnic lines, albeit in an environment with a great deal of fear of coercion.

In Mozambique, the ideological war ended in stalemate, but with the governing party Frelimo enjoying the upper hand militarily. Frelimo cast blame on its rebel rival Renamo, sought to spin its own violence as justified, and emphasized its commitment to stability. Joaquim Chissano's 'party's programme aimed to create harmony among all Mozambican tribes by consolidating national unity' and centring on 'national reconciliation'. Chissano donned 'both the clothes of a Catholic priest and a Muslim religious leader' to cast a net over a broad constituency. Frelimo further sought to offset its past wrongs by pointing to its successes in achieving peace. Chissano expressed: 'Frelimo's mistakes had the weight of a feather while its achievements weighed far more than all the world's elephants'.[11] Frelimo's tactics proved successful; the party won 53% of the presidential vote in the founding post-war elections, even seemingly some cross-ethnic votes.[12]

Facing Frelimo and also non-coercive parties' message that 'Renamo only knew how to rule by weapons',[13] Renamo displayed its commitment to the system and peaceful governance, arguing that it was the 'father of democracy'[14] and the 'champion of democracy'. 'Other parties do not know what they are saying when they claim Renamo's hands are soiled with blood',[15] Afonso Dhlakama, Renamo's presidential candidate, declared. 'I have saved the nation'.[16] The party sought to expand its appeal to a broad electorate and signal restraint, offering posts to all tribes in an eventual Renamo government.[17] Renamo secured 33.7% of the vote in the founding election, again with some votes across tribal lines.[18]

[9] *WestAfrica*, 4 August 1997, quoted in Harris (1999).
[10] *Africa Confidential*, 20 June 1997, quoted in Harris (1999).
[11] Radio Mozambique, Maputo, 9 October 1994, cited in BBC Summary of World Broadcasts, 'The Election Campaigns'
[12] It won 44% of the legislative vote.
[13] Maximo Dias, presidential candidate for the Mozambican Nationalist Movement – Mozambican Social Democratic Party (Monamo-PMSD), Radio Mozambique, Maputo, 9 October 1994, cited in BBC Summary of World Broadcasts, 'The Election Campaigns', 12 October 1994.
[14] Deutsche Presse-Agentur (1994).
[15] TVM television, Maputo, 1800 GMT, 10 October 1994, cited in BBC Summary of World Broadcasts, 'The Election Campaigns', 12 October 1994.
[16] Deutsche Presse-Agentur (1994).
[17] TVM television, Maputo, 1800 GMT, 10 October 1994, cited in BBC Summary of World Broadcasts, 'The Election Campaigns', 12 October 1994.
[18] It won 37.7% of the legislative vote.

An additional example can be found in Iraq's 2018 elections. Despite fomenting a decade of sectarian conflict against Sunnis, Shiite cleric Muqtada al-Sadr's political list Sa'iroun (Moving Forward) and the Da'wa Shia sectarian party appealed across ethnic belligerent lines to Sunni voters. To do so, it ran on its effective fight against and victory over ISIS and on rebuilding war-torn social services (Jalabi and Georgy 2018). To render credible the party's political transformation from a protector of only Shias to a leader of all Iraqis, including Sunnis, Sadr established an unlikely alliance with communists and secular Iraqis, a costly move, to demonstrate to the public his formal renunciation of sectarian politics and his adoption instead of an overarching Iraqi civic nationalism (Al-Marashi 2018). Large numbers of Sunnis crossed ethnic lines and voted for this party. It received almost 30% of its votes from Sunnis and won the 2018 elections (Coker 2018; Kaltenthaler 2018).

10.4.2 Wars fought over territory

The situation is different following wars fought over territory. In these contexts, electorates may become segregated or bifurcated, and swing voters may not cross ethnic belligerent lines with their ballots. Instead, for co-ethnics of war-losing armed groups, non-combatant parties constitute viable alternatives for voters, particularly compared to the war-losing parties or to crossing the ethnic divide to vote for the non-co-ethnic war winner. On the winning belligerent party side, co-ethnic non-belligerent parties who lack a history of war-time coercion still push the belligerent successors to reckon with their violent past and to make plausible promises that they will not revictimize in the future. In these cases, how the war ends may influence whether voters choose a belligerent or instead a non-belligerent party. In other words, voters are likely to flock to a war winner (if co-ethnic), but to a non-belligerent party if their ethnic belligerent loses the war. Undecided voters seem to rarely cross ethnic lines in the founding elections following wars over territory, but they still swing between belligerent and non-belligerent (co-ethnic or multi-ethnic) parties; war outcomes matter to this decision.

I touch on several cases that illustrate this dynamic. The 1995 election in Croatia was called 'after Operation Storm, obviously with the intention of exploiting the military gains, ... [and] the advent of peace in 1995' (Matic and Ramet 2007: 47), and 'to capitalize politically on the Croatian Army's victories in retaking occupied territory' (CSE 1995: 1).[19]

[19] The May invasion saw the HDZ's popularity increasing from about 32% to about 40% in newspaper polling. The August invasion saw a further jump in HDZ popularity, for the first time topping 50% through August and the first half of September. The HDZ used this opportunity to call early elections (Gagnon 2004: 170).

Following the military defeat of Serb separatism in Croatia, many Serbs did not cross over belligerent (ethnic) lines to vote for the ethno-nationalist, Croat government belligerent successor party Croatian Democratic Union (HDZ) (i.e. they did not augment the victor's vote share), yet they still voted *against* the vanquished (co-ethnic) Serb belligerent successor, reducing its share of the vote. These Serb voters instead 'supported non-ethnic parties, especially the SDP and the HSLS' (Social Democratic Party of Croatia [Socijaldemokratska partija Hrvatske] and Croatian Social Liberal Party [Hrvatska socijalno-liberalna stranka]), deeming these non-belligerent parties better able to secure the country's political future. 'It would be wrong to assume that members of the Serb ... communities uniformly support[ed] the political parties that claim[ed] to speak in their name' (CSCE 1995) instead, war outcomes—their ethnic side's military loss—guided whether they voted *against* their co-ethnic combatant parties and rather *for* non-combatant ones.

At the same time, the war winner Croat-HDZ sought to appeal beyond its radical core supporters to undecided and opposition co-ethnic Croat voters who were more closely aligned politically with moderate, non-belligerent parties. Because these non-belligerent parties could raise 'human rights concerns related to [HDZ's] Operation Storm'—the ethnic cleansing that resulted in the death of 200,000 Serbs—HDZ opted to spin its violent past as justified and brandish its Leviathan credentials to appeal to these voters.[20] It did not, however, seek non-Croat votes; these were successfully pursued by non-belligerent Serb parties or multi-ethnic parties.

Croat victor HDZ's propaganda asserted that, 'We are forced to listen to the "theory" of common guilt, of two "sides in war"', and claimed that it was actually a 'Homeland War' of 'heroic defense' against one-sided terrorism. HDZ scapegoated all the 'murderous and destructive components' of the war on the Serbs.

> A war of words took place through magazines, journals, newspapers, and books, as well as on television, the radio, and the internet. All modern means of communication were actively subordinated to the goals of ethnic nationalist leaders in Serbia and Croatia, seeking to promote revised images of their respective histories . . . Images of Serbian, Croatian, Bosnian Moslem, and Kosovar Albanian genocides and 'holocausts' frequently appeared in the popular media, and the reader, listener, or internet surfer was berated with a continuous stream of material, all seemingly arguing the same thing: 'we are the victims first and foremost—our war is legitimate because we are fighting against annihilation'. (MacDonald 2003: 2).

[20] These observations are based on fieldwork conducted in Croatia and Bosnia, June–July 2019. Most quotations in this paragraph, unless otherwise noted, come from the museum exhibition, 'Dubrovnik during the Homeland War, 1991–1995', Empire's Fort, Dubrovnik. The exhibit includes over 500 original photographs, documents, and objects from the war.

The emphasis in the HDZ's discourse in this period was on the threats to innocent Croats and the bombing by Serb paramilitary groups of Croatian cities and cultural monuments (Gagnon 2004: 152).

The HDZ's own violence, although targeted disproportionately against non-co-ethnics, assumed atrocious forms and broadly impacted Croats too. It justified its violence with the boast that it had achieved war termination, the 'final defeat of the enemy'. HDZ 'succeeded in defending the territorial integrity of Croatia, and in this regard could legitimately claim to have led Croatia to victory in "the Homeland War"'. In the election campaign itself, the HDZ 'portrayed itself as bearing the sole responsibility for ... winning the war' and as capable of maintaining domestic security (Gagnon 2004: 156).

HDZ campaign posters showed 'a newborn baby in the muscular arms of a Croatian bodybuilding champion' labelled, 'in the arms of a safe future' (Swain 1995).[21] It 'hoped to capitalize on the success in retaking the Krajina region in the campaign rather than have any genuine policy debates about the future course of the country', focusing narrowly on issues of peace and security (CSCE 1995: 15). 'The focus of the election was predominantly on the feeling of relief among Croatian citizens that the conflict was effectively behind them' (CSCE 1992: 16). The opposition parties were obliged to play along, focusing their campaigns on similar themes (CSCE 1992: 16). Polling prior to the October 1995 elections confirmed the consistency of opinion: when asked to identify the top three problems in Croatia, 66.9% listed social justice and security, 48.6% listed lower unemployment, and 44.5% listed ensuring individual rights and freedoms (Gagnon 2004: 170–171).

The HDZ's war win and electoral strategy earned it the support of many Croat swing and security voters, but not of non-Serb voters who moved away from their co-ethnic belligerent parties to non-combatant parties. According to Kasapović (1997: 273–274), the military politics—particularly the war outcome—directly influenced the civil politics in general: 'the content and the course of electoral campaigns, the electoral prospects of the ruling party and the opposition, the electoral preferences of the voters and the electoral results. In this way, the military politics indirectly influenced the parliamentary party system and the type of government in general'.

At the same time, rather than ethnic mistrust, 'those who called for respecting basic human rights of everyone who lived in Croatia regardless of nationality, or the right to cultural autonomy in Croatia, also remained high, at about 83 percent' (Gagnon 2004: 170–171). Therefore, while HDZ won its hardcore

[21] Adoption of non-equilibrium electoral strategies seems to have engendered election results off the regression line in wars over autonomy. In Kosovo, for example, the Kosovo Liberation Army (KLA) carried the prestige 'of having led [and won] the war of liberation against Serbia', but nonetheless lost to non-belligerent Democratic League of Kosovo [Lidhja Demokratike e Kosovës] (LDK) in the founding elections because KLA's successor (PDK) failed to moderate, stretch its constituency, or signal restraint (International Crisis Group 2001).

ethnic supporters and some swing and security co-ethnics, a significant minority voted for non-belligerent and multi-ethnic parties in the founding post-war elections, defying a pure ethnic voting model.

Moving across the world, in Sri Lanka, after the Liberation Tigers of Tamil Eelam's (LTTE) military defeat, Tamils did not cross ethnic lines and choose to vote for the war-winning Sinhalese belligerent successor party. Instead, they cast their votes for non-belligerent, co-ethnic Tamil National Alliance (TNA) (however, no successor party to the belligerent Tamil emerged to contest the elections). Sinhalese swing and security voters, meanwhile, did shift disproportionately to the Sinhalese government combatant party, the United People's Freedom Alliance, which had been indiscriminately violent (mostly against Tamils), and thus rewarded the government's military victory and security provision despite its ethnic violence.

In wars over territory that end not in government victory (like those in Croatia and Sri Lanka) but instead in a draw, belligerent successor parties become likely to share the vote, squeezing out non-belligerent parties. In this sense, we would expect voting to occur along ethnic lines. In Bosnia, for example, under stalemate, in the 1996 Parliamentary and Presidential Elections, while 49 political parties participated, the belligerent Party of Democratic Action (Bosniak), Serb Democratic Party, and the Croatian Democratic Union of Bosnia and Herzegovina dominated the elections. These three parties reflected the continuation of belligerent ethnic politics in post-war Bosnia. In fact, one could say that the elections boil down to what Benjamin Reilly calls 'ethnic-style census-voting' (Reilly 2006: 815). The election in Bosnia was not about the economy, education, or unemployment. While the consociational institutions also have been blamed for having 'a centrifugal effect and promoting ethnic parties as the building blocks of the system' (Touquet 2011:455), stalemate made the belligerent parties equally competent on peace and security, with convergent strategies to compete in the elections, and with little reason to reach across ethnic lines. Thus, 'the elections resemble an ethnic census and those politicians playing the ethnic card perform best' (Du Pont 2000: 302).[22] Non-belligerent parties, including the United List, a joint ticket grouping five multi-ethnic opposition parties that spanned the political spectrum from liberal, Western-trained intellectuals to former communists, proved relatively uncompetitive, as did the Social Democratic Party of Bosnia, consisting of 65% Bosniaks, 20% Serbs, and 15% Croats (Vuletíc 2007).

Finally, at times, territorial wars end in rebel victory: successful secession. In this (rarer) set of cases, the electorate becomes not singular but *bifurcated*. In such cases, the rebels' co-ethnics significantly bolster the rebel victors' electoral fates

[22] The ethnic rallying call is clear when one sees that 'the election itself was effectively presented as . . . an opportunity for the people of Republika Srpska to demonstrate their faith in the SDS, its leaders and in particular the indicted war criminal Radovan Karadzic' (International Crisis Group 1996).

(for example, Fretilin in Timor Leste and South West Africa People's Organisation in Namibia), while co-ethnics of the government belligerent appear, on average, less likely to cast their ballots for successors to the rebel belligerent and vote instead for non-belligerent parties (such as Namibia's Democratic Turnhalle Alliance). In such contexts, the voters only swing so far (and not across ethnic lines) and belligerent parties do not face a shared and unitary electorate after mass violence is violated but must contend with segregated and multiple electorates across new international borders.

10.5 Cross-national analysis

Building on this theoretical framework, I test two key hypotheses using original, cross-national data:

H1: War victors (both rebel and government) will receive higher vote shares than losers across both ethnic and non-ethnic wars, as victory enhances perceived competence on security.

H2: Belligerent successor parties will perform worse following territorial conflicts than in those fought over government control, as territorial conflicts create bifurcated electorates with less voter crossover.

The logic underlying these hypotheses derives from the unitary versus divided electorate mechanism. In conflicts fought over state takeover, unified electorates create incentives for belligerents to appeal across ethnic lines, potentially winning votes from groups they previously victimized. In territorial conflicts, bifurcated electorates mean voters more rarely cross ethnic divides, limiting belligerents' ability to expand support beyond core constituencies.

To evaluate these implications, I analyse cross-national data on belligerent successor party performance. I use the Civil War Successor Party dataset, which traces successor parties of all belligerents—rebels and government—that transitioned from civil conflict between 1970 and 2015. It determines the founding elections following the termination of their armed struggles and records the legislative vote share of the successor parties. This results in a dataset of 205 civil war belligerents across 57 different states (Daly 2021).

The primary outcome of interest is the legislative vote share of belligerent successor parties in the first post-conflict elections. This variable captures the extent of electoral support for parties with roots in war-time armed organizations. Following the classification of Cederman et al. (2010), conflicts are coded as ethnic if they seek ethnic aims, predominantly recruit fighters from leaders' ethnic group, and forge alliances on ethnic affiliation. Using the Uppsala Conflict Data Program (UCDP) coding, I distinguish between conflicts fought over government control and those fought over territory (secession or autonomy).

To capture war outcome, I employ data from the UCDP dataset on conflict termination and create an ordinal variable with the UCDP outcome variable which ranges from 0 (government victory) to 3 (rebel victory). 'No activity' (a rebellion that petered out) assumes a value of 1, and conflicts that ended in 'peace agreements/ceasefire' I coded as 2 (Daly 2022a).

I control for several confounders. One, *war-time violence*: the cost of war in human lives is found to influence stable termination likelihood (Mason et al. 2011; Walter 2004). I use a relative atrocities index capturing whether belligerents used severe civilian abuse forms—'massacres; scorched earth campaigns; cleansing of a particular ethnic or religious group; or deliberate bombing and shelling of civilian targets'—or instead made 'deliberate efforts to avoid attacking civilian targets' (Stanton 2016: 67). Two, I control for *veto players*. Cunningham (2006) demonstrates that more veto players make bargaining more challenging and wars longer. I use his count of such veto players in war. Three, I control for *development levels*. Economic development is posited to aid post-war democratization (Fortna and Huang 2012), while higher development correlates with sustainable peace (Fearon and Laitin 2003; Walter 2004). I include in the analyses the Varieties of Democracy (V-Dem) indicators for logged gross domestic product per capita (*e_migdppcln*). Four, I control for *democracy scores* as democratic rights may further help prevent war recurrence (Walter 2004). Specifically, I include the V-Dem clean election index (*v2xel_frefair*) (Lindberg et al. 2014). Five, I control for *power-sharing* as formal power-sharing arrangements may facilitate conflict termination by enabling internal guarantees of the peace terms. I use the Peace Agreement Dataset's *shagov* variable (Högbladh 2011), indicating the presence of such power-sharing provisions.[23] Finally, I include a variable, *UN intervention*, derived from Brancati and Snyder (2012),[24] because intervention may provide external guarantees to ease the commitment problem, enabling the actors to end their armed struggles (Fortna 2008; Gilligan and Sergenti 2008; Howard 2008; Walter 2002). Intervention is also posited to render elections and successor parties more likely, because belligerents' participation in politics has become part of the UN's peacebuilding recipe (United Nations Peacebuilding Commission 2009).

10.5.1 War outcomes and post-war politics

As the dependent variable, this research uses the valid vote share of a successor party. My main specifications use ordinary least squares. A number of countries in the dataset have experienced multiple civil wars. I account for the

[23] For missing cases, I use data on political power sharing from Hartzell and Hoddie (2015) and the Power- Sharing Event Dataset (Ottmann and Vüllers 2015).

[24] The variable captures whether and how the UN intervened, through mediation, observation, peacekeeping, or enforcement.

non-independence of these observations within countries by presenting robust standard errors clustered on the country unit.

As displayed in Figure 10.1, the cross-national data reveal a robust positive relationship between favourable war outcomes and electoral performance following ethnic conflicts. Notably, this correlation is nearly indistinguishable from the pattern observed in non-ethnic conflicts. This finding supports the theoretical expectation that war outcomes significantly shape electoral performance regardless of conflict's ethnic character. Victorious parties—whether in ethnic or non-ethnic conflicts—successfully leverage their military success to build electoral support, often by casting themselves as competent security providers. The similar patterns across ethnic and non-ethnic conflicts suggest that the security competence mechanism operates consistently across different conflict contexts.

10.5.2 War incompatibility and electoral performance

Figure 10.2 illustrates the relationship between war outcomes and vote share across conflicts fought over government control versus territory. The results demonstrate that, while the positive relationship between favourable war outcomes and electoral performance holds in both conflict types, important differences emerge in the magnitude of support. The lower average performance of belligerent parties in territorial conflicts supports the hypothesis that bifurcated electorates in these contexts limit belligerents' ability to expand beyond their core ethnic constituencies. This finding aligns with the illustrative case studies presented earlier showing that voters in territorial conflicts rarely cross ethnic belligerent lines with their ballots. Instead, co-ethnics of losing belligerents tend to support non-belligerent parties rather than crossing over to support non-co-ethnic winners.

These findings enhance our understanding of post-conflict electoral dynamics by demonstrating that, beyond ethnic identities, strategic considerations stemming from war outcomes and conflict incompatibilities significantly shape political behaviour. While ethnicity remains important, particularly in territorial conflicts, voters respond to security considerations and make strategic choices based on war's aftermath.

Furthermore, the data reveal that belligerent parties' electoral strategies—whether to seek votes across ethnic lines or focus on core constituencies—may be shaped by structural factors emerging from the conflict itself. This helps explain variation in ethnic voting patterns across post-conflict contexts without resorting to primordial explanations of ethnic identity.

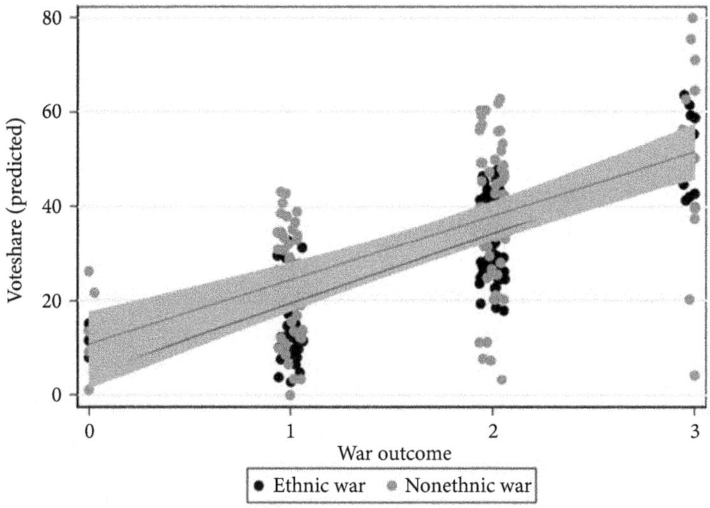

Figure 10.1 War outcomes and vote shares in founding elections following ethnic and non-ethnic conflicts

Note: The war outcome variable is reversed for government belligerents such that war outcome ranges from defeat (0) to victory (3) for all observations.

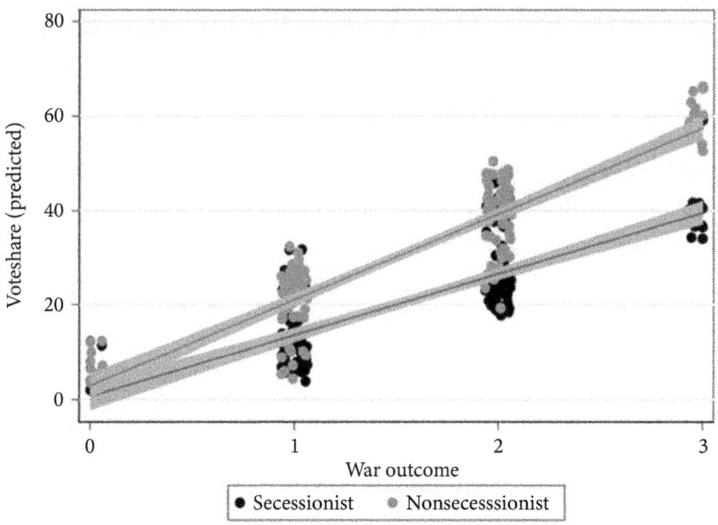

Figure 10.2 War outcomes and vote shares in founding elections following wars fought over territory (secessionist) and government (non-secessionist)

Note: The war outcome variable is reversed for government belligerents such that war outcome ranges from defeat (0) to victory (3) for all observations.

10.6 Conclusion

This chapter has examined the complex dynamics of political life after ethnic wars, focusing on how societies navigate toward stability and reconciliation through post-war elections. While previous research has illuminated the effects of violence on civic engagement and political participation, this study addresses a crucial knowledge gap regarding who victimized populations vote for and why, particularly in the immediate aftermath of ethnic conflicts.

The central argument advanced here is that two factors—the nature of the violent incompatibility (government control versus territory) and military outcomes (victory, defeat, or stalemate)—fundamentally shape post-war electoral dynamics. In government-focused conflicts, the electorate remains unitary, creating incentives for winning belligerents to reach across ethnic lines and appeal to voters they previously victimized. In territorial conflicts, electorates become bifurcated, with voters rarely crossing ethnic divides; instead, they choose between co-ethnic belligerent and non-belligerent parties based on the war outcomes.

The cross-national evidence strongly supports these theoretical expectations. War outcomes consistently predict electoral performance, with victors receiving significantly higher vote shares than losers across both ethnic and non-ethnic conflicts. However, belligerent successor parties perform worse following territorial conflicts than government-control conflicts, confirming the importance of the unitary versus bifurcated electorate mechanism. The illustrative case studies further demonstrate how these mechanisms operate in diverse post-conflict settings.

These findings significantly advance our understanding of post-conflict politics in several ways. First, they challenge primordial views of ethnic identity by demonstrating that violence does not inevitably harden ethnic divisions. Instead, institutional settings and strategic considerations stemming from conflict outcomes can facilitate cross-ethnic voting under certain conditions.

Second, this research offers a synthesis of institutional and interest-based explanations of ethnic politics. The findings acknowledge that formal institutions (like electoral systems) matter but demonstrate that another factor is also strongly important: the legacies of conflict itself. Specifically, whether a war was fought over government control or territory creates distinct patterns of voter accessibility and incentives for parties. These conflict-produced structures help explain when voters prioritize security and economic interests over ethnic identity, and when ethnic voting remains entrenched despite institutional design efforts to discourage it.

Third, the chapter reveals an important but underappreciated mechanism in post-conflict democratization: the relationship between military performance and perceived governance competence. War victors transform battlefield success into electoral advantage by positioning themselves as capable security providers, a dynamic that operates consistently across different conflict types (Daly 2022a).

Several promising areas for future research emerge from this study. First, additional work should explore parties' political strategies for reckoning with violent pasts and positioning to secure countries' futures across different contexts. This requires more fine-grained disaggregated data on individual preferences and behaviour, particularly examining how citizens of different ethnicities vote and how victims and non-victims vote.

Second, longitudinal studies tracking voting patterns and political engagement over extended periods would reveal whether initial post-war behaviours persist or evolve over time, shedding light on the durability of war's political legacies.

Third, research should investigate how inter-group relations are affected by post-war political developments. Do certain electoral outcomes exacerbate intergroup tensions, or can they improve relations between previously conflicting ethnic groups?

Fourth, future work should examine the role of international actors and interventions in post-ethnic war politics. How do foreign aid, peacekeeping missions, and diplomatic efforts impact political stability and reconciliation trajectories?

Fifth, given the importance of narrative control in the case studies, further research should analyse media and information dissemination in post-conflict electoral processes, examining how narratives about the violent past influence voter choices and political outcomes.

The study of political life after ethnic war remains vital for understanding democratic development in divided societies. By highlighting how conflict incompatibility and war outcomes structure electoral dynamics, this research contributes to both scholarly debates and practical efforts to promote peace, stability, and meaningful reconciliation in the aftermath of devastating ethnic violence.

References

Abdelal, R., Y. M. Herrera, A. I. Johnston, and R. McDermott (2009). *Measuring Identity: A Guide for Social Scientists*. Cambridge: Cambridge University Press. https://doi.org/10.1017/CBO9780511810909

Adida, C. L. (2015). 'Do African Voters Favor Coethnics? Evidence from a Survey Experiment in Benin'. *Journal of Experimental Political Science*, 2(1): 1–11. https://doi.org/10.1017/XPS.2014.26

Adida, C., J. Gottlieb, E. Kramon, and G. McClendon (2017). 'Reducing or Reinforcing in-group Preferences? An Experiment on Information and Ethnic Voting'. *Quarterly Journal of Political Science*, 12(4): 437–477. https://doi.org/10.1561/100.00017018

Africa Confidential (1997). *Africa Confidential*, 20 June. Quoted in Harris, D. (1999) 'From "warlord" to "democratic" president: how Charles Taylor won the 1997 Liberian elections'. *The Journal of Modern African Studies*, 37(3): 431–455. https://doi.org/10.1017/S0022278X99003203

Aha, K. (2019). 'Resilient Incumbents: Ethnic Minority Political Parties and Voter Accountability'. *Party Politics*, 27(4): 680–691. https://doi.org/10.1177/1354068819881125

Alexander, M., and F. Christia (2011). 'Context Modularity of Human Altruism'. *Science*, 334(6061): 1392–1394. https://doi.org/10.1126/science.1202599

Al-Marashi, I. (2018). 'How Iraq's Elections Proved "Status Quo" Expectations Wrong'. *Aljazeera*, 14 May.

Bakke, K. M., X. Cao, J. O'Loughlin, and M. D. Ward (2009). 'Social Distance in Bosnia-Herzegovina and the North Caucasus Region of Russia: Inter and Intra-ethnic Attitudes and Identities'. *Nations and Nationalism*, 15(2): 227–253. https://doi.org/10.1111/j.1469-8129.2009.00363.x

Bakke, K. M., K. G. Cunningham, and L. J. M. Seymour (2012). 'A Plague of Initials: Fragmentation, Cohesion, and Infighting in Civil Wars'. *Perspectives on Politics*, 10(2): 265–283. https://doi.org/10.1017/S1537592712000667

Balcells, L. (2012). 'The Consequences of Victimization on Political Identities. Evidence from Spain'. *Politics & Society*, 40(3): 311–347. https://doi.org/10.1177/0032329211424721

Barry, B. (1975). 'Political Accommodation and Consociational Democracy'. *British Journal of Political Science*, 5: 477–505. https://doi.org/10.1017/S0007123400008322

Bar-Tal, D. (2003). 'Collective Memory of Physical Violence: Its Contribution to the Culture of Violence'. In E. Cairns and M. D. Roe (eds), *The Role of Memory in Ethnic Conflict*. London: Palgrave Macmillan UK. https://doi.org/10.1057/9781403919823_5

Bates, R. H. (1974). 'Ethnic Competition and Modernization in Contemporary Africa'. *Comparative Political Studies*, 6(4): 457–484. https://doi.org/10.1177/001041407400600403

Bellows, J., and E. Miguel (2009). 'War and Local Collective Action in Sierra Leone'. *Journal of Public Economics*, 93(11–12): 1144–1157. https://doi.org/10.1016/j.jpubeco.2009.07.012

Blattman, C. (2009). 'From Violence to Voting: War and Political Participation in Uganda'. *American Political Science Review*, 103(2): 231–247. https://doi.org/10.1017/S0003055409090212

Bose, S. (2002). *Bosnia after Dayton: Nationalist Partition and International Intervention*. London: Hurst & Company.

Brady, H. E., and Sniderman, P. M. (1985). 'Attitude Attribution: A Group Basis for Political Reasoning'. *The American Political Science Review*, 79(4): 1061–1078. https://doi.org/10.2307/1956248

Brancati, D., and J. L. Snyder (2012). 'Time to Kill: The Impact of Election Timing on Post-conflict Stability'. *Journal of Conflict Resolution*, 57(5): 822–853. https://doi.org/10.1177/0022002712449328

Bratton, M., and M. S. Kimenyi (2008). 'Voting in Kenya: Putting Ethnicity in Perspective'. *Journal of Eastern African Studies*, 2(2): 272–289. https://doi.org/10.1080/17531050802058401

Brehm, H. N., and N. Fox (2017). 'Narrating Genocide: Time, Memory, and Blame'. *Sociological Forum*, 32(1): 116–137. https://doi.org/10.1111/socf.12319

Burgess, R., R. Jedwab, E. Miguel, A. Morjaria, and G. Padró I Miquel (2015). 'The Value of Democracy: Evidence from Road Building in Kenya'. *American Economic Review*, 105(6): 1817–1851. https://doi.org/10.1257/aer.20131031

Burleigh, M. (2014). *Small Wars, Far Away Places: The Genesis of the Modern World 1945–65*. London: Penguin.

Butler, D. M., and D. E. Broockman (2011). 'Do Politicians Racially Discriminate Against Constituents? A Field Experiment on State Legislators'. *American Journal of Political Science*, 55(3): 463–477. https://doi.org/10.1111/j.1540-5907.2011.00515.x

Butt, N. (2023). 'Voting for Former Collaborators of Insurgent Groups: Evidence from Afghanistan' Paper Presented at the Annual Meeting of the American Political Science Association, Montreal, 29 August.

Carlson, E. (2015). 'Ethnic Voting and Accountability in Africa: A Choice Experiment in Uganda'. *World Politics*, 67(2): 353–385. https://doi.org/10.1017/S0043887115000015

Cederman, L.-E., A. Wimmer, and B. Min (2010). 'Why Do Ethnic Groups Rebel? New Data and Analysis'. *World Politics*, 62(1): 87–119. https://doi.org/10.1017/S0043887109990219

Chandra, K. (2001). 'Cumulative Findings in the Study of Ethnic Politics'. *Comparative Politics*, 33(1): 1–25.

Chandra, K. (2004). *Why Ethnic Parties Succeed: Patronage and Ethnic Head Counts in India*. Cambridge: Cambridge University Press. https://doi.org/10.1017/9781108573481

Chandra, K. (2012). *Constructivist Theories of Ethnic Politics*. Oxford: Oxford University Press. https://doi.org/10.1093/acprof:oso/9780199893157.001.0001

Christia, F. (2012). *Alliance Formation in Civil Wars*. Cambridge: Cambridge University Press. https://doi.org/10.1017/CBO9781139149426

Coker, M. (2018). 'U.S. Takes a Risk: Old Iraqi Enemies Are Now Allies'. *The New York Times*, 11 May.

Conroy-Krutz, J. (2013). 'Information and Ethnic Politics in Africa'. *British Journal of Political Science*, 43(2): 345–373. https://doi.org/10.1017/S0007123412000300

CSCE (Commission on Security and Cooperation in Europe) (1992). *Parliamentary and Presidential Elections in an Independent Croatia*. Washington, DC: U.S. Government Printing Office.

CSCE (Commission on Security and Cooperation in Europe) (1995). *Croatia: Implications of the Conflict and Peacekeeping Efforts*. Washington, DC: U.S. Government Printing Office.

Cunningham, D. E. (2006). 'Veto Players and Civil War Duration'. *American Journal of Political Science*, 50(4): 875–892. https://doi.org/10.1111/j.1540-5907.2006.00221.x

Daly, S. Z. (2019). 'Voting for Victors: Why Violent Actors Win Post-War Elections'. *World Politics*, 71(4): 747–805. https://doi.org/10.1017/S0043887119000091

Daly, S. Z. (2021). 'Political Life after Civil Wars: Introducing the Civil War Successor Party Dataset'. *Journal of Peace Research*, 58(4): 839–848. https://doi.org/10.1177/0022343320920905

Daly, S. Z. (2022a). *Violent Victors: Why Bloodstained Parties Win Postwar Elections*. Princeton Studies in International History and Politics Series. Princeton, NJ: Princeton University Press. https://doi.org/10.23943/princeton/9780691231334.001.0001

Daly, S. Z. (2022b). 'A Farewell to Arms? Election Results and Lasting Peace after Civil War'. *International Security*, 46(3): 163–204. https://doi.org/10.1162/isec_a_00429

Davies, S., G. Engström, T. Pettersson, and M. Öberg (2024). 'Organized Violence 1989–2023, and the Prevalence of Organized Crime Groups'. *Journal of Peace Research*, 61(4): 673–693. https://doi.org/10.1177/00223433241262912

Deutsche Presse-Agentur (1994, 29 October). 'Voting Nears Close in Mozambique Elections'.

Du Pont, Y. (2000). 'Levelling the Political Playing Field: Democratization Through Supporting a Pluralistic and Moderate Party System in Bosnia and Herzegovina'. In IFSH (ed.), *OSCE Yearbook 1999*. Baden-Baden: Nomos.

Dyrstad, K. (2012).; After Ethnic Civil War: Ethno-nationalism in the Western Balkans'. *Journal of Peace Research*, 49(6): 817–831. https://doi.org/10.1177/0022343312439202

Elster, J. (1999). *Alchemies of the Mind.* New York: Cambridge University Press. https://doi.org/10.1017/CBO9781139173308

Elster, J. (2004). *Closing the Books.* Cambridge: Cambridge University Press. https://doi.org/10.1017/CBO9780511607011

Fearon, J. D., and D. D. Laitin (2003). 'Ethnicity, Insurgency, and Civil War'. *American Political Science Review*, 97(1): 75–90. https://doi.org/10.1017/S0003055403000534

Ferree, K. E. (2006). 'Explaining South Africa's Racial Census'. *The Journal of Politics*, 68(4): 803–815. https://doi.org/10.1111/j.1468-2508.2006.00471.x

Ferree, K. E. (2011). *Framing the Race in South Africa: The Political Origins of Racial Census Elections.* Cambridge: Cambridge University Press. https://doi.org/10.1017/CBO9780511779350

Fjelde, H., and D. Nilsson (2012). 'Rebels Against Rebels: Explaining Violence Between Rebel Groups'. *Journal of Conflict Resolution*, 56(4): 604–628. https://doi.org/10.1177/0022002712439496

Flores, T. E., and I. Nooruddin (2012). 'The Effect of Elections on Postconflict Peace and Reconstruction'. *Journal of Politics*, 74(2): 558–570. https://doi.org/10.1017/S0022381611001733

Fortna, V. P. (2008). *Does Peacekeeping Work? Shaping Belligerents' Choices after Civil War.* Princeton, NJ: Princeton University Press. https://doi.org/10.1515/9781400837731

Fortna, V. P., and R. Huang (2012). 'Democratization After Civil War: A Brush-clearing Exercise'. *International Studies Quarterly*, 56(4): 801–808. https://doi.org/10.1111/j.1468-2478.2012.00730.x

Gagnon, V. P. (2004). *The Myth of Ethnic War: Serbia and Croatia in the 1990s.* Ithaca, NY: Cornell University Press.

Gerdes, F. (2015). 'The Interplay of Domestic Legitimation and Foreign Relations: Contrasting Charles Taylor and Ellen Johnson Sirleaf of Liberia'. *Civil Wars*, 17(4): 446–464. https://doi.org/10.1080/13698249.2015.1115576

Gilligan, M. J., and E. J. Sergenti (2008). 'Do UN Interventions Cause Peace? Using Matching to Improve Causal Inference'. *Quarterly Journal of Political Science*, 3(2): 89–122. https://doi.org/10.1561/100.00007051

Gleditsch, N. P., P. Wallensteen, M. Eriksson, M. Sollenberg, and H. Strand (2002). 'Armed Conflict 1946–2001: A New Dataset'. *Journal of Peace Research*, 39(5). https://doi.org/10.1177/0022343302039005007

Hadzic, D., D. Carlson, and M. Tavits (2020). 'How Exposure to Violence Affects Ethnic Voting'. *British Journal of Political Science*: 50(1): 345–362. https://doi.org/10.1017/S0007123417000448

Harris, D. (1999). '). 'From "Warlord" to "Democratic" President: How Charles Taylor Won the 1997 Liberian Elections. *Journal of Modern African Studies*, 37(3): 431–455.

Hartzell, C. A., and M. Hoddie (2015). 'The Art of the Possible: Power Sharing and Post-Civil War Democracy'. *World Politics*, 67(1): 37–71. https://doi.org/10.1017/S0043887114000306

Heath, O., G. Verniers, and S. Kumar (2015). 'Do Muslim Voters Prefer Muslim Candidates? Co-Religiosity and Voting Behaviour in India'. *Electoral Studies*, 38:10–18. https://doi.org/10.1016/j.electstud.2015.01.005

Högbladh, S. 'Peace Agreements 1975–2011—Updating the UCDP Peace Agreement Dataset'. In T. Pettersson and L. Themnér (eds), *States in Armed Conflict.* Uppsala: Uppsala University, Department of Peace and Conflict Research Report.

Horowitz, D. L. (1985) *Ethnic Groups in Conflict.* Berkeley, CA: University of California Press.

Horowitz, D. L. (1990). 'Presidents vs. Parliaments: Comparing Democratic Systems'. *Journal of Democracy*, 1(4): 73–79. https://doi.org/10.1353/jod.1990.0056

Horowitz, D. L. (1991). 'Making Moderation Pay: the Comparative Politics of Ethnic Conflict Management'. In J. V. Montville (ed.), *Conflict and Peacemaking in Multiethnic Societies*. New York, NY: Lexington Books.

Horowitz, D. L. (1993). 'The Challenge of Ethnic Conflict: Democracy in Divided Societies'. *Journal of Democracy*, 4(4): 18–38. https://doi.org/10.1353/jod.1993.0054

Howard, L. M. (2008). *UN Peacekeeping in Civil Wars*. Cambridge: Cambridge University Press. https://doi.org/10.1017/CBO9780511840593

Hutchings, V. L., and N. A. Valentino (2004). 'The Centrality of Race in American Politics'. *Annual Review of Political* Science, 7(1): 383–408. https://doi.org/10.1146/annurev.polisci.7.012003.104859

IHS Global Insight (2003). 'Election 2003: Rwanda's Historic Presidential Poll Undermined by Allegations of Foul Play', 25 August.

International Crisis Group (1996). 'Elections in Bosnia and Herzegovina'. International Crisis Group. Available at: https://www.crisisgroup.org/europe-central-asia/balkans/bosnia-and-herzegovina/elections-bosnia-and-herzegovina (accessed 9 April 2025).

International Crisis Group (2001). 'Kosovo: Landmark Election'. Balkans Report 120. Available at: https://www.crisisgroup.org/europe-central-asia/balkans/kosovo/kosovo-landmark-election (accessed 6 May 2025).

International Foundation for Electoral Systems. (2005). 'Burundian Presidency 2005'. Available at: https://www.electionguide.org/elections/id/1979/ (accessed 9 April 2025).

Jalabi, R., and M. Georgy (2018). 'Cleric Moqtada Al-Sadr's Bloc Wins Iraq Election'. *Reuters*, 18 May.

Kalinaki (2003). 'Rwanda: Presidential Elections: The Good, the Bad and the Ugly'. *AllAfrica* News, 25 August. Available at: https://allafrica.com/stories/200308250452.html (accessed 9 April 2025).

Kaltenthaler, K. (2018). 'Some Sunnis Voted for a Shiite—and 3 More Takeaways from the Iraqi Election'. *The Conversation*, [Online], 24 May. Available at: https://theconversation.com/some-sunnis-voted-for-a-shiite-and-3-more-takeaways-from-the-iraqi-election-86904 (accessed March 29, 2026).

Kalyvas, S. N. (2008). 'Ethnic Defection in Civil War'. *Comparative Political Studies*, 41(8): 1043–1068. https://doi.org/10.1177/0010414008317949

Kao, K., and M. R. Revkin (2023). 'Retribution or Reconciliation? Post-Conflict Attitudes toward Enemy Collaborators'. *American Journal of Political Science*, 67(2): 358–373. https://doi.org/10.1111/ajps.12673

Kaplan, R. D. (1994). *Balkan Ghosts: A Journey through History*. New York: Vintage Books.

Kasapović, M. (1997). '1996 Parliamentary Elections in Bosnia and Herzegovina'. *Electoral Studies*, 16(1): 117–121. https://doi.org/10.1016/S0261-3794(97)83122-8

Kasfir, N. (1979). 'Explaining Ethnic Political Participation'. *World Politics*, 31(3): 365–388. https://doi.org/10.2307/2009994

Kinzer, S. (2008). *A Thousand Hills: Rwanda's Rebirth and the Man Who Dreamed It*. Hoboken, NJ: John Wiley & Sons.

Kramon, E., and D. N. Posner (2011). 'Kenya's New Constitution'. *Journal of Democracy*, 22(2): 89–103. https://doi.org/10.1353/jod.2011.0026

Kuran, T. (1991). 'Now out of Never: The Element of Surprise in the East European Revolution of 1989'. *World Politics*, 44(1): 7–48. https://doi.org/10.2307/2010422

Laitin, D. D. (1986). *Hegemony and Culture: Politics and Religious Change Among the Yoruba*. Chicago, IL: University of Chicago Press.
Lerner, J. S., and L. Z. Tiedens (2006). 'Portrait of the Angry Decision Maker: How Appraisal Tendencies Shape Anger's Influence on Cognition'. *Journal of Behavioral Decision Making*, 19(2): 115–137. https://doi.org/10.1002/bdm.515
Levy, G. (2022). 'Evaluations of Violence at the Polls: Civilian Victimization and Support for Perpetrators after War'. *Journal of Politics*, 84(2). https://doi.org/10.1086/715248
Levitsky, S. R., and L. A. Way (2012). 'Beyond Patronage: Violent Struggle, Ruling Party Cohesion, and Authoritarian Durability'. *Perspectives on Politics*, 10(4): 869–889. https://doi.org/10.1017/S1537592712002861
Lindberg, S. I., M. Coppedge, J. Gerring, and J. Teorell (2014). 'V-Dem: a New Way to Measure Democracy'. *Journal of Democracy*, 25(3): 159–169. https://doi.org/10.1353/jod.2014.0040
Liu, S. X. (2022). 'Control, Coercion, and Cooptation: How Rebels Govern After Winning Civil War'. *World Politics*, 74(1): 37–76. https://doi.org/10.1017/S0043887121000174
Lupu, N. (2015). 'Party Polarization and Mass Partisanship: A Comparative Perspective'. *Political Behavior*, 37: 331–356. https://doi.org/10.1007/s11109-014-9279-z
Lupu, N., and L. Peisakhin (2017). 'The Legacy of Political Violence across Generations'. *American Journal of Political Science*, 61(4): 836–851. https://doi.org/10.1111/ajps.12327
Lyons, T. (2016). 'The Importance of Winning: Victorious Insurgent Groups and Authoritarian Politics'. *Comparative Politics*, 48(2): 167–184. https://doi.org/10.5129/001041516817037745
MacDonald, D. B. (2003). *Balkan Holocausts?: Serbian and Croatian Victim-centred Propaganda and the War in Yugoslavia*. Manchester: Manchester University Press. https://doi.org/10.7228/manchester/9780719064661.001.0001
Manning, C. (2008). *The Making of Democrats: Elections and Party Development in Postwar Bosnia, El Salvador, and Mozambique*. New York: Palgrave Macmillan. https://doi.org/10.1057/9780230611160
Martin, P. A., G. Piccolino, and J. S. Speight (2021). 'Ex-rebel Authority After Civil War: Theory and Evidence from Côte d'Ivoire'. *Comparative Politics*, 53(2): 209–232. https://doi.org/10.5129/001041521X15923094954447
Matanock, A. M. (2017). *Electing Peace: From Civil Conflict to Political Participation*. New York: Cambridge University Press. https://doi.org/10.1017/9781316987179
Mason, T. D., M. Gurses, P.T. Brandt, and J. M. Quinn (2011). 'When Civil Wars Recur: Conditions for Durable Peace After Civil Wars'. *International Studies Perspectives*, 12(2): 171–189. https://doi.org/10.1111/j.1528-3585.2011.00426.x
Matić, D., and S. P. Ramet (2007). *Democratic Transition in Croatia: Value Transformation, Education & Media*. College Station, TX: Texas A&M University Press.
McLauchlin, T., and W. Pearlman (2012). 'Out-group Conflict, In-group Unity? Exploring the Effect of Repression on Intramovement Cooperation'. *Journal of Conflict Resolution*, 56(1): 41–66. https://doi.org/10.1177/0022002711429707
Meierhenrich, J. (2006). 'Presidential and Parliamentary Elections in Rwanda, 2003'. *Electoral Studies*, 25(3): 627–634. https://doi.org/10.1016/j.electstud.2005.10.003
Muzej Domovinskog Rata Dubrovnik (n.d.). *Dubrovnik during the Homeland War, 1991–1995* [Exhibition]. Empire's Fort, Dubrovnik.
Nindorera, W. (2012). 'The CNDD-FD in Burundi: The Path from Armed to Political Struggle'. Berghof Transitions Series, 10. Berlin: Berghof Foundation.
Niyoyita, A. (2005). 'Polls Close in Parliamentary Elections in Burundi'. *Associated Press*, 4 July.

Ottmann, M., and J. Vüllers (2015). 'The Power-Sharing Event Dataset (PSED): A New Dataset on the Occurrence of Power-Sharing in Post-Conflict Countries'. *Conflict Management and Peace Science*, 32(3): 327–350. https://doi.org/10.1177/0738894214542753

Petersen, R., and S.Z. Daly (2010). 'Anger, Violence, and Political Science'. In M. Potegal, G. Stemmler, and C. Spielberger (eds), *International Handbook of Anger: Constituent and Concomitant Biological, Psychological, and Social Processes*. New York: Springer.

Posner, D. N. (2004). 'The Political Salience of Cultural Difference: Why Chewas and Tumbukas Are Allies in Zambia and Adversaries in Malawi'. *American Political Science Review*, 98(4): 529–545. https://doi.org/10.1017/S0003055404041334

Posner, D. N. (2005). *Institutions and Ethnic Politics in Africa*. Cambridge: Cambridge University Press. https://doi.org/10.1017/CBO9780511808661

RadioMozambique (1994). *[Broadcast]*, Maputo, 9 October. Cited in *BBC Summary of World Broadcasts*, 'The Election Campaigns'.

Ramet, S. P., and I. Goldstein (2019). 'Politics in Croatia since 1990'. In S. P. Ramet, C. M. Hassenstab (eds), *Central and Southeast European Politics since 1989*. Cambridge: Cambridge University Press. https://doi.org/10.1017/9781108752466

Reilly, B. (2001). *Democracy in Divided Societies: Electoral Engineering for Conflict Management*. Cambridge: Cambridge University Press. https://doi.org/10.1017/CBO9780511491108

Reilly, B. (2006). 'Political Engineering and Party Politics in Conflict-Prone Societies'. *Democratization*, 13(5): 811–827. https://doi.org/10.1080/13510340601010719

Rozenas, A., S. Schutte, and Y. Zhukov (2017). 'The Political Legacy of Violence: The Long-Term Impact of Stalin's Repression in Ukraine'. *Journal of Politics*, 79(4): 1147–1161. https://doi.org/10.1086/692964

Rudloff, P., and M. G. Findley (2016). 'The Downstream Effects of Combatant Fragmentation on Civil War Recurrence'. *Journal of Peace Research*, 53(1): 19–32. https://doi.org/10.1177/0022343315617067

Sartori, G. (1976). *Parties and Party Systems: A Framework for Analysis*. Cambridge: Cambridge University Press.

Schumpeter, J. A. (1976). *Capitalism, Socialism, and Democracy*. London: Allen & Unwin.

Sindre, G. M. (2016). 'In Whose Interests? Former Rebel Parties and Ex-combatant Interest Group Mobilisation in Aceh and East Timor'. *Civil Wars*, 18(2): 192–213. https://doi.org/10.1080/13698249.2016.1205564

Söderberg Kovacs, M. (2007). 'From Rebellion to Politics: the Transformation of Rebel Groups to Political Parties in Civil War Peace Processes'. PhD Dissertation. Uppsala: Uppsala University.

Staniland, P. (2012). 'Between a Rock and a Hard Place: Insurgent Fratricide, Ethnic Defection, and the Rise of Pro-state Paramilitaries'. *Journal of Conflict Resolution*, 56(1): 16–40. https://doi.org/10.1177/0022002711429681

Stanton, J. A. (2016). 'Violence and Restraint in Civil War: Civilian Targeting in the Shadow of International Law'. Cambridge: Cambridge University Press. https://doi.org/10.1017/9781107706477

Steinmo, S. (1989). 'Political Institutions and Tax Policy in the United States, Sweden, and Britain'. *World Politics*, 41(4): 500–535. https://doi.org/10.2307/2010528

Swain, J. (1995). 'Exultant Croatia Heads for Murderous Election'. *The Sunday Times*, 22 October.

Tedeschi, R. G., and L. G. Calhoun (2004). "Posttraumatic Growth: Conceptual Foundations and Empirical Evidence." *Psychological Inquiry* 15 (1): 1–18. https://doi.org/10.1207/s15327965pli1501_01.

Thaler, K. M. (2018). 'From Insurgent to Incumbent: State Building and Service Provision After Rebel Victory in Civil Wars'. Doctoral Dissertation. Cambridge, MA: Harvard University.
The Canadian Press (2003). 'Commission Declares Former Rebels Winners of Burundi Parliamentary Elections'. *Canadian Press*, 5 July.
The Carter Center (1997). *Observing the 1997 Special Elections Process in Liberia*. Atlanta, GA: The Carter Center.
The Economist (2003). 'Kagame Won, a Little Too Well; Rwanda's Presidential Election'. *The Economist*, 30 August.
Touquet, H. (2011). 'Multi-Ethnic Parties in Bosnia-Herzegovina: Naša Stranka and the Paradoxes of Postethnic Politics'. *Studies in Ethnicity and Nationalism*, 11(3): 451–467. https://doi.org/10.1111/j.1754-9469.2011.01134.x
United Nations Peacebuilding Commission (2009). *Report of the Secretary-General on Peacebuilding in the Immediate Aftermath of Conflict: Report of the Peacebuilding Commission*. New York: General Assembly Security Council.
Vuletić, D. (2007). 'Internal Party Democracy in Bosnia-Herzegovina: An Interaction Between Crises and Development'. In G. Karasimeonov (ed.), *Reshaping the Broken Image of Political Parties: Internal Party Democracy in South Eastern Europe*. Sofia: Gorexpress.
Walter, B. F. (2002). *Committing to Peace: The Successful Settlement of Civil Wars*. Princeton, NJ: Princeton University Press. https://doi.org/10.1515/9781400824465
Walter, B. F. (2004). 'Does Conflict Beget Conflict? Explaining Recurring Civil War'. *Journal of Peace Research*, 41(3): 371–388. https://doi.org/10.1177/0022343304043775
Waters, M. C. (1999). *Black Identities: West Indian Immigrant Dreams and American Realities*. Cambridge, MA: Harvard University Press. https://doi.org/10.4159/9780674044944
Wilkinson, S. (2004). *Votes and Violence: Electoral Competition and Ethnic Riots in India*. Cambridge: Cambridge University Press. https://doi.org/10.1017/CBO9780511510458
Zhukov, Y. M., and R. Talibova (2018). 'Stalin's Terror and the Long-term Political Effects of Mass Repression'. *Journal of Peace Research*, 55(2): 267–283. https://doi.org/10.1177/0022343317751261

PART IV

IS THERE A ROLE FOR EXTERNAL INTERVENTIONS?

11
States of disorder
An ecosystems approach to state-building in conflict-affected countries

Adam Day

11.1 Introduction

Since the end of the Cold War, the West has developed something of an obsession with failed states. Countries suffering from chronic violence, deep poverty, and endemic corruption are 'the single most important problem for world order' (Fukuyama 2004: 92), 'weak links' (Stewart 2011) in the international system, and 'black holes' that threaten the rest of the world (Rotberg 2003: 9). In this narrative, the project of fixing failed states is more than a development concern; it has grown to become a central pillar in Western concepts of world order and global governance.

However, over the past 30 years, there are very few examples of successful international state-building or peacebuilding interventions (see e.g., Paris 2004; Doyle and Sambanis 2006). Despite hundreds of billions of dollars invested in countries like Somalia, the Democratic Republic of the Congo (DRC), and Mali, they remain embroiled in conflict, unable to build the kind of effective, legitimate institutions envisaged by interveners. In 2013, the United Nations (UN) was forced to abandon its ambitious state-building project in South Sudan after a new civil war broke out. And most recently, the US withdrawal from Afghanistan signalled an end to a multi-decade attempt to shore up the Afghan state. These experiences support the growing evidence that international interventions are not only unlikely to transform fragile states into strong ones but may in fact work to undermine their overriding goal of improved stability (see e.g., Barnett and Zürcher 2009; Day et al. 2021; Paris and Sisk 2009; von Billerbeck and Tansey 2019). At worst, we may be learning that state-building could be one cause of state failure, rather than its cure (Woodward 2017; Call 2008).

Explanations for the failure of state-building can be broadly categorized into three lines of scholarship. Perhaps the most well-known can be termed the 'ivory tower' problem of international intervention. As Severine Autessere has astutely pointed out, international interventions tend to fail due to ignorance of the local

Adam Day, *States of disorder*. In: *Institutional Legacies of Violent Conflict*. Edited by: Patricia Justino, Oxford University Press. © United Nations University World Institute for Development Economics Research (UNU-WIDER) (2026).
DOI: 10.1093/9780197904077.003.0011

conflicts that may drive instability in settings like the DRC (Autessere 2010). At worst, Susan Woodward argues, such interventions do more to bolster the skills of Western intervenors, rather than building local or national capacities (Woodward 2017). Leading a call for a 'local turn' in international interventions, authors like Mac Ginty and Richmond have suggested that the shortcomings of peacebuilding can be addressed by better understanding of local dynamics, and indeed an enabling of local conflict resolution capacities (Leonardsson and Rudd 2015; Mac Ginty and Richmond 2013).

A second explanation for this failure derives from post-colonial studies, which have illuminated how Western-driven concepts of state-building, peacebuilding, and stabilization all have a strong tendency to impose a European model of statehood and state formation on settings which have a much different history. Pointing to deeply engrained patterns of patronage, violence, and colonial structures, scholars like Bayart, Chabal, and Daloz suggest that the Western project of state-building is very unlikely to take hold in post-colonial settings where the bulk of interventions have occurred over the past 30 years (Bayart 1993; Chabal and Daloz 1999; Herbst 2000; Reno 1998; Ayoub 1996). Roland Paris similarly cautioned against a 'mission civilisatrice' by the international community, which has continued to push largely European models of the state into post-colonial settings around the world (Paris 2002: 637).

A third and increasingly influential critique of state-building arises in the field of non-state governance. Rather than adopting a Weberian view of governance as residing purely in a state–society relationship, this scholarship explores how a range of non-state actors deliver basic protections, services, and goods to populations, often with a higher degree of legitimacy and effectiveness than the state (Cheng 2018; Hall and Bierstecker 2009; Jackson 2003; Mampilly 2011; Risse 2013; Rosenau and Czempiel 2010). This view understands governance as an 'active process' rather than a set of institutions; governance can be produced by traditional leaders, businesses, chiefs, civil society groups, armed militias, and ordinary citizens (Raeymaekers et al. 2008). Indeed, the growing field of 'hybrid governance' suggests that states and non-state actors can compete for, collaborate, and share governance roles in a variety of ways, forming 'complexes of power' (Vlassenroot and Raeymaekers 2004), 'arenas of negotiation' (Hagmann and Péclard 2010), 'twilight institutions' (Lund 2006), and/or 'negotiated statehood' (Hagmann and Péclard 2010). Common across these concepts is the understanding that governance is contested and relational, the product of a network of relationships rather than the sole purview of state institutions. The power to govern is, as Alex de Waal writes, the product of negotiation in the political marketplace (de Waal 2016).

This chapter expands upon the notions of non-state governance and the political marketplace to offer a more holistic and empirically grounded explanation for the failures of state-building. It argues that governance in these settings is best understood as part of a complex ecosystem, one where change is the result of the evolution of the underlying rules and patterns of the system itself. Taking South Sudan as a paradigmatic case of failed state-building, this chapter explores how its system of governance evolved through decades of war to the point of independence in 2011. It argues that the South Sudanese system was dominated by an ethno-military set of relations that grew out of Sudan's civil war, one where basic security and services for the population were generated via a network of relations that stretched across the rebel army, traditional leaders, and a range of private actors.

The chapter further argues that the South Sudanese governance system developed deeply entrenched patterns—feedback loops and strong attractors, to use the language of complexity theory—that allowed it to resist the kind of top-down, institutionally based state-building envisioned by the UN mission and its partners. It concludes that the South Sudanese experience offers insights into all settings where international intervention is attempting to address longstanding conflict dynamics and build more effective state institutional capacities. From DRC to Somalia to Afghanistan, complex ecosystems of governance exist, systems that strongly resist the kind of state-centric approaches typical of the UN and Western actors. By better understanding the rules and patterns that stabilize these systems, we can design more effective approaches in the future.

11.2 What is complexity theory?

Thinking of the world in complex systemic terms is not new. Pre-Socratic thinkers like Heraclitus viewed the world as composed of a network of relations (Boulton et al. 2015), while Darwin's theory of evolution was likewise founded on the understanding that change in life forms was the result of patterning variations in complex systems (Bonner 1988). The fields of physics, mathematics, and economics have developed advanced notions of complexity (Boulding 1981; Boulton 2010; Mitchell 2009; Veblen 1898), as has literary criticism (Cilliers 1998; Lyotard 1984).

In straightforward terms, a complex system is one where its constituent elements interact together to create effects different from the sum of what each element would produce on its own. These interactions are *non-linear* and cannot be reduced to input–output models. The systems are *open*—they interact with their environment and are in a state of constant change. And they *self-organize*, often by feeding activities back onto themselves in a way that generates adaptation over time (so-called 'emergent behaviour') (Cilliers 1998). It is helpful to think of complex systems as opposed to complicated ones: a car engine may have an enormous number of parts that must be fitted perfectly together, but each part performs a discrete function in a linear input–output manner. A car engine, like a traditional computer, is *complicated*, not complex. In contrast, our immune system's constituent elements produce something wholly different together than each would on their own; they feed back their activities into the system in a way that allows it to adapt to new conditions and generate outcomes beyond the sum of their parts. Our immune system is complex, as are bee colonies, economies, and, I argue, human societies.

Complex systems may feel chaotic, but they evolve around patterns that stabilize over time. For example: ant colonies organize into structures that appear to demonstrate a 'collective intelligence' capable of building viable structures well beyond their own individual understanding; inter-related patterns of behaviour of neurons in the brain produce thoughts and emotions that go well beyond what each electric impulse generates; and significant research has been directed at economic activity as a complex system with emergent qualities (Mitchell 2009). Adaptation in complex systems is non-linear, but a system's self-organization does follow discernible patterns that can be predicted over time (Chandler 2014). And while systems built of human beings are not always wholly equivalent to those in the natural sciences, the modalities for self-organization are often analogous.[1]

One of the most important ways in which systems self-organize is through 'feedback loops'. Simply put, a feedback loop is a way that information is directed back into the system to generate an effect. A positive feedback loop reinforces itself and the pattern in the system: the more people catch the flu in a community, the more will continue to catch it; the more soil erodes, the less vegetation can grow, leading to fewer root structures and greater erosion.[2] In contrast, a negative feedback loop is best thought of as a corrective: it works against the process that caused it. When humans get hot, the resulting sweat cools us down; as prices in an economy increase, demand tends to decrease and stabilizes the market. In a conflict setting, inter-ethnic animosity can function as a positive feedback loop: tensions increase, the risk of violence between the communities grows, which reinforces enmity between the communities.[3] Corruption can also create positive feedback loops: informal networks gain traction and build relationships, undermining formal, state-owned enterprise, stripping it of resources and authority, which in turn strengthens the influence of the illicit actors.

Over time, patterns can entrench themselves, creating what are called 'strong attractors' in a given system. Intractable conflicts between two parties offer a good example of this dynamic: each party's thoughts and actions tend to become attached to the idea of the other party as an enemy, thus intensifying the conflict and reinforcing the negative view of the other side (Coleman 2011). Nearly anything the Palestinians do can be seen as provocative to the Israelis, and vice versa,

[1] For a description of agency in complex systems, see Brusset et al. (2017).
[2] Examples drawn from Meadows (1999).
[3] For an application of systemic thinking to inter-ethnic disputes, see Splinter and Wustehube (2011).

thus reinforcing the negative perceptions of each side. As Peter Coleman has described, 'the attractor serves as a valley in the psychological landscape into which the psychological elements—thoughts, feelings and actions—begin to slide' (Coleman et al. 2011: 42). Once trapped in such a valley, escaping over its steep sides requires the kind of intention and energy that may appear impossible from within the system.

Complexity thinking has enormous implications for state-building. Unlike traditional approaches, which assume that a gradual increase in institutional capacities will lead to a corresponding improvement in stability, a systemic approach suggests that change is generated by some kind of rewriting of the underlying rules. Systems evolve by shifting the gravitational pull of the attractors, resulting in new ways for governance powers to be generated, negotiated, and exercised. The system must self-organize differently, finding new patterns around which to stabilize itself (de Coning 2016). In protracted conflicts, this may involve the creation of new narratives that begin to undo the vicious cycles of stigmatization and hatred of the other, or it may require incentives that move actors away from illicit networks that have sustained the system for decades. In some societies, change can happen with surprising rapidity: Mohamed Bouazizi set himself on fire in Tunis in December 2010, and less than one month later, protests that became the Arab Spring had snowballed (a term that refers to a rapid positive feedback loop), toppling the Tunisian government and spreading across the region. Similarly, severe shocks to a system can trigger an almost instantaneous leap into a new 'phase space' (Richardson 2006) where patterns of behaviour are radically altered, new possibilities rapidly emerge, and the contours of the system may take time to reshape (for example, the stops and starts in Egyptian rule following the Arab Spring).

In contrast, deeply entrenched patterns of behaviour can also persist for generations, suffering apparent reversals before any shift may take hold (see e.g. Vimalarajah 2011). In the DRC, for example, it appears that decades of state-building by the UN have had little effect on the underlying patterns of patronage linking powerbrokers in Kinshasa to the peripheries of the country. A non-linear notion of change 'requires that interveners have humility, because specific changes are often unpredictable and uncontrollable ... [it] suggests we attend to temporality and trends, not specific outcomes' (Coleman et al. 2011: 39). Ideas of 'fixing failed states' gain little traction here because there is no end-state (de Coning 2018: 312); systems do not 'break down'—as much of the state failure literature suggests—they reorganize and reach new equilibria, often at great human cost (Rhodes et al. 2011).

Complexity thinking does more than merely challenge traditional notions of linearity; it also offers tools for researchers to map change in socio-political systems (Körppen 2011). Robert Jervis did ground-breaking work applying complexity to political science (Jervis 1997). David Byrne used complexity to understand the impacts of health, education, and urban governance policies in England, while a range of other scholars have suggested complexity-driven approaches to public policy (Byrne 1998; Geyer and Rihani 2010; Morçöl 2012; Rhodes et al. 2011; Room 2010). Michael Woolcock, Duncan Green, Rachel Kleinfeld, and Ben Ramalingam have drawn from complexity thinking to suggest innovative approaches to international development and humanitarian assistance (Green 2013; Kleinfeld 2015; Ramalingam 2013; Woolcock 2009). Bousquet and Curtis have persuasively argued for a more concerted application of complexity thinking to international relations, a call that was taken up by Emilian Kavalski in his analysis of world politics (Bousquet and Curtis 2011; Kavalski 2015). Similar applications of complexity thinking have now been suggested for international policing efforts (Hunt 2015), humanitarian delivery (Ramalingham and Jones 2008), military operations, and studies of social resilience in conflict (Moe and Müller 2017; Richardson et al. 2009). Most relevant, Brusset, de Coning, and Hughes curated an exploratory volume on the potential application of complexity thinking to post-conflict peacebuilding, arguing that external attempts to 'fix' local governance systems may 'undermine and interfere with the self-organising process' (Brusset et al. 2017: 17).

What is missing, and what this article attempts to offer, is how complexity thinking can be applied in the context of state-building. This is the topic of the following section.

11.3 State-building from scratch: the case of South Sudan

In July 2011, 40 heads of state gathered in Juba to celebrate the creation of the world's newest country. Standing before a celebrating crowd, President Salva Kiir declared, 'The Republic of South Sudan is like a white paper – *tabula rasa*!'.[4] This view was echoed across the international community. President Obama spoke of a 'new dawn'[5] after a period of darkness, while the World Bank suggested 'South Sudan must build its institutions *from scratch*' (World Bank 2013a). Here, state-building in South Sudan was comparable to filling a void, writing over a blank space where state institutions were utterly absent. Indeed, the newly established UN Mission in South Sudan (UNMISS) was given a billion-dollar mandate to fill this institutional vacuum, to constitute and strengthen state governance capacities.[6] Taking the helm of UNMISS in 2011, Hilde Frafjord Johnson wrote that the UN's task was 'literally building a country' (Johnson 2016: 98).

[4] President Salva Kiir's Martyr's Day Speech, 30 July 2011 (Salva Kiir 2011).

[5] Statement of President Barack Obama on Recognition of the Republic of South Sudan, 9 July 2011 (White House 2011). See also Statement of UN Secretary-General Ban Ki-Moon on the Independence of the Republic of South Sudan (United Nations 2011).

[6] United Nations Security Council Resolution on South Sudan, S/RES/1996 (8 July 2011), para. 3.

Only two years later, this optimism about building up South Sudan evaporated as the country descended into a brutal civil war, causing the death of nearly 400,000 people and the displacement of more than four million (Checchi et al. 2018). The nascent army and police were prime actors in this conflict, driving large populations from their homes, killing, looting, and raping civilians, and obstructing humanitarian aid to vulnerable populations.[7] Recognizing that a complete shift was needed, the UN Security Council quickly halted the state-building mandate of UNMISS, cutting off enormous resources that had been dedicated to supporting state institutions across the country, and calling on UNMISS to focus on protecting the civilians still in harm's way.[8] In only a few months, the UN had pivoted from the role of building the state to one of protecting the people from it. State-building had failed.

The remarkable apparent takeaway within the international community was that South Sudan had suffered from *too little* state-building. Special Representative of the Secretary-General Johnson suggested that capacity development of the South Sudanese state had been conducted in a 'patchy and uncoordinated' manner, 'not done in the comprehensive and systematic way needed to build a functioning state' (Johnson 2016). The World Bank reported that dysfunction and corruption within the state meant that public expenditures had not delivered the kind of institutions needed to prevent the war (Adiebo et al. 2013). Capturing a sentiment held across many in the donor community, Richard Dowden suggested that South Sudan had become independent too early, before the international community was able to help it build effective state institutions that would be resilient in the face of ethnic divisions (Dowden 2014). If the problem was poorly functioning state governance, then the solution should have been to invest more in the state.

This chapter offers an alternative—and in some ways directly opposed—explanation of the failure of state-building in South Sudan. Its central argument is that governance in South Sudan is best understood as an ecosystem, a set of relations across actors that evolved over the course of the 20-year civil war with Khartoum. This system exhibits 'strong attractors', deeply entrenched patterns that create powerful tendencies and tend to stabilize the system over time (Coleman et al. 2007). In the case of South Sudan, the strongest attractor was what I term an 'ethno-military' network composed of the former rebel army (the Southern People's Liberation Army (SPLA)), traditional leaders, and powerbrokers in Juba, which over time was able to absorb extraordinary shocks and continue on. The patterns underlying this system, I argue, meant that energy and resources directed

[7] Letter dated 20 November 2017 from the Panel of Experts on South Sudan addressed to the President of the Security Council, S/2017/979.

[8] United Nations Security Council resolution, S/RES/2155 (2014).

towards state institutions were pulled in other directions, captured by the gravitational pull of the system, even when it appeared that South Sudan was making progress.

11.3.1 The evolution of South Sudan's governance system

The South Sudanese governance system in 2011 was in large part the outcome of the structures put in place during the colonial period and their evolution through twenty years of brutal civil war against Khartoum.[9] Anglo-Egyptian rule was based in large part upon a form of 'native administration' in which traditional leaders in southern Sudan were recognized as legitimate state authorities, able to levy taxes and impose rules upon their communities. At the same time, traditional authorities (chiefs, mainly) continued to govern via their own long-established structures, which were largely based on kinship and ethnic identity.

The result was a system in which urban areas (themselves created to support the slave trade) became nodes in an extractive governance system that fed the political centre in Khartoum/Omdurman. As Cherry Leonardi describes, towns became the place where the mediation role of the chief played out:

> [A] whole range of people in and around the towns have made claims upon the state and/or their chief, often employing notions of a contract, transaction or reciprocal deal to demand guarantees of their rights in property or persons. In its most basic expression ... this was a bargain of protection from the threat of the same state from which the guarantee was obtained (Leonardi 2013: 3).

As a result of the colonial instrumentalization of local customary roles, wealth and administrative authority were inextricably linked to the ethnic affiliation of the traditional leader. Access to resources was negotiated as between a community and the colonial power through the intermediary of the traditional authority, who maintained local legitimacy through kinship. As Volker Boege has pointed out in other settings, traditional leaders had to 'adopt an ambiguous position with regard to the state, appropriate state functions and "state talk", but at the same time pursu[e] their own agenda under the guise of state authority and power' (Boege et al. 2008).

Following independence in 1956, Sudan's trajectory was largely shaped by two civil wars. In simplified terms, the wars arose out of attempts by Khartoum to assimilate and control its southern territory, making it economically dependent on the centre, while the southern population fought for greater autonomy. Indeed,

[9] Indeed, one could trace these structures back further to the Turco-Egyptian and Mahdiyya regimes, as I do in *States of Disorder, Ecosystems of Governance: Complexity Theory Applied to UN Statebuilding in the DRC and South Sudan* (Day 2022).

at the close of the first civil war in 1972, a key aspect of the Addis Ababa agreement was to give southern Sudan greater executive and legislative powers and political representation in Khartoum. However, economic dependence on Khartoum was maintained by keeping a strong hold on revenues and only transferring funds to the south via government positions. Indeed, for most of the twentieth century, the most reliable way for a southerner to attract resources from Khartoum was not through any national budgetary process, but rather by obtaining a government post. Up to 96 per cent of government expenditures in southern Sudan at the time went on government salaries and wages, creating a highly dependent and ethnically stratified set of relationships governing the south.

As a result, local government positions—distributed along traditional kinship lines—were the exclusive recipients of resources from the centre, creating what Edward Thomas has called the 'ethnic homogeneity of administrative units' given their strong tendencies to distribute resources within their own communities (Boege et al. 2008: 131). When Khartoum experienced economic downturns, the government transmitted the costs first and foremost southwards, increasing southern dependency on the north over time. For example, as late as 2003, peripheral dependency on the centre was still increasing, even as the southern government had created apparently independent governance capacities across the southern territory (IMF 2012).

Sudan's second civil war (1983–2005) witnessed a militarization of these structures. Leading the rebellion, the Southern People's Liberation Movement/Army (SPLM/A) gradually took over all major governance functions, subordinating the role of traditional authorities to the war effort. However, from birth, the SPLA considered itself a movement aspiring to alter how Sudan was governed as a whole, not as a future government of a southern Sudanese state. In fact, prior to the Comprehensive Peace Agreement (CPA) period in 2005, it never set up the kind of shadow ministries or provisional government structures typical to an autonomous region, but instead largely assumed the structures of the Anglo-Egyptian native administration (IMF 2012). Traditional chieftaincies continued to be recognized as the custodians of customary law within communities, and they were expected to perform state-like activities such as tax collection and infrastructural projects on behalf of the SPLA. But customary authorities were subjected to the military exigencies of the movement in a variety of ways: SPLA officers often played a supervisory role over the chiefs, including the selection of chieftaincies; in rural areas, SPLA commanders carved out fiefdoms where they overruled community leadership and extracted resources; and rural communities were forced to contribute to SPLA upkeep via taxes in kind, such as grains, livestock, and cattle (Pinaud 2014).

The SPLA's governance role created a symbiotic relationship between the rebel group and the communities, mediated by traditional authorities.[10] On the one

[10] For an in-depth use of symbiotic relations in peacebuilding, see Hunt (2017).

hand, the SPLA gained material resources—food, shelter, recruits, and different forms of rent—from their territorial control of many parts of southern Sudan. Operating in concert with traditional authorities allowed the SPLA to maintain some degrees of legitimacy within communities; there were even instances where traditional authorities were given SPLA military ranks to ensure compliance and guarantee that SPLA presence was seen as part of the community governance structure (Podder 2014). The ethno-military aspect of the SPLA allowed it to provide to its communities as well: because the network was maintained along ethnic lines, the SPLA was seen as a protector of community interests, directing land, natural resources, and representation at the centre in favour of the community in which they were deployed. Here, traditional chiefs were a mediation point, articulating community needs and demands upwards, while expressing the SPLA's power downwards. This symbiotic relationship operates as a strong pattern that became even more entrenched during and after the CPA period.

An important outcome of the militarization of the governance system in southern Sudan was the lack of attention to economic development in the region. Roads, government offices, communications, and basic services, none of which was particularly well delivered at any point in the South's history, fell into further disrepair. 'The nucleus of the political system', Sukanya Podder writes, 'was confined to garrison towns ... while the rural areas served as the base for planning and launching war operations' (Podder 2014:213). As chieftaincy structures were incorporated into the SPLA's military chain of command in these garrison towns—and indeed as the SPLA took on a more direct role in appointing chieftaincy positions—local governance was redirected in support of the rebellion rather than providing for the communities of the region. Resource flows reflected this dynamic as communities received very little in exchange for the food, taxes, and resources provided to the SPLA (LeRiche 2018).

The SPLA's failure to govern effectively or fairly is one of the most cited reasons for the series of splits and infighting that characterized southern dynamics in the civil war from the mid-1980s through the 1990s. Anne Walraet's research has shown that a combination of predatory practices of the SPLA—including its forcible takeover of lucrative agricultural resources, forced taxation, and looting—deepened distrust and fomented rebellions within the South (Walraet 2008). Stripped of the means to govern effectively other than by the authority vested in them by the SPLA, local governors and chiefs were thus caught between their roles as representatives of the communities and recipients of patronage from above. Cherry Leonardi describes this role in bargaining terms, where people in and around towns in southern Sudan entered into deals with chiefs to secure guarantees around land rights and also protection from predation by the state itself (Leonardi 2013).

Here, it is important to highlight the nexus between the economic and the security aspects of governance in southern Sudan, as it demonstrates early patterns that later became the country's deeply entrenched patronage network. As noted above, the SPLA largely assumed the Anglo-Egyptian structures of customary authorities but placed chieftaincies within the SPLA's military chain of command. This meant that traditional mechanisms of governance were repurposed for war aims, allowing for high degrees of predation and abuse by the SPLA, especially in rural areas. But it also led the SPLM/A leadership to use the military network across southern Sudan to maintain coherence in the face of splits, rebellions, and mutinies by communities during the war with Khartoum.

This coherence was achieved, in blunt terms, by purchasing loyalty: Faced with divisions and rebellions by southern communities, SPLM leader John Garang tended to offer integration into the SPLA and/or leadership positions within the movement, where a secure paycheck hedged against future disloyalty. Given that Khartoum's principal method for weakening the rebellion was to foment discord within the SPLA, preventing the collapse of the group was often Garang's overriding strategic objective. As Matthew LeRiche notes, 'managing the political economy of factional dynamics in the region became the main vehicle through which Garang and many of his commanders conducted the war' (LeRiche 2018: 22) The military chain of command, laid over the traditional authority structures from the colonial era, thus became the conduit to maintain the communities of southern Sudan in a unified fight against the north.

This meant that communities wishing to express dissatisfaction with the SPLM/A found that the most expedient act was armed rebellion. Groups capable of threatening the SPLM/A leadership with violence could establish a bargaining position, extract concessions for ending their uprising, and create new economic opportunities for their communities. Those without the ability to confront the military strength of the SPLA were either quashed or ignored. Major insurrections—such as the uprising of the Nasir faction in 1991—not only exhibited the willingness of Khartoum to instrumentalize ethnic divisions within the South but also presaged a sort of continual disintegration and reintegration of the SPLM/A over decades, including through the CPA period. Dozens of insurrections appeared across southern Sudan, with some commanders defecting so frequently it became a joke in Juba trying to count the number of rebellions by a single leader.[11] As John Garang himself wrote, 'the marginal cost of rebellion in the South became very small, zero to negative; that is, in the South it pays to rebel' (Ali et al. 2005: 193).

However, as Matthew LeRiche's authoritative study on factionalism in southern Sudan has uncovered, the continual process of fracturing and reconstituting the SPLA was not a purely military venture. LeRiche found that the levels of violence did not determine whether a rebellion would be rewarded with an integration

[11] In 2010, for instance, the commander Peter Gatdet had defected more than a dozen times, each time receiving a reintegration deal back into the SPLA.

deal; instead, it was the combination of some military threat along with a high degree of political authority that created bargaining position (LeRiche 2018). This points to one of the dominant patterns that emerged through the SPLA's role in governance: southern communities expressed their political needs militarily. Describing a dynamic that spans the periods before and after the CPA, LeRiche writes:

> Governance in South Sudan is a continual process of negotiating, brokering and mediating between a wide range of leaders and between communities, many of whom have well-armed followers that either are, or could be, a threat to the state, at least in a localized area. (LeRiche 2018: 38)

Here, governance is expressed, not merely as a relationship in which legitimacy is exchanged for protections and services, but as a mode of survival. In order to resist the attempts of Khartoum to fracture the SPLM/A along ethnic lines, its leadership continually brokered deals with communities via military integration. With its leaders integrated into the SPLA, a community could be assured of basic protections (though also subjected to the predations of the troops), while disenfranchised communities would rebel in the hope of gaining more resources via the next integration deal.

The outcome of the continual disintegration and reintegration of the SPLA was the growth of a patronage network expressed through the military chain of command, layered over existing traditional governance structures. Here, the mode of negotiation between communities and the SPLA was insurrection, where bargains were struck in accordance with the political and military threat posed by a local leader. Largesse was dispensed militarily, in the form of integration deals that included the right to SPLA command positions over specific territories. As Sukanya Podder notes, a form of 'wartime governance' arose during this period, privileging and legitimizing the rebel SPLA in ways that allowed it to permeate the social and economic spheres of southern Sudan, becoming what Clémence Pinaud has called a 'military aristocracy' in the South (Podder 2014).

11.3.2 Cash floods the system

In 2005, the SPLM and the Sudanese government signed the CPA, ending twenty years of civil war and bringing to a close nearly fifty consecutive years of war in Sudan. Overnight, the SPLM became a recognized regional government within Sudan, given significant legislative and judicial autonomy and the rights to 50 per cent of the oil revenues generated from southern Sudan (United States Institute of Peace n.d.). This arrangement resulted in a staggering influx of cash to the region, both in the form of oil revenues and development support.

In the year following the 2005 CPA, Juba's annual budget jumped one hundred-fold, from US$14.5 million to US$1.3 billion, as the south received roughly half of the US$100 million per month in oil revenues (Shankleman 2011). However, rather than helping to build more viable state institutions or transforming the rebel group into a liberal governing structure, this flood of cash tended to strengthen the existing ethno-military network. The result was a southern government synonymous (quite literally) with the rebel force that had fought for twenty years, a ruling SPLM/A that deployed its new administrative authority into a sprawling patronage system.

The most obvious example of this dynamic was the southern security forces, which received the bulk of the new revenues (Biong and Kuol 2019). Military wages made up nearly 70 per cent of government salaries, with soldiers receiving roughly US$150 per month, much more than neighbouring countries with similar budgets (Biong and Kuol 2019). These enormous outlays were in part driven by dramatic increases in oil production from the 1990s through the early 2000s, but also a concern within the SPLM leadership that a robust military was the best hedge against renewed confrontation with Khartoum (Patey 2010; Shankleman 2011). In 2006, SPLM eagerness to pour resources into wages meant that it actually overspent its annual revenues by more than US$200 million (Overseas Development Institute 2010). This fiscal policy, violating every accepted norm for dealing with resource windfalls (van der Ploeg and Venables 20011), was a stark demonstration of the SPLM's overriding priority on its own military strength and its use of military structures to maintain loyalty across South Sudan.

Governance via ethno-military networks aligns with what Alex de Waal has called 'the hegemonic power of the SPLM-SPLA patronage-coercion nexus' (de Waal 2014: 349). This network was formed by a pattern of exchange: loyalty to the SPLM in return for rents that could be extracted from communities as a member of the SPLA. However, the system did not just run on cash: ethnicity was a crucial currency that also flowed through it, shoring up relationships when money was short. Ethnicity was the means for the patronage network to extend from the urban centres to the largely cashless hinterlands.[12] 'Tribalizing' issues was a cheap way to ensure loyalty, as evidenced by the widespread practice of SPLA soldiers marrying within the families of their chain of command (Pinaud 2014). For example, when SPLA General Paulino Matiep died, his 47 wives and 102 children were not just a sign of his status and wealth within South Sudan but also a network of soldiers and loyalists with a clear function in the southern governance system (Sudan Tribune 2012).

Spending on the SPLA meant that the army tended to co-opt all other forms of governance, as it had done to sustain itself during the civil war. While the

[12] Pendle and Anei (2018) (noting that the patronage network grew weaker as it extended beyond urban centres).

2005 interim constitution (and indeed the 2009 Local Act) gave formal powers to traditional leaders and community chiefs (Leonardi 2013), these legal measures were easily disregarded by an SPLA (Branch and Mampilly 2005). Instead, the distribution of southern revenues via ethno-military networks rather than institutionalized administrative authorities created a heavily dependent periphery within the governance system of South Sudan. Stripped of any capacity to meaningfully collect taxes, and without funding from the centre, local institutions beyond the major towns relied almost entirely on Juba for their existence and communicated those needs through the SPLA. According to the World Bank, most southern counties could meet less than 20 per cent of their budgets from their own tax revenues, while the SPLA stepped in to take local roles of administrating land and cattle markets (Thomas 2015; World Bank 2010).

The result was a reinforcing (positive) feedback loop within the governance system of South Sudan: during the early years of the CPA period, the states' formal ability to generate revenue actually declined, making them less able to develop institutional infrastructure or maintain staff, leading to a further decline in their revenue generation (IMF 2012). Consequently, the formal state structures were only somewhat involved in the distribution of power and resources across South Sudan, more like rocks in a stream dampened by the flows around them but unable to influence the current. Meanwhile, the SPLA absorbed nearly all of the oil revenues, strengthening the ethno-military network that had evolved through the civil war.

However, by maintaining the ethno-military network, southern resources were never channelled into administrative institutions (Lacher 2012). The SPLM fed cash into their personal and community networks, often using government sinecures to ensure the dominance of their own ethnic group in local government. In places like Upper Nile State, salaries for state security services approached 80 per cent of the state budget, while funding for formal administrative structures in those locations hovered close to zero (Lacher 2012). The result was an empty shell of state government at the county and local level. In 2007, 15 government institutions representing 80 per cent of the government's payroll at the time could present no records of their staff (Johnson 2016). By the end of the interim period in 2011, half of the statutory positions within ministries of South Sudan still had not been filled, while the region ranked near or at the bottom of every governance indicator worldwide (Johnson 2016; Mores 2013).

11.3.3 UNMISS in the South Sudanese ecosystem

While the 2011 independence of South Sudan was a major turning point for the world's newest country, the dynamics on the ground actually changed very little. Deeply entrenched ethno-military patronage remained the dominant governance system, even while the South Sudanese government spoke in increasingly liberal,

Western terms about their own leadership of the country. As I briefly describe here, the UN's support to the South Sudanese state, if anything, appeared to bolster some of the more dangerous aspects of the underlying governance system.

The Government of South Sudan's discourse resonated well with UNMISS. For example, the government-led South Sudan Development Plan for 2011–2013 articulated state-building goals in an uncannily similar way to the UN and major donors. Referring to itself as 'the nation's response to core development and state-building challenges', the plan described good governance as a key priority and allocated 25 per cent of the annual budget to building state capacity across the country (Government of the Republic of South Sudan 2011). This, however, is best understood as a form of 'isomorphic mimicry' in which state actors adopt the forms of traditional state structures while actually pursuing different objectives (Larson et al. 2013). By speaking in the same terms as international partners, the government was able to 'tick the boxes' (Snowden 2012: 16) for international donors and secure continued support, while the actual resources and political energy were directed elsewhere. In fact, the government appeared to maintain a 'fake ministry' that dealt with international actors and reported on progress according to the development plan, while the 'real ministry' funnelled resources elsewhere (Larson et al. 2013). This resulted in extraordinary revelations of corruption. In 2012, President Kiir sent an open letter to 75 of his current and former ministers demanding that they return roughly US$4 billion that was 'unaccounted for or, simply put, stolen' (Aleu 2011). But one should not merely think of this as large-scale graft (though it was also that); instead, as I have described above, the 'real ministries' were part of the ethno-military network in South Sudan. So-called 'corruption' was the system of governance persisting and evolving to new inputs.

A good example of this dynamic was UNMISS's support to extension of state authority in the peripheries of the country. UNMISS was mandated to help to build institutional capacities beyond the major urban areas, including by improving the state's rule of law capacities across the country. The mission deployed 900 police to the ten states of South Sudan with a mandate to train the state's security services, dedicating a majority of its civilian resources to capacity-building. Here, the government's development plan aligned almost flawlessly with UNMISS, laying out a decentralization of resources to build state institutions. However, in practice, South Sudanese resources were directed into salaries for SPLA commanders that were supporting their respective communities (South Sudan Ministry of Foreign Affairs 2011). In fact, rather than a distribution of funds across other administrative functions, there was a *rise* in salaries to the SPLA in the immediate post-independence period, alongside cuts to fiscal transfers to other state institutions (de Waal 2014). To the extent they received any resources at all, decentralized administrative structures 'function[ed] above all as patronage instruments', rather than meaningful efforts to establish institutions in the peripheries (Lacher 2012: 349).

There was a mismatch between what UNMISS appeared to be supporting (extension of state authority and increase in formal governance capacities) and reality. In fact, by pouring resources and political legitimacy toward state institutions, UNMISS appeared to reinforce the top-down, centre–periphery dynamic in which the Dinka-dominated SPLA was the primary benefactor. 'UNMISS put its finger on the scales, it only helped the Dinka. That's what capacity development means to us', one South Sudanese expert told me.[13] In speaking to dozens of South Sudanese, I often heard the view that UNMISS's capacity-building work from 2011 to 2013 was directed at a government controlled by President Kiir (a Dinka) and employed in the service of shoring up Dinka interests across South Sudan.[14] Others have similarly noted that external efforts to reform the political structures of South Sudan appeared to result in the 'progressive consolidation of an elite-centred and Dinka-dominated decision-making structure that remains top-down and personality driven' (Podder 2014: 7).

A similar form of isomorphic mimicry took place in the arena of security sector reform (SSR), which was a key objective for UNMISS. The mission planned to help reduce the size of the army by 80,000 troops during the post-independence period, offering training for up to 150,000 demobilized soldiers to return to civilian life (UNMISS 2014). This work aligned with the government's own SSR plan (DFID 2012), which was budgeted at US$1.3 billion (Snowden 2012). Incredibly, UNMISS predicted that the security sector could be reformed extremely quickly; in its 2011–2012 budget, the mission suggested that within three years, resources for SSR were likely to be no longer needed.[15]

On paper, the government made real progress towards the central goals of SSR during its first two years. A Department for International Development (DFID) study found that between 2011 and 2013, indicators of progress included: the government's passage of a draft National Security Plan; a Training Strategy under which the SPLA conducted its own basic military training; a logistics capacity for the army; and an IT training facility (DFID 2012). On the police side, hundreds of trainings for newly recruited police suggested that internal security might shift away from the army to the police, while newly passed legislation on the security sector indicated that South Sudan might be moving in a positive direction.[16] UNMISS regularly reported on its support to these reforms, placing emphasis on their role in building a viable state.[17]

[13] Interview with head of South Sudanese NGO, Juba, 13 December 2018.

[14] Interviews, Juba, 1–15 December 2018.

[15] Budget for the United Nations Mission in South Sudan for the period from 1 July 2011 to 30 June 2012: report of the Secretary-General, A/66/532 (2011), para 14.

[16] 'Rule of Law and Security Institutions Support', United Nations Mission in South Sudan, UNMISS, 1 July 2014.

[17] Report of the United Nations Secretary-General on the situation in South Sudan, S/2012/486 (2012), paras 71–73; Report of the United Nations Secretary-General on the situation in South Sudan, S/2013/140 (2013), para 58. Not all were so positive, see, e.g. Malan and Hunt (2014).

However, this apparent progress towards the stated goals of both UNMISS and the government belied the actual trajectory of the security services in South Sudan, which continued to rely on an ethnically driven patronage system. In fact, instead of shrinking the army in line with established plans, SPLA ranks actually swelled before and immediately following independence (de Waal 2017; Weber 2013). In Unity State, for example, the SPLA conscripted roughly 7000 new recruits following independence (Snowden 2012). Promotion of dozens of new major and brigadier generals added to the already top-heavy structure of the national army at a time when the government was publicly calling for massive reductions in support of its SSR plan (Rands 2012).

By 2013, the World Bank estimated that the SPLA and southern militias accounted for more than 300,000 troops, a near doubling of the figure during the CPA period (World Bank 2013b). The creation of the South Sudan National Police Service offered further evidence that SSR was not resulting in a transformation from the existing system: dramatically underfunded and clearly unable to replace the army as the providers of internal security, the newly-formed police was only really notable for its overwhelmingly Dinka leadership (Snowden 2012). Other evidence, such as the deployment of the SPLA across the entire territory of South Sudan rather than areas of most acute violence, pointed to the inescapable conclusion that the security services remained what they had been for decades: a means to ensure that the centre could generate the loyalty of the periphery.

11.3.4 A systemic explanation

When South Sudan descended into its own civil war in 2013, there was widespread hand wringing about the failure of the state-building project. UN leadership suggested that not enough resources had been given to the new state; donors lamented a lack of coordination amongst efforts; everyone blamed the South Sudanese leadership for corruption and infighting. These explanations offer only a small part of the story. Thinking in systemic terms, however, we can see that governance in South Sudan had come to depend on the SPLA as the conduit for influence from the centre to the periphery. Integration into the SPLA was the way in which Juba addressed potential rifts in its network, meaning that efforts to downsize the army ran against well-established patterns that acted to stabilize the system. Equally, efforts to build independent state institutions across the country threatened to destabilize the highly effective network of relations that depended upon the SPLA to secure rights and resources to various communities. As South Sudan underwent successive shocks to its system—in particular the 2012 oil shut-off—reliance on the SPLA to hold the network together became even more urgent. Austerity was passed on to the formal institutions, not the SPLA network; generals were promoted rather than retired; patterns of purchasing loyalty proved too deep to be overcome by superficial legislation and occasional training regimes (Snowden 2012).

If anything, these dynamics demonstrate that UNMISS's state-building may have bolstered the more dangerous elements of the underlying governance system in South Sudan. The combination of a Juba-focused, legislatively driven attempt to build formal institutions appeared to contribute to what Sukanya Podder has called 'the progressive consolidation of an elite-centred and Dinka-dominated decision-making', and an embedding of the elite's dependence upon the SPLA to maintain its web of control (Podder 2014: 216). In dozens of interviews conducted with South Sudanese—including former government officials and members of civil society—I heard a consistent theme around the topic of national reform and state-building: UN support to the government ran with the grain of patronage, not against it, offering resources and political support that were channelled into the existing network rather than changing how it functioned (Day 2019). 'There was no 'reform' in SSR', one expert told me, 'only more money for Kiir to pay his commanders'.[18]

11.4 Conclusion

This chapter is not meant to offer a comprehensive application of complexity thinking to UN state-building but is instead designed to show the promise of a systemic approach to settings like South Sudan. While many scholars have astutely pointed to the shortcomings of UN-led efforts in fragile settings, these have tended to focus on lack of resources, poor coordination, and isolation from local dynamics. These are all valid criticisms of the UN, but they do not offer a way forward. As the above mini-case study demonstrates, fixing all of these faults would not have solved the South Sudanese challenge. The UN could have had far more resources, could have coordinated flawlessly across donors, and could have had a granular understanding of local conflict dynamics (indeed, many of the UN staff I met did have such an understanding). But none of that would have addressed the reality in South Sudan, the presence of a deeply interconnected, highly adaptive system of governance that stretched across the rebel army, traditional leaders, and powerbrokers in Juba. This system proved capable of adapting to new inputs, able to evolve around its strongest attractors—a resilient network that had sustained the region through decades of war.

[18] Interview with senior member of South Sudanese think tank, Juba, 13 December 2018.

References

Adiebo, K., L. Bandiera, and P. Zacchia (2013). 'Public Expenditures in South Sudan: Are They Delivering?'. World Bank Economic Brief, Issue 2. Washington, DC: World Bank.

Aleu, P. T. (2011). 'South Sudan Ministers Invited to Answer Questions on $2 Billion Missing Grain Scandal'. *Sudan Tribune*, 16 June. https://sudantribune.com/article38819/ (accessed 2 December 2022).

Ali, A. G., I. A. Elbadawi, and A. El-Batahani (2005). 'Sudan's Civil War. Why Has it Prevailed for So Long?'. In P. Collier and N. Sambanis (eds), *Understanding Civil War: Evidence and Analysis, Vol. 1 – Africa*. Washington, DC: World Bank.

Autessere, S. (2010). *The Trouble with the Congo: Local Violence and the Failure of International Peacebuilding*. New York: Cambridge University Press. https://doi.org/10.1017/CBO9780511761034

Ayoub, M. (1996). 'State Making, State Breaking, and State Failure: Explaining the Roots of "Third World" Insecurity'. In L. van de Goor, K. Rupesinghe, and P. Sciarone (eds), *Between Development and Destruction: An Enquiry into the Causes of Conflict in Post-Colonial States*. The Hague: Clingendael. https://doi.org/10.1007/978-1-349-24794-3_4

Barnett, M., and C. Zürcher (2009). 'The Peacebuilder's Contract: How External Statebuilding Reinforces Weak Statehood'. In R. Paris and T. Sisk (eds), *The Dilemmas of Statebuilding: Confronting the Contradictions of Postwar Peace Operations*. London: Routledge Press.

Bayart, J. F. (1993). *The State in Africa: The Politics of the Belly*. London: Longman Press.

Biong, L., and D. Kuol (2019). 'The Federalism-Decentralisation-Peace Nexus in South Sudan'. In L. Biong, D. Kuol, and S. Logan (eds), *The Struggle for South Sudan: Challenges of Security and State Formation*. London: I.B. Tauris. https://doi.org/10.5040/9781788316361.ch-005

Boege, V., A. Brown, K. Clements, and A. Nolan (2008). *On Hybrid Political Orders and Fragile States: State Formation in the Context of Fragility*. Berlin: Berghof Research Center for Constructive Conflict Management.

Bonner, J. T. (1988). *The Evolution of Complexity by Means of Natural Selection*. Princeton, NJ: Princeton University Press.

Boulding, K. (1981). *Evolutionary Economics*. London: Sage.

Boulton, J. (2010). 'Why is Economics Not an Evolutionary Science?'. *Emergence, Complexity and Organisation*, 12(2): 41–69.

Boulton, J. G., P. M. Allen, and C. Bowman (2015). *Embracing Complexity: Strategic Perspectives for an Age of Turbulence*. Oxford: Oxford University Press. https://doi.org/10.1093/acprof:oso/9780199565252.001.0001

Bousquet, A., and S. Curtis (2011). 'Beyond Models and Metaphors: Complexity Theory, Systems Thinking and International Relations'. *Cambridge Review of International Affairs*, 24(1): 43–62. https://doi.org/10.1080/09557571.2011.558054

Branch, A., and Z. C. Mampilly (2005). 'Winning the War, But Losing the Peace? The Dilemma of SPLM/a Civil Administration and the Tasks Ahead'. *Journal of Modern African Studies*, 43(1): 1–20. https://doi.org/10.1017/S0022278X04000588

Brusset, E., C. de Coning, and B, Hughes (eds) (2017). *Complexity Thinking for Peacebuilding Practice and Evaluation*. London: Palgrave Macmillan. https://doi.org/10.1057/978-1-137-60111-7

Byrne, D. (1998). *Complexity Theory and the Social Sciences: An Introduction*. New York: Routledge Press.

Call, C. T. (2008). 'The Fallacy of the "Failed State"'. *Third World Quarterly*, 29(8): 1491–1507. https://doi.org/10.1080/01436590802544207

Chabal, P., and J.-P. Daloz (1999). *Africa Works: Disorder as Political Instrument*. Oxford: James Currey Press.

Chandler, D. (2014). *Resilience: The Governance of Complexity*. Abingdon: Routledge. https://doi.org/10.4324/9781315773810

Checchi, F. et al. (2018). 'South Sudan: Estimates of Crisis-attributable Mortality'. London: London School of Hygiene and Tropical Medicine. https://crises.lshtm.ac.uk/wpcontent/uploads/sites/10/2018/09/LSHTM_mortality_South_Sudan_report.pdf.

Cheng, C. (2018). *Extralegal Groups in Post-Conflict Liberia: How Trade Makes the State*. Oxford: Oxford University Press. https://doi.org/10.1093/oso/9780199673346.001.0001

Cilliers, P. (1998). *Complexity and Postmodernism: Understanding Complex Systems*. London: Routledge.

Coleman, P., R. Vallacher, A. Bartoli, A. Nowak, and L. Bui-Wrzosinska (2011). 'Navigating the Landscape of Conflict: Applications of Dynamical Systems Theory to Addressing Protracted Conflict'. In D. Körppen, N. Ropers, and H. J. Giessmann (eds), *The Non-Linearity of Peace Processes: Theory and Practice of Systemic Conflict Transformation*. Opladen: Verlag Barbara Budrich. https://doi.org/10.2307/j.ctvbkjz66.6

Coleman, P. T., R. R. Vallacher, A. Nowak, and L. Bui-Wrzosinska (2007). 'Intractable Conflict as an Attractor: A Dynamical Systems Approach to Conflict Escalation and Intractability'. *American Behavioral Scientist*, 50(11): 1454–1475. https://doi.org/10.1177/0002764207302463

Day, A. (2019). 'Assessing the Effectiveness of the UN Mission in South Sudan (UNMISS)'. Report 2/2019. Oslo: Norwegian Institute of International Affairs. Available at https://effectivepeaceops.net/unmiss/ (accessed 2 December 2022).

Day, A. (2022). *States of Disorder, Ecosystems of Governance: Complexity Theory Applied to UN Statebuilding in the DRC and South Sudan*. Oxford: Oxford University Press. https://doi.org/10.1093/oso/9780192863898.001.0001

Day, A., S von Billerbeck, O. Tansey, and A Al Maleh (2021). *Peacebuilding and Authoritarianism: The Unintended Consequences of UN Intervention in Post-Conflict Settings*. New York: United Nations University.

de Coning, C. (2016). 'From Peacebuilding to Sustaining Peace: Implications of Complexity for Resilience and Sustainability'. *Resilience*, 4(3): 166–181. https://doi.org/10.1080/21693293.2016.1153773

de Coning, C. (2018). 'Adaptive Peacebuilding'. *International Affairs*, 94(2): 301–317. https://doi.org/10.1093/ia/iix251

de Waal, A. (2014). 'When Kleptocracy Becomes Insolvent: Brute Causes of the Civil War in South Sudan'. *African Affairs*, 113(452): 347–369. https://doi.org/10.1093/afraf/adu028

de Waal, A. (2016). *The Real Politics of the Horn of Africa: Money, War and the Business of Power*. London: Polity Press.

de Waal, A. (2017). Peace and the Security Sector in Sudan, 2002–11'. *African Security Review*, 26(2): 180–198. https://doi.org/10.1080/10246029.2017.1297582

DFID (2012). 'Annual Review Security Sector Development & Defence Transformation'. Report 200329, Development Tracker, DFID 16–27 July 2012. London: Department for International Development.

Dowden, R. (2014). 'South Sudan's Leaders Have Learnt Nothing from 50 Years of Independence in Africa'. *African Arguments*, 22 January. https://africanarguments.org/2014/01/south-sudans-leaders-have-learnt-nothing-from-50-years-of-independence-in-africa-by-richard-dowden/ (accessed 2 December 2022).

Doyle, M., and N. Sambanis (2006). *Making War and Building Peace.* Princeton, NJ: Princeton University Press. https://doi.org/10.1515/9781400837694

Fukuyama, F. (2004). *State-building: Governance and World Order in the 21st Century.* Ithaca, NY: Cornell University Press.

Geyer, R., and S. Rihani (2010). *Complexity and Public Policy: A New Approach to 21st Century Politics, Policy and Society.* New York: Routledge.

Government of the Republic of South Sudan (2011). *South Sudan Development Plan (2011–2013): Realising Freedom, Justice, Equality, Prosperity and Peace for All.* Juba: Government of the Republic of South Sudan.

Green, D. (2013). *From Poverty to Power: How Active Citizens and Effective States Can Change the World.* Oxfam e-books. https://policy-practice.oxfam.org/resources/from-poverty-to-power-2nd-edition-how-active-citizens-and-effective-states-can-249411/ (accessed 2 December 2022).

Hagmann, T., and D. Péclard (2010). 'Negotiating Statehood: Dynamics of Power and Domination in Africa'. *Development and Change*, 41(4): 539–562. https://doi.org/10.1111/j.1467-7660.2010.01656.x

Hall, R. B., and T.J. Bierstecker (eds) (2009). *The Emergence of Private Authority in Global Governance.* Cambridge: Cambridge University Press.

Herbst, J. (2000). *States and Power in Africa.* Princeton, NJ: Princeton University Press.

Hunt, C. T. (2015). *UN Peace Operations and International Policing: Negotiating Complexity, Assessing Impact and Learning to Learn.* London: Routledge. https://doi.org/10.4324/9781315813486

Hunt, C. T. (2017). 'Beyond the Binaries: Towards a Relational Approach to Peacebuilding'. *Global Change, Peace & Security*, 29(3): 209–227. https://doi.org/10.1080/14781158.2017.1360855

IMF (2012). 'Sudan: Selected Issues Paper'. IMF Country Report 12/299. Washington, DC: International Monetary Fund. https://www.imf.org/external/pubs/ft/scr/2012/cr12299.pdf (accessed 2 December 2022).

Jackson, P. (2003). 'Warlords as Alternative Forms of Governance'. *Small Wars and Insurgencies*, 14(2): 131–150. https://doi.org/10.1080/09592310412331300716

Jervis, R. (1997). *System Effects: Complexity in Political and Social Life.* Princeton, NJ: Princeton University Press. https://doi.org/10.1515/9781400822409

Johnson, H. F. (2016). *South Sudan: The Untold Story from Independence to Civil War.* London: L.B. Tauris.

Kavalski, E. (2015). *World Politics at the Edge of Chaos: Reflections on Complexity and Global Life.* Albany, NY: State University of New York.

Kleinfeld, R. (2015). 'Improving Development Aid Design and Implementation: Plan for Sailboats Not Trains'. Carnegie Endowment for International Peace. https://carnegieendowment.org/files/Brief-Kleinfeld_Development_Aid_Design.pdf (accessed 2 December 2022).

Körppen, D. (2011). 'Space Beyond the Liberal Peacebuilding Consensus – A Systemic Perspective'. In D. Körppen, N. Ropers, and H. J. Giessmann (eds), *The Non-Linearity of Peace Processes: Theory and Practice of Systemic Conflict Transformation.* Opladen: Verlag Barbara Budrich. https://doi.org/10.2307/j.ctvbkjz66

Lacher, W. (2012). 'South Sudan: International State-Building and Its Limits'. SWP Research Paper. Berlin: German Institute for International and Security Affairs. https://www.swp-berlin.org/fileadmin/contents/products/research_papers/2012_RP04_lac.pdf (accessed 2 December 2022)

Larson, G., P. Ajak, and L. Pritchett (2013). 'South Sudan's Capability Trap: Building a State with Disruptive Information'. HKS Working Paper RWP13-041. https://papers.ssrn.com/sol3/papers.cfm?abstract_id=2366894 (accessed 2 December 2022)

Leonardi, C. (2013). *Dealing with Government in South Sudan: Histories of Chiefship, Community and State.* Cambridge: Boydell & Brwer.

Leonardsson, H. and G. Rudd (2015). 'The "Local Turn" in Peacebuilding: A Literature Review of Effective and Emancipatory Local Peacebuilding'. *Third World Quarterly*, 36(5): 825–839. https://doi.org/10.1080/01436597.2015.1029905

LeRiche, M. (2018). 'Conflict Governance: The SPLA, Factionalism, and Peacemaking'. In S.E. Roach and D. K. Hudson (eds), *The Challenges of Governance in South Sudan.* London: Routledge. https://doi.org/10.4324/9781315158464-2

Lund, C. (2006). 'Twilight Institutions: An Introduction'. *Development and Change*, 37(4): 673–684. https://doi.org/10.1111/j.1467-7660.2006.00496.x

Lyotard, J.-F. (1984). *The Postmodern Condition: A Report on the Knowledge (Theory and History) of Literature.* Minneapolis, MN: University of Minnesota Press.

Mac Ginty, R., and O. P. Richmond (2013). 'The Local Turn in Peace Building: A Critical Agenda for Peace'. *Third World Quarterly*, 34(5): 763–783. https://doi.org/10.1080/01436597.2013.800750

Malan, M., and C. T. Hunt (2014). 'Between a Rock and a Hard Place: The UN and the Protection of Civilians in South Sudan'. ISS Paper 275. Pretoria: Institute for Security Studies.

Mampilly, Z. C. (2011). *Rebel Rulers: Insurgent Governance and Civilian Life during War.* Ithaca, NY: Cornell University Press.

Meadows, D. (1999). 'Leverage Points: Places to Intervene in a System'. Hartland, VT: The Sustainability Institute. http://donellameadows.org/archives/leverage-points-places-to-intervene-in-a-system/ (accessed 2 December 2022).

Moe, L. W. and M.-M. Müller (2017). *Reconfiguring Intervention: Complexity, Resilience and the 'Local Turn' in Counterinsurgent Warfare.* London: Palgrave MacMillan. https://doi.org/10.1057/978-1-137-58877-7

Mores, M. (2013). 'Overview of Corruption and Anti-corruption in South Sudan'. Transparency International. https://www.transparency.org/files/content/corruptionqas/371_Overview_of_corruption_and_anti-corruption_in_South_Sudan.pdf (accessed 2 December 2022).

Paris, R. (2002). 'International Peacebuilding and the "Mission Civilisatrice"'. *Review of International Studies*, 28(4): 637–656. https://doi.org/10.1017/S026021050200637X

Mitchell, M. (2009). *Complexity: A Guided Tour.* Oxford: Oxford University Press.

Morçöl G., (2012). *A Complexity Theory for Public Policy.* New York: Routledge.

Overseas Development Institute (2010). 'Planning and Budgeting in South Sudan: Starting from Scratch'. Overseas Development Institute Briefing Paper 65. https://cdn.odi.org/media/documents/6093.pdf (accessed 2 December 2022).

Paris, R. (2004). *At War's End: Building Peace after Civil Conflict.* Cambridge: Cambridge University Press.

Paris, R., and T. Sisk (eds) (2009). *The Dilemmas of Statebuilding: Confronting the Contradictions of Postwar Peace Operations.* London: Routledge Press. https://doi.org/10.4324/9780203884836

Patey, L. (2010). 'Crude Days Ahead? OIL and the Resource Curse in Sudan'. *African Affairs*, 109(437): 617–636. https://doi.org/10.1093/afraf/adq043

Pendle, N. and C. M. Anei (2018). 'Wartime Trade and the Reshaping of Power in South Sudan: Learning from the Market of Mayel Rual'. South Sudan Customary Authorities Project. Nairobi: Rift Valley Institute.

Pinaud, C. (2014). 'South Sudan: Civil War, Predation and the Making of a Military Aristocracy'. *African Affairs*, 113(451): 192–211. https://doi.org/10.1093/afraf/adu019

Podder, S. (2014). 'Mainstreaming the Non-state in Bottom-up State-building: Linkages Between Rebel Governance and Post-conflict Legitimacy'. *Conflict, Security & Development*, 14(2): 213–243. https://doi.org/10.1080/14678802.2014.889878

Raeymaekers, T., K. Menkhaus, and K. Vlassenroot (2008). 'State and Non-State Regulation in African Protracted Crises: Governance Without Government?'. *Afrika Focus*, 21(2). https://doi.org/10.21825/af.v21i2.5045

Ramalingam, B. (2013). *Aid on the Edge of Chaos: Rethinking International Cooperation in a Complex World*. Oxford: Oxford University Press.

Ramalingham, B., and H. Jones (2008). 'Exploring the Science of Complexity: Ideas and Implications for Development and Humanitarian Efforts'. ODI Working Paper 285 (2008). London: Overseas Development Institute.

Rands, R. (2012). 'In Need of Review: SPLA Transformation in 2006–10 and Beyond'. Small Arms Survey Working Paper 23. Geneva: Small Arms Survey.

Reno, W. (1998). *Warlord Politics and African States*. Boulder, CO: Lynne Rienner Publishers.

Rhodes, M. L., J. Murphy, J. Muir, and J. A. Murray (2011). *Public Management and Complexity Theory: Richer Decision-making in Public Services*. London: Routledge.

Richardson, K. A. (2006). 'Complex Systems Thinking and Its Implications for Policy Analysis'. In G. Morçöl (ed.), *Handbook on Decisionmaking*. Pennsylvania, PA: Penn State University Press.

Richardson, K. A., G. Mathieson, and P. Cilliers (2009). 'Complexity Thinking and Military Operational Analysis'. In K. A. Richardson (ed.), *Knots, Lace and Tartan: Making Sense of Complex Human Systems in Military Operations Research*. Litchfield Park, AZ: ISE Publishing.

Risse, T. (2013). *Governance Without a State: Policies and Politics in Areas of Limited Statehood*. New York: Columbia University Press.

Room, G. (2010). *Complexity, Institutions and Public Policy: Agile Decision-making in a Turbulent World*. Cheltenham: Edward Elgar.

Rosenou, J. N., and E.-O. Czempiel (2010). *Governance without Government: Order and Change in World Politics*. Cambridge: Cambridge University Press.

Rotberg, R. I. (2003). *When States Fail: Causes and Consequences*. Princeton, NJ: Princeton University Press. https://doi.org/10.1515/9781400835799

Salva Kiir (2011). 'Martyr's Day Speech'. https://pachodo.org/latest-news-articles/pachodo-english-articles/36363-full-transcript-of-dr-gen-salva-kiir-mayardit-s-mas sage-on-martyr-s-day (accessed 2 December 2022).

Shankleman, J. (2011). 'Oil and State-building in South Sudan'. Special Report 282. Washington, DC: United States Institute of Peace.

Snowden, J. A. (2012). 'Work in Progress: Security Force Development in South Sudan through February 2012'. HSBA Working Paper 27. Geneva: Small Arms Survey.

South Sudan Ministry of Foreign Affairs (2011). *Multi Annual Strategic Plan South Sudan 2012–2015*. Available at: http://extwprlegs1.fao.org/docs/pdf/ssd148386.pdf (accessed 2 December 2022).

Splinter, D., and L. Wustehube (2011). 'Discovering Hidden Dynamics: Applying Systemic Constellation Work to Ethnopolitical Conflict'. In D. Körppen, N. Ropers, and H.J. Giessmann, (eds), *The Non-linearity of Peace Processes: Theory and Practice of Systemic Conflict Transformation*. Opladen: Verlag Barbara Budrich. https://doi.org/10.2307/j.ctvbkjz66.10

Stewart, P. (2011). *Weak Links: Fragile States, Global Threats and International Security.* Oxford: Oxford University Press.

Sudan Tribune (2012). 'Paulino Matip Nhial Nyaak, General'. [Online article – no longer available]. Paris: Sudan Tribune.

Thomas, E. (2015) *South Sudan: A Slow Liberation.* London: Bloomsbury Publishing. https://doi.org/10.5040/9781350222717

United Nations (2011). 'Statement of UN Secretary-General Ban Ki-Moon on the Independence of the Republic of South Sudan'. https://news.un.org/en/story/2011/07/381102 (accessed 2 December 2022).

United States Institute of Peace (n.d.) 'Comprehensive Peace Agreement, Wealth Sharing Agreement, articles 4.5 and 4.3'. Washington, DC: USIP.

UNMISS (2014). 'Disarmament Demobilization and Reintegration'. United Nations Mission in South Sudan, 17 July 2014. http://unmiss.unmissions.org/Default.aspx?tabid=4055&language=en-US (accessed 2 December 2022).

van der Ploeg, F., and A. J. Venables (20011). 'Harnessing Windfall Revenues: Optimal Policies for Resource Rich Developing Economies'. *The Economic Journal*, 121(551): 1–30. https://doi.org/10.1111/j.1468-0297.2010.02411.x

Veblen, T. (1898). 'Why is Economics Not an Evolutionary Science'. *The Quarterly Journal of Economics*, 12(4): 373–397. https://doi.org/10.2307/1882952

Vimalarajah, L. (2011). 'Thinking Peace: Revising Analysis and Intervention in Sri Lanka'. In D. Körppen, N. Ropers, and H. J. Giessmann, (eds), *The Non-linearity of Peace Processes: Theory and Practice of Systemic Conflict Transformation.* Opladen: Verlag Barbara Budrich. https://doi.org/10.2307/j.ctvbkjz66.11

Vlassenroot, K., and T. Raeymaekers (2004). *Conflict and Social Transformation in Eastern DR Congo.* Ghent: Academia Press Scientific Publishers.

Von Billerbeck, S., and O. Tansey (2019). 'Enabling Autocracy? Peacebuilding and Post-conflict Authoritariansm in the Democratic Republic of Congo'. *European Journal of International Relations*, 25(3): 1–29. https://doi.org/10.1177/1354066118819724

Walraet, A. (2008). 'Governance, Violence and the Struggle for Economic Regulation in South Sudan: The Case of Budi County (Eastern Equatoria)'. *Afrika Focus*, 21(2). https://doi.org/10.21825/af.v21i2.5044

Weber, A. (2013). 'Transformation Backlog in South Sudan: Security Sector Reforms Stall in the Face of Growing Autocracy'. SWP Comments 20. Berlin: German Institute for International and Security Affairs.

White House (2011). 'Statement of President Barack Obama Recognition of the Republic of South Sudan'. https://obamawhitehouse.archives.gov/the-press-office/2011/07/09/statement-president-barack-obama-recognition-republic-south-sudan (accessed 2 December 2022).

Woodward, S. L. (2017). *The Ideology of Failed States: Why Intervention Fails.* Cambridge: Cambridge University Press.

Woolcock, M. (2009). 'Towards a Plurality of Methods in Project Evaluation: a Contextualised Approach to Understanding Impact Trajectories and Efficacy'. *Journal of Development Effectiveness*, 1(1): 1–14. https://doi.org/10.1080/19439340902727719

World Bank (2010). 'Southern Sudan: Enabling the State: Estimating the non-Oil Revenue Potential of State and Local Governments'. Report 54795. Washington, DC: World Bank.

World Bank (2013a). 'South Sudan Overview'. www.worldbank.org/en/country/southsudan/overview (accessed 2 December 2022).

World Bank (2013b). 'International Development Association and International Finance Corporation: South Sudan – Interim Strategy Note (FY2013–2014)'. Report 74767-SS. Washington, DC: World Bank.

12
Revisiting community-driven reconstruction in fragile states

Cyrus Samii

12.1 Introduction

This chapter argues that amid debates about their institutional impact and how they relate to imperatives for localization, 'community-driven' reconstruction strategies stand as a highly appealing option for infrastructural reconstruction and service delivery in war-affected and fragile states. Community-driven reconstruction (CDR) is a strategy for reconstruction and institution building in civil war-affected and otherwise 'fragile' states (Cliffe et al. 2003; King and Samii 2014; Samii et al. 2011). CDR is an application of the more general 'community-driven development' (CDD) concept (Mansuri and Rao 2012; Wong and Guggenheim 2018). CDD is motivated by a logic of decentralization: local actors know best about local priorities. CDR is further motivated by the need to rehabilitate or even invent institutions for reconstruction and service delivery, given that state institutions have been weakened by civil war (De Regt et al. 2013; King and Samii 2014). CDD and CDR programmes are 'community-driven' in that they have village-level or neighbourhood-level councils define reconstruction priorities and co-finance reconstruction or development projects. CDD has been a widely applied development strategy in fragile- and non-fragile-state contexts alike. The current literature strikes a rather pessimistic tone regarding its institution-building effects (Casey 2018). This chapter argues that such pessimism is unwarranted.

I review evidence to show that CDR interventions have demonstrated an impressive level of efficiency. CDR interventions have generated institutional networks that are durable and adaptable for achieving goals of both infrastructure reconstruction and sustainable service delivery. CDR does so in a manner that is consistent with imperatives for contributing to local institution building and handing over reconstruction programmes to locally accountable institutions. For those who have maintained interest and faith in CDR, the accomplishments will not come as a surprise. But for the many who have been drawn to scepticism about CDR by findings about the limited impact on collective action capacity, embezzlement, or winning 'hearts and minds', this chapter will hopefully revise

Cyrus Samii, *Revisiting community-driven reconstruction in fragile states*. In: *Institutional Legacies of Violent Conflict*. Edited by: Patricia Justino, Oxford University Press. © United Nations University World Institute for Development Economics Research (UNU-WIDER) (2026). DOI: 10.1093/9780197904077.003.0012

the prevailing wisdom that informs such scepticism. I propose a logic of 'decentralized oversight' to conceptualize the value of CDR strategies in fragile states as the basis of a multipurpose institutional network. When contrasted with strategies that are either more centralized or that rely on more conventional governance frameworks, CDR appears as a striking example of institutional engineering done right.

This chapter draws on general arguments as well as original field research in Afghanistan (prior to the Taliban takeover in 2021). I will argue that in fragile states, which are marked by weak state institutions, CDR has been a demonstrably effective approach for both short-term infrastructure reconstruction and for building out accountable institutional networks for sustained service delivery. My emphasis on CDR is also informed by the current strategic shift in major donors' aid policy towards localization and institution building as a goal for aid. The value of CDR, both as an emergency measure and an institution-building measure, is consistent with this localization agenda (Glennie et al. 2012). Considering CDR as part of the localization process also allows us to expand our thinking of institution building beyond the current focus on centralized state capacity and towards strategies that empower citizens at the local level.

The chapter will proceed in three parts. First, I will briefly state a key problem that I see CDR as helping to address in fragile states—–namely, what I call the handover imperative for post-conflict reconstruction aid. This problem statement is informed by the current localization discourse, although it also draws on general accountability ideals and domestic political realities within states recovering from conflict.

Second, I will briefly review the current wisdom about CDR's institutional effects, which is pessimistic about its potential for institutional development or stabilization. In doing so, I will raise some questions about the appropriateness of the standards used in recent evaluations to gauge CDR's institutional impact.

I will then turn to the logic of decentralized oversight, both for one-off infrastructure projects and, as a more novel contribution, for sustained service provision. I will explain the appeal of decentralized oversight as a reconstruction and service delivery strategy in fragile states. I will then use the logic to reinterpret the successes of CDR, focusing on three pieces of evidence: (1) efficient project delivery with little indication of local-level corruption in contexts marked by high levels of corruption in central state agencies; (2) durability of CDR institutions in contexts that have seen the collapse of other governance institutions; and (3) adaptability for overseeing ongoing administration of basic services (namely, in the case of Afghanistan, primary education).

To conclude, I will draw a connection to the localization agenda, which is the dominant theme in current foreign aid discourse. I will discuss how the localization agenda currently places too much emphasis on highly centralized state-building and overlooks the potential for decentralized strategies such as the one that was tested in Afghanistan.

12.2 Aid handover dilemmas and CDR

One of the problems motivating the current analysis is the dilemma in fragile states that foreign aid agencies face in working through host-country institutions. On the one hand, concern for immediate basic needs motivates supporting those who can operate expediently and can efficiently translate funds into services. By definition, 'fragile-state' contexts are those in which central government institutional capacities are limited in their ability to mobilize or transmit resources so as to serve basic needs throughout the territory. State capacity is simply lacking, due to physical destruction, displacement, or ongoing contestation over fundamental political questions. International non-governmental organizations (NGOs) have developed specialized capacities to operate in such difficult settings and deliver high-quality basic services. Relative to domestic state counterparts, NGOs can rely on a combination of advantages in terms of resources and mission-motivated personnel. NGO services are often high quality (for an example relevant to the discussion below, see Burde and Linden 2013), although there are, of course, cases of corruption and exploitative practices.

On the other hand, a number of factors motivate an imperative to hand over service provision to institutions operating under the host country's government. A long line of social science literature has put this in terms of the 'Samaritan's dilemma', whereby offers of external assistance can induce dependency in ways that leave citizens in both aid-recipient and aid-donor societies worse off (Gibson et al. 2005). The current 'localization' discourse that predominates among donors echoes such sentiments. In an agenda-setting piece for the aid community, Glennie et al. (2012) summarize the logic of channelling development and reconstruction support through host-country institutions to facilitate 'learning by doing'. In the longer run, the hope is that this promotes locally governed and locally accountable institutions' capacity to operate autonomously. One may trade off short-term efficiency in the hope of generating longer-term domestic capacity.

Such analyses still leave open the question as to why such transfer to localized institutions is desirable. Here, we must appeal to norms of accountability and sovereignty. Nussbaum (2019) develops a normative framework that supports the idea of localization under the logic of accountability. Assuming a right to have basic needs provided for, one must consider those claiming those rights and those who stand to service the associated needs. Each step that obscures the ability of those claiming rights from holding the service providers accountable (through, for example, directing their replacement or changes in priorities) deviates from the ideal. These normative arguments are buttressed by empirical observations that the accountability pressures that do operate on the international aid sector in fragile states are often misaligned with or oblivious to the interests and concerns of citizens in aid-recipient countries (Autesserre 2010; Campbell 2018).

The question remains of *how* to navigate the dilemma: are there ways to soften the trade-offs between efficiently servicing material needs versus contributing to accountability and local institution building? Reconstruction strategies based on CDR have been motivated by the premise that 'local communities possess the core skills, incentives, and unity to implement a large range of projects provided that they are given the resources and a management support system' (Cliffe et al. 2003). Ostensibly, the handover and localization challenges can be overcome by recognizing and bringing in contributions that communities might offer. These contributions complement and significantly expand the capacities that central ministries offer. CDR and CDD strategies give respect to intended beneficiaries' autonomy in establishing priorities (Tanasoca and Dryzek 2021). Decentralization and devolution to communities may help to unwind the legacies of authoritarian and exclusionary centralization that perpetuate conflict. On this basis, decentralization can lessen the risk that external donors inadvertently favour present-day political incumbents at the expense of others and at the expense of pluralism more generally (Ferguson 1994; Murtazashvili and Murtazashvili 2020).

12.3 Assessing current pessimism on the institutional impact of CDR in fragile states

The proposition that CDR could expediently service material needs, contribute to institution building, and operate under local accountability has been the subject of a rigorous research programme. King and Samii (2014) and Casey (2018) offer a thorough review of a set of randomized controlled trials (RCTs) that sought to test the material and institutional impacts of CDR interventions. Such RCTs have been undertaken in Liberia (Fearon et al. 2015), Sierra Leone (Casey et al. 2012), the Democratic Republic of the Congo (DRC) (Humphreys et al. 2012, 2019), Afghanistan (Beath et al. 2013), and Sudan (Avdeenko and Gilligan 2015). Across the studies, and as summarized by King and Samii (2014) and Casey (2018), CDR interventions are shown quite generally as delivering effectively on immediate material reconstruction needs. An exception is the DRC intervention (Humphreys et al. 2012), for which reasons might have to do with the relatively low levels of resources applied per community (Casey 2018). Authors tend to take these immediate material contributions to be an unremarkable, almost mechanical contribution of CDR. These material accomplishments deserve much more attention, and in Section 5.1 I explain why.

The research programme offers a more pessimistic take when it comes to institution building. The studies have emphasized two types of outcomes when studying institutional impact. The first type of outcome is bottom-up collective action capacity, which the researchers have operationalized in terms of community member contributions to collective initiatives that require individuals to look beyond their immediate private interests. The studies use measures that include economic games (Avdeenko and Gilligan 2015; Fearon et al. 2015) as well as structured community activities such as submitting applications for future rounds of social fund grants (Casey et al. 2012). The second type of outcome is social inclusiveness, and in particular inclusion of historically marginalized groups such as women or minorities in resource allocation decisions. Researchers have operationalized this outcome through specially designed programmes to distribute centrally provided material goods such as food or agricultural production inputs within communities (Beath et al. 2013; Casey et al. 2012; Humphreys et al. 2012). As detailed in King and Samii (2014) and Casey (2018), as a whole, the studies find null or weak effects on these two types of institutional outcomes. The conclusion is that CDR is not an effective strategy for post-conflict *institution building*.

The emphasis on these outcomes was motivated, in part, by the idea that CDR can contribute to social cohesion, perhaps reducing the potential for conflict (Cliffe et al. 2003; King and Samii 2014). Given the null effects on institutional outcomes, the studies do not suggest optimism regarding CDR's contribution to cohesion or stability. The SIGAR (2018) review of the CDR programme in Afghanistan, the National Solidarity Programme (NSP), comes to a similar conclusion: despite the effective administration of infrastructure projects, NSP was limited in its contribution to stability, defined in terms of the Afghan government's ability to exercise authority and ward off threats from the Taliban.

I do not think these results should be taken as the final word on the institution-building impact. Preliminarily, I note that Anderson and Magruder (2022) demonstrate that Casey et al.'s conclusions regarding null institutional impact in Sierra Leone are sensitive to alternative specifications. (Specifically, they show that it is likely that null would have been rejected if the study considered a panel data specification and a split sample approach to determine whether to use it.) But my concerns are not based on questioning the methodological merits of the findings. Rather, I want to argue that on empirical and conceptual grounds, the type of institution building that these studies emphasized may have been inappropriate. Mine is a different take than, for example, King (2013) or Bennett and D'Onofrio (2015), who propose revisions to CDR programme design under the assumption of wanting to improve collective action capacity and social cohesion.

First, it is not clear that there were problems of cohesion and bottom-up collective action in these settings. As Casey (2018: 157–158) notes in her review of the RCTs listed above,

> [L]evels of social capital appear to be fairly high in these communities already . . . Thus, it seems plausible that there is already sufficient social capital to facilitate collective action within the community. While these studies find no evidence that CDD enhances measures of such localized social capital, like trust and social networks, this may be a moot point.

An intervention can only contribute to addressing a problem when that problem is itself present. The processes and cleavages that animated the violent conflicts in the countries in question were not driven to any meaningful extent by a lack of within-community social cohesion.

The second point is that it is not clear that bottom-up collective action capacity or social inclusion are reasonable standards for judging the success of CDR. In a war-torn context, is it even a reasonable goal to try to put communities into a position to solve their own problems without facilitation that comes from the top down? Mansuri and Rao (2012), in their evaluation of more development-oriented CDD programmes in much more institutionally stable contexts, proposed a 'sandwich model' through which community councils could operate as partners for a central government, rather than setting things up for communities to fend for themselves. While within-community social inclusion is a worthy goal, it is a goal that runs orthogonally to issues of effective service provision or even the cleavages animating the conflicts in the respective countries. In a sense, my conclusion is similar to that of Avdeenko and Gilligan (2015): social cohesion can be a sensible goal, but in so far as it is, one might consider programmes that try to address it directly (as discussed in, for example, King et al. 2010) rather than hoping for it to emerge as a byproduct of activities that are really intended to address more immediate, material concerns.

I appreciate that each of these studies developed its analysis plans and outcome definitions as part of a deliberative process that included a variety of stakeholders. Through such deliberations, and in consulting project documentation justifying the CDR programmes themselves (King and Samii 2014), these studies decided to focus on collective action capacity and inclusiveness as the way to test institutional impact. So we cannot entirely blame the study authors for leading us to pessimistic conclusions that I am trying to argue are unwarranted. I would chalk this up to excessive ambition on the part of those drafting project justification documents for major agencies such as the World Bank and to researchers wanting to define outcomes in a way that spoke directly to such ambition. The unfortunate consequence is an overly pessimistic take on what CDR has, in fact, accomplished.

In light of these empirical and conceptual arguments, my goal is to restore attention to and appreciation of CDR's accomplishments as a 'decentralized oversight' mechanism. In this regard, I view it as a remarkably successful example of institutional design. The following sections elaborate.

12.4 The logic of decentralized oversight

Decentralization is often motivated on the basis of an informational rationale. If one wants to decide how to allocate resources over a set of localities for infrastructure, it makes sense to give individuals within those localities control over the process, given that they will tend to know the needs and priorities of their respective locality. A canonical reference is Oates (1972), who argues for decentralizing to the furthest extent that still allows for effectively managing externalities or reaping economies of scale (Casey 2018).

CDR interventions also invoke another logic, what I call decentralized oversight. Yes, CDR project selection was granted to local councils, on the basis of the classical information rationale (local communities know best). However, project selection is only half of the challenge; the other half is implementation. Implementation of CDR projects themselves is often put under the oversight authority of the local councils. Local councils are answerable to their community members, creating bottom-up accountability pressures. This is distinct from traditional implementation bureaucracy, in which accountability is primarily from the top-down, starting at the ministry and then linking downward through provincial and then district agents. Such decentralized oversight helps to overcome a problem that is particular to fragile states: limited state capacity to monitor implementation over this top-down chain of command and, perhaps due to problems of transport or communication infrastructure, high costs of such monitoring.

Regardless of whether the motivation for decentralization is based on the logic of local information or oversight (or both, as seems to be the case for CDR interventions), scholars point to possible hazards of decentralization, with emphasis given to risks of elite capture or embezzlement. Particularly in situations where local elites are put in charge of using funds sent out from the centre, neither officials at the centre nor citizens within localities may be able to monitor leaders' use of funds well. This leaves local elites with space within which to redirect funds in ways that could make local citizens worse off than if central authorities were fully in control (Bardhan and Mookherjee 2005, 2006; Gadenne and Singhal 2014).

Given such potential risks, a large recent literature has examined strategies of decentralized 'social accountability' to mitigate risks of elite capture and allow for decentralization processes to deliver. We can view the social accountability literature as contributing to our understanding of how decentralized oversight can be made to work. While early work on social accountability was pessimistic (e.g. Olken 2007), a wave of research in recent years has pointed to strategies that can work. Fox (2015) offers a review and synthesis, arguing that the findings point to the role of both increasing local community members' access to performance information and, crucially, investing in community-level mobilization. The latter helps to ensure that citizens can take action to hold elites and service providers accountable.

Social accountability is not the only mechanism through which decentralized oversight can work. Indeed, decentralized control over resource allocation can be invulnerable to capture if those who are put in charge do so on the basis of their own intrinsic interest in the local public good being provided. Any redirection of funds away from community member interests by elites would be attributable to interests being misaligned (Bardhan and Mookherjee 2005). That said, such misalignment is not always given. Interest in basic infrastructure or services such as primary education may be widely shared by local elites and citizens alike (Galiani et al. 2008). Moreover, local deliberation can help to increase such alignment between those in positions of authority and citizens who are the ostensible beneficiaries (Barr et al. 2012).

CDD has long put these principles into practice (Mansuri and Rao 2012), and CDR, as an adaption of CDD, maintains these principles as well (Cliffe et al. 2003). A central feature of CDR is the investment in using collective processes, such as elections, to nominate local authorities to oversee projects, strengthening local-level collective oversight institutions, and giving such institutions access to information regarding project performance. This is in stark contrast to traditional, top-down state-building, in which agents are appointed from the capital and downward through the provincial and district levels. CDR projects tend to be focused on satisfying basic needs (basic infrastructure, health, and education), on which leaders' and local citizens' preferences are mostly aligned, even if there may be some scope for disagreement over precisely how resources should be distributed. CDR programmes include deliberation processes for selecting projects, with the potential to align interests. As such, CDR would seem to abide by best practices identified from the theoretical and empirical literature to establish local oversight and bottom-up accountability for managing risks from decentralization.

12.5 Evidence on CDR and decentralized oversight

In this section, I review three types of evidence to support the claim that CDR is a demonstrably effective decentralized oversight mechanism that has succeeded where more traditional state-building approaches have failed. I review evidence on the efficiency of infrastructure delivery, durability of CDR institutions, and repurposing of CDR institutions from project selection and oversight for infrastructural reconstruction to basic service delivery (in this case, primary education). The analysis draws on existing reviews as well as fieldwork in Afghanistan conducted by a team led by Dana Burde, Joel Middleton, and myself.

12.5.1 Evidence point 1: efficient delivery

As introduced above, King and Samii (2014) and Casey (2018) offer detailed reviews of the evidence from a set of high-quality RCTs evaluating the effects of CDR interventions in fragile-state contexts—specifically, Afghanistan, DRC, Liberia, Sierra Leone, and Sudan. As reported by Casey (2018), evidence from the short-term impact evaluations in Afghanistan and Sierra Leone clearly supports the conclusion that CDR can deliver infrastructure, although the evidence from DRC and Liberia does not. Longer-term follow-up in Sierra Leone by Casey et al. (2021) found that infrastructure was better maintained in CDR communities than in places where infrastructure projects were implemented through more traditional, centralized approaches. Contrary to findings from the short-term evaluation, a longer-term follow-up by Mvukiyehe and Van der Windt (2020) found that certain measures of infrastructure (school and hospital quality), which reflected areas of investment under the CDR programme, were in better shape eight years after programme initiation. That said, the longer-term effects in DRC appear to be smaller than those found in Sierra Leone Casey et al. (2021).

The conclusion from these evaluations is that CDR can deliver infrastructure, and the Afghanistan and Sierra Leone projects appear to have done so especially well. These two programmes were distinct from the programmes in DRC and Liberia in at least two important ways King and Samii (2014: table 2). First, in Afghanistan and Sierra Leone, overall programme implementation was administered through national ministries with the assistance of NGOs for implementation, whereas in DRC and Liberia, the CDR programmes were more wholly NGO-managed and implemented. This is actually good news for the idea of using CDR as part of a localized institution-building strategy. Second, the per capita investments in Afghanistan and Sierra Leone were about double those in DRC and Liberia. Thus, from the Afghanistan and Sierra Leone studies, one finds that decentralized oversight under CDR delivered infrastructure as part of a well-financed, ministry-managed process. This, again, is good news for those advocating localization: ministry management was relatively more successful in cases where allocations were larger.

Studies reporting on the impact of CDR interventions tend not to dwell on this evidence about project delivery. Infrastructure delivery and project completion are sometimes taken to be mechanical outcomes of the programme (although the lack of indication of short-run effects in Liberia and DRC would be a puzzle). The emphasis in the evaluations of these programmes quickly turns to questions of measurable effects on welfare and the other institutional effects. I think this gives too little weight to what was accomplished, particularly in challenging post-war settings. It is not a given that the processes would result in successful project implementation and material improvement of infrastructure. The case of Kenya's Arid Lands Resource Management Project (ALRMP), discussed by Ensminger (2017) and to which I return below, is an example of CDR failing to deliver even on these 'mechanical' benefits. That these programmes, in Afghanistan and Sierra Leone especially, were able to yield meaningful infrastructural improvements, despite general institutional weakness and through national institutions, is remarkable.

The findings on project delivery raise a second question about efficiency. As discussed above, decentralization, and the transfer of authority that it involves, generates opportunities for local authorities to misappropriate resources or duplication of administrative efforts. Even if this does not amount to wholesale graft and projects being delivered, such misappropriation would increase costs and undermine efficiency.

Among the studies that are the focus here, the Afghanistan NSP project offers the most complete evidence regarding the incidence of embezzlement or other misappropriation of resources. At least from this evidence, it seems that CDR provides an institutional network for the delivery of projects and services that can also operate with minimal misappropriation or redirection of funds. NSP was subject to audit reporting by the United States Special Inspector General for Afghanistan Reconstruction (SIGAR) from 2003 through 2017 (SIGAR 2018). A 2011 audit (SIGAR 2011) evaluated the application of over US$1.5 billion in donor contributions, of which 72 per cent were allocated to the block grants, 19 per cent to facilitation, and 9 per cent to administration. Costs that were identified as potentially ineligible or unsupported amount to only a tiny fraction (less than 1 per cent) of the US$1.5 billion total, and only one instance of outright fraud was identified (involving a US$2.8 million transaction that was misdirected due to a hawala dealer). The SIGAR report pointed specifically to 'community participatory monitoring' and 'local ownership' as mechanisms through which the use of funds was held in check. Complementing the SIGAR reports is Beath et al.'s (2018) study of a food aid delivery programme in which community leaders were enlisted to coordinate village-level delivery. The question that they sought to answer was whether NSP institutions helped to reduce embezzlement and improve targeting to the most vulnerable. They found that in NSP communities, indicators of embezzlement were slightly lower, although these effects were not statistically significant (Beath et al. 2018: table 5). But this was off of a baseline of very little apparent embezzlement overall (less than 10 per cent of localities appeared to show any indication that leaders redirected food aid). In so far as embezzlement has been a concern during the internationally aided reconstruction process in Afghanistan, the roots appear to be more in higher levels of state authority than at the level of local communities. By empowering local communities and circumventing more centralized channels for implementing projects, NSP helped to bypass the sites in which redirection of funds was most likely.

The relatively clean implementation of NSP was certainly not a given: the context in Afghanistan was challenging, and CDR programmes had not always succeeded in the past. SIGAR (2018) notes that NSP managed to apply 72 per cent of funds to projects and 28 per cent to administrative costs, whereas other stabilization initiatives in Afghanistan during this same period applied up to 75 per cent of funds to administration. The USAID-sponsored District Delivery Program, launched in 2010, had similar local-level reconstruction and development goals as NSP but sought to do so by increasing the capacity of district-level governments and channelling resources through them. In this way, the District Delivery Program was a more traditional top-down state-building programme. It was cancelled in 2013, with less than 6 per cent of project funds disbursed, due to concerns about corruption (although such concerns were questioned in subsequent reports) and bureaucratic inefficiency.

It is not a given that things would work out this way for a CDR programme. It is important to acknowledge progress in the design of CDR in reducing the scope for misappropriation. Ensminger (2017) contrasts the poorly performing ALRMP CDR programme in Kenya, implemented from 1996 to 2010, to Indonesia's Kecematan Development Programme (KDP), implemented from 2007 to 2015 and among the world's largest CDR programmes. A World Bank forensic audit report found the vast majority of transactions associated with ALRMP CDR implementation to be suspicious or fraudulent, resulting in the Kenyan government having to pay back substantial sums to the World Bank. Ensminger's own fieldwork revealed that funds were often appropriated by local elites for their private benefit rather than being applied to projects with broad benefits. By contrast, in the KDP, only a small minority of transactions or funds appear to have been subject to fraud or misappropriation. Beyond social accountability and aligned interests of local authorities, Ensminger points to other CDR design features that can help to minimize misappropriation. These include embedding the programme in a ministry or top-level agency with a culture of performance, steering clear of known 'centres of corruption' in government, being careful about how discretion is given in selecting projects or beneficiaries, and establishing mechanisms for transparency and monitoring.

In the design of the NSP in Afghanistan, one could see these lessons being put into effect. The World Bank has long invested in a learning network through its series of reports on CDR strategies (Mansuri and Rao 2012; Wong and Guggenheim 2018). Advisers to the Indonesian government, including Scott Guggenheim and others connected to the World Bank, assisted in the design and operation of the KDP and also contributed to the design of NSP and related programmes in Afghanistan (Banerjee 2019; Cliffe et al. 2003). And, as noted throughout this chapter, CDR programmes have been subject to rigorous evaluation and testing even in the most challenging of contexts.

My sense is that the suite of available evaluations does too little to celebrate these accomplishments in efficient project delivery. The contexts in which the CDR-based reconstruction initiatives were operating represent, after all, among the very most difficult institutional environments imaginable. To have arrived at an institutional intervention to service infrastructural needs, in situations where other interventions have failed, is an important win for institutional engineering.

12.5.2 Evidence point 2: durability of the institutions

Interventions are of limited value when they fail to establish a beneficial legacy, and rather serve only to generate value during periods of intensive facilitation and application of resources. What can we say about the durable impact of CDR-based reconstruction? Three recent studies have looked into durable impacts of CDR, and the results suggest that CDR may do more for institution building than the first wave of RCT studies conveyed. These recent studies include long-term follow-ups by Casey et al. (2021) in Sierra Leone and Mvukiyehe and Van der Windt (2020) in the DRC, as well as a descriptive study led by Dana Burde, Joel Middleton, and myself in Afghanistan (Burde et al. 2017). The Sierra Leone and DRC studies show that certain benefits last, although they do not substantially revise the received wisdom about institutional effects. The Afghanistan study approaches the question differently, looking at whether the CDR institutions in Afghanistan exhibit a high degree of formalization after the completion of facilitated projects and whether they might be adaptable to provide oversight on new tasks, such as basic service provision.

We begin by considering the results of long-term follow-up studies in Sierra Leone and DRC, for which the Sierra Leone study showed promising results while the DRC study, in a manner that was similar to the short-term follow-up, did not. In Sierra Leone, Casey et al. (2021) evaluated long-term outcomes in 2016–2018, approximately a decade after the period of facilitated CDR activities in 2005–2009. Village development committees remained operational in 60 per cent of localities that participated in the treatment group that received intensive facilitation in 2005–2009, as compared to 43 per cent in control areas. This is indicative of facilitation investments translating into meaningful long-term differences in institutional capacity. The study also found that the substantial gains in access to local infrastructure and other public goods persisted into the long run. When considering these persistent effects in comparative perspective, they note that the CDR-based infrastructure investments exhibited more durability than a comparable European bilateral infrastructure programme in Kenya. As Casey et al. (2021: 13) put it, such durability is 'consistent with CDD [CDR] advocates' claims about the value of local participation in aligning investments with demand and thereby bolstering utilization and maintenance over time'. Finally, contrary to the null effects on institutional capacity-building found in the short-term follow-up study, the long-term follow-up shows that the CDR intervention produced a small positive improvement in average long-run institutional quality at the local level. The long-term follow-up also showed a modest improvement in the local response actions to the 2014 Ebola crisis in Sierra Leone. Mvukiyehe and Van der Windt's (2020) long-term assessment in DRC showed fewer long-term gains. They document that the infrastructure and upgrades built under the programme endured, but these did not translate into meaningful effects on the quality of services or welfare. It is worth recalling that Humphreys et al. (2019) found little in terms of short-run impact as well. One sense is that this programme was hampered by the relatively small size of its per-community allocations (as described above) or other limitations of the intervention.

Research in Afghanistan by Burde et al. (2017) looks at the sustainability question differently. Rather than looking at the long-term impacts of the CDR intervention, we focused on the descriptive questions of whether the community councils established under NSP (1) could demonstrate their formal institutionalization after ministry-facilitated NSP activities concluded in 2015, and (2) had the capacity to adapt by going beyond overseeing occasional infrastructure projects to overseeing sustained service provision. The specific goal of the analysis was to assess whether the NSP-generated CDR institutions could provide a reliable institutional network for sustaining primary schools in remote communities in Afghanistan after the international NGOs that launched the schools withdrew. To do this, we carried out capacity assessments of councils in 179 villages in late 2016. With regard to the first question (the institutional formality of CDR councils), in all communities, representatives from the councils could be summoned upon request. In 80 per cent of communities, the councils were able to furnish documentation and describe activities during the two years prior to the assessment, which was the tail end of the last period of ministry-facilitated projects. Their activity was concentrated on infrastructure projects, which were the central focus of the NSP. Consistent with NSP's goals for inclusion and accountability, 63 per cent of councils could present their procurement documents, and 85 per cent were able to display records from social audits. As noted in Burde et al. (2017: 23), the social audits were a formal requirement under NSP for administering grants, and the high rate of demonstrable compliance with such formal requirements indicated well-functioning institutions in a setting where examples to the contrary had been unfortunately common (SIGAR 2018).

In addressing the second question of adaptability to a new role in overseeing service provision, it is important to note that our assessment work was carried out in collaboration with the Afghan presidency in their 2016 launch of the Citizen's Charter National Priority Programme (CCNPP). The Citizen's Charter was issued by Afghan President Ashraf Ghani and established that 'access to clean drinking water, quality education in government schools, and delivery of Basic Package of Health Services' were basic rights for all Afghan citizens (GIRoA 2016). To operationalize this commitment, the CCNPP sought explicitly to employ the institutional network created under NSP for administering basic services. Our research was designed to inform how that strategy might be carried out. While NSP operated exclusively under the Ministry of Rural Reconstruction and Development, the CCNPP was proposed as a multi-ministry initiative for basic service provision in rural and urban areas of the country. Moreover, the NSP community councils were augmented to enhance their capacity for overseeing service provision. For primary education, this included the creation of an Education Subcommittee. It also meant linking the Ministry of Education's (MoE) existing regional School Management Shuras with the community councils.

Burde et al. (2017) employed state-of-the-art assessment methods from the literature on firm and public sector managerial capacity (Bloom and Van Reenen 2007; Bloom et al. 2016; Lemos and Scur 2016) to assess the capacities of the community councils and the supporting institutions (Educational Subcommittees and School Management Shuras) to oversee the administration of village primary schools. The assessment used a rubric to define capacity levels in various domains as 'low', 'moderate', 'adequate', and 'high'. Our assessment showed that the NSP councils were positioned as decision-making and problem-solving bodies in their respective communities, with the potential to oversee the Education Shuras and School Management Shuras, which were more specifically trained to manage education and linked to the formal MoE system. On average across the 179 villages, the community councils scored lower than the Education Shuras and School Management Shuras on seven school management practices, achieving 'adequate' competency only on the problem-solving capacity. The Education Shuras and School Management Shuras achieved at least 'adequate' competency in five of seven school management practices. This reflects differences in each institution's originally intended purpose: recall that the councils were created through NSP to oversee grants targeted primarily at infrastructure projects, rather than to serve as school management bodies. The capacity assessment suggested that CDR institutions offered a network of decision-making institutions that could oversee sustained service delivery, but that their role would have to come amid a network of more specialized bodies (the Education Shuras and School Management Shuras) with ongoing support from above by relevant ministries.

To conclude, evidence on the long-term impacts of CDR from Sierra Leone, and to some extent DRC, shows that gains in institutional capacity endure, even if the gains themselves are not of tremendous magnitude. The evidence from Afghanistan shows that the CDR institutions organized through the NSP were formalized, enduring, and potentially adaptable to new tasks. To realize this promise, central governments and their partners would have to commit to continued capacity-building and facilitation, along the lines of Mansuri and Rao's (2012) 'sandwich' model. But the very fact that the NSP generated a ready-to-employ institutional network should be counted as an institution-building success.

12.5.3 Evidence point 3: successful adaption to new oversight tasks

I now turn to the last evidence point, which concerns the performance of CDR in tackling problems beyond the oversight of infrastructure projects. The long-term evidence from Casey et al. (2021) and Mvukiyehe and Van der Windt (2020) demonstrated that infrastructure upkeep can be better in places receiving investments in CDR council oversight. This already points to the potential for CDR to service ongoing needs. In this section, I look at evidence from Afghanistan that speaks even more directly to CDR institutions' potential as networks to oversee sustained service delivery, and in particular primary education.

I focus on research led by Burde, Middleton, and myself to study the potential for CDR institutions to serve as a network of decentralized service administration in Afghanistan from 2016 to 2019. The research sought to test whether the CDR institutional network could provide a foundation for sustainably administering basic services. This served as an empirical test of the concept informing the CCNPP, described in the previous section. The study was conducted as an RCT, with encouraging findings. The details are covered in Burde et al. (2022). Here, I highlight results relevant to this chapter's broader argument—namely, that CDR represents a durable and adaptable institutional investment.

Before turning to the results of the Burde et al. (2022) study, it is worth noting that our RCT was not the first time CDR institutions in Afghanistan have been utilized for purposes other than project delivery under NSP. USAID's Local Governance and Community Development Program and the Alternative Development Program worked with the CDR councils to target basic services, economic growth, and infrastructure development programmes in rural areas. Like NSP, these programmes successfully executed many projects, but they accomplished little in establishing a strong link to local and national levels of government (as per discussions with USAID officials, reported in Burde et al. 2017). These projects were also forced to close down due to the worsening security situation in Afghanistan.

The Burde et al. (2022) RCT built on the capacity assessment findings summarized in the previous section. Community councils were recognized in their leadership and decision-making roles, and, along with their Education Subcommittees, were given capacity refreshment training to prepare them to oversee the application of funds transmitted directly to them by the MoE to sustain the operations of a primary school in their village.

Along with the Citizens Charter, the context of the study was a recognition that the handover of international NGO programmes to the Afghan government administration had not fared well in recent years. Throughout the reconstruction period following the 2001 US-led invasion, international NGOs established and ran programmes to service basic needs in education and health. When NGO programme cycles ended, such services were handed over to Afghan ministries, in line with the localization and handover imperatives discussed in the opening section of this chapter. In a survey that we undertook in 2014 (reported in Burde et al. 2017), we documented troubling problems with such handover. We studied 209 villages that hosted community-based primary schools that had been established as part of an international NGO-run programme from 2004 to 2011. A previous study by Burde and Linden (2013) used an RCT to estimate impacts from the 2007–2008 programme cycle, showing that these NGO-run schools produced tremendous gains in children's educational access and learning. But in 2014, three years after the end of the NGO programming and ostensible handover to the national ministry to sustain these children's access to school, only 48 villages had schools that either continued to operate within their village or to operate within a reasonable daily walking distance (2 km or less, based on the results from Burde and Linden 2013). This 77 per cent 'failure' rate in handover prompted a need to test new strategies for sustaining service provision after NGO programme cycles ended.

Thus, in line with the Citizen's Charter idea of utilizing the NSP-initiated councils, and motivated by the imperative to find a better approach to handing over NGO-run schools to a sustainable local administration model, Burde et al. (2022) used an RCT to study how well the NSP-created community councils would fare in overseeing primary school administration. The treatment condition in this study was a model through which community councils were put in charge of school administration in their respective villages. Using the school management capacity assessments described above as a guide, councils and their Education Subcommittees received training on primary school administration. The councils and their Education Subcommittees liaised directly with local MoE institutions (including the School Management Shuras and district offices) to request and receive materials necessary for running the school. Payments to cover teacher salaries and materials were wired directly to community council leaders, and the councils were responsible for issuing teacher salaries and procurement of materials for the school. The control condition was ongoing NGO administration of the village-level schools. The treatment–control comparison reflected the true choice at hand: given the failure of the status quo 'handover' policy, the real question was whether there existed an alternative handover model that could sustain a level of quality comparable to NGO administration. If not, then ethically it would seem necessary to maintain NGO administration until a workable handover model could be figured out.

Given the nature of the comparison, Burde et al. (2022) use a 'non-inferiority equivalency design' to evaluate whether the novel community council-based model could meet a performance benchmark established by the NGOs. Thus, rather than testing whether the community councils performed significantly better than the NGOs, the test was whether the community councils' performance was within a range that was deemed to be roughly equivalent to NGO performance. This analysis allows for the community councils to do worse than the NGOs, but not too much worse. An explicit inferiority threshold was established based on a cost comparison between community council administration and NGO administration; what Burde et al. (2022) test is whether the community council's performance was significantly better than what one would achieve was that performance degraded with an elasticity (in terms of dollars spent) of 1. Performance was assessed after one academic year based on children's attendance and test scores and household assessments of the quality of the school; the study also assessed whether there were any indications of bias or misuse of funds.

The findings were highly encouraging for giving councils authority to oversee school administration. Per-village costs under the community council model were only 53 per cent of the costs under NGO administration. We used this cost ratio to establish a minimally acceptable performance benchmark, and the community model over-performed relative to the benchmark concerning student attendance (only a 2 percentage point difference), test scores (only a 0.016 standard deviation difference), and household satisfaction (only a 0.013 standard deviation difference). There was no indication of biases based on ethnicity or gender, and in terms of the use of funds, we found that teachers were actually paid more regularly, and therefore expressed even higher satisfaction under community council administration as compared to NGO administration.

The Burde et al.'s (2022) study offers rigorous evidence of the lasting value of NSP's institutional network for service delivery. This approach served as the basis of the broader Citizen's Charter initiative, including in the domains of health and water/sanitation. After the Taliban takeover in 2021, the NSP network continued to function as a service delivery and oversight mechanism through the newly registered non-profit, the Community-Driven Development Organization (CDDO), which sought to institutionalize the capacities developed to support the NSP programme.[1] This attests to the robustness of the NSP institutional network despite the political upheavals.

The findings from Afghanistan, along with the findings regarding infrastructure maintenance in Sierra Leone and DRC, are indicative of how institutional investments through CDR can produce a robust and sustainable network for longer-term oversight of service delivery. At least in the Afghanistan case, such performance in service delivery depended on working with relevant line ministries—contrary to the types of local collective action tasks that had been used previously to evaluate the institutional effects of CDR, the idea is not to transfer responsibility to CDR councils to fend for themselves in pursuing development goals. This would seem to be a realistic but meaningful way (given the failure of other decentralization initiatives, discussed in the previous section) to recognize the lasting impact of CDR.

12.6 Conclusion

This chapter has sought to revise the current take on the institutional impacts of CDR. A rigorous research programme has tended to undersell the successes of CDR in establishing a localized network for administering reconstruction aid, and instead focused on weak effects on bottom-up collective action capacity and social

[1] This is based on discussions with CDDO leadership and partners working with them as of January 2023.

inclusiveness. I argue that such conclusions are unduly pessimistic about the value of CDR as a strategy for addressing both short-term material needs and longer-term institution-building needs. It is not clear whether issues of collective action capacity were themselves problems, nor is it clear that enabling communities to 'fend for themselves' is a reasonable goal in post-conflict reconstruction. Social inclusiveness is a worthy goal, but it is quite distinct from the need to develop institutions for material reconstruction and service provision. Rather, I argue that CDR can be viewed as a remarkable success, given that it served as the basis of *efficient* delivery of infrastructural reconstruction, the resulting institutional network has been *durable*, and the institutional network has been *adaptable* to the servicing of new needs, such as overseeing ongoing administration of basic services such as primary education. In reviewing detailed evidence from Afghanistan, these achievements stand in contrast to challenges experienced with other strategies that have tried to run through more centralized government channels.

CDR has already helped to manage several dilemmas in reconstruction assistance and in transitioning from more 'emergency' modes of NGO-led implementation to approaches that are more directly subject to local accountability. The successes of CDR bring to the forefront considerations of respecting the autonomy of local communities. CDR is an approach that uses local empowerment as a complement to centralized state capacity in achieving reconstruction and development goals. Further policy research could build on the lessons from the Afghanistan research described above, looking into ways of making use of the institutional networks created by CDR. The localization agenda emphasizes using aid to contribute to institution building in aid-recipient countries (Glennie et al. 2012). Those working on this agenda should take a lesson from this success, and consider how to balance between building centralized state capacities versus empowering local communities.

References

Anderson, M.L., and J. Magruder (2022). 'Highly Powered Analysis Plans'. Working Paper 29843. Cambridge, MA: National Bureau of Economic Research. https://doi.org/10.3386/w29843

Autesserre, S. (2010). *The Trouble with the Congo: Local Violence and the Failure of International Peacebuilding*. Cambridge: Cambridge University Press. https://doi.org/10.1017/CBO9780511761034

Avdeenko, A., and M.J. Gilligan (2015). 'International Interventions to Build Social Capital: Evidence from a Field Experiment in Sudan'. *American Political Science Review*, 109(3): 427–449. https://doi.org/10.1017/S0003055415000210

Banerjee, N. (2019). 'Community-Driven Development as a Mechanism for Realizing Global Development Goals: The National Solidarity Programme and Citizens' Charter Afghanistan Program'. In F. Baqie, N. Banerjee, and S. Yaya (eds), *Better Spending for Localizing Global Sustainable Development Goals*. London: Routledge. https://doi.org/10.4324/9780429322327-9

Bardhan, P., and D. Mookherjee (2005). 'Decentralizing Antipoverty Program Delivery in Developing Countries'. *Journal of Public Economics*, 89: 675–704. https://doi.org/10.1016/j.jpubeco.2003.01.001

Bardhan, P., and D. Mookherjee (2006). 'Decentralisation and Accountability in Infrastructure Delivery in Developing Countries'. *The Economic Journal*, 116: 101–127. https://doi.org/10.1111/j.1468-0297.2006.01049.x

Barr, A., F. Mugisha, P. Serneels, and A. Zeitlin (2012). 'Information and Collective Action in Community-Based Monitoring of Schools: Field and Lab Experimental Evidence from Uganda'. Working Paper. Available at: https://www.dartmouth.edu/neudc2012/docs/paper_277.pdf (accessed 23 January 2023).

Beath, A., F. Christia, and R. Enikolopov (2013). 'Randomized Impact Evaluation of Afghanistan's National Solidarity Programme'. Report. Washington, DC: World Bank.

Beath, A., F. Christia, and R. Enikolopov (2018). 'Do Elected Councils Improve Governance? Experimental Evidence on Local Institutions in Afghanistan'. CEPR Discussion Paper 13053. London: CEPR.

Bennett, S., and A. D'Onofrio (2015). 'Community-Driven Development in Conflict-Affected Contexts: Revisiting Concepts, Functions and Fundamentals'. *Stability: International Journal of Security and Development*, 4(1): art. 19. https://doi.org/10.5334/sta.ff

Bloom, N., and J. Van Reenen (2007). 'Measuring and Explaining Management Practices Across Firms and Countries'. *The Quarterly Journal of Economics*, 122(4): 1351–1408. https://doi.org/10.1162/qjec.2007.122.4.1351

Bloom, N., R. Lemos, R. Sadun, D. Scur, and J. Van Reenen (2016). 'International Data on Measuring Management Practices'. *American Economic Review*, 106(5): 152–156. https://doi.org/10.1257/aer.p20161058

Burde, D., and L.L. Linden (2013). 'Bringing Education to Afghan Girls: A Randomized Controlled Trial of Village-Based Schools'. *American Economic Journal: Applied Economics*, 5(3): 27–40. https://doi.org/10.1257/app.5.3.27

Burde, D., M. Lisiecki, J. Middleton, O. Okhidoi, M.A. Sadiqi, C. Sage, and C. Samii (2017). 'The Assessment of Learning Outcomes and Social Effects of Community-Based Education: A Randomized Field Experiment in Afghanistan, Phase Two Baseline Report'.

Burde, D., J. Middleton, R. Rahnama, and C. Samii (2022). 'Can Communities Take Charge? A Randomized Controlled Trial on Sustaining Schools in Afghanistan'. Report. New York: New York University.

Campbell, S.P. (2018). *Global Governance and Local Peace: Accountability and Performance in International Peacebuilding*. Cambridge: Cambridge University Press. https://doi.org/10.1017/9781108290630

Casey, K. (2018). 'Radical Decentralization: Does Community-Driven Development Work?'. *Annual Review of Economics*, 10: 139–163. https://doi.org/10.1146/annurev-economics-080217-053339

Casey, K., R. Glennerster, and E. Miguel (2012). 'Reshaping Institutions: Evidence on Aid Impacts Using a Preanalysis Plan'. *The Quarterly Journal of Economics*, 127(4): 1755–1812. https://doi.org/10.1093/qje/qje027

Casey, K., R. Glennerster, E. Miguel, and M.J. Voors (2021). 'Long Run Effects of Aid: Forecasts and Evidence from Sierra Leone'. Working Paper 29079. Cambridge, MA: National Bureau of Economic Research. https://doi.org/10.3386/w29079

Cliffe, S., S. Guggenheim, and M. Kostner (2003). 'Community-Driven Reconstruction as an Instrument in War-To-Peace Transitions'. CPR Working Paper 7. Washington, DC: World Bank.

De Regt, J., S. Majumdar, and J. Singh (2013). 'Designing Community-Driven Development Operations in Fragile and Conflict-Affected Situations: Lessons from a Stocktaking'. Working Paper 83022. Washington, DC: World Bank.

Ensminger, J. (2017). 'Corruption in Community-Driven Development. A Kenyan Case Study with Insights from Indonesia'. *Chr. Michelsen Institute: U4 Issue* 2017: 9.

Fearon, J.D., M. Humphreys, and J.M. Weinstein (2015). 'How Does Development Assistance Affect Collective Action Capacity? Results from a Field Experiment in Post-Conflict Liberia'. *American Political Science Review*, 109(3): 450–469. https://doi.org/10.1017/S0003055415000283

Ferguson, J. (1994). *The Anti-Politics Machine: "Development," Depoliticization, and Bureaucratic Power in Lesotho*. Minneapolis, MN: University of Minnesota Press.

Fox, J.A. (2015). 'Social Accountability: What Does the Evidence Really Say?'. *World Development*, 72: 346–361. https://doi.org/10.1016/j.worlddev.2015.03.011

Gadenne, L., and M. Singhal (2014). 'Decentralization in Developing Economies'. *Annual Reviews of Economics*, 6(1): 581–604. https://doi.org/10.1146/annurev-economics-080213-040833

Galiani, S., P. Gertler, and E. Schargrodsky (2008). 'School Decentralization: Helping the Good Get Better, But Leaving the Poor Behind'. *Journal of Public Economics*, 92: 2106–2120. https://doi.org/10.1016/j.jpubeco.2008.05.004

Gibson, C.C., K. Andersson, E. Ostrom, and S. Shivakumar (2005). *The Samaritan's Dilemma: The Political Economy of Development Aid*. Oxford: Oxford University Press. https://doi.org/10.1093/0199278857.001.0001

GIRoA (2016). *Citizens' Charter National Priority Programme*. Kabul: Government of the Islamic Republic of Afghanistan (GIRoA).

Glennie, J., A. Ali, M. King, A. McKechnie, and G. Rabinowitz (2012). 'Localising Aid: Can Using Local Actors Strengthen Them?' Working Paper 352. London: Overseas Development Institute.

Humphreys, M., R.S. de la Sierra, and P. Van Der Windt (2012). 'Social and Economic Impacts of Tuungane: Final Report on the Effects of a Community Driven Reconstruction Program in Eastern Democratic Republic of Congo'. Report. New York: Columbia University.

Humphreys, M., R.S. de la Sierra, and P. Van der Windt (2019). 'Exporting Democratic Practices: Evidence from a Village Governance Intervention in Eastern Congo'. *Journal of Development Economics*, 140: 279–301. https://doi.org/10.1016/j.jdeveco.2019.03.011

King, E. (2013). 'A Critical Review of Community-Driven Development Programmes in Conflict-Affected Contexts'. Report. London: DFID/International Rescue Committee.

King, E., and C. Samii (2014). 'Fast-Track Institution Building in Conflict-Affected Countries? Insights from Recent Field Experiments'. *World Development*, 64: 740–754. https://doi.org/10.1016/j.worlddev.2014.06.030

King, E., C. Samii, and B. Snilstveit (2010). 'Interventions to Promote Social Cohesion in Sub-Saharan Africa'. *Journal of Development Effectiveness*, 2(3): 336–370. https://doi.org/10.1080/17449057.2010.504552

Lemos, R., and D. Scur (2016). 'Developing Management: An Expanded Evaluation Tool for Developing Countries'. Working Paper London 16/007. London: London School of Economics, Centre for Economic Performance. https://doi.org/10.35489/BSG-RISE-WP_2016/007

Mansuri, G., and V. Rao (2012). 'Localizing Development: Does Participation Work?'. Policy Research Report. Washington, DC: World Bank. https://doi.org/10.1596/978-0-8213-8256-1

Murtazashvili, J., and I. Murtazashvili (2020). 'Bottom-Up State-Building'. In S. Haeffele and V.H. Storr (eds), *Bottom-up Responses to Crisis*. New York: Springer.

Mvukiyehe, E., and P. Van der Windt (2020). 'Assessing the Longer Term Impact of Community-Driven Development Programs: Evidence from a Field Experiment in the Democratic Republic of Congo'. Policy Research Working Paper 9140. Washington, DC: World Bank. https://doi.org/10.1596/1813-9450-9140

Nussbaum, M.C. (2019). *The Cosmopolitan Tradition*. Cambridge, MA: Harvard University Press. https://doi.org/10.2307/j.ctv24w65jk

Oates, W. (1972). *Fiscal Federalism*. New York: Harcourt Brace Jovanovich.

Olken, B.A. (2007). 'Monitoring Corruption: Evidence from a Field Experiment in Indonesia'. *Journal of Political Economy*, 115(2): 200–249. https://doi.org/10.1086/517935

Samii, C., A. Brown, and M. Kulma (2011). 'Evaluating Stabilization Interventions'. Working Paper. London: International Initiative for Impact Evaluation.

SIGAR (2011). *Afghanistan's National Solidarity Program Has Reached Thousands of Afghan Communities, but Faces Challenges that Could Limit Outcomes*. Washington, DC: Office of the Special Inspector General for Afghanistan Reconstruction (SIGAR).

SIGAR (2018). *Stabilization: Lessons from the U.S. Experience in Afghanistan*. Washington, DC: Office of the Special Inspector General for Afghanistan Reconstruction (SIGAR).

Tanasoca, A., and J.S. Dryzek (2021). 'Democratic Altruism'. *International Theory*, 13(2): 205–230. https://doi.org/10.1017/S1752971920000342

Wong, S., and S. Guggenheim (2018). 'Community-Driven Development: Myths and Realities'. Policy Research Working Paper 8435. Washington, DC: World Bank. https://doi.org/10.1596/1813-9450-8435

13
Final remarks
Prospects for state-building in post-conflict countries

Patricia Justino

13.1 Overview and core themes

This volume has explored how the institutional dynamics that emerge during violent conflicts profoundly shape post-conflict trajectories of state-building, governance, and development. The chapters collectively provide a nuanced understanding of the dual-edged nature of these legacies. While some wartime institutions and governance arrangements create opportunities for stability and resilience, others perpetuate cycles of violence, mistrust, and institutional fragility. This concluding chapter distils the key themes of the book, presents an overarching synthesis of its policy and theoretical implications, and suggests pathways for future research.

Armed conflict constitutes one of the most significant catalysts of social, political, and institutional transformation within societies, leaving long-lasting effects that influence a country's trajectory toward peace and development (Arjona 2016; Arjona et al. 2024; Justino 2009, 2012; Justino and Stojetz 2018). Many of the violent conflicts witnessed today—from Sudan and DRC to Gaza and Ukraine—are rooted in, or are continuations of, disputes that began decades earlier. Violent conflicts cause unmeasurable destruction, but also lead to profound forms of institutional transformation as new political and social orders emerge, pockets of resistance arise, power hierarchies are reimagined, and identities take on new meanings. Violent conflicts may dismantle pre-existing institutions, but also give rise to new structures of authority, collective identities, and forms of economic and political organization. These wartime arrangements can have lasting effects, some of which are overlooked in efforts by the international community supporting state-building frameworks in the aftermath of war. However, if we do not recognize the complexities of such legacies, we risk at best missing opportunities to build lasting peace and at worst channelling financial and human resources towards interventions that unintendedly reinforce patterns of violence. This volume represents a collaborative effort to shed new light on how and why violent

Patricia Justino, *Final remarks*. In: *Institutional Legacies of Violent Conflict*. Edited by: Patricia Justino, Oxford University Press. © United Nations University World Institute for Development Economics Research (UNU-WIDER) (2026). DOI: 10.1093/9780197904077.003.0013

conflicts persist, how and why their legacies endure across time, and what can be done to support state-building efforts in societies emerging out of war.

The volume's central argument is that the legacies of wartime governance are neither wholly destructive nor entirely constructive but represent a spectrum of outcomes contingent on specific contexts. Across the chapters, three interrelated themes emerge around: (i) the role of local institutions; (ii) governance adaptability; and (iii) the interplay between local and national dynamics.

13.1.1 Role of local institutions

A central theme emerging across this volume is the critical role played by local institutions in shaping governance during conflict and in the post-conflict recovery phase. As several chapters demonstrate, local institutions are not peripheral to these processes. Rather, they are often the primary arenas where power is contested, negotiated, and reconstituted. In contexts of state fragility or collapse, local institutions, whether formal or informal, frequently become co-opted or reshaped into *de facto* governing structures by armed groups. They become the mechanisms whereby armed groups mediate access to resources, provide security, and deliver basic services. They can also act as sources of civic resistance and rebellion.

Gafaro, Ibáñez, and Justino examine the case of Colombia, where the strength of local governance institutions significantly conditioned the strategies of armed groups. Where local governments were relatively effective and legitimate, armed actors were more likely to pursue collaborative or embedded forms of governance. Conversely, in areas where state presence was weak or contested, armed groups sought to replace local institutions altogether, imposing coercive governance strategies and seeking to capture community loyalty through a mix of violence and service provision. Similarly, Steele and Weintraub show how rebel groups selectively engage with local governance structures in ways that aim to legitimize their authority and facilitate civilian compliance, including the use of community assemblies and traditional justice mechanisms. Cyrus Samii brings a post-conflict lens to this discussion, offering a reassessment of community-driven reconstruction (CDR) programs. He argues that CDR mechanisms, by vesting authority in local councils and leveraging decentralized oversight, can not only deliver infrastructure efficiently but also foster durable and adaptable local governance networks. Contrary to earlier scepticism about their institution-building effects, Samii highlights how CDR institutions have proven more resilient and less prone to corruption than many centralized efforts, especially in contexts like Afghanistan. These institutions endure even amid severe state breakdown and, crucially, have shown capacity to repurpose themselves for new service delivery needs.

However, this volume also cautions against idealizing local institutions, and some chapters illustrate the fragility and ambivalence of localized governance. Bakke and Rickard emphasize how wartime legacies can distort trust and undermine post-war local governance. Where local institutions were co-opted by violent actors or aligned with particular ethnic or political factions, rebuilding trust in their impartiality and legitimacy proved exceptionally difficult. Roxana Gutierrez-Romero, focusing on Mexico, shows how the war on drugs entrenched networks of corruption within local police and municipal governments. Rather than serving as bulwarks against violence, these local institutions became complicit in its reproduction, often incentivized by illicit economies and political opportunism.

Taken together, these findings underscore how local institutions are shaped by their wartime experiences, pre-existing legitimacy, relationships with armed actors, and the institutional design of post-war interventions. A recurring insight is that conflict does not simply destroy institutions—it transforms them. Wartime governance often gives rise to new institutional configurations that persist well into peace. These legacies can be enabling or obstructive, depending on the context and how post-war policies engage with them. By shifting the analytical focus from destruction to institutional transformation, the chapters in this volume emphasize how conflict reorders governance from below. Recognizing the foundational role of local institutions—and critically assessing their strengths and vulnerabilities—is essential for designing peacebuilding strategies that are both context-sensitive and sustainable.

13.1.2 Governance adaptability

Several chapters highlight the adaptability of wartime institutions to external shocks, such as the COVID pandemic or post-conflict political transitions. These institutions, initially formed for survival or domination, often evolve into complex governance systems capable of responding to contemporary challenges. However, this adaptability does not always equate to inclusivity or long-term stability, and the same institutions can foster resilience in some contexts while perpetuating fragility in others. Marta Fulan explores how pre-existing rebel governance structures adapted rapidly to the COVID pandemic. Drawing on cases where armed groups had already developed bureaucratic capacity, taxation systems, and public health services during wartime, the chapter shows that these groups were able to swiftly implement lockdowns, distribute aid, and communicate health directives. These actions were not only strategic—intended to assert control or gain legitimacy—but also indicative of the institutional evolution that occurs under conflict. Wartime governance, originally rooted in survival and coercion, often morphs into complex systems of rule that can respond dynamically to crises. Similarly, Sarah Zuckerman Daly highlights how successor parties to armed groups or ethnic militias often continue to influence politics long after the guns fall silent. In post-ethnic war contexts, wartime institutions shape voting behaviour, identity formation, and political allegiance. Former belligerents and their political offshoots learn to navigate formal democratic processes, often by rebranding their appeals, forming cross-ethnic coalitions, or leveraging their wartime legitimacy. Yet, as Daly notes, this evolution is not inherently progressive or stabilizing. In some cases, these institutions perpetuate exclusive ethno-political agendas, entrenching identity cleavages and undermining inclusive governance. As Adam Day emphasizes, governance in conflict-affected settings is best understood as a complex ecosystem, where actors—state, non-state, and hybrid—interact within a set of evolving feedback loops. Adaptability in this context means not linear progression, but constant negotiation and self-organization, often around 'strong attractors' such as ethnic allegiances, patronage systems, or coercive power structures. These attractors can be stabilizing in one moment and destabilizing in another.

Importantly, this adaptive capacity does not necessarily result in inclusive or democratic governance, and institutions that adapt successfully to conflict may also develop entrenched exclusionary logics or become embedded in illicit economies. For instance, Roxana Gutiérrez-Romero shows how criminalized governance structures in the context of the drug war in Mexico exhibited adaptability by reshaping local power configurations, often co-opting municipal authorities and embedding violence in everyday life. This form of adaptive governance can achieve order and predictability but at the cost of democratic accountability and citizen trust.

These findings resonate with broader debates in development and in political science on the nature of state-building. A growing body of literature emphasizes the need for autonomous and capable state institutions that are not only responsive but also grounded in legitimacy and accountability (Slater 2010; Wimmer 2018). Adaptive institutions are not always inclusive institutions, and short-term functionality may come at the cost of long-term transformation. From a policy perspective, recognizing the adaptability of governance institutions means more than identifying whether they function; it means understanding *how* and *for whom* they function. Adaptive governance can sustain service delivery and social order, but it may also reinforce exclusion, reproduce violence, or inhibit reform. The challenge lies in engaging institutions without either idealizing their effectiveness or dismissing them as obstacles to peace. This calls for policy approaches to post-conflict state-building that are historically grounded, context-sensitive, and attuned to the dual nature of wartime institutions: as sources of both resilience and fragility.

13.1.3 Interplay between local and national dynamics

A third key theme emerging from this volume is the often-contentious interplay between local governance systems and national state-building efforts. Several chapters emphasize that post-conflict governance is not merely a matter of rebuilding state institutions from the top down, but a complex negotiation between national agendas and local realities. This dynamic tension raises fundamental questions about legitimacy, sustainability, and the appropriate scale of governance in fragile and conflict-affected settings. For instance, Marine Gassier draws on fieldwork from Ethiopia and Somalia to show how localized governance systems, such as clan-based leadership, informal courts, and religious authorities, fill institutional vacuums left by weak or predatory states. These local systems often provide security, dispute resolution, and even basic services more effectively than state institutions. However, their legitimacy is not uniformly recognized by national actors or international donors, leading to tensions in peacebuilding strategies. Attempts to overlay centralized structures atop deeply embedded local arrangements often generate resistance, fragmentation, or renewed violence. Similarly, Adam Day critiques conventional state-building interventions through an 'ecosystems' lens. He argues that external actors frequently impose institutional blueprints that ignore the adaptive, negotiated nature of local governance systems that have evolved during conflict. These wartime systems, composed of traditional authorities, rebel bureaucracies, informal markets, and civil society actors, operate according to their own logics and feedback loops. Rather than collapsing into disorder, they often stabilize into new equilibria that resist centralized reengineering. Efforts to 'fix' fragile states without engaging the underlying local governance ecology risk not only failure but also further destabilization. Cyrus Samii advances this critique by presenting CDR as a more grounded and effective model. Based on extensive evidence from Afghanistan and other post-conflict settings, Samii demonstrates how local councils and community assemblies, when given oversight authority and resources, can deliver services efficiently and with greater accountability than centralized bureaucracies. This is especially true when these CDR institutions are not designed to replace the state but to complement it. This approach allows local institutions to act as intermediaries, translating national policies into locally meaningful action while maintaining the trust of the populations they serve.

Beyond institutional configurations, several chapters in the volume underscore the central role of *civilian agency* in mediating the local–national interface. Civilians are not merely passive recipients of governance but active participants who shape its content and form. They negotiate with armed actors, align with or challenge local elites, and use both compliance and resistance as strategies to survive and influence. For instance, Steele and Weintraub detail how civilians engage with rebel governance by participating in community meetings, voting in rebel-administered elections, or shaping the terms of taxation and justice provision. Such interactions shape the legitimacy of armed groups and influence their capacity to govern. This civilian agency is not confined to wartime. In the post-conflict phase, local communities play a crucial role in sustaining institutions created through external assistance. Samii's analysis of Afghanistan's National Solidarity Programme (NSP) highlights how local councils maintained service delivery even after the withdrawal of NGOs, and in some cases, adapted to oversee new functions such as education. These findings reveal that the durability of governance institutions depends as much on their embeddedness in civilian life as on their formal design.

Taken together, the chapters in this volume call for a recalibration of how we understand the relationship between local and national governance. Top-down state-building approaches often fail to appreciate the institutional legacies and social contracts forged during wartime. Conversely, overly localized approaches may struggle to address macro-political challenges or scale up successful interventions. The key lies in recognizing that effective governance must be both vertically and horizontally legitimate, and able to coordinate across scales while remaining responsive to the lived experiences of communities (Balcells and Justino 2014). Sustainable peace and development will depend not on choosing between these levels, but on managing their tensions and building bridges between them.

13.2 Lessons for policy and practice

This volume has argued that a better understanding of the legacies of wartime institutional change can improve strategies aimed at supporting stability, peace, and state-building in post-conflict countries. Many aspects of conflict can have long legacies on post-conflict society. We contend that this is especially the case for institutional changes that occur during conflict. This generates important policy implications.

Policy interventions in post-conflict settings in the last decade or so have taken a strong institutional approach intended to strengthen state capacity, supporting political stability, and promoting democracy (World Bank 2011, 2017). This approach, which has come under heavy criticism since the withdrawal of the US military and NATO forces from Afghanistan, tends to portray countries emerging from internal armed conflicts as blank slates where new institutions can be built from scratch. There is also an underlying assumption in the academic and policy debates on state-building and peace-building that conflict-affected countries are not capable of autonomous recovery without external intervention.

The focus on wartime governance as a key mechanism shaping state-building trajectories in post-war countries reveals how institutional change is in fact endogenous to conflict dynamics and how the mechanisms that shaped such institutional change will also determine—both in negative and in positive ways—state-building trajectories in the aftermath of civil wars. Tackling these endogenous processes also provides insights into civilian agency and its role in shaping wartime governance and armed group behaviour. The forms of governance that result from these complex interactions between competing authorities and civilians in wartime provide, in turn, entry points to understand the potential for state-building and governance options in post-conflict countries, especially their implications for the institutional capacity of governments formed in the immediate post-conflict period and the strength of social contracts formed between ruling elites and ordinary citizens emerging from wars.

Given the lacklustre record to date of external state- and democracy-building interventions, it is important that the international community understands more systematically how internal institutional dynamics may be harnessed to secure peace and stability in post-war countries. One key takeaway of the framework proposed in this volume for state-building policy in post-conflict settings is the combined need to enhance both governmental capabilities and the role of civil society after conflict ends—while remembering that, in many cases, paths toward rebuilding the state may continue to involve the use of violence, and militarized ways of thinking may linger. Policymakers should avoid assuming that transitions from civil war to stable statehood will follow a clear or predictable route, especially when it comes to moves towards democratic governance.

While curbing violence, reinforcing the social contract, and expanding institutional capacity are all vital, they do not, on their own, guarantee democratic consolidation. In fact, robust wartime governance across these areas can sometimes pave the way for armed movements to evolve into political parties during the post-conflict phase, whether they form governments or serve in opposition. In certain contexts, experience with governing during war may lay the groundwork for democratization (Huang 2016). However, more commonly, we see former armed groups that win elections eventually slipping into authoritarianism, an outcome witnessed in several African nations following independence-era conflicts (Levitsky and Way 2022). Elsewhere, political fragmentation tends to prevail, as seen in countries like Somalia, South Sudan, and Iraq. Such outcomes do not necessarily mean that efforts at state-building have failed, but rather point to the complexity and duration of forming cohesive nation states. Moreover, liberal democracy may neither be feasible nor desired by all societies emerging from war. Therefore, supporting post-conflict state-building calls for moving beyond rigid notions of what 'good governance' entails and toward a more nuanced understanding of how diverse (often armed) actors negotiate, strike bargains, build alliances, and attempt to shape political authority and resource distribution.

As highlighted in almost every chapter in this volume, it is also important to remember that, in the short term, the formal end of a conflict (through a peace agreement, for instance) may be associated with a vacuum of power in many post-conflict regions. In these circumstances, myriad political actors may use social, economic, and political networks established during the conflict for their benefit, some with positive consequences for state formation, others with negative outcomes, particularly if corrupt, rent-seeking, and predatory behaviours persist and political competition (and fighting) between opposing factions continues into the post-conflict period. Strengthening state capacity and institutional reach in the post-conflict period may then be hindered by how the losing side continues to operate their own institutions, how those are absorbed into the new state, and whether processes of capture and co-option continue to operate at the local level. Although strengthening the reach of state institutions in the aftermath of violent conflicts is a necessary condition to support state-building trajectories towards inclusive democracies, these interventions require caution and an understanding that informal institutions may still have key roles to play until other conditions (such as legitimacy, social organization, and political inclusiveness) are met.

The findings of this volume suggest several critical lessons for policymakers, practitioners, and international actors involved in post-conflict recovery in terms of (i) engaging with wartime institutional legacies, (ii) strengthening local economic and social capacities, and (iii) promoting inclusive state-building.

13.2.1 Engagement with wartime legacies

A key lesson from this volume is that wartime governance does not simply dissolve with the end of armed conflict. Rather, it leaves behind a dense fabric of institutions, power relations, and norms that continue to shape the post-war political landscape. Recognizing and engaging with these legacies—rather than erasing them—is essential to effective state-building. Armed groups often fill critical governance gaps during conflict, providing justice, security, and basic services. These experiences influence how communities perceive authority and legitimacy after war. Ignoring them can lead to policy failure or renewed instability.

State-building efforts that overlook the embedded authority of wartime actors often underestimate the persistence of informal institutions. As several chapters in this volume show, from local taxation mechanisms in the DRC to rebel-led dispute resolution systems in South Sudan, wartime institutions often maintain relevance long after violence ceases. Policymakers must, therefore, understand how wartime actors governed, whom they governed, and how those experiences influence citizen expectations and trust in public authority today.

Rather than imposing ideal-typical state institutions from the top down, international and domestic actors should identify and work with the structures that communities continue to rely on. For instance, if a former rebel group has developed credible dispute resolution mechanisms, these could be integrated into hybrid justice systems that blend customary and formal institutions. If community members view wartime health systems as more effective or fair than post-war state provision, there may be value in incorporating these actors into decentralized service delivery models.

At the same time, engagement must be cautious and strategic. Not all wartime institutions are benign. Some actors accrued power through coercion, exclusion, or criminal activity. Policymakers must differentiate between structures that offer opportunities for building legitimacy and those that entrench impunity or reinforce violence. This requires detailed local political economy analysis, grounded research, and sustained dialogue with civil society organizations and local leaders.

Concrete policy actions could include:

- Conducting legacy mapping of wartime governance actors and institutions at the subnational level as a first step in all post-conflict state-building programs.
- Establishing inclusive dialogue forums between national authorities, wartime actors, and local communities to determine which wartime structures should be transformed, adapted, or dismantled.
- Supporting transitional governance arrangements that incorporate trusted wartime actors into temporary administrative positions, coupled with clear exit strategies and oversight.
- Creating hybrid governance arrangements, such as joint service delivery between state and non-state actors, where wartime institutions continue to provide public goods.
- Building adaptive legal frameworks that allow for plural systems of justice, with mechanisms to gradually harmonize customary or wartime systems with formal law.
- Developing training programs for civil servants and donor staff on how to engage constructively with wartime legacies rather than working around them.

Ultimately, meaningful engagement with wartime legacies challenges conventional assumptions about what the state should look like and how legitimacy is built. This volume underscores that legitimacy is often relational, earned through practice, and shaped by history. Efforts to build peace, democracy, and state capacity must begin not from blank slates, but from the complex institutional and social terrain left behind by war.

13.2.2 Strengthening local capacities

A central theme that emerges from this volume is the critical role of local institutions and social dynamics in shaping long-term peace and development outcomes. While national-level reforms often dominate post-conflict policy agendas, sustainable governance and resilient state-building are forged in the everyday interactions, trust relations, and problem-solving capacities of local communities. Strengthening these local capacities is not simply about decentralizing authority; it is about recognizing, supporting, and integrating the pre-existing institutional ecosystems that have emerged through and despite conflict.

Several chapters highlight how community-driven approaches that build on local knowledge, norms, and networks often outperform externally imposed governance models. Such approaches are more attuned to the lived realities of conflict-affected populations and more capable of navigating complex social divisions. They also contribute to two essential conditions for sustainable peace: trust and cooperation across social groups, and perceived legitimacy of governing authorities rooted in a renewed social contract.

Post-conflict societies are often marked by deep social fragmentation. Conflicts may harden ethnic, religious, or class-based divisions, while years of violence erode the interpersonal trust and norms of reciprocity needed for collective action. At the same time, the legacies of wartime governance, whether inclusive or extractive, shape how citizens view authority and their own civic roles in its aftermath. In this context, rebuilding local governance capacity requires more than technical interventions; it requires social repair and political reintegration. This means investing in policies that rebuild horizontal cohesion among citizens and vertical trust between citizens and institutions. As documented in chapters examining local reconciliation processes in Colombia, Syria, and the DRC, local initiatives that facilitate inter-group dialogue, acknowledge historical grievances, and allow communities to co-create governance solutions are central to restoring civic trust. These spaces also enable communities to reimagine their roles in the political order and can contribute to more responsive and inclusive governance arrangements.

Importantly, the nature of wartime governance shapes post-conflict civic resilience. Communities governed inclusively during war often demonstrate stronger post-war civic engagement, while those subjected to coercive rule may remain wary of authority. As such, local capacity-building efforts must be sensitive to the wartime experiences of communities and avoid one-size-fits-all templates through policy actions such as:

- Institutionalizing participatory local planning, where citizens shape priorities for reconstruction, service delivery, and dispute resolution.
- Funding community-based reconciliation programs, including truth-telling projects, memory initiatives, and platforms for inter-group exchange.
- Supporting local governance structures that emerged during conflict where they retain community legitimacy, including informal councils, customary courts, or civilian arms of armed groups.
- Providing flexible funding to civil society organizations that promote local accountability, monitor corruption, and advocate for inclusive policies.
- Training local officials in conflict sensitivity, trauma-informed governance, and adaptive leadership, especially in areas previously governed by non-state actors.

- Linking local governance initiatives to national frameworks, through tiered coordination mechanisms that maintain local autonomy while feeding into broader planning.

Strengthening local capacities also entails shifting the assumptions and incentives of donors and central governments. Rather than focusing solely on vertical state-building from the centre outward, policy must support polycentric governance: systems where authority is negotiated across multiple levels and actors. This reflects the reality of many post-conflict contexts, where governance is already hybrid, and legitimacy is dispersed.

13.2.3 Promoting inclusive state-building

This volume makes clear that inclusive state-building is not just a normative aspiration—it is a practical necessity for creating resilient post-conflict governance. As several chapters underscore, the exclusion of local actors, perspectives, and institutions from state-building processes has consistently undermined legitimacy, weakened accountability, and, in many cases, contributed to renewed cycles of violence. A more inclusive approach—one that balances national cohesion with local autonomy—offers a path toward governance that is both functional and legitimate.

State-building is fundamentally about rebuilding the relationship between citizens and the state—the social contract. While asserting state authority and reestablishing control over violence remain essential, these actions must be situated within broader efforts to foster reciprocal trust, participation, and social accountability. Violent conflict disrupts these dimensions, fracturing the social contract and distorting the norms and practices that sustain civic engagement. The goal of post-conflict policy, then, should not be to impose an abstract model of governance, but to reweave this torn fabric by drawing on both pre-existing and wartime structures, and supporting citizens' agency in shaping how they are governed. This calls for a multi-scalar approach to inclusion, grounded in three principles: political inclusion and participation; economic inclusion and attention to post-war livelihoods; and institutional inclusion and the role of hybrid governance.

Improved political inclusion and participation implies encouraging broad-based political engagement, both formal (such as elections and institutional representation) and informal (including grassroots organization and support for local councils, when appropriate). Where identity-based exclusion played a role in conflict, meaningful political representation is essential to mitigating grievances. Reforms to electoral systems, political party formation rules, and decentralization frameworks should aim to create incentives for power-sharing and cooperation rather than domination and exclusion. Importantly, citizens must see political participation as a viable alternative to violence. This requires that public institutions be not only open, but also responsive. Measures that facilitate citizen feedback, protect civil liberties, and create avenues for accountability—such as local ombudsman offices or participatory budgeting—can help build this perception over time.

Economic inclusion is another key principle of inclusive state-building. Post-conflict societies often face the challenge of transitioning away from wartime economies built on networks of illicit trade, patronage, and survival-based transactions that flourished during conflict. Rather than rely on punitive or extractive strategies, successful state-building transitions will require cooperative economic reintegration. This means identifying ways to legalize and regularize informal livelihoods, including those tied to ex-combatants or rebel-held territories, and investing in community-level economic development that addresses material grievances. This may involve supporting public works and cash-for-work schemes that employ local populations and ex-combatants in rebuilding infrastructure, legalizing and regulating informal markets to create sustainable sources of income, or creating cooperatives or social enterprises rooted in local needs and capacities, with initial financial support and business training.

Finally, post-conflict state-building must be rooted in the lived institutional landscape of affected communities. This often includes customary authorities, religious leaders, rebel-era governance bodies, and informal dispute-resolution mechanisms. These actors are not always in competition with the state and can be, under some circumstances, collaborators in extending legitimacy and responsiveness. Rather than enforce a rigid centralization of power, hybrid governance arrangements can bridge the gap between state and society. This may include recognizing customary courts and integrating them into the formal legal system with human rights safeguards, creating joint governance councils at the municipal level that include state representatives and local leaders, or supporting local security arrangements that blend community policing with national oversight mechanisms.

These inclusive frameworks must be adaptive and iterative. Community needs and power dynamics shift over time, and so must the institutional arrangements that serve them. Pilot programs, learning cycles, and regular feedback loops should be integrated into the design of state-building interventions. Some examples of potential policy actions include:

- Constitutional or legal reforms that mandate political representation for historically excluded groups (such as ethnic minorities, women, and youth).
- National–local forums that allow civil society actors to feed into national peacebuilding and policy discussions.

- Subnational peace and development plans that are co-designed by local communities and line ministries.
- State recognition and support for local governance structures, including transitional arrangements where former rebel authorities hold local legitimacy.
- Independent monitoring bodies that track inclusivity and responsiveness in post-conflict institutional development.

Ultimately, promoting inclusive state-building means working with the grain of post-conflict societies. It requires an understanding that legitimacy is earned through participation, that authority is relational, and that peace is sustained not by coercion but by connection. As shown across this volume, successful state-building is not imposed—it is negotiated.

13.3 Closing reflections

The institutional legacies of violent conflict present both formidable challenges and critical opportunities for post-conflict recovery. As the chapters in this volume demonstrate, wartime governance structures—whether in the form of rebel administrations, informal justice systems, or localized service provision—do not vanish with the end of hostilities. They persist, shaping the architecture of post-war political life. In some cases, they entrench divisions and perpetuate exclusion. In others, they foster social cohesion, local legitimacy, and institutional resilience. What distinguishes one outcome from the other is not merely the institutional form of these legacies, but how they are engaged with, transformed, or integrated during the post-conflict period.

This volume calls for a fundamental rethinking of how peace is conceptualized and pursued. Durable peace is not synonymous with military victory or the formal cessation of violence. It involves the creation of a legitimate political order—one that responds to citizens' needs, enables non-violent modes of conflict resolution, and earns the trust of its constituents. Central to this challenge is understanding that war does not only destroy—it also creates. It creates new institutions, power relations, and governance practices. These wartime formations endure, shaping post-conflict trajectories in ways that international policy has too often overlooked.

The core contribution of this book lies in offering an alternative lens to dominant post-conflict policy paradigms. Instead of assuming that peacebuilding must begin from scratch, or that legitimacy stems solely from state-centric models of authority, this volume emphasizes the need to engage with wartime legacies constructively. This engagement requires grappling with the realities of local institutional authority, the adaptive nature of governance in wartime and post-war contexts, and the interplay between local and national dynamics. Together, these themes help reframe state-building as a negotiated, iterative, and context-dependent process.

Three core propositions emerge from this work. First, post-conflict recovery must begin with an honest accounting of what war has left behind. Conflict does not just dismantle but also reorganizes. Effective interventions must recognize the institutional and social reordering produced by war, including the new modes of authority, legitimacy, and resource distribution that have emerged. Ignoring these realities risks reintroducing fragility under the guise of reform. Second, governance is not only about capacity, but also about legitimacy. Institutional strength must be assessed not merely in terms of bureaucratic reach or technical efficiency, but in terms of public trust, accountability, and responsiveness. This means valuing and engaging with local institutions even when they diverge from normative models of 'good governance'. It also means building inclusive processes that rebuild social cohesion and address the grievances that fuelled conflict. Third, state-building is not a technocratic exercise but rather a political process of reconstituting—and often renegotiating—the social contract. Effective peacebuilding must move beyond a focus on central government institutions and instead support hybrid, multi-level governance arrangements. This includes empowering civil society, enabling political participation, and reinforcing the autonomy of local actors to co-construct their political futures.

International actors must adopt a posture of humility and flexibility in this work. Too often, peacebuilding efforts falter not because of a lack of resources or effort, but because they impose rigid institutional blueprints that ignore local histories and power dynamics. As the cases of Afghanistan, Colombia, Somalia, and elsewhere show, sustainable peace emerges from locally anchored processes that build on the realities of post-war life. Supporting these processes requires space for experimentation, dialogue, and long-term commitment.

While this volume advances important insights into the role of wartime governance in shaping post-conflict trajectories, it also raises critical questions that remain underexplored. Addressing these gaps will be essential to building a more complete, comparative, and actionable understanding of post-conflict governance. In many ways, the research presented here should be seen not as the endpoint, but as a foundation for a broader intellectual and policy agenda that treats war-to-peace transitions as deeply political, historically contingent, and globally entangled processes.

First, to date, much of the literature on wartime governance and post-conflict state-building has concentrated on a handful of high-profile cases, such as South Sudan, Afghanistan, DRC, Iraq, and Colombia, where international presence has been extensive and data more readily available. However, the patterns identified in these contexts may not fully reflect the diversity of wartime institutions and recovery trajectories globally. There is a pressing need for systematic comparative research across under-studied regions, particularly Southeast Asia, Central

America, and parts of the Sahel and Horn of Africa, where conflict dynamics, political economies, and cultural institutions follow distinct trajectories. Such comparative work would enable scholars to distinguish between context-specific phenomena and more generalizable dynamics, while avoiding the overrepresentation of cases shaped by international intervention. Future research should adopt comparative historical approaches and utilize cross-national datasets alongside ethnographic fieldwork to map how different configurations of conflict, ideology, and governance—such as ethno-nationalist insurgencies, criminalized violence, or revolutionary state-building—leave distinctive institutional legacies.

Second, while this volume provides valuable snapshots of wartime governance and its immediate post-conflict effects, far less is known about the long-term evolution of wartime institutions across generations. How, for example, do rebel-established education or legal systems evolve once integrated, or resisted, by national authorities over a 20–30 year period? What happens to the civic habits and political values instilled during wartime governance as generations pass? How does trauma, memory, and myth-making about wartime institutions shape local identity and political participation decades after the fighting has stopped? To answer these questions, future research must move beyond post-war 'windows of opportunity' and invest in deep longitudinal studies that track institutions, social norms, and community governance strategies over time. Such studies could draw from archival research, oral histories, and panel surveys to better understand how institutional memory and intergenerational transmission of trust or resistance toward authority impact the resilience or fragility of peace settlements.

Third, a forward-looking research agenda must engage more seriously with the intersections between wartime legacies and global systemic challenges. Climate change, public health crises, technological disruptions, and large-scale migration flows are increasingly reshaping the governance landscape in fragile and post-conflict settings. How do wartime institutions adapt to or falter under these pressures? Can wartime governance systems enhance local climate resilience or pandemic response, or do they become sources of new vulnerabilities? How do digital technologies (such as mobile justice platforms or encrypted wartime communication networks) transform the durability and adaptability of non-state governance? By forging interdisciplinary collaborations with fields such as environmental governance, digital sociology, and public health, future research can develop a more nuanced picture of how the legacies of war interact with global forces to shape the future of governance. This also opens space for exploring how non-traditional actors—like diaspora communities, multinational corporations, or transnational activist networks—engage with or influence post-war institutions.

Finally, there is an urgent need to critically revisit the role of external actors in post-conflict settings, not simply in terms of their technical effectiveness, but in how they shape, suppress, or amplify the agency of local actors.

How can international donors, peacekeeping missions, and international non-governmental organizations move from a model of directive intervention to one of embedded accompaniment that supports endogenous trajectories of change—something that may become more and more necessary as aid budgets continue to reduce? What does a legitimate external role look like in contexts where the state's authority is historically contested, and trust in formal institutions remains fragile? This also demands greater attention to the politics of knowledge production: whose definitions of peace, development, and good governance are being applied, and who benefits from them? How do global governance regimes (such as aid conditionalities or counterterrorism frameworks) constrain the flexibility needed to engage with wartime institutions on their own terms? Answering these questions requires a more reflexive and collaborative research approach that treats communities not just as sites of data extraction, but as co-producers of knowledge and co-designers of policy. The field must grapple with the ethical implications of research and policy in spaces still shaped by deep power asymmetries.

This volume does not seek to provide a prescriptive roadmap for peace. Rather, it invites a reorientation towards a more grounded, pluralistic understanding of how post-conflict societies reconstruct authority and legitimacy. Peace, as argued throughout these chapters, is not a destination but a process marked by negotiation, adaptation, and contestation. It is not defined solely by the absence of war, but by the presence of justice, accountability, and civic participation. In the years ahead, the success of post-conflict interventions will depend on our ability to embrace this complexity. By acknowledging the generative, as well as destructive effects of war, and by centring the voices and agency of those living through its aftermath, we can move closer to models of peace- and state-building that are not only more inclusive, but more enduring.

References

Arjona, A., J. C.Cárdenas, A. M. Ibáñez, P. Justino, and J. A. Vallejo (2024). 'The Long-Term Economic Legacies of Rebel Rule in Civil War: Micro Evidence from Colombia', *Journal of Conflict Resolution* 68 (9): 1825–1855. https://doi.org/10.1177/00220027231170569

Arjona, A. (2016). *Rebelocracy: Social Order in the Colombian Civil War.* New York: Cambridge University Press. https://doi.org/10.1017/9781316421925

Balcells, L., and P. Justino (2014). 'Bridging Micro and Macro Approaches on Civil Wars and Political Violence: Issues, Challenges and Way Forward', *Journal of Conflict Resolution* 58 (8): 1343–1359. https://doi.org/10.1177/0022002714547905

Huang, R. (2016). *The Wartime Origins of Democratization: Civil War, Rebel Governance, and Political Regimes.* New York: Cambridge University Press. https://doi.org/10.1017/CBO9781316711323

Justino, P., and W. Stojetz (2018). 'On the Legacies of Wartime Governance', HiCN Working Paper no. 263, The Households in Conflict Network.

Justino, P. (2012). 'War and Poverty', in M. Garfinkel and S. Skaperdas (eds.), *Handbook of the Economics of Peace and Conflict*. Oxford: Oxford University Press, Chapter 27, pp. 676–705. https://doi.org/10.1093/oxfordhb/9780195392777.013.0027

Justino, P. (2009). 'Poverty and Violent Conflict: A Micro-Level Perspective on the Causes and Duration of Warfare', *Journal of Peace Research*, 46(3): 315–333. https://doi.org/10.1177/0022343309102655

Levitsky, S., and L. Way (2022). *Revolution & Dictatorship: The Violent Origins of Durable Authoritarianism*. Princeton, NJ: Princeton University Press. https://doi.org/10.2307/j.ctv2drhcnf

Slater, D. (2010). *Ordering Power: Contentious Politics and Authoritarian Leviathans in Southeast Asia*. New York: Cambridge University Press. https://doi.org/10.1017/CBO9780511760891

Wimmer, A. (2018). *Nation Building: Why Some Countries Come Together While Others Fall Apart*. Princeton, NJ: Princeton University Press. https://doi.org/10.2307/j.ctvc77kjx

World Bank (2011). *World Development Report 2011: Conflict, Security, and Development*. Washington, DC: The World Bank. https://doi.org/10.1596/978-0-8213-8439-8

World Bank (2017). *World Development Report 2017: Governance and the Law*. Washington, DC: The World Bank.

Index

Tables and figures are indicated by an italic *t* and *f*, following the paragraph number.